ABOUT THE AUTHOR

© DAVID ISRAEL

The travel bug bit Val Mallinson early, in the back of a 1972 Mercury station wagon with fake wood paneling. On family road trips, and on her own, she has avidly explored all 50 states, a dozen European countries, Mexico, and the Caribbean. She's hiked the Swiss Alps, snorkeled in Hawaii, bungee jumped in British Columbia, eaten Belgian chocolate in Belgium, and discovered how to ask for public facilities in more than six languages.

Val's love of dogs began even earlier, thanks to her childhood companion Keegan, who waited with his nose pressed to the window for her to come home from kindergarten. Her favorite bedtime story was *The Pokey Little Puppy*, which also forecast an early love of dessert. After a passing puppy love with wrinkly shar-peis as a teenager, she adopted two miniature dachshunds, Cooper and Isis, as an adult.

Before devoting herself to the position of chauffeur and stenographer for the Wonder Wieners, Val survived medical policy and procedure documentation, wrote a screenplay, and spent a decade in the fast-paced and glamorous world of advertising and marketing copywriting. She penned snappy copy for dot coms that no longer exist, as well as for a large software company in Redmond, Washington. She is also a contributing author to the stylish travel guide *Moon Metro Seattle*. With her husband, Steve, she has lived in Seattle for ten years.

In the course of writing *The Dog Lover's Companion to the Pacific Northwest*, Val has figured out how to set up a tent in the dark and sleep in a mummy bag with two burrowing hounds. She has honed her reflexes avoiding road hazards flying out of the backs of pickup trucks. Most importantly, she's learned what poison oak looks like, and not to set up at campsites located near roaming bears or wandering boys carrying .22 rifles.

To Dread Pirate Steve,
for saying As you wish
to every demand
made of him.

The Dog Lover's Companion to the Pacific Northwest

1ST
EDITION

Val Mallinson

AVALON
TRAVEL

THE DOG LOVER'S COMPANION TO THE PACIFIC NORTHWEST
THE INSIDE SCOOP ON WHERE TO TAKE YOUR DOG

Published by
Avalon Travel Publishing
1400 65th Street, Suite 250
Emeryville, CA 94608, USA

Avalon Travel Publishing
A member of the Perseus Books Group
Printing History
1st edition—May 2005
5 4 3

ISBN-10: 1-56691-773-5
ISBN-13: 978-1-56691-773-5
ISSN: 1553-135X

Editors: Amy Scott, Kay Elliott
Series Manager: Kathryn Ettinger
Acquisitions Manager: Rebecca K. Browning
Copy Editor: Valerie Sellers Blanton
Designer: Jacob Goolkasian
Graphics Coordinator: Tabitha Lahr
Production Coordinators: Gerilyn Attebery, Amber Pirker
Layout Artist: Mary Gilliana
Map Editor: Kat Smith
Cartographers: Kat Kalamaras, Mike Morgenfeld
Indexer: Valerie Sellers Blanton

Cover and Interior Illustrations by Phil Frank

Printed in the United States by Malloy

CONTENTS

Introduction 1

The Paws Scale 4
He, She, It 5
To Leash or Not to Leash 5
There's No Business
    Like Dog Business 6
Etiquette Rex:
    The Well-Mannered Mutt 7
Safety First 8

The Ultimate Doggy Bag 9
Bone Appétit 10
A Room at the Inn 11
Natural Troubles 12
The Price of Freedom 14
A Dog in Need 15
Keep in Touch 15

WASHINGTON 17

1. Olympic Peninsula 19

Joyce 21
Port Angeles 22
The Sequim-Dungeness Valley . . . 23
Port Townsend 26
Port Hadlock and
    Marrowstone Island 31
Forks 32
La Push 34

Kalaloch 35
Lake Quinault 37
West Hood Canal 38
Pacific Beach 40
Copalis Beach 41
Ocean City 42
Ocean Shores 43
Aberdeen-Hoquiam 45

2. Kitsap Peninsula 49

Kingston, Hansville,
    and Port Gamble 50
Poulsbo 52
Silverdale and Seabeck 55
Bremerton 57
Bainbridge Island 59

Port Orchard 63
Vashon and Maury Islands 65
East Hood Canal 67
Gig Harbor 70
Key Peninsula 72

3. The Islands 75

Orcas Island 77
San Juan Island 79
Shaw Island 83
Lopez Island 84
Guemes Island 87

Fidalgo Island and Anacortes 88
North Whidbey 90
Central Whidbey 93
South Whidbey 95
Camano Island 98

4. Everett and Vicinity 101

Stanwood 102
Arlington 104
Marysville. 105
Granite Falls 106
Everett 108
Mukilteo. .113
Snohomish. 115
Gold Bar .117
Edmonds 118
Lynnwood 120

5. Greater Seattle 123

Shoreline 125
North Seattle. 126
Green Lake 127
University District and Ravenna. . 128
Ballard 130
Magnolia 132
Fremont and Wallingford. 133
Queen Anne 135
Downtown. 136
Capitol Hill 140
Madison and Montlake 141
Madrona and Leschi. 142
West Seattle 143
South Seattle. 145
Kirkland 147
Redmond. 148
Bellevue. 150
Mercer Island 151

6. North Cascades. 155

Blaine and Birch Bay 157
Lynden. 159
Ferndale 161
Mt. Baker. 163
Bellingham-Fairhaven 164
Mount Vernon and La Conner. . . 172
Sedro Woolley 174
Concrete 175
Rockport 177
Marblemount 179
Newhalem. 180

7. Southwest Washington 183

Kent 185
Federal Way 186
Tacoma 187
Black Diamond 190
Olympia. 191
Centralia and Chehalis. 195
Westport 196
Grayland and Tokeland 198
Long Beach Peninsula 199
Mossyrock 202
Kelso-Longview. 203
Battle Ground 204
Vancouver 205
Camas and Washougal 206
Skamania. 207
Stevenson 208

8. Central Washington 211

Leavenworth 213
Issaquah. 216
Snoqualmie and North Bend . . . 217
Snoqualmie Pass. 219
Easton 220
Salmon La Sac. 221
Roslyn 222
Cle Elum 222

Ellensburg	224	Carson	235
White Pass and Chinook Pass	226	Bingen-White Salmon	236
Naches	227	Lyle	238
Yakima	228	Dallesport	239
Union Gap	232	Maryhill	240
Toppenish	233	Goldendale	240
Trout Lake	234		

OREGON 243
9. North Coast 245

Astoria-Warrenton	246	Garibaldi	260
Gearhart	250	Tillamook	261
Seaside	251	Cape Meares	263
Cannon Beach	252	Oceanside	263
Manzanita	257	Netarts	264
Wheeler and Nehalem	258	Pacific City	265
Rockaway Beach	259	Neskowin	268

10. Central Coast 271

Lincoln City	273	Seal Rock	286
Gleneden Beach	277	Waldport	287
Lincoln Beach	279	Yachats	289
Depoe Bay	279	Florence	292
Otter Rock and Cape Foulweather	281	Mapleton	295
Newport	281	Reedsport	296
		Scottsburg	297
South Beach	285	Winchester Bay	297

11. South Coast 301

The Bay Area	302	Port Orford	312
Coquille and Myrtle Point	306	Gold Beach	315
Bandon	308	Brookings-Harbor	317

12. Greater Portland 322

North Portland	326	Southwest Portland	340
Northwest Portland	328	Southeast Portland	342
Nob Hill	330	Milwaukie	347
Downtown and Historic Waterfront	332	Lake Oswego	348
		West Linn	349
Northeast Portland–Airport	335	Beaverton	350
Tigard	339	Gresham	352

13. Willamette Valley 355

Wilsonville 357
Newberg 358
McMinnville 360
Canby 361
Estacada 361
Dallas 363
Salem–Keizer 364
Silverton 368
Lyons 369
Albany 370
Corvallis 371
Alsea 375
Sweet Home 376
Eugene–Springfield 376
Blue River and McKenzie Bridge . . 379
Cottage Grove 381

14. Central Oregon 383

Troutdale 385
Corbett 386
Cascade Locks 388
Hood River 389
Lost Lake 392
The Dalles 392
Mt. Hood 395
Parkdale 396
Maupin 397
Madras–Culver 398
Sisters 399
Redmond 401
Bend 402

15. Southern Oregon 409

Roseburg 411
Merlin and Galice 413
Grants Pass 415
Jacksonville 417
Medford 420
Ashland 422
Shady Cove and Prospect 426
Union Creek 427
Crescent Lake 428
Diamond Lake 430
Fort Klamath and Crater Lake . . . 431
Klamath Falls 432

CANADA 437
16. British Columbia 438

Whistler 439
Squamish 443
West Vancouver 445
North Vancouver 446
Kitsilano 447
Point Grey 449
West End 450
Downtown Vancouver
and Gastown 451
Granville Island 453
Cambie 454
Kerrisdale 456
Tri-Cities Area 457
Chilliwack and
Harrison Hot Springs 459
Sidney and the
Saanich Peninsula 460
Victoria 463
Sooke 467

RESOURCES 471

Emergency Veterinary Clinics . . . 472
Pet-Friendly Chain Hotels 477
Transportation. 497
Extended Trails 499
Useful Organizations 501

INDEXES 504

Accommodations Index 505
Restaurant Index. 512
General Index 519

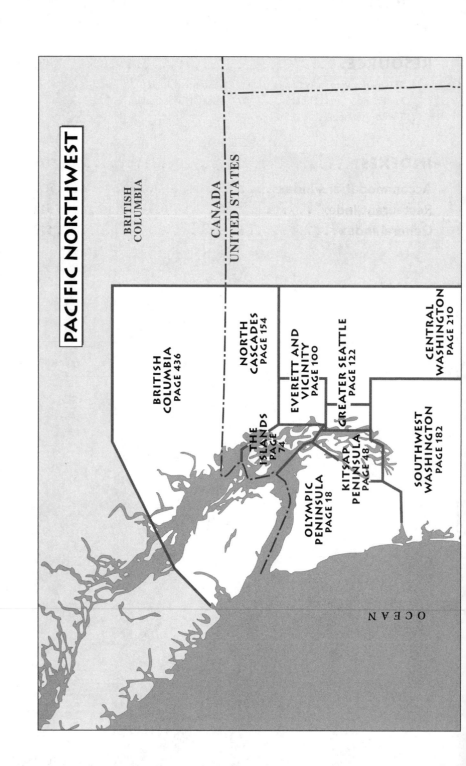

PACIFIC NORTHWEST

BRITISH COLUMBIA

CANADA
UNITED STATES

BRITISH COLUMBIA
PAGE 436

NORTH CASCADES
PAGE 154

THE ISLANDS
PAGE 74

EVERETT AND VICINITY
PAGE 100

GREATER SEATTLE
PAGE 122

OLYMPIC PENINSULA
PAGE 18

KITSAP PENINSULA
PAGE 48

SOUTHWEST WASHINGTON
PAGE 182

CENTRAL WASHINGTON
PAGE 210

OCEAN

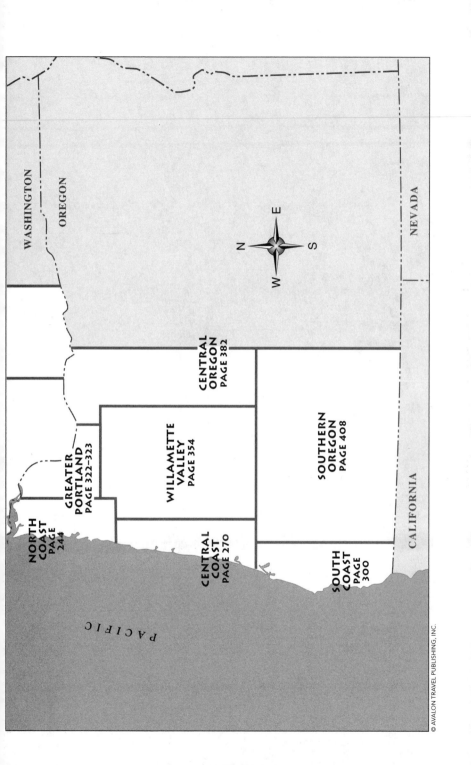

WASHINGTON

OREGON

NEVADA

CALIFORNIA

PACIFIC

NORTH
COAST
PAGE
244

GREATER
PORTLAND
PAGE 322–323

CENTRAL
COAST
PAGE 270

WILLAMETTE
VALLEY
PAGE 354

CENTRAL
OREGON
PAGE 382

SOUTH
COAST
PAGE
300

SOUTHERN
OREGON
PAGE 408

N
W E
S

Introduction

In our demand-driven lives, filled with rules and requirements for what we must do, the faithful creatures who sit at our feet expect so little of us. In exchange for lifelong devotion, all they ask is to be fed and to have some-place warm and dry to sleep. For bringing joy and laughter into our lives, all they hope for in return is an occasional tummy rub and some playtime. For unconditional love, they demand only to remain glued to our sides, always, always, always allowed to go wherever we are going. That is, unless, we are going to the v-e-t.

At our house, going on a trip without the dogs is rarely an option. For start-ers, we can't handle the guilt. Copernicus Maximus the Red, a.k.a. Cooper or Coop for short, mourns our departure from his perch at the picture window, his devastation clearly visible in his hangdog posture. The Goddess Isis is much more direct in expressing her displeasure. At the first key jangle, she runs to the door to the garage. As soon as the door closes behind us, she protests, using a high-pitched, staccato bark reserved for these occasions. "I-can't-be-lieve-you-are-leav-ing-with-out-ME!" We know that as soon as we're out of sight, she happily returns to composing squeak toy symphonies and he resumes his post as protectorate of the realm from squirrel and crow intruders. Yet, in our hearts, we torture ourselves endlessly for having left them behind.

Why shouldn't they protest? They know the big wide world out there holds more wonders than they can possibly fit into their short dog lifetimes. They have to make up for lost time—before being rescued, Cooper spent the first year of his life in a cage in a barn, and in her former life, Isis got left behind while her siblings went to dog shows. For the Dachsie Twins, even a trip to the dry cleaners is full of new sensory pleasures.

Truth be told, we don't want to go anywhere without the kids, for the dogs are our children, hairy, four-legged, and speech-challenged though they may be. Seeing the Pacific Northwest through the eyes of the Wonder Wieners makes the region's natural beauty and endless recreation opportunities seem even more wondrous. They are right, there are marvels out here.

Native Americans treasured the secrets of the Pacific Northwest for thousands of years. Their oral legends and petroglyphs tell of its abundance. Of giant forests sheltering elk and wildlife to hunt, hillsides thick with brambles yielding sweet blackberries, and oceans and rivers teeming with steelhead and the sacred salmon. The Lewis and Clark Expedition of 1805–1806 brought the mysteries of what was called the Oregon Territory to the attention of European settlers back east. Meriwether Lewis explored Washington and Oregon with his faithful Newfoundland named Seaman at his side, and his journals are bursting with drawings and details of native flora, fauna, and natural phenomenon the likes of which the Corps of Discovery had never seen. From 1843 to 1869, hundreds of thousands of pioneers endured dangerous journeys and immense hardships to reach this promised land at the end of the Oregon Trail.

Thanks in part to this book, our hope is that you don't have to suffer any hardships traveling the Pacific Northwest with your pets. Coop 'n' Isis worked their weenie hindquarters off for you, to sniff out romps with the highest fun factor, the choicest eats where dogs are allowed, and the nicest digs for slumber parties. They discovered, more often than not, that dogs are a natural fit into the relaxed, casual, outdoor lifestyle of the region. On their journey, the Dachshund Duo met dogs who hike, bike, kayak, fish, and ride river rafts and motorcycles with their humans. International outdoor outfitters are headquartered here, such as Eddie Bauer, REI, and Nike. REI even allows you to bring your leashed and well-mannered dog into its flagship store in Seattle while you equip for your adventures.

What will you find on your travels in the Pacific Northwest? Steve, dad of Cooper and Isis, declares his love for the region because it has "big water *and* big mountains." The marine heritage of the Northwest Coast is everywhere: ferries, lighthouses, beaches, islands, inland waterways, bridges, marine parks, and people who live on houseboats. No matter how many times you see it, the power of the Pacific Ocean never diminishes. As for the mountains, despite 150 years of logging, there are deep forests and wilderness areas with towering conifers that will astound you. This combination of surf and turf yields the highest concentration of parks, beaches, and recreation opportunities we think you'll find anywhere. That doesn't include the off-leash areas (OLAs) centered on the major metropolitan areas—close to 50 in Seattle and Portland alone!

For at least half of the year, you'll also find mud. It is said that the Eskimo peoples of the world have a hundred names for different qualities of snow. So, too, do residents of the Pacific Northwest have many ways to describe rain, from mist and drizzle on through to showers with sun breaks and raining cats and dogs. This precipitation nourishes the greenery and flowers that give the region its nicknames: Evergreen State for Washington, Emerald City for Seattle, and City of Roses for Portland. Embrace mud, jump in mud puddles, take a therapeutic mud bath, and make mud pies. Enjoy it without judgment, as your dog does, or like you did when you were a kid. Bring raincoats and towels for everybody, and cover your car seats.

If you simply cannot stand the wet dog smell a minute longer, don't despair—simply head east. Starting at the eastern slope of the Cascade Mountains, it is typically warm and dry. In this book, you can count on the locations in the Central Washington and Central Oregon chapters to have an average of 300 sunny days a year. Some even say Pacific Northwesterners exaggerate reports of rainfall to prevent more people from moving here, thus keeping all of the region's desirable qualities to themselves. Honestly, the sun starts peeking through in April, and it can be dry and temperate through Indian Summer in September.

While rumors of rain may be exaggerated, everything you've ever heard about the regional obsession with coffee is true. No matter how backwoods or one-horse a town, there will be an espresso shack, even if it doubles as the post office, grocery store, and gas station. It's not just a beverage, it is a way of life.

Which brings us back to the reason we are here. Cooper and Isis hope that this guide will help make traveling with your dogs a way of life. Every park, place to eat, and place to stay has passed the inspection of these hounds' fine-tuned senses. Coop 'n' Isis dug up dog events, unearthed the fanciest pet boutiques, and scratched under the surface of dog day care centers to include a few they deemed most worthy. Each pupportunity has been carefully rated and described to make your travels easier. You can fit your dog into your favorite outdoor passion, whether it's hitting every farmers market and roadside fruit and vegetable stand in sight, climbing every mountain, or fording every stream. As we researched this book, we fell in love with the region's beauty over and over again, from the mountains, to the prairies, to the oceans white with foam. The Wonder Wieners hope your discoveries in the Pacific Northwest will be no less wonderful.

The Paws Scale

At some point, we've got to face the facts: Humans and dogs have different tastes. We like eating chocolate and smelling lavender and covering our bodies with soft clothes. They like eating roadkill and smelling each other's unmentionables and covering their bodies with slug slime.

The parks, beaches, and recreation areas in this book are rated with a dog in mind. Maybe your favorite park has lush gardens, a duck pond, a few acres of perfectly manicured lawns, and sweeping views of a nearby skyline. But unless your dog can run leash-free, swim in the pond, and roll in the grass, that park may not deserve a very high rating from your pet's perspective.

The lowest rating you'll come across in this book is the fire hydrant ♟. When you see this symbol, it means the park is merely "worth a squat." Visit one of these parks only if your dog can't hold it any longer. These pit stops have virtually no other redeeming qualities for canines.

Beyond that, the paws scale starts at one paw 🐾 and goes up to Four Paws 🐾🐾🐾🐾. A one-paw park isn't a dog's idea of a great time. Maybe it's a tiny park with only a few trees and too many kids running around. Or perhaps it's a magnificent national park that bans dogs from every inch of land except paved roads and a few campsites. Four-paw parks, on the other hand, are places your dog will drag you to visit. Some of these areas come as close to dog heaven as you can imagine. Many have lakes for swimming or hundreds of acres for hiking. Some are small, fenced-in areas where leash-free dogs can tear around without danger of running into the road. Many four-paw parks give you the option of letting your dog off-leash (although most have restrictions, which are detailed in the park description).

In addition to finding paws and hydrants, you'll also notice an occasional foot symbol 👣 in this book. The foot means the park offers something special for humans. After all, you deserve a reward for being such a good chauffeur.

This book is not meant to be a comprehensive guide to all of the parks in the Pacific Northwest. This region suffers from a happy problem of excessive recreational opportunities. We struggled not to become overwhelmed or jaded as we selected the best, largest, most convenient, and dog-friendliest parks to include in the guide. Most areas have so many wonderful parks that we had to make tough choices about which to include and which to leave out. A few places have such a limited supply of parks that, for the sake of dogs living and visiting there, we listed parks that wouldn't otherwise be worth mentioning.

Since signposts are spotty and street names are notoriously confusing, we've given detailed directions to all the parks from the nearest major roadway or city center. If you ask, Pacific Northwesterners have a reputation for being as helpful as they are adventurous, all too glad to give you directions that will get you hopelessly lost on their favorite backdoor route to somewhere obscure. It certainly can't hurt to pick up a detailed street map before you and your dog set out on your travels.

He, She, It

In this book, whether neutered, spayed, or au naturel, dogs are never referred to as "it." They are either "he" or "she." Cooper and Isis insisted we alternate pronouns so no dog reading this book will feel left out.

To Leash or Not to Leash...

This is not a question that plagues dogs' minds. Ask just about any normal, red-blooded American dog if she'd prefer to play off-leash, and she'll say, "Arf!" (Translation: "That's a rhetorical question, right?") No question about it, most dogs would give their canine teeth to frolic about without that cumbersome leash.

Whenever you see the running dog 🐕 in this book, you'll know that under certain circumstances, your dog can run around in leash-free bliss. Some parks have off-leash hours, marked by the time ⏰ symbol. Fortunately, the Pacific Northwest is home to dozens of such parks, and the trend is growing. The rest of the parks require leashes. We wish we could write about the parks where dogs get away with being scofflaws. Unfortunately, those would be the first ones animal control patrols would hit. We can't advocate breaking the law, but if you're tempted, please follow your conscience and use common sense.

Also, just because dogs are permitted off-leash in certain areas doesn't necessarily mean you should let your dog run free. Unless you're sure your dog will come back when you call or will never stray more than a few yards from your side, you should probably keep her leashed. An otherwise docile homebody can turn into a savage hunter if the right prey is near. A curious wet-nose could perturb the rattlesnakes that are common in high desert areas or run into a bear or cougar in the woods. In pursuit of a strange scent, your dog could easily get lost in an unfamiliar area.

Crowded or popular areas, especially beaches, can be full of unpredictable children and other dogs who may not be as well behaved as yours. It's a tug of war out there. People who've had bad experiences with dogs are demanding stricter leash laws everywhere or the banning of "those mongrels" altogether from public places. When faced with increasing limits, dog lovers want more designated places where their pets can play without fear of negative consequences. The rope is stretched thin and tensions are tight. Even as this book went to press, there were horrible incidents of dogs being deliberately poisoned with tainted meat left in parks and on beaches where dogs were roaming free despite leash laws.

In short, be careful out there. If your dog needs leash-free exercise but you don't have her under complete voice control, she'll be happy to know that several beaches permit well-behaved, leashless pooches, as do a growing number of beautiful, fenced-in dog exercise areas.

As for general leash restrictions, Washington State Parks require dogs to be on an 8-foot or shorter leash. Oregon State Parks limit it to a 6-foot or shorter lead, and this is the standard that is rapidly being adopted throughout the region.

There's No Business Like Dog Business

There's nothing appealing about bending down with a plastic bag or a piece of newspaper on a chilly morning and grabbing the steaming remnants of what your dog ate for dinner the night before. It's disgusting. Worse yet, you have to hang onto it until you can find a trash can. Blech! It's enough to make you wish you could train your pooch to sit on the potty. But as gross as it can be to scoop the poop, it's worse to step in it. It's really bad if a child falls in it, or—gag!—starts eating it. The funniest name for poop we heard on our travels was WMDs, Wanton Mongrel Defecations, but there's nothing funny about a poop-filled park. Have you ever walked into a park where few people clean up after their dogs? You don't want to be there any more than anyone else does.

Unscooped poop is one of a dog's worst enemies. Public policies banning dogs from parks are enacted because of it. Good Pacific Northwest parks and beaches that permit dogs are in danger of closing their gates to all canines because of the negligent behavior of a few owners. A worst-case scenario is already in place in several communities—dogs are banned from all parks. Their only exercise is a leashed sidewalk stroll. That's no way to live.

Be responsible and clean up after your dog everywhere you go. Stuff plastic bags in your jacket, purse, car, pants pockets—anywhere you might be able to pull one out when needed. Don't count on the parks to provide them. Even when we found places with bag dispensers, they were more often empty than not. If it makes it more palatable, bring along a paper bag, too, and put the used plastic bag in it. That way you don't have to walk around with a plastic bag whose contents are visible to the world. If you're squeamish about the squishy sensation, try one of those cardboard or plastic bag pooper-scoopers sold at pet stores. If you don't like bending down, buy a long-handled scooper. You get the point—there's a pooper-scooper for every preference.

And here's one for you: If your dog does his business in the woods, and nobody is there to see it, do you still have to pick up? Yes! Unless you carry a bivouac shovel to bury the doo 6–8 inches deep, and can guarantee your pet won't relieve himself within 200 yards of a water source, you should pack out what you pack in, and that includes the poop. As forest lands get ever increasing usage, the only way to keep them pristine is to do your part.

Etiquette Rex:
The Well-Mannered Mutt

While cleaning up after your dog is your responsibility, a dog in a public place has his own responsibilities. Of course, it really boils down to your responsibility again, but the burden of action is on your dog. Etiquette for restaurants and hotels is covered in other sections of this chapter. What follows are some fundamental rules of dog etiquette. We'll go through it quickly, but if your dog's a slow reader, he can read it again: no vicious dogs; no jumping on people; no incessant barking; no leg lifts on kayaks, backpacks, human legs, or any other personal objects you'll find hanging around beaches and parks; dogs should come when they're called; and they should stay on command.

Nobody's perfect, but do your best to remedy any problems. It takes patience and consistency. For example, Isis considers it her personal duty to vocally defend the car from passersby. So, we keep a squirt bottle on hand to quench her tendency to bark. In Cooper's mind, he's obeying the "Come!" command as long as he's vaguely and eventually headed in the right direction, and you can forget about it altogether if there are squirrels in the general vicinity, which means he's on leash more often than not. Every time there's a problem between someone's dog and someone else, we all stand to lose more of our hard-earned privileges to enjoy parks with our pets. Know your dog's limits or leash him. If you must, avoid situations that bring out the worst in your best friend.

The basic rules for dog parks are fairly consistent as well, and we've compiled a master list from our experience: No puppies under four months or

females in heat; keep dogs from fighting and biting; leash your pets on entry and exit and in parking lots; be aware and keep your dog under voice control; ensure that your dog is properly vaccinated and licensed; and, you guessed it, pick up poop.

Safety First

A few essentials will keep your traveling dog happy and healthy.

Beat the Heat: If you must leave your dog alone in the car for a few minutes, do so only if it's cool out and you can park in the shade. Never, ever, ever leave a dog in a car with the windows rolled up all the way. Even if it seems cool, the sun's heat passing through the window can kill a dog in a matter of minutes. Roll down the window enough so your dog gets air, but also so there's no danger of your dog getting out or someone breaking in. Make sure your dog has plenty of water.

You also have to watch out for heat exposure when your car is in motion. Certain cars, particularly hatchbacks, can make a dog in the backseat extra hot, even while you feel okay in the driver's seat.

Try to time your vacation so you don't visit a place when it's extremely warm. Dogs and heat don't get along, especially if your dog is a true Pacific Northwesterner who thinks anything over 80 degrees is blistering. The opposite is also true. If your dog lives in a hot climate and you take him to a cold and rainy place, it may not be a healthy shift. Check with your vet if you have any doubts. Spring and fall are the best times to travel, when parks are less crowded anyway.

Water: Water your dog frequently. Dogs on the road may drink even more than they do at home. Take regular water breaks, or bring a bowl and set it on the floor so your dog always has access to water. We use a thick clay bowl on a rubber car mat, which comes in really handy on Oregon's curvy roads. When hiking, be sure to carry enough for you and a thirsty dog. Those folding cloth bowls you can find at outdoor stores are worth their weightlessness in gold.

Rest Stops: Stop and unwater your dog. There's nothing more miserable than being stuck in a car when you can't find a rest stop. No matter how tightly you cross your legs and try to think of the desert, you're certain you'll burst within the next minute…so imagine how a dog feels when the urge strikes, and he can't tell you the problem. There are plenty of rest stops along the major freeways. We've also included many parks close to freeways for dogs who need a good stretch with their bathroom break.

How frequently you stop depends on your dog's bladder. Cooper can hold it all day, whereas Isis is whining for a potty stop at every park. If your dog is constantly running out the doggy door at home to relieve himself, you may want to stop every hour. Others can go significantly longer without being uncomfortable. Our vet says stop every two hours as a matter of course. Watch for any signs of restlessness and gauge it for yourself.

Car Safety: Even the experts differ on how a dog should travel in a car. Some suggest dog safety belts, available at pet-supply stores. Others firmly believe in keeping a dog kenneled. They say it's safer for the dog if there's an accident, and it's safer for the driver because there's no dog underfoot. Still another school of thought says you should just let your dog hang out without restraint, and hey, the dogs enjoy this more anyway.

Because of their diminutive stature, Isis and Cooper have a car seat in the back that lifts them to the level of the car window and secures their harnesses to the seat belt. That way, they can stick their snouts out of the windows to smell to world go by with some level of security. There's still the danger that the car could kick up a pebble or a bee could buzz by, so we open the car window just enough to stick out a little snout.

Planes: Air travel is even more controversial. We're fortunate that our tiny bundles of joy can fly with us in the passenger cabin, but it still costs $75 a head each way. We'd rather find a way to drive the distance or leave them back at home with a friend or at the pampered pets inn. Val lost a childhood dog due to a heat-induced stroke from being left on the tarmac too long in his crate. There are other dangers, such as runway delays, when the cargo section is not pressurized on the ground, or the risk of connecting flights when a dog ends up in Auckland, New Zealand, while his people go to Oakland. Change can be stressful enough on a pet without being separated from his loved ones and thrown in the cargo hold like a piece of luggage.

If you need to transport your dog by plane, it is critical to fly nonstop, and make sure you schedule takeoff and arrival times when the temperature is below 80°F and above 35°F. All airlines require fees, and most will ask for a health certificate and proof of rabies vaccination.

The question of tranquilizing a dog for a plane journey causes the most contention. Some vets think it's insane to give a dog a sedative before flying. They say a dog will be calmer and less fearful without a disorienting drug. Others think it's crazy not to afford your dog the little relaxation she might not otherwise get without a tranquilizer. Discuss the issue with your vet, who will take into account the trip length and your dog's personality. Cooper prefers the mild sedative effect of a children's antihistamine.

The Ultimate Doggy Bag

Your dog can't pack her own bags, and even if she could, she'd fill them with dog biscuits and squeaky toys. It's important to stash some of those in your dog's vacation kit, but other handy items to bring along are bowls, bedding, a brush, towels (for those inevitable muddy days), a first-aid kit, pooper-scoopers, water, food, prescription drugs, tags, treats, toys, and, of course, this book.

Make sure your dog is wearing her license, identification tag, and rabies tag. We advocate a microchip for your dog in addition to the ever-present collar. On a long trip, you may want to bring along your dog's rabies certificate. We pray it'll never happen, but it's a good idea to bring a couple of photos of your dog to show around, should you ever get separated.

You can snap a disposable ID on your dog's collar, too, showing a cell phone number and the name, address, and phone number of where you'll be staying, or of a friend who'll be home to field calls. That way, if your dog should get lost, at least the finder won't be calling your empty house.

Some people think dogs should drink only water brought from home, so their bodies don't have to get used to too many new things at once. Although Cooper and Isis turn up their noses at water from anywhere other than a bottle poured in their bowl, we've never heard of anyone having a problem giving their dogs tap water from any parts of the Pacific Northwest. Most vets think your dog will be fine drinking tap water in U.S. cities.

Bone Appétit

In many European countries, dogs enter restaurants and dine alongside their folks as if they were people, too. (Or at least they sit and watch and drool while their people dine.) Not so in the United States. Rightly or wrongly, dogs are considered a health threat here. Health inspectors who say they see no reason clean, well-behaved dogs shouldn't be permitted inside a restaurant or on a patio are the exception, rather than the rule.

Fortunately, you don't have to take your dog to a foreign country in order to eat together. Despite a drippy sky, the Pacific Northwest has restaurants with outdoor tables and many of them welcome dogs to join their people for an alfresco experience. The law on outdoor dining is somewhat vague, and you'll encounter many different interpretations of it. In general, as long as your dog doesn't go inside a restaurant to get to outdoor tables in the back and isn't near the food preparation areas, it's probably legal. The decision is then up to the restaurant proprietor. The most common rule of thumb we find is that if the patio is fully enclosed, dogs are discouraged from dining. Coop 'n' Isis have included restaurants with good takeout for those times when outdoor tables are stacked and tucked away.

The restaurants listed in this book have given us permission to tout them as dog-friendly eateries. But keep in mind that rules can change and restaurants can close, so we highly recommend phoning before you set your stomach on a particular kind of cuisine. Since you can safely assume the outdoor tables will move indoors for a while each year, and some restaurants close during colder months or limit their hours, phoning ahead is a doubly wise thing to do. Even for eateries listed in this book, it never hurts to politely ask the manager if your dog may join you before you sit down with your sidekick. Remember, it's the restaurant proprietor, not you, who will be in trouble if someone complains to the health department.

Some fundamental rules of restaurant etiquette: Dogs shouldn't beg from other diners, no matter how delicious the steak looks. They should not attempt to get their snouts (or their entire bodies) up on the table. They should be clean, quiet, and as unobtrusive as possible. If your dog leaves a good impression with the management and other customers, it will help pave the way for all the other dogs who want to dine alongside their best friends in the future.

A Room at the Inn

Good dogs make great hotel guests. They don't steal towels, burn cigarette holes in the bedding, or get drunk and keep the neighbors up all night. In the Pacific Northwest, we've seen a positive trend in the number of places that allow pets. This book lists dog-friendly accommodations of all types, from affordable motels to bed-and-breakfast inns to elegant hotels, and even a few favorite campgrounds—but the basic dog etiquette rules apply everywhere.

Our stance is that dogs should never, *ever* be left alone in your room, even if crated. Leaving a dog alone in a strange place invites serious trouble. Scared, nervous dogs may tear apart drapes, carpeting, and furniture. They may even injure themselves. They might bark nonstop or scare the daylights out of the housekeeper. Just don't do it.

Bring only a house-trained dog to a lodging. How would you like a house-guest to relieve himself in the middle of your bedroom?

One of the hosts we met recommended always entering a new place with your dog on a short leash or crated, unless you've inquired ahead otherwise. We think that's a splendid idea. There are too many factors beyond your control.

Make sure your pooch is flea-free. Otherwise, future guests will be itching to leave. And, while cleanliness is not naturally next to dogliness, matted hair is not going to win you any favors. Scrub your pup elsewhere, though; the new rule we've heard quoted frequently is not to bathe your dog in a lodging's bathroom.

It helps to bring your dog's bed or blanket along for the night. Your dog will feel more at home having a familiar smell in an unfamiliar place, and will be less tempted to jump on the hotel bed. If your dog sleeps on the bed with you at home, bring a sheet or towel and put it on top of the bed so the hotel's bedspread won't get furry or dirty.

After a few days in a hotel, some dogs come to think of it as home. They get territorial. When another hotel guest walks by, it's "Bark! Bark!" When the housekeeper knocks, it's "Bark! Snarl! Bark! Gnash!" Keep your dog quiet, or you'll find yourselves looking for a new home away from home.

For some strange reason, many lodgings prefer small dogs as guests. All we can say is, "Yip! Yap!" It's ridiculous. Isis, bless her excitable little heart, is living proof that large dogs are often much calmer and quieter than their tiny, high-energy cousins.

If you're in a location where you can't find a hotel that will accept your big brute, it's time to try a sell job. Let the manager know how good and quiet your dog is (if he is). Promise he won't eat the bathtub or run around and shake all over the hotel. Offer a deposit or sign a waiver, even if they're not required. It helps if your sweet, immaculate, soppy-eyed pooch sits patiently at your side to convince the decision-maker.

We simply cannot recommend sneaking dogs into hotels. Accommodations have reasons for their rules. It's no fun to feel as if you're going to be caught and thrown out on your hindquarters or charged an arm and a leg and a tail if discovered. You race in and out of your room with your dog as if ducking the dogcatcher. It's better to avoid feeling like a criminal and move on to a more dog-friendly location. The good news is that many hotel chains are realizing the benefits of courting canine travelers. For sure bets, see Hotel Chains in the Resources section of this book.

Unless you know it's a large facility with plenty of availability, call ahead to reserve a dog room and always get prior approval to bring your pets to bed-and-breakfasts and private inns. Listed rates for accommodations are for double rooms, unless otherwise noted. They do not include AARP, AAA, or other discounts you may be entitled to. Always ask about discounts and specials. Likewise, pet fees listed are nonrefundable, per pet, per night unless we say otherwise. The places that don't charge a pet fee are few and far between, but where we haven't listed one, you can assume there's no canine upcharge unless damage is done.

Natural Troubles

Chances are your adventuring will go without a hitch, but you should always be prepared to deal with trouble. Know the basics of animal first aid before you embark on a long journey with your dog.

The more common woes—ticks, burrs, poison oak and ivy, and skunks—can make life with a traveling dog a somewhat trying experience. Ticks are hard to avoid in parts of the Pacific Northwest. Although Lyme disease is rarely reported here, you should check yourself and your dog all over after a day in the country. Don't forget to check ears and between the toes. If you see an attached tick, grasp it with tweezers as close to your dog's skin as possible and pull straight out, gently but steadily, or twist counterclockwise as you pull. Disinfect before and after removing the pest.

The tiny deer ticks that carry Lyme disease are difficult to find. Consult your veterinarian if your dog is lethargic for a few days, has a fever, loses her appetite, or becomes lame. These symptoms could indicate Lyme disease. Some vets recommend a new vaccine that is supposed to prevent the onset of the disease. If you spend serious time in the woods, we suggest you carry a tick collar and have your dog vaccinated.

As for mosquitoes, a medical professional told us that West Nile is expected to reach this region by 2005 or 2006. Our vet hasn't heard of a dog contracting the disease, but *you* are going to want some repellant for yourself.

Burrs and seeds—those pieces of nature that attach to your socks, your sweater, and your dog—are an everyday annoyance. In rare cases, they can be lethal. They may stick in your dog's eyes, nose, ears, or mouth and work their way in. Check every nook and cranny of your dog after a walk in dry fields.

Poison oak and ivy are very common menaces in our woods. Get familiar with them through a friend who knows nature or through a guided walk. Dogs don't generally have reactions, but they easily pass the oils on to people. If you think your dog has made contact with some poison plant, avoid petting her until you can get home and bathe her (preferably with rubber gloves). If you do pet her before you can wash her, don't touch your eyes and be sure to wash your hands immediately. There are several good products on the market specifically for removing poison oak and ivy oils.

If your dog loses a contest with a skunk (and he always will), rinse his eyes first with plain warm water, then bathe him with dog shampoo. Towel him off, then apply tomato juice. If you can't get tomato juice, try using a solution of one pint of vinegar per gallon of water to decrease the stink instead.

Sea water may not seem sinister, but a dog who isn't accustomed to it may not restrain himself from gulping down a few gallons, which makes him sick as a dog, usually all over your car. Keep him hydrated to avoid temptation, and when you arrive at the beach, don't let him race to the sea and drink.

DOG BEACH
DOGS PERMITTED OFF LEASH BEYOND THIS POINT

The Price of Freedom

Dog parks in the Pacific Northwest have yet to pick up on the trend of paying for off-leash play, but most state parks and national forests require daily parking fees unless you are also camping overnight. A $30 annual Northwest Forest Pass is good for all Forest Service (USFS) sites except a few with private concessions. They are available online at www.fs.fed.us/r6/feedemo or at ranger stations. All Washington State Parks charge a $5 daily fee, or require an annual $50 Natural Investment permit available at www.wa.parks.gov/parking/permitmenu.asp or at staffed park booths. Only 26 of Oregon's nearly 200 parks charge a $3 day-use fee. Oregon's annual pass is $25, available with a credit card by phone at 800/551-6949. Various Army Corps of Engineers sites, Bureau of Land Management (BLM) sites, and Fish and Wildlife locations may charge $1 to $10 per day for parking and/or camping.

The comprehensive Washington and Oregon Recreation Pass, new in 2004, is by far the best deal of all for frequent users. For $85 per year, about the cost of a single night's hotel stay, you can get an annual pass that covers you for all Oregon State Parks, 20 participating Washington State Parks, and all other BLM, USFS, Fish and Wildlife, and Army Corps of Engineers recreation sites. Hopefully, more of Washington's State Parks will get with the program in 2005 and beyond. The Washington and Oregon Recreation Pass is available at www.naturenw.org.

Washington fishing, shellfish harvesting, and hunting licenses can be purchased online at www.greatlodge.com. You can also find a store near your destination that sells permits using the Washington Department of Fish and Wildlife's online search engine at http://wdfw.wa.gov. For Oregon, go to www.dfw.state.or.us and click the Licensing and Regulations link.

A Dog in Need

If you don't currently have a dog but could provide a good home for one, we'd like to make a plea on behalf of all the unwanted dogs who will be euthanized tomorrow—and the day after that and the day after that. Cooper came from a rescue organization and Isis from previous owners who knew they couldn't give her the personal attention she deserved. In their extended family, Coop 'n' Isis have a grandmother with two more dachshunds, an uncle with a boxer, and an aunt with a corgi mix, all rescued. Animal shelters and humane organizations are overflowing with dogs who would devote their lives to being your best buddy, your faithful traveling companion, and a dedicated listener to all your tales. We also strongly support efforts to control the existing dog population—spay or neuter your dogs! Just do it.

Keep in Touch

Readers of *The Dog Lover's Companion to the Pacific Northwest* mean everything to us. The Wonder Wieners explore the Pacific Northwest so you and your dogs can spend true quality time together. Your input is very important. We can't wait to hear from many wonderful dogs and their people about new dog-friendly places or old dog-friendly places we simply didn't know about. If you have any suggestions or insights to offer, please contact us using the information listed in the front of this book.

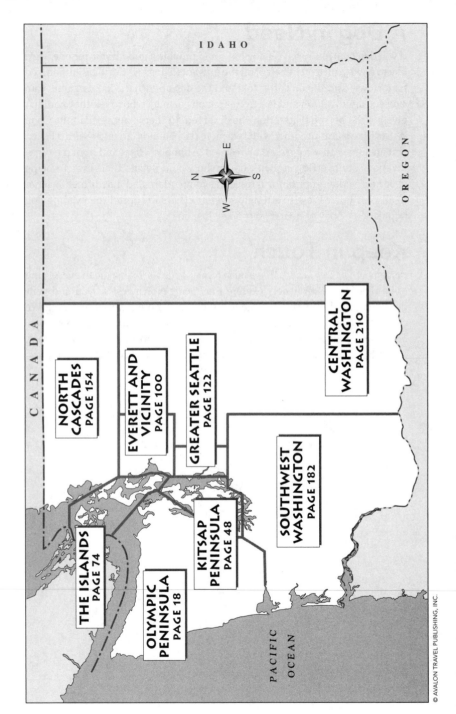

IDAHO

OREGON

CANADA

N E
W S

NORTH CASCADES
PAGE 154

EVERETT AND VICINITY
PAGE 100

GREATER SEATTLE
PAGE 122

CENTRAL WASHINGTON
PAGE 210

THE ISLANDS
PAGE 74

OLYMPIC PENINSULA
PAGE 18

KITSAP PENINSULA
PAGE 48

SOUTHWEST WASHINGTON
PAGE 182

PACIFIC OCEAN

© AVALON TRAVEL PUBLISHING, INC.

WASHINGTON

Washington is nicknamed the Evergreen State, not because of the greenbacks that line the pockets of billionaire Bill Gates, but because of its abundance of majestic conifers, nurtured by our infamous rains. While money may not grow on trees, fun sure does—and on the state's beaches, in city and county parks, national forests, and more than 125 state parks. In the Emerald City of Seattle and its suburbs alone, there are a dozen off-leash parks that make other cities' dogs green with envy.

Washingtonian dogs are happy to let the world at large think of the state for its famous, high-ticket exports—Microsoft software, Boeing airliner jets, and Starbucks coffee, to name a few—while they go about enjoying the natural riches of the region that can't be exported, bought, or sold.

For starters, you can't get very far in Washington without running into a mountain and all the great outdoor activity that implies. The Olympic Mountain Range dominates the western skyline, and the Cascades line the east. Mt. Rainier, Mt. Adams, and Mount St. Helens tower to the south, and Mt. Baker to the north. As you take a ferry to the islands, cross Puget Sound bridges to the peninsulas, or walk a remote beach on the Pacific Ocean, you realize how much water shapes the landscape, and not just the gray stuff from above. While many people wait out the drizzle in more bookstores, movie theaters, and coffeehouses per capita than anywhere else in the country, there are as many who put on microfiber, grow webbed feet, and get out "24/7/365." You'll find these people and their dogs in the best places, on, say, the Mountains to Sound Bicycling Greenway, or kayaking and canoeing the Cascade Marine Highway, or on extensive Rails-to-Trails multi-use pathways.

While you're at it, Washington's 24 scenic byways prove the theory that getting there is half the fun. A Department of Transportation Scenic Byway Map, free at visitors centers, shows you how to make your journey as worthwhile as your destination.

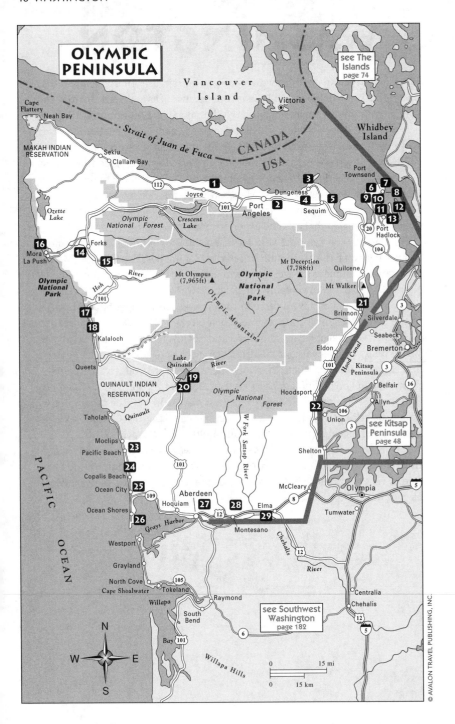

© AVALON TRAVEL PUBLISHING, INC.

CHAPTER 1
Olympic Peninsula

First, the bad news. The core of the Olympic Peninsula, and about half of its coastline, consists of 922,651 acres of wilderness where dogs are forbidden on trails, in buildings, or anywhere in the backcountry. This is the **Olympic National *Park*** (ONP). Dogs are allowed in national park campgrounds and they may stay in the car if you travel up to Hurricane Ridge or into the Hoh Rainforest.

Now for the good news. That still leaves 632,324 acres of **Olympic National *Forest*** (ONF), surrounding the national park where your dog is allowed, on leash. The ONF offers countless recreation opportunities for pups with boundless energy. In many cases, the only things that restrict a dog's life, other than an eight-foot tether, are high tides that limit the amount of beachfront real estate at seaside parks. You may want to consult a tide table before you head out, available for a few bucks at most convenience stores.

It gets better. In addition to state, county, and city parks that are lively, beautiful, and dog-friendly, the peninsula is host to 101 campgrounds; a few of the best are listed here. Lest this paints too rosy a picture, you will have to

PICK OF THE LITTER—OLYMPIC PENINSULA

BEST PARKS
Chetzemoka, Port Townsend (page 28)
Fort Flagler, Marrowstone Island (page 31)

BEST BEACHES
Rialto Beach, La Push (page 34)
Griffiths-Priday, Copalis Beach (page 42)

BEST TRAIL
Quinault Loop, Lake Quinault (page 37)

BEST PLACE TO EAT
Macadoo's Barbeque, Port Townsend (page 30)

BEST PLACES TO STAY
Sunset Marine Resort, Sequim (page 25)
Palace Hotel, Port Townsend (page 30)
Ocean City State Park Camping, Ocean City (page 43)

prepare yourself and your sad-eyed basset hound for the sight of clear-cut forests in some areas—forestry is the area's largest industry and the majority of land not protected by the federal government belongs to logging companies.

NATIONAL FORESTS

Olympic National Forest

ONF is divided into two ranger districts, Hood Canal and Pacific, with four offices around the Olympic Peninsula. At each ranger station, you can get current information about campground listings, weather, and road conditions. Trail descriptions include trailhead directions, highlights, length, elevation gain, and latest reported conditions. If the office is closed, pertinent information is posted on a bulletin board and online. Even if you've been to a specific destination before, stop by or call ahead, as frequent closures and restrictions are reported due to fallen trees, landslides, spring floods, and other whims of Mother Nature. ONF trails are serious business, all of which can be described as backcountry; know your limits, register at trailheads, and take the essentials. Forks: 437 Tillicum Ln.; 360/374-6522; Quilcene: 295142 Hwy.

101 S.; 360/765-2200; Hoodsport: 150 N. Lake Cushman Rd.; 360/877-5254; Quinault: 353 Southshore Rd.; 360/288-2525. www.fs.fed.us/r6/olympic.

Joyce

The town is tiny, the views huge. The Strait of Juan de Fuca Highway, Highway 112, is an American Scenic Byway that hugs the jagged cliffs and cedar forests on one side and the ocean on the other. It winds 60 miles from west of Port Angeles to the Makah Indian Reservation at Neah Bay. Across the water is Vancouver Island, British Columbia.

PARKS, BEACHES, AND RECREATION AREAS

◼ Salt Creek Recreation Area

🐾 🐾 🐾 (See Olympic Peninsula map on page 18)

Salt Creek/Tongue Point/Crescent Beach/Fort Hayden is known by four names, with three paws, and two campgrounds, for one park. Salt Creek Recreation Area is the name you'll see on the signs. For starters, there's a playground and immense fields designed for RV camping that also happen to be a blast for dogs to run around on. There are fun trails; the shortest follows the bluff past two heavily camouflaged concrete bunkers that are simultaneously creepy and cool, built before World War II for the Fort Hayden military reservation. Just behind the main gate to the right are more trails: a 1.1-mile jaunt to a cove, and a longer, rockier, narrower 2.4-mile path to the vista at Striped Peak nearby (that makes five names, doesn't it?).

Isis feels they use the term "beach access" too liberally. Out of the five "walkways," four are concrete stairs that end in the sky over rocky, slippery, dangerous cliffs. Not very inviting. The only practical way is to drive out the main entrance to the west and pay $5 a head at the private Crescent Beach RV Park for all-day access to the most pristine section of sand. Once there, you can walk around Tongue Point to study the tide pools.

Turn north on Camp Hayden Road, 13 miles west of Port Angeles on State Route 112.

PLACES TO STAY

Crescent Beach RV Park: Cooper isn't in the habit of recommending RV parks, but this one is different. First of all, the folks here own a half mile of pristine beachfront. People and pets happily shell out $5 a head for the privilege of hanging out for the day. The lot is a field, shaded by large trees with nearby deer and bald eagles, and every site has an ocean view. It costs $30 a night for a tent site, plus $5 per pet. 2860 Crescent Beach Rd.; 360/928-3344 or 866/690-3344; www.olypen.com/crescent.

Port Angeles

While it's true that dogs are not allowed in the Olympic National Park, you'd deserve a "bad human" scolding if you left out a drive up to Hurricane Ridge. Starting in Port Angeles, it takes about 45 minutes to drive up the cliff-hanging, gasp-at-every-turn road to the top of the Northwestern world. The bird's-eye panorama of the wilderness and mountains elicits the kind of "ooohs" and "aaahs" normally reserved for Fourth of July fireworks. The friendly park ranger said that no one will hassle you if you let your dog out at the top, on leash, as long as you don't go in the building with him or on the trails. Your pup will spend some quality hang time with his head out the car window.

PARKS, BEACHES, AND RECREATION AREAS

2 Jesse Webster Park

🐾🐾🐾 (See Olympic Peninsula map on page 18)

There's nothing here except lush green grass and really tall trees for two whole city blocks, the doggie definition of divine. Okay, there is a dirt trail cutting diagonally across and a bench or table or two, but your field spaniel will be too busy noticing the forest for the trees. Bordered on all sides by residential homes, this refuge is quiet and shady.

From U.S. Highway 101, go west on Eunice for two blocks and turn right onto 2nd Street for streetside parking. Open 5 A.M.–11 P.M.

PLACES TO EAT

Bonney's Bakery: Snag an order sheet at the To Go counter and build the sandwich of your dreams to enjoy on the large front patio or next door in Veteran's Memorial Park. Bonney believes there's more to life than pastry—omelettes and quiches provide protein at breakfast and daily soups and fruit smoothies add zest to lunch. The staff makes whole New York–style pizza pies to go, too. 215 Lincoln St., Port Angeles; 360/457-8992.

Van Goes: Maybe it takes a crazy person to put pizza and Mexican food together in one takeout joint, but his pies and burritos are works of art. Your choice of pizza sauces includes red, ranch, pesto, curry, BBQ, and teriyaki. Toppings can be equally unusual, or not—it's up to you. Burritos, nachos, quesadillas, and huge tacos are more traditional, enjoyed at the table out front or "to goes." 814 S. C St., Port Angeles; 360/417-5600.

PLACES TO STAY

Northwest Manor: This isn't your grandmother's frou-frou bed-and-breakfast, it's a contemporary home with an extensive collection of Northwest Coast Native American art. From the balcony of your second-floor suite, you have commanding views of the Olympics and downtown. Host Rich knows every good fishing hole and playground on the peninsula. Hostess Bonita is half-Makah Indian. She makes her authentic smoked salmon quiche and fry bread with homemade blackberry jam for breakfast. Über-friendly black Lab Griff greets you at the door. The room rate is $95–110 per night plus a $15 pet fee. 1320 Marie View Drive; 360/452-5839 or 888/229-7052; www.nwmanor.com.

More Accommodations: Please look under Chain Hotels in the Resources section for additional places to stay in this area.

The Sequim-Dungeness Valley

Sequim sits in the Banana Belt, a crescent of land in the shape of the fruit that escapes the soggy fate of the Pacific Northwest, averaging 300 sunny days each year (see its Website at www.visitsun.com). The biggest deal each year is the Irrigation Festival, celebrating its 110th annual in 2005. Sequim reuses 100 percent of reclaimed water in upland areas to grow its famed lavender, strawberry, and raspberry crops. The region is also home to a migrating herd of nearly a hundred elk, which gives the city no small share of headaches when it wanders through town.

Dungeness is home to the Dungeness crab, a tasty delicacy you should try at the famous **Three Crabs** restaurant (alas, no patio seating). If you're looking for a nice scenic drive, but your dog whines about being trapped in the car all day, the Dungeness Scenic Loop is a perfect compromise. It's short, you get to see the scenery, and there are three pet-worthy parks to stop at along the way.

PARKS, BEACHES, AND RECREATION AREAS

3 Dungeness Recreation Area

🐾🐾🐾 (See Olympic Peninsula map on page 18)

This is another place where a technicality could get you into trouble. Dogs *are* allowed in the 216-acre Dungeness Recreation Area, which consists of marshland, sand dunes, and cliffs leading up to the Dungeness Spit. Dogs *are not* allowed in the **Dungeness National Wildlife Refuge,** the land that makes up the seven-mile spit itself, the longest natural spit in the United States.

The mile-long scenic bluff trail offers phenomenal vistas that will give even your dog goose bumps. You'll come upon them suddenly as you make your way through tall dune grasses. Keep dogs on leash and stay behind the fence to avoid tumbling hundreds of feet to the beach below; go over that ledge and Lassie herself won't be able to rescue you.

In season, hunting dogs can strut their stuff as they flush out and retrieve quail and other migratory birds on Wednesday, Saturday, Sunday, and holidays. Camping is available year-round.

From U.S. Highway 101, turn north on Kitchen-Dick Road, turn left on Lotzgesell Road, and left again on Voice of America Road leading into the park. Open 7 A.M.–7 P.M. 360/683-5847; www.clallam.net/countyparks.

4 Robin Hill Farm

🐾🐾🐾 (See Olympic Peninsula map on page 18)

It would be enough if this county park had only its six miles of trails winding through 150 acres of managed forest. The 20 acres of open grass fields would be satisfactory. The five acres of wetlands are fine. Put it all together, and add in experimental gardens, pastures, crops, an orchard, and the occasional farm animal, and you've got the wonder known as Robin Hill. About 3.5 miles of trails are leveled, gravel footpaths; the rest, designated as equestrian trails, are narrower and have a wood chip or dirt surface and a greater variety of elevation changes. Your dog is allowed to walk the horse trails as long as he's not a "yippy" dog, according to park rules. Although the humans found it disconcerting, Cooper and Isis didn't mind the "pop, pop, pop" sound of rifles from the nearby shooting range.

From U.S. Highway 101, turn north on Kitchen-Dick Road, west on Old Olympic Highway, left on Vautier Road, and right on Pinnell Road. There you'll find the parking lot and a garbage can.

5 Carrie Blake Park

🐾🐾 (See Olympic Peninsula map on page 18)

Like pearls before swine, or in front of shelties for that matter, much of the beauty of this park may be lost on your pet. She can still enjoy walking the paved paths with you around the impeccably landscaped gardens, ponds, fields, streams, and recreation areas. City planners recognized this fact and conveniently placed garbage cans and doggie bag dispensers at several locations throughout.

While your dog is getting her daily exercise, you'll view the Zen rock garden and a native wetland plants display. Most beautiful is the Friendship Garden and Lantern, donated by Yamasaki, Japan, Sequim's sister city. You'll see sculpture, totems, and the bronze bust of local-boy-made-good Matt Dryke, 1984 Olympic gold medalist and international skeet shooting champion. The winding walkways take you past several water features, including bridges over streams, waterfalls, and ponds—all a part of the park's progressive water reclamation program. It's a good place to meet locals who are deservedly proud of their park and come often.

Take the Washington Avenue exit from U.S. Highway 101 and follow the signs to turn right on North Blake Street.

PLACES TO EAT

Candy Depot and Depot Deli: A candy store, coffee shop, ice cream parlor, and sandwich shop each occupy real railroad cars, painted in bright candy colors, on an elevated platform with umbrella-covered tables. Owner Bruce gave the dogs bites of roast beef. You should try biting into a mesquite chicken sub. 282023 Hwy. 101, Discovery Bay; 360/385-9490.

Cone Heads: Order at the window for gourmet ice cream, espresso, and signature sausage dogs. The breakfast wrap is so good it'll make you weep, with sausage, eggs, onions, cheese, garlic, and mild peppers wrapped in a tortilla. The gal at the drive-through gave the dogs biscuits, which didn't do much to ease the pain of watching their owner chow down on all the rest. 291 Washington Ave., Sequim; 360/683-1232.

PLACES TO STAY

Dungeness Recreation Area Camping: There are 67 campsites in two loops, each loop with bathroom and shower facilities. All sites are hard-packed sand with picnic tables and fire pots. There are no electric or water hookups, but water is provided on the campground. Fees are $14 for non-county residents, $12 for residents, available on a first-come, first-served basis. 554 Voice of America Rd. W.; 360/683-5847.

Groveland Cottage: The Secret Room behind this 115-year-old bed-and-breakfast is open to traveling pets and their weary companions. The kitchen-and-bath unit is tucked away on grounds featuring lovely gardens where a dog can get out and smell the roses. It rents for $85–95 per night plus $10/day for pets. Owner Simone is a realtor who can hook you up with dog-friendly vacation rental properties in the area as well. 4861 Sequim-Dungeness Way, Dungeness; 360/683-3565 or 800/879-8859; www.sequimvalley.com.

Sunset Marine Resort: The resort has been around since the 1930s and some of the regulars have been coming since then. The property's cabins, ancient boat sheds, and rickety docks have that priceless weathered look that can't be faked, whereas cottage interiors are bright and new. You'll feel right at home, except that this home includes waterfront cabins on a private beach! The Clam Cottage, Boat House, and Landing allow pets. Dogs also tag along in the kayaks available for rent for $35 for four hours. Rates are $145–165, plus $15 per pet. 40 Buzzard Ridge Rd., Sequim; 360/681-4166; www.sunsetmarineresort.com.

More Accommodations: Please look under Chain Hotels in the Resources section for additional places to stay in this area.

Port Townsend

Port Townsend wins the award for the dog-friendliest downtown in Washington. The sheer number of dogs walking the historic district will tell you they are welcome here, then there are the dog bowls outside nearly every shop and plenty of outdoor places to eat, sit, and relax. Several stores, including April Fool's and Ancestral Spirits Gallery, have resident canines. The buildings of the core shopping and hotel district, along Water Street, feature restored Victorian and Romanesque architecture. It's a pretty maritime town, perched on the northeast tip of the peninsula. As a dog lover, you can appreciate it all the more, knowing that your pets can enjoy so much of it with you. For a complete list of parks in the area, more than 25, check out www.ptguide.com/recreation.

PARKS, BEACHES, AND RECREATION AREAS

🐾 North Beach

🐾🐾🐾 (See Olympic Peninsula map on page 18)

North Beach is technically only an acre, but you'd never know it, because once you're on the sand, you can walk and beachcomb for miles. The beach at this county park connects to Fort Worden, which connects to Chetzemoka, to create an extensive swath of coastline. An upland trail through waist-high dune grass and eventually into the woods also connects North Beach to Fort Worden. Even better, there's no fee to park at this public access point, unlike

DIVERSION

Your dog can and should come with you for healing retreats at the **Annapurna Center For Self Healing (ACSH),** in Port Townsend, if she doesn't mind sleeping in her kennel in your room. After all, dogs are healers, proven to lower blood pressure, prevent heart attacks, and lengthen the lives of their owners. ACSH is a feng shui environment, created in an 1881 Victorian home built by seafarer Captain Sewell, a couple of blocks from the beach. ACSH incorporates live, organic, vegan food with a multitude of therapies to heal your body, mind, and spirit. Massage, yoga, reflexology, colonics, iridology, Turkish steam baths, a sauna, and long walks on the beach are among the treatments designed to create a healthier you, inside and out. As you practice your Downward Facing Dog and Upward Facing Dog yoga poses, don't be surprised if you find yourself relaxing your dogma and embracing the Zen-like existence dogs have already perfected. 538 Adams St., Port Townsend; 360/385-2909; www.theannapurna.com.

NATURE HIKES AND URBAN WALKS

It's easy to get your daily dose of exercise walking the **Waterfront Trail** in Port Townsend. This paved trail extends 2.5 miles in either direction from the center of the city. The northern half is more developed; alongside the asphalt are lawn plots with picnic tables or viewing benches. The southern section is more scenic, passing through a lagoon and circling the inner harbor on the way out to the Coast Guard Station at Ediz Hook. Through the center of town, the path switches to sidewalk, then returns to a wider pavement. Park at the Art Fiero Marine Life Center at the bottom of Lincoln Street and be sure to check out the octopus topiary before taking to the trail.

the $5 you pay in the state park. Above the beach, there's a mowed lawn area, picnic shelter, water, and restrooms.

From Sims Way, take a left on Kearney Street, left on Blaine Street, and a sharp right on San Juan Avenue. Stay on San Juan past Admiralty Avenue to turn left on 49th Street and right on Kuhn Street to the end.

7 Fort Worden

🐾🐾🐾 (See Olympic Peninsula map on page 18)

White clapboard buildings lined in soldierly order on a high bluff offer clues to the past of this former military installation. Fort Worden, along with Fort Flagler on Marrowstone Island and Fort Casey on Whidbey Island, formed a three-fort defense system dubbed "The Triangle of Death," designed to protect the entrance to Puget Sound. The main asset to protect was the shipbuilding yard at Bremerton, but the potential enemy changed, from 1898, through two world wars, up to the mid-1950s. In the end, all the defense buildup proved unnecessary. Twelve massive gun batteries never fired shots in battle, and all such fortifications have since been decommissioned and transformed into state parks.

The park is huge, encompassing everything from forested hiking trails to sand dunes. The excellent beach curves around a point from the north to the east and connects to other beaches north and south. Peace Mile Trail, Artillery Hill, and other headland trails keep hike-minded dogs busy. The parade grounds, five blocks long, is perfect for games of Red Rover, and an entire scout troop can play a thrilling game of Capture the Flag in and around the overgrown remains of the batteries.

From Sims Way, turn left up the hill on Washington Street, and immediately left again on Walker Street. Walker takes a sharp bend to the right and becomes Cherry Street, which leads straight into the park entrance. Parking is $5 per day. 360/902-8844.

🖪 Chetzemoka

🐾🐾🐾🐾🐆 (See Olympic Peninsula map on page 18)

The dog rule at this fabulous city park is a perfectly reasonable policy that Cooper thinks should be adopted worldwide: "Dogs must be on leash of eight feet or less, *unless* under voice or signal control of a competent person." It goes on to say dogs shouldn't be allowed to rummage in the flower and tropical water gardens and they should refrain from running in packs, especially in the play areas, where they would alarm the children.

This community gathering place is named for a Native American who befriended European settlers. The bandstand, a replica of the first in 1904, regularly features barbershop quartets, brass brands, and weddings to be enjoyed on the wide lawns that slope down to the water. The beach and extensive tidelands connect northward to Fort Worden's stretch of sand.

Go all the way into town along Water Street until one block before it ends. Turn left on Monroe Street, go up the hill eight blocks, and turn right on Blaine Street. It's one block to the park entrance and angled parking. 360/344-3055.

🖪 Kah Tai Lagoon

🐾🐾 (See Olympic Peninsula map on page 18)

Coop 'n' Isis have come to love places with the words lagoon, marsh, or wetland in their titles because there are so many fascinating distractions for dogs. Although short, the .3-mile path along the southwest shore of the lagoon is a feast for dog senses. It's a good idea to apply a spritz of bug spray or dab of citronella lotion to you and your hairy beast before heading to the lagoon. The bugs can get a bit thick.

The protected area includes 80 acres maintained to protect and encourage waterfowl nesting and use. Bird watchers and bird dogs will be thrilled, watching from a respectful distance. In other words, no harassing or hunting the wildlife! A rough-hewn wood bench and bridge across the lagoon give you spaces for quiet moments of reflection.

From Sims Way, turn left onto Haines Street, then right at the stop sign at the Haines Place parking lot behind the McDonalds.

🔟 Larry Scott Memorial Trail

🐾🐾🐾 (See Olympic Peninsula map on page 18)

Built by the paper mill, which also built a water pipeline for the city in 1928, this 3.5-mile-and-growing trail wanders through fields along the highway until it breaks out and hugs the hill around the bay to end up at the boat haven in downtown Port Townsend. The trail is gravel, and it was created from forest service roads and railroad beds, so it is comfy, wide, and level. Plus, there's a good variety of flora and fauna to hold a dog's interest for the duration.

Along the way, you'll pass the mill, which is still in operation making brown paper grocery bags out of scrap sawmill dust and recycled corrugated boxes. Even though you'll see steam billowing out of its stacks and strange pools of milky water, this mill is on the cutting edge of environmental protection. North of the mill is the best section of trail, with views of Admiralty Inlet and Port Townsend Bay.

To reach the southern end, turn right on Frederick Street from State Route 19 northbound, and right again onto Otto Street. There is limited roadside parking. Other trailhead options are on Mill Road and Thomas Street, both right turns off of S.R. 19.

🐾 Old Fort Townsend

🐾🐾🐾 (See Olympic Peninsula map on page 18)

Fort Townsend was built in 1853 to protect Port Townsend from a Native American uprising, but it was such a poorly planned effort that, should a battle have ever occurred, the Port would have had to protect the Fort. Guess no one told them a couple of well-trained German shepherds would've done the trick.

Although the half-mile beach is okay, it's the 6.5 miles of trails through wooded glades that perk up shaggy ears. The main road bisects the park, with trailheads snaking out in either direction. At the end of the road, the spacious fields of the former encampment are good for a roll in the grass, a game of fetch, or the toss of a Frisbee. Two of the trails that start at the beach have self-guided interpretive markers—one for nature, the other for historic highlights. If you can score one of four impromptu parking spaces at the entrance, you'll be closer to the rest of the hiking paths.

From State Route 20, turn east on Old Fort Townsend Road approximately two miles south of Port Townsend. Open 8 A.M.–dusk. Parking is $5 a day. Forty campsites are available in the summer on a first-come, first-served basis. 360/902-8844.

PLACES TO EAT

Dos Okies: A hulking steel grill and a trailer on wheels are all these two good ole boys from Oklahoma need to create phenomenal, mouth-watering, pit-barbecued ribs, chicken, and salmon for you to take on your picnic. Their zippy sauce will make your lips buzz; mild sauce is available in case you forgot your antacids. It almost made Isis miss Texas. Almost. Cash only please. Okie Uno is Larry and Okie Dos is Ron; true to form, they advise you never to buy barbecue from a skinny man. 5309 Kuhn St.; 360/301-0120.

Lehani's Café & Coffee: It is refreshing to find a place that emphasizes light, healthy, all natural fare. Lehani's makes daily salads, vegetarian dishes, couscous, and "live" fresh veggie pizza, all necessary to balance out their rich, thick cakes, pastries, coffee, and locally made chocolates. 221 Taylor St.; 360/385-3961.

Macadoo's Barbeque: Isis fought for Dos Okies, Cooper for Macadoo's, and the only way we could tear these two off each other is to include both. Macadoo is the pet name for the owner's pound mutt Max. They have a large outdoor patio and a tub of dog biscuits waiting on the bar. It looks too respectable for a rib joint, but don't worry, the pulled pork, jalapeño-cheese cornbread, beans, and slaw are for real, worth begging for. Chef/Owner Jeff hails from Tennessee; pull up a chair and he'll pour you a drink "for medicinal purposes." 600 W. Sims Way; 360/379-1619.

PLACES TO STAY

Aladdin Motor Inn: By far the best deal in town, this motel's rooms go for $85 for a view, $75 without, plus a $7 per pet daily fee. It is outside the hustle and bustle of the historic district and thankfully quieter. The beach is practically yours, with a waterside picnic table. The rooms are decent and continental breakfast is included. 2333 Washington St.; 360/385-3747 or 800/281-3747.

Big Red Barn: This romantic retreat is perfectly located, one block from the wonders of Fort Worden State Park. Every detail is perfect, details such as warm wood walls and floors, a gas fireplace, jetted tub for two, fluffy bed, garden patio, and coffee, muffins, and fresh fruit for breakfast delivered to your barn door. The pet fee is a little steep, $30 per dog. The nightly rate of $135 is more reasonable, considering the amount of pampering your hosts provide. 309 V St.; 360/385-4837; www.bigredbarngetaway.com.

Bishop Hotel: All the rooms in this boutique are non-smoking, and all are suites with kitchenettes, private baths, and separate bedrooms. For character, some rooms have the original brick walls and all are decorated in antiques, which are for sale if you get the itch. Formal gardens and an open field surround the property. Rates range $99–199; the pet fee is $15 per day. 714 Washington St.; 360/385-6122 or 800/824-4738; www.bishopvictorian.com.

Palace Hotel: This gorgeous Richardson Romanesque building with 14-foot ceilings and soaring windows has a colorful history as a brothel 1925–1933, among other things. Each room is extensively decorated with antiques, each different, and each named after a girl who worked in The Palace of Sweets, as it was known. The Madam's Room, restored with red velvet wallpaper and deep green woodwork, is the favorite. Rates range $49–139 by size and season, plus $10 per pet, per night. The lowest-priced rooms share a hall bath. 1004 Water St.; 360/385-0773 or 800/962-0741; www.palacehotelpt.com.

Port Hadlock and Marrowstone Island

Archaeological digs establish this area as one of the oldest continuously occupied areas of Washington, with evidence of Coastal Salish inhabitants dating back at least 12,000 years. Three dominant tribes, S'Klallam, Duwamish, and Suquamish, shared the area in relative harmony only after they had removed members of the Chemakum tribe—an effort led by Chief Sealth, after whom Seattle is named. Tribes would gather from the entire region for Potlach (share the wealth) celebrations of competition and feasting.

PARKS, BEACHES, AND RECREATION AREAS

❶❷ Fort Flagler

🐾🐾🐾🐾 (See Olympic Peninsula map on page 18)

Even wet-nosed visitors have trouble knowing where to begin when describing all the wonders of this former military installation turned state park. There is so much to do and see, they won't even notice that they're not allowed in the environmental learning center, interpretive museum, hostel, vacation homes, or dorm-style camps.

Starting with the beaches, there's almost four miles of saltwater shoreline with three access points. Turn right and drive past the gun emplacement when you first enter the park to hit the south beach, favored by Isis. The second beach curves around the Western Fisheries Research Center at Marrowstone Point. It's got the best views, including Mt. Baker, Mt. Rainier, and the Cascades. Here, a map shows where the nine gun emplacements are located and gives a little history lesson. Short climbs to the top of cannon embankments provide the highest, choicest vistas.

The third beach is the windiest, where you'll find the kite-flying fanatics. It's also the most crowded, with RV camping right on the sand. A concession stand operates in the summer, thank goodness, because the Popsicles and ice cream won't keep in a cooler. People are busy water skiing, fishing, and power boating, or not so busy with their butts parked in lawn chairs. It's one enormous block party from Memorial Day straight on through to Labor Day. A forest trail loops the 784-acre park, with three shortcuts across to the beaches, totaling five miles of trails altogether.

Take State Route 19 to the four-way stop in Chimacum, turn right onto Chimacum-Center Road, right on Oak Bay Road in Port Hadlock, and left onto State Route 116. Fort Flagler is at the end of S.R. 116 on Marrowstone Island. Parking is $5 per day. Open 6:30 A.M.–10 P.M. 360/385-3701.

13 South Indian Island Parks

😻😻😻 (See Olympic Peninsula map on page 18)

This is the local moniker for two waterfront parks connected by a quarter-mile headland trail. The first park you come upon is also called Lloyd L. Good Memorial Park. This meadow on a slope recalls those fond memories of when you were a kid and found that perfect hill to roll down, getting so dizzy that you couldn't stand up. With a view across the water to Old Fort Townsend, it's brilliant for picnics. This is where Cooper met a fox terrier named Duke who's been traveling on the back of a motorcycle in his own carrier for 11 years.

The second stop's official name is the Jefferson County Day-use Park. A dirt road leads down to parking and picnicking on a wide, flat beach. You can take the trail between the two, or when the tide is low, walk along the oyster shell beach.

The first park entrance is immediately to your right as you cross the first bridge on State Route 116 to Indian Island, the second is a couple hundred yards farther. Parks close at dusk.

PLACES TO STAY

Fort Flagler State Park: Camping is available March–October. There are 47 campsites, suited only for tents, in the woods, with some water views through the trees, and 54 sites on the open beach, with easy water access and full views, populated mainly by RV users. Cost is $16 for non-utility sites, $22 for hookup sites. Reserve a space up to 90 days in advance by calling 888/CAMP OUT (888/226-7688) or online at www.camis.com/wa. 10541 Flagler Rd., Nordland.

Forks

On U.S. Highway 101 from Port Angeles to Forks, you'll drive a spectacular 12-mile road that skirts the southern coast of glacier-carved Lake Crescent. Forks is the only true commercial center on the coast, with the honor of having the only stoplight on a 160-mile stretch of highway. If you don't stop here for groceries at the **Thriftway,** you're at the mercy of a few, scattered trading posts and mercantile stores for more than a hundred miles. It's also the best place to stay if you prefer the reliability of a modern motel to the quirks of historic lodges and backwoods cabins. The Forks Timber Museum and Loggers Memorial give you an excellent perspective on the industry that shaped this entire region.

PARKS, BEACHES, AND RECREATION AREAS

14 Tillicum Park

😾 😾 😾 (See Olympic Peninsula map on page 18)

The City of Forks maintains this 15-acre park, which features two tennis courts, three ball fields, a playground, horseshoe pits, a covered picnic area, and open spaces. It's that last one, open spaces, that particularly appeals to Isis. Her favorite sport is soccer, which she plays by alternately biting, nudging, and dribbling on the ball in frenzied circles until she collapses, panting with glee. She played here on the natural turf and no one as much as said "boo" about her being off-leash. Kids get a kick out of the playground and looking at the real Shay steam engine train and Vietnam-era tank on display behind safety fences.

The city park is on the east side of N. Forks Avenue, which is also U.S. Highway 101, on the north end of town. 360/374-2531.

15 Bogachiel River Trail

😾 😾 😾 (See Olympic Peninsula map on page 18)

The hosts at Miller Tree Inn raved about this 1.5-mile section of moderately difficult hiking. It's basically the only place where dogs are allowed to experience the Hoh, the world's sole coniferous rainforest. It is an otherworldly trip through a deep and mysterious river valley, dripping with vegetation. Cooper believes that scat sniffing along this trail is far more exotic than the run-of-the-mill fare he's used to on his usual around-the-neighborhood walks. There is a colloquialism about this remote region: "This isn't the end of the world, but you can see it from here." World's end looks good from a dog's-eye view.

You'll feel like you're going to the ends of the earth to get there. Go south on U.S. Highway 101 from Forks for five miles, look for mile marker #188, then immediately turn east on Undie Road. Travel another five miles to the trailhead, where there is plenty of parking.

PLACES TO EAT

Pacific Pizza: The grilled panini sandwiches and gourmet pizzas are just about the only things you can get to go in this town, made from "Monteleone Family Recipes." 870 S. Forks Ave., Forks; 360/374-2626.

PLACES TO STAY

Dew Drop Inn: Dogs may join you at this motel, so clean that your bichon frise will stay winter white. Rooms are extra large, and there's a huge lawn for morning ablutions, rolling around in the previous night's dew drops. Pets are $10.95 per stay (.95 for tax, so they say). The most you'll pay is $80 a night in the high season, as low as $42 in the winter. 100 Fern Hill Rd.; 360/374-4055 or 888/433-9376; www.dewdropinnmotel.com.

Manitou Lodge: Handsome Romeo, the massive but docile Great Dane/Doberman mix, will welcome you to stay at either the Eagle ($90 per night) or Owl ($100 per night) cottages next to the main building. The lodge is an oasis of luxury in thick, primal rainforest. It is absolutely the Wieners' favorite place to stay on the peninsula, six miles from Rialto Beach. The pet fee is $10 per night. 813 Kilmer Rd.; 360/374-6295; www.manitoulodge.com.

Miller Tree Inn: An 80-year old cherry tree towers several stories high outside the window of the Orchard Suite, where dogs are welcome as long as they don't chase the cat. The bed-and-breakfast is nicely situated away from the center of town in an apple orchard. A hot tub and hammock are outside your separate entrance; inside are a king-size bed, queen-size hide-a-bed, full bath, and kitchenette. Hearty breakfasts feature treats such as blueberry French toast or gingerbread pancakes. Rates are $95–115 plus a total of $10 per night for pets. 654 E. Division St.; 360/374-6806 or 800/943-6563; www.millertreeinn.com.

La Push

The Pacific Ocean is only 12 miles from Forks, near La Push. The land is the home of the Quileute First Nations people. The water is home to migrating gray whales, seals, and harbor porpoises, all frequently sighted from the beaches. Dogs will be ecstatic to learn that the abundant wildlife in the region includes an overabundance of squirrels, chipmunks, seagulls, and crows, all of whom are fair game for chasing.

PARKS, BEACHES, AND RECREATION AREAS

16 Rialto Beach

🐾🐾🐾🐾 (See Olympic Peninsula map on page 18)

In a glorious exception to the Olympic National Park rule stated above, dogs are allowed on Rialto Beach to the north, bordered by Ellen Creek. If you get to only one beach in Washington, this is the one you should see. Photographers pilgrimage to its shores, the definition of dramatic, pounding waves on a windswept coast.

Trails of river rock lead you through the driftwood, and as you approach the beach, the stones get smaller, turning into pebbles, and finally the smoothest of sand. Intense storms carve and shape a unique landscape, with sea-stack rock formations offshore and driftwood sculptures on the beach. Hole-in-the-Wall is perhaps the most famous feature, a tunnel carved out of the cliff-side big enough to walk through.

Isis says to ignore the humans blathering on about beauty, for the seashore is long enough to give even big dogs a workout and the sniffscape is excellent, even if the surf is often too heavy for swimming. The local ranger is a Dudley Do-Right type with a reputation for throwing the book at dogs caught off-leash.

Signs to the beach are easy to follow from U.S. Highway 101, simply head toward Mora/La Push.

PLACES TO EAT

River's Edge: It's likely that the halibut, cod, salmon, oysters, and crab are caught the same day they are served at this dockside restaurant on the Quileute Reservation. Excellent breakfast, lunch, and dinner are served at outdoor tables at a remodeled boat launch building on First Beach. You may be serenaded by seals and soared over by eagles as you dine. The pie slices are gargantuan and so fine. 41 Main St., La Push; 360/374-5777.

Kalaloch

It's wild, wet, wonderful Pacific Ocean as far as a dog can smell, and that's pretty far. In one more rule-breaking bonanza, dogs are allowed on all Olympic National Park beaches between the Quinault and Hoh Indian Reservations. That's 33 miles of smooth sand, sun, and surf. There are a handful of beach access points, simply called Beach 1, Beach 2, Beach 3, and so on, up to Beach 6. The fifth is difficult to find, and the sixth is only a viewpoint, so most people stick to the first four.

PARKS, BEACHES, AND RECREATION AREAS

🐾 Ruby Beach

🐾🐾🐾 (See Olympic Peninsula map on page 18)

This is one of those jaw-dropping ocean vistas complete with crashing waves, haystack rocks formed by water erosion, and trees clinging to cliffs above. In the distance, you can see the lighthouse perched on Destruction Island, named for the massacre of British explorers nearby by natives in 1787. In March, you can also catch glimpses of migrating gray whales spouting offshore.

This beach escapes the numbering convention, named for tiny garnets that can be found in the sand. It could just as easily refer to the jewel-colored evening sky; locals recommend it as the best place on the entire coast to experience an ocean sunset. Winter storms are equally dramatic, as the wind whips the waves into frenzied peaks.

After an easy trail, you'll have to cross those pesky driftwood logs again to get to the sand. If you love sparkly things as much as Isis does, you'll be glad you did. Ruby Beach is on U.S. Highway 101 at milepost 164.

🔲 Beaches 1–4

🐾🐾🐾 (See Olympic Peninsula map on page 18)

This stretch of ocean is so gorgeous it leaves people at a loss for words, which may explain why the access points are simply numbered. All in all, the beaches look about the same and you can walk the miles between them. Just remember where you started, because there are no markers on the beach to remind you how to get back up! Isis recommends you pick one, get to the bottom, and camp out all day, engaging in her favorite activities: running from surf foam and chasing seagulls until you collapse, panting and spent, for a nap.

All access points are along U.S. Highway 101, and some are hard to find. Your best marker is Kalaloch, two are south of this point and two north. For Beaches 1–3's access points, parking is a roadside pullout affair. The cars are easier to see than the signs, so follow their lead. Each access has about a half-mile trail leading to the sand, at the bottom of which is a minefield of driftwood logs you'll have to navigate to reach the water. Isis will tell you this is no mean feat for miniature Dachsie legs.

Beach 4 is easier to get to, if only by a little bit. This is the only one of the four to have a parking lot, a latrine, and a bridge at the bottom of the trail. The bridge doesn't quite get you to the beach, but you can climb down a manageable rocky ridge to do that. None of the areas are wheelchair-accessible, but Beach 4 does have a viewing platform that wheelchairs can reasonably reach. Of the four, this one is reputed to have the best tidepools at low tide for sniffing out the starfish, hermit crabs, clams, and so on that live in the shallows.

PLACES TO STAY

Kalaloch Campground: In summer, availability at 175 campsites disappears faster than Jack Russells after a lure. There are six loops of sites, some on the cliffs with ocean views, some hidden in groves of moss-covered trees spooky enough to inspire campfire stories. There are two, 1.25-mile forest hikes along the Kalaloch River and an easy climb down to the beach from the day-use area. No water or electric hookups are available. Cost is $16 per night. On Highway 101, 35 miles south of Forks. Make reservations at 800/365-CAMP (800/365-2267) or http://reservations.nps.gov/.

Kalaloch Lodge: Dogs are not allowed in the lodge, but they are welcome in the cabins on the cliffs overlooking the ocean, real log cabins with two rooms, wood stoves, showers, and kitchenettes. A pricey $174–264 per night buys comfort, instant beach access, and the best ocean views in the state. The Lodge's restaurant and mercantile are your only options for food. Cooper says their chowder is the clammiest! 157151 Hwy. 101, Kalaloch; 866/525-2562.

Lake Quinault

More than 65 percent of the world's temperate rainforests line the coasts of Washington, British Columbia, and Alaska. On the southern end is the Quinault Rainforest, where 140 inches of rain can fall in an average year. Lake Quinault is a glacier-fed oasis nestled among the evergreens and old-growth cedars. It's a long way from anywhere, a perfect antidote for city-weary canines. The northern shore of the lake is an ONP boundary, off-limits to dogs. The south shore is A-OK, so look for the Lake Quinault South Shore Recreation Area sign.

PARKS, BEACHES, AND RECREATION AREAS

19 Quinault Loop

🐾🐾🐾🐾 🐾 (See Olympic Peninsula map on page 18)

This four-mile hike starts across the street from your boathouse room at Lake Quinault Lodge. Along the way, and on short spurs that intersect, you'll encounter cascading waterfalls, Douglas firs that grow 200 feet tall, ferns and mushrooms of *Alice in Wonderland* proportions, and blankets of moss, lichen, and mold rivaling the shag carpets of the '70s. It is a magical place. Isis wouldn't have been surprised if a unicorn had stepped out of the forest to greet her. At the very least, you have a good chance of seeing a Roosevelt elk or a black-tailed deer. Keep watch for river otters as well, and osprey that dive more than 80 feet from their treetop nests to grab fish from the lake.

Take the .3-mile jaunt off the main trail to see the giant Sitka spruce tree, a magnificent specimen estimated to be at least 1,000 years old. Talk about your old-age spread—the base of the trunk is 58 feet in diameter.

The loop is accessible from several points along the South Shore Road. Good map signs are posted along the trail. Stop in at the ranger station next to the lodge for more information if you don't want to wing it.

20 Rainforest Nature Trail

🐾🐾 (See Olympic Peninsula map on page 18)

This is a miniaturized half-mile version of the Quinault Loop and connects to it if your dog is still dragging you on after the first four miles. You may have that extra burst of energy to manage it, thanks to the oxygen-enriched air of the jungle. Head rushes, rosy cheeks, excessive tail wagging, and nose twitches in overdrive are common side effects of a walk through this forest primeval. It feels like time travel; the world of dinosaurs is easy to imagine.

Follow the Olympic National Forest signs, 1.5 miles to the park from U.S. Highway 101 on the South Shore Road. Paved parking, picnic tables, and restrooms are available at the trailhead. Parking is $3 per day.

PLACES TO STAY

Lake Quinault Historic Lodge: Teddy Roosevelt loved it here when he visited in 1937 to talk about creating a national park on the peninsula. It is not known if his dogs Pete or Sailor Boy joined him on this visit. The lodge retains its 1926 character and charm, lent by designer Robert Reamer, who also built Old Faithful Inn in Yellowstone. Rustic rooms with private baths and a top-floor suite are available in the adjacent boathouse for travelers with pets. View rooms are $80 in winter, $130 in the summer. 349 South Shore Rd., Quinault; 360/288-2900 or 800/562-6672; www.visitlakequinault.com.

West Hood Canal

Slivers of human habitation are lean on the west side of the canal, sandwiched in between the water and the Olympic National Forest. There's only one road, and if it's blocked, you're not going anywhere. Land, rock, and mudslides happen infrequently, and when they do, the DOT will put up signs to let you know exactly how far you can get before you have to turn around. Oysters are the regional delicacy, and the waters of the canal are also home to the largest recorded octopus species in the world.

At the southern end of the canal, Hoodsport is the modern equivalent of a frontier town. It's your last big opportunity to gear up and lay in provisions for your adventures in the forest or along the canal. Divers, campers, and fisherfolk stop in for vital supplies: sunscreen and bug spray, batteries, stove fuel, ice cream.

PARKS, BEACHES, AND RECREATION AREAS

🐾 Dosewallips State Park

 (See Olympic Peninsula map on page 18)

Fishing and shellfish harvesting are popular pastimes at this unique park that offers both 5,500 feet of saltwater shoreline along the Hood Canal and 5,400 feet of freshwater fun along the Dosewallips River. The campgrounds are huge, a series of meadows with good shade trees to host the hundreds of people who come in the pursuit of edible things that live in shells. A popular pastime for the kids is riding their bikes on the paved roads through camp. This particular park is more popular with the RV crowd, as tent campers usually go into the Olympic National Forest nearby.

The campground is on the west side of the highway, day-use areas are on the east. To reach the beach trail, park at the northernmost day-use area. The beach is a marsh, the Dosewallips River Delta, very popular with dogs for the waterfowl sightings and fowl smells. An elevated pea gravel walkway winds through the grass, leading to a viewing platform and to the water. There are up to five miles of rough beach hiking and biking, but only if the tide is all the

DIVERSION

The western shores of the Hood Canal have the best spots in the state for digging for your dinner, and we haven't met a dog yet who doesn't love to dig. Salty dogs might consider giving up their bones in exchange for oysters, razor clams, Geoducks, and mussels buried in the sand, waiting to be shucked and slurped. If mollusks don't move you, then how about the fishing? Both freshwater and salt-water fishing is in abundance throughout the Olympic Peninsula, some of the best in the country.

There are a few things that you have to keep in mind to enjoy food found in the wild: permits, limits, and toxicity warnings. The **Washington Department of Fish and Wildlife** issues permits and sets limits for shellfish harvesting and fishing. You can get information online at http://wdfw.wa.gov. They have a great search engine you can use to find a store near your vacation spot that will sell licenses, or you can buy them ahead of time at www.greatlodge.com/wa. Limits and toxicity warnings will be posted at each fishing or shellfishing location. Main Office: 360/902-2200; License Division: 360/902-2464.

way out. Another trail leads through the woods above the main camp, where you can see evidence of rail beds where logs were hauled down from the forest to be floated to sawmills or ships.

Dosewallips is 20 miles south of the State Route 104 intersection on U.S. Highway 101. There are three separate entrances to the park, two to day-use areas and one to the main campground. Parking is $5 per day. Hours are 8 A.M.–dusk. 360/902-8844.

22 Potlach State Park

🐾🐾 (See Olympic Peninsula map on page 18)

The day-use area is a bump-out from the highway on the water. Sunny days and low tides bring out the people for oyster harvesting, clam digging, crabbing, and fishing. High tides bring out the divers, and the winds pull in the kite flyers. The rocky beach is accessed easily from the long north/south manicured grounds, where the Skokomish Native Americans set their winter villages and held gift-giving ceremonies called Potlaches. Oysters must be shucked on the beach, and their shells left for future generations of baby oysters to occupy. This leaves natural beach debris of high merit for the explorations of curious wet noses.

The campground and hiking trails are on the opposite side of the highway. The shorter hike, the half-mile Lower Loop has a great viewpoint from which you can almost see the whole canal spreading north. The Upper Loop is a bit longer, .75 miles, winding through the forest.

Potlach is on U.S. Highway 101, south of Hoodsport. Parking is $5 per day. 360/902-8844.

PLACES TO EAT

Hood Canal Seafood and Dabob Café: People swear by the seafood stew, made fresh from crustaceans, fish, and shellfish probably caught out back the morning they are served. Regulars insist you try an oyster burger with one of 31 flavors of milkshakes. Breakfasts are basic. The elevated, outdoor patio is reserved for humans; you can order takeout. 294963 Hwy. 101, Quilcene; 360/765-3857.

PLACES TO STAY

Mike's Beach Resort: Mike's has mastered the laid-back, seaside, summer camp vibe. There's a private gravel beach, kayak and paddleboat rentals, boat launch, playground, laundry room, and beachside showers. You and your hound can hang with the PADI people; dive instructors from all over the region bring trainees to Mike's for open water certification. Rates and amenities range widely, from $45 for budget rooms in the main building (think very budget) to $95 for a swank waterfront cabin with kitchen, Jacuzzi, fireplace, and picture window on the water. A one-time $10 fee covers your pet. Campground sites also available for $20 per night. N 38470 Hwy. 101, Lilliwaup; 360/877-5324 or 800/231-5324; www.mikesbeachresort.com.

Mount Walker Inn: "Bring your family, pets too," they say, right on the front of their brochure. Tasteful standard and kitchenette rooms sit on a peaceful plot of land just off the highway within walking distance of the Quilcene River. Rates range $55–85, plus $10 per pet, per night. Checks and cash only. Highway 101, Quilcene; 360/765-3410; www.mountwalkerinn.com.

Pacific Beach

The towns that include Pacific Beach, Copalis Beach, and Ocean City are known as the North Beaches, heading north on State Route 109, not to be confused with the beaches at Kalaloch and La Push further north. This strip of sand travels 30 miles before reaching the Quinault Indian Reservation, which is off-limits to public access. These shores are more accessible and inviting, if not as dramatic as their northerly neighbors.

PARKS, BEACHES, AND RECREATION AREAS

23 Pacific Beach

🐾🐾 (See Olympic Peninsula map on page 18)

This waterfront state park doesn't waste real estate on nonessentials. There's a small parking-lot style campground and an even smaller day-use area, both of which are situated for one purpose: to get you onto the beach ASAP. Once up and over a tiny hill, you and your dog can travel all 30 miles of coastline from this one access point. The sand is brilliant for castle building, fine and soft and moist enough to hold together for hours.

In Pacific Beach, turn west on Main Street and south on Second Street to enter the park. Parking is $5. 360/902-8844.

PLACES TO EAT

Zany Zebra: A drive-in with two picnic tables, the Zebra has summer food down pat. The selection includes fishwiches, chili, salmon burgers, bacon burgers, fries, onion rings, chicken burgers, tuna sandwiches, and grilled cheese. The treats outnumber the meals two to one: hot fudge sundaes, banana splits, Italian sodas, lattes, soft and hard cones, malts, and shakes. 28 Main St., Pacific Beach; 360/276-4755.

PLACES TO STAY

Sand Dollar Inn and Cottages: There are two pet-friendly rooms in the Inn, but Isis highly recommends the four cottages. Each is uniquely furnished; they all have decks, tubs in the bath, and easy beach access next door to the state park. Periwinkle and Sea Perch are charming and bright, Star Fish and Sandal Shores are newer, with more contemporary wood floors and furnishings. $119–135; $10 each pet. 53 Central Ave.; 360/276-4525; www.sanddollarinn.net.

Sandpiper: This beach resort wins the vote for the best ocean views from every room, the coolest gift and kite shop crammed with stuff, and the fastest access to a private beach. Suites are huge and newer than many on the coast, with fully equipped kitchens and fireplaces. They provide pick-up bags and a wash station for dogs at the beach. Pets are $10 each per day; rates range $90–110, $165 for the whirlpool tub suite. 4159 Rte. 109; 360/276-4580 or 800/567-4737; www.sandpiper-resort.com.

Copalis Beach

What is so cool about this shoreline is that when the signs say "Beach Access," they're not fooling around—you turn off the main road and drive your car right onto the hard-packed sand. Areas of motorized beach alternate with strips that are pedestrian only, marked clearly with signs. In Ocean City, the terrain is fairly flat; when you get to this area, you'll see pine and cedar trees clinging to wind-carved sandstone cliffs.

PARKS, BEACHES, AND RECREATION AREAS

🐾 Griffiths-Priday

🐾🐾🐾🐾 (See Olympic Peninsula map on page 18)

While it is much easier to get to the beach at Ocean City or Pacific Beach, dogs will give you several reasons why this state park is more fun. Cars are not allowed, it's not as crowded, and best of all, you have to hike through the tall grasses and along the cliffs of sand dunes to reach the beach. Following the paths carved by foot traffic through the dunes leads to all kinds of adventures, including thorough inspection of the smells and textures that nesting birds have left behind.

If it looks like you may never reach the beach, don't lose hope! Keep going to the point of land, past where the Copalis River curves out to empty into the ocean, over a pile of driftwood, and there you are. Watch for aggressive geese protecting their fledglings in the spring—they'll eat your dog alive. Turn west on Roosevelt Beach Road from Highway 109 in Copalis Beach. Parking is $5. 360/902-8844.

PLACES TO STAY

Iron Springs Ocean Resort: Mention this part of the coast, and dog lovers will tell you to stay at Iron Springs. Although the resort seemed a bit run-down to us, its popularity could be due to a central location, low-key friendliness, and instant private beach access. Twenty-eight cottages are dotted throughout the woods—all have ocean views, kitchenettes, baths, and fireplaces or stoves. Prices range $78–156, plus a $12 charge per pet. Three miles north of Copalis Beach on Highway 109; 360/276-4230; www.ironspringsresort.com.

Ocean City

There are bunches of funky, destination beach resorts that are dog- and kid-friendly up and down this coast. They have more personality than the resort hotels on Ocean Shores. Cooper and Isis also prefer these beaches to the ones down south.

PARKS, BEACHES, AND RECREATION AREAS

🐾 Ocean City

🐾🐾🐾 (See Olympic Peninsula map on page 18)

Ocean City is the most popular park on the strip, with the best combination of beach access and secluded camping. To reach the beach, you drive over an estuary, past the ranger's house and four camping loops to the right fork in the road. A gravel beach trail transitions to sand, through the dunes and shore pines across a little stream to the beach. For canine entertainment, there are scented treasures to be found: crab and mollusk shells and stranded seaweed and kelp strands. Not to mention hundreds of sandpipers! The dogs were no match for these tiny, long-legged birds that sprint along the leading edge of the waves. There are covered picnic shelters in clearings in the trees, not on the beach. Restrooms are located in the center of the camping loops.

From State Route 109, turn south on State Route 115. Farther south, on Chance a la Mer Street in Ocean Shores, there is a parking lot with restrooms and drive-on beach access that is technically a part of this state park. Parking is $5. 360/902-8844.

PLACES TO STAY

Ocean City State Park Camping: Four loops separate the tents from the RVs (three for tents, one for RVs), and everyone has good tree cover for privacy. There are trails to the beach from the two closest loops. The site's 178 spaces go unbelievably fast in the summer, so reserve ahead. 888/CAMPOUT (888/226-7688); www.camis.com/wa.

Ocean Shores

Ocean Shores' 6,000 acres are Washington's most popular seaside destination. The entire peninsula is incorporated as a resort city. The beach itself is a public highway, with a posted speed limit of 25 mph, and unlimited travel from Labor Day through April 15. In the summer, parts of the beach are limited to foot, horse hoof, and dog paw traffic only.

However, Ocean Shores isn't for every dog. They'll have to compete with cars, mopeds, and horse riders on the long, flat beaches. Big hotels and resort homes are tightly stacked together on the dunes, limiting unspoiled views. And, as inviting as the ocean may be, the rip tides and undercurrents may be too strong for swimming in all but the shallowest places. That said, you can walk, beachcomb, rockhound, dig for clams, fly kites, and so on for six miles on uninterrupted sand beaches with endless ocean horizons. Many hotels take pets, so we've limited our list to a few word-of-mouth favorites.

PARKS, BEACHES, AND RECREATION AREAS

26 Damon Point/Protection Island

🐾🐾 (See Olympic Peninsula map on page 18)

Damon Point is a half-mile wide, mile-long example of accreted land, where sand has piled up over the years to create walkable earth where once there was none. The spit is also called Protection Island, a fitting name now applied to protecting the endangered bird species the snowy plover. The park is limited to select pedestrian use only March 15–August 31. The trail to the beach is always open, as is the moist sand along the shore. There are excellent views of

NATURE HIKES AND URBAN WALKS

In Ocean Shores, there are eight **Public Beach Access Points,** not including the state parks, to get you onto six miles of uninterrupted shoreline. Some roads lead right onto the sand, making it as easy as stepping out of your car onto the beach. Other spots are walk-on only, over a dune or two. A few have parking lots and restrooms, and some are nothing more than trails through the grass. Here's the list, in order from north to south.

Damon Road, drive-on, paved parking

Chance a la Mer, drive-on, restrooms, paved parking ($5)

Pacific Street, drive-on

Ocean Lake Way, drive-on, paved parking, restroom

Taurus Boulevard, drive-on, no amenities

Butter Clam Street, walk-on, gravel parking, protected dune, dogs on leash

Driftwood Street, walk-on, roadside parking, protected dune, dogs on leash

South Jetty, walk-on, paved parking, latrine

shipping lanes, Westport across the bay, and windswept land that is beautiful, stark, and quiet. People are serious about surf fishing here, even though they have to don heavy cold weather gear to do it. Dogs must always be leashed to prevent them from plundering plover nests.

Take Point Brown Avenue to the end, and take the right fork in the road onto Marine View Drive. Turn left onto Protection Island Road; there is minimal parking at a circular driveway. Parking is $5 unless you can fit into a couple of roadside spaces before the official park entrance. Open 8 A.M.–5 P.M. 360/902-8844.

PLACES TO EAT

Peppermint Parlor: It's a common sight at the parlor, a dog with bated breath, attached to the hip of a child, waiting for a scoop to fall from a teetering cone into his open maw. So common, in fact, there is a sign, next to the one advertising 53 ice cream flavors, that says replacement scoops are $2 each. They serve bagels also, and if there's enough demand, they'll fire up a cotton candy machine. Oh, sugar-induced bliss! 748 Point Brown; 360/289-0572.

Picnic Table Bistro and Deli: The cooks at this deli make up potato, pea, and macaroni salads; several daily hot entrees like lasagna, chicken enchiladas, meatloaf, and mac 'n' cheese; and the fattest sandwiches on the shore. Finish up with one of a half-dozen wicked-looking dessert bars. There are a couple of picnic tables out front, but why not take your goodies to the beach? 821 Point Brown Ave.; 360/289-0900.

Sand Castle Drive In: Local seafood doesn't get any more authentic than the Castle's razor clam chowder in a sourdough bread bowl. Because not everyone appreciates the salty, chewy texture of a cooked clam, this joint is well known for its burgers and fries as well. 788 Point Brown Ave.; 360/289-2777.

PLACES TO STAY

Grey Gull: The gull is another big favorite of dog owners by reputation. Individually owned condos are tastefully furnished and include gas fireplaces and dune- and ocean-view patios. Rates range $120–235. The pet fee is $10. The building is an unmistakable landmark, a gray building in two wings that does indeed look like it could take off. 651 Ocean Shores Blvd. N.W.; 360/289-3381; www.thegreygull.com.

Westerly Motel: Allen and Jeanne have managed this motel for 31 years and they plan to keep it that way as long as they're able. Rooms are truly tiny, but the pillow top beds are comfy. Room rates are $50–90 per night, plus a $10 pet fee. Cooper insisted we include the fabulous quote on their business card: "Dogs or cats are welcome in this motel. We have never had a dog or cat that smoked in bed and set fire to the blankets…that stole our towels and played the TV too loud or had a noisy fight with his traveling companion…that got drunk and broke up the furniture. So, if your dog or cat can vouch for you, you are welcome here." 870 Ocean Shores Blvd.; 360/289-3711.

Aberdeen-Hoquiam

Aberdeen and Hoquiam are sister cities on either side of a river, like Minneapolis-St. Paul. They make up the biggest pocket of civilization on the way to Washington's lower ocean beaches. The main highways through town are complicated with twists and turns and are all one-way, which makes navigating especially interesting.

The deep-water port at Aberdeen is the largest on the Washington coast. The tall ship the *Lady Washington* is moored here, the only real vessel used in making the films *Star Trek Generations* and *Pirates of the Caribbean.* Recreation centers on area lakes and rivers, as do scores of migrating birds. These smaller inland towns are supported by logging, fishing, and tourists, whether human or canine. Between the city of Olympia and the ocean, there's a string of small towns—McCleary, Satsop, Brady, Elma, and Montesano—with a few quickie park options along the way.

PARKS, BEACHES, AND RECREATION AREAS

27 Joseph Stewart Park

🐾🐾🐾 (See Olympic Peninsula map on page 18)

Coop 'n' Isis butted in on a game of ring toss with a couple of dogs on the lawn at this city park. Just when they thought things couldn't get any better, they discovered a wooden bridge on the north side of the picnic area and play-ground leading to a great trail. Within a few steps, you are deep in the forest, and the city instantly disappears. It's a miniature great escape, with bridges over streams, wooden staircases up and down hills, and an elevated board-walk over the lush vegetation of the valley floor. Stumps of giant trees show logging activity of a century before. Isis especially liked the bird-watching in the Stewart forest. It definitely gets muddy after a good rain.

From U.S. Highway 101 westbound, turn right on F Street, immediately right on Market Street, and left on B Street. Follow B Street as it turns and take the left fork in the road to enter the park. Eastbound, turn left on G Street, right on Market Street, and left on B Street.

28 Lake Sylvia

🐾🐾🐾 (See Olympic Peninsula map on page 18)

Around Lake Sylvia State Park, people will look at you funny if you don't have a fishing pole and tackle box. There are picnicking fishing areas, camping fishing areas, pier fishing areas, and shoreline fishing areas. The only place where there aren't any anglers is on the trails, several miles of them along the lake, on the stream below the dam, and a scenic path on a ridge overlook-ing the whole works. The trails are accessed on the far side of the lake from the parking lot, over a floating dock and a dam bridge. The park used to be a logging camp, and you'll see the stumps of giant trees as you hike. It feels removed, but you don't have to go far to get there, only two miles from the highway outside Montesano.

From State Route 8, take the Montesano exit onto Main Street, turn on Pioneer Way, go through town, turn north on Third Street, and go straight through the stop sign onto Lake Sylvia Road. Parking is $5 per day. Fishing licenses are extra. 360/902-8844.

29 Vance Creek

🐾🐾 (See Olympic Peninsula map on page 18)

There are two lakes at this county park stocked for public fishing. The first is the tot pond, for kids, seniors, and handicapped fishermen (and fisher-women). This lake has an accessible paved trail all the way around and a small designated swimming beach. The second lake is longer and more secluded, with a gravel path along the north side that loops around a slough along the highway. You can hear the traffic, but you are protected from it by fencing and tree cover. This lake is more secluded, and there are several informal access areas where your dog can hop in for a quick swim without getting hassled as long as you don't disturb boats drifting nearby. Practice your "leave it" or "drop it" command before you go; salmon and trout carcasses may contain organisms hazardous to your dog's health.

From State Route 8, take the Elma Exit, turn south on Wakefield Road, and right on Wenzel Slough. Open 8 A.M.–dusk.

PLACES TO EAT

Anne Marie's: This downtown stop is the place for full breakfasts and lunches to go. A long list of omelettes and pancakes tempts your palate and an equally lengthy lunch list includes sandwiches named after the owner's handsome, grown sons. Of the daily specials, the taco soup is all the rage. 110 South I St., Aberdeen; 360/538-0141.

Deidra's Deli: Deidra runs an excellent sandwich place that's located in the same building as the farmer's market, so you can stock up on the best fruits and veggies while you lunch. There's a picnic table outside and a piece of play equipment to keep the kids busy while you squeeze the pears and sniff the melons. 1956 Riverside Ave., Hoquiam; 360/538-9747.

PLACES TO STAY

Guesthouse International Inn and Suites: Without question, this is the only upscale choice for lodging between Olympia and the ocean. They've scored a great location along the Riverfront Walkway downtown, sweetening the deal with good-looking rooms and an excellent list of services and amenities. A standard queen double goes for $82–88, plus $10 per pet. 701 E. Heron St., Aberdeen; 360/537-7460 or 800/214-8378.

Monte Square Motel: Every room is big and non-smoking in this new 2002 motel in downtown Montesano near Lake Sylvia. The lower floor is retail; the rooms are upstairs. Rates are $49 in winter, $89 in summer. Pets are $10 per visit. 1000 Brumfield Ave. W.; 360/249-4424.

More Accommodations: Please look under Chain Hotels in the Resources section for additional places to stay in this area.

KITSAP PENINSULA

Olympic

National

Forest

Olympic

National

Park

Quilcene

Brinnon

Seabeck **5**

Eldon

Holly

Potlatch

Tahuya

Union

Dewatto

Shelton

Capitol State
Forest

104

101

Port Ludlow

Shine

Lofall

Poulsbo

Silverdale

Kitsap
Lake

Bremerton

Kitsap

Peninsula

Belfair

Allyn

106

Dabob Bay

Hood Canal

3

101

Tahuya

Potlatch

3

Case Inlet

Lakebay

Longbranch

Anderson
Island

Olympia

3

Port Gamble

Hansville **1**

2

3

Squamish

4

10

Bainbridge
Island

6

11

12

Winslow

7

13

8

14

15

9

16 **17**

Port
Orchard

25

21

22

23

24

28

27

26

302

16

Gig
Harbor

McNeil
Island

Kingston

Puget

Sound

Seattle

Vashon
Island

Vashon

18

19

20

Maury
Island

Tacoma

Parkland

Spanaway

525

Clinton

99

5

305

see The
Islands
page 74

see Greater
Seattle
page 122

see Olympic
Peninsula
page 18

see Southwest
Washington
page 182

8

7

507

5

N

W E

S

0   5 mi

0   5 km

© AVALON TRAVEL PUBLISHING, INC.

CHAPTER 2
Kitsap Peninsula

The Kitsap Peninsula, and surrounding islands Bainbridge and Vashon, have the largest accessible coastlines in the state, not as dramatic and remote as the ocean, but equally fun to frolic on. The south end of the peninsula is accessed from Tacoma, across the Tacoma Narrows Bridge. In 1940, the original bridge wobbled, twisted, and collapsed due to wind-induced vibrations; the spectacular demise of Galloping Gertie was captured in a famous black-and-white silent video. There was one fatality, sadly: Tubby the dog. The upper end of the peninsula is reached by ferry from Edmonds (just north of Seattle) to Kingston.

The bottom half is dominated by the Hood Canal, an 80-mile stretch of saltwater that divides the Kitsap and Olympic Peninsulas. Mounds of white shells are piled at the side of the road, used as seedbeds for oyster farms cultivated in the canal's tideland basins. The canal is a playground for boating, scuba diving, and shellfish digging.

The center retains a strong military presence with the Naval Undersea Warfare Center in Keyport (a.k.a. Torpedo Town, U.S.A.), the Puget Sound Navel

PICK OF THE LITTER—KITSAP PENINSULA

BEST PARKS
Battle Point Park, Bainbridge Island (page 60)
Twanoh State Park, East Hood Canal (page 68)

BEST DOG PARK
Bandix Dog Park, Gig Harbor (page 70)

BEST BEACH
Point No Point Lighthouse, Hansville (page 51)

BEST EVENT
Posing Pets with Santa, various locations (page 55)

BEST PLACE TO EAT
Stray Dog Café, Vashon Island (page 66)

BEST PLACES TO STAY
Sandy Hook Beach Shack, Poulsbo (page 54)
Holly Lane Gardens, Bainbridge Island (page 63)

Shipyard in Bremerton, and the Bangor Trident Submarine Base outside of Silverdale. In the upper peninsula, most of the lumber mills are gone and the land is returning to nature, with plenty of perk-up-your-ears opportunities.

Kingston, Hansville, and Port Gamble

Kingston, a rip-roaring lumber town a hundred years ago, is a more mild-mannered ferry town today, built around the commuters and visitors who travel back and forth from Edmonds on the mainland. There are a bunch of good places to eat here; the farther you go out onto the peninsula, the leaner the pickings get. Anglers come from the world over to Hansville to net salmon around this thumb of a peninsula that sticks straight north. Port Gamble is a restored mill town that looks much the same as it did in the 1850s. It's the National Historic Site of the Pope & Talbot Mill, New England Victorian homes, a general store, and church. You pass through Port Gamble on the way to the Hood Canal Bridge, which leads to the Olympic Peninsula.

PARKS, BEACHES, AND RECREATION AREAS

🄰 Point No Point Lighthouse

🐾🐾🐾🐾 (See Kitsap Peninsula map on page 48)

There's no point in denying that we love walking the point at Point No Point. The sound of the water lapping against the shore, the silky sand extending for a couple of miles, and the sight of fishing boats trolling just offshore soothe the souls of human and hound. Views extend 180° west to east, from the Olympics across Whidbey Island to Everett. The Native Americans call this low sand spit *Hahd-skus,* which means Long Nose. Isis and Cooper's long noses had a field day on the beach.

Onshore, the little whitewashed building with the red roof is the oldest operating lighthouse in Puget Sound. When the Fresnel lens and glass panes for the lantern failed to arrive in time for the scheduled exhibit on New Year's Eve in 1879, the first keeper hung a kerosene lamp in the dome.

Cooper wants to clue you in to a local secret: There's a back entrance with better parking, a half-mile forest trail, and railroad tie steps down to the beach.

Turn north on Hansville Road (about two miles from the ferry terminal on State Route 104). Drive 6.4 miles and turn right on Gust Halvor Road, then left at the T-intersection onto Thors Road to the end. Open daylight hours only. You can tour the lighthouse (without food, drink, or your dog) noon–4 P.M., Saturday and Sunday, April 15–September 29; 360/337-5350.

🄱 Salisbury Point

🐾🐾 (See Kitsap Peninsula map on page 48)

Although the beach may be too rocky to enjoy, the lawn is lovely at this tidy county park. Your Doberman can dream of chasing the cars crossing the Hood Canal Bridge looming to the left—the best view of the bridge you'll find. Salisbury Point is a good family park, with clean restrooms, public showers, a lively playground, a boat launch, and the ever-present picnic tables. Dogs are welcome on leash.

From State Route 104, turn right on Wheeler Street, then right on Whitford Road. 360/337-5385.

PLACES TO EAT

The Coffee Exchange: When all else fails, you can always count on a coffee shop in the Northwest to satisfy the grumblings of a hungry tummy. This Kingston grinder has milkshakes, soup, sandwiches, espresso, and baked goods. There's one lone table out front covered by an umbrella, and a deck for about a dozen people, pets welcome, out back. It's right on the main avenue to the ferry terminal, for that last cup o' joe before you go. 11229 Hwy 104, Kingston; 360/297-7817.

NATURE HIKES AND URBAN WALKS

Port Gamble is a perfectly preserved mill town that dates back to 1853. Pick up a brochure at the Kitsap Peninsula Visitor Center in town and head out on a self-guided tour of the buildings and grounds, cemetery, and shops with your pup. Each 150-year-old building has a sign with pertinent names and dates. The buildings don't languish in antiquity, however. Today, one might be a chocolate shop, another a bed-and-breakfast; many are private residences. Most of Port Gamble's original settlers came from Maine, the first bi-coastal couples. If your border collie gets bored with this stroll through history, there are shorefront picnic tables and large manicured lawns to give him a break. Dogs need to stay on leash. When you take Highway 104 toward the Hood Canal, the road will lead you directly through Port Gamble. Hop out and gambol about.

J'aime les Crêpes: This is a new trend in Northwest fast food, although crepes themselves date back to 16th-century France. Savory crepes have fillings like smoked salmon, ham and Swiss, or veggies, and sweet ones drip with fruit, chocolate, butter, sugar, and whipped cream. Order at the window and relax at one of many outdoor tables. Espresso, ice cream, and Italian sodas are available, too. 11264 H.E. Hwy. 104, Kingston; 360/297-5886.

Port Gamble General Store: It's a bona fide general store in the original 1853 historic building. A full breakfast buffet will cost you $5.95, the same price for the lunch special of the day. Your dogs can lie about the picnic tables and the kids can go crazy in the candy jar isle while you check out the internationally famous seashell museum upstairs (free admission). 32400 Rainier Ave. #3, Port Gamble; 360/297-7636.

Poulsbo

Dogs, please pardon us for a moment while we get carried away with a strictly human pursuit, for downtown shopping in the historic district of this Scandinavian town known as "Little Norway" is absolutely fabulous. From window shopping to serious retail therapy, boutiques of enticing clothes, gifts, and knickknacks pack the streets. Now that we've got that out of our systems, you'll be pleased to know that this hamlet has its own tiny dog park. Besides, it's on the way to almost anywhere you want to get on both of the peninsulas.

PARKS, BEACHES, AND RECREATION AREAS

3 Frank Raab Municipal Park

🐾🐾🐾 (See Kitsap Peninsula map on page 48)

When you get to Frank Raab, you'll wind up the hill to the parking lot. With your dog on leash, take the exercise trail around the main field past the half court basketball blacktop, skateboard park, fire pit, horseshoe pits, sand volleyball, picnic shelter, swing set, and jungle gym. Just before you get to the amphitheater and the P-patch, you'll see the fenced off-leash area to your left.

They call this strip of wood chip–covered ground the Bark Park. It is fenced on one side and the rest is surrounded by thick blackberry and thistle bushes that cover a steep hill. You don't want any dog that's even vaguely fluffy to get into these brambles. Amenities include picnic benches, a water pump, and doggie bag dispensers. There are restrooms in the park for you and decent views of Liberty Bay and the Olympic Mountains.

From State Route 305, turn east (up the hill) on N.E. Hostmark Street, and turn right on Caldart Avenue. The park is farther up the hill and around to the right. Open dawn–dusk. 18349 Caldart Ave. N.E., Poulsbo.

4 Old Man House

🐾🐾 (See Kitsap Peninsula map on page 48)

The old man lending his name to this park is Chief Sealth, the same whose roughly translated moniker is the name of Washington's largest city, Seattle. This is the ancestral home and communal gathering place of one of the most influential Native Americans in the Pacific Northwest. About an acre of his land is now yours to enjoy, from the shady hillsides to the sunny beach.

It is a teeny swath of beach that is particularly pleasant, looking out on Bainbridge Island across Agate Pass. The sand is bright white and silky soft, unusual for this area. A display board gives you some history of the cedar longhouse, and a log bench under a canopy provides respite. The park is relatively unknown, giving you a quiet place to play.

Immediately west of the bridge to the peninsula, turn north on Suquamish from State Route 305, go 1.8 miles and turn right on Division Street, which dead-ends into the park. There are two spaces where you can park your car in luxury for $5 per day, or some street parking nearby.

PLACES TO EAT

Liberty Bay Bakery and Café: Choose from a yummy array of baked goods, soups, and sandwiches at the counter and then park your buns on the bench-booth outside. Sandwich specials come with a salad and your choice of a drink or a piece of pie (apple, cherry, blackberry, or strawberry-rhubarb). Guess you'll be thirsty. 18996 Front St. N.E.; 360/779-2828.

Magnolia Café: The restaurant's food is so good because they keep it light and simple. The menu lists a page of salads, one of wood-fired pizzas, and pasta entrées for dinner, all excellent. They taste even better because they have an outdoor patio tucked under a huge Magnolia tree where your dog is welcome to sit with you. 18830 Front St.; 360/697-1447.

Sluy's Poulsbo Bakery: This Norwegian bakery has one of those window-front pastry displays that will have your tongues flapping before you enter the store. They are most famous for their potato bread and a traditional potato flatbread called *lefse* (looks like a tortilla, tastes like a 'tater). Isis is fond of the elephant ears, a flat sugary cinnamon confection that's bigger than her head. Cooper'll take the cheese sticks any day. 18924 Front St. N.E., Poulsbo; 360/779-2798.

PLACES TO STAY

The Beach House: The house is a roomy wood-shingle affair with two suites and an entire apartment for rent on a sugar sand beach with views of Agate Pass and Bainbridge Island. Unusual tile mosaic art lines the walls at a home where everything you could possibly need is provided for you. Bliss can be yours for $125–175, plus $10 per pet, per night. Heck, go in with a bunch of pet-loving pals and rent the whole joint for $350–425 per night. 17922 Angelina S. Ave., Suquamish; 360/779-7093; www.thebeachbb.com.

Brauer Cove: The entire lower floor of this farmhouse is yours, and your dog's, including the grill on the back patio over the water, a California King-size bed, jetted tub, wood stove, and bay windows that give you an actual bay view of the Poulsbo marina. Historic Poulsbo is a mile away by car or a half hour by paddle-powered canoe. $125 per night (no pet fees!). 16709 Brauer Rd., Poulsbo; 360/779-4153; www.brauercove.com.

Poulsbo Inn: This motel is a practical, reasonably priced roadside place to stay for pup lovers visiting the peninsula. Fees are $10 per pet, per night, and rates range $76–99. Limit of two pups. 18680 Hwy. 305, Poulsbo; 800/597-5151; www.poulsboinn.com.

Sandy Hook Beach Shack: The property around and including Le Shack, as it is affectionately known, is held in trust with the express wishes to keep this vacation getaway affordable for future generations. That is why, for only $75 per night (no dog fees), you can enjoy a room with a queen-size bed, two twin-size beds in the living area, fireplace and wood stove, a fully equipped kitchen, full bath with tub, banks of windows facing a deck with amazing views, private beach, hammock, treehouse, patio picnic table with gas grill, and saltwater swimming pool (unheated, summer only). You must have reservations, booked as early as a year in advance. Your only requirement is to make the bed and clean up for the next guest. Devotees come year after year, not minding to put in a little sweat equity for the rewards it brings. Dogs are welcomed with bowls, biscuits, and extra towels. 14532 Sandy Hook Rd. NE; 360/394-3632.

More Accommodations: Please look under Chain Hotels in the Resources section for additional places to stay in this area.

Silverdale and Seabeck

Since the 1970s, Silverdale has been the West Coast's Trident Submarine base, where scenes from the movie *Hunt for Red October* were filmed. The subs continue to go out on 60- to 90-day deterrent patrols; you may sight them coming and going in the Hood Canal. In the 1850s, Seabeck was a logging town with a bigger population than Seattle. Now, it's a mere shadow of its former self; the only reminders are a general store, post office, and Scenic Beach, a gorgeous state park.

PARKS, BEACHES, AND RECREATION AREAS

5 Scenic Beach

🐾🐾🐾 (See Kitsap Peninsula map on page 48)

While it's true that you can see the Olympic Mountains from many vantage points in the Northwest, at this state park, they are *right there*—up close and personal, larger than life, take-your-breath-away huge. They take you by surprise as you come out of the dense trees onto the gravel beach, littered with oyster shells. On the shore, the shipwrecked remains of a dinghy with a tree growing through its middle marks the southern boundary of the park.

Every distinct area of the park is a discovery, hidden from the others by dense forest canopy. In 1911, Joe Emel opened his homestead as a scenic resort. The restored Emel house has ADA-accessible wild rhododendron gardens, with a quaint bridge and gazebo with water views along the path. In another area is the deserted cabin and picnic grounds of the Frank Dupar

---

DOG-EAR YOUR CALENDAR

When 'tis the season to be jolly, get your jollies **Posing Pets with Santa** at various locations throughout Kitsap County. You know your family loves to get the holiday cards with your adorable dog on the cover! Kitsap Humane Society holds this holiday tradition, where not only dogs, but cats, gerbils, rats, ferrets, ducks, llamas, horses, and everything in between are welcome to sit on Santa's lap. Poor Santa.

Yes, you can pose with your pets, too. Dates and times are announced in flyers posted at locations throughout the peninsula, and on the website at www.kitsaphumane.org. Call 360/692-6977, ext. 113.

family, who built a summer camp here that has grown into the state park. It just looks like a state park should.

One of the nicest features of the park is its bulletin board, no kidding. The park ranger has gone out of his way to make it educational, posting information about everything you could possibly want to know: guides to Pacific Northwest trees, Northwest Coastal invertebrates, and parks and backyard birds; maps of the Olympics marked with the peaks you can see from the park; stories of the local bald eagles, the salmon life cycle, and more.

The signs to Scenic Beach are easy to follow from State Route 3 to Anderson Hill Road, which becomes the Seabeck Highway. Open 8 A.M.–9 P.M. in the summer, until 5 P.M. in winter. Parking is $5 per day. 360/902-8844.

6 Island Lake

🐾🐾 (See Kitsap Peninsula map on page 48)

The phrase "to while away an afternoon" could very well have been coined at Island Lake. It's all very civilized, from the long, paved walkway along the western shores to the dock lookout over the water. It is the only lakefront park in the county that allows dogs. Although it is primarily used for fishing, there is a designated swimming beach and a couple of playgrounds, and for once, we didn't see any signs saying that dogs have to stay out of these areas. Of course, your dog may prefer to play on the sloping lawns of this three-paw park, it's up to her.

Take Highway 3 and turn east on Wilcox Road, then south on Central Valley Road, which becomes Hillcrest Street. From there, you'll see the signs to the park from Island Lake Road. Open 9 A.M.–9 P.M.

PLACES TO EAT

Lighthouse Café and Wine Bar: One of those rare and wonderful places where your dog can hang out with you at an outdoor table until 10 P.M. as you order a merlot or chardonnay by the glass and eat such civilized delicacies as prosciutto-wrapped melon balls and parmesan-artichoke dip. Fancy salads, light sandwiches, and a decent bottled beer list round out the menu. 3388 N.W. Byron St., Silverdale; 360/698-WINE (360/698-9463).

Waterfront Bakery and Café: Across the street from Silverdale's Waterfront Park and at the center of the known universe is this spot for coffee and comfort. Our world revolves around the panini and focaccia sandwiches, daily wraps, and frosted fruit bars. The gourmet box lunches include a half sandwich, salad, fruit, chips, drink, and dessert. Open for breakfast and lunch. 3472 Byron St., Silverdale; 360/698-2991.

Bremerton

Bremerton was chosen as the site for a naval shipyard in 1889, a decision that led to significant military buildup in the region that continued through World War II. This, in turn, led to a large number of seaside state parks in the latter half of the century when all of those ports were decommissioned. President Truman gave his famous "Give 'em Hell Harry" speech here on the docks. The Puget Sound Naval Shipyard serves as moorage for the Navy's Inactive Mothball Fleet, including the Vietnam-era destroyer U.S.S. *Turner Joy,* which is open to the public. If you don't want to drive around to the south end of the peninsula and up Highway 16 to reach the city, there is a 45-minute ferry crossing to Bremerton from Seattle that is a beautiful trip through Sinclair Inlet and Rich Passage, around Bainbridge, and across the Sound. Dogs will experience as much headwind sticking their noses out the car window on the ferry deck as they would if car was moving. Now that's cool.

PARKS, BEACHES, AND RECREATION AREAS

7 Illahee State Park

🐾🐾🐾 (See Kitsap Peninsula map on page 48)

Illahee gives you a bittersweet glimpse of what the entire peninsula looked like at one time as the only remaining stand of old growth forest on Kitsap. One of the largest yew trees in the nation grows here. The road through the trees takes a series of curves, down a steep hill to the beach, with sweeping vistas of Port Orchard Passage and Bainbridge Island on the way down. You can watch the Bremerton to Seattle ferry crossing Rich Passage to the south. From the beach, you can hike a half mile straight up the hill to the

DOG-EAR YOUR CALENDAR

Grab a leash and your walking shoes and join people and their pets at the **PetsWALK Benefit** for the Kitsap Humane Society (KHS). Many of the dogs walking are KHS alums, now in happy families. Walkers collect donations and walk a 1K or 5K course, the last Saturday in June. Demonstrations, displays, vendors, and contests cater to the canine lover in us all.

People only, please, come to the **Animal Krackers Gala Dinner and Auction,** held annually in October in Bremerton. Dinner, wine, a silent auction, and a live auction keep the festivities going all night, for a great cause. All proceeds benefit KHS.

For information on these events, call 360/692-6977; or visit www .kitsaphumane.org.

campgrounds and the playground for a serious aerobic workout. Huff, puff up; pell-mell down. Illahee is a popular park for shellfish harvesting and crabbing; rules and limits are posted at the dock.

From the ferry, turn left on Burwell Street and right on Warren Avenue. Shortly after you cross the bridge, the road becomes Wheaton Way, and you'll see the signs to turn right on Sylvan Way. Parking is $5 per day, but if you want to see the views without coughing up the dough, there are 10-minute free parking spaces down by the beach. Open 8 A.M.–dusk. 360/902-8844.

8 Lent Landing

 (See Kitsap Peninsula map on page 48)

As proof that good things come in small packages, this tiny plot has the greenest, most perfect lawn Isis has ever seen, lined with a row of dogwood trees leading down to the water. Three benches, two picnic tables, and one viewing gazebo add symmetry to nature. It's so pretty and almost perfect, a picnic spot befitting her royal dogness. We humans loved it as well; Cooper was the only one who was a bit underwhelmed.

Cross the Manette Bridge, turn left and follow Wheaton Way to Lebo Boulevard. If you hit the Lions Park ball fields, you've gone just a dog hair too far.

9 Evergreen Park

 (See Kitsap Peninsula map on page 48)

Whether you're a sun worshipper, or break out in hives with anything less than SPF 50 on, Evergreen has got you covered. The north half of the park is forested with old evergreens, lending cool shade on hot days. The treed half has the playground, volleyball court, horseshoe pits, and restrooms. The south half is wide open, where they've planted small trees that won't block the sun for at least 10 years and a couple of picnic shelters thrown in for good measure. The views of the Washington Narrows and the Manette and Warren Bridges are only slightly marred by a hulking power tower. Cooper didn't even notice it as he chased the squirrels.

From the ferry, turn left on Burwell Street, and almost immediately right on Pacific Avenue, which will lead you to the southern parking lot on the sunny side. Another, larger parking lot is accessible on Park Avenue between 14th and 16th Streets. A leash law is in effect and they're known for being sticklers about enforcing it. 360/478-5305.

PLACES TO EAT

Café Destino: Across the street from Evergreen Park, this Italian eatery has more outdoor seating than indoor. Lunch dishes include a tuna wrap, pastrami and Swiss on rye, curried egg salad, and several salads and soups. The daily pasta special is a good bet for dinner, and salmon, lamb, and asparagus ravioli are regular menu items. Beer and wine; reservations recommended. 1223 McKenzie Ave.; 360/782-0711.

Goodies: Soups, wraps, and sandwiches are on the blackboard behind a counter covered with chocolates, candies, and gift cards. It's on the way to Evergreen Park and wouldn't you know it, they serve ice cream and espresso, too. 409 Pacific Ave., 360/373-6272.

PLACES TO STAY

Illahee Manor Vacation Rentals: The Cottage (sleeps four) and the Beach House (sleeps eight) are pet-friendly, for a $25 per visit fee. Both have water-view windows, sun porches, kitchens, and baths, plus use of a deck hot tub and six acres of waterfront with private beach access. Llamas and fallow deer live on the property, separately fenced for those dogs who can't resist giving chase. The Cottage is $190 per night, the Beach House is $250. 6680 Illahee Rd. N.E.; 360/698-7555; www.illaheemanor.com.

Illahee State Park Campground: There are 24 discreet, wooded tent sites way up on the hill above the beach with a slide, swings, and a baseball field nearby for family fun. All sites are available on a first-come, first-served basis for $16 per night. www.parks.wa.gov.

More Accommodations: Please look under Chain Hotels in the Resources section for additional places to stay in this area.

Bainbridge Island

Bainbridge is packed with fun parks for pups, all with well-marked signs. There were dogs everywhere we looked—sitting by the side of the road, running up to greet us, tearing past us down hiking trials, galloping along beaches, and just a few heeling by their owners on leashes. They all seemed happy, as did their humans, perhaps because of an island philosophy we saw on a bumper sticker: "Slow down, this isn't the mainland." Leash-law enforcement seems lax on the island, except at the state parks. The northwest access to Bainbridge is a drive across the Agate Passage from Poulsbo, and on the southeast from a Seattle ferry.

PARKS, BEACHES, AND RECREATION AREAS

🔟 Fay Bainbridge State Park

🐾🐾🐾 (See Kitsap Peninsula map on page 48)

Come with your lunch, or catch it while you're here. Dozens upon dozens of picnic tables parked on the beach offer water views, and a sign lists the seasons and limits for hauling in Dungeness crab, Rock crab, oysters, steamer clams, Horse clams, mussels, and Geoducks (a giant local clam oddity counter-intuitively pronounced GOO-ee-duck).

When you're full, thread your way through the driftwood logs piled on the 1,420 feet of saltwater shoreline to a rocky beach with great skipping stones. Two prominent volcanoes, Mt. Baker to the north and Mt. Rainier to the south, are visible on clear days, with the entire Cascade Mountain Range in between. Of historical note, the Port Madison Bell is here, brought from San Francisco by Captain Jeremiah Farnum in 1883, and used to proclaim important events.

From either direction on State Route 305, you'll see the big brown signs to the park. Turn onto Day Road N.E., travel about two miles to a T-intersection and turn left onto Sunrise Drive N.E., then go another couple of miles to the park entrance. There is a $5 day parking fee. Pets must be leashed. Open 8 A.M.–5 P.M. Oct.–Mar. and 6:30 A.M.–10 P.M. Apr.–Sept. 15446 Sunrise Dr. N.E., Bainbridge Island; 360/902-8844.

11 Battle Point Park

😺😺😺😺 (See Kitsap Peninsula map on page 48)

The center of this great city park is busy with kids playing soccer, baseball, basketball, roller hockey, tennis, and on the playground. While parents go apoplectic over the ref's last call, Cooper recommends you sneak away to the fringes of the park. This is where things really go to the dogs. There's a 1.5-mile paved loop trail that circles the entire park and from here, you can find wide fields, ponds with geese and ducks, hidden picnic tables and viewing benches, rolling hills, and rough trails winding through unkempt wild blackberry bushes—all pleasures dogs enjoy. Many of these areas are blocked from the supervised activities in the park's center by trees and clumps of tall vegetation left to the wild. Although it's not officially sanctioned, people take this opportunity to let well-mannered pets off the leash to play ball and wander more freely. It is a versatile and popular park, much loved by the community.

From the north end of Highway 305, turn on West Day Road, and immediately look for the arrow to follow Miller Road. From the south, turn on Lovgren Road to Miller. From Miller, turn west on Arrow Point Drive, and you'll see the sign for the park. Open 7 A.M.–dusk.

12 Grand Forest

😺😺😺 (See Kitsap Peninsula map on page 48)

It's strictly follow your nose on the trails of Grand Forest. There's no development in this 240-acre park other than two trailhead signs and a bridge somewhere in the middle of the 240-acre old growth forest. One sign at Miller Road leads to a one-mile trail that parallels the road. The second at Mandus Olson Road marks a two-mile trail, and there are unmarked trails that wind through, to, and in between these "official" paths. A river runs through it, providing atmosphere and navigation pointers. Trails are multi-use, designated for mountain bikes and horses as well as leashed pets and their people. Dogs and nature purists dig it.

Parking is equally ad hoc; simply pull over onto the side of the road. To find your way to Grand Forest, turn left on High School Road from I-305, turn right on Fletcher Bay Road and follow it until it becomes Miller Road. Watch for the sign on the right. To access the Mandus Olson section, take New Brooklyn Road to Mandus Olson Road and go north. Watch for the sign when the road makes a 90-degree turn. You're on your own finding your way through. 206/842-2306; www.biparks.org.

13 Eagledale Park

🐾🐾🐕 (See Kitsap Peninsula map on page 48)

Of the 6.7 acres at Eagledale, one acre is a devoted off-leash area. A six-foot-high chain-link fence with a double gate protects the area, as much to keep deer out as dogs in. On the left is a playing field, stocked with tennis balls generously donated by the Island Racquet Club. On the right is a miniature forest with a winding trail. Plastic chairs and tables are strewn about and a couple of bag dispensers hang from the fence, but you're on your own for water. To reach the off-leash area, walk up the roped-off street to the top of the hill and around to the left.

In addition to the dog park, Eagledale has a meditation walking maze. At the top of the plateau is a design of concentric circles laid with stones in the grass. Following the path to the center leads you to a sitting rock, with a view of Mt. Rainier to the south framed by the trees. The remainder of the park includes a playground, sand volleyball court, picnic shelter, and pottery studio for community classes. The restrooms are in the pottery studio building.

You'll travel over hill and dale to get to this park with an off-leash area. It's well removed from the center of anything on the island. From Winslow Way, turn right on Madison Avenue, then left on Wyatt Way, which becomes N.E. Eagle Harbor Drive when it turns to the south. Take the left fork in the road at the Eagledale sign, go 1.5 miles, and turn right on N.E. Rose Avenue. Residents kindly ask that you obey the 25 mph speed limit on your way to the park to protect their kids and dogs. 5055 Rose Ave. N.E., Bainbridge Island; 206/842-2306; www.biparks.org.

14 Fort Ward State Park

🐾🐾🐾 (See Kitsap Peninsula map on page 48)

Three cheers, or paws, for another decommissioned military installation converted to a day-use state park. We thoroughly enjoyed walking the one-mile loop trail around Fort Ward, half on a paved road following the shoreline, half on gravel and dirt paths through the woods. You can hear seals barking in the harbor, watch the ferries headed to and from Seattle along Rich Passage, and check out the overgrown remains of two gun batteries. For kids, the upper gun battery in the woods along the trail is a really cool place to play hide-and-seek.

The beach location is just right for swimming, walking, jogging, picnicking, and whatever other activities get your Pekinese panting for joy.

There are two entrances to this 137-acre park that lead to separate picnic areas. The upper picnic area and entrance are closed October–April, but the lower picnic grounds, on the beach, are open year-round. It's a short walk from the 25 parking spots to the tables, barbecue grills, and vault toilets.

The signs will direct you to turn west on High School Road from State Route 305, south on Grow Road to Wyatt Way W., then right at the fork in the road. Once you reach Pleasant Beach Drive N.E., follow the signs toward the boat launch entrance—it's the easier of the two to find and the only one open year-round. Parking is $5 per day. Dogs must be leashed. Open 8 A.M.–dusk. 360/902-8844.

PLACES TO EAT

Bainbridge Bakers: Travel through the center of town to Winslow Green, a new shopping area, to find this casual eatery serving sandwiches on warm focaccia bread, soups, salads, and baked goodies. It's popular and crowded; with luck you can find a place at one of a handful of benches or half-dozen tables under protected awnings on the broad tile patio. 140 Winslow Way W., Bainbridge Island; 206/842-1822.

Emmy's VegeHouse: It's really a veggie window, through which you order fabulous Vietnamese specialties for $5 a plate, with nothing over $7. Fried rice, spring rolls, stir-fry noodles, kabobs, golden tofu noodle salad, and more are made without meat, eggs, fish, poultry, or MSG. Wash it all down with hot green tea while sitting at a covered table warmed by an outdoor heater. 100 Winslow Way, Bainbridge Island; 206/855-2996.

Treehouse Café: There's a soft spot in our hearts for this classic sidewalk café near Fort Ward because it offers a selection of bottled artisan beers and hand-dipped ice cream along with the hefty Plowman's lunch, Cobb salads, and fancy baguette sandwiches. 4569 Lynnwood Center Rd. N.E., Bainbridge Island; 206/842-2814.

PLACES TO STAY

Bainbridge House: This top-floor, two-bedroom rental property in downtown goes for $150 per night, with a two-night minimum rental. It is fully equipped, spacious, and modern, has a private deck, and doesn't discriminate against dogs. There are no extra charges for well-behaved pets. 130 Knechtel Way, Bainbridge; 206/842-1599; www.bainbridgehouse.com.

Fay Bainbridge State Park Campground: While the 17-acre park is open year-round for day use, campers can stake a claim April–October on one of 10 tent sites or 26 utility sites that share a couple of restroom buildings with hot showers. A paved, wheelchair-accessible site has a prime location on the beach. Camping fees are $16 to $22 and are occupied on a first-come, first-served basis. 888/CAMPOUT (888/226-7688); www.camis.com/wa.

Holly Lane Gardens: Cooper gets so excited when we stay at places that include farms, hearty breakfasts, and bumpy country lanes. Patti asks for a $25 refundable pet deposit when your pet joins you in the picture-perfect cottage with French doors leading to fields, flowers, and herb gardens. A dog could really get used to lying about on the grand deck and in the fireplace-warmed parlor. Cost is $110–125 per night, depending on the season. 9432 Holly Farm Lane, Bainbridge Island; 206/842-8959; www.hollylanegardens.com.

Island Country Inn: It's the only hotel on the island and a step above the norm with pine furniture and pleasant décor that doesn't come out of the same catalog everyone else must use. It's smallish, offering only four rooms for dogs, and prefers smallish dogs (under 40 pounds). Rooms are $89–109, plus $10 per pet, per night, maximum two furry friends. 920 Hildebrand Lane N.W., Bainbridge; 800/842-8429; www.nwcountryinns.com.

Port Orchard

Where Bremerton is all business, Port Orchard across the bay is all play, water play. The marina is bigger than the town, filled with boats mostly under sail power. The contrast is interesting as you look across the inlet to the hulking gray battleships of the naval yard. Port Orchard embraces the spirit of play for pets with several off-leash parks, sea legs not required.

PARKS, BEACHES, AND RECREATION AREAS

15 Manchester State Park

😺😺 (See Kitsap Peninsula map on page 48)

The waterfront at Manchester is just average, most of the fun here comes from walking the trails and examining the remains and exhibits related to the park's Naval history. Beginning in 1901, Manchester was a coastal defense installation designed to protect the entrance to Rich Passage and the Bremerton Naval Shipyard. An underwater minefield was laid across the channel, monitored from a gun battery tower. You can use this lookout point to take in a great view of Puget Sound and Bainbridge Island.

The former torpedo warehouse is now the park's largest picnic shelter. Your sheepdog can sniff around the mining casement too, where men sat in cramped quarters, waiting to push the button to detonate the nearest bomb. The park buildings are on the register of National Historical Monuments.

A drive along Beach Drive from Port Orchard is the easiest and most scenic route to the park. Follow the signs to Hilldale Road to reach the park entrance. Parking is $5 per day. Dogs must be leashed. Hours are 8 A.M.– dusk. 360/902-8844.

16 South Kitsap Community Park

🐾🐾🐕 (See Kitsap Peninsula map on page 48)

If you ask locals for this park by name, fuggedaboudit, all you'll get are quizzical looks. Around these parts it's called Jackson Park, for the street it's on. There are plenty of clearly marked areas where dogs aren't allowed at all. As for the rest, the rule is that your dog has to be under your control, not necessarily on leash. You and your Lhasa apso are left with an unfenced field to roam alongside the playground, ringed with picnic shelters and an informal walkway. You can also wander those small trails through the woods at Camp Sinclair across from the field.

Of special interest to the kids, the Kitsap Live Steamers runs a model railroad train ride every second and fourth Saturday, 10 A.M.–4 P.M., April–October. Call 360/871-6414 or visit www.kitsaplivesteamers.org.

The park is at the corner of Jackson and Lund. From Highway 16, take Tremont Street east until it curves south to become Lund Avenue. Shortly thereafter, turn north on Jackson. The parking lot and off-leash entrance will be to your left.

17 Howe Farm

🐾🐾🐾🐕 (See Kitsap Peninsula map on page 48)

Every day, dogs are romping happily through the fields of Howe Farm, oblivious to the hullabaloo swirling around them. For years, the county allowed dog owners free rein with their dogs on this undeveloped property. In 2004, they put up signs declaring that dogs had to be on leash, which caused a great uprising among the people and pets of the land. At press time, discussions were still underway to designate anywhere from 3 to 50 acres of the 83-acre property as off-leash with fencing and facilities.

Dogs, put your paws together and pray that as much of this land stays off-leash as possible. There are few joys more precious than to let loose and let your paws take you where they will through wide open, tall grass fields of unbroken splendor and through wooded trails.

Turn south on Long Lake Road at the intersection with Mill Hill Road. Travel .2 mile and immediately look for the unmarked dirt road to your left. You'll know it's the dog park because there are grocery bags tied to the fence to be given a recycled life as poop bags. At present, there are no other facilities. Check www.kitsapdogparks.org for the park's status before you visit.

PLACES TO EAT

Hideaway Café: Dogs are enthusiastically welcomed on the deck out back behind all the activity along the main street of old town Port Orchard. The menu doesn't hold any surprises, simply low-key breakfasts of eggs, bacon, and pancakes and stress-free lunches of soup, salad, sandwiches, and burgers. 807 Bay St.; 360/895-4418

PLACES TO STAY

Manchester State Park Campground: Reserve one of Manchester's 50 forested campsites in the summer, or occupy one in the off-season on a first-come, first-served basis. The restroom and shower facility on the beach is especially nice. We cleaned off and changed clothes in there after falling into a lake at a different park, but that's a story for another time. 888/CAMPOUT (888/226-7688); www.camis.com/wa.

More Accommodations: Please look under Chain Hotels in the Resources section for additional places to stay in this area.

Vashon and Maury Islands

Although larger than Bainbridge, these two islands connected by a narrow causeway have a smaller population because they're more remote, accessible only by ferry from Southworth on the Kitsap Peninsula and West Seattle or Tacoma on the mainland. This community is dog-friendly and dog-smart. The Vashon Park District has installed pet waste disposal systems for your convenience, and many local businesses hand out treats including the True Value Hardware store, Pandora's Box Pet Supplies, and the Fair Isle Animal Clinic. Karen at the Vashon Bookstore is especially pleased to welcome well-behaved pets and will dote on them while you browse. There are large areas of preserved lands on Vashon that are not accessible—yet. Isis hopes to include them in future editions of the book.

PARKS, BEACHES, AND RECREATION AREAS

18 KVI Beach

🐾🐾🐾🦮 (See Kitsap Peninsula map on page 48)

As long as you don't mind a radio tower planted on *your* beach, Fisher Broadcasting Corporation doesn't mind you hanging out, in leash-free bliss, on theirs. It's privately held land, not on any map, nor is it marked, except for a tiny sign when you get to the path that says the public is welcome. So please enjoy the beach, but don't tell anyone else about this well-kept secret! The main path loops around a bog on the way to the sand, and many impromptu footpaths have been worked through the driftwood. When the tide is out, your dog can run for about four miles to the north, looking for the perfect fetch stick. Swim and dog paddle to your heart's content and take in the views of the tip of Rainier and the mainland south of Seattle. If there's no burn ban in effect and you get a permit in town before heading out, you can even build a beach bonfire below the high tide line.

Don't be intimidated by the directions; it's worth the journey. From Vashon Highway, turn left on Bank Road, right on Beall Road, left on 184th Street, and right on Ridge Road until just before it goes around the bend and becomes Chataqua Road. When you can see the red-and-white radio tower, you should be able to see the path to the beach.

19 Lisbuela Park

🐾🐾 (See Kitsap Peninsula map on page 48)

This is a gem of a beach with a sign at the entrance, "Dogs off leash ONLY if not disturbing others." Seems like a reasonable rule. Five and a half acres of sand and gravel beach lead to a sheltered bay of water. There's a rudimentary boat launch (meant for carry-in kayaks and canoes only) and some odd sculptures on the beach of wooden planks nailed to large pieces of driftwood.

It is quiet enough here to be unspoiled. We saw an otter run from the bushes into the water. Once he realized that Coop 'n' Isis wouldn't follow (water dogs they are not), he turned over on his back and taunted them as he floated along. Basic services include a gravel parking lot, recycling bins, a portable potty, and a couple of picnic tables on a patch of grass.

Take Vashon Highway to Cemetery Road, which winds around and becomes Westside Highway. Turn right onto 220th Street, which becomes Lisbuela Road, a windy, narrow, single lane leading directly into the park. Open from dawn to dusk.

20 Point Robinson Lighthouse

🐾🐾🐾 (See Kitsap Peninsula map on page 48)

This 12-acre park is a perennial favorite, with good reason. The walk along the rocky beach was our favorite of the day, and if the number of paw prints in the sand is any indication, that of many others. The views across the water to Tacoma are great, and there's lots of boat traffic to watch. We saw a famous Foss tugboat chug along.

A tiny white lighthouse with a red roof and its flashing light sits at an apex, kept for show. Nowadays, it's dwarfed by a massive radar tower—certainly more technically effective, if not as aesthetic.

There are two parking lots. From the upper lot, you can look out over the water while sitting on a grassy hillside with some picnic tables and a couple of fire pits. Follow the sign that says Trail (why mince words?) down a few stairs to the beach. Careful, they're slick when wet! The lower lot leads more directly to the beach and to the lighthouse, past the Keepers Quarters.

To get to Maury, you have to go through Vashon, with the only link being a single road along a narrow spit of land. To reach Point Robinson, take Vashon Highway to Quartermaster Drive, go east on Quartermaster Drive, and follow the left fork, which becomes Point Robinson Road, leading directly to the park.

PLACES TO EAT

Stray Dog Café: Here's a fine dining establishment where dinner is served to your outdoor table, with your pal at your side. The Stray Dog is named in homage to the original in St. Petersburg, Russia, of the 1930s and 1940s, a safe and fertile ground for the era's poets, artists, and free thinkers. The breakfast, lunch, and dinner menus are full of rich entrées with a twist, things like lemon ricotta pancakes, chicken crepes and Croque Monsieur, gazpacho risotto with peppers, and bacon-wrapped filet mignon and gorgonzola potatoes—with a glass of house red or white grape. 17530 Vashon Hwy. S.W.; 206/463-7833.

Sound Food: This favorite haunt has been around forever, and people believe you haven't really "done" Vashon until you've eaten here. A bag of Sadie's Happy Dog Snacks is just one of the many treats you can get to go at this restaurant and counter bakery. Call ahead to order from the restaurant's menu with emphasis on healthy, local specialties such as halibut, eggplant terrine, and poached pear salad. Or, pop in to the to-go counter at the bakery for fare that is simpler and equally delicious. 20312 Vashon Hwy. S.W.; 206/463-0888.

PLACES TO STAY

Castle Hill: There are no fees or pet restrictions when you stay on the south end of the island in Ron's suite with a full kitchen and bath with shower. The décor is light blue and bright, and the five acres of property benefit from the host's green thumb. He makes reservations for properties all over the island and can help you in a pinch if his room is taken. Isis, with her tricky back, says the only disadvantage is that it's not handicapped accessible; it's above his garage, reached by a long set of stairs. A reasonable rate of $85 per night includes a breakfast that is "heavy, heavy fuel." 26734 94th Ave. S.W., Dockton, Maury Island; 206/462-5491; www.vashonislandlodging.com.

Swallow's Nest Guest Cottages: The folks at Swallow's Nest have eight cottages in four separate island locations. The small, rustic units near the golf course have fields for a dog run and are unequivocally dog friendly. The Edson House, with art by the photographer and artist Norman Edson, is a two-story Victorian in the Burton harbor with a clawfoot tub and antiques. It's available for dogs with hair rather than fur, who are accustomed to in-town living. If your dog isn't a cat chaser, you may talk your host into letting you stay in The Ladybug, a cozy place with unforgettable views of Mt. Rainier. Rates vary from $85 to $170. Pet fees are $10 each pet. 6030 SW 248th St; 800/ANY-NEST (800/269-6378); www.vashonislandcottages.com.

East Hood Canal

Small towns—Belfair, Sunset Beach, Allyn, and Union—line scenic State Route 106 along the east side of the Hood Canal. Technically, it's not a canal at all, it's a fjord, a long, narrow body of water open to the ocean and bordered by steep cliffs or hills. The native tribes who lived here were considered some of the world's wealthiest. The area's abundant wildlife produced more than they could use, which they traded for goods up and down the coast. For domesticated dogs who visit, the wealth comes in the form of beaches, lakes, rivers, and trails to explore.

PARKS, BEACHES, AND RECREATION AREAS

🐾 Belfair State Park

 (See Kitsap Peninsula map on page 48)

This is supreme, windblown kite flying territory at the tip of the inner hook where the canal begins. The day-use area is a field of tall marsh grasses with a playground and a swimming lagoon formed by a natural inlet that the kids love. The water is relatively warm, canal waters are the warmest saltwater bodies in the state. A dirt trail follows along 3,700 feet of saltwater shoreline through the fields or you can pick your way along the sometimes-rocky beach. The view of the canal to the south, framed by forested hills, is excellent.

From State Route 3 in Belfair, turn west at the Safeway onto State Route 300, North Shore Road, and travel about three miles to the park. 360/902-8844.

🐾 Allyn Waterfront Park

🐾🐾 (See Kitsap Peninsula map on page 48)

The nicest feature of this community park is a tall link fence that protects the people and dogs enjoying it from the busy highway (even so, pets are supposed to be on leash). It has a boat launch, dock, and play area that didn't warrant a glance from the wieners, who were drawn to the arbors, lawn, and picnic rotunda while visions of lunch, play, and naps danced in their heads. Isis was puzzled by a topiary gone to the wild, trying to figure out what it was supposed to be. The case was solved when the park's gardener said he wished he knew someone practiced in the art of topiary trimming who could return the ivy beast to its former glory as a giraffe.

The park is on the water, to your left as soon as you come into town on State Route 3, with views of Case Bay.

🐾 Twanoh State Park

 (See Kitsap Peninsula map on page 48)

Twanoh enjoys a choice waterfront location, with 3,200 feet of beachfront real estate along the canal. Two parking lots are big out of necessity to hold the trucks and trailers of boaters who put in at Twanoh's launch. Open and covered picnic tables are everywhere; some of them are shelters with kitchens, fireplaces, and sinks in handsome brick, stone, and log shelters crafted by the Civilian Conservation Corps in the 1930s. Cooper met a man who has been coming here since then, as a child of six or seven when his Dad worked in the corps. When asked if anything was different, the man said, "Yes. The trees are bigger."

The gravel beach is split by a creek that filters down from rainforest lakes. Berms create natural wading tide pools for youngsters to explore and swim. The water here is probably warmer than anyplace else in the state, so get your fins out and start dog paddling! The campground is on the opposite side of the highway from the beach, and it leads deep into an old growth forest. The park continues farther into the woods with a two-mile loop trail. The northern part of the trail is the prettiest, winding along the creek and up the side of a canyon through huge trees dripping with moss.

Twanoh is on State Route 106, about 10 miles south of Belfair. It's technically closed from mid-October through March, but you can still pull off the highway and enjoy the beach. Parking is $5 per day. 360/902-8844.

24 Mason Lake

🐾🐾 (See Kitsap Peninsula map on page 48)

Cooper wasn't sure if he should include this county park at first. It's out of the way and really small. But as he hung out there, it grew on him. The deal was cinched when he saw Riley, the chocolate Lab, take a flying leap off the dock into the cool water. According to Riley's human, the park is well kept, quiet, and a good place for dogs to come take a bath because no one will bother them about being off-leash. The restroom is almost bigger than the lawn, with showers for humans to bathe as well. Most importantly, the beach is good for retrieving—clean, smooth, and no water hazards.

From State Route 3, go west on the Mason-Benson Road and follow the signs to the park. Parking is across the road from the lake.

PLACES TO EAT

Big Bubba's Burgers: From the size of these whoppers, it oughta be called Bubba's Big Burgers. Cheap, too. Breakfast sandwiches are only $.99. Big Bubba's Attack (could that be heart attack?) is a double burger with double cheese, large fries, and an extra large soda. A family of four—kids and dogs—can chow down for the price of a $23 Family Pack, and that includes soft dip ice cream cones. Garden burgers, onion rings, and BLTs are also available; cash only. Right across the street from Allyn Waterfront Park. 18471 E. State Route 3, Allyn; 360/275-6000.

PLACES TO STAY

Alderbrook Resort: This stunning spa, dining, and relaxation hotel re-opened in June 2004 after such extensive renovation that it might as well be brand new. It would be the toast of the town, if there were a town. You won't mind that there isn't, being too busy getting massages and body treatments to bother with civilization…that is, when you're not busy absorbing the Hood Canal and Olympic Mountains views. One or two small pets are allowed in ground floor Marina View rooms, with rates of $170–250 per night, plus a refundable $200 deposit authorized to your credit card. 10 East Alderbrook Drive, Union; 360/898-2200; www.alderbrookresort.com.

Robin Hood Village: The cottages have been around since 1934 and the exteriors look straight out of Sherwood Forest. The interiors, however, have been constantly updated, and they are gorgeous. Fireplaces, big beds, private hot tubs, kitchens, entertainment centers, and lofts are among the amenities that make this Cooper's favorite place to stay on the canal. The private beach and liquor store (aptly named Friar Tuck's Grog Shoppe) help, too. Rates are $85 to $165 with a $12 pet fee. 6780 E. Hwy. 106; 360/898-2163; www.robin-hoodvillage.com.

Twanoh State Park Campground: Twanoh has 25 beautiful tent spaces and 22 RV sites nestled under huge trees, some along the winding creek that will sing you to sleep. Camping is on a first-come, first-served basis and is only available Apr. 1–Oct. 12 for $16–21 per night. East Hwy. 106; 360/902-8844.

Gig Harbor

A maritime city that retains its fishing-village character, Gig Harbor is a place to boat sightsee, people watch, and window shop for antiques, crafts, and gifts. Sorry, dogs, make that seagull sightsee, crotch watch, and shrubbery shop for the latest in designer fragrances. Grab some pup grub, toys, and treats at **Green Cottage Pets** (3024-A Harborview Dr.; 253/851-8806; www.greencottagepets.com). Owners Tom and Anna have pictures of regulars posted everywhere and an unruly Rolodex full of their canine and cat clients' preferences, with more than 500 cards at last count. They carry only human-grade, holistic pet food. Isis talked her mom into buying her a new collar with daisies on it.

PARKS, BEACHES, AND RECREATION AREAS

25 Bandix Dog Park

🐾🐾🐾🐾 🦴 (See Kitsap Peninsula map on page 48)

In 2004, Kitsap dogs celebrated independence a day early, when the peninsula's first exclusive canine country club opened its gates on July 3. The organization that created this dedicated off-leash park, Kitsap Dog Parks, Inc. (KDP), was formed when the city of Tacoma closed access to the Tacoma Narrows Airport Landing Buffer, an unofficial off-leash area for more than 10 years. KDP immediately set out to create an official dog park, and boy, oh boy, have they succeeded masterfully!

Bandix is a full 33 acres devoted entirely to life as an unleashed dog, worth the ferry trip over if only to come and play for the day. There are a couple of quickie wooded trails and at least three open play areas, called the landing strip, the old log clearing, and the meadow, linked by other trails. Six-foot fences and gates protect the front entrance; a fully enclosed central area, more trails, and grass seeding are in the works. Maps on the bulletin board show the different open areas and trails in the park, and, until they get knocked down or mauled, there are signs throughout the park as well. There is a portable potty in the parking lot, a picnic table, and bag dispensers throughout the park. You are required to carry a leash in the park at all times, to leash up if necessary.

Feel free to patronize the businesses that advertise at the park, to support its ongoing success and to help build other OLAs. While you don't have to pay membership dues to use the park, an individual membership to KDP is only $10 a year. Go to www.kitsapdogparks.org.

Bandix is in a prime location, easy to reach from Bremerton, Port Orchard, and Gig Harbor. From State Route 16 at milepost 20, turn east on S.E. Olalla Road, travel .6 mile, turn right on Bandix Road S.E., and continue .3 mile to the entrance on your right. Open 8 A.M.–dark.

26 Sunrise Beach

🐾 🐾 (See Kitsap Peninsula map on page 48)

This 80-acre park is a meadow clearing in the woods on a hill, with a gravel path curving down to a pebble beach that only exists when the tide is out. It is used primarily by divers, so you have a good chance of being the only ones enjoying it above water's surface. The beach faces south, with Tacoma in the distance. A decaying shelter looks as though it could have been left behind by Robinson Crusoe. Cooper doesn't mind having a deserted park to himself, he rather enjoys it as long as he can be home in time for dinner.

Take Harborview Drive through town, turn right to continue on Harborview, then right on Vernhardson Avenue. At the series of T-intersections, turn left on Crescent Valley Drive, right on Drummond Drive, right on Moller Avenue, and left onto Sunrise Beach Drive. Closes at dusk.

PLACES TO EAT

Kelly's Café: Kelly's makes great, fat deli sandwiches with fresh-cut meats and cheeses to devour at sidewalk tables. The hot sandwiches, burgers, and fish 'n' chips come with fries in a basket, and you can top it off with ice cream or intensely flavored handmade chocolates. They have a carousel horse, pinball machine, and jukebox to keep the restless natives happy while you relax under the red-and-white striped awning. 7806 Pioneer Way; 253/851-8697.

Le Bistro: Pick something from the extensive full-service breakfast menu or a traditional soup-salad-sandwich trio for lunch to enjoy at an outdoor table on the front porch. Watch the boats in the marina as you sip a Snapple or indulge in a Yoguccino nonfat frozen yogurt dessert or not-so-nonfat slice of famous Schwarz Brothers cake. It's all good. 4120 Harborview Dr., Gig Harbor; 253/851-1033.

PLACES TO STAY

Gig Harbor Motor Inn: Set aside your pre-conceived notions of what a strip motel looks like to embrace this log cabin lodge on 14 acres, set back from the road. The cheapest rooms are also the best for dog travelers, with king-size beds and sliding glass doors leading out to a lawn, pond, and wooded trails for $81 a night, plus $10 each pet. 4709 Point Fosdick Dr. N.W.; 253/858-8161.

Inn at Gig Harbor: Isis feels right at home at this contemporary hotel with cherry wood furniture, a fitness room, and excellent restaurant on site. Standard rooms are $129, plus a $15 one-time pet fee and $5 per night. 3211 56th St. N.W.; 253/858-1111; www.innatgigharbor.com.

No Cabbages Bed and Breakfast: Jamee and her dog Trout have created a spare and serene place where they hope you will relax and renew. Her three acres, including a labyrinth and backyard deck, connect to 80 acres of county park land. The suite, done in neutral colors, is $135 per night and the rooms in the main house that share a bath are $80 per night, including breakfast. There is no extra charge for the privilege of bringing your dog with you. 10319 Sunrise Beach Dr. N.W.; 253/858-7797; www.nocabbages.com.

More Accommodations: Please look under Chain Hotels in the Resources section for additional places to stay in this area.

Key Peninsula

You are welcome to camp, but there's no place to lodge out here "in the sticks," as residents self-effacingly say. Your best bet is in town, meaning nearby Gig Harbor.

PARKS, BEACHES, AND RECREATION AREAS

27 Penrose Point

🐾🐾 (See Kitsap Peninsula map on page 48)

Dare the dogs say it's just another beach, with just another great view? Forgive them for getting jaded; it's hard not to, with so many to choose from. The large picnic area is barely reclaimed from the swamp, a bit squishy in the rainy season. Doesn't matter much, because your dog has probably just come from a splendid romp in the mud along the tidal flats. Your only hope of staying dry is a grass bluff walk above a breakwater wall, where there are more picnic tables and a short trail down to the boat moorage and campground. Benches line the slope, facing the water to take in the views of Tacoma and nearby islands.

From the Key Peninsula Highway, turn left on Cornwall Road, right on Delano Road, and left on 158th Avenue. $5 daily parking fee. Open 8 A.M.–dusk. 360/902-8844.

28 Joemma Beach

😸😸😸 (See Kitsap Peninsula map on page 48)

This state park is diplomatically named after Joe and Emma Smith, regional renaissance merchants who operated a trading store, newspaper, flower bulb business, and impromptu beach resort on the land from 1917 to 1932. They started the tradition of coming to enjoy the broad sand and gravel beach on Puget Sound.

The Seattle Shellfish Company owns the right to farm the mollusks that live on the beach, and you have the right to walk among them and smell them to your doggie heart's content. A grassy picnic hill leads to a long pier, which is the extent of the park at high tide. When the tide is out, the beach goes on a ways, down to YMCA's Camp Coleman, and they'll share their beach with you, should you want to go farther.

From the Key Peninsula Highway, turn right on Whiteman Road, and follow the little brown signs. Take the left fork of the road, turn right on Bay Road, and you'll see the sign for Camp Coleman next door. This park may be called Robert Kennedy Park on older maps. $5 daily parking fee. Hours are 8 A.M.–dusk. 360/902-8844.

PLACES TO EAT

Lisa's Fresh Express Deli: The address is officially Gig Harbor, but it's located out of town on the Key Peninsula. Make a run through the drive-through on your way to Penrose Point or Joemma Beach. Watch for Lisa's daily specials, including pulled-pork barbecue subs, chicken cordon bleu, and good-looking, good-tasting pasta salads. Lisa herself is usually behind the counter, working hard. Evenings, she heads up the street to run Blondie's, her restaurant and bar. 5501 N.W. 38th St.; 253/884-3354.

PLACES TO STAY

Penrose Point State Park Campground: With 82 tent spaces in the woods, all shaded or partially shady, Penrose Point has reliable availability. Tent sites are steps away from the beach. Reserve yours, for $16 per night, by calling 888/CAMPOUT (888/226-7688) or online at www.camis.com/wa.

THE ISLANDS

Bellingham

Lake Whatcom

Waldron Island

Orcas Island

Eastsound

1

Morgan State Park

2

Bellingham Bay

Lummi Island

Lake Samish

Stuart Island

Olga

Orcas

3

Cypress Island

Samish Bay

4

Shaw Island

8

Blakely Island

12

San Juan

5

9

10

Guemes Island

Anacortes

6

Island

Friday Harbor

Lopez

Decatur Island

13

14

see North Cascades page 154

7

11

Lopez Island

15

Richardson

Fidalgo Island

Rosario Strait

Mount Vernon

Conway

16

Skagit Bay

17 20

18

Whidbey Island

19

Oak Harbor

Utsalady

27

Strait of Juan de Fuca

20

San de Fuca

Camano Island

see Everett and Vicinity page 100

21

Coupeville

Camano

Port Susan

28

22

525

Greenbank

Saratoga Passage

Dungeness

Port Townsend

23

Mabana

Sequim

Sequim Bay

Langley

24

101

Freeland

26

see Olympic Peninsula page 18

20

25

Clinton

N
W—E
S

Olympic National Forest

Port Ludlow

104

Puget Sound

Hansville

Olympic National Park

0   5 mi

0   5 km

Shine

101

see Kitsap Peninsula page 48

CANADA
UNITED STATES

CHAPTER 3

The Islands

There's nothing quite like an island to give you the feeling that you're getting away from it all, and if you believe some of the tourist literature, the San Juan Archipelago, or group of islands, has 743 of them at low tide. That number sinks to 428 at high tide; only 60 of those rocks are inhabitable; unless you own or charter a boat, you can only get regular ferry service to four of them: Orcas, San Juan, Shaw, and Lopez. When you add in Whidbey Island, the second longest island in the U.S., and Camano Island, you have more recreational opportunities than you and your pup can, well, shake a stick at.

The San Juans sit in the rain shadow of Vancouver Island. All the rain dumps on Vancouver, leaving the islands typically sunny and dry. It is a welcome change from Portland or Seattle in the winter, but can cause droughts and water restrictions come summer.

The key to enjoying a trip to the islands is to plan ahead. Two things come in very handy: a Washington State ferry schedule and a tide table. The San Juans are accessible only by boat, plane, or a Washington State Ferry that leaves from Anacortes. Ferry schedules limit when you can come and go from the

PICK OF THE LITTER—THE ISLANDS

BEST PARKS
Moran State Park, Orcas Island (page 77)
Camano Island State Park, Camano Island (page 99)

BEST DOG PARK
Marguerite Brons Memorial Park, South Whidbey
(page 97)

BEST BEACHES
Young's Park, Guemes Island (page 87)
Double Bluff, South Whidbey (page 96)

BEST PLACES TO EAT
Flying Burrito, San Juan Island (page 82)
Love Dog Café, Lopez Island (page 86)

BEST PLACES TO STAY
Cottages at Cayou Cove, Orcas Island (page 79)
Spencer Spit State Park Campground, Lopez Island (page 86)
Camano Cottages, Camano Island (page 99)

islands, and lines of waiting cars can be brutally long on summer weekends. Plan to travel at off-peak times or park your car in line early and leave it there while you sightsee nearby. Dogs are welcome on ferries but must stay in the car or on the car decks.

For camping and lodging in the high season, May 15–September 15, make reservations well in advance to score your favorite site or room. Many of the restaurants and services on the islands are closed or have limited hours in the off-season. Call ahead for availability. For all state parks on the islands, the contact phone number is 360/902-8844.

Whale-watching, sailing, kayaking and cycling are the most popular island pastimes. You can rent bicycles and kayaks, charter boats, and book whale-watching tours on all the islands except Shaw. Most importantly, relax—you're on island time.

Orcas Island

At 60 square miles, Orcas is the largest and the hilliest of the San Juans. Its beautiful state park, Moran, takes full advantage of both of these features, including the towering Mt. Constitution with a viewpoint many would say is the best in the state. You'll find pockets of activity on the island centered in the small hamlets of Deer Harbor, Olga, Doe Bay, and the Orcas ferry landing. The center of commerce is Eastsound Village, with good restaurants and shops highlighting local artists.

PARKS, BEACHES, AND RECREATION AREAS

1 Eastsound Waterfront Park

🐾🐾 (See The Islands map on page 74)

You've been on the ferry for an hour, and, as you follow the trail of cars off the boat into the center of town, you realize that a pit stop for your pit bull would be a really good idea right about now. Eastsound Waterfront Park is your first, best bet for a potty break and provides the bonus of a decent bay view. A lawn with a few picnic tables and a bike rack are about it for niceties. Its sliver of beach isn't passable due to the amount of driftwood piled up.

You'll be on Orcas Road from the ferry headed into Eastsound until you turn right on Main Street, where you'll immediately find the half dozen parking spaces and the park on your right, but no signs.

2 Moran State Park

🐾🐾🐾🐾 (See The Islands map on page 74)

Moran is a four-paw park all the way, with something for everyone. Driving into the park, a grand stone archway welcomes you to more than 5,000 acres of forest, five freshwater lakes, a couple of waterfalls, majestic old-growth trees, and 30 miles of hiking trails. Shipbuilder and one-time mayor of Seattle Robert Moran and his wife Millie donated the first 2,700 acres to the state to open the park in 1921, adding another 1,000 acres to their gift in 1928. It has gradually grown over the years to become Washington's fourth largest park.

The first thing you'll see is the day-use area along the shores of Cascade Lake, which features a designated swimming beach. Dogs are not allowed in the roped-off area. No visit to the park is complete without a drive or hike up to the 2,409-foot peak of Mt. Constitution. From the sandstone observation tower built by the Civilian Conservation Corps in 1936, the view extends easily 100 miles in every direction.

Trail maps, available at the ranger station, identify 15 separate trails rated as easy, challenging, or difficult depending on elevation gain. Cooper and Isis adored the flat Cascade Loop and Mountain Lake Loop and found that even the Cold Springs Trail, with its 2,000 feet of elevation gain, was possible with their vertically challenged legs.

Getting here is easy—turn left when you get off the ferry and follow the signs 14 miles to the park entrance. There is a $5 parking fee. Hours are 6:30 A.M.–10 P.M. in the summer, 8 A.M.–dusk in winter.

🔳 Obstruction Pass

🐾🐾🐾 (See The Islands map on page 74)

This remote, primitive area was acquired by the State Parks and Recreation department in April of 2003. After a moderate half-mile hike, you'll come upon 10 rough campsites, distinguishable from the thick woods only by tiny markers, picnic tables, and fire pits. It's rugged and unkempt, which adds to its unspoiled, natural beauty. There is a rock worthy of note here, a sitting rock, on a promontory overlooking the water and at least a dozen other islands. On each side of the bluff are two tiny coves, and around to the east are stairs leading down to a wider beach, covered in tiny pebbles. In crystal clear waters, Isis saw a starfish hanging out at low tide. Other than a latrine, there are no amenities. Camping is on a first-come, first-served basis for $11 per night, payable by check or cash at the self-pay station at the trailhead. Pack out what you pack in.

To find this out-of-the-way wonder, follow Olga Road through Moran State Park, turn left on Point Lawrence Road, right on Obstruction Pass Road, and right on Trailhead Road.

PLACES TO EAT

Bilbo's Festivo: If your dog can wait for you calmly just outside the wall, you owe it to yourself to sit on the patio and cool off with a marionberry margarita while you spice it up with chicken molé or another fabulous authentic Mexican dish for lunch or dinner. The carved wooden tables and knickknacks were inspired by the restaurant's Hobbit namesake, 20 years before the *Lord of the Rings* movie craze. 310 A St., Eastsound; 360/376-4728.

Portofino Pizzeria: Its claim to being "the best pizza on the island" is akin to you telling your only sibling he's your favorite brother. Fortunately, the only pizza available on the island is really good, and the salad bar's not half bad either. It's unbelievably busy on weekend nights; order for takeout or delivery an hour before you get hungry. 274 A St., Eastsound; 360/376-2085.

PLACES TO STAY

Bartwood Lodge: Friendly owners Kenny and Shelley welcome you to their 18-room lodge. Half of the rooms face a landscaped patio; the others sit on a deck over the water, with views of Victoria, Vancouver, and Mount Baker. You'll pay as little as $59 for a standard room to $189 for a kitchen/fireplace suite plus a $15 one-time pet fee for these view rooms, a real steal. Guest dogs have their own lawn, complete with a baggie dispenser. Please keep pets on leash on the property. 178 Fossil Bay Dr., Eastsound; 866/666-2242; www.bartwoodlodge.com.

Cottages at Cayou Cove: These two free-standing cottages (three by spring 2005) are cozy and perfect in every detail. How do we love them? Let us count the ways: wood fireplaces, down duvets, fully equipped kitchens, decks with hot tubs with views of Deer Harbor marina, DVD/VCR/CD/satellite cable, clawfoot tubs and two-person showers, antique furnishings, continental breakfast delivered to your door, and an organic garden that guests are welcome to raid for their meals. Resident pooches Coco, Pancho, and Bruno live in the inn next door. Owner Valerie welcomes dogs with biscuits and asks only that they be kept off of the furniture. They are welcome to wander the property unleashed as long as they don't bother other guests and are under voice control. Rates range $195–285 plus a one-time $25 pet cleaning fee. Closed December through Valentine's Day. Call for directions; there's no sign. Deer Harbor; 888/596-7222; www.cayoucove.com.

Doe Bay Village: Pets are welcome in the campsites for no extra fee. They are also allowed in most cabins for an additional fee of $20 per pet, per night. Accommodations are simple, without TVs, phones, or Internet. To further help you unplug and unwind, relax in the mineral springs pools and in a huge sauna, where everyone hangs out in the buff. Very refreshing. Rates range $75–185, open weekends only Oct.–Apr. 107 Doe Bay Rd., Olga; 360/376-2291; www.doebay.com.

Moran State Park Campground: Tent camping is available at five different sites, three in the woods, one on the shores of Cascade Lake, and one at Mountain Lake, for a total of 150 available spaces. Fees are $16 per night for a standard site and $22 for a utility hookup site. May 15–September 15, reserve a space in advance by calling 888/CAMPOUT (888/226-7688) or online at www.camis.com/wa. Only a few campsites are available in the off-season, and reservations are not required.

San Juan Island

San Juan, the largest of the islands, has the most developed tourist facilities, shopping, and to our delight, the best-maintained parks. Much of the island's wealth came from a hundred years of mining lime from rich limestone deposits for use in steel production, paper, cement, and plaster.

The island is most famous for its role in history as the location of The Pig War, a conflict between the United States and Britain over the Oregon Territories, which included parts of Oregon, Washington, Idaho, Wyoming, and Montana. In 1859, as the two countries haggled over the San Juans, the last bits of real estate to be divvied up, an American farmer killed a British pig.

NATURE HIKES AND URBAN WALKS

Which came first, the nature preserve or the sculpture garden? No matter, your dog will think you're treating him to a walk through the forest, meadows, ponds, and wetlands of **Wescott Bay Reserve** on San Juan Island, while you enjoy 85 works of art by Pacific Northwest sculptors. Discovering the sculptures in a 19-acre natural setting adds to their appeal, and each piece created in bronze, wood, stone, metal, glass, or ceramic is placed for maximum effect. The reserve is maintained using only native plant landscaping designed to attract more than 120 bird species. It is an excellent pairing that makes for a special treat.

The area is fenced, although dogs should be kept on leash to protect the art and natural habitats. There is a suggested $3 donation at the entrance and maps to guide you through the maze of artwork. Most of the pieces are for sale if you find something you can't live without. Open dawn–dusk. 360/370-5050; www.wbay.org.

It was the final straw that nearly plunged the two countries into war. Troops of the two nations were sent to opposite ends of the island for a time out to await the decision over territorial rights. The U.S. was awarded ownership of the islands in 1872. The former garrisons of the two armies, English Camp and American Camp, were brought together to form the San Juan National Historical Park. Armed with this little bit of history, you and your Havanese may better appreciate the legacy of the parks all this activity left behind.

PARKS, BEACHES, AND RECREATION AREAS

4 English Camp

🐾🐾 (See The Islands map on page 74)

When the Americans were awarded ownership of the San Juans by peaceful arbitration, the British abandoned their garrison on the northwest side of the island, and James Crook and his family settled on the property. He lived on the island for 93 years and maintained the buildings, gardens, and parade grounds in excellent condition, preserving the area's history for us to enjoy.

Pick up a historical interpretive guide at the parking lot, which will provide detailed background on the log house, barracks, commandant's house, and formal gardens on the wide field that served as the parade grounds. It's a nice area for bird-watching, flying a kite, and gazing across Garrison Bay to Vancouver Island. There are two trails to hike, a 1.25-mile hill climb past the cemetery and up to Young Hill. At 650 feet, it is the highest elevation on the island. The other is a loop of similar length that leads to a bluff viewpoint.

Turn right on Blair Avenue from Spring Street, left on Guard Street, and right on Beaverton Valley Road, which will become West Valley Road leading into the park. Park hours are dawn–11 P.M. 360/378-2240; www.nps.gov/sajh.

5 San Juan Island County Park

🐾🐾🐾 (See The Islands map on page 74)

Bring your binoculars, because this is prime whale-watching territory. Unofficially called West Side Park, this pretty, pint-sized 12-acre county property on the sunny side of the island includes a beach, rocky bluff, and a campground with unobstructed water views of the migratory path of orca whale pods. On the gravel beach, you'll see an ancient madrona tree arching out over the water and a stream that runs down from the hills. From there, you can walk a path up and over the bluff that leads to strategically paced picnic benches for maximum views, and onto a soft, grassy slope for picnicking and even more ocean lookouts.

From West Valley Road, turn onto Mitchell Bay Road, and then left on West Side Road. Hours are 7 A.M.–10 P.M. 360/378-8420; www.co.san-juan.wa.us/parks.

6 Lime Kiln Point

🐾🐾🐾 (See The Islands map on page 74)

Getting to Lime Kiln is almost as much fun as the park itself, winding along the coast on the scenic West Side Road. This is another choice location for whale-watching, overlooking Haro Strait where orcas and minke whales travel May–October. From the parking area, an ADA-accessible trail leads 300 yards down to a viewing platform and several other trails branch out from there. The interpretive trail continues for a one-mile loop (not handicapped-accessible beyond the viewing platform) and leads to the lighthouse (built in 1919) and an interesting reproduction of a lime kiln operation. On the way, you'll pass large groves of madrona and Douglas fir trees. A steep wooden staircase leads down to the kiln for a closer look. Throughout the trail, educational signs tell the stories of marinelife and the lime industry that shaped the island. It's well done, the best interpretive trail we've hiked.

In the opposite direction along the park's 2,500 feet of coastline is the .3-mile hike to Deadman Bay. It's steep, narrow, and on the edge of a cliff, not for those who get woozy at the sight of heights. The reward is a rocky beach with exciting surf and more amazing views.

From Spring Street at the ferry, take San Juan Valley Road, turn left on Douglas Road, and right on Bailer Hill Road, which becomes West Side Road. The fee for parking is $5 per day. Park hours are 8 A.M.–dusk.

7 American Camp

🐾🐾🐾🐾 (See The Islands map on page 74)

Somewhat in parallel to the two countries themselves, English Camp is small, green, and tidy while American Camp is large and more untamed, with wide plains, grandiose forests, and long beaches, totaling 1,223 acres occupying the entire southeast tip of the island.

There's so much to see and do here, you might want to start at the visitors center to put together your game plan. Meanwhile, the following are some of our top recommendations: Drive the length of Cattle Point Road through the park to take in the views and see the lay of the land. Build a bonfire on Fourth of July Beach, on the quiet side of the bay. Take a walk on the wild and windy side, for miles and miles and miles, along South Beach, the longest public beach on the island. Not tired yet? Hike the old dirt road trail, covered by a forested canopy of fir, cedar, and maple to Jakle's Lagoon and Mount Finlayson. Finally, wade through the grasslands to the Redoubt, a buried gun battery.

If you and your pup enjoy a dose of education with your exercise, there are exhibits featuring the American-British boundary dispute, archaeology, and camp life. Historical tour guidebooks are available to borrow in boxes at the top of each trailhead. One-mile self-guided walks start at the visitors center and Jakle's Lagoon parking lot.

From Spring Street off the ferry, turn left on Mullis Street. Mullis becomes Cattle Point Road, and you can follow the road's twists and turns and the signs directly to the park entrance. Park hours are dawn–11 P.M.; 360/378-2902 or 360/378-2240; www.nps.gov/sajh.

PLACES TO EAT

The Doctor's Office: Walk off the ferry and across the street into this self-proclaimed "treatment café" and treat yourself to espresso, homemade hard-pack ice cream, a juice bar, daily pastries, sandwiches, and breakfast burritos. A convenient walk-up window makes it easy—just what the doctor ordered. Breakfast and lunch; 85 Front Street, Friday Harbor; 360/378-8865.

The Flying Burrito: Sorry, we don't buy it—these puppies are too big and heavy to get airborne. The burritos, tacos, and house specials do make for good eating if not flying, on a large, sunny patio where dogs are welcome for lunch and dinner. Stuffings range from traditional chicken, beef, and pork to exotic wild salmon, steak, and tofu. Add your favorite sauce and a beer or margarita, and you are good to go. It's right on the way to American Camp, too. 701 Spring St., Friday Harbor; 360/378-1077.

PLACES TO STAY

Friday Harbor Inn: This inn welcomes pets most warmly and provides sensible, non-smoking rooms on the first floor. It has the largest number of rooms available for pets on the island. Extra touches include fresh-baked cookies in the lobby and a designated dog lawn. Its location is ideal, easy to get to the ferry and perfect as a jumping-off point for your San Juan adventures. Rates are $69–140, plus a one-time $15 fee per pet. 410 Spring St., Friday Harbor; 800/793-4756; www.theinns.com.

Lakedale Resort: This private, 82-acre property is a vacation unto itself, with about 200 tent sites, a grand lodge, waterfront cabins, a general store, and three lakes stocked with rainbow trout and wide-mouth bass. Campsites on Dream Lake and Neva Lake are $21–26 per night depending on the season, plus an extra $1 per pet, per night. Log Cabin No. 1 welcomes pets also; it features two bedrooms, two full baths, fireplace, lakeside deck, full kitchen, linens, and cookware. It looks like L. L. Bean or Eddie Bauer had a hand in decorating. You might as well take a dip in the lake or grab a pole and catch some dinner. Nightly rate for the cabin is $160 in the low season up to $265 in July and August. 4313 Roche Harbor Rd.; 800/617-2267; www.lakedale.com.

San Juan County Park Campground: The campgrounds are up on a slope, and because they're placed for your viewing pleasure when you look out of your tent, there's nothing to stop anyone from looking in, either. Advance reservations are your only hope of getting one of the 23 sites in the summer. Water, real flushing toilets, picnic tables, fire rings, and firewood are available. Cost is $23 per night, plus a $6 reservation fee. West Side Road; 360/378-1842; www.co.san-juan.wa.us/parks.

Shaw Island

This tiny island of 7.7 square miles, with a population of less than 200, has one grocery store at the ferry landing, a library, and a county park with camping and a lovely sandy beach as its only public amenities. It often gets overlooked by the hordes of summer island tourists, meaning you stand a good chance of being one of only a handful of people enjoying gorgeous views and peaceful country roads. Until 2004, the ferry and convenience store were run by a local order of Franciscan nuns; now the Masons take care of business.

PARKS, BEACHES, AND RECREATION AREAS

8 Shaw Island County Park

🐾🐾🐾 (See The Islands map on page 74)

You'll hear the locals call this South Beach, a beautiful spot that meets our every requirement for a perfect beach. It is secluded, with great views of Canoe and Lopez Islands. The sand is soft for squishing between paws and toes, and there are comfortable observation rocks and driftwood logs to sit upon and watch the waves. The beach is accessed by two steep wooden staircases that descend from the campground and day-use area. A picnic shelter, some tire swings, and a small lawn make up the area above the beach.

From the ferry landing, Gratzer Road will lead you to Blind Bay Road. From there, it's less than a mile before you turn left on Squaw Bay Road, then right on Indian Cove Road and the park to your right. 360/378-8420.

PLACES TO STAY

Shaw Island County Park Campground: There are 11 campsites, #1–6 with water views for $11 per night and #7–11 on the hillside for $9 per night. Each site has a picnic table and a fire pit, and some privacy provided by tree cover. Camping is by reservation only April–October for an additional $6 per reservation. Call 360/378-1842 up to 90 days in advance, and pay by VISA or MasterCard. Campsites are first-come, first-served the rest of the year, and you pay by cash or check at self-pay stations in the park. There's one vault toilet and running water, but no shower facilities. 360/378-1842; www.co.san-juan.wa.us/parks.

Lopez Island

Although Lopez is lacking in pet-friendly accommodations, it is otherwise the friendliest and most casual of the San Juans. The mostly agricultural island is open and pastoral. We knew a dog named Lucia who barked only at cows and bicycles; she would have been hoarse and happy here. There is a tradition to greet everyone you pass in the car with a wave, typically a finger lifted off the steering wheel (index finger, *not* middle finger). It's easy enough to hop a quick ferry from Orcas or San Juan to come for the day. Lopez Village is the town center, with shops, restaurants, a good-sized grocery, and the only public showers available on the island.

PARKS, BEACHES, AND RECREATION AREAS

🐾 Odlin

🐾🐾 (See The Islands map on page 74)

This county park offers 80 acres of near-instant gratification, only one mile south of the ferry landing. You can park your car on the beach and step out onto the sand. Picnic tables are lined up along the waterfront, with views across Upright Channel to Shaw Island. When you've had your fill of the beach, you can hike the dense, narrow, winding Little Bird Trail, accessible from behind a small meadow. Be prepared to get muddy in the rainy season—some puddles were deep enough for Cooper to swim through! On a unique note, we discovered our first beachfront baseball field here and wondered how many foul balls have been retrieved from the surf over the years.

FETCHING NECESSITIES

It's a rare and special place where literature and dogs get equal billing, as they do at **Islehaven Books & Borzoi** in Lopez Island Village. Owner Phyllis has six of these Russian beauties, who alternate coming with her to the shop every day. Skye, Reefer, Nita, Trader, Apollo, and Fiesta are their casual names. You can ask her about their show names and see their winning ribbons on the wall behind the counter. Please leave your pets to bask in the sun on the deck out front while you browse, to avoid any potential conflicts of interest. Talk to Phyllis a while, let her get to know you a bit, and then have her recommend a book for you. She's positively psychic in her perfect picks. Perhaps that's one reason her customers return again and again over the 17 years she's been in business—and to visit the dogs. #2 Village Center, Lopez Village; 360/468-2132.

10 Spencer Spit

🐾🐾🐾 (See The Islands map on page 74)

The spit is a symmetrical triangular sandbar, created by the action of waves eroding sand from cliffs to the north and south and transporting sand along the shoreline. In the middle of the spit is a protected lagoon. This unique land feature is named for Theodore Spencer, who built a house for his family on the hillside and a log cabin at the tip of the spit for guests sometime between 1913 and 1920. The park was acquired in 1967, and a replica of the cabin was built in 1978 from materials washed up on the beach. The rest of the site was developed 1981–1983 and dedicated in 1983.

The first parking you see is a view lot with a 10-minute limit. Continue past the restrooms to the second parking area, for spots with no time limit. From there, it's a short hike down and onto the spit itself. You'll want a sweater or jacket, even in good weather, to defend you against the brisk winds. Picnic benches and fire pits are lined up along the north edge of the sandbar. You're welcome to swim if you have the fortitude. You can go crabbing and clamming for your sustenance as did the island's first Native American inhabitants, but you must have a state license to do so.

To make your way to Spencer Spit, follow the signs from Center Road to Cross Road, turning right on Port Stanley Road and left on Bakerview Road.

11 Shark Reef Sanctuary

🐾🐾🐾 (See The Islands map on page 74)

It is absolutely vital that you respect the signs cautioning you to keep dogs on leash and stay on the trails. After a quick, half-mile trot through the woods, the trail ends abruptly on a cliff, high above big waves crashing against the rocks. It would be way too easy for your English setter to run right over the edge in his enthusiasm. Shark Reef gets its name from rocks as chiseled as a shark's teeth. It is dangerous, dramatic, and stunning. Once you arrive at that first arresting viewpoint, the trail continues along the cliff's edge, presenting you with viewpoint after viewpoint of islands with equally dangerous names such as Mummy Rocks and Deadman Island, and just when you think you've passed the last good view, you come upon another. There are plenty of opportunities to put down a blanket, perhaps to enjoy a packed picnic, inspired by the views of the surrounding islands and the Strait of San Juan de Fuca. This gorgeous, wild sanctuary is preserved with the joint efforts of the Department of Natural Resources and the San Juan County Parks department. Take the proper precautions to fully enjoy the drama it presents.

When you reach the park boundary at the southern end of the cliff trail, Cooper recommends retracing your steps back to the main trail. The rest of the paths through the park are barely discernable through the brush, and it is easy to get lost (or so he heard, not willing to admit that as a hound, he couldn't pick up the scent of the track).

To reach the park, take the right fork in the road from Ferry Road to Fisherman Bay Road, turn right on Airport Road, and then left on Shark Reef Road to the end, where you'll see a trailhead with room for about four cars, a latrine, and a trash can. The trail to the bluff is right at the park sign.

PLACES TO EAT

Love Dog Café: According to owner and chef White Bear Woman, her restaurant's name comes from a quote by mystic poet Rumi, "There are love dogs in this world no one knows the name of. Give your life to be one of them." She believes in the power of good food to comfort and soothe the soul, and she certainly made believers out of Coop 'n' Isis. A grilled cheese sandwich with tomatoes and onions was doggone good, and the homemade desserts all looked lovely. Buy a bag of the homemade, heart-shaped peanut butter dog treats for the road. #1 Village Center; Lopez Village; 360/468-2150.

Vita's Wildly Delicious: Vita is a caterer with a fancy shop that caters to picnickers who want to put together a gourmet spread of wine, cheese, bread, and other delicacies to take on the road or home for a patio supper. Daily specialties are made with quality ingredients. Vita has wildly good taste and high style. 77 Village Road, Lopez Village; 360/468-4268.

PLACES TO STAY

Spencer Spit State Park Campground: Sites at this 138-acre park are available March 5–October 26, and they are some of the best we've encountered. They are spacious, level, paved with gravel, and spaced much farther apart than usual, offering complete privacy. In addition, there are seven walk-in sites right on the beach just south of the spit, with the ocean just outside your tent flap. There are no showers or utility hookups. Camping is $16 per night. 888/CAMPOUT (888/226-7688).

Guemes Island

Cooper and Isis felt the spirits of distant ancestors here on "Dog Island," nicknamed for the companions raised by the Samish Indian Nation whose fur was used to weave blankets when goat hair was sparse. Guemes (GOO-eh-mus) Island, a tiny oasis reached by a seven-minute ferry ride from Anacortes, is the place to go to get your island fix if you don't have the time or money to head to the San Juans. The county ferry, a different boat than the state ferry to the San Juans, leaves from the intersection of 6th and I streets in Anacortes and costs only $5.25 round-trip. The island retains its character of peace and quiet; at only four miles from bottom to top, it's too small to draw much attention. You have one choice for lodging, one for food, and two public beaches. In short, Dog Island is perfect for a dog's day out.

PARKS, BEACHES, AND RECREATION AREAS

12 Young's Park

🐾🐾🐾🐾 (See The Islands map on page 74)

Generations of people have enjoyed this plot of land since 1925. It is the place to go for fishing, crabbing, clamming, beachcombing, stick throwing, swimming, sunbathing, kite flying, boating, exploring, sniffing...we could go on, but you get the idea. You and your pooch can pick your pleasure on land and in the waters around the island.

The area immediately south of the park is private, but you can walk around the island to the north just about as far as you want. You'll pass in front of the Guemes Island Resort and a group camp; they don't mind sharing. The beach is a combination of sand and gravel, easy on the paws. Views to the north are prettier than those on the island's south side, looking out on Canada, with snow-capped Mt. Baker hogging center stage.

The county has maintained the park since 1977, providing a comfortable lawn, a few picnic tables, trash, and a portable potty. By the way, there is one more county park in the center of the island, Schoolhouse Park, but we've left it off the list because there's nothing there of interest to a dog other than soft grass in an emergency.

The way to Young's Park is idiot-proof. From the ferry, drive four miles, go straight past the park sign to the end of the road, bear right, and park in the gravel parking lot. Day use only. 4243 Guemes Island Rd.; 360/336-9414; www.skagitparksfoundation.org/youngs.htm.

PLACES TO EAT

Anderson's General Store and Kitchen: The kitchen serves up huevos rancheros, omelettes, yogurt parfaits, and legendary cinnamon rolls for breakfast. Burgers, hot dogs, Greek salad, and pesto chicken sandwiches dominate the lunch menu. The Andersons also offer ice cream, espresso, and, as they say, free advice. Outdoor seating is on a wraparound porch overlooking the ferry terminal. The general store shelves are well stocked with unusual treats. This is your only choice for island groceries—the tongue-in-cheek motto is "If we don't have it, we'll explain how to get along without it." 7885 Guemes Island Rd.; 360/293-4548; www.guemesislandstore.com.

PLACES TO STAY

Guemes Island Resort: It seems as though everyplace is called a resort on the islands, harkening back to quainter days when people were in the habit of summering here. These five cozy cabins and two homes share the driveway that leads to Young's Park and a stretch of sandy beach. The cabins are heated by woodstove only. The Mt. Baker house has furnace heat and is wheelchair accessible. They do not provide TV, phones, or radio—who needs them when every window frames a view of Mt. Baker and the islands? Cabins are $120–140 per night, and the Mt. Baker house is $138–165. Barbecues and rowboats are provided to guests at no charge. Pets are $5 per night. 4268 Guemes Island Rd.; 800/965-6643; www.guemesislandresort.com.

Fidalgo Island and Anacortes

The channel of water separating Fidalgo Island from the mainland is so narrow that most people don't even realize that the city of Anacortes is on an island. Recreational opportunities are overshadowed by the city's blue-collar reputation and people rushing through town to get on the next ferry to the San Juans. We say "phooey"—dogs don't discriminate. In town, all retail activity centers appropriately on Commercial Avenue.

PARKS, BEACHES, AND RECREATION AREAS

13 Washington Park

🐾🐾🐾 (See The Islands map on page 74)

Everyone we talked to in Anacortes said, "Have you been to the loop yet? Isn't it great?" We quickly learned that the loop is a two-mile paved trail around the beachhead of Fidalgo Island in Washington Park. And, sure enough, it is great. It is the social circle for high-paw society in Anacortes, and debutante dogs happily drag their humans on leashes behind them as they meet and greet. Let's just say there's a whole lot of sniffing going on.

Peek-a-boo views of Rosario Strait, Fidalgo Head, Burrows Bay, and the surrounding islands through the trees keep you occupied while your dog works the crowd. At several points along the loop, unpaved .1-mile spurs stick out to take you to less obstructed views, particularly at Green Point. The rest of the 220-acre park includes a campground, playground, 24-hour boat launch, and waterfront picnic tables off to the right at the entrance to the loop. The loop is restricted to walkers 6 A.M.–10 A.M., after which it is open to cars until the park closes at 10 P.M. However, dogs looked down their noses at us and walkers gave us the big stink eye when we tried to drive around, it is obviously local custom to walk.

Take the Highway 20 Spur all the way through town and out Oakes Avenue. At the fork in the road where all the cars go right to get on the ferry, take the left fork instead onto Sunset Avenue and straight into the park.

14 H & 38th Reservoir Site Dog Park

🐾🐾🐾 (See The Islands map on page 74)

The city of Anacortes is mapped on an alphanumeric grid (east/west streets numbered 1–41 and north/south avenues A–Z), which is how you get a park named the "H & 38th." Fidalgo Islanders for Dogs Off-leash, or F.I.D.O., is the local organization that worked hard to get their very own dog park opened in late 2003. It is a plain, two-acre, rectangular exercise yard with a postage stamp–sized separate area for small, timid, and older dogs. It's funny that the little dog area has a six-foot fence with barbed wire at the top, while the larger area has a plain, low, chain-link border surrounding it. Maybe it's because of those Jack Russell Terriers, like Cooper's neighbor Millie, with their astounding vertical leaps. All that matters is that it is fenced and leash-free.

Scattered straw does little to cut the mud, which never slowed down any dog we know. Poop bags, garbage cans, and a portable potty are provided. Bring your own drinking water and a towel. From Commercial Avenue, turn west onto 32nd Street, and left onto I Avenue, which curves to become H Avenue a block later. Just south of 38th, you'll see a dirt road on the left, and the double-gated entrance to the park down the lane. For more information, call F.I.D.O. at 360/293-9658.

15 Anacortes Community Forest Lands

🐾🐾🐾 (See The Islands map on page 74)

We were pleasantly surprised to learn of an extensive network of trails on protected land managed through the ACFL program. Unless you're lucky enough to stumble upon trail markers for the 2,200 acres of ACFL lands, your best bet is to buy a set of maps at the visitors center for $10 (Corner of 9th Street and Commercial Avenue; 360/299-1953). You'll find out where to park and where main trail access points are located. Other handy map information includes elevation gain, mileage, trail usage restrictions, and difficulty ratings. Map-loving geeks, like Cooper's dad Steve, are in heaven.

It's a big, messy maze of lakes, forests, ponds, wetlands, forests, and mountains, but don't let that scare you off. Trails are short, all of them less than two miles, and remember, you're on an island. You can't get far without bumping into civilization or the water. Speaking of water, in attempt to put some kind of framework around ACFL lands, trails are grouped around the three biggest inland bodies of it: Cranberry Lake, Heart Lake, and Whistle Lake. What the locals call Little Cranberry Lake, not to be confused with Big Cranberry Lake in Deception Pass State Park, is the perennial favorite. Another highlight is the summit of Mt. Erie at 1270 feet, which can be reached from either Heart Lake or Whistle Lake. The only drawback is that some trails are open to horses, mountain bikes, and even a few to off-road motorbikes. We didn't encounter anyone in the winter, and hopefully everyone will share and share alike. ACFL's Conservation Easement Program continues to add acreage to protected lands as donations allow. 360/288-1953.

PLACES TO EAT

Rockfish Grill: The pub grub pleases and the Anacortes Ales and Lagers go down nice and easy on the side patio. Nachos, tostadas, fish and chips, vegetarian specialties, and wood-fired brick-oven pizzas are the biggest crowd-pleasers for lunch and dinner. 320 Commercial Ave., Anacortes; 360/588-1720; www.anacortesrockfish.com.

PLACES TO STAY

Fidalgo Country Inn: Pine furniture and French country patterns soften the look of an otherwise standard motel. Freshly baked cookies and a gas fireplace in the lobby didn't hurt either. It's ideally located halfway between the Anacortes ferry and Deception Pass State Park. Pets under 40 pounds are allowed for an additional $20 per night. Standard room rates are $89; suites are $169. 7645 SR 20, Anacortes; 360/293-3494 or 800/244-4179; www.nwcountryinns.com.

North Whidbey

The top of Whidbey Island is reached via the Deception Pass Bridge, the most-photographed span in the state. The bottom of the island, 45 linear miles later, can be reached by the Clinton/Mukilteo ferry just north of Seattle. Halfway in between, you can take a ferry from Port Townsend on the Olympic Peninsula.

Whidbey is the second longest island in the U.S., after Manhattan, and the list of beaches and parks at which to play with your pet is equally long, so we've divided the island into its three commonly used regions: North, Central, and South.

PARKS, BEACHES, AND RECREATION AREAS

16 Deception Pass

🐾🐾🐾 (See The Islands map on page 74)

Based on the number of annual visitors, Deception Pass consistently ranks as the most popular state park in Washington. From a dog's point of view, that's a deceiving statistic, because the majority of people are merely driving through, stopping for a snapshot at the famous bridge and to take in the views. Isis doesn't mind if they leave the beach and 38 miles of hiking trails to her.

The park straddles the bridge from Fidalgo to Whidbey, but most activity is on the Whidbey side. One thing worth checking out on the north side is the Maiden of Deception Pass totem at Rosario Beach, depicting the lives of the Samish Indian Nation. On the south side, the main beach and picnic area cover a spit of land between the ocean and the lake. Foggy mornings are quite something as the mists lift over the lake and get swept out to sea. On the trails, really ambitious hikers can cover cliffs, forests, sand dunes, and wetlands in one day.

The Park starts 10 miles north of Oak Harbor on Highway 20. Parking is $5 per day.

17 Clover Valley

🐾🐾🐕 (See The Islands map on page 74)

This dog park is a popular hangout for local dogs and visiting pooches are welcome to join in the fun. About two acres of the off-leash area is a rocky open field, basic for ball tossing and retrieving and generally chasing each other around. Another third is a wooded area off to the east side, good for a quick walk and sniff. The area is fully fenced with a single wooden gate. One side borders along a busy street—fortunately the park has its own private driveway and parking away from the hustle and bustle.

There's a portable potty for human comfort and a single picnic table under a covered awning in center field, but it's B.Y.O. water and waste bags. There are other truly amazing off-leash areas on the island by comparison, so Cooper rates this one as just okay.

Getting here is a simple matter and the sign to the driveway is easy to see. Just take Highway 20 to Ault Field Road going west, and you'll see the park off to your right just past the Clover Valley Baseball Park. 360/321-4049; www.whidbey.com/fetch.

18 Oak Harbor

🐾🐾🐕 (See The Islands map on page 74)

This little one-acre, off-leash area is literally down the street from Clover Valley and is not used as frequently, so it's an ideal park for small or timid dogs to enjoy some off-leash time without getting bowled over by the rowdier pups at the "big" park. It is a bit rough around the edges, with some uneven, rocky ground and a couple of scrawny trees. The park is next to a noisy welding warehouse, too.

On the plus side, the park is fully fenced and gated at the end of a cul de sac with a half dozen parking spots. Concrete pipes are laid out to run through; rock landscaping, a covered picnic bench, and running water add to the niceties. It opened very recently; it'll improve over time.

Take Highway 20 to Ault Field Road, go west on Ault Field Road and turn left on Goldie Road. Pay close attention to find Technical Drive on your left a couple of blocks down the road, and go to the end of the lane to get to the park, past a small industrial area. 360/321-4049; www.whidbey.com/fetch.

19 Joseph Whidbey State Park

 (See The Islands map on page 74)

The park, like the island, is named for a nautical figure, Master Joseph Whidbey, the first mate of the *Discovery* sailed by explorer George Vancouver in 1792 with orders to chart the Pacific Northwest for Britain. It's got what other island parks have, namely a good beach on 3,100 feet of shoreline, views of the Strait of San Juan de Fuca, and 112 acres of general picnic stuff. It's not one of the state parks in highest demand by the general public, which makes it all the better for its unofficial purpose, a regular coffee klatch for the canine set. Dog people from the Oak Harbor area with their dogs to the lower level of the park, down by the pebbly beach, and on a couple of miles of okay trails. You can come and mingle with the locals while your mutt finds new playmates.

Take State Route 20 south through Oak Harbor, and just past town, turn right on Swanton Road for three miles. Parking is $5. The park is officially closed October–April. Uh huh. You'll have to improvise on parking when the gates are closed.

PLACES TO EAT

The Pot Belly Deli: Versatility is the name of the game at this diner, and the choices will surprise you. Sure, they've got hot and cold sandwiches, soups, and burgers, but things really heat up after 4 P.M. That's when you can get the good stuff, such as steak, prime rib, chicken ravioli, and crab cakes. Call ahead and pick-up at the drive-through window. 32070 S.R. 20, Oak Harbor; 360/675-5204.

PLACES TO STAY

Deception Pass State Park Campground: There are 251 campsites, most of them located near Cranberry Lake, which, by the way, is a *different* Cranberry Lake than the one in Anacortes. Seven restrooms and six showers are sprinkled throughout the campground. Call for reservations. Cost is $16–22 for overnight camping. 888/CAMPOUT (888/226-7688); www.camis.com/wa.

More Accommodations: Please look under Chain Hotels in the Resources section for additional places to stay in this area.

Central Whidbey

The island has an extensive naval military history evident in retired bases that have been given second lives as state parks (hooray!), and the Naval Air Station remains the island's largest employer today. A high ratio of soldiers on the island must be what lends it a general air of strict discipline, extending even to the enforcement of leash laws, to the tune of a $500 fine if you're caught running free where you're not supposed to be.

In Coupeville, take a moment to stop by **The Stray Dog Co.,** a gift store with a unique collection of antique dog and cat collectibles (12 Front St.; 360/678-4826).

PARKS, BEACHES, AND RECREATION AREAS

20 Patmore Pit

🐾🐾🐾 🐕 (See The Islands map on page 74)

As Pavlov's bell suggested to his dog that it was time to eat, the front fence and gate at Patmore Pit suggest to yours that he shouldn't go too far. The rest of the park is only partially fenced, and it's not exactly clear how much of the 40-acre parcel is officially off-leash, but suffice it to say that it's big enough not

THINK GLOBALLY, BARK LOCALLY

The local pro-pup organization on Whidbey Island is called **FETCH!,** Free Exercise Time for Canines and their Humans! Membership is $10 a year, and from the looks of things, the organization does a great job of keeping up the local dog parks and promoting more off-leash opportunities for four-legged islanders. You can pick up a copy of its quarterly newsletter, *Daily Wag,* at any of the off-leash parks. To contribute, go to www.whidbey.net/fetch or call 360/321-4049.

The island rescue organization is called **WAIF,** for Whidbey Animals' Improvement Foundation. Shop for bargains and help homeless animals at the same time at WAIF's two thrift stores on the island, in Freeland at 1651 Main St., 360/331-2818; and in Oak Harbor at 1036 SE Pioneer Way, 360/279-9504.

Together, the organizations have published a cookbook to raise money. If your dog could speak, he would tell you to buy a copy of *Culinary Tails: Recipes and Whimsy from Whidbey Island,* available for $19.95 at select island merchants or online at www.waifanimals.org.

to have to worry about it. There's plenty of scrubby brush, trees, and crab grass for everybody in a field wide enough to stretch all four legs.

In addition to land, lots of land, under starry skies above, Patmore Pit features an agility course, with a few tired pieces of equipment to set up in the desired configuration. This smaller area is completely fenced, and a nearby sign suggests this secured spot for dogs in training, young and foolish dogs, and dogs new to the whole off-leash idea. We're not sure how practical that is, because you have to walk the gauntlet of off-leash dogs all the way across the wide field and down a short road before you can even reach the fenced area. Other than a portable potty and some water in gallon jugs, we didn't see any facilities at the park, just room to roam.

To reach the pit from Highway 20, turn left on Patmore Road, and follow it just past Keystone Hill Road. 360/321-4049; www.whidbey.com/fetch.

21 Fort Ebey and Kettles Park

🐾🐾🐾 (See The Islands map on page 74)

If you're willing to share the trails with mountain bikers and the bluffs with model glider enthusiasts, Fort Ebey State Park is another one of many options on Whidbey created from former military defense posts.

A winding road into the 645-acre park forks to the right for access to the beach and Lake Pondilla and to the left for the campground and remains of the gun battery. A mile-long walking trail along a ridge leads between the two. The beach is unremarkable, too rocky and rough on the paws for walking and too much kelp growing in the water to swim. However, if you park at the gun battery, you can walk out onto a series of wide, grassy steppes with commanding views. This is where you'll see the warning signs, "Caution: Model Glider Low Approach." Picnic tables are available at both the beach and on the slopes.

Adjacent to Fort Ebey is access to Kettles Park, named for a geological formation visible in the area. The "kettles" are large indentations left in the ground from melting ice as the glaciers retreated and shaped the landscape 15,000 or so years ago. The labyrinth of 30 miles of trails is most frequently used by mountain bikers, maybe too rattling on the nerves of some dogs. Otherwise, the trails are fairly wide, well marked, short, hilly, and well kept. There's a worn map posted on the board at Fort Ebey.

From Highway 20, two miles north of Coupeville, turn left on Libbey Road, and then left of Hill Valley Drive to enter the park. Parking is $5 per day.

22 Fort Casey

🐾🐾🐾 (See The Islands map on page 74)

The park is part three of the "Triangle of Death," along with Fort Worden on the Olympic Peninsula and Fort Flagler on Marrowstone Island (both in the first chapter). Of the three, this state park has the best-preserved display of firepower, of definite interest to history buffs. The concrete platforms of the William Worth Battery are a restored exhibit featuring four guns that were operational from 1898 to 1942. That's guns as in cannons, and they are daunting. Nearby, the Admiralty Head Lighthouse now houses an interpretive center; pets are not allowed inside. Dogs are also not likely to join divers at the underwater scuba park. Cooper and Isis preferred chasing each other across the parade grounds and lying in the sun by the picnic tables, watching the ferries go back and forth to Port Townsend.

Highway 20 West, one of the island's main roads, leads directly to the park. Parking is $5 day. Open 8 A.M.–dusk.

PLACES TO EAT

Greenbank Farm and Whidbey Pies Café: On the 522 acres of the largest loganberry farm in the U.S., you can get quiche, roasted vegetable salad, savory popovers, a sandwich, and some fabulous pie, and take it all outside to the picnic benches by the pond for a relaxing meal. Afterwards, you can participate in wine tasting or walk across the fields to visit the alpacas. If you're really lucky, you can buy some of the loganberry liqueur–filled chocolates before they disappear each season. The farm is right off the mainline of Highway 525. 765 Wonn Rd., Greenbank, Whidbey Island; 360/678-1288; www.greenbankfarm.com.

South Whidbey

Whidbey and Camano Islands have a joint motto that is immortalized in the URL of their official website, www.donothinghere.com. It's amazing how tired you can get doing nothing, especially when there's so much of nothing to do. The southern end of the island is prettier than the north, with better off-leash parks.

PARKS, BEACHES, AND RECREATION AREAS

23 South Whidbey State Park

🐾🐾🐾 (See The Islands map on page 74)

With names like Mutiny Bay and Smuggler's Cove, the roads to South Whidbey make you think the island was dominated by pirates, not the Navy. The park covers 347 acres of old-growth forest down to a 4,500-foot shoreline on Admiralty Inlet. A relaxing .8-mile trail leads through the woods to an ancient cedar tree; another .7-mile trail down to the beach is steep, making for a good workout on the way back up. The beach area is fairly small, with good views of Puget Sound and the Olympics. The dogs enjoyed the trails here more than the water.

To reach South Whidbey by land, turn west on Fish Road from Highway 525, take a right on Mutiny Bay Road, and then a left on Bush Point Road, which becomes Mutiny Bay Road as it heads toward the park. Follow the signs from there. Parking is $5 per day.

24 South Whidbey Community Park

 (See The Islands map on page 74)

Okay, we know that many of you think of your pets as kids. If you happen to have children of the two-legged variety, this park is a must. It has the coolest playground we've ever encountered, with a huge castle like something straight out of Disneyland. A maze of corridors, towers, slides, bridges, turrets, and dungeons carved of wood provide countless hours of climbing, sliding, and hide-and-seeking opportunities. Each piece is marked with the names of the people and organizations in the community who donated time and money to make the play kingdom possible.

Pets are not allowed on the playground itself, but while the kids are releasing their pent-up energies, dogs can enjoy some beautifully maintained grass. Or, grab a map on-site and walk a mile and a half of short trails around the park and between various playing fields. The whole park is a shining example of community effort and pride.

South Whidbey is halfway between Langley and the ferry terminal on Maxwelton Road, right off of Highway 525, just past South Whidbey High School.

25 Double Bluff Beach Access

(See The Islands map on page 74)

Isis couldn't help but hum the tune to *Born Free* as she ran along the beach at Double Bluff, with her ears flapping in the breeze and no leash to tie her down. While most dog parks are finite, fenced-in areas by necessity, this strip of soft sand goes on for at least two miles. What a joy! On one side is a cliff too steep to climb, and on the other, the water, keeping the area naturally protected for off-leash beachcombing. Views from the beach look out onto the shipping channel of Admiralty Inlet and across to the Kitsap and Olympic Peninsulas. We raise our paws in salute to the people responsible for designating this great beach an off-leash area. Of course, everybody loves it here, so it gets really crowded and parking is a pain in the tail. You're allowed to park on Double Bluff Road as long as your car is completely outside of the white border line.

You must keep your dogs on leash, strain as they might, from the parking area until you pass the first 500 feet of beach. Remember, the $500 fine applies if you're caught off guard and off leash (hey, that's about a $1 a foot). There are signs and a big windsock on a pole that mark the start of the free-roam sand. Après surf, there is a dog-rinse station with fresh water against the wall, near the park entrance. For fun in the sun, head south on Double Bluff Road from Highway 525. 360/321-4049; www.whidbey.com/fetch.

26 Marguerite Brons Memorial Park

🐾🐾🐾🐾🐕 (See The Islands map on page 74)

This park is really two parks in one, offering the best of both worlds. At the center of the plot of land is a fully fenced, two-acre field, with a couple of entry gates. It's a wide, open square tailor-made for running, tussling, and tossing the soft flying disks provided for you in a nearby bucket. Mud-management is well handled, with plenty of gravel and grass. Then, surrounding the field, accessible from two separate gates, are 13 additional acres of fenced leash-free forest. The woods are dense, with trails winding through them, giving you the sensation of leaving civilization behind completely within a few feet. Word on the street is that it is typically less crowded here than at Double Bluff.

The park is pretty well stocked with the basics, including a covered picnic area, waste bags, shovel, portable potty, and garbage. Water is carried in and may not be reliable. Stop by the community bulletin board to see a picture of Dr. Alvin Brons, who donated this land in honor of his late wife, and his adorable dog Tuffy. To get to the Brons, turn south onto Bayview Road from Highway 525; the driveway is about a block past the cemetery on the left. The sealed gravel parking lot has room for about 20 cars. 360/321-4049; www.whidbey.com/fetch.

PLACES TO EAT

Langley Village Bakery This bake shop serves grilled panini sandwiches, soup, quiches, and vast shelves full of baked goods. Homemade dog bones in three sizes are a hit with the critters, and people rave about the *trés leches,* a three-milk cake. Courtyard tables offer seating for you near your pooch. 221 2nd St., Langley; 360/221-3525.

Sfoglio Gourmet and Fresh Pasta: Blink and you'll miss it, so ask a local to guide you to this storefront that's been around for a decade. They'll heat up ready-made meals on the spot or pack you a picnic basket full of pasta salads and goodies to go. There are a couple of tables out back in the organic garden where they pick greens for summer salads. On weekends, a local fisherman sells his catch of the day out of the shed next door, which might include crab, shrimp, and clams. 1594 Main St., Freeland; 360/331-4080.

PLACES TO STAY

Blue Willow By the Sea: This is a classic bed-and-breakfast, lovingly appointed, elegant, and charming. Resident cat Lily and dog Darcy are kind enough to share their very civilized home with guest dogs. The Captain's Chamber is $125 per night and the Olympic Suite, with a clawfoot tub and balcony, is $135. Breakfasts are amazing! 6342 Apple Lane, Freeland; 360/331-7420; www.bluewillowbythesea.com.

Island Tyme: This little bed-and-breakfast is a Victorian beauty on 10 wonderfully secluded acres, conveniently located two miles from the quaint town of Langley and 10 minutes from the Clinton/Mukilteo ferry back to the mainland. From the Keepsake Room, you have a private patio with access to free grounds for your dog. Herding dogs will enjoy chatting with the pet pygmy goats behind the fence on the property. The room's gas fireplace provides a welcome hearth on damp winter nights. A rate of $95 per night includes breakfast, with no extra fees or restrictions for pets. 4940 S. Bayview Rd., Langley; 800/898-8963; www.islandtymebb.com.

South Whidbey State Park Campground: The campground is secluded in the forest, with 54 sites that are close together, with enough forest cover to provide modest privacy. Ice ($1.50/bag) and firewood ($4/bundle) are available at the pay station. Campsites are closed December and January. Rates are $16–22; reserve ahead in summer; first-come, first-served in the winter. 888/CAMPOUT (888/226-7688); www.camis.com/wa.

Camano Island

The fishing, logging, and trading industries have been replaced by beach homes, art galleries, boat launches, and driftwood-strewn beaches. It's an island you can drive to, which means no inconvenient ferry schedules or fees. Simply take Highway 532 from I-5 over the General Mark Clarke Bridge. Stop by the Camano Gateway Information Center or go to www.donothinghere.com to find out the latest happenings. Places to eat out are rare on the island, but there are plenty of great spots in Stanwood, just across the bridge. Pop into the Camano Animal Shelter Association (C.A.S.A.) and come home with another member of the family (call 360/387-1902 for more information). Your experience at many of the waterfront parks will depend on how high the tide, and how muddy and wet you're willing to get. Bring waders if you've got 'em!

PARKS, BEACHES, AND RECREATION AREAS

27 Utsalady Point Vista

🐾🐾 (See The Islands map on page 74)

This tiny gem is a vest pocket–sized park with three gravel parking spots, two picnic tables, and one barbecue grill. But, oh, the views! To the north, it is islands, bays, and the Skagit Valley as far as the eye can see. This park is cute—there's no better way to describe it. It's been carefully landscaped, and a tall, chain-link fence protects you and your dogs from going over the cliff down to the sea. You have a reasonably good chance of getting the whole place to yourself for a picnic, and the groomed grass is a lovely place to lay down a blanket for a nap in the sun. For something more strenuous, read about the history of island lumber production on the storyboard at the park entrance.

When you reach the island, take the right fork in the road to North Camano Drive, turn right on Utsalady Point Road, and go about 150 feet to the bluff.

28 Camano Island State Park

🐾🐾🐾🐾 (See The Islands map on page 74)

This stunning park has an amazing history. The original 93 acres came into being in a single day on July 27, 1949, when 900 volunteers showed up with trucks, tractors, hoes, rakes, spades, saws, and digging equipment to make trails, build roads, develop campsites, set up picnic areas, clear and level parking lots, construct buildings, and reach a spring for a water source.

It's grown into 134 acres with 6,700 feet of beachfront along the Saratoga Passage, looking out on Whidbey Island and the peaks of the Olympic Mountains. The North Beach day-use area has picnic tables on a grassy, sheltered bluff, with parking, restrooms, fire pits, and sheltered picnic areas. Lowell Point is a second day-use area, where the picnic benches are right on the rocky, windy beach just inches from the water.

If you can tear yourself away from the water, a five-mile loop trail leads along the beach for about a mile, then up through some steep sections that reward your efforts with tantalizing water views, and finally into deep, quiet woods. We saw two bald eagles on the day we visited, although Cooper thought they might be eyeing him as a potential snack.

From I-5, take Highway 532 through Stanwood. Once on the island, take the left fork onto East Camano Drive, keep going straight when it becomes Elger Bay Road, turn right on Mountain View Road, and then left on Lowell Point Road, which dead-ends into the park. Open 8 A.M.–dusk. Parking is $5 per day.

PLACES TO STAY

Camano Cottages: These two extravagant cottages on a ten-acre wildlife preserve include all the goodies: king-size beds, fireplaces, kitchens, soaking tubs, TV/VCR/CD player, fresh flowers, and view decks facing sunsets over the water. Owner Christina says she usually charges $10 extra for pets during flea season, in case she needs to flea bomb the place. To protect the privacy of the property, they don't publish the address; they'll give you directions when you make a reservation. Rates are $125–195. 360/387-4050; www.camanocottages.com.

Camano Island State Park Campground: The campground offers 88 sites that are surprisingly private thanks to the wooded canopy. Isis has a Shih Tzu friend, Sweetheart, who prefers Site #70 in the woods, while we liked #9 for its water view. Sites are first-come, first-served and range from $15 for a standard site to $21 for one with utility hookups. 888/CAMPOUT (888/226-7688); www.camis.com/wa.

EVERETT AND VICINITY

20

Sedro Woolley

20

Mount Vernon

Big Lake

5

Conway

9

McMurray

see North Cascades page 154

Mt Baker-
Snoqualmie
National Forest

Stanwood **1**

532

Bryant

River

530

Oso

Stillaguamish

Arlington **3**

Warm Beach

Mt Baker-
Snoqualmie
National Forest

2

Camano Island

5

9

5 Robe

92

TULALIP INDIAN RESERVATION

Granite Falls

4 Marysville

92

Clinton

6
8 **7** Everett

Lake Stevens

Roesinger Lake

18

Whidbey Island

9

19 *Flowing Lake*

16 **10**
11 **12**

Mukilteo

2

17 526

13

Snohomish

14

15

Sultan

22

23

20 Monroe

2

Gold Bar

Lynnwood

21

24 **26**

9

Skykomish River

Edmonds

524

27

25 104

Mountlake Terrace

Snohomish

River

Bothell

N

Lake Washington

405

see Greater Seattle page 122

Duvall

W E

99

203

S

5

Kirkland

Redmond

River

0   5 mi

0   5 km

Lake Sammamish

Carnation

© AVALON TRAVEL PUBLISHING, INC.

CHAPTER 4
Everett and Vicinity

Everett is the seat of county government, the second-largest freight port on the West Coast, and the home of Paine Field, the Boeing manufacturing facility building the world's largest 747, 767, and 777 airplanes. The city hosts Naval Station Everett, home of the aircraft carrier USS *Abraham Lincoln* when it returns from overseas deployment. The city reflects the hardworking, patriotic, practical side of its inhabitants. In contrast, the parks of the region are showy, centered on the theme of water—lakes, rivers, creeks, streams, or the saltwater of Puget Sound. Two major intercity trails can show you the region on foot and on paw, following railroad and trolley lines long abandoned.

Centennial Trail: This paved avenue extends for seven miles between Snohomish and Lake Stevens, winding through a country valley. It's jam-packed with speed cyclists, so Coop and Isis recommend the smaller soft-surface trail that runs alongside. Centennial is best for dogs trying to get their owners in shape with a long-distance jog or in-line skate session, rather than a place to stop and sniff the bushes. As money and time permits, the trail will be extended to total 44 miles to county lines north and south, following

PICK OF THE LITTER—EVERETT AND VICINITY

BEST PARKS
Kayak Point, Stanwood (page 103)
River Meadows, Arlington (page 104)
Meadowdale, Edmonds (page 118)

BEST DOG PARKS
Loganberry Lane, Everett (page 111)
Marina Park, Edmonds (page 119)

BEST EVENT
Bark in the Park, Aquasox Baseball, Everett (page 109)

BEST PLACE TO EAT
Ezell's Famous Chicken, Lynnwood (page 121)

BEST PLACES TO STAY
Inn at Port Gardner, Everett (page 112)
Countryman Bed and Breakfast, Snohomish (page 117)

former railroad lines. The southern end of the trail begins in Snohomish at the intersection of Maple Street and Pine Avenue, but the best place to hit the trail is outside Snohomish in the town of Machias. There's a replica of an 1890s railroad depot, expansive parking, a covered picnic shelter, restrooms, and a trail marker that lets you know just how far it is to each stop along the way. 425/388-6600.

Interurban Trail: The current six-foot-wide paved path extends from Everett south 15 miles to Lynnwood. From there, the cities of Mountlake Terrace and Shoreline are adding to the trail, eventually making non-motorized access available from Seattle to Everett. The north end is easiest to find: Take Everett Mall Way to West Mall Road to the end, and park in the fringes of the mall lot behind Sears.

Stanwood

The local greeting is *Vilkommen til Stanwood* (Welcome to Stanwood) in this Norwegian stronghold, where Lutheran churches, dairy farms, and bakeries carry on the traditions of their Viking ancestors. You'll love the farm country views, and your dog will go crazy for the smells, mostly manure, if you exit

I-5 at Marysville and drive the Pioneer Highway through the valley north to town. For an intimate glimpse into Norwegian culture, stop at the **Scandia Bakery and Lefse Factory** (8706 271st St.; 360/629-2411) or the **Uff Da Shoppe** ("Uff Da!" is the Norwegian equivalent of "Oy Vey!"; Viking Village; 360/629-3006) Artists are forging new traditions here as well at the internationally acclaimed Pilchuck Glass School, formed by Dale Chihuly. Stanwood is a good place to eat before heading across the bridge to Camano Island, where choices are limited.

PARKS, BEACHES, AND RECREATION AREAS

1 Church Creek Park

🐾🐾 (See Everett and Vicinity map on page 100)

This 16.5-acre city park is so popular with the summertime picnicking crowd that parking in the lot is limited to 90 minutes. Tall trees and rolling hills are complemented by a smattering of tables, horseshoe pits, a basketball court, a cool rocketship slide, and some rocking horses. Short trails lead to a picnic shelter, down to the creek side, and back to a little league field.

The park seemed to be suffering from a gopher problem when we visited. Cooper and Isis were captivated, sniffing furiously at the mounds of dirt, disappointed when none of the rodent residents came out to play.

From I-5, take Exit 212 and go west on State Route 532. Turn north on 72nd Avenue N.W. for a couple of blocks. The park is on the right. Open 9 A.M.–dusk, but the park is only open on Saturday and Sunday October–March. Restroom facilities are also closed in the winter.

2 Kayak Point

🐾🐾🐾 (See Everett and Vicinity map on page 100)

This regional favorite used to be a private resort, and much of that refinement shines through the impeccably groomed 428-acre county park. Sheltered picnic tables line up neatly along 3,300 feet of saltwater shoreline, offering ideal views of Port Susan. Clamming, fishing, crabbing, and windsurfing are popular pastimes for people, while pets probably prefer lounging or running on the huge beachfront lawn that leads right up to the water. We also wandered on the hiking trails up and around the campsites and a little ways into the woods. The real star here is the beach, and that's where you'll probably want to spend most of your time soaking up the views, the sunshine, and the antics of the sailboarders. Dogs are not allowed on the fishing pier.

From I-5, take Exit 206 and go west on State Route 531, Lakewood Road. Turn south onto Marine Drive, go two miles, and turn right on Kayak Point Road. The park is open 7 A.M.–dusk. Dogs must be leashed. There is a $5 fee for parking or use of the boat launch. 15610 Marine Dr., Stanwood; 360/652-7992.

PLACES TO EAT

The Cookie Mill: Don't let the name fool you. In addition to making many breeds of cookies, they serve gourmet waffles, croissants, and smoothies for breakfast. Lunch includes a dozen salads and creative sandwiches with goofy names like Weekend Gardener (veggie) and Aunt Jemima (peanut butter, honey, and bananas). An awning protects a few outdoor tables, and there is a drive-through. Cash or check only. 9808 S.R. 532; 360/629-2362.

PLACES TO STAY

Kayak Point Park Campground: The campground is well situated up the hill from the water. This gives each of 30 sites wooded seclusion and privacy from the RV, bus, trailer, and boat parking. Sadly, dogs are not allowed in Yurt Village. The staffed office and information center includes a vending machine, hot drinks and snacks, and a pay phone (cell service here is spotty). Campsites are $20 in the summer, and $10 Oct.–March. 15610 Marine Dr., Stanwood; 425/388-6601.

Arlington

More people probably know what Arlington looks like from the air than on the ground because this town hosts the annual **Arlington Fly-In** around the Fourth of July, the third-largest exhibition of experimental aircraft in the United States. Much of the area's recreation focuses on "The Stilly," or the Stillaguamish River, including the Annual Duck Dash to determine the fastest floating rubber duck. Hey, don't laugh—the winner nets $5,000! Okay, go ahead and laugh anyway.

PARKS, BEACHES, AND RECREATION AREAS

🐾 River Meadows

🐾🐾🐾🐾 (See Everett and Vicinity map on page 100)

This county property merits the highest paw rating, with an extra tail wag thrown in during the off-season, when it's not crowded. Imagine 200 acres of pasture to bound through, without having to worry about those pesky cows or stepping in any cow pies. This former dairy farm is tucked into a bend of the Stillaguamish River, giving boaters water recreation opportunities, although the river runs too fast for dogs to swim during spring runoff.

When no one is camped out, people have been known to bring their dogs for hours of no-leash fun without being hassled. Unless your pooch is a champion sniffer-outer, you have to be willing to lose a tennis ball or two in the deep grass. Cooper and Isis literally disappear into the fields, known as "going on safari." As if endless prairie isn't enough, there are six miles of trails winding along the river and around the meadows into nearby forests.

Take State Route 530 east through Arlington and turn right onto Arlington Heights Road. Bear right onto Jordan Road and go approximately three miles to the park entrance. Open 6 A.M.–dusk. 20416 Jordan Rd., Arlington; 360/453-3441.

PLACES TO STAY

Arlington Motor Inn: At this convenient motel with a friendly staff, the gal behind the counter giggled as she said that they tend to charge a one-time fee of $10–25, based on the "size and hairiness" of the dog or dogs joining you for your stay. Rates are $58–69. 2214 Rte 530; 360/652-9595.

River Meadows Campground: It's every tent for itself out in the unmarked fields of this huge pasture. For $14 a night, you can pick a spot and lie under the stars, searching for Sirius by Orion's side as the burbling river lulls you to sleep (by this time, your dog's already snoring). No reservations, no showers, and no out-of-county checks. Come early, come clean, and bring cash. 20416 Jordan Rd., Arlington; 360/453-3441.

Marysville

Many of the Native American reservations in Washington run casinos, and the Tulalip Casino across the highway from Marysville is one of the fanciest, with a good reputation for being fun, fast, and loose. Drop your dog off for a day or an overnight at the securely fenced, fully licensed, five-acre **Bone-a-Fide Dog Ranch** in Snohomish (7928 184th St.; 206/501-9247; www.bone-a-fide.com) and she'll romp while you roll the dice. When she's tired, she sleeps in their house, not a kennel, and when you've won the jackpot, you can buy her a diamond dog collar.

DIVERSION

Bridges Pets in Lake Stevens is one of the largest and strangest pet stores Cooper and Isis have ever seen. The back half of the store rivals the Seattle Aquarium, with floor-to-ceiling displays of exotic fish living in tanks with elaborately designed ocean and lake environments. The front half of the store is a hodgepodge of gifts, pet supplies, water gardens, and pond equipment and supplies. Store owner Dan Eylander took all of his passions and put them in one place. The result is quirky and wonderful, a direct contrast to the practical if somewhat sterile environment of retail chain pet stores. For dogs, Bridges carries holistic and premium-grade food, crates and carriers, and an entire aisle of toys. 701 Hwy 9 N.E. #42A; 425/344-7557; www.bridgespets.com.

PARKS, BEACHES, AND RECREATION AREAS

🐾 Jennings Memorial and Nature Park

🐾🐾🐾🐾 (See Everett and Vicinity map on page 100)

The memorial part of the park is 51 acres of fun, the nature side is 17 acres of wetland observatory, and altogether it's an impressive city park. They've got the bases covered with a ball field, basketball court, and picnic shelters with heavy-duty barbecue grills, and that's just the beginning.

The varied topography includes hills, dales, ponds, bridges and wetland observation platforms, grass slopes, and a creek, all of which you wander through on gravel and wood chip trails. It's enough to keep even the most attention-span-challenged puppy occupied for hours. Oh, and did Isis mention the trees? Big, beautiful trees, and ducks, and frogs, and so on, and so forth.

Kids rave about the display cannon, miniature steam engine, Kiwanis Youth fishing pond, and most frequently, Dinosaur Park, where they can crawl all over a 23-foot-long Stegosaurus, a 17-foot Salamander-saurus, a Pterodactyl swing, T-Rex, Triceratops, and a baby Brontosaurus.

You'd never know it's close to the highway. Take Exit 199 from I-5, go six blocks and turn left on 47th Avenue N.E., which bears to the right and becomes Armar Road, and shortly thereafter, the park entrance is on your right at 6915 Armar Rd.

PLACES TO EAT

Oosterwyk's Dutch Bakery: You don't have to be able to pronounce it to enjoy it. They were here long before the low-carb craze, and they'll likely be here long after. If it is sticky, sweet, or filling, you'll find it behind the long, tempting counter. Cash or check only. 1513 3rd St.; 360/653-3766.

PLACES TO STAY

In this area, chain hotels offer the best choices for dogs and their owners; please look under Chain Hotels in the Resources section.

Granite Falls

What used to be a provision town for miners and loggers is now the gateway to the recreation along the Mountain Loop Highway. It's not a loop at the moment, as $6 million in flood damage shut down the road in an October 2003 storm. The road is closed at Barlow, which still leaves you free to recreate along 36 miles of gorgeous mountains, rivers, and valleys. You and your pal with his nose to the ground have access to the Big Four Ice Caves and the mining ghost town of Monte Cristo, plus dozens of campgrounds and hikes in the Mt. Baker-Snoqualmie National Forest.

PARKS, BEACHES, AND RECREATION AREAS

5 Robe Canyon Historic Park

🐾🐾🐾 (See Everett and Vicinity map on page 100)

When you hike through Robe Canyon, your footsteps will follow the trail of the Monte Cristo, a narrow gauge railroad built in 1892, connecting the frontier town of Granite Falls to the mines. Hopeful prospectors found plenty of trouble, but little gold.

It's a mile from the road to the river, with inspiring canyon views on the way. After winding down some steep and narrow switchbacks to get to the valley floor, the trail levels out through a canopy of trees and along the sandy banks of the Stillaguamish river. It's a little rough around the edges. Floods wiped out the railroad time and again; they'll do the same for the trail occasionally. It's a blast if you're willing to get your paws wet in errant streams and if you can jump over and under fallen logs. Isis noted that it's almost like agility trials, complete with tunnels at about 1.4 miles in, only these arches are carved through rock and big enough for a steam engine to travel through.

From the town of Granite Falls, follow the Mountain Loop Highway for seven miles. Look for a low brick wall with the sign "Old Robe Trail" across the street from Green Mountain Road. Parking is a roadside affair. There are a couple of picnic tables; you're on your own for everything else. Signs warn that the area is hazardous to unleashed dogs.

PLACES TO EAT

Mountain View Restaurant, Cocktail Lounge, and Robe Store: People come from miles around for the trout (flown in from Idaho) and hand-cut steaks. The only big screen TV lounge within a 100-mile radius is another huge draw, as is Russia, the cat, who sits on a bar stool and checks IDs at the door. Outdoor dining at umbrella-covered tables is available in the summer. The store carries basic conveniences, and it's all run by the same hardworking folks at the Inn. 32005 Mtn. Loop Hwy.; 360/691-6668.

PLACES TO STAY

Mountain View Inn: It's a tiny place, simple and spare, the only lodging between Marysville and Darrington, and it's a good 'un; hand-carved log furniture from Montana inside, view of Mt. Pilchuck outside, and less than a mile from the Snoqualmie-Mt. Baker National Forest. Hosts Vince and Diana have turned getting away from it all into an art form. Just $59 covers you and your pets for the night. 32005 Mtn. Loop Hwy.; 360/691-6668.

Everett

You've got to hand it to Everett for having the most parks with the best views. You can hit a bunch of them in one trip if you start at Mukilteo Lighthouse Park and drive north on Mukilteo Boulevard. In Everett, there's one off-leash area we can recommend wholeheartedly, and that's Loganberry Lane.

PARKS, BEACHES, AND RECREATION AREAS

6 American Legion Memorial

🐾🐾 (See Everett and Vicinity map on page 100)

Although much of the park is designated for specific uses that don't involve dogs, there's room to hang out, enjoy the harbor view, and comb the grass for a beetle or spider to pester and then eat (one of Cooper's favorite activities). You could probably convince your pooch to walk the gravel trails of the Evergreen Arboretum and Gardens with you. This elaborate and educational series of planted landscapes includes the Fernery, Conifer forest, Dahlia garden, Japanese maples, and more. It's at the south end of the park, next to the golf course.

Follow Marine View Drive north around to the crest of the hill and turn on Alverson Boulevard. 145 Alverson Blvd.; www.evergreenarboretum.com.

7 Langus Riverfront Trail

🐾🐾🐾 (See Everett and Vicinity map on page 100)

As hard as it is to find this park, you'd think it would always be peaceful and uncrowded. However, when the salmon are running the river, usually in August and September, there are so many boaters and anglers it's hard to get a dog in edgewise. Stick to the rest of the year, and you'll have enough room to throw a stick for your pooch along this excellent riverfront pathway.

Three miles of paved avenue wind along the mouth of the Snohomish River around the perimeter of Smith Island. Some of the trail is more interesting than picturesque, such as underneath the I-5 highway, past grain elevators and a sawmill, and around the sewage treatment plant. If the wind is blowing the wrong way, you might get a whiff—as far as your dog is concerned, that's akin to stepping into a French perfume boutique. The river is lovely for the majority of the trail and the picnic grounds are as well groomed as a New York Fifth Avenue poodle. Tall fencing protects you from the industrial areas along the way. Bring a towel in case either of you decides to swim, and be prepared for muddy river banks or use the row boat launch as your entry point.

You can only access the Frontage Road from I-5 Southbound, exit 198. You'll see the signs for Riverfront Park, but you'll still need some guidance. Bear left onto 35th Avenue, left onto Ross Avenue, wind through Dagmars Marina and some industrial warehouses, keep going, and finally, bear right

DOG-EAR YOUR CALENDAR

It's dogs and frogs and a human-sized hot dog named Frank at **Bark in the Park** night at the Everett Aquasox, a class-A farm team for the Seattle Mariners baseball club. Webbly is the team mascot, a pop-fly catching toad. This ball club is the movie *Bull Durham* come to life. Your pet can enjoy America's pastime with you at Homer Porch, a lawn behind right field. Tickets are a steal at $6 per person, no charge for the dogs. The stadium has a policy of no outside food. Cooper had no problem polishing off the stadium's way-better-than-average concession food, including chowder or chili in sourdough bread bowls. All dogs' eyes will be riveted on Frank, who tosses free frankfurters into the crowd. To find out which night the ballpark goes to the dogs, call 800/GO FROGS (800/463-7647). Order tickets by phone or get them online at www.aquasox.com.

onto Smith Island Road. As a side note, Dagmars has one of the largest collections of pleasure craft on the coast. You may be tempted to window shop, or even buy a Bayliner, if you've got a couple hundred thousand bucks lying around unused.

🗊 Grand Avenue Park

 (See Everett and Vicinity map on page 100)

The homes are grand, the immaculate grass grander, and the view grandest. At the turn of the 20th century, Everett was proud of its mill and shingle town status, when this park overlooked the factories of an industrial boomtown. The smokestacks are gone, replaced with one of the largest pleasure craft moorages on the Pacific Coast and Naval Station Everett. Bordering three city blocks, this park is befitting of the stately Colonial-style homes along the avenue. It's what Europeans would call formal gardens, with precise trees and flower beds, trimmed hedges, and strategically placed benches. Ideal for a Sunday stroll, perhaps, rather than a place to let your tongue hang out. Isis lifts her nose a little higher and revels in her purebred, blue-blood lineage; Cooper straightens his collar and tries to look respectable. On Grand Avenue between 16th and 19th Streets.

🗊 Howarth Park

 (See Everett and Vicinity map on page 100)

This is one of three parks in Everett that's advertised as having an off-leash area. Isis gives it a lowly fire hydrant rating for many reasons. First of all, the north end of the beach is supposed to be off-leash, but she couldn't find any sign or boundary saying so. The unmarked OLA is the rockiest and least-accessible section of the park. Getting there requires navigating a rickety bridge over a muddy stream, dozens of flights of concrete stairs, and a high bridge over the railroad tracks. If that doesn't spook your dogs, the hurtling steel of trains rattling by will. Fencing is minimal and in many places there is nothing to separate the beach from the rails at all. The park has a great water view, but there are better beaches nearby, preferable even if Lassie has to be leashed on them.

From Mukilteo Boulevard (41st Street) in Everett, turn right on Olympic Boulevard and follow it into Howarth Park. Leave your car in the first lot, a hard right turn at the bottom of the hill, to access the beach trail. The second parking lot is for the playground and other designated areas where dogs are not allowed. Open 6 A.M.–10 P.M. 1127 Olympic Blvd.; 425/257-8300.

10 Harborview

 (See Everett and Vicinity map on page 100)

You can easily fool your pup into thinking that you are stopping for her because there is plenty of room to run around, when in fact you are coming here for the all-encompassing views of Port Gardner Bay and Everett. From the wide promontory, you can see Whidbey, Hat, Jetty, and Camano Islands; the port, naval station, and city of Everett; the Tulalip Indian Reservation; Mt. Baker; and Saratoga Passage leading to Deception Pass and the Pacific Ocean. While your darling putters around, you can watch ferries cross the water, trains roll by hugging the shoreline, and industrial ships being tugged out to sea. The park is on Mukilteo Boulevard at the intersection of Hardeson Road.

11 Forest Park

(See Everett and Vicinity map on page 100)

It amuses Cooper that most of what draws people to Forest Park isn't forest, but a pool, playground, animal farm, tournament-quality horseshoe field, tennis courts, day care, meeting hall, and classrooms. There are a few trails through a tall grove of trees, perhaps a half mile total. You can find them if you park at the top of the hill and walk just behind the playground to the west. Or, grab a map at the park office, clearly marked next to the parking lot.

From I-5, take Exit 192 and go west on Mukilteo Boulevard to the park on your left. Open 6 A.M.–10 P.M. 802 Mukilteo Blvd.; 425/257-8300.

12 Lowell Park

(See Everett and Vicinity map on page 100)

Poor Lowell Park. It's hot, dusty, tiny, and jam-packed. The gates require two hands to operate, which is an exercise in frustration when you have two dogs with you and others trying to make a break for it when you enter or leave. That said, it's one of the few options local dogs have for freedom, and they'll take it any way they can get it.

Regulars come here in shifts, nothing official, but patterns that have developed over time. It's like a small town—everybody knows, and has got their noses into, everybody else's business. People are busy chatting each other up, leaving the pup playground unsupervised in a state of mild chaos. It's a blast for any Maltese looking to see how much mischief she can get into before being called onto the carpet. Isis can recommend it if you're not dogmatic about discipline and your canine can comport herself in a crowd.

Take Exit 192 from I-5, and go east at the bottom of the ramp instead of west toward town. Turn right onto 3rd Avenue and follow it down to 46th Street. You'll see the park on the left and angled parking in front of the tennis courts, with the off-leash area to the north. Open 6 A.M.–10 P.M. 46th St. and S. 3rd Ave.; 425/257-8300; www.everettwa.org/parks.

13 Lowell Riverfront Trail
🐾🐾🐾 (See Everett and Vicinity map on page 100)

The river you're fronting in this case is the Snohomish, nicely framed by a backdrop of Cascade Mountains and the remains of the Ebey frontier farmstead on the opposing bank. From the ample parking lot, the paved boulevard travels two miles north, hugging the river. The level, smooth trail is a hugely popular spot for young families to go strolling, socializing, and tricycling or training-wheeling, with a few hard-core joggers whooshing by. Along the path are landscaped bump-outs, peppered with square picnic tables, barbecue stands, and garbage cans. Lowell is highly walk-worthy in Cooper's estimation. He fondly remembers chasing a remote-control car brought by a couple of teenagers and being mesmerized by a tiny garter snake slithering across his path.

Take exit 192 from I-5 going east. You'll be on 3rd Street, which curves around south and becomes 2nd street. Turn left on Lenora and follow the signs to Lowell River Road. Parking lot will be on your left. Open 6 A.M.–10 P.M.

14 Loganberry Lane
🐾🐾🐾🐕 (See Everett and Vicinity map on page 100)

Loganberry wins best in show for Everett's off-leash areas. The lane offers a merry jaunt through a strip of woods sandwiched between the W. E. Hall golf course and playfields of Kasch Park. A couple of decent trails wind through cool shade trees, thick undergrowth, and brush for about a half mile. The entrance is not gated, but the remaining park borders are effectively secured by adjacent fences. It's a welcome contrast to the typical rectilinear, blockhead dog park.

There are a couple of parking spots available in a clearing laid with gravel. Don't be misled by the sign that says pets must be leashed. As soon as you pass the concrete barriers into the park, you are welcomed into the dog area by a sign and a baggie dispenser. Bring your own water to avoid a couple of brackish ponds in the park that look decidedly non-potable for pets.

From I-5, take Exit 189 to State Route 526 west, and turn left on Evergreen Way, right on 100th Street, and right on Loganberry Lane (18th Avenue). Drive until it dead-ends into the park. Open 6 A.M.–10 P.M. 425/257-8300; www.everettwa.org/parks.

⅏ Picnic Point

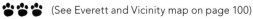 (See Everett and Vicinity map on page 100)

Picnic Point's got picnic tables, six of them, on a small green plot overlooking the water. They're nifty, but that's nothing compared to the beach below. At low tide, the sandy shore is a real winner, a huge expanse of tidal flats tailor-made for dog-day afternoons. Unlike Howarth Park, which Isis whined about earlier, the beach is wheelchair-accessible by means of a gentle ramp and pedestrian overpass over the railroad tracks. Trains are separated from the land by a decent fence.

The park is north of Edmonds and can be reached by heading west on Shelby Road from State Route 99, then taking the right fork in the road onto Picnic Point Road. 13001 Picnic Point Rd., Edmonds; 425/388-6600.

PLACES TO EAT

Meyer's: This half-bistro/half-bar is next to the Inn at Port Gardner and the Everett Marina, with outdoor tables on the pier, a dog biscuit jar on the counter, and several choice beers on tap. The yuppie pub grub keeps hotel patrons happy, and they do decent breakfast and lunch, too. 1700 W. Marine View Dr.; 425/259-3875.

Pavé Bakery: This is the home of the Cake Therapist, who will create tasty, artistic cakes for any dessert crisis. Even if your needs aren't urgent, or your tooth sweet, you'll love the quiches, soups, salads, sandwiches, and lunch specialties such as southwestern chicken chops and warm goat cheese salad. The sidewalk seating is on the most fashionable street in town. 2613 Colby Ave.; 425/252-0250.

PLACES TO STAY

Inn at Port Gardner: This boutique hotel is sleek and upscale, inside and out. Most rooms have marina views, and Jacuzzi and fireplace suites are available. Its choice location puts you right on the waterfront near the city's best dining, and that fact is reflected in the rates of $109–299 per night, plus a $30 nonrefundable pet fee. Reservations are a must; the inn's 33 rooms go quickly. 1700 W. Marine View Dr.; 425/252-6779; www.innatportgardner.com.

Welcome Motor Inn: As long as you aren't on the fashion police squad and your dog is under 25 pounds, you'll be okay staying at this style-challenged motel that is affordable and close to everything. There is a $10 pet fee, and double units are $47–57. Kitchenette units are available. 1205 N. Broadway; 425/252-8828.

More Accommodations: Please look under Chain Hotels in the Resources section for additional places to stay in this area.

Mukilteo

Old Town Mukilteo, as it is known locally, is tucked inside greater incorporated Everett. There are neat bistro-style eateries and lovely shops (for example, Rose Hill Chocolate Company) in this tiny waterfront village. It's the Eastern Terminus of the Clinton/Mukilteo ferry, taking you and your pup to the wonders of Whidbey Island.

PARKS, BEACHES, AND RECREATION AREAS

16 Mukilteo Lighthouse Park
🐾🐾 (See Everett and Vicinity map on page 100)

This site has historic significance as the location of the signing of the Point Everett Treaty, where 2,000 members of dozens of regional tribes met with Isaac Stevens, Superintendent of Indian Affairs, in 1855. The parking lot is bigger than the park to provide plenty of boat trailer parking, but that is the only thing that disappoints at this prime waterfront location. It's one of the few places where you can reach the beach within a short distance from I-5.

Next door, the grounds of Light Station Mukilteo, the lighthouse built by the U.S. Army Corps of Engineers in 1905, are open noon–5 P.M. Saturday, Sunday, and Holidays, Apr.–Sept. (no pets in the lighthouse). The rest of the park is open year-round. From this site, you are looking out over Whidbey and Camano Islands across Port Gardner Bay.

Picnic tables are lined in soldierly order along the beach, each with a huge fire pit and standing grill. Behind them, there is a field wide enough to roam, and in front, plenty of rocky beach to walk.

Take the Mukilteo Speedway to the water, staying in the left lane, and turn left into the park at the ferry dock. Parking is limited to four hours. 609 Front St.; 425/355-4141.

17 92nd Street Park
🐾🐾 (See Everett and Vicinity map on page 100)

It's like the putt-putt equivalent of a state park, without the camping, shrunk to city-size to fit in a crowded suburban area. There are a few ponds to sniff around, groomed grass to roll in, and a maze of miniature trails through the woods to walk. Probably the only ones who'll get any exercise are the kids, who can romp in two play areas. It is hilly, so you could run your dog up and down to mellow him out for the ride home. The park has made it easy to pick up after yourself, thoughtfully providing poop bag dispensers, seemingly every few feet, and each picnic table has its own garbage can.

At the intersection of 92nd Street and the Mukilteo Speedway, turn south on 92nd street to enter the parking lot.

PLACES TO EAT

Amici Italian Deli and Pizzeria: You know it's the real deal when you can hear heated arguments in Italian coming from the kitchen. The list of authentic specialties seems to go on forever including *insalata* (salads), *zuppa* (soups), panini, pizzas, and calzones. Don't pass up the finer things in life with gelato, wine, cannoli, and tiramisu to go. Sidewalk tables sit on the sunny side of the street. 649 5th St.; 425/438-2995.

Philly Ya Belly: Everett-ites must have a thing for Philly Cheese Steaks, because Cooper saw lots of places that offer them, and this is one of the best, right down the street from 92nd Street Park. The home of the Belly Buster serves up hot beef, chicken, pastrami, egg, and Portobello cheese steaks on French rolls with globs of grilled onions and green peppers (hold the onions for the dogs, please). 9800 Harbor Pl.; 425/349-1316.

Whidbey Coffee Company: Coffee tastes better when sipped at your table on the garden terrace, looking out over the bay. Oatmeal, granola, bagels, and croissants are featured for breakfast along with fresh-squeezed juices and foamy lattes. Lunch is also light, including salads, a few sandwiches, and hot specials. 619 4th St.; 425/348-4825.

PLACES TO STAY

Hogland House: This bed-and-breakfast is a classically styled and furnished romantic Victorian that's listed on the Register of Historic Places. There is a hot tub deck overlooking Puget Sound, and there are trails to the beach. Rates of $95 for the Rose Room and $105 for the Lilac Room include a hearty breakfast. Or, you can make your own meals—with in-room refrigerators, microwaves, and coffee—and pay only $75 (Rose) or $85 (Lilac) per night. There is a two-dog limit, and each dog is $10 per night. 917 Webster St.; 425/742-7639; www.hoglandhouse.com.

More Accommodations: Please look under Chain Hotels in the Resources section for additional places to stay in this area.

Snohomish

Snohomish is famous as the antiquing capital of the Northwest. Historic First Street is packed with shops bearing gifts, collectibles, furniture, and really good food. Stop by **Firehouse Tails,** a pet boutique, and visit customer service representative Barkley, a golden retriever with his own line of homemade pet treats (127 Avenue A; 360/568-4154; www.firehousetails.com).

Only an hour from downtown Seattle, the Snohomish Valley is rural, with farm country scenery and prime lakeside parks. You're heading into country where you'll see Tractor Crossing signs, where pickup trucks rule the road, and nearly every car you pass has a dog with his head stuck out the window, tongue flapping in the breeze.

PARKS, BEACHES, AND RECREATION AREAS

18 Lake Roesinger

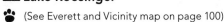 (See Everett and Vicinity map on page 100)

You wouldn't know by looking that Lake Roesinger is actually bigger than Flowing Lake. Roesinger's park is much smaller, and the lake goes around a steep bend out of sight. A sloped hillside leads to the beach access for boating, fishing, and swimming (for dogs, outside of the roped area). It's a decent fallback plan if Flowing Lake is too crowded or you don't want to shell out the $5 for parking there. Here, a dozen parking spots across the road from the park are free.

Take the Snohomish exit off I-5 onto Highway 2 and go toward Monroe. At milepost 10, turn left onto 100th Street S.E. (Westwick Road), which will eventually make a sharp turn to the north and become 171st Avenue S.E. Turn right on Dubuque Road, travel six miles, and turn left onto Lake Roesinger Road. Stay to your right at the Y-intersection, and go another mile to the park. 1608 S. Lake Roesinger Rd., Snohomish; 360/568-2274.

19 Flowing Lake

(See Everett and Vicinity map on page 100)

Once the Dachsie Twins got comfortable on a lawn blanket facing the lake, they thought they might never want to get up again. They were happily hypnotized by the boats making lazy circles on the water and the swish, click, and whir of anglers' fishing poles on the pier and shore. Summer also brings out the swimmers, water-skiers, volleyball players, and more kids for a rowdier atmosphere. There are too many expensive homes along the shores to get away from it all, yet it is forested and rural enough to induce a tranquil spell.

Take the Snohomish exit off I-5 onto Highway 2 and go toward Monroe. At milepost 10, turn left onto 100th Street S.E. (Westwick Road), which will eventually make a sharp turn to the north and become 171st Avenue S.E. Turn right onto 48th Avenue S.E. into the park. Parking is $5 for the day. Open 7 A.M.–dusk.

20 Lord Hill

🐾🐾🐾🐾 (See Everett and Vicinity map on page 100)

This 1,300-acre upland nature preserve is a great trail-dog destination, and dogs of the region probably lord that fact over others. Six miles of roughly groomed trails lead you past ponds, marshes, lakes, rivers, and evergreens, leading to a series of viewpoints that give you a distinct feeling of being a lord or lady, surveying your kingdom and perhaps watching for invading foes. The origin of the park's name isn't quite so dramatic, just from some dude named Mitchell Lord who bought the land for a dairy farm in 1879.

To get to the bulk of the trails, you must cross a series of long boardwalks built over a swamp—Isis thinks this part of the park is especially nifty. Beavers are the ruling class of wildlife at Lord Hill; your dog might see one at work, or at least the evidence of their handiwork. You'll share the trail with horses, mountain bikes, and especially joggers; even so, it doesn't seem crowded. 12921 150th St. S.E.; 360/568-2274.

PLACES TO EAT

Chuck's Seafood Grotto: The grotto took over an auto body shop; basically, when they roll up the garage doors, it's all outdoor seating. It's all seafood as well—the good, the fried, and the fresh. Try salmon, halibut cheeks, and catfish; seafood wraps; or shrimp and chips, scallops and chips, calamari and chips, fish and chips…well, you get the gist of it. 1229 1st St., Snohomish; 360/568-0782.

City Deli and Wine: To eat is human, but to dine with wine in the sunshine is divine. The experience is complete when you can sit with your dog at the European café tables, looking over the river, feasting on soup du jour, chicken almond salad, or sandwiches made with homemade bread fresh from the oven. 102 Avenue D, Snohomish; 360/568-0369; www.citydeliandwine.com.

Dee Bee's Sandwich and Soup Café: Dee Bee's is a spin-off of the Snohomish Valley Ice Cream and Candy Company, styled like an old-fashioned soda fountain serving treats and the traditional trio of soup, salad, and sandwiches. Cooper, usually a stubborn cuss, will do any trick you ask of him for a bite of the homemade caramel corn. 902 1st St., Snohomish; 360/568-1133.

Snohomish Pie Company: Oh lordy, there are few stronger temptations than chocolate pecan pie à la mode. That's merely one of a dozen specialty pies you can order by the slice, or whole, and wolf down at a sidewalk table. Soup, sandwich and a slice of pie are yours for $7.25. If you start with the garden or chef salad, you'll save more room for apple pie. 915 1st St., Snohomish; 360/568-3589.

PLACES TO STAY

Countryman Bed and Breakfast: Beautiful antiques and handmade quilts grace this 1896 restored Victorian home. Dogs are welcome without extra charge, as long as there's no extra wear and tear on the room when you leave. "But, please," says owner Sandy, "be honest with me. If you've got a big dog, just say so. I'd like to know." Rates are $85–105. 119 Cedar Ave.; 360/568-9622; www.countrymanbandb.com.

Flowing Lake Park Campground: There are 30 extra-wide campsites in the woods surrounding Flowing Lake, seven of which are handicapped-accessible. Ten are tent sites at $14 per night, and the rest are hookup sites for $20. For the ultimate in luxury, there are tidy cabins, one of which is designated for pets and their owners, furnished with a bed, futon, lights, and a heater. Ask for Cabin #4, which accommodates up to five people for $40 a night, plus $5 per pet. 17900 48th St. N.E., Snohomish; 425/388-6601.

Inn at Snohomish: This motel on the edge of historic downtown is bright, sunny, and tidy. Rooms are named after famous local historical figures, with photographs and a short history lesson about that person in framed pictures on the walls, a unique touch that impressed us. Pet policies include not leaving dogs unattended and not bathing pets in the room. "It's hard on the tub drainage system," said the gal at the counter. Your $100 pet damage deposit is returned in full when you leave the room in good condition. Standard rooms are $65; suites with whirlpool tubs are $105. 323 2nd St.; 800/548-9993; www.snohomishinn.com.

Gold Bar

PARKS, BEACHES, AND RECREATION AREAS

2.1 Gold Bar Dog Park

🐾 🦮 (See Everett and Vicinity map on page 100)

Gold Bar's off-leash area is a smidgen of land between the railroad tracks and the highway. The only thing separating the grass from the traffic is a small ditch, so you must have control of your dog at all times, physically or verbally, for her safety. It has trees, soft grass, and blackberry bushes to sniff. For dogs, it ain't much, but it is all theirs. Bring your own everything; there are no services or amenities, but you can throw your pickup bags in the trash can at the gas station across the street.

It's on the south side of U.S. Highway 20 at the intersection of 6th Street in Gold Bar. A couple of cars can park in a gravel lane bordering the OLA.

22 Wallace Falls State Park

🐾🐾🐾🐾 (See Everett and Vicinity map on page 100)

The park's name is the Anglicized version of *Kwayaylsh,* for Skykomish Native Americans Jack and Sarah, the first homesteaders in the area. Wallace is a tremendously popular 4,735-acre park specifically for hiking and, through word of maw, has cultivated a dogmatic following of canine climbers. The main footpath is the Woody Trail, a moderately difficult trek, gradually climbing from 500 to 1700 feet in elevation, past nine falls of more than 50 feet each, the largest of which tumbles 265 feet through a narrow gorge. It's 1.8 miles to the Skykomish Valley Overlook and Picnic Shelter at the Lower Falls, 2.4 miles to the top of Middle Falls, and 2.7 miles to the Upper Falls. You'll cross several bridges and navigate stairs along the way. The round-trip trek takes about three hours if you're going at a steady clip. We won't tell you how long it took Cooper. Cougars have been sighted near the falls, so leashes are a really good idea. Leashes are even more important on summer weekends, when the crowds are a more frightening prospect than some big cat. Seven primitive walk-in tent sites are available, from 50 to 150 feet from the parking area, for $15 per night on a first-come, first-served basis.

From U.S. Highway 2 in Gold Bar, turn north on 1st Street, travel .5 mile, turn right on May Creek Road, follow the left fork when it becomes Ley Road, and the left fork again at Wallace Lake Road into the park. Parking is $5. Open 8 A.M.–dusk.

Edmonds

The city of Edmonds is an overgrown seaside resort town that's not particularly Fido-friendly. The party line is that dogs are not allowed in city parks, except on trails. Fair enough. We discovered plenty of parks within the city limits that have trails, and some truly wonderful county parks that do allow pets. When you've exhausted the possibilities in Edmonds, catch the ferry over to Kingston, leading to all the wonders of the Kitsap and Olympic Peninsulas.

PARKS, BEACHES, AND RECREATION AREAS

23 Meadowdale

🐾🐾🐾🐾 (See Everett and Vicinity map on page 100)

This awesome park on the northern border of Edmonds is a cheerful, muttlike breeding of half-forest and half-beach that's pure fun. From the parking lot, a 1.25-mile trail leads down a moderate incline to the beach, wandering through groves of old-growth trees and alongside a bubbling stream. The gravel path is tidy and wide, manageable for everyone from toddlers to seniors. We could feel the tension melting away as we walked, and the wonder wiener twins had grins on their faces the whole time.

At the bottom of the trail is a loop surrounding the promised meadow and dale, dotted with covered and open picnic tables. Past that is a tunnel, maybe 15 feet long, that leads to the beach. What a beach! It's wide, flat, sandy, and long, broken only by the marine estuary formed by the stream as it empties into the ocean. More picnic tables are tossed in between the driftwood. Our only caution is that you remember to save some strength for the one-mile walk back to the car. We exhausted ourselves playing on the *playa del sol* and had to take advantage of every bench as a rest stop on the climb back up to the parking lot. Those with limited mobility can make prior arrangements with the Park Ranger to take the service road directly to the beach.

The directions make getting there sound worse than it really is. Exit onto 164th Street from I-5 and follow 164th, turning right to cross Highway 99. Turn right onto 52nd Avenue, left onto 160th Street, right onto 56th Avenue, and finally left onto 156th Avenue to the park entrance at the end of the road. 6026 156th S.W.; 425/338-6600.

🐾🐾🐾 Southwest County Park

🐾🐾🐾 (See Everett and Vicinity map on page 100)

The term park is used loosely in this case to describe 120 acres of open space on either side of Olympic View Drive. Old logging skid roads are now trails, grouped in concentric loops, with shortcuts in between. The outer loop is seven miles, following the road. The inner path is four miles, passing through ravines and along Perrinville Creek. You'll pass through time, seeing the history of second-growth forest and buckboard notches in old-growth stumps where loggers stood to muscle the mighty saws. Cooper will take a hilly trail in dense woods over a sidewalk walk any day.

Parking is at the corner of 180th St. S.W. and Olympic View Drive.

🐾🐾 Marina Park

🐾🐾🐾🐾 (See Everett and Vicinity map on page 100)

It's puny, hard to find, and surrounded by parks with cruel No Dogs Allowed signs, but none of that matters to aquatic-minded animals who just want to take a dip in cool ocean waters. As long as you keep your dog in the Marina Beach South off-leash area, south of the pier beyond the fence, he's free to roam the sand dunes and swim in the sound with abandon. Go north of the fence, and McGruff the Crime Dog will be on your tail faster than you can say, "Take a bite out of crime."

When you should come depends on what you want to do. At high tide, there's more water for dog paddling and water retrieving exercises. Low tide expands the beach area for ball playing, digging, and sand castle building. Fences separate the dog park from the hillside and the pier, but the area is not gated. Saltwater is plentiful; drinking water is not. Driftwood and a bench serve as seating for weary toy-tossers.

Take Highway 104, Sunset Avenue, all the way to the ferry terminal at the Port of Edmonds, but instead of getting in the ferry lane, turn left onto Dayton Street at the light. Dayton curves right onto Admiral Way. You'll see signs to Marina Park—turn left at the stop sign and continue to follow the signs all the way to the end of the marina. Parking is limited to three hours. Open 6 A.M.–10 P.M.

PLACES TO EAT

5th Avenue Grill: At 5th Avenue, dogs are treated as first-class citizens, soaking up the sun on the huge sidewalk dining patio with its own fountain pond. Humans are treated to generously hand-poured double martinis. Steak, lobster, and pork chops from the grill are accented with fresh vegetables and healthy salads. They offer box lunches to go for $5 on weekdays. 610 5th Ave.; 425/776-1976; www.5thavegrillhouse.com.

Old Milltown Pizza: Nosh on New York–style pizza by the slice while your dog tries to get the toppings to slide off by the sheer force of his stare. Picnic tables under a gondola provide summer shade and protection from winter wet. Whole pies are available to go. This pizza's not only for pepperoni; creative toppings include zucchini, artichoke hearts, pesto, fire-roasted red peppers, and spinach. 201 5th Ave.; 425/670-6702.

Waterfront Coffee Company: If you get stuck waiting for a ferry, wander over to Waterfront for daily soups, croissants, pastries, espresso, and ice cream. The store manager, who goes by the nickname Tree, will serve your pooch a scoop of ice cream with a humongous dog bone for $1.50. It's much nicer to bask in the sun at the outdoor tables than bake in your car until the next boat arrives. 101 Main St.; 425/670-1400.

PLACES TO STAY

Edmonds Harbor Inn: With this one notable exception, motels in the immediate area are low on the respectability scale. This appealing hotel is down by the waterfront, near the ferry terminal, offering many types of rooms with an extensive list of niceties. Rates range from $89 for standard rooms to $169 for all-out suites. 130 W. Dayton St.; 425/771-5021; www.nwcountryinns.com.

More Accommodations: Please look under Chain Hotels in the Resources section for additional places to stay in this area.

Lynnwood

Lynnwood, essentially a Seattle suburb, is welcoming to whelps as long as they are on leash.

PARKS, BEACHES, AND RECREATION AREAS

26 Wilcox Park

🐾🐾 (See Everett and Vicinity map on page 100)

This is the civilized neighbor to Scriber Park across the street. While the huddled masses stick to the playground area, a.k.a. tot lot, you can enjoy seven acres of lush lawn, bordered by a couple of tree groves. There's not much else to speak of, other than picnic tables, a clean restroom, and enough space to lay down a tablecloth and eat fried chicken from Ezell's just down the street.

The dogs like to sneak in the back entrance to avoid the crowds. Take 196th Street west from I-5 and turn right on 52nd Avenue, then left on 194th Street into the parking lot. Open dusk to dawn.

27 Scriber Park

🐾🐾🐾 (See Everett and Vicinity map on page 100)

If a dog were a landscape architect (A dogscaper?) and she were asked to design a park solely for the purposes of an ideal walkabout, Scriber Park would be the result. It is a simple place with 20 acres of trees surrounding a lake—no fuss, no frills, and as close to nature as you can get in an otherwise suburban, strip-mall environment.

A series of paved and soft-surface trails lead you on a magical mystery tour; one trail ends up at a viewing platform over Scriber Lake, another at a multi-trunked tree, a third to another park called Mini Park, and on it goes. The best part is a series of floating bridges on the lake itself. Isis commented that it would be perfect if dogs were allowed to swim, but she understands the need to preserve such enjoyable natural habitats for future generations of dogs to enjoy. No chasing the waterfowl, please.

You'll pass the park on the left on 196th Street before turning left on Scriber Lake Road, then almost immediately left on 198th Street. It looks like you are entering a shopping mall; past that, you'll see the park entrance to your left.

PLACES TO EAT

Ezell's Famous Chicken: Cooper says Ezell's is the best fried chicken in the solar system, including that 10th planet they just discovered. This is the stuff Oprah had flown to Chicago. You can die and go to heaven content after eating their crisp, not-too-greasy, secret-recipe spicy chicken; lumpy gravy and mashed potatoes; and crunchy, sugary, buttery peach cobbler. Don't forget a side order of liver and gizzards for the pups. 7531 196th Ave. S.W.; 425/673-4193.

PLACES TO STAY

In this area, chain hotels offer the best options for dogs and their owners; please look under Chain Hotels in the Resources section.

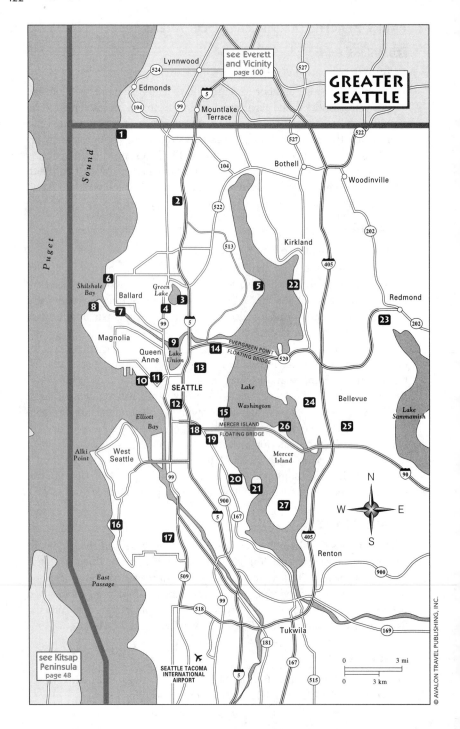

see Everett and Vicinity page 100

GREATER SEATTLE

Lynnwood

524

Edmonds

104

99

Mountlake Terrace

5

527

522

1

Bothell

104

Woodinville

527

2

522

202

513

Kirkland

405

Shilshole Bay

6

Green Lake

3

5

22

Redmond

Ballard

4

8

7

23

202

99

5

Magnolia

9

14

EVERGREEN POINT FLOATING BRIDGE

520

Queen Anne

Lake Union

13

SEATTLE

10 11

12

Lake Washington

24

Bellevue

Lake Sammamish

Elliott Bay

15

25

18

MERCER ISLAND FLOATING BRIDGE

26

19

Alki Point

West Seattle

Mercer Island

20

21

27

90

N

W   E

S

16

900

5   167

17

405

Renton

509

East Passage

900

518

99

169

Tukwila

181

see Kitsap Peninsula page 48

0   3 mi

0   3 km

167

SEATTLE TACOMA INTERNATIONAL AIRPORT

5

515

CHAPTER 5

Greater Seattle

Dogs of Seattle owe much to John C. Olmsted and Frederick Olmsted Jr., sons of famed Central Park architect Frederick Law Olmsted. The Olmsted brothers are the master planners behind a connected string of 20 of Seattle's most beloved parks, and their work set the tone for a continued respect and priority for city greenery. In the Emerald City, being green also refers to the inhabitants' environmental bent, reportedly recycling more than any other major metropolis.

For quintessential Seattle, walk with your dog through the Pike Place Market, the country's oldest continually operating open-air market, and in Pioneer Square, the core of early Seattle with its preserved Richardsonian-Romanesque buildings. Don't forget the Eastside, which is what Seattleites call anything east of Lake Washington, the region's Silicon Forest, home of high technology, led by giants including Microsoft and Nintendo.

In Seattle city parks, dogs are not allowed, even on leash, on beaches, in playgrounds, or on organized sports fields. For areas to call their own, the needs of dogs in the greater metro area are looked after by Citizens for Off-Leash Areas (COLA), www.coladog.org.

PICK OF THE LITTER—GREATER SEATTLE

BEST PARKS
Green Lake Park, Green Lake (page 127)
Discovery Park, Magnolia (page 132)

BEST DOG PARKS
Magnuson Park at Sand Point, University District (page 128)
Marymoor Park, Redmond (page 149)

BEST BEACH
Richmond Beach, Shoreline (page 125)

BEST EVENTS
Bark in the Park and PAWSwalk, University District
(page 129)

BEST PLACES TO EAT
Le Pichet, Downtown (page 138)
Three Dog Bakery, Downtown (page 139)
Cactus, Kirkland (page 142)
St. Clouds, Madrona (page 142)

BEST PLACES TO STAY
Alexis Hotel, Downtown (page 139)
W Hotel, Downtown (page 140)
Bellevue Club Hotel, Bellevue (page 151)

Burke-Gilman Trail: This paved, multi-use trail hugs the shores of Lake Washington after passing Lake Union and the University of Washington. It is heavily used by cyclists and in-line skaters as well as walkers with leashed dogs. There are six park rest stops along the way. At the top of the lake, in Kenmore Logboom Park, the trail connects to the Sammamish River Trail. For an excellent interactive map, go to www.cityofseattle.net/parks/burkegilman/bgtrail.htm.

Sammamish River Trail: The transition between Burke-Gilman and this trail is so seamless, people usually think they are one and the same. This segment adds 9.4 miles through the valleys on the east side of the lake, ending at the dog mecca of Marymoor.

Shoreline

This quiet residential area is a young city, having only split from Seattle to incorporate in 1995. Canines can rest assured that city leadership has its priorities straight. Two of the largest projects in progress are building the section of the multi-use Interurban Trail to connect Seattle to Lynnwood, and adding greenery, landscaped medians, and wide sidewalk promenades to improve walking along Aurora Avenue, the main north-south commercial strip.

PARKS, BEACHES, AND RECREATION AREAS

1 Richmond Beach Saltwater Park

🐾🐾🐾🐾 (See Greater Seattle map on page 122)

Isis and Coop's buddies Holly and Hailey "The Comet" Pengelly turned the dogs onto this city park on Puget Sound, which might be easy to miss if you don't live in the neighborhood. It is worth every minute of the 10-mile drive north from downtown, for the views and the multiple options, without the masses of humanity you'll find on beaches closer in.

The park comes in layers, starting on the top of the bluff with a gravel trail that leads around the point. The water views from here are high enough to give you a good case of vertigo. Halfway down the hill is a covered picnic shelter, and closer to the bottom, a circular lawn with parking, a playground, and the basic handy stuff, including restrooms and water fountains.

Now, if your dog hasn't heard a word we've said up to this point, it's because he only cares about the bottom layer, the beach. Shoreline doesn't have the strict rule of prohibiting dogs from park beaches as Seattle does, merely the standard leash and scoop provisions. After crossing over the railroad tracks on a cement footbridge, thar' she blows, with a berm built of river rock and gravel that gives way to sandier spots north and south.

From I-5, take Exit 176, and go west on N.W. 175th Street, turn right on Aurora Avenue (State Route 99), and turn left on N.W. 185th Street. You'll travel west on 185th for two miles, as it becomes N.W. Richmond Beach Road, and then N.W. 195th Street, then turn left on 20th Avenue N.W. into the park. 2021 N.W. 190th St.

PLACES TO EAT

Hotwire Café: Milo the Chihuahua is the CEO of this enterprising Internet café. He ensures that a water bowl is in front by the outdoor tables and that dog biscuits can be found in a jar nearby. Dog T-shirts are for sale ($15), in addition to coffee beverages, smoothies, sandwiches, low-carb wraps, salads, doughnuts, and s'mores, cooked over a miniature table fire. Live music, local art, and free wireless Internet are a few of the coffeehouse's perks. 17551 15th Ave N.E., Shoreline; 206/957-2000. www.hotwirecoffee.com.

North Seattle

North Seattle is the home base for a very active dog agility club, the Sno-King Agility Club. The organization promotes the fun and competition of agility for dogs in Snohomish and North King counties (www.snokingagility.org).

PARKS, BEACHES, AND RECREATION AREAS

2 Northacres

🐾🐾🐾 🐕 (See Greater Seattle map on page 122)

It's an unoriginal name for 20.7 acres of park just north of Seattle, the home of one of the city's off-leash areas along with picnic tables and grills, baseball fields, a playground, wading pool, and groomed trails. Strict signs warn that dogs are not allowed in the children's play area or on the athletic fields, so keep your pals under control until you reach the designated romping grounds. The off-leash area occupies a fraction of the acreage, but it is a little jewel worth exploring in the middle of a forest of fir trees. Within the fenced area are smaller fenced-in Habitat Protection Areas, leaving the play space looking like an off-road rally course with plenty of sharp turns. Cooper and his pug friend Mr. Peabody like to chase each other around the figure eights, pick up sticks, and poke their noses into the ferns.

Northacres is very progressive when it comes to waste disposal, providing biodegradable pick-up mitts and a doggy latrine. No, your Pekinese doesn't sit on the potty, but you can use the pooper-scooper to toss the waste into a compost bin. Traditionalists will also find spare bags attached to the community bulletin board. No matter how much gravel and wood chips volunteers spread around, you're bound to encounter mud puddles here during three seasons out of four. As far as Cooper is concerned, that's a bonus. Because he's such a low rider, he gets treated to a warm washcloth rubbed over his dirty underbelly when we get home—and Cooper will do anything for a tummy rub.

Take the 130th Street exit from I-5 North (145th Street exit if you're going south), then a left on 130th, a left on 1st, a left on 125th, and a left on 3rd to the end of the cul de sac. 12718 1st Ave. N.E.

PLACES TO EAT

Qdoba: We're cheating, because this is a chain—but it has the best outdoor seating, fresh make-your-own burritos, quesadillas, and *tres-queso* nachos the size of a Chihuahua. 10002 Aurora Ave. N.; 206/528-1335; www.qdoba.com.

PLACES TO STAY

In this area, chain hotels offer the best choices for dogs and their owners; please look under Chain Hotels in the Resources section.

Green Lake

All life in this neighborhood revolves around the 300-acre body of water named for the algae blooms which give it a characteristic jade color.

PARKS, BEACHES, AND RECREATION AREAS

🐾 Green Lake Park

🐾🐾🐾🐾 (See Greater Seattle map on page 122)

Without a doubt, the paths around this natural lake see more dog-walking action than anywhere else in the city. Brave souls never fear to tread the 2.8-mile paved inner pathway, flinching not an inch when in-line skaters and speed cyclists buzz by. The meek can inhabit the 3.2-mile outer ring, a soft-surface path preferred by the joggers. The lake is visible throughout, where you can watch scullers drill and ducks dawdle. There are wide expanses of lawn encircling the whole shebang, plus playgrounds, wading pools, a community center, and the list goes on. Dogs with masterful socialization skills will thrive in this canine cosmopolis. If your dog can handle Green Lake, she could probably pass the Canine Good Citizenship test without lifting a paw. Leashes are mandatory—don't leave home without them.

From I-5, take Exit 169 and go west on N.E. 50th Street for .7 miles. Turn right onto Green Lake Way. Go north on Green Lake Way and park along the street surrounding the lake or in one of several small, free parking lots. 7201 East Green Lake Drive.

🐾 Woodland Dog Park

🐾🐾🐾🐕 (See Greater Seattle map on page 122)

In 1889, lumber baron Guy T. Phinney bought the land for his estate and an exotic animal menagerie, which he opened for public viewing. The city acquired his estate in 1899, and 90 acres of woods are now home to a certified rose test garden, a popular summer concert series, and the world-famous Seattle Zoo. Your dogs will undoubtedly enjoy indulging their animal instincts in the leash-free zone.

The one-acre off-leash area is swank, hilly, and thick with trees. It's surrounded by a six-foot, rubber-coated chain-link fence, with double gates at three entrances. Railroad tie steps on two sides lead up to a plateau where everyone hangs out in a very well-behaved fashion. If you or your dog get bored, Green Lake Park's three-mile loop trail is right down the hill.

There is running water and a few picnic tables and benches. In addition to waste bag dispensers, a portable waste composter, and scoopers, there is a whimsical fire hydrant, painted yellow and blue with dog bones.

From I-5, take Exit 169 and go west on N.E. 50th Street for .7 miles. Turn right onto Green Lake Way, and take the next available left at .2 miles. Turn left in the next driveway at the sign for Woodland Park, and follow the road up the hill to the right of the tennis courts. Parking and the off-leash area will be on your left. 1000 N. 50th Street.

PLACES TO EAT

Blu Water Bistro: At this open-air dining establishment, across the street from Green Lake, the summer menu fills up with salads, and come winter, meatloaf goes back on the menu along with heartier soups. Dogs tie up to a tree alongside your patio tables, and the staff will bring out a water bowl for them. 7900 E. Green Lake Dr. N.; 206/524-3985; www.bluwaterbistro.com.

Mighty O Doughnuts: This is where dogs of Green Lake go after a run and where Isis and Cooper rendezvous with their friend Blue, who goes for the hard-core cake doughnuts in all their gut-bomb glory. 2110 N. 55th; 206/547-0335.

University District and Ravenna

Dogs will feel right at home in the home of the Dawgs, the University of Washington Huskies. About 40,000 students come to party—oops, we mean study—at U-Dub annually. The heart of the U-District is a good source for second-hand shopping and ethnic eats ordered through walk-up windows.

PARKS, BEACHES, AND RECREATION AREAS

5 Magnuson Park at Sand Point

🐾🐾🐾🐾🐾🦴 (See Greater Seattle map on page 122)

This is the land that doggie dreams are made of, a nine-acre site with winding trails, several open areas, and the only paw-approved water access within city limits, along Lake Washington. Your canine will never lack for companionship at this dog park, between the puppy play dates, mutt meet-ups, dog-walker outings, and regulars who spend quality time in Seattle's largest pet playground. Cooper, who is both shy and small, is pleased to announce that Magnuson has a separate Small and Shy Dog Area. Despite the best efforts of the wood-chip patrol, the OLA's main field is often mud soup, so you'll be pleased to know that there is a dog wash station at the main entrance.

The OLA is completely fenced, with several double-gated entry points. To reach the beach, you have to leave the main fenced section and cross a trail to enter another gated area. Water is plentiful, but the bag supply is sporadic. Magnuson is Seattle's second-largest park, a 350-acre former Navy facility with many uses, but frankly, once you've seen the dog park, you've seen all there is to see.

The off-leash area is straight east from the 74th Street entrance. Open 4 A.M.–10 P.M. 7400 Sand Point Way N.E.; 206/684-4946.

DOG-EAR YOUR CALENDAR

You might wish you, too, had fur when running or walking the **Furry 5K** around Seward Park in Seattle. It's often still chilly when this race is run in April, to benefit the Help the Animals Fund, providing veterinary care to shelter animals. Register early for $20 to get your T-shirt, $15 if you want to get the lead out but don't need the shirt. One fee covers you and your dog, who must run on an 8-foot or shorter leash. This is seriously fun business—results are timed and winners posted. 206/615-0820; www.furry5k.com.

Have a ball raising money for the Seattle/King County Humane Society at the annual **Tuxes and Tails** benefit, one of many events and activities sponsored by SHS. This dinner and auction brings out celebrities and high society in packs to promote a wonderful cause. For the highlight of the evening, dogs in the latest designer attire walk the runway in a Celebrity Pet Fashion Show. Tuxes and Tails is held annually in April, at different venues in downtown Seattle. Top Dog Tickets are $175 for front-row seats at this evening of super-stars. 425/373-5384; www.seattlehumane.org.

It's the biggest doggone party with a purpose every September at **Bark in the Park and PAWSwalk** at Sand Point in Seattle. The festivities include a 1K and a 5K walk, music, food (human and canine), and nearly a hundred booths of dog-related products and vendors. The point is to have a blast while raising money for PAWS. Coop 'n' Isis came home with enough treats and food samples to last a month. Upwards of 5,000 people plus pets attend. Pre-registration is $20 per person, $25 at the door. You get a T-shirt and your dogs wear sporty bandanas. 425/742-4009, ext. 262; www.barkinthepark.com.

Calling all ghostbusters, ghouls, and ghost dogs to the annual **Dog-O-Ween** costume contest at South Seattle's Genesee off-leash area. While some dogs have been known to sulk when placed in costume, at least they'll get to mix and mingle with their friends while you raise money for COLA, Citizens for Off-Leash Areas, Seattle's pro-pup-park organization. The festive fundraiser is held, rain or rain, 11 A.M.–2 P.M. with food and fashion, door prizes, a silent auction, and vendor booths. The suggested donation for your pet to enter the costume contest is $5, and bring your checkbook to bid on auction items. Call for event dates. 206/264-5573; www.coladog.org.

PLACES TO EAT

Agua Verde Paddle Club and Café: In addition to serving some of the best authentic tacos north of the Mexican border, this unique establishment in the University District rents sea kayaks by the hour. Munch on the renowned yam or portobello mushroom Tacos de la Casa with pineapple-jicama salsa, and work off the calories paddling past Seattle's famous houseboats on Lake Union. Kayak rentals are available March–October; the cafeteria-style restaurant is open year-round. Order at the counter or the to-go window and relax at the picnic tables in the waterfront park next door. 1303 N.E. Boat St., Seattle; 206/545-8570; www.aguaverde.com.

60th Street Desserts and Delicatessen: This kitchen bakes the cakes for the pastry cases of the finer grocery stores in town. It's a quick stop for good takeout lunch foods, across the street from the entrance to Sand Point. 7401 Sand Point Way N.E.; 206/527-8560.

PLACES TO STAY

University Inn: Legendary for the staff's quality of service, this hotel bills itself as the "hotel with a heart," which extends a warm welcome to pets under 25 pounds, as many as you like, for $10 per pet, per night. Pets are allowed in 20 traditional rooms, much too modern and stylish to be called such. Rates are $95–105. 4140 Roosevelt Way N.E.; 206/632-5055 or 800/733-3855; www.universityinnseattle.com.

Ballard

Still fondly referred to as "Little Scandinavia," this neighborhood struggles to retain the flavor of its mariner and millwork settlers, even as it becomes the next best new place to open an art gallery, shop, or sidewalk café. Market Street is the one to stroll along for people-watching, and if you follow this arterial all the way around the point past yacht-packed Shilshole Marina, it leads to a popular beach with its own rowdy dog park.

PARKS, BEACHES, AND RECREATION AREAS

6 Golden Gardens

🐾🐾🦴 (See Greater Seattle map on page 122)

The masses of Seattle flock to the beach at Golden Gardens to capture elusive sun rays and unbeatable views of Puget Sound and the Olympic Mountains. Dogs are not allowed on the beach or playground, but that's no great loss because it's usually crowded. Leashed dogs are allowed on the paved beach trail and in the picnic areas, but you might want to opt instead for the off-leash area a little ways up the hill.

The off-leash area is a rough and tumble park, with a bunch of rambunctious regulars who rule the turf. If you've got an outgoing pup with too much energy on your hands, this is the place to bring him, and he'll nap like a baby afterwards. Cooper thinks it's the WWF of the dog world; we think some owners could be in better control of their animals.

Two gates open into a wide, fenced enclosure, with a gently sloping hill with a few benches, a couple of tables, a water pump, and some dog bowls. A covered enclosure and lighting for dark evenings are particularly nice features. It's wood chips and mud with plenty of room for rompin' and stompin'.

From the south, take N.W. Market Street through downtown Ballard, which becomes 54th Street N.W. and then Seaview Ave. N.W. At the entrance to the park, turn right on Seaview Place N.W., go under the railroad trestle and up the hill to the dog park. Open 6 A.M.–11:30 P.M. 8498 Seaview Pl. N.W.

⁊ Hiram M. Chittenden Locks and Carl S. English Jr. Botanical Gardens

😺😺😺 ◄● (See Greater Seattle map on page 122)

More than 85,000 vessels pass through the two navigation locks each year, allowing passage between the saltwater of Puget Sound and the freshwater ship canal to Lake Union and Lake Washington. Opening day of boating season, May 1, is a sight not to be missed at the locks. The giant oil tankers, each one taking up an entire lock, are another fascinating sight.

In the seven-acre park surrounding the locks, 500 species of plants and 1,500 varieties of flowers were planted to transform the mounds of dirt left over after the construction of the locks in 1913. The gardens are separated into small, distinct beds with concrete pathways throughout. Dogs on leash are welcome as long as you bring your own bags to pick up after them. The only areas dogs are not allowed are in the visitors center and underground in the fish-viewing windows. Hand off your leash to a friend for a moment to see a rare glimpse of salmon migrating through the 22-step fish ladder.

On either side of the locks, there are stepped hills, shaped for the sole purpose of picnicking; you just have to watch out for goose droppings at migratory times of the year.

From I-5, take Exit 166 westbound on Denny Way, which curves around to become Elliott Avenue, and then 15th Avenue N.W. Continue north across the Ballard Bridge, turn left on N.W. Market Street, and follow it through Ballard. Take the left at the Y-intersection onto N.W. 54th Street, and the locks are a hundred yards or so past that point. 3015 N.W. 54th St.; 206/783-7059. The grounds are open 7 A.M.–9 P.M.; the visitors center hours vary by season.

PLACES TO EAT

Dish Urban Market: The Dish has ready-made entrées, salads, breads, and desserts, plus shelves of gourmet food items to pack a picnic lunch to take to the Locks. The Cuban pork and the green beans with olive oil and Meyer lemon belong in the culinary hall of fame. 2052 N.W. Market St.; 206/297-1852.

Totem House: This seafood and chowder house by the locks has been around forever; its distinctive totem poles make it easy to spot. There are a few token chicken items for the non-seafood lovers and excellent Caesar salads. 3058 N.W. 54th St.; 206/784-2300.

Magnolia

This old-money peninsula grew out of a summer home enclave. It stands out from other communities for the pruning, grooming, landscaping, and manicuring of its lawns and gardens. There are poodles who would give their canine teeth to be this tricked out. A sidewalk stroll around Magnolia Bluff gives your heeler a chance to hobnob with local purebreds, while you watch the ferry boats in Elliott Bay and snap a shot of the Space Needle with Mt. Rainier hulking in the background.

After an afternoon of new delights at Discovery Park, pop around the corner to **PJ's Paws and Claws,** in Magnolia Village for handmade gifts and premium treats, toys, and accessories (3320 W. McGraw St.; 206/281-WOOF (206/281-9663); www.pjspawsandclaws.com).

PARKS, BEACHES, AND RECREATION AREAS

8 Discovery Park

🐾🐾🐾🐾 (See Greater Seattle map on page 122)

The young city of Seattle donated 500 acres to the federal government in 1894 for an army base on the tip of the Magnolia peninsula. More than a million troops were shipped out to Europe from Fort Lawton during World War I and World War II, with up to 10,000 a day headed to Korea in the early 1950s. Seventy years later, the land was returned to the city, and Discovery Park was born.

Every trip to these largely untamed woods is an adventure, with two miles of tidal beaches, grassy meadows, shifting sand dunes, forested groves, and plunging sea cliffs. The southwest entrance is closest to the former parade grounds, perfect for kite flying, picnics, picking blackberries in August, and taking in sweeping views of the Olympic Mountains and Elliott Bay. Down the trail to South Beach, you can harvest clams on 50 yards of mudflats at low tide and check out the lighthouse.

The east entrance leads to the visitors center, and North Beach, a picnic spot with a birds-eye view of the yachts at Shilshole Bay Marina. Down a winding driveway is the Daybreak Star Indian Cultural Center, telling of the Duwamish people who fished here more than 4,000 years before Scandinavian settlers came for the region's gold, timber, and salmon.

No bones about it: We love this place. Our favorite is the three-mile loop trail, a moderate hike that leads you through the park's highlights. Dogs must be leashed, and this is especially important on the bluffs, where entire hundred-yard sections of the hillside have recently slid back into the sea.

It's challenging to get here but worth the effort. From downtown, take Denny Way, which becomes Elliott Avenue and then 15th Avenue. Take the Nickerson/Emerson exit and loop around onto W. Emerson Place past Fisherman's Terminal. Turn right onto Gilman Avenue, and follow it around until it becomes Government Way and leads directly into the park's east entrance. Park closes at dusk; 3801 W. Government Way; 206/386-4236.

PLACES TO EAT

Celebrations To Go: Every meal is a celebration of good taste, and every day is a little different, according to the whims of the wonderful chef, whose catering is in high demand throughout Magnolia peninsula. People probably talked her into putting her dishes out daily because they couldn't host enough parties to get their fill of her yummy food. 2434 32nd Ave. W.; 206/286-8755.

Fremont and Wallingford

Left-of-center and just a little bit off-kilter, Fremont is a free-spirited community with a high concentration of artists and a few software engineers thrown in for good measure. Even before it starts officially at Gas Works Park, you can pick up the Burke-Gilman trail anywhere along the waterfront to watch the boats going through the Montlake Cut. Street-corner art is everywhere. Walk your pup past *Waiting for the Interurban* at 34th Street and Fremont Avenue, the troll under the Aurora Bridge, a rocket that "takes off" everyday at noon at 35th Street and Evanston Avenue, and a statue of Lenin rescued from a ditch in Poland and placed at 36th Street and Fremont Avenue.

East of Stone Way, Wallingford is toned down a bit, unless there's food involved at festivities such as Bite of Wallingford and the Wallingford Wurst Festival. Cooper's got a soft spot in his belly for this restaurant-heavy neighborhood.

DIVERSION

Dogs are welcome to come on the **Sunday Fremont Ice Cream Cruise,** but no, that's not why they call it the poop deck. If your dog is calm and sea worthy, at the captain's discretion, she's welcome to test her sea legs on board the MV *Fremont Avenue,* a small ferry plying the waters of Lake Union.

The tour cruises the inside passages of Seattle's canals and lakes for about 45 minutes, giving you the best views of resident houseboats, glass artist Dale Chihuly's studio, and the city skyline. The captain keeps bacon-flavored treats on board, knowing that ice cream is not always the best for canine stomachs. Tours depart summer Sundays, on the hour 11 A.M.–5 P.M. Adults are $7, kids are $4, and four-leggeds are free. Ice cream treats are extra. Reservations are accepted, but not required. The vessel departs from Fremont, under the Aurora Bridge. Watch for the sandwich board signs, flags, and balloons, to the lower Adobe parking lot. Contact Capt. Larry Kezner; 801 N. Northlake Way; 425/889-0306 or 206/713-8446; www.seattleferryservice.com.

PARKS, BEACHES, AND RECREATION AREAS

🟨 Gas Works Park

🐾🐾 (See Greater Seattle map on page 122)

There is one day a year you should avoid bringing a dog to this city park, at all costs. First and foremost, dogs typically despise and fear fireworks, and secondly, several hundred thousand people crawl all over the 20-acre hill on Independence Day to watch the Fourth of JulIvar's fireworks shot off a barge in Union Lake (Ivar's is a clam restaurant chain started by colorful historical figure Ivar Haglund).

Any other day, there are a bunch of reasons to visit Gas Works. Come to check out the hulking remnants of the pipelines that provided natural gas to early residents and give the park its name. Watch people fly kites on the breezy hill and take in choice views of downtown and the houseboats, including the one made famous as Tom Hank's pad in *Sleepless in Seattle.* This park is the official starting point for the Burke-Gilman multi-use trail and the best place to find free parking to get on the trail.

On a recent visit, we watched a couple trying to get their new golden retriever puppy to sit-stay long enough to take a picture of him against the city backdrop, for a New Baby Arrival announcement to family and friends—hilarious.

From I-5, take Exit 169, go east on N. 45th Street eight blocks, turn right on University, go seven long blocks and turn right on N. Pacific Street. As the road curves right, the park is on your left. The park is open 4 A.M.–11:30 P.M., the parking lot only from 6 A.M.–9 P.M. 2101 N. Northlake Way.

PLACES TO EAT

Essential Baking Company: This is an essential stop when you're in the neighborhood. The artisan bakers that supply bread to many local, upscale grocery stores also make luscious soups (Isis loves the ginger and carrot puree), pizza, salads, select sandwiches, and entrées. The pastries are works of art, and the coffee is superb. As if that's not enough, they hand-craft elegant chocolates. The patio is smallish with four tables for two and one long bench, but it captures the warm afternoon sun. Breakfast, lunch, and supper with counter service to stay or to go. Near Gas Works Park and the Burke-Gilman Trail. 1604 N. 34th St., Seattle; 206/545-3804; www.essentialbaking.com.

Norm's Eatery and Ale House: Pictures of Norm and Polly the goldens are plastered on the walls, the drinks are named after them, and the dog theme is carried out in every aspect of the bar's décor. Norm and Polly welcome guest dogs at patio tables and recommend the cumin-chipotle meatloaf, creamy tuna casserole, and steak sandwiches for canines. If you sit quietly and don't beg, they may allow you to share. 460 N. 36th St.; 206/547-1417.

Queen Anne

This neighborhood comes in two flavors, Lower Queen Anne and Top of Queen Anne, the latter up the steepest street in the city, known in local parlance as the Counterbalance. Dividing the plateau on one of Seattle's few remaining original hills is Queen Anne Avenue, a chic shopping and dining destination.

PARKS, BEACHES, AND RECREATION AREAS

10 Elliott Bay–Myrtle Edwards Park

🐾🐾 (See Greater Seattle map on page 122)

This 4,100-foot strip of waterfront property is the closest real greenspace to the downtown core, with a 1.25-mile winding bike and pedestrian path bordered by rolling lawns and Puget Sound. Every step awards views of Mt. Rainier and the Olympics across the water. You'll start at the skyscrapers of downtown, and end at working docks and fishing piers of the wharf in Magnolia. You'll come close to the Port of Seattle's working grain elevators; hopefully, you'll get the chance to watch one load up with grain.

Your dog will find likely walking partners with the many downtown dogs who frequent the trails and lawns. Watch out for the in-line skaters and cyclists who may provide some unintentional agility training for you and your dog.

To reach Myrtle Edwards, think right-left-right-left-right: From I-5 north-bound, take the left Exit 165 onto Seneca Street. Turn right onto 1st Avenue, left onto Battery Street, right onto Western Avenue, left onto Wall Street, and right on Alaskan Way, .3 mile into a metered parking lot. Open 24 hours, with an afterglow provided by the city lights. 3103 Alaskan Way W.

PLACES TO EAT

Chinoise: For pan-Asian specialties, this café and sushi bar consistently ranks in Seattle's top favorite polls. We swear, when Isis tried her first rain-bow roll, we saw her eyes widen in delight. It's doubtful you'll suffer from the hungry-two-hours-later syndrome if you try the soup pots or noodle bowls. Patio dining is weather permitting, and there's always those little white to-go boxes. 12 Boston St.; 206/284-6671; www.chinoisecafe.com.

Downtown

After several boring decades in which people only came downtown to work, and Seattle was infamous for rolling up its sidewalks at 9 P.M., the downtown core is fashionable again after the bull market and dot-com boom of the 1990s gave a financial boost to the city. The bursting of the dot-com bubble seems to have had little effect on an area where a new courthouse, luxury condos, symphony halls, sculpture gardens, and office buildings continue to rise. For top

DIVERSION

Within seconds of opening, well-to-do downtown dogs who'd had enough of high-rise loft living were crawling all over the **Downtown Dog Lounge.** Within its first year, this doggie day-care center was voted the best in Seattle and had to open two additional locations to handle the volume of dogs scratching at the door.

This hip spot has separate play pens for different sizes and temperaments of dogs. The dog lounge features play care, overnights, and adventures, and that's just the beginning. Walks, hiking trips, herbal baths, healing massages, pawdicures, obedience training, pooch parties, and a rush-hour doggie valet are among the services offered. Your four-legged loved ones are pampered and preened while you do the same at the spa, or go out for dinner or perhaps to a museum or movie. Lounges are conveniently located in Belltown, one right across the street from Regrade Dog Park, but if that's not good enough, the lounge will come to you. The business has estab-lished relationships with the W Hotel, Hotel Monaco, and others for in-room pet sitting. The original location is at 3131 Western Ave., #301, Seattle; 206/282-3647; www.downtowndoglounge.com.

designer boutiques, head to Pacific Place and Nordstrom, founded in Seattle. At lunchtime, Westlake Plaza is the place to be for free summertime concerts and simply absorbing the city. Seattle's waterfront piers are another good choice for a city walk, always bustling with a mix of tourist and working port activities.

PARKS, BEACHES, AND RECREATION AREAS

11 Seattle Center Grounds

🐾🐾🔹 (See Greater Seattle map on page 122)

Since it was created for the 1962 World's Fair, the Seattle Center continues to house more cultural attractions per square foot than any other plot in the city. There are so many things for people to see: the Space Needle, the colorful blob of the Experience Music Project, the Monorail, and the spires of the Children's Museum, to name a few. Walking by all of these must-sees is good for a spot of exercise, and a tug of the leash in the right direction will lead to the center square of grass surrounding the International Fountain. The size of a small mountain, the dome spouts water-jet shows choreographed to classical music. Kids delight in being caught off-guard and getting drenched when the fountain bursts to life; dogs will have to settle for stray spray.

Seattle Center hosts the city's oldest and biggest event traditions, including the Folk Life Festival, Bite of Seattle, and Bumbershoot. These are the times when being a dog in the park is a drag, and as a human, you may get dragged by the crowds in directions you had no intention of going.

From I-5, take Exit 167 and follow Mercer Street straight west. There are multiple paid parking lots around the center.

DIVERSION

What do you get for the girl who has everything? A feather boa collar from **High Maintenance Bitch,** of course! Run by Lori and Ryan, a sister and brother from Seattle, this business with the tongue-in-cheek name is nationally famous for its Pet Feathers, a line of ultra-glam accessories for furry fashionistas. There's the Martini Collection for cocktail parties, Everyday Ensembles for jaunts about town, and Fru Fru Feathers for casual days. Dogs in the know have been seen sporting them at such high-society events as the Pug Gala, the Tuxes and Tails Celebrity Fashion Show, and the Furry 5K run. The boas made it into the 2004 Golden Globe presenter gift baskets, and Jessica Simpson's dog adores hers.

If you can't afford a diamond dog collar, stop by the store at 619 Broadway in Capitol Hill to get your baby a boa, call 206/709-9050, or check them out online at www.highmaintenancebitch.com.

12 Regrade Dog Park

🐾🐾🐕 (See Greater Seattle map on page 122)

Rarely has so small a space generated such huge excitement. More than 100 dogs packed the quarter city block when this off-leash area opened in March 2004. Not only is this park a sight for the sore eyes of downtown dogs trapped on the patios of high-rise condos and apartments, but it helped clear up a city eyesore of illegal activity.

The ground is alternating patches of concrete and wood mulch. Because it was converted from a former use, there's probably more cement than is desirable, but at least it's not mud! Even though the rubber-coated chain-link fence that surrounds the area is five feet tall, you'll still have to watch how far and high you throw balls and fetch toys to avoid hitting parked cars and pedestrians on the adjacent bustling city streets. City bicycle cops have also hinted that they'll be extra strict about enforcing the leash laws until you get your pet into the park. Two double-gated entrances on either side of the park provide extra room for leash maneuvers.

Regrade Park borders the ultra-hip and pricey Belltown neighborhood, the address of choice for up-and-coming urban professionals. This could be an interesting place to scout for a date while your Scout tries to mate. At the very least, a little extra grooming couldn't hurt. Open dawn–dusk. On the corner of Bell and 2nd. 2251 3rd Avenue.

PLACES TO EAT

Fish Club: Down by the waterfront, at the Marriott Hotel, the patio at this restaurant has at least 20 tables in the summertime and a few scattered tables around a heat lamp in the winter. Dogs are welcomed with open arms, biscuits, and water bowls. The menu's fish and seafood preparations come from sustainable sources around the world. For the best variety, try a bunch of Small Bites and be sure to let Fido lick your fingers between each course. 2100 Alaskan Way; 206/256-1040; www.fishclubseattle.com.

Le Pichet: This multi-award-winning gourmet French bistro takes the European approach by allowing dogs on the patio—but of course—and they confess they'd let them belly up to the bar for a glass of house red if the health codes would allow it. This isn't small and fussy food; it's rich and hearty and moderately priced. The chef believes that elegant dining should be an everyday experience. 1933 1st. Ave.; 206/256-1499.

Macrina Bakery and Café: This bake shop's breads and pastries are sold in high-falutin' grocery stores and touted all over the city. Equally heavenly vegetable dishes are available only in the café—salads of baby spring greens in light vinaigrette dressing, and roasted vegetables with mascarpone cheese on ciabatta rolls or flaky pie crusts. Small, perky downtown dogs are frequently spotted at Macrina's sidewalk tables. 2408 1st Ave.; 206/448-4032.

Three Dog Bakery: Dogs, bring your owners and come sniff around the most extraordinary just-for-dogs bakery in Seattle, where everything everything on the Munchers and Crunchers menu is made from scratch using all-natural ingredients. The Dachsie Twins appreciate that the folks at Three Dogs are very active in dog events throughout the community. Aw, who are we kidding? All the dogs care about are treats and toys in this jam-packed store. 1408 1st Ave.; 206/364-9999.

PLACES TO STAY

Ace Hotel: The super-short name of this boutique hotel often goes to waste. People instead choose to describe it as "that futuristic, minimalist, all-white hotel down by the water." Standard rooms, which share a bath, are $85; deluxe rooms with their own baths are $95. Most rooms have water views. There are no dog restrictions or fees; Astro never had it so good. 2425 1st St.; 206/448-4721; www.theacehotel.com.

Alexis Hotel: This elite hotel is a member of the Kimpton group, a select few stylish urban hotels in desirable major metropolises. The Alexis is so dog-friendly that you may feel jealous at the quality of treatment your pet receives, including treats, doggie in-room dining menus, a designer pet bed, and a blackboard that greets them, by name, when they check in. If you can't stay at this hotel, which is on the National Register of Historic Places, go into the lobby to see the glass sculpture by Dale Chihuly. Rates start at $165 for standard guest rooms. The Alexis is unique in the number of specialty suites, which range $215–550. 1007 1st Ave.; 866/356-8894; www.alexishotel.com.

Edgewater Hotel: "No dog restrictions or fees" are music to a dog's ears, especially when they apply to a premier waterfront hotel. The Edgewater is on a dock over Puget Sound, and it looks like a mountain lodge as seen through the eyes of a modern designer from Milan. Every room has a guard teddy bear and bear ottomans, which Isis barked at. Rates range $189–359. 2411 Alaskan Way; 206/728-7000 or 800/624-0670; www.edgewaterhotel.com.

Hotel Monaco: It is so hard to choose among Seattle's dog-friendly Kimpton hotels with their different vibes; the Monaco is on the edge of avant-garde. Hotel Monaco's list of dog amenities, packages, and services is longer than most hotels' lists for people. You'll be equally pampered, and this hotel will even lend you a pet goldfish for your stay if you fail to bring a pet of your own. No dog restrictions or fees. Rates are $215–315. 1101 4th Ave.; 206/621-1770 or 800/715-6513; www.monaco-seattle.com.

Hotel Vintage Park: Each room is dedicated to celebrating a different Washington winery and vineyard. This four-star hotel gives dogs the five-star treatment, above and beyond what any pooch can expect, with no fees or restrictions. Rates range $139–259. 1100 Fifth Ave.; 800/853-3914; www.hotelvintagepark.com.

Vagabond Inn: An affordable choice close to Seattle Center and the Space Needle. Rates range $49–79; the pet fee is $15 per pet, per stay. 325 Aurora Ave. N.; 206/441-0400.

W Hotel: At this ultra-sleek hotel, the staff goes out of its way to make dogs feel like members of the family. "Dear Doggie," begins a letter addressed specifically to them, "Kick back and enjoy your visit!" The lobby is decked out in suede, leather, and polished aluminum; the rooms are subtle and tasteful. You might even rub noses with the mastiff named Lucius who's a regular bar hound. Rates are $199–399. Dogs are an additional $25 per pet, per night, which barely covers all the wonderful things pets receive in their care package. 1112 4th Ave., Seattle; 800/WHOTELS (800/946-8357); www.whotels.com.

Capitol Hill

Pioneers optimistically named this mound, hoping it would become the site of the state capital. Instead, it has become the city seat for counterculture, a thriving gay and lesbian community, and seemingly more hair colors and body piercings than anywhere else in the city. Broadway, the main drag, has lots of foot traffic, more than its fair share of homeless kids asking for change, and designer collars on dogs, cats, and a few humans. Leash up tight and keep an eye out for potential pet skirmishes on crowded sidewalk cafés and when window-shopping for vintage clothing and retro home furnishings.

PARKS, BEACHES, AND RECREATION AREAS

🐾 Volunteer Park

🐾🐾🐾 (See Greater Seattle map on page 122)

Called City Park at its dedication in 1887, this 48-acre hilltop was renamed in 1901 to honor the volunteers in the Spanish-American War. The park is a landscape legacy of the Olmsted Brothers, with a 106-step tower leading to views of Lake Union and an exhibit about the green-thumbed brothers. Sun worshipers dot the hillside, kids stay busy at a playground and summertime wading pool, and local musicians and Shakespeare productions regularly entertain park goers. Your pal will be pleased to indulge in this highly cultured park with you, also home to the Seattle Asian Art Museum (sorry, no pets inside). In the summer, don't miss the local Dahlia Society's display of these tall flowers with their fat, colorful blooms. Management kindly asks that dogs observe the flowers from a respectful distance. Dogs are not allowed in the Conservatory. Directly north is the Lake View Cemetery, where Jimi Hendrix, Bruce Lee, and Seattle pioneers enjoy eternity in the sun.

From I-5, take Exit 166, east on E. Olive Way, which merges into E. John Street. At the T-intersection, turn left on 15th Avenue E. The park entrance will be on your left after .75 miles. Open 6 A.M.–11 P.M. 1247 15th Ave. E.

PLACES TO EAT

Broadway New American Grill: Dog lovers, lovers, and the film and theater festival crowd elbow in to the Grill for slight twists on American comfort food, such as mashed sweet potatoes, bleu cheese burgers, and Chinese chicken salad. Each tiny sidewalk table is placed for maximum people-watching pleasure. 314 Broadway E.; 206/328-7000.

Café Septieme: A bistro with ambience to spare, Septieme serves fresh salads and soups, espresso in bowls, breakfasts that gently massage away a hangover, and desserts that'll replace it with a sugar high. Sidewalk seating appears when it's nice out, with only a thread of a rope to divide you and your dog from the active sidewalk street life. 214 Broadway E.; 206/860-8858.

Madison and Montlake

These two communities on Lake Washington are generally quiet, with an air of charm created by tree-lined boulevards and the old Seattle-style brick and wood-frame combination homes of the early 20th century, bought up by baby boomers and meticulously restored.

PARKS, BEACHES, AND RECREATION AREAS

14 Washington Park Arboretum

🐾🐾 (See Greater Seattle map on page 122)

To walk through the arboretum is to see the forest for the trees, more than 5,500 varieties of them in a 230-acre living museum. Opened in 1934, the woodland was designed by James F. Dawson, of the Olmsted Brothers landscape architecture firm. Every one of the 40,000 trees and shrubs is deliberately placed, grouped by species. Money and manpower shortages have left the park overgrown and a bit like a faded rose, which doesn't dampen your dog's enthusiasm for a walk through areas with quaint names like Honeysuckle Hill, Azalea Way, and Loderi Valley. During any given season, there are a half dozen species in full glory. Isis chooses fall, when Japanese maples and Chilean fire trees are ablaze with color.

You can do a drive-by through the park on Lake Washington Boulevard or Arboretum Drive East. Or stop by the visitors center to get a trail map for several miles of bark mulch trails and find out which gardens are not to be missed when you visit. Dogs are not allowed in the Japanese garden.

From I-5, take Exit 168B onto State Route 520 and immediately take the first exit off S.R. 520 to Montlake Boulevard. Go straight across Montlake Boulevard to E. Lake Washington Boulevard; at the next left, turn onto E. Foster Island Road to reach the Graham Visitors Center. Hours are 10 A.M.–4 P.M.; the park is open dawn–dusk. 2300 Arboretum Dr. E.; 206/543-8800; http://depts.washington.edu/wpa/.

PLACES TO EAT

Cactus: Like its counterpart in Kirkland, this Southwestern restaurant is close to the water, makes great cocktails, and has outdoor tables, all against the fence on the sidewalk, which allows your dog to sit near you, although on the other side of the fence. 4220 E. Madison St.; 206/324-4140; www.cactus-restaurants.com.

Madrona and Leschi

In 1975, the Historic Seattle Preservation and Development Authority hired architectural expert Victor Steinbrueck to inventory the homes of these old Seattle neighborhoods. The report found Victorian, bungalow, colonial, Tudor cottage, California cottage, ranch house, medieval mansion, early northwest regional, and contemporary structures, which gives you and your dog an interesting and varied neighborhood in which to take walks.

PARKS, BEACHES, AND RECREATION AREAS

15 Lake Washington Boulevard

🐾🐾🐾 (See Greater Seattle map on page 122)

The alternating gravel and sidewalk paths along scenic Lake Washington are populated with walkers in any weather and the winding road is a regular training ground for Seattle cyclists and pleasure cruisers. Starting all the way south in Seward Park, or at the Genesee Dog Park if you prefer, you can choose the length of your walk past Sayres Park, Mt. Baker Park, and Day Street Park. The lakeside walking trails continue up to Leschi Park and Madrona Park. Views of Bellevue and the Cascades are reflected in the water. It's a lovely dog walk, pure and simple.

Lake Washington Boulevard trails parallel the road from Seward Park on the South to Mt. Baker Park on the north, then becomes Lakeside Avenue north of U.S. Highway 90. Restrooms and parking are available at most parks along the way. You're on your own for doggie supplies.

PLACES TO EAT

St. Clouds: This neighborhood bistro is named after the orphanage in John Irving's *The Cider House Rules*. An orphan himself, Cooper rates this spot as his number-one favorite in the entire book. Of course, he may be biased because he knows the owner and one of the restaurant's best chefs. A gated courtyard allows you and your dog to enjoy full service outdoors for dinner or heavenly weekend brunch. The menu mixes comfy favorites like mac 'n' cheese, fried chicken and mashers, and burgers with more trendy fare such as seared Ahi tuna, goat cheese and pear bruschetta, and market fish of the day. The bartender, Rob, mixes a mean Metaxa sidecar and will amuse you with card tricks on the side. The kids' menu was designed by kids for kids. Ever had a fluffernutter (a.k.a. Cloudy Day) sandwich? Kids, make your parents order you one. Did we mention they regularly feature local bands? Doggone it, you simply can't pass up this place. 1131 34th Ave., Madrona; 206/726-1522; www.stclouds.com.

Verité Coffee: The skeptics among you may be saying, "Not another coffeehouse." Ah, but this is the home of the Cupcake Royale, gourmet buttercream-frosted cupcakes. Verité also serves gourmet grilled paninis, has outdoor sidewalk chairs, and is next to the Madrona playground. 1101 34th Ave.; 206/709-4497; www.cupcakeroyale.com.

West Seattle

A peninsula unto itself! Catch the ferry to Vashon Island and Southworth on the Kitsap Peninsula. Dogs are not allowed on the beach at Alki, but you can walk the sidewalk promenade around the tip for fab views. When in West Seattle, do as West Seattle dogs do, and get a watercolor portrait painted by local artist and theater personality Ada McCallister. Her unique paintings capture the essence of your pet's personality; see examples of her work online at www.adapetportraits.com.

PARKS, BEACHES, AND RECREATION AREAS

16 Lincoln Park

🐾🐾 (See Greater Seattle map on page 122)

Put together by piecemeal acquisitions over the years since 1922, the park suitably reflects the varied nature of West Seattle residents, who take great pride in being perceived as eclectic. Rather than giving a laundry list of the park's features, Coop 'n' Isis direct you to the picnic areas, the wooded trail that defines the perimeter of the park, and the long beach walk on Puget Sound in this 135-acre park. The trail is refreshing, a level one-mile walk in and out of the forest and then along the water. It's a fine line between walking the waterfront trail and being on the beach in the water, one that dogs are not supposed to cross. If your dog stays on leash and generally behaves herself, you should be fine.

From I-5, take Exit 163A, the West Seattle exit, follow the signs to Fauntleroy Way S.W. and stay on Fauntleroy, almost the length of the peninsula, until you come to park on the right-hand side of the street. If you end up in line for the Vashon Ferry, you've gone too far. Open 6 A.M.–11 P.M. 8011 Fauntleroy Way S.W.

DIVERSION

Isis faced a crisis of canine conscience trying to pick only a few dog boutiques to include from among the Greater Seattle area's many wonderful choices. She resorted to closing her eyes and pointing to one for each paw.

In Bellevue Square Mall, **Urban Dogs** has unique artwork, books, and gifts celebrating the bond between humans and their pets, plus fancy couture du jour, unusual toys, and tempting treats for your bow-wow. 2036 Bellevue Square; 425/456-0009; www.urban-dogs.com.

Next to Nature in West Seattle is the largest and roomiest of the pet boutiques and carries the best selection of natural and raw foods as well as treats and toys. 4543 California Ave. S.W.; 206/935-1134.

There are more elegant sweaters and collar charms than Isis could wear in a month packed into **Bark!**, a tiny boutique in Ballard. You'll love their collection of breed-specific refrigerator magnets. 5338 Ballard Ave. N.W.; 206/738-4972; www.barknaturalpet.com.

Railey's Leash & Treat in Fremont will tempt even penny-pinching pets to blow their mad money on fabulous toys and accessories and frivolous, but healthy, delicacies. 513 N. 36th St.; 206/632-5200.

17 Westcrest Dog Park

 (See Greater Seattle map on page 122)

At Westcrest, all roads lead to the dog park. Eight gates lead from wooded trails to the fully enclosed off-leash area, including our favorite, the Greenbelt Trail, which can be enjoyed on leash. But you could stay within the confines of the off-leash area and be content to never venture farther. Often, the dogs come in clumps, with an overseer from a dog-sitting or dog-walking service. Within the four-acre OLA, there are trails that lead to several open spaces, including a hillside. It's obvious that some thought and money went into creating a quality dog park here in the bohemian West Seattle neighborhood. For the dogs, there is a drinking fountain, trees, and open space. For people, there are benches and chairs, a covered shelter, and restrooms nearby outside of the fence.

From I-5, take Exit 163A onto the West Seattle Bridge. Take the Delridge Way S.W. exit, and stay in the left lane on the exit ramp to get onto Delridge Way. Go south for 3.3 miles on Delridge, turn left on S.W. Trenton Street, go .6 miles, turn left on 9th Avenue S.W., and take the next right on S.W. Cloverdale Street. Go four blocks and turn right into the parking lot on 5th Avenue S.W. This is the main entrance into the dog park. 8806 8th Ave. S.W. Open 4 A.M.–11:30 P.M.

PLACES TO EAT

Cat's Eye Café: This offbeat little sandwich place near Lincoln Park has healthy food, picnic tables, and really nice people. 7301 Bainbridge Pl. S.W.; 206/935-2229.

Husky Ice Cream and Deli: You can't go wrong at a place named for a dog. These DAWG fans make dozens of ice cream flavors, scooping generous globs of it into homemade waffle cones. Cold and grilled specialty sandwiches feature exotic flavors like marinated artichokes with turkey, cashew chicken, liverwurst and pickle, or olive loaf and cream cheese on dark rye. To top it all off, there's an eye-popping selection of imported, gourmet foods, chocolates, and cookies. Order to go. 4721 California Ave S.W., West Seattle; 206/937-2810; www.huskydeli.com.

PLACES TO STAY

In this area, chain hotels offer the best choices for dogs and their owners; please look under Chain Hotels in the Resources section.

South Seattle

PARKS, BEACHES, AND RECREATION AREAS

🔟🔋 Dr. Jose Rizal Park

🐾🐾🐕 (See Greater Seattle map on page 122)

Dr. Rizal was a Filipino Renaissance man who made lasting contributions to the fields of social and political reform, engineering, medicine, art, and literature before he was executed in 1896 for participating in the Philippine Revolution. During the 1900s, people of Filipino descent formed the second-largest minority population in Seattle, after the Chinese, and this 10-acre park is in their honor.

The off-leash area may be the only known dog park that's busier during workdays than evenings or weekends because it's right across the street from the headquarters of Amazon.com, an employer that allows people to bring their pooches into work with them. Rumor has it there are 90-plus dogs who are office regulars.

Four acres of open and wooded areas follow a short trail. Running water, pooper-scoopers, and a compost bin are provided. A full fence with a double gate surrounds the area, which is largely brush, although the city is working on landscaping it with native plants and trees and getting rid of invasives (translation: overgrown blackberry bushes).

From here, you have the most amazing views of the city from any Seattle dog park. You're close to Seahawks Stadium, SAFECO field, south downtown, and Elliott Bay. It's noisy, because the park borders the I-90 highway interchange.

Take exit 165A toward James Street, stay straight onto 6th Ave, then turn left onto Yesler Way. Turn right onto Boren Avenue, then bear right onto 12th Avenue South. After the Jose P. Rizal Bridge, immediately turn right onto Charles Street, which continues as 12th Avenue. You'll see the park off to your right up the hill. Park up the hill in the parking lot and walk back down to the off-leash area entrance. Parking is limited to two hours 6 A.M.–10 P.M. 1008 12th Ave. S., Beacon Hill.

19 Blue Dog Pond

🐾 🐕 (See Greater Seattle map on page 122)

Is it: a) A rainwater detention basin? b) A sculpture garden? c) An off-leash dog park? If you guessed d) All of the above, you would be correct! To say it is damp here occasionally would be an understatement—during storms this big hole in the ground is designed to hold water until the city's drainage system can handle it. But it doesn't always rain in Seattle, honest, and the area gets put to good use when it's not flooded. Who better than dogs to fully appreciate playing in the mud?

The area is fully fenced and gated. It has a water pump, and a couple of benches. They're doing some landscaping with small trees and marking a few areas for marsh recovery; otherwise, it's an open field with steep sides.

The park is on the northwest corner of S. Massachusetts Street and Martin Luther King Jr. Way S. You can leave your car along 26th Avenue S., a dead-end street alongside the park's west edge. Open 4 A.M.–11:30 P.M.

20 Genesee Dog Park

🐾 🐾 🐾 🐕 (See Greater Seattle map on page 122)

Genesee Park is a wide field that extends about five city blocks. To the south are kids' ball fields, with the off-leash area taking up the entire north end. Three acres of open space have been lovingly designed by landscaped architects for maximum canine enjoyment. It all sits elevated on a slight plateau, created by a garbage landfill, which tends to keep it drier than many of its local counterparts. Small trees, rocks, benches, and sitting logs are strategically placed for maximum comfort around the gravel play area. A community bulletin board and doggie drinking fountain round out the details.

Two double-gated entrances give you places to deal with leashes, which are extremely important until you get into the fenced area because roadside parking is along an extremely busy thoroughfare. Genesee is a popular area, conveniently located in South/Central Seattle. In October, pups strut their stuff in the annual Dog-O-Ween costume contest to benefit Seattle's off-leash areas. The park shares lakeside borders with Lake Washington Boulevard, making it a great launching point for a day's walk along the water.

Take Rainier Avenue South to Genesee Street, and go east to 46th Street. Open 4 A.M.–11:30 P.M. 4316 S. Genesee St.; 206/264-5573; www.coladog.org.

21 Seward Park

🐾🐾🐾 (See Greater Seattle map on page 122)

Most of this city park's 300 acres are left in their natural state, an old-growth forest where eagles are frequently sighted in the tops of the trees. The forest and fern canopy in the core of the park is so thick that hiking the internal trails of the park can be downright spooky. That's just one reason most park-goers stick to the 2.5-mile perimeter trail, a wide road suitable for wheelchair-users. The other main motivator for using that particular trail is the continuous view from all angles of the park, a peninsula that sticks out into Lake Washington. And, if you haven't had your fill by the time you make it around, the trail continues north on Lake Washington Boulevard for many more miles.

From I-5 southbound from Seattle, take Exit 163A, and keep left at the fork in the ramp onto Columbian Way S. Follow the arterial road as it weaves, to the right on 15th Avenue S., to the left on S. Columbian Way, and to the right on S. Alaska Street. Turn right onto Rainier Avenue S (State Route 167), and left onto S. Orcas Street into the park. Open 4 A.M.–11:30 P.M. 206/684-4396; www.sewardpark.net.

Kirkland

Crowded and lively Kirkland keeps the feel of a waterfront resort town, even within spitting distance of mega-Microsoft. Dogs are allowed on leash in Kirkland's parks, which are all waterfront, but not at the park beaches at any time during the year. Party animals should stop by **Denny's Pet World** (12534 120th Ave.; Totem Lake Mall; 425/821-3800), a 17,000-square-foot pet store.

PARKS, BEACHES, AND RECREATION AREAS

🐾 Lake Washington Boulevard–Eastside

🐾 (See Greater Seattle map on page 122)

Join the throngs of people walking the sidewalk of this waterfront promenade. It takes you past all of the prime real estate in town, the outdoor restaurants, galleries, and four beachfront city parks along its 1.2-mile length. If your dog wonders why you're making such a big deal about the views of Seattle and the lake, tell her you don't understand why she loves sniffing so much, but you don't give her grief about it.

Take the State Route 520 bridge across the lake to Exit 14, follow the directions to Lake Washington Boulevard N.E., and stay in the left lane to continue straight on the boulevard. Free parking is available at the north end of the trail at the Kirkland Municipal Library Parking Garage.

PLACES TO EAT

Cactus: Cactus' Mexican specialties have a Santa Fe style to them, with black beans and chipotle peppers making star appearances on the menu. The staff will put out water bowls on the sidewalk patio for the canine crowd, and they suggest that humans stick to the fresh-squeezed juice margaritas and Cuban mojitos. 121 Park Ln.; 425/893-9799; www.cactusrestaurants.com.

Marina Park Grill: This marina cantina's popularity is of mastiff proportions. Reservations are recommended for this bistro in downtown Kirkland on the waterfront. To make room, your dog may have to sit just outside the fence next to your table. 89 Kirkland Ave.; 425/889-9000; www.marinaparkgrill.com.

PLACES TO STAY

Willows Lodge: The Willows combines Japanese influences, Native American art, and extravagant luxury into an appealing package. Augustus Walker the basset hound—your dog can call him Gus—sits in his basket by the front desk to greet new pals at check-in. Rooms are rated nice ($260), nicer ($290), and nicest ($340); a $200 refundable deposit is required for your pets. It's about 15 minutes north of Kirkland in the village of Woodinville. 14580 N.E. 145th St.; 425/424-3900 or 877/424-3930; www.willowslodge.com.

Redmond

There are only two words you need to know about Redmond: Microsoft and Marymoor, the software giant and the dog park by which all others are judged, respectively. Across the highway is the Redmond Town Center, where all good dogs go first to the information center for a free biscuit, and then to **Eastside Dog** for a new toy or any number of wonderful designer doggy duds, gifts, treats, and natural pet food lines (7533 166th Ave. N.E.; 425/497-9487). Redmond Town Center, across the highway from Marymoor Park, is an outdoor mall with abundant outdoor seating and a number of upscale food court options.

PARKS, BEACHES, AND RECREATION AREAS

23 Marymoor Park

🐾🐾🐾🐾🐕 (See Greater Seattle map on page 122)

Marymoor is massive and crowded, a live wire, the Big Apple for the doggie jet set. At last count, more than 650,000 carloads of dogs visit this 40-acre off-leash area each year, and that doesn't include the 600 acres of the county park reserved for other uses.

The park's acreage is naturally divided into many separate play spaces by the Sammamish River, as well as a long gravel promenade running the length of the southern edge of the dog park, bridges over marshes and wetlands, clumps of trees and dense blackberry bushes, and a multitude of bark-dust trails. It's a mad, mad, mad, mad dog world, but even on the zaniest days, your dog should be able to find a territory to mark as his own for the day. There are at least four separate dog beaches, with steps leading down to them to prevent bank erosion, lined along the gravel trail.

There's no end to the things a dog can do at this off-leash area, from shaking a leg to sowing some wild oats. During salmon spawning season, mid-August through November, water activities are curtailed only slightly by fences that allow dogs into the river but restrict access to the main channel.

Every big city has its drawbacks, and here the downsides are water that gets a bit stinky and cases of kennel cough that make the rounds once in a while. Otherwise, for the phenomenal usage it gets, Marymoor is kept in impeccable condition by people and dogs who take great pride in it, most of them volunteer members of Serve Our Dog Areas (www.soda.org). Marymoor is not fully fenced or gated. Dogs are expected to heed voice control and you are expected to exercise it. If you get to visit only one dog park in the city (heaven forbid!), make Marymoor the one.

Take State Route 520 east, turn right on West Lake Sammamish Parkway, and left onto N.E. Marymoor Way. To find the OLA, stay on Marymoor for .3 mile, turn right at the stop sign, and proceed to Parking Lot D. When you pass the community garden, you'll know you're almost there. Parking is $1 in self-pay automated stations. 6046 W. Lake Sammamish Parkway. Open 8 A.M.–dusk.

PLACES TO STAY

In this area, chain hotels offer the best choices for dogs and their owners; please look under Chain Hotels in the Resources section.

Bellevue

Bellevue has the most skyscrapers outside of Seattle and a slightly more relaxed policy of allowing dogs on park beaches September 15–May 31; full dog codes and other park rules can be found at www.cityofbellevue.org/departments/parks.

PARKS, BEACHES, AND RECREATION AREAS

24 Downtown Park

🐾🐾🐾 (See Greater Seattle map on page 122)

A stroll through this gorgeous city park is a study in urban wildlife. You'll encounter Baby Gap–clad tots in strollers; power-walking, earpiece-talking execs on lunch break; MP3 player–equipped runners; and talented individuals who can juggle a latté, a leashed pet, a PDA, and their shopping bags from Bellevue Square next door. Even without the live visual stimuli, the park has unique architecture, sculpture, ponds, waterfalls, kelly-green lawns, and a ring of mature trees.

The walking path is wide with a sand-and-crushed rock surface, dotted with benches every few feet and periodic bag dispensers. Dogs who are stuck downtown shopping with their people are happy to have the distraction.

From I-5, take Exit 13, go west on N.E. 8th Street, turn left on 100th Avenue N.E.; and left on 1st Street. Parking is in a lot in the center of the park on N.E. 1st Street. Open dawn–dusk.

25 Robinswood Community Park

🐾🐾🐕 (See Greater Seattle map on page 122)

This city park full of after-school activities has two designated off-leash areas, former horse corrals with picket fences fortified with chain-link. If a horse shows up, it has first priority, but in reality, these practice rings have gone completely to the dogs.

Together, the dog corrals add up to about an acre. Which one you saddle up to depends on your priority for the day. The southwest OLA has better security, not as many holes under the fence, and a double gate with a big leash-up area. Parking is close by, just a few yards north. What little grass there is won't save you from mud in the rainy season. The big boys like to congregate here.

Smaller dogs tend to socialize at the southeast OLA, which is funny, considering they're the ones who can squeeze under the fence, which doesn't quite reach the ground. Keep an extra eye out if you've got a Houdini dog. However, this area is more removed from the hustle of other park activities and the bustle of the main street. Parking is farther away, a walk of a hundred yards or so on leash, south past the tennis courts, before you reach the single, swinging gate. This lot has much better ground cover, at least during the season Cooper and Isis visited. Each area has a bag dispenser and garbage can right outside the gate. Bring your own water source, or fill 'er up from a park drinking fountain before you step into the ring. No spurs, please.

From U.S. Highway 90, take exit 11, and carefully follow the signs to go north on 148th Ave S.E. Turn right on S.E. 24th Street, .8 mile from the beginning of your highway exit, to park for the Southwest OLA. Continue two more blocks on 148th to turn right on S.E. 22nd Street, and right again on 151st Place to park for the Southeast OLA. 2430 148th Ave. S.E.

PLACES TO EAT

Byblos Deli: Byblos is a Mediterranean food market and deli with falafel, gyros, and garlic chicken on Coop's Top-10 list. It shares outdoor seating with Casa D's Taqueria, in the other half of the building. Both are a block down from Downtown Park. 102 Bellevue Way; 425/455-4355; www.byblosdeli.com.

Fatburger: This gourmet, cook-to-order burger joint serves up only Grade A Prime, artery-hardening grub. Chow down on one-third-pound burgers with all the fixings, hot dogs, fries, onion rings, chili, and hand-scooped, real ice cream shakes. A half dozen aluminum tables are set out on the sidewalk when the weather suits. If not, you can always get the goods to go. You'll enjoy the classic 1950s music drifting from inside and even the best-behaved heeler will be straining at the leash for another whiff from the grill. 120 Bellevue Way N.E.; 425/213-1428; www.fatburger.com.

PLACES TO STAY

Bellevue Club Hotel: Isis knew she was right at home before we even entered the place, looking at all the Lexus, Infiniti, and BMW autos in the parking lot. A member of Small Luxury Hotels of the world, this class-act combines high style and high tech. Isis couldn't get over the fact that the lights come on automatically when you open the door to your room. The textures and colors of the rooms, and private courtyard gardens, will win over the toughest critics. Rates range $230–315 weekdays. Because it's primarily a business hotel, weekend rates are actually cheaper, at $130–235. One or two pets under 30 pounds are welcome for a flat fee of $30 per stay. 11200 S.E. 6th St.; 425/454-4424; www.bellevueclub.com.

Mercer Island

Upscale Mercer Island is a bastion for lawyers and doctors. It has the third-largest Sephardic Jewish community in the United States. The only island commerce is straight down Island Crest Way. It's fun to take twisty, curvy Mercer Way around the island and ogle all the fancy homes tucked in the trees.

PARKS, BEACHES, AND RECREATION AREAS

26 Luther Burbank Park

🐾🐾🐕 (See Greater Seattle map on page 122)

The off-leash area of Luther Burbank is a small, soggy patch of ground, but it can be forgiven much because it has its own waterfront property. Dogs are welcome to wade right in, as long as they wait at least a half hour after eating (kidding!). The area is roughly designated by a couple of signs and a split-rail fence but is otherwise unsecured and has no other facilities or services. Railroad tie steps lead down to the beach. There's a bit of grass and some tree cover, and everything is squishy this close to the water. This park should be rated for two rubber boots in addition to two paws.

A stroll on leash around the groomed trails of the park is enjoyable, with great views of Seattle, Bellevue, and Microsoft millionaires' homes across the water in Medina. Undeveloped areas of the 77-acre park foster wildlife including beavers, muskrats, raccoons, rabbits, and loud tree frogs.

Take the 77th Avenue S.E. exit (#7A) from I-5. Turn left onto 77th, right at the stop sign onto N. Mercer Way, go through the light at 80th Avenue, immediately turn left on 81st Avenue S.E., and then right on S.E. 24th Street to the end. The dog park is at the north end; please walk your pets on leash until you reach the area. 2040 84th Ave. S.E.; 206/236-3545.

27 Pioneer Park

🐾🐾🐾 (See Greater Seattle map on page 122)

Pioneer Park captures the feel of backcountry hiking in the midst of a dense population. The city divides the 113-acre park into three distinct areas called quadrants, containing 6.6 miles of trails.

Cooper hiked the most popular Northwest Quadrant, which follows Island Crest Way down the center of the island for a while, then wanders off into the forest. The best parking for this park section is on 84th Avenue S.E., on the north end of the park off Island Crest Way.

The woods are denser in the Northeast Quadrant, with trails that skirt past a ravine, wetlands, and a stream, with a neat bridge suspended 15 feet over the water. Parking is on S.E. 68th Street in the middle of the block near a large maple tree.

The Southeast Quadrant is maintained specifically for equestrian use, but you and your non-skittish dog are welcome to join the horseback riders in this section. Many of the Douglas firs in this area have root rot, and the fallen, decayed trees provide some extra padding underfoot, lending this forest a hushed quality.

Park on the east side of Island Crest Way, south of S.E. 68th Street. Open 6 A.M.–10 P.M. Island Crest Way and S.E. 68th St.; 206/236-3503.

PLACES TO STAY

In this area, chain hotels offer the best choices for dogs and their owners; please look under Chain Hotels in the Resources section.

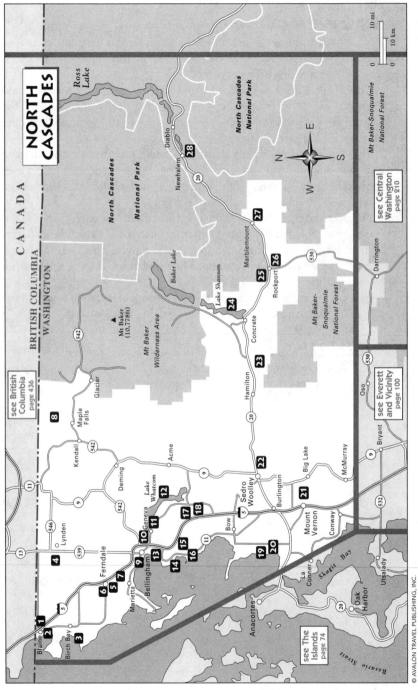

NORTH CASCADES

CANADA

BRITISH COLUMBIA
WASHINGTON

see British Columbia page 436

see Central Washington page 210

see Everett and Vicinity page 100

see The Islands page 74

Ross Lake

North Cascades National Park

Mt Baker-Snoqualmie National Forest

Mt Baker (10,778ft)

Mt Baker Wilderness Area

Baker Lake

Lake Shannon

Diablo
Newhalem

Marblemount

Rockport

Concrete

Hamilton

Sedro Woolley

Burlington

Mount Vernon

Conway

Darrington

Oso

Bryant

McMurray

Big Lake

Acme

Deming

Lake Whatcom

Geneva

Bellingham

Ferndale

Marietta

Lynden

Birch Bay

Brainerd

Anacortes

Oak Harbor

Utsalady

La Conner

Bow

Kendall

Maple Falls

Glacier

Skagit Bay

Rosario Strait

© AVALON TRAVEL PUBLISHING, INC.

CHAPTER 6

North Cascades

The inroads are few and far between in the 10-million-acre core of the North Cascades protected ecosystem. Most dogs are not going to lose any sleep at night over the fact that they're not allowed in those acres of the North Cascades National Park Complex. At least 93 percent of the park is pure wilderness, with no accessible roads. Regarding the two exceptions, the Ross Lake and Lake Chelan Recreation Areas, the former can only be reached by a tiny inroad from British Columbia, and the latter only by boat, upriver from Chelan to Stehekin. There are many other wonderful opportunities in this extensive mountain range to keep your pooch busy during the day.

You can start a day on one of Bellingham's many off-leash trails and finish with a potty stop on the Canadian side of Peach Arch Park. Once in the mountains, your two corridors for recreation are U.S. Highway 2 and State Route 20. The northernmost of the two, State Route 20 takes you past the most glaciers outside of Alaska. It is one of Washington's most scenic byways, to be enjoyed fully in the summer. Parts of the road close for the winter due to the high danger of avalanches, rock slides, flooding, and washouts. Wintertime

PICK OF THE LITTER—NORTH CASCADES

BEST PARK
Rasar State Park, Concrete (page 175)

BEST DOG PARKS
Post Point Lagoon and Dog Park, Bellingham (page 168)
Lake Padden Dog Park, Bellingham (page 169)

BEST OFF-LEASH TRAIL
North Lake Whatcom Park–Hertz Trail, Bellingham
(page 167)

BEST EVENT
Dog Days of Summer Fun Run and Festival, Bellingham
(page 165)

BEST PLACE TO EAT
Colophon Café, Bellingham-Fairhaven (page 170)

BEST PLACES TO STAY
Smuggler's Inn, Blaine (page 159)
Hotel Bellwether, Bellingham (page 171)
Fairhaven Village Inn, Bellingham (page 171)

travel on the roads that remain open may necessitate traction tires, and over
the passes, snow chains are sometimes required. Check www.wsdot.wa.gov/
traffic for travel conditions.

NATIONAL FORESTS AND RECREATION AREAS

Wenatchee National Forest

This forest covers 2.2 million acres, an overwhelming figure to contemplate.
Fortunately, the Leavenworth and Lake Wenatchee Ranger Stations break it
down for you with fun pamphlets including Take a Hike!, Hikes on Highway
2, and Family Day Hikes. In the districts in this chapter, dogs must be under
control at all times, which includes voice control, although rangers strongly
advise leashes, especially during hunting seasons. Dogs are prohibited in the
Enchantments Area and Ingalls Lake.

Leavenworth: 600 Sherbourne; 509/548-6977; Lake Wenatchee: 22976 S.R.
207; 509/763-3103; www.fs.fed.us/r6/wenatchee.

Mt. Baker–Snoqualmie National Forest

At least 62 percent of the population of Washington is within 70 miles of the recreation opportunities in this massive forest, which extends 140 miles from the Canadian Border to Mt. Rainier on the western slope of the Cascade Mountains, through five counties. For recreation on the north side of the area, along State Route 542, the Mt. Baker Highway, check into the Ranger Station at Glacier, 360/599-2714. Dogs are not allowed at Artist's Point, nor on the Table Mountain and Picture Lake Trails. For hiking and general recreating on the southern slope, along the North Cascades Scenic Byway, your best bet is the single-page Recreation Guide to State Route 20 Corridor Points of Interest, which has a good map, and a list of trails and campgrounds. It's available at the Ranger District Office in Sedro Woolley, 810 S.R. 20; 360/856-5700; www .fs.fed.us/r6/mbs. Special site for the Mt. Baker National Recreation Area: www.fs.fed.us/r6/mbs/recreation/special/mtbaker_nra.shtml.

Blaine and Birch Bay

Blaine is the town on the American side of the most frequently used border crossing between Washington and British Columbia, Canada. Southerly neighbor Birch Bay is the epitome of a summer seaside retreat, with a great water slide park for the kids—sorry, no dogs.

PARKS, BEACHES, AND RECREATION AREAS

1 Peace Arch Park

🐾🐾 🐾 (See North Cascades map on page 154)

Half of this park is on U.S. soil as a state park; the other half is a Canadian provincial park. The arch, which straddles the two counties, was dedicated in 1921 to commemorate the lasting peace and friendship of the two nations. True to form, after September 11, Canadians gathered at the park to offer moral support and free coffee and food to traumatized Americans waiting in long lines to cross the border.

The grass is so perfect at this park, your dog may feel guilty using it as a restroom, but she may recover from her pee shyness once she realizes she can anoint two countries in one trip. The gardens are equally incredible, including Canadian and American flags done in flowers and colorful shrubs. Every year, the park hosts an International Sculpture Exhibition May–September, adding to the stunning things to see at this historically significant park. Your dog can dream of chasing cars across the international boundaries and contemplate whether or not the grass really is greener on the other side.

From I-5 take Exit 276 (don't miss the exit, or you'll automatically be in line for Canada). At the bottom of the exit ramp, go straight on 2nd Street into the park. Parking is $5. Open 6:30 A.M.–dusk, Apr.–Sept.; 8 A.M.–dusk Oct.–March. 206/332-8221; www.peacearchpark.org.

❷ Semiahmoo Spit

🐾🐾 (See North Cascades map on page 154)

This natural landform was a site for canneries, warehouses, and a boat repair yard for the legendary Alaska Packers Association, which dominated the Puget Sound salmon industry from 1890 through the 1960s. The area has been completely transformed and reborn as a posh golf resort, with prime real estate, a boutique hotel, and a spa.

The spit trail is an easy-access paved path for users of all interests and abilities. It runs .8 mile on the skinny part of the 1.5-mile sand spit, dividing Semiahmoo Bay and Canada from Drayton Harbor. Leashes are important; the paved trail closely parallels the roadway. Walking the beach along both sides, for a loop of 1.6 miles, is prettier and more fun your dog, though she needs to stay on leash. Beachcombing, digging for clams, bird-watching, and picnicking are hot tickets on the spit.

From I-5, take Exit 270, west on Birch Bay-Lynden Road, turn right on Harborview Road, and left on Lincoln Road, which becomes Semiahmoo Parkway. Limited parking is available in lot next to the museum on the south end. 9261 Semiahmoo Pkwy.; 360/733-2900.

❸ Birch Bay State Park

🐾🐾🐾 (See North Cascades map on page 154)

Cars on Birch Bay Drive have to share the road with the many dog-walkers and bicyclists alongside two miles of beach, dogs, and people who come for views of the water and Canadian Gulf Islands on one side and the Cascades on the other. The park is in between 8,000 feet of saltwater shoreline and 14,000 feet of freshwater estuary of the Terrell Creek Marsh. Choose your pleasure—beachfront property for dog paddling and stick retrieving, a patch of lawn to call your own, or, when the headwinds are too cold, picnic tables up on the hill in the tree cover.

From I-5, take Exit 266, head west on State Route 548 for 6.8 miles, turn right on Jackson Road; after .7 mile, take a left on Helweg a final .4 mile. Parking is $5 per day.

PLACES TO EAT

Blackberry House: This café and coffeehouse is a warm and inviting place that focuses on light foods, bagels, wraps, and salads, until you get to the hearty daily soups and giant pumpkin cookies. Unobtrusive pets on leash may join you on the deck. 321 H St.; 360/332-9556.

The C Shop Summertime: This candy store and café is straight out of a child's fantasy. The shop is open weekends mid-May to mid-June and daily mid-June to Labor Day and closed the rest of the season. The litany of clapboard signs on the storefront say it all: bagels, muffins, pizza after 5 P.M., brownies, cookies, floats, sundaes, pop, espresso, baked goods, salads, soups, cinnamon rolls, breads, baked goods, candy, fudge, caramel, snow cones, cotton candy, ice cream, cheese corn, caramel corn, and chocolate. 4825 Alderson Rd.; 360/371-2070.

Truffles by the Sea: Truffles, as in the mushroom, not the chocolate, serves tapas, cocktails, and seafood for dinner only, on a sidewalk patio, prepared by a culinary wizard transplanted from Chile. 442 Peace Portal Way; 360/332-2528; www.trufflesbythesea.com.

PLACES TO STAY

Birch Bay Campground: All campsites, 147 for tents and 20 with full utilities, are in the woods above the beach. Rates are $15–22; reserve by calling 888/CAMPOUT (888/226-7688) or online at www.camis.com/wa.

Resort Semiahmoo: The emphasis is on the ahhh at this seaside golf resort, lodge, and spa, from ocean sunsets viewed on your patio or balcony to the warmth of your wood-burning, river-rock fireplace. If money is no object, the elegance and luxury of the hotel are unsurpassed. Small and medium-sized dogs are allowed at the manager's discretion for an additional $50 per pet, per stay. Rates range $99–409. 9565 Semiahmoo Pkwy.; 800/770-7992; www.semiahmoo.com.

Smuggler's Inn: Motley, the golden retriever who runs this bed and breakfast, is internationally famous for voluntarily deciding to inform the border patrol of kids trying to sneak pot across the border in backpacks. Five feet of the property's lawn is over the Canadian border, and Motley won't leave the yard unless he's following suspicious kids around who won't play with him. The Mounties notice Motley's away from home and something odd must be up. Motley will also take the leash of small dogs in his mouth and walk them along the cul de sac by the house and leave his toys in a line outside the door to your room if he takes a shine to your dog. The inn is a casual affair, where kids and pets feel comfortable and welcome, yet it also has extensive collections of art and antiques. Rates are $100 for rooms, $175–350 for suites. No pet fee. 9910 Canada View Dr.; 360/332-1749; www.smugglersinnblaine.com.

Lynden

At least 50 percent of the population of this small community is of Dutch heritage, and historic downtown Lynden celebrates all things from Holland. Take your pup for a stroll past windmills, gardens, and bakeries to window-shop and sightsee along Front Street downtown and then take a side trip to the excellent community park.

PARKS, BEACHES, AND RECREATION AREAS

4 Berthusen Park

 (See North Cascades map on page 154)

The Berthusens were an industrious family of homesteaders and farmers who emigrated from Norway, and patriarch Hans was an admired founder of the Lynden community. Hans kept 20 acres of virgin timber on his farm; when his children passed away, this old-growth forest and the 236 acres of farmland around it were willed as a memorial park for the benefit of future generations.

You can walk through the farm buildings and through the tractor club display, although your dog will likely prefer the trails in the old-growth and second-growth stands of trees. From the picnic area, cross the ball field to the fire road to reach 2–3 miles of looped trails in addition to the developed areas of the park. Perhaps the only bummer is that Bertrand Creek, which wiggles through the park, is too stagnant for a swim. In the old growth, a short interpretive trail is led with brochures created by the Girl Scout Troop. The park manager is fond of signs, including several that state dogs must be on leash.

From I-5, take Exit 270, turn east on Lynden Road, travel eight miles, turn left on Guide Meridian for two miles, then left on Badger Road for one mile, and left on Berthusen Road for .2 mile. Closes at dusk. 8837 Berthusen Rd.; 360/354-2424; for camping reservations, call 360/354-6717.

PLACES TO EAT

Dutch Mothers: If you and your friend with the snout can score a tiny sidewalk table, you'll enjoy heaping plates of home cooking, served by waiters in traditional Dutch attire. Cooper considered changing his nationality after sampling *krenten brood met erwen soep,* a bun stuffed with ham and Gouda cheese served with pea soup. 405 Front St.; 360/354-2174.

The Famous Lynden Dutch Bakery: If it's in the name, it must be so, and this must be the place for famous, authentic pastries, soups, sandwiches, salads, and more pastries. The folks behind the counter wear traditional garb and the shop's sidewalk tables are a nice spot to take off your clogs and rest awhile. 421 Front St.; 360/354-3911.

PLACES TO STAY

Windmill Inn: The owners of this tiny motel are not Dutch, which hasn't stopped them from running away with the theme in the exterior décor. The rooms' interiors, where small pets are allowed, are more standard. Rates range $55–65. The pet fee is $5. 8022 Guide Meridian Rd.; 360/354-3424.

Ferndale

This town of 10,000 or so keep busy at two oil refineries and the Alcoa Intalco Aluminum plant. Don't let all this heavy industry scare you away from some of the biggest off-leash areas in the region.

PARKS, BEACHES, AND RECREATION AREAS

5 Hovander Homestead and Tennant Lake

🐾🐾🐾🐕 (See North Cascades map on page 154)

On the National Register of Historic Places, this county park has carefully preserved an early 20th century farmhouse, big red barn, and two-mile riverbank dike trail. Alert to dogs with high prey drives: There are horses, cows, pigs, sheep, and farm fowl in pens around the barn. A great amount of thought and planning went into creating a park that users of all abilities can enjoy. The River Dike Trail, an old dirt road, is 2.2 miles one-way along the Nooksack River, but you can't really see the river through the trees and bushes. The Tennant Lake Loop is a 1.4-mile elevated boardwalk loop through a native marsh; it starts at the Tennant Lake Tower behind the Fragrance Garden. There are great views of Mt. Baker from the park, especially from the top of the tower, and if you are not able to climb, there's a live video camera feed at the bottom.

The Fragrance Garden is a unique and very special feature of the park. It was created specifically for park patrons without sight. The plants are meant to be touched and smelled, set in planters at a height convenient for wheelchair users, and there are detailed Braille descriptions of each plant species.

From I-5, take Exit 262 west on Main Street, go .5 mile and turn left immediately under the railroad overpass on Hovander Road and turn right on Nielsen road and follow the signs. Open 8 A.M.–7 P.M. 5299 Nielsen Rd.; Hovander Homestead: 360/384-3444; Tennant Lake and Fragrance Garden: 360/384-3064.

6 F&W Boat Launch OLA

🐾🐾🐕 (See North Cascades map on page 154)

In Tennant Lake Park, south of the Fragrance Garden parking lot, there is a bulletin board called the Canine Corner, with detailed maps of the off-leash areas on the Hovander Homestead property, including this boat launch and off-leash area. The smaller of the two off-leash areas, this field is 28 acres with a .3-mile section of the River Dike Trail, and water access at the Nooksack River boat ramp. This OLA, and its larger partner to the south, are intended primarily for the training of hunting dogs. The fields are left in their natural state, and there's a garbage can, a mutt mitt dispenser, and a latrine.

From I-5, take Exit 262 west on Main Street for .5 mile. Turn left on Hovander Road under the railroad pass and immediately turn right at the Nooksack River Access sign. A Washington Fish and Wildlife Access vehicle-use permit is required to park. Daily permits are free with the purchase of a fishing license, or annual permits are $10 at any sporting goods store, or at Wal-Mart, Kmart, and Fred Meyer. Open dawn–dusk. 360/384-3444.

7 Tennant Lake Wildlife Area

🐾🐾🐕 (See North Cascades map on page 154)

Approximately half of the total acreage the Hovander Homestead and Tennant Lake Wildlife Area allows pets off-leash. This section of the property is 313 acres bordered by Slater Road, the Nooksack River, the railroad tracks, and the bottom fourth of Tennant Lake. That's the good news. The bad news is that the area is a wildlife preserve in its natural state, primarily used to train hunting dogs. The only developed area of the fields and wetlands is a one-mile trail on an old road leading to Hovander Homestead Park. Going anywhere else might require waders, the ability to navigate through five-foot-tall native ground cover, and a keen sense of smell for retracing your footsteps to your car. There are no facilities at this site.

From I-5, take Exit 260, and go west on Slater Road for 1.1 miles to the Public Access Area sign on the north side of the road. A Washington Fish and Wildlife Access vehicle-use permit is required to park. Daily permits are free with the purchase of a fishing license, or annual permits are $10 at any sporting goods store, Wal-Mart, Kmart, and Fred Meyer. 360/384-3444.

PLACES TO EAT

Mount's Café: Save room for Leona Mount's homemade pies. Heck, skip the main course altogether—the lasagna, fish and chips, and a few Mexican specialties—and head straight for the pies. The café's outdoor tables are on a covered stone patio, which makes it easier for your pooch to lick up whatever fruit pie slips off your fork. 1860 Main St.; 360/380-4638.

Mt. Baker

In the winter of 1998–1999, Mt. Baker set a new world record for the highest seasonal snowfall of 1,140 inches. This winter wonderland of a volcano, at 10,778 feet, is not the site of the actual ski resort, which is on an arm of adjacent 9,127-foot Mt. Shuksan. When other ski areas were shunning snowboarders, Mt. Baker welcomed them. By maintaining a funky, non-corporate style, the area continues to build an international reputation as the friendliest place for snowboarding and the burgeoning sport of snowshoeing. In the summertime, there are plentiful hiking opportunities and rafting and fishing on the Nooksack River. Pre-ski, the towns of Glacier and Maple Falls sprung up around gold mining and coal mining activities.

PARKS, BEACHES, AND RECREATION AREAS

🐾 Silver Lake

🐾🐾🐾 (See North Cascades map on page 154)

This 180-acre lake looks like a painting come to life, ringed with mountain peaks and complete with lily pads and cattails. Nearly every form of legal outdoor recreation is possible at this 411-acre county park, provided dogs are on leash and don't go in the water on the designated beach.

There's a campground, horse camps, picnic areas, swimming beaches, trails, and rentals of paddleboats, rowboats, and canoes. There are immaculate lawns and au naturel forests. There's a concession stand in the summer, a lodge, and planned family activities. One way or another, someone is going to see to it that you have a good time at this retreat. As you can imagine, it gets hectic on summer weekends.

The Black Mountain Trail, 1.7 miles one-way, is hip with the horse crowd. The one-mile Lookout Mountain Loop is reserved for hikers and bicyclists—no horse play. It can be reached near campsite #10, or from the park entrance.

From I-5, take Exit 255 and drive 28 miles east on the Mt. Baker Highway, State Route 542, to Maple Falls. Turn left on Silver Lake Road and continue 3.4 miles to the park. Parking is $4 for non-county residents. 9006 Silver Lake Rd.; 360/599-2776.

PLACES TO EAT

Everybody's Store: There's something for everyone crammed into this tiny general store that's been around for more than 100 years. Try the famous Landjaeger, a dry sausage, or select from organic and gourmet goodies to put together a picnic. Grab an order form on top of the deli case and design your own sandwich. There are a couple of picnic tables out back, or you can walk across the highway to Josh Vander Yacht Memorial Park behind the Community Hall. 5465 Potter Rd., Hwy. 9, Van Zandt; 360/592-2297; www.everybodys.com.

North Fork Brewery: It's a brew pub, and a pizza place, and a beer shrine... oh, and the owner, Vicki, is an ordained minister licensed to perform wedding ceremonies. If the weather doesn't allow the lawn-chair seating to be set up for you and your dog, you must stop anyway at this local institution for pizza and a jug of the finest daily brew to go. 6186 Mt. Baker Hwy.; 360/599-2337.

PLACES TO STAY

Mt. Baker Lodging: If you're looking for a place to stay anywhere near Mt. Baker, Dan Graham is your go-to guy. He has at least 25 different pet-friendly rental properties, including condos, cabins, and complete houses that sleep 2–8 people and up to two pets. Rates range $85–265 with a two-night minimum, three nights on holidays and during special events. There are no pet fees if you sign a rental contract and pay by credit card. The website shows the properties in all their glory and clearly states which ones allow pets. Office: 7463 Mt. Baker Hwy.; 360/599-2453 or 800/709-SNOW (800/709-7669); www.mtbakerlodging.com.

Silver Lake Campground: There are 89 well-sheltered campsites in six loops, in a quiet setting under the shadow of Mt. Baker. Open April–October. Rates are $13–21. 360/599-2776.

Bellingham-Fairhaven

The largest city in the region wears its industrial maritime heritage proudly on its sleeve. Working ports, railways, mills, and canneries sit side by side with the fanciest boutique hotels and restaurants. The city has earned the designation of Trail Town USA from the American Hiking Society and the National Park Service for making excellent trails an integral part of its hardworking community. It is rumored that people move to Bellingham just because there are so many places to walk their dogs.

Bellingham certainly wins the blue ribbon for the largest number of off-leash hiking and walking opportunities in the region, *if* you know where to look, which, thanks to Isis and Cooper's super sleuthing, you will. None of the city's off-leash trails are marked as such, but never fear! The Wonder Wieners will tell you where to go and what landmarks to watch for. Bellingham wins again for the most leash-free water frolicking—again, hard to find and

DOG-EAR YOUR CALENDAR

Dogs and the people who love them pound the pavement on the first Saturday in September to benefit the Whatcom Humane Society at Bellingham's **Dog Days of Summer Fun Run and Festival.** For those who would rather not run unless chased by a mean dog, pet-related booths and festivities pack pooches into the off-leash area of Lake Padden Park from 10 A.M.–2 P.M. The festival is free, and the entry fee for the race is $25. 360/733-2080; www.whatcom-humane.org.

worth the hunt. For questions and updates, call the Bellingham Parks and Recreation office at 360/676-6985 or look on the Web at www.gratefuldogs .org, Bellingham's group promoting off-leash opportunities.

The Fairhaven Historic District, south of Bellingham, draws people from all over the country to the southern terminal for the Alaska Marine Highway (dogs allowed!), a cruise through the Inside Water Passages of Skagway in the Land of the Midnight Sun (360/676-8445; www.alaska.gov/ferry or www.akferryadventures.com). Alas, if you've ever heard of the famed Doggy Diner, it has gone out of business, but Fairhaven remains one of the dog-friendliest districts in an already dog-friendly city.

Chuckanut Mountain Trail System: County, state, and DNR agencies jointly manage this labyrinth of interconnecting trails on 8,000 acres of public land. Larrabee State Park is the easiest access point for several hikes. Whatcom County has a decent map of the most popular hikes, but your best resource is the DNR Chuckanut Mountain System Brochure and Map, available at the Whatcom County Parks office (3373 Mt. Baker Hwy.; 360/733-2900).

Interurban Trails: This seven-mile walk is a finely crushed gravel bed on an old transit rail system pathway, connecting Fairhaven to Larrabee State Park and the Chuckanut Mountain System. It's wide enough for you and your dog to walk abreast and leave room for the cyclists whizzing by. Convenient trailhead parking is located at the intersection of Old Fairhaven Parkway and 20th Street.

PARKS, BEACHES, AND RECREATION AREAS

9 Little Squalicum Park

🐾🐾🐾 (See North Cascades map on page 154)

There are some dogs—such as the Dachsie Twins' uncle-dog Sam the chocolate Lab—for whom the call of the water pulls more strongly than a bowl of beef with gravy. For these dogs, an off-leash beach is nirvana, even if it's one that exists only at low tide and is rocky and plastered with seaweed and kelp. This beach is a largely undeveloped site, and the locals who've been coming here for years don't mind it that way. It is tough to find, unglamorous, and has a brilliant view of sunsets over Bellingham Bay and its working marina. You can walk around the point of the beach, and just before you reach the pier, there are a series of trails that wind through a gulley of woods. All of it may be enjoyed off-leash.

From I-5, take Exit 253 to Lakeway westbound, bear to your right on Holly Street, through town and along the water until it becomes Eldridge Avenue. At 2.5 miles, turn left on Seaview Avenue, and right on Roeder Avenue under the railroad trestle in front of Mt. Baker Plywood. The city has plans to create a legitimate parking lot and improved infrastructure in 2005, but dogs aren't holding their breath. Open dawn–dusk.

10 Whatcom Falls Park

🐾🐾🐾🐾 (See North Cascades map on page 154)

It's easy to figure out which trails are designated off-leash in this 209-acre city park—if you're north of Whatcom Creek, your dog is free and clear. Some pathways are level, wheelchair-accessible gravel; others are single-track hikes through the woods. Citizens are understandably proud of this treasure. From the main parking area, walk down to the falls, cross the bridge and view the water cascade, and as soon as you are on the other side, pick a direction and disconnect. The gal at the visitors center said this city park is gorgeous enough to be a state park, and that's about right.

From I-5, take Exit 253 east on Lakeway Drive for 1.5 miles and turn left on Silver Beach Road, then continue to the end. 1401 Electric Ave.

11 Bloedel-Donovan

🐾🐾🐾 (See North Cascades map on page 154)

Yes, water-frenzied canines, this city park on Lake Whatcom is another splashdown landing pad, allowing dogs off-leash on the beach at certain times of the year. Dogs are limited to the sand between the marked swimming beach and the parking lot, on the north end of the park, 6–11 A.M., Nov.–April. That leaves plenty of territory of the park's 18 acres for training water retrievers and ad hoc bathing. Bring the whole family, as there are picnic tables with standing grills, a playground, a volleyball pit in the area, and a marked people's beach. The lawn is wide enough to shake off the water and play fetch on land as well.

From the south side of Bloedel-Donovan's parking lot, you can take the gravel trail, cross the street, and continue over to Whatcom Falls Park. Once past the bridge over the creek, you can hike unleashed there.

From I-5, take Exit 253 east on Lakeway Drive and continue 1.6 miles, turn left to go down to Electric Avenue, and then you'll take it further, .9 mile to the entrance on the right. 2214 Electric Ave.

12 North Lake Whatcom Park—Hertz Trail

🐾🐾🐾🐾🐕 (See North Cascades map on page 154)

The Dachsie Twins can't say enough about this perfect hike. It begins with a pretty shore drive along Lake Whatcom to reach the county park. A vault toilet and bag dispensers are provided right up front, and then there's the sign that says, "If you don't have voice control of your dog, it will need to be on a leash." Thus, the converse is also true: Your dog may be off-leash if you have voice control at all times. After a .25-mile connecting trail from the gravel parking lot through the woods and over a boardwalk, a grand entrance arch ushers you onto the main trail, and it keeps getting better from that point onward.

The wide, level gravel path is fanatically maintained, smooth enough for easy wheelchair access. There's a separate, closer parking lot and spur trail for disabled users. The trail is right on the shores of the sparkling lake, and there are many convenient areas for happy hounds to leap into the water. At the same time, humans are ogling the gorgeous mountain and lake views. It's 3.1 miles one-way, following the old Blue Canyon mine railroad, tucked between the lake and Stewart Mountain.

Dogs are required to be on leash in Whatcom County parks, unless there is a sign allowing otherwise. At the moment, dogs are permitted off-leash on the Hertz Trail if you have excellent voice control of your pet. When we spoke with the folks at the park office, they stressed that this policy could change at any time, so if the sign isn't there when you visit, leash up.

From I-5, take Exit 254, go east on Iowa Street for .6 mile, take a soft left onto Yew Street, not the hard left onto Woburn. Continue .5 mile, take a right on Alabama, continue one mile and turn left at the T-intersection onto North Shore Drive. Follow North Shore Drive seven miles, turn left at the sign for the trailhead and continue .5 mile. 360/733-2900.

13 Sehome Hill Arboretum

🐾🐕 (See North Cascades map on page 154)

You and your dog can join Western Washington University kids crawling all over the 180-acre natural forest habitat on the hill, but the Dachshund Duo were at a loss to figure out which of the 5.9 miles of trails are off-leash and which aren't. In fact, they weren't able to determine which paths worn through the woods were technically trails at all, and which were simply footpaths worn by students taking shortcuts to class. Even after we spoke with park staff, the information didn't translate to the unmarked trails on the hill. The official word is dogs must be on leash on paved trails, along Jersey Street, and on the Arbor Walkway. Our suggestion is to drive to the top, walk on leash from the parking lot to your right toward the observation tower about a quarter mile, climb the stairs for fabulous views of the port, the city, and the marina, and call it good.

From I-5, take Exit 252 west on Samish Way, turn left at the second light on Bill McDonald Parkway (the first left puts you back on the highway southbound), continue .8 mile, take a right on 25th into the Arboretum. Open 6 A.M.–sunset.

14 Post Point Lagoon and Dog Park

🐾🐾🐾🐾🐕 (See North Cascades map on page 154)

This off-leash area is a brilliant use of land that might otherwise go to waste (pun intended), next to the sewer plant south of the city. It isn't fully fenced or gated; however, it is in a valley effectively hemmed in on all sides by steep hills covered with impassable blackberry bushes, by water, and by the tall fences of the water treatment facility and a rail yard. From the gravel trail that leads down into the area, the park just keeps going and going, opening out onto several large fields and finally down to the lagoon, where the majority of dogs play. The lower field is a soggy mess—oh, the joy.

From I-5, take Exit 250 west on State Route 11, turn right on 12th Street, left on Harris, and watch closely to turn left on 4th Street. The OLA is on the right, .1 mile after you turn onto 4th. It's not marked, so watch for the parked cars on the side of the road, the bag dispenser and trash can, and the gravel path leading down into the patch of dog heaven. Bring drinking water.

15 Arroyo Park

🐾🐾🐾🐕 (See North Cascades map on page 154)

Arroyo Park is a piece of forested land managed by the city, connecting the Interurban Trail to Chuckanut Mountain Trails in Larrabee Park lands. Dogs are allowed off-leash on the .75-mile connector trail that winds through Arroyo, and even better yet, Chuckanut Creek courses through for crystal-clear water play. Be prepared to be brushed aside by hounds running hell-bent for water down the gradual slope to the streambed, followed by sheepish owners apologizing as they run to catch up. The hike alone is great, hilly and narrow but manageable, across the creek on a footbridge. It will definitely be muddy in the rainy season. The city vanishes instantly when you step into the trees, and you're likely to meet locals who've been bringing dogs here for decades. Occasionally, horses and their riders take to the trail, and every few years salmon come up the creek to spawn. From Arroyo, you can leash up and hike for miles on the Hemlock and North Lost Lake trails. There are no facilities.

From I-5, take Exit 250 west on State Route 11, turn left on 12th Street, and left again on Chuckanut Drive. Continue for one mile and turn left on Lake Samish Way. The first parking area is .1 mile after the turn on the right, a second lot is .3 mile after the turn. There's an additional parking area .4 mile south of mile marker 19 for North Chuckanut Mountain on Chuckanut Drive.

16 Larrabee State Park

🐾🐾🐾 (See North Cascades map on page 154)

The 8,100 feet of saltwater shoreline along Larrabee are geared to a dog's sensibilities. While humans might prefer soft sand to tan on, canines are thrilled with this state park's smelly tidepools, gravel beaches, and piles of driftwood and seaweed to sort through. Humans tag along for the scenery, sunsets, and 2,683 acres of hiking trails through a forest so deep and enchanting, it had Cooper happily chasing shadows. Larrabee is a convenient access point for some choice treading ground on an additional 8,000 acres in the Chuckanut Mountain Trail System.

Fragrance Lake is the easiest to reach, with a trailhead right across the street from the main entrance to the state park. It's a 1.8-mile climb to the top, with a level lake loop to bring your heart rate down to normal before you descend. Take the quick detour to an overlook at the start of the trail for a breather and a great Puget Sound vista. Or, from the state park's main entrance, you can walk north on the Interurban Trail to Teddy Bear Cove Trail. At the bottom of this .9-mile switchback descent is a white sand beach from centuries of crushed clam shells. We can't recommend tent camping at Larrabee, because there's too much train and highway noise.

From I-5, take Exit 250 west on State Route 11, at 1.2 miles, take a left on 12th Street, and at the next block, take a soft left onto Chuckanut Drive. There's limited trailhead free parking at roadside pullouts. Parking is $5 at Larrabee's main entrance and at the Clayton Beach lot. Open 6:30 A.M.–dusk. 360/676-2093.

17 Lake Padden Dog Park

🐾🐾🐾🐾🐕 (See North Cascades map on page 154)

In addition to more than five miles of off-leash trails, the 900-acre Lake Padden Recreation Area and Public Golf Course has the city's only fully fenced and gated off-leash exercise area. On the trails, it's another one of those places where it can be confusing to figure out where your dog is allowed off-leash. That just means you'll have to visit more often, darn it, until it becomes second nature.

The off-leash area is a circular field with a cyclone fence and a clump of trees in the middle. It's big, several acres, and worth a visit for playtime, whether or not you take to the trails. There's a nearby restroom, garbage can and bags, and a water fountain if you've got a dish to fill.

The 2.5-mile trail around the lake, on leash, is a lovely walk on a level gravel path. On a narrow strip of marked beach adjacent to the ball field fence, dogs are allowed into the water. Essentially, the rest of the trails are off-leash on the south end between the golf course power lines and the trailhead on Samish Way and in the woods west of Padden Creek Dam from the Ruby Creek entrance into the lake.

From I-5, take Exit 246; turn east onto Samish Way. At 1.3 miles, there is an unmarked, gravel trailhead parking lot for immediate access to the off-leash trails. The East Entrance, the road to the golf course and to the fenced dog park, is at 2.5 miles. After you turn left into the park, follow the right fork in the road to the picnic area, .5 mile to the end, past the ball fields, to the OLA. The West Entrance is at 2.7 miles, and the last entrance, at Ruby Creek, is at 3.0 miles. Open 6 A.M.–10 P.M. 4882 Samish Way.

18 Squires Lake

🐾🐾🐾 (See North Cascades map on page 154)

The toughest part of the hike is the first .3 mile, huffing up the connector trail from the parking lot to the remote, miniature lake. At the top, you are treated to a three-mile loop around a pretty lake, removed from all else. A short piece of the trail follows the dirt road of an abandoned rail bed, and you can connect to the slightly more challenging South Ridge loop and the easy Beaver Pond circle. The water is a bit too scummy for swimming, even for dogs, and hard to reach through the marsh. The hike is great, in the kind of place you can have the peaceful forest and the wildlife to yourselves.

From I-5, take Exit 242 and turn east onto Nulle Road, continue .6 mile to the gravel parking lot on the left. A portable potty and a garbage can are the only amenities. Bring water and bags.

PLACES TO EAT

Colophon Café: The Dachshund Duo thoroughly enjoyed chowing down at a restaurant whose legendary founder and mascot is Mama Colophon, the cow. This deli, dairy, and ice cream counter is legendary for its dog-friendliness and its unique and delicious daily soups. The soups are so varied, the restaurant has a menu and monthly soup calendar. There are tables on the sidewalk at the upper café level, patio seating downstairs for the more elaborate restaurant, and grass nearby in Fairhaven Square Park. 1208 11th St.; 360/647-0092; www.colophoncafe.com.

Little Cheerful: Probably the most popular breakfast spot in town, this café succeeds with a simple formula: great food and large portions. You might consider borrowing some friends' dogs to add to your own when you eat at Cheerful's sidewalk seating. You'll need lots of help polishing off the café's legendary mountains of mixed hash browns. 133 Holly St.; 360/738-8824.

Mallard Ice Cream and Café: This parlor with a single sidewalk table serves daily soups, fresh-pulled espresso, and unusual flavors of homemade ice cream in sizes small, medium, and "inner child." Have a brownie sundae with mocha brevé à la mode, for example, or an apricot ice. It's a crowded place, and everyone is happy to be there. 207 E. Holly St.; 360/734-3884.

Swan Café: This eatery, with a nice row of sidewalk tables, is the deli arm of the Community Food Co-op, so the food is understandably healthy and typically organic. 1220 N. Forest St.; 360/734-8158.

PLACES TO STAY

Fairhaven Village Inn: At this refined vintage hotel, two rooms are reserved for people with pets for a $20 fee. The designated dog rooms have washable cotton comforters on the beds, the only difference from standard rooms. If those two rooms are booked, the hotel will open up its other rooms for a $30 fee, to cover dry cleaning for the down bedspreads. This property is worthy on its own merits. It becomes irresistible when you discover it's within walking distance of the city's best dog park and all of the Interurban and Chuckanut Mountain Trails. Rates are $109–159; save money with Park View rooms, just as nice as Bay View rooms, only without fireplaces or balconies. 1200 10th St.; 360/733-1311 or 877/733-1100; www.fairhavenvillageinn.com.

Hotel Bellwether: This marina-view hotel rivals the finest European boutique hotels, decked out in marble and granite and mahogany with imported Italian antiques, Hungarian and Austrian linens, and distinctly American decadent luxury. After a stroll with your pet through the seaside rose garden, you should sit by your roaring fire, soak in a thermo-masseur jetted bathtub, and tipple from the well-stocked mini-bar. Isis says it brings new meaning to the words lap of luxury, and she loves naps in laps. Rates range $107–499, and there is a $65 nonrefundable fee per stay for one or two pets. For the lodging experience of a lifetime, save your pennies for the 900-square-foot Lighthouse Condominium, $299–725 per night, plus optional butler service, champagne, and caviar. All rooms are nonsmoking. One Bellwether Way; 360/392-3100 or 877/411-1200; www.hotelbellwether.com.

Val-U-Inn: This central motel is an excellent value. For rates of $56–74, plus a $5 pet fee, you get tidy, modern rooms and a good list of amenities including indoor hot tub, laundry facilities, continental breakfast, and high-speed wireless Internet. 805 Lakeway Dr.; 360/671-9600 or 800/443-7777.

More Accommodations: Please look under Chain Hotels in the Resources section for additional places to stay in this area.

Mount Vernon and La Conner

The Lower Skagit Valley is home to the largest fields of tulips outside of Holland. In April, visitors flock here from all parts of the globe to drive through the colorful fields during the Skagit Valley Tulip Festival. To avoid the crowds, you might enjoy coming earlier, in March, when the fields are full of bright yellow daffodils, or even in late February, when thousands of snow geese make a migratory pit stop in the valley. A bird dog might think she's died and gone to heaven when she sees thousands of geese take flight in noisy waves. La Conner is known for its many art galleries and boutique shopping.

PARKS, BEACHES, AND RECREATION AREAS

19 Bay View State Park

🐾 🐾 (See North Cascades map on page 154)

Before it was a popular bay picnic meadow, the Skagit County Agricultural Association developed a racetrack and baseball diamond to entertain the valley's hardworking farmers. Before that, it was a Native American village, home of Pat-The-Us, a prominent chief and one of the signers of the 1855 Point Elliott Treaty.

Down the hill and under the road is a picnic meadow and the Joe Hamel Beach. You have views of Fidalgo Island from the gravelly beach, a nice picnic stop on a tour of the valley. There are facilities for both species, in the form of vault toilets and bag dispensers.

From I-5, take Exit 226 west into Mount Vernon, follow the signs to stay on State Route 536 (Memorial Highway) for five miles, turn left on State Route 20, continue 1.7 miles, turn right on Bay View-Edison Road, continue 3.6 miles. Open 8 A.M.–dusk. Parking is $5. 360/757-0227.

20 Padilla Bay Shore Trail

🐾 🐾 🐾 (See North Cascades map on page 154)

Coop 'n' Isis don't think the views of the oil refinery towers across the bay on Fidalgo Island spoil this great walk in the least. The wide, finely graded gravel trail is 2.2 miles one-way, along the edge of the Padilla Bay Estuarine Reserve and a demonstration farm. It's a good area for birding and simply a really fine walk.

THINK GLOBALLY, BARK LOCALLY

The world would be a better place if all animal shelters were as loving and beautiful as the **Northwest Organization for Animal Health,** or NOAH, Center. It is a luxurious animal adoption center, a low-cost spay/neuter clinic, a training and grooming facility, and much more. You must come see the wonderful things they are doing here if you are in the vicinity. Tours are free and take only about 15 minutes. There are many ways to give to NOAH. You can become a member, sponsor a dog or cat suite, place a tile on the friendship wall, and more.

The NOAH Center is at Exit 215 on I-5. Hours are 11 A.M.–6 P.M. Mon.–Fri. and 11 A.M.–5 P.M. Sat. and Sun.; 360/629-7055; www .thenoahcenter.org.

From I-5, take Exit 226 west, follow the signs to stay on State Route 536 for five miles, turn left and continue 1.7 miles west on State Route 20. Take a right on Bay View-Edison Trail and continue .8 mile for the south parking area, where there's room for a couple of cars. The north trailhead is on the left, 2.2 miles farther on Bay View-Edison Road. Parking for the north trailhead is in an overflow lot, .1 mile past the trailhead, right on 2nd Street. Be extra careful crossing the road to get back to the trailhead. 360/428-1558; www.padillabay.gov.

21 Little Mountain City Park

🐾🐾🐾 (See North Cascades map on page 154)

You'll see said mountain off to your right as you drive toward the park. Once in the park, on the drive to the top, there's a grab bag of parking pullouts and trails that wind through. None of the trails are marked, but the largest loop is only 1.5 miles, so pick a direction and go for it. At the top, there are two phenomenal viewpoint towers, and, oh, what views there are. You can see the whole valley, and in April, it looks like a patchwork quilt with all the colors of tulips in the fields. You can drive to the top, straight to a couple of picnic tables perched on the lawn and the towers. A dog bag dispenser is provided at the entrance.

From I-5, take Exit 226, turn west into Mount Vernon on Kincaid Street, turn left on 2nd Street, continue .7 mile, turn left on Blackburn Road and continue 1.4 miles, veer right on Little Mountain Road for .2 mile. Open 10 A.M.–dusk, weather permitting. 360/336-6215.

PLACES TO EAT

Conway Skagit Barn: The deli sandwiches and salads in the cold case are made daily, and our recommendations include the homemade fudge and salmon chowder and generous scoops of ice cream, slurped on a wooden deck with a half dozen plastic patio tables. Discover the answer to the age-old question, "How many licks does it take a dog to get to the center of a waffle cone?" 18729 Fir Island Rd.; 360/445-3006.

The Lunch Box: Check out the large collection of lunch boxes while you order your soup, salad, and sandwich combo to eat in the brick courtyard with tons of outdoor seating. Can't decide? Try the chicken cranberry salad with homemade focaccia bread. 311 Pine St. in Pine Square; 360/336-1603.

PLACES TO STAY

Bay View Campground: The higher the number, the more secluded the site, with 46 tent spaces and 32 utility spaces. Rates are $15–22; 10905 Bay View-Edison Rd.; 888/CAMPOUT (888/226-7688); www.camis.com/wa.

Country Inn: The eight pet-friendly rooms of this cheerful inn are cozy, gracious, and warm, each with a gas fireplace. There is a one-time cleaning fee of $25 for pets. Rates range $82–119; S. 2nd St.; 360/466-3101; www.laconnerlodging.com.

South Fork Marina Bed and Breakfast: This cool rental is more accurately described as a boat-and-breakfast. From April through September, for $90 per night, plus a $10 pet fee, you and your salty dog can be lulled to sleep on the Tea House, a tidy houseboat moored on the South Fork of the Skagit River, beside the Skagit Wildlife Area. Your pooch can play with the year-round tenant dogs who live on the docks. Winter rentals are typically monthly, for $700, if water levels are safe. 21357 Mann Rd.; 360/445-4803; www.virtualcities/wa/southfork.htm.

More Accommodations: Please look under Chain Hotels in the Resources section for additional places to stay in this area.

Sedro Woolley

Historically an important trading post and lumbering town, Sedro Woolley is now the last large outpost before heading into the woods.

PARKS, BEACHES, AND RECREATION AREAS

22 Cascade Trail

🐾🐾 (See North Cascades map on page 154)

This 22-mile hiking and bicycling trail starts next to the highway, but doesn't stay next to it, which is nice. From Sedro Woolley on the west, it skirts behind farms and along the Skagit River, and winds gradually up a hill before ending east in Concrete. This banked railway is a fine-gravel multi-use path for pedestrian, equestrian, and cyclestrian users. It's kept in beautiful condition by Skagit County Parks and Recreation.

Park at the gravel lot at the intersection of Fruitdale Road and State Route 20, .1 mile west of milepost 67 on the south side of the highway. 360/336-9414; www.skagitparksfoundation.com.

PLACES TO EAT

Double Barrel BBQ: The three picnic tables in front of this joint have red-and-white checkered tablecloths. You can also drive-through ("honk if you're hungry") and get food to-go ("have ribs, will travel"). The namesake double-barreled barbecue sits hulking and smoking under a tent outside. Burlington Blvd. and Avon Avenue; 360/757-RIBS (360/757-7427).

PLACES TO STAY

Three Rivers Inn: The three rivers are the Sauk, the Cascade, and the Skagit. The three top reasons to stay here are convenience, cleanliness, and affordability. Medium or small pets only, please. Rates range $69–79. The pet fee is $10 per pet, per stay. 210 Ball St.; 360/855-2626.

Concrete

Named for a cement plant now defunct, this small town is working hard to preserve its interesting heritage. East of Concrete, the population thins out drastically, replaced by alternating forest and scattered farmland.

PARKS, BEACHES, AND RECREATION AREAS

23 Rasar State Park

🐾🐾🐾🐾 (See North Cascades map on page 154)

Rasar, as in speed racer, is the newest all-season park in the state system. Open since 2000, it has only been on the camping reservation system since 2004. Everything's new and nice, especially the restrooms, covered shelter, and playground. Trails throughout the park include a paved, wheelchair-accessible path to the banks of the Skagit River. On the Skagit Trail Loop, after a quarter mile of woods, the path breaks out into a farming valley, surrounded by hills, and the trail becomes simply a mowed path through the field grass. It's about a half mile to the wide river and a big sandy beach with a smattering of river rocks, which instantly upgrades the park to four paws as far as Isis is concerned. It's a compact park, only 128 acres, a quick and easy mountain playground that is rapidly growing in popularity. Eagle-watching is excellent in fall and early winter.

NATURE HIKES AND URBAN WALKS

On a walking tour of the **Fairhaven Historic District** in Bellingham, there are 24 historical markers and dozens of brick and sandstone buildings circa 1890–early 1900s. The Victorian architecture and character of the area's buildings are very appealing, filled with restaurants, galleries, and gift shops where trading posts, bordellos, and saloons once ruled a rowdy frontier town. Look for the Walking Tour Map of the Fairhaven Historic District.

The mountain village of **Concrete** is a fascinating aggregate of living, breathing community and eerie ghost town. Local deposits of limestone and clay became the basis of the cement industry, thriving by 1905, and closing finally in the 1960s. The name remains, as do abandoned, poured concrete buildings dating back to the 1920s and the massive concrete silos that welcome you into town, as unusual a "Welcome to" sign as you're likely to see. For the Concrete Heritage Museum Association and guided tours with Sockeye Express, call 360/853-7009. Self-guided walking tour brochures are available at 7460 S. Dillard St.; 360/853-7042.

From State Route 20, .1 mile west of milepost 81, turn south on Lusk Road, go .5 mile, take a left on Cape Horn Road, and go an additional mile to the park entrance. Parking is $5. Open 8 A.M.–dusk.

24 Mt. Baker–Snoqualmie National Forest—Baker Lake Trail

🐾🐾🐾 (See North Cascades map on page 154)

The nine-mile Baker Lake journey is for those who prefer a hands-on approach to their nature experiences—schlepping through shallow streams, crawling up, over, and under fallen logs, hopping a few boulders, that kind of thing. This is eco-tourism at its most personal. Trail conditions vary wildly season to season, even month to month; it's never really the same trail twice. The tree cover is thick, and you usually can't see the lake until you're right up on it. There's a suspension bridge over the river at the north end that's thrilling if you don't suffer from vertigo. Also on the north end, you can hike up to a spot called Sulfite Camp, to a clearing where the sky is filled with the glaciers of Mt. Baker and Mt. Shuksan in all their glory.

If you are camping at Baker Lake, stay at one of the forest service campgrounds. The folks at Baker Lake Resort, run by Puget Sound Energy, are not dog enthusiasts. For the trail, check conditions at the ranger station before you go, layer clothing, and bring extra water and food.

To reach the south trailhead from State Route 20, turn north on Baker Lake Road at .6 mile west of milepost 83, and travel 13.7 miles to Baker Lake Dam

Road, Forest Road 1106. Turn right and continue 2.8 miles on the dirt road and over the dam to the trailhead. Parking is $5.

PLACES TO EAT

Birdsview Burgers: Owners Kevin and JoAnn claim to have the best burger on this side of the Cascades. As far as Cooper is concerned, when it comes to burgers, there is no good, better, best—there is only best, best, best. What we liked best are the dozen turquoise and purple picnic tables on a patio, in a gravel lot, on a lawn, more than enough outdoor seating for any dog. That, and the Cascade Glacier ice-cream cones. 39974 Hwy. 20; 360/826-3553.

PLACES TO STAY

Rasar State Park Campground: This new park has 18 standard sites, 20 utility sites, and eight walk-in sites in the woods about a half mile from the Skagit River. Rates are $10–22; reserve by calling 888/CAMPOUT (888/226-7688) or online at www.camis.com/wa.

Rockport

Somewhere between 300 and 400 bald eagles come to the Upper Skagit area from mid-December to mid-January to snack on salmon that have come upriver to spawn. Starting in Rockport, there are four miles of wildlife viewing pullouts on State Route 20. Maps of the staffed viewing areas are available in Rockport at the Skagit River Bald Eagle Interpretive Center, one block sough of S.R. 20 on Alfred Street; 360/853-7283; www.skagiteagle.org.

PARKS, BEACHES, AND RECREATION AREAS

25 Rockport State Park

🐾🐾🐾 (See North Cascades map on page 154)

The old growth in this 670-acre park was never logged, leaving you with the rare experience of hiking and camping under a forest canopy so thick that sunlight might not reach the ground. Isis says a blessing for the people at the Sound Timber Company who refused to log these giants, selling the land to the state instead for the princely sum of $1.

Use the small picnic area (which has dog hitching posts!) as a staging ground for a hike on the Evergreen Trail or on the ambitious Sauk Mountain Trail. Evergreen begins to the east of the restrooms in the picnic area and ends near site #28 in the campground. It's .7 mile to a rest stop called Broken Fir, 1.5 miles to a water break at Fern Creek, and 2.6 miles total to the campground, by way of Egypt through China (the campground sits next to the picnic area; the trail takes you on a long detour).

The Sauk Mountain Trail starts at about 2,000 feet and climbs to 5,400 feet. You'll huff and you'll puff over 30 some-odd switchbacks in three miles and sit yourself down on plenty of resting benches before attaining the prized summit views you've earned.

The entrance to Sauk Mountain Road, Forest Road 1030, is at milepost 96, immediately west of the state park, and .4 mile from the campground and picnic area entrance to Rockport. The eight-mile gravel road to the trailhead can be pretty rough. Parking is $5 at the state park and the trailhead.

26 Howard Miller Steelhead Park

🐾 🐾 🐾   (See North Cascades map on page 154)

This county park's 1.4-mile trail is a manageable way to explore the backcountry without getting too deep or steep into it. The path begins on the west side of the park, past campsite #36. You'll walk on a railway grade and across a footbridge to enter a big meadow with a view of snow-capped Sauk Mountain. For the first .5 mile, the trail follows the south side of the meadow to reach the water at the confluence of the Sauk and Skagit Rivers. The second half of the trail parallels the river through an old-growth forest, looping back to the footbridge. Underfoot, you can still see the railroad timbers embedded in the ground. It's a sample of much of the beauty the region offers.

Camping is an open-meadow affair on the banks of the Skagit River. What it lacks in privacy, it makes up for in river and mountain views. Tent sites are $10, sites with electricity $15, and full hookup sites cost $18. Call 360/853-8808 for reservations.

From State Route 20, turn south on Alfred Street, .1 mile west of the intersection of S.R. 20 and State Route 530.

PLACES TO EAT

Cascadian Farms: Make a beeline for the seasonal berry shortcake, and worry about the soups, deli case sandwiches, and ice cream if you have room left over. This all-organic farm store specializes in jams and jellies and carries enough other foods to put together a splendid picnic lunch. Outside is a nice restroom, a shelter, umbrella-covered picnic tables, and lots of parking. Three miles east of Rockport on U.S. Hwy. 20; 360/853-8173.

PLACES TO STAY

Clark's Skagit River Resort: Robert De Niro stayed here, and Ellen Barkin, too, while filming the movie *A Boy's Life* nearby. Your pet can join this prestigious list of guests, if, and only if, he can handle being around rabbits. We're not talking a couple of bunnies in a hutch, we're talking hundreds of them, of all different colors and sizes, tamely lounging around on the lawns all over the 125-acre property. One or two pets are allowed in all of the 35 cabins, chalets, lodge rooms, and an Airstream trailer, each slightly different, decorated with themes that aren't overdone. Cabins range $59–109, with a $10 pet fee. 58468 Clark Cabin Rd.; 360/873-2250 or 800/273-2606; www.northcascades.com.

Gracehaven: After a couple of days in one of these deluxe cabins, you may remember what it feels like to live without stress. Two of the five nearly identical cabins are pet-friendly (#4 and #5). The only difference is that they have vinyl floors instead of hardwood, and #4 has a tub in addition to a shower. The woodwork is beautiful in each log cabin, and the buildings are tucked away in a bend by the river. Please let them know you are bringing pets and keep your dogs on leash on the property. Rates are great, $65–90, and each pet is $5 per night—bring as many as you want, within reason. This is a Christian retreat, open to the public. 9303 Dandy Pl.; 360/873-4106; http://wordofgraceministries.homestead.com/gracehaven.html.

Rockport State Park Campground: There are eight tent sites, 50 utility sites, two restrooms, and four showers nestled in the really, really big trees of an ancient forest. Campsites are rented first-come, first-served at rates of $15–22. Milepost 96 on Hwy. 20; 360/902-8844.

Marblemount

This tiny burg has the last major services for 69 miles, and even they aren't very major. You can get gas and coffee, fuel for your machine and your metabolism. Named for a nearby quarry, it began as a gold rush camp at the time of the Civil War.

PARKS, BEACHES, AND RECREATION AREAS

27 Pressentin Park

😺😺😺 (See North Cascades map on page 154)

Pressentin Park should be called Pressentin Meadows, and most of the one-mile trail is a mowed path through an open field. Chances are unlikely you'll meet anyone else traipsing through the wildflowers, and you'll certainly never have to fight for room. You'll pass through the fields, a bit of forest, and get a peek at the river and connecting slough besides. If you have a member of a short species, your only risk is losing your pet if they leave the trail for the unmowed fields. Pressentin is a natural park with no amenities, unless you count the gas station's bathroom next door.

On State Route 20 in Marblemount, park at the Shell station and you'll see the signs for the park on the southwest side of the road.

PLACES TO EAT

Marblemount Drive In Good Food: Yes, the Good Food is part of the name at this order window. The offerings include pizza, mountain burgers, fish and seafood baskets, Philly cheesesteaks, and Cindy's soups. Eat at picnic tables on the grass—if you can tear your pal away from the dog run on the premises and Junior, the blue heeler who will pace-set for your pet in the exercise area. There's no point in going inside to eat, because everybody's outside. 59924 S.R. 20; 360/873-9309.

Newhalem

The mountain outpost of Newhalem is the last inhabited place you can reach on the Scenic North Cascades Byway before the road closes for the winter, usually between the end of October and sometime in May. Listed on the National Register of Historic Places, it's a working company town for the Skagit Hydroelectric Project, which extends 40 miles along the Skagit River from Newhalem to the Canadian Border. In addition to supplying the greater part of the electric power for Greater Seattle, the town has been a tourist destination since the 1930s, when people arrived by train from Rockport. It took two days to reach and tour the facility back then; you should be able to do it in a couple of hours with a self-guided tour brochure from the visitors center. Seattle City Light; 206/684-3000; www.cityofseattle.net/light, Skagit Tours link.

PARKS, BEACHES, AND RECREATION AREAS

28 Newhalem Trails

🐾🐾🐾 (See North Cascades map on page 154)

The core of town is one big park, a legacy of the power plant's first manager and his love for exotic greenery. There are a couple of short walks worthy of some tail-wagging time.

The Trail of the Cedars starts with a suspension bridge over the Skagit, which can be slippery when wet. The whole thing is a half-mile at most—it seems like some of the trees are taller than the trail is long. This easy stroll has good interpretive markers telling stories of the trees and the power plant. From the company store in the center of town, walk straight back through the parking lot until you see the big arch that declares the trail.

Ladder Creek Falls also starts with a trek over a suspended bridge, and here the similarity with Trail of the Cedars ends. This quarter-mile trip through an elaborate garden involves navigating many, many stairs, wooden bridges, rock steps, a tunnel, and steep, narrow trails, to view gardens clinging to cliffs behind the powerhouse. The falls is an exciting series of chutes and ledges, and you can get close enough to feel the spray. Showcasing the spark of electricity provided by the project, this unique garden is fully illuminated so you may walk at night. Even so, Isis warns you to watch your step.

To find Ladder Creek Falls, walk east to your left from the company store until you are in front of the powerhouse building. Cross the suspension bridge to the right of the powerhouse to begin the trail.

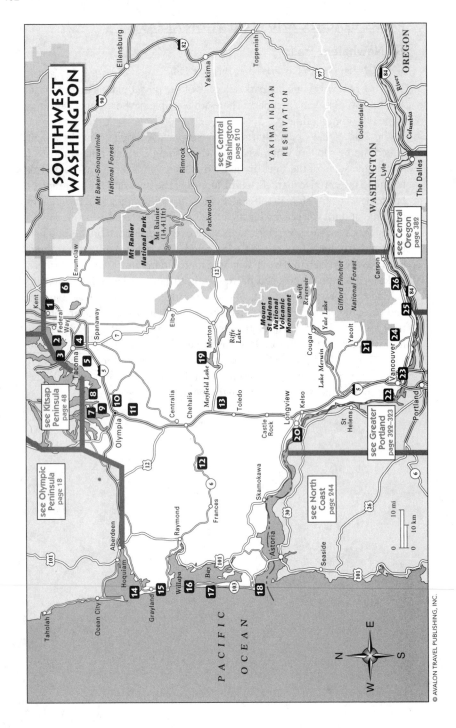

CHAPTER 7

Southwest Washington

This is volcano country. The most renowned of Washington's active peaks, Mt. Rainier, towers a staggering 14,410 feet above sea level. On a clear day, when it looms large in Seattle, people say, "The mountain is out." Mount St. Helens, the most active of the volcanoes, blew her top on May 18, 1980, losing 1,300 feet off the summit and leaving everything coated with ash for hundreds of miles. In September of 2004, as Cooper and Isis researched this book, Mount St. Helens started rumbling again. At its current rate, the lava oozing and bulging in the crater is predicted to rebuild the mountain within a decade. Mt. Rainier National Park and Mount St. Helens National Volcanic Monument are off-limits to dogs. Considering volcanoes' unpredictable nature, perhaps it's best to admire them from afar anyway! At 12,276 feet, Mt. Adams has been the least active of the trio in the last several thousand years, but it will surely come to life again.

PICK OF THE LITTER— SOUTHWEST WASHINGTON

BEST PARKS
Point Defiance Park, Tacoma (page 188)
Flaming Geyser State Park, Black Diamond (page 190)
Lake Sacajawea, Kelso-Longview (page 203)

BEST DOG PARKS
Grandview Dog Park, Kent (page 185)
Fort Steilacoom Park, Tacoma (page 188)

BEST BEACHES
Grayland Beach, Grayland (page 198)
Cape Disappointment, Long Beach Peninsula (page 200)

BEST EVENT
Canine Fest, Puyallup (page 187)

BEST PLACES TO EAT
Red Barn Café, Mossyrock (page 202)
Tiger's Garden Take-Out, Vancouver (page 206)

BEST PLACES TO STAY
Russell House Bed and Breakfast, Grayland (page 198)
Columbia Gorge Riverside Lodge, Stevenson (page 209)

BEST CAMPING
Millersylvania State Park Campground, Olympia (page 194)

As you leave these volatile mountains behind, you'll pass through old-growth and second-growth forests, butting right up against the state capitol in Olympia. You'll skirt around the bottom of Puget Sound on your way out to Washington's lower beaches, flat stretches of unbroken sand, sea, and sky. On Long Beach Peninsula and Grays Harbor, the beaches are long and wide, without the power and drama of those farther north. On the other hand, you won't have to chase your tail in frustration trying to get to them, and they are much more hospitable for playing on the sand and in the ocean.

NATIONAL FORESTS

Gifford Pinchot National Forest

The Dachshund Duo didn't spend much time exploring this national forest for you, partly because it's between two national parks where dogs aren't allowed to go, and partly because a volcano was in the process of erupting about 20 miles away as they were sniffing around! Gifford Pinchot is one of the oldest forests in the United States, starting with land set aside as early as 1897, now consisting of 1.3 million acres, including the 110,000-acre Mount St. Helens National Volcanic Monument. This is definitely one of those areas you'll want to check out ahead of time for conditions and closures, online and at the Ranger Station in Randle. 10024 U.S. Hwy. 12; 360/497-1100; www.fs.fed.us/gpnf.

Kent

For the first time in recreational history, eight cities and one county joined together to form a regional off-leash park, providing the fencing and capital improvements to open 37-acre Grandview. The park is in Kent, and the winning cities that ponied up for dogs are SeaTac, Kent, Auburn, Renton, Burien, Des Moines, Federal Way, and Tukwila, along with King County. The park is close to SeaTac International Airport, halfway between Seattle and Tacoma. All of the many chain hotels in the area are listed under SeaTac in the Resources section at the back of this book.

PARKS, BEACHES, AND RECREATION AREAS

1 Grandview Dog Park

🐾🐾🐾🐾🐕 (See Southwest Washington map on page 182)

This regional off-leash park is grand, and the view of Mt. Rainier and the Kent Valley is not half bad either. No afterthought carved out of an existing park, this is a stand-alone masterpiece custom designed for dog revels. It's two plateaus, a grassy area for ruff-and-tumble play up top and a trail down around to a lower playfield, the more dog-spectacular of the two. Level, smooth, sandy playgrounds are bordered by big logs where people sit and chat while their dogs chase each other into exhaustion. Most of the hillside has been cleared and seeded with grass, with steps leading between the main play areas. Even more greenery surrounds the sand pits. We're not grandstanding when we say that the place is immense.

The park is fully fenced, although the two entrances are not gated. The lower entrance leads down a long fenced pathway before it opens up to a secure area. A former road serves as a trail into the upper park area. The parking lot is down a long driveway from the busy street.

Thick rolls of plastic bags, the same ones in the produce section of the grocery, are mounted onto five dispenser stations, next to trash cans. A covered shelter, benches, and picnic tables are placed for maximum views. The only water fountain is up top. The park, like Marymoor in Redmond, is managed by Serve Our Dog Areas; www.soda.org.

Go to Grandview, and go often, by taking the Kent/Des Moines exit (#149) from I-5. Turn left at the bottom of the ramp, and take a left at the next light, Military Road. A couple of blocks up, past the Metro bus park-and-ride, you'll see the sign to your right at 228th Street. Open dawn–dusk.

PLACES TO EAT

Taco del Rey: The food is so authentic, the regulars who frequent this restaurant almost daily simply call it "Going to Mexico." Hispanic cooks at a taco chain to remain unnamed across the street sneak over here to eat. The chef-owner is from Acapulco, and he makes an unforgettable chicken molé (think Olé! with an m). Even dogless, you'll probably want to sit outside, at least for lunch, to escape the throngs inside. 330 S.W. 43rd, Tukwila; 425/251-0100.

PLACES TO STAY

In this area, chain hotels offer the best choices for dogs and their owners; please look under Chain Hotels in the Resources section.

Federal Way

PARKS, BEACHES, AND RECREATION AREAS

🐾 Dash Point State Park

🐾🐾 (See Southwest Washington map on page 182)

Dogs can make a quick dash for the beach at this state park if you don't have time to get to the islands or all the way out to the Pacific. From the parking lot, a tunnel leads out onto the flat, quiet shoreline. The dogs engaged in a study of sealife, as the park brochure recommends, pestering a miniscule crab until it escaped safely under a tidepool rock.

If you want Cooper's two scents' worth, the 11 miles of trails here are the real draw. Heading north from the parking lot is a path that used to loop the entire 398-acres but now is stopped in the middle by a wrecked bridge over an impassable ravine. The state hasn't budgeted to fix the bridge anytime soon. That's okay; it takes a couple of miles just to get to the dead end, and four miles round-trip is plenty for us for one day. The little section of trail from the beach to the campground is steep enough to take your breath away. Dash Point is a quick getaway in Federal Way.

Take Highway 99 to Highway 509, also called S.W. 320th Street and S.W. Dash Point Road at varying points. Follow it all the way west to the water, and turn onto 47th Ave S.W. to enter the park. $5 per day for parking. Hours are 8 A.M.–dusk.

PLACES TO STAY

In this area, chain hotels offer the best choices for dogs and their owners; please look under Chain Hotels in the Resources section.

Tacoma

Revitalized downtown Tacoma has some attractions you should not miss, such as the Museum of Glass, Tacoma Art Museum, Pantages Theatre, Washington History Museum, and **Urban Dogs,** a boutique of high-end fashion and design for our four-legged significant others in a gallery setting (1717 Dock St.; 253/573-1717; www.urban-dogs.com). Isis loves the shop's advertising slogan: PLAYhard, EATright, LOOKsharp, SLEEPtight.

The times, they are a changin' for dogs in Tacoma, decidedly for the better. The city's first neighborhood dog park opened in 2004, and hopefully by the time you read this, there will be a Free-Roaming Program, for limited off-leash hours in certain areas of several city parks. Details weren't finalized in time for this edition, but you can look online at www.metroparkstacoma.org or call 253/305-1000. We'll keep our floppy ears to the ground for more news in the future.

DOG-EAR YOUR CALENDAR

When you hear people say, "Do the Puyallup," they're talking about the State Fair at the Puyallup Fairgrounds in September. Think of the amorous French skunk in those old cartoons to correctly pronounce the town's name (PEW-ahl-up). After the stampede has moved on, the dogs take over for **Canine Fest** at the fairgrounds, the second or third Saturday in October. This dog day is a family affair, where individuals with one dog each get in for $5, or the whole family and pack can come for $15. In addition to booths and a pet parade, the fair elects a Mr. and Mrs. Canine Fest canine king and queen, and some lucky, unkempt mutt gets a Mad Mutt Makeover. There are pet comedians, communicators, and trainers. You can also adopt a dog or get yours washed, microchipped, and blessed. Proceeds benefit the local 4-H Club and Pullayup Mainstreet. 253/840-2631; www.puyallupmainstreet.com.

PARKS, BEACHES, AND RECREATION AREAS

🗷 Point Defiance Park

🐾🐾🐾🐾 (See Southwest Washington map on page 182)

We defy you to find a better urban park in any city in Washington. At 696 acres, it's just a shade under New York Central Park's 843 acres and has been around almost as long, approved as a public park by President Grover Cleveland in 1880, whereas Central Park officially opened in 1878.

A five-mile drive around the perimeter includes five viewpoints, each with a few picnic spots. Our favorites are Owen Beach, with an unobstructed view of Mt. Rainier, and the Bridge Viewpoint, looking at the Tacoma Narrows Bridge.

The diversity of this park keeps us coming back for more. A Japanese Garden with a pagoda, a rhododendron garden, and the lawn that looks out over the Talequah ferry terminal are some high points. A bunch of trails crisscross the park, each anywhere from .25 mile to four miles. There are two outdoor museums where your dog is allowed to join you: the Camp 6 Logging Museum and Fort Nisqually, a fur-trading post dating from the 1850s. Kids rave about Never Never Land, a playground and picnic area with a six-foot-tall, pre-fall Humpty Dumpty at the entrance. Finally, this park is home to the city's zoo and aquarium, which are not dog-friendly.

Take Exit 132 off I-5 to State Route 16 and turn north on 6th Avenue. Exit to State Route 163 (Pearl Street) and turn right, leading you directly into the park. Closes a half hour after sunset. 5400 N. Pearl St.

🗷 Rogers Dog Park

🐾🐾🐕 (See Southwest Washington map on page 182)

The first of Tacoma's official dog parks is no less groundbreaking for its small one-acre size. The grass is green and level, the area is fully fenced, and there are two entry points with double-gates, one of which is wheelchair-accessible. There's a bag dispenser, garbage, and a functioning water source in the shape of a water hydrant with a stylin' flame paint job.

From I-5, take Exit 132 and follow the signs to go east on S. 38th Street for .4 mile. Turn left on M Street, travel four blocks, and turn right on S. 34th Street a block to the park on your left. Park along the street.

🗷 Fort Steilacoom Park

🐾🐾🐾🐕 (See Southwest Washington map on page 182)

The unofficial off-leash space at this 340-acre regional park is the last big land of the free for Greater Tacoma dogs, and it's been used by the community as such for at least 15 years. Reactions are mixed to plans for a fenced-off legitimate dog park, mostly because the fenced area will undoubtedly be much smaller than where dogs are roaming now. Highly tentative plans, which involve money that doesn't currently exist, are to start development of the official dog park in 2005.

The only sign of dogdom at present is an empty bag dispenser in front of a wide field of natural groundcover, with many weaving paths. The area is bordered by tall trees, and dotted with a couple pines in the expanse. If you do take advantage of this space off-leash, have good control of your dog, don't go into developed areas of the park, and especially don't go jump in the lake. Dogs disturbing the waterfowl in the park's Waughop Lake is what started the whole controversy over whether or not a dog area has to be enclosed to be effective in an urban park with many other users. The area is bordered by Dresden Lane, Angle Lane, and Elwood Drive.

From I-5, take Exit 129, go west on 74th Street W. for 3.4 miles, which curves south to become Custer Road. Turn right on 88th Street S.W. for 1.2 miles, which merges into Steilacoom Boulevard. Turn left on 87th Avenue S.W. and right on Dresden Lane. The OLA will be off to your left, with gravel parking in front of white pillars and garbage cans that mark the area. Open 7:30 A.M.–dusk. 8714 87th Ave. S.W.

PLACES TO EAT

Antique Sandwich Company: This sandwich shop with a healthy bent is right on the way to Point Defiance Park. You can find salami or sardine sandwiches, hummus and pitas, spinach lasagna, and fresh juices. A daily selection of desserts features treats like huckleberry cheesecake and peanut butter fudge. Outside is the Garden of Eatin'—a large, fenced garden with tables outside where dogs are welcome to bask in the sun with you. 5102 N. Pearl; 98407; 253/752-4069.

Dock Street Sandwich Company: For Jack Sprat, who could eat no fat, sandwich innards are available tucked into low-carb wraps. For his wife, who could eat no lean, the same and more are placed between herbed focaccia bread and grilled. For Sam I Am, there are green eggs and ham, the "green" being pesto. Relax at sidewalk or courtyard seating next door to Urban Dogs and the Museum of Glass, or order a boxed lunch with all the trimmings to go. 1701 Dock St.; 253/627-5882.

Tatanka Take Out: This wacky establishment claims that buffalo is "America's Original Health Food." The menu includes bison burgers, bison burritos, bison chili, bison…well, you get the point. In keeping with the healthy theme, other selections include free-range chicken, tofu dishes, and yogurt shakes. Lest we forget, there are raw, frozen buffalo bones for dogs, with good meat still clinging to them. Two outdoor tables wear cowboy boots on their legs and counter seats are pulled off the nearest John Deere tractor. 4915 N. Pearl; 253/752-8778.

PLACES TO STAY

In this area, chain hotels offer the best choices for dogs and their owners; please look under Chain Hotels in the Resources section.

Black Diamond

This tiny hamlet is one of the few remaining coal mining communities in the state.

PARKS, BEACHES, AND RECREATION AREAS

6 Flaming Geyser State Park

🐾🐾🐾🐾 (See Southwest Washington map on page 182)

One of the things Coop 'n' Isis like so much about the Pacific Northwest is that you get out in the country so quickly from the city. People escape to this park, less than 20 miles from the highway, for many reasons. With three miles of freshwater shoreline on the Green River, many folks come to raft, kayak, float, and fish for steelhead and salmon. The Flaming Geyser Flyers come with remote-control aircraft to an RC airport complete with a windsock, spectator benches, and a covered shelter. You and your companion can try flat meadow walks or steep forested hikes and spend some time in and around the river.

The park's featured attractions are fueled by methane gas seeping from 40 feet of an un-mined coal seam. In the 1960s, the Flaming Geyser regularly burned at 6–8 feet, now it manages about the same in inches. The Bubbling Geyser is a bit anticlimactic, popping bubbles not much more than Isis can manage when she's eaten too much peanut butter or cheese. From this area, a moderate and muddy and kick-tail trail loops about three miles through the park's 480 acres of woods.

A smooth stone beach and the river are "right there" when you enter and go to the left. To the left of the RC airport is also a meadow trail, marked only with a dog bag dispenser, that parallels the river for about a half mile. The presence of bags confirms the suspicion that this trail, close to the water in many places, is a winner with the canines.

From I-5, take Exit 142 to State Route 18 toward Auburn, then take the exit for Auburn-Black Diamond Road. Take a right on 218th Avenue S.E., at 1.3 miles, take a left on Green Valley Road, travel another .5 mile, and turn right onto S.E. Flaming Geyser Road. Parking is $5.

PLACES TO EAT

Famous Black Diamond Bakery and Deli: The brick oven for baking Black Diamond's bread was built in 1902. (How's that for a tongue teaser?) It has grown into a "bone-a-fide" tourist attraction. You can order from the full-ser-

DIVERSION

Ever heard of the B.A.R.F. diet? The Bones and Raw Food movement is gaining strength as people discover that their pets may have as many food allergies and sensitivities as humans. **Tonita Fernandez** has studied canine nutrition for more than a decade, and she is devoted to switching your dogs over to the diet nature intended. Her philosophy is that the key to feeding your dog is to feed your head with knowledge. Tonita offers individual counseling by appointment if you are interested in exploring this alternative to better your loved one's health. The fee for an hour and a half session is $75, but she is such a passionate advocate, the sessions usually go on much longer.

Tonita plans to open **The Pampered Paw,** a canine spa for the too many dogs who suffer from back and hip problems; she may already have done so by the time you read this. In a purpose-built building, your furrkids can come for rehabilitation, recovery, conditioning, or plain old pampering. Afterward, there are doggie videos to watch, a fireplace to dry in front of before going home, and gourmutt treats.

Call Tonita at 360/802-4888 to arrange for your private nutrition counseling and canine spa package.

---

vice restaurant, a deli, an espresso stand, and the bakery. There are benches out front for you and your buddy. 32805 Railroad Ave.; Bakery: 360/886-2741; Restaurant: 360/886-2235; www.blackdiamondbakery.com.

Olympia

"Bowser is welcome," read the bag dispensers this city has thoughtfully placed in all city parks. It goes on to say your dog can have fun, while keeping you on an eight-foot or shorter leash and requesting that you pick up after him. Olympia is the state capital, located at the base of Puget Sound.

PARKS, BEACHES, AND RECREATION AREAS

7 Burfoot County Park

😺😺😺 (See Southwest Washington map on page 182)

This county park is one of those out-of-the-way places in a residential area where you often have the run of the place. Several easy trails connect a big picnic meadow with a 1,000-foot pebble beachfront on Budd Inlet. The Rhododendron Trail is the over-the-bridge-and-through-the-woods trail to the water. The Beach Trail is no-nonsense and gets you to the water in .25 mile or less; there's a set of railroad tie steps and a boardwalk at the

NATURE HIKES AND URBAN WALKS

At the Washington State Capitol in Olympia, many of the attractions are outside, making a self-guided tour of the **Capitol Campus** a great walk for you and your dog. The buildings, outdoor art, gardens, memorials, and monuments cover 100 landscaped acres. The grounds were designed by the famed Olmsted Brothers architecture firm from New York, and the fountains include a replica of the famous Roman-style fountain located at Tivoli Park in Copenhagen, Denmark. Maps and information are available at the visitors center, which is in a handy location in a corner of the campus. 360/586-3460; www.ga.wa.gov/visitor.

end. The .25-mile Horizon Trail is a wheelchair-accessible and braille interpretive loop in the woods. Until you get to the beach, stay on the trails to avoid poison oak. Come out a ways to get some fresh air and watch a sunset.

From I-5, take Exit 105B, bear right onto Plum Street, stay on the road when it becomes East Bay Street and then Boston Harbor Road, seven miles from the highway to the park. Open 9 A.M.–dusk. 360/786-5595.

8 Tolmie State Park

 (See Southwest Washington map on page 182)

This 105-acre park is named for Dr. William Frazer Tolmie, a surgeon, botanist, and fur trader who spent 16 years with the Hudson Bay Company at Fort Nisqually, which, by the way, you can tour with your dog at Point Defiance Park in this chapter. This multi-tasking Renaissance man also studied Native American languages during the Indian wars of 1855–1856 to improve communication and bring about peace.

Underwater enthusiasts have built a scuba park at Tolmie. Unless your dog can hold his breath for a good long time, he might prefer hiking the 1.25-mile Four Cedars or the .75-mile Twin Creeks Trails. Of course, there are always the simple pleasures of snooping around the tidal flats or selecting a driftwood fetch stick from the cobble and shell beach. Four Cedars climbs almost straight up from the lower parking lot, offering views of Anderson and McNeil Islands. Twin Creeks has fewer views, more trees, and little elevation changes.

From I-5, five miles north of Olympia, take Exit 111 onto Marvin Road N.E. and stay in the right lane to continue straight on Marvin through a series of roundabouts. Turn right on 56th Ave. N.E., left on Hill St., and turn left down the hill at the sign into the park. 8 A.M.–dusk.

🄴 Priest Point Park

🐾🐾🐾🐾 (See Southwest Washington map on page 182)

At this centerpiece wooded city park, only two miles from downtown, you can glimpse what the area looked like before French Catholic missionaries came in 1848, when Native Americans gathered for *potlatch* feasts. The 320-acre park is wild and woody and woolly with moss, a jungle thick enough to provide secluded picnic spots. Bring your machete—even if you don't need it to hack through the brush, you could use it to open oyster shells from the mud flats.

On a hill to the east are short trails, picnic shelters, and the Samarkand Rose Garden. Ah, but go west, young dog, go west, to the Ellis Cove Trail along Budd Inlet. This 2.4-mile moderately easy path mixes boardwalks, steps, gravel, and dirt to take you past towering trees of nesting osprey, gravel beaches with water access, mud flats at low tide, and watershed marshes before ending on the shore of south Puget Sound. It's for hikers only, and it couldn't be more fun.

From I-5, take Exit 105B, go straight onto Business 101, and bear to the right onto Plum Street through downtown, which becomes East Bay Drive leading to the park entrance, 2.5 miles from the highway. Start at the north trailhead to get to the gravel beaches faster. Pass up the main entrance into the park, continue north .5 mile, turn left on Flora Vista N.E., and parallel park along the side of the road. Open 7 A.M.–10 P.M. Apr.–Oct., 7 A.M.–7 P.M. Nov.–March. 2600 East Bay Dr N.E.

🔟 Capitol Lake Park

🐾🐾 (See Southwest Washington map on page 182)

If you know someone who's begging to go for a walk, take her royal dogness to the 1.5-mile trail encircling the reflecting pond for the State Capitol Building. The six-foot-wide alternating gravel and concrete path is a favorite lunchtime stroll; maybe you'll meet your state representative and have the chance to make sure she's representing the constituency. In concentric circles around the pond are the trail, a ring of viewing benches, narrow lawns, and finally young cherry trees that show off in April.

From I-5, take Exit 105B west to Plum Street, left on Legion Way, continue nine blocks, and turn left on Water Street into the parking lot. Three-hour metered parking is available for $.50 per hour. There's a dog bag dispenser a few feet from the parking lot. 5th & Water Streets.

🄻🄻 Millersylvania State Park

🐾🐾🐾 (See Southwest Washington map on page 182)

It may sound like someplace vampires inhabit, but the only thing that'll want to suck your blood is a mosquito or two, and even those are pretty rare in these tall, cool fir trees on the shores of Deep Lake. This state park is considered one of the finest accomplishments of the Civilian Conservation Corps, formed to get Depression-era men back to work. An interesting pictorial history board tells of the 200 men living on the grounds 1933–1939 who created the park and built sturdy rock and log buildings used as restrooms, kitchen shelters, picnic areas, and a concession stand. A fat white duck was greeting everyone who came to the park with loud quacks, and Cooper and Isis created a stir by responding. Several kids joined in, shouting "AFLAC" at the top of their lungs. The park brochure says it is an "842-acre hushed forest." So much for the hushed. For that, you'll have to hike the 8.6 miles of easy trails through the towering old growth. Dogs are not allowed between the buoys in the swimming areas or on the grounds of the environmental learning center.

From I-5, take Exit 95, turn right on Maytown Road S.W., travel three miles, and take a left on Tilley Road S. into the park. Parking is $5.

PLACES TO EAT

Traditions Café and World Folk Art: Tell your server there's no rush when making your light, healthy, and slightly exotic sandwich or salad. You'll want time to look through the connected shop of folk art products from more than 50 countries around the world. Everything is made available through equitable trade arrangements with low-income artisans and farmers. Traditions is also a center for concerts, public forums, and workshops promoting a worldwide community. The café's outdoor tables are across the street from Capitol Lake Park. 300 5th Ave. S.W.; 360/705-2819; www.traditionsfairtrade.com.

Wagner's European Bakery and Café: Like a good German deli should, Wagner's will make you a liverwurst and pickle sandwich or offer you a selection of knockwurst and kielbasa sausages. Save room for dessert from a pastry case filled with delicacies almost too beautiful to eat. Isis, being of German descent, reminds you that the "W" in Wagner's is pronounced like a "V" (VAHG-ners). 1013 Capitol Way S.; 360/357-7268.

The Whale's Tail: This deli adds deluxe hot meals—pizza, pasta, lasagna, and so on— to the traditional made-to-order sandwich and salad menu. Your canine will have the best seats in the house, dockside at the marina on Percival Landing. 501 N. Columbia; 360/956-1928.

PLACES TO STAY

Millersylvania State Park Campground: This is an exceptional campground, quiet and sheltered, only 12 miles from Olympia. There are 128 tent spaces and 48 utility spaces. Rates are $15–22. Reserve sites May 15–Sept. 15, at 888/CAMPOUT (888/226-7688) or online at www.camis.com/wa. A limited number of sites remain open on a first-come, first-served basis in the winter. 12245 Tilley Rd.

Puget View Guesthouse: A couple of small to medium pets are allowed in this adorable cottage, with advance approval from your hosts. It's only 200 yards from the front door of your painted hardwood hideaway to Tolmie State Park, and far fewer steps to a water-view hammock or wooden lawn chair. A continental (and then some) breakfast is served to your door, leaving no worries as to what to do with the dog while you eat. Rates range $99–149. The pet fee is $10. 7924 61st Ave. N.E.; 360/413-9474; www.bbonline.com/wa/pugetview.

Centralia and Chehalis

Lewis county is an antique-seeker's destination. In these two towns, and on the road between them, called the "miracle mile," there are close to 350 antique dealers in 20 shops and three antique malls. The major state parks in the area give the stores a run for their money in terms of classic style. Each park features towering old-growth forests and the timeless rock wall and timber-framed building built by the Civilian Conservation Corps (CCC) in the 1930s.

PARKS, BEACHES, AND RECREATION AREAS

🔢 Rainbow Falls State Park

🐾🐾🐾 (See Southwest Washington map on page 182)

This park, Lewis and Clark, and Millersylvannia are the three CCCs, parks built 1933–1942. During the week, even in the summer, Coop 'n' Isis are surprised at how empty many of these parks are, so if you can manage weekday travel, you'll have quite a bit of freedom and privacy. In addition to the stands of old-growth forest and the Corps' log buildings, Rainbow Falls has 3,400 feet of freshwater shoreline on the Chehalis River, with the namesake falls, and a garden displaying 40 varieties of fuchsia flowers.

Winding through it all are a total of 10 miles of hiking trails, including an interpretive loop and an easy two-miler through the old growth. Ask for a map from the campground host.

From I-5, take Exit 77, travel west on State Route 6 for 17 miles to the park entrance. Parking is $5. 360/291-3767.

🔢 Lewis and Clark State Park

🐾🐾🐾 (See Southwest Washington map on page 182)

This CCC-legacy park focuses on the kids, teaching them about the forest with fun activities and displays. There is a forest life cycle exhibit, information about the Cowlitz Indians, an interesting story about the tallest flagpole in the world, and regular activities scheduled at the amphitheater such as the Mount St. Helens Explosion movie and ever-popular slug races. On the way to the park, stop by the Jackson House, a homestead built in 1844, which became a famous resting stop for pioneers on the Oregon Trail.

For dogs who would rather blaze trails than read bulletin boards or watch movies, there are eight miles of trails through the park's old-growth Douglas firs and red cedar. Although 8.5 million board feet of trees were blown down in one tremendous storm in 1962, the remaining 5 million board feet are impressive enough. This storm wasn't the first time the big trees fell. Pioneers who traveled the Oregon Trail, which passed through the current site, had to build bridges over the logs because there were no saws big enough at the time to cut them. The Deer Trail is an easy walk through the hushed forest, starting from the far end of the parking area. Your dog needs to stay on leash to protect this game sanctuary.

From I-5, take Exit 68, and travel 3.6 miles east on U.S. Highway 12. Turn right on Jackson Highway, which will lead you directly into the park after another 2.8 miles. The park is closed for day use Oct.–March. 360/864-2643.

PLACES TO EAT

Centralia Perk: At this café and antique store, available outdoor seating changes regularly, and they'll sell your seat right out from under you, along with everything else you see in the place. Whatever your perch, you'll be treated to pesto panini sandwiches, daily soups, 14 flavors of ice cream, and at least 15 different desserts daily. At least your dog doesn't have to worry about them selling the sidewalk where he's resting. 101 N. Tower St.; 360/330-1470.

PLACES TO STAY

Rainbow Falls Campground: Under the tall, tall trees are 47 standard sites and three primitive walk-in sites. Rates are $10–16. Reserve by calling 888/CAMPOUT (888/226-7688) or online at www.camis.com/wa.

More Accommodations: Please look under Chain Hotels in the Resources section for additional places to stay in this area.

Westport

Grays Harbor, including the towns of Raymond, Westport, Grayland, and Tokeland, is referred to as the Cranberry Coast, home to the world's largest cranberry bogs. It is especially pretty in the summer, when the bogs are blanketed with pale pink blossoms. The fields are flooded in the fall to make the berries bob to the top for easy harvesting. You can see much of it along 50 miles of Scenic Highway from Aberdeen to Westport and Raymond. Another interesting sight are metal sculptures that line the roadways, commissioned to portray the heritage of the area, along Highway 101, State Route 6, and in Downtown Raymond.

Westport is best known for deep-sea fishing. From the marina at the tip of the peninsula, you can watch the boats head out and return from an excellent viewing tower, walk past the docks of working boats, and check out the warehouses with stacks of crab traps.

PARKS, BEACHES, AND RECREATION AREAS

14 Westport Light State Park and Westhaven

🐾🐾🐾 (See Southwest Washington map on page 182)

It takes the smallest bit of effort to get to the beach at Westport. The trick is to pick an existing footpath that looks reliably worn through the dune grasses and walk a few hundred yards due west. You can also walk right up to the 107-foot-tall Westport Lighthouse at Grays Harbor, the tallest on the Washington Coast. For expansive views, walk some more, along the popular 1.3-mile paved dune trail that connects Westport Light with Westhaven, a popular surfers' beach. When your tootsies are tired of walking, the sand is soft and the water is cold and refreshing. Very refreshing. Bring your binoculars and watch for brown pelicans and gray whales.

From the sign in Westport on State Route 105, go west almost a mile on Ocean Avenue. There's a long row of angled parking before the park entrance that does not require a parking fee. The smaller lot inside the park is $5 per day. There are restrooms and picnic tables and covered braziers sheltered by windbreak walls near the parking lot. Open 6 A.M.–10 P.M. summer; 8 A.M.–6 P.M. winter.

PLACES TO EAT

Original House of Pizza: Cooper showed great restraint by not including a pizza place in every city in this book. He put his paw down for this one, insisting it be included, even though you'll have to order to go (no outside seating). If you've had enough delivery pizza to last a lifetime, there are other options: salads, seafood platters, and hot chicken, fish, or pastrami sandwiches. 1200 N. Montesano; 360/268-0901.

Whale of a Cone: The whale's got 31 flavors of ice cream and 50 flavors of nonfat yogurt, which ceases to be nonfat when you put it in a fresh-made waffle cone, but, hey, life is about balance, right? Kids will love the candy, corn dogs, and soda pop. Ice cream practically begs to be eaten outside, while walking the docks of the marina. Two locations, twice the pleasure: 2435 Westhaven Dr., 360/268-9261; 1200 N. Montesano St. (in the same building as Original House of Pizza); 360/268-2676.

PLACES TO STAY

Breakers Motel and Condos: There's an on-site Go-Kart track at the Breakers—wahoo! Other than a bias against pit bulls and rottweilers, this motel allows two pets per room for $8 per pet, per night. Standard room rates are $49–79, fireplace and jetted tub suites are $135–175. 971 N. Montesano St.; 360/268-0848 or 800/898-4889; www.westportwa.com/breakers.

Grayland and Tokeland

If you are seeking solitude, this is the area of the coast to come to for 18 miles of undisturbed, undiscovered beaches. Much of the area seems as though time has passed it by. The Grayland Community Hall, built by the Finnish community as a dance hall and meeting place in the 1930s, is still used for community events. Another Finnish dance hall—those Finns do like their dancing—is now the Cranberry Museum. Every so often, you'll see little brown Beach signs with arrows. Pick one. You can't go wrong.

PARKS, BEACHES, AND RECREATION AREAS

15 Grayland Beach

🐾🐾🐾🐾 (See Southwest Washington map on page 182)

Captain Robert Gray is a pretty popular guy in these parts, one of the very first to explore the area by ship. As much as he could get away with it, he named everything he discovered modestly after himself. Isis is partial to simple beaches, and this one fits the bill perfectly. When you turn onto the beach road, it looks like you are driving straight into the sky, and you can, almost, drive straight onto the beach. Grayland has 7,500 feet of soft sand, light surf, and sun to greet you. The brave, stunted trees show you the direction of the wind, so you'll know which way to launch your kite.

Watch for the park signs on State Route 105 in Grayland. There's a restroom in the parking lot. Parking is $5. 360/268-9717.

PLACES TO EAT

Local Bar and Grill: This bar and takeout window is the home of the Local Burger and juicy broiled chicken. It's on the only street in town, it's the only red building in town, and it's your only option until Westport. 2183 S.R. 105; 360/267-5071.

PLACES TO STAY

Russell House Bed and Breakfast: The house is a Victorian confection, perched on the highest hill overlooking Willapa Harbor. Built in 1891 as an anniversary gift, it is listed on the National Register of Historic Places. If you appreciate the sheer opulence and romanticism of full-on Victorian style, it would be worth your while to come out of your way to South Bend, about a half hour south of Tokeland. Two small dogs or one medium-sized dog are allowed in the Russell, Rose, and Captain Rooms. Rates are $90–125; the pet fee is $10. 902 E. Water St.; 360/875-6487 or 888/484-6907; www.russellhouse.com.

Tokeland Hotel: This historic hotel was established in 1886, and it is an antique, with creaks and groans and a bit of chipped paint here and there. By the same token, the antiques are originals, and staying here is an experience in the rich character and history of the community you won't find anywhere else. One dog is allowed, preferably under 15 pounds, larger if well-behaved. The 17 rooms share four bathrooms. The two resident dogs are Whitey, a three-legged springer spaniel and Otto Von Bismarck, whose papers say is a mini-dachshund, but whose owners believe is a large standard. Rates are $45–95, with no dog fee. 100 Hotel Rd.; 360/267-7006; www.tokelandhotel.com.

Tradewinds-on-the-Bay Motel: This small motel is simple and super-friendly. The staff enthusiastically welcomes all pets, with pats and treats, for a $5 pet fee. Rates range $55–75; all rooms have water views, and the lawn out back is big and secluded. 4305 Pomeroy Ln.; 360/267-7500; www.westportwa.com/tradewinds/index.html.

Long Beach Peninsula

Long Beach marks the most northwesterly point reached by the Lewis and Clark Expedition in 1805. The beach here is 26 miles long, flat and wide. It's ideal for family fun and absolute dog heaven. You do need to be careful not to allow your pet to eat rotting fish on the beach, usually salmon, which give off toxins that can be very harmful. In addition, cars are allowed on the beach with restrictions in the summer, so watch kids and pets around the autos.

Long Beach is an unpretentious community. A popular pastime for locals is to bring a six-pack and a pickup with a winch to the beach to relax and watch people who are unfamiliar with hard-pack driving get stuck in the sand. At the least, the unofficial truck towers get to play hero of the moment; at best, they might get a tip for the tow. Pop into **Unique Petique** for pet supplies and gifts (2103 Pacific Ave. N.; 360/642-1202).

PARKS, BEACHES, AND RECREATION AREAS

16 Leadbetter Point

😸😸😸 (See Southwest Washington map on page 182)

Bird dogs, look up! This state park is on the Pacific Flyway, the main thoroughfare for migrating waterfowl in spring and fall. While everyone, including the cars, crowd the main beaches on the peninsula, you and your dog can come close to the tip, along marshy Willapa Bay and butting up against the Willapa National Wildlife Refuge.

Without going into the refuge, dogs can hike three trails: the two-mile Loop Trail along the bay side, a half-mile Green Trail along the beach, and the 1.3-mile southern route on the Blue Trail from the bay to the ocean. Once you've worked your way through the lowland forests and grass dunes, some serious beach romping is in order.

Getting away from it all and getting to Leadbetter requires some zigzag maneuvers. Take State Route 103 to Ocean Park. Turn east onto Bay Avenue and drive nearly a mile before turning left onto Peninsula Highway/Sand Ridge Road. Continue four miles, turn west onto Oysterville Road, and in 0.25 mile, turn right onto Stackpole Road. Continue to the park entrance, about three miles. Park at the first parking area. Parking is $5.

17 Pacific Pines

 (See Southwest Washington map on page 182)

Concerned citizens rescued this beach from development hell, ensuring that it would remain as permanent public beach access. Perhaps they named it after the proposed development as a reminder.

Digging dogs, this beach is for you. The wind works the sand up into piles, not quite big enough to be called dunes, but certainly big enough to hide a dachshund. It's prime, smelly territory for your dog to excavate crab shells, kelp bits, or the perfect salty driftwood stick to use as leverage when pleading with you for a game of toss. It's much harder to resist those puppy dog eyes when he's got the stick already in his mouth, isn't it? On this pure beach, there's nothing between you and the water except the pines and a few seagulls. There are five unsheltered picnic tables and a restroom.

Take State Route 103 to Ocean Park. When S.R. 103 turns right, continue straight onto Vernon Avenue, and turn left on 271st Place. Parking is $5.

18 Cape Disappointment State Park

(See Southwest Washington map on page 182)

When he failed to find inner passage to the Columbia River on a 1788 sailing exploration, Captain John Meares named this nearby headland. After life as an active military installation until 1957, this state park hasn't disappointed anyone since. If you and your dog were to put your heads together and come up with a list of what you wanted in a beachfront park, 1,882-acre "Cape D" would likely fit the bill. It's got bluff views, access to 27 miles of beach to the north, hiking trials adding up to seven miles, and the Cape Disappointment and North Head Lighthouses.

Above all the other attractions, Beard's Hollow receives the most favorable puppy press. A level walking road leads to the beach through a marsh, with old-growth trees draped in moss, spooky enough to be interesting, not so much as to be scary. From the hollow, you can hike a naturally steep, muddy, and slippery trail 1.3 miles to the first lighthouse, 4.3 miles to the tip and the end.

From U.S Highway 101 into Illwaco, turn left onto South Highway 101. At 1.8 miles, take a right on Spruce Street W., State Route 100, go another 1.8 miles to Beard's Hollow, or a total of three miles to the end of the park. Dogs are not allowed in the Lewis and Clark Interpretive Center. Parking is $5.

PLACES TO EAT

Kelly's Deli and Chowder House: Your dog will be trying his telepathic powers on you—"Burger, go for the burger," which would be fine, as would Kelly's big salad combinations and signature wraps. 411 S. Pacific Ave.; 360/642-0555.

Surfer Sands: There are three foods surfers seem to gravitate to above all else—fruit smoothies, veggie sandwiches, and pizza. As soon as she saw the Carnivores' Corner on the menu, Isis gravitated right on over to the yellow-and-blue picnic tables. Order from the window, then relax under the awning. 1113 S. Pacific Hwy.; 360/642-7973.

PLACES TO STAY

Beach It Rentals: Two pet-friendly houses, The Sundowner ($110–130) and Tinker House II ($150–175), are available for rent. A couple of big pets is all each house can manage, but there are no pet fees. 11409 Pacific Way; 360/642-4697; www.vacationparadise.com/Washington.

Cape Disappointment Campground: Cape D has 152 standard sites, 83 utility sites, eight restrooms, and 14 showers. Reservations are absolutely necessary in the summer. Rates are $15–22. 888/CAMPOUT (888/226-7688); www.camis.com/wa.

Charles Nelson Guest House: You'd never guess that this stately home was originally purchased from a 1920s-era *Sears and Roebuck* catalog. Rates range $130–150, in the off-season all nights after the first are 50 percent off. 26205 Sandridge Rd.; 360/665-3016 or 888/862-9756; www.charlesnelsonbandb.com.

Chautauqua Lodge: This oceanfront lodge is big, a staple fixture on Long Beach for as long as most people can remember, and it has always been a pet-friendly place. Rooms range $70–130, suites $110–170. Limit two pets; the fee is $8 per pet, per night. 304 14th St. N; 360/642-4401 or 800/869-8401; www.ocean-front-hotel.com.

Historic Sou'wester Lodge: Sou'westers are the winds that push treasures ashore during spring and winter storms. This collection of eclectic lodging options is a treasure for those who can appreciate its quirky nature. You stay in cabins or 1950s trailers, bringing your own bedding. There are no dog restrictions or fees. It's an unusual getaway for people who have a sense of adventure that a motel can't tame. Rates range $58–139; On Beach Access Rd. (38th Place), the first street on the left as you enter Seaview from U.S. Highway 101; 360/642-2542 or 800/269-6378.

Moby Dick Hotel, Restaurant, and Oyster Farm: There are plenty of mega-motels on the beaches, so Coop 'n' Isis decided to pick some options for you that are just a little different and that exude a Bohemian charm. At Moby Dick's, each room is a little different; all allow two pets. A three-course breakfast is included. You should try the Japanese sauna in the woods and explore the rambling grounds and forest paths with your pooch. Rates range $85–140; the pet fee is $10; 25814 Sandridge Rd., Nahcotta; 360/665-4543; www.mobydickhotel.com.

More Accommodations: Please look under Chain Hotels in the Resources section for additional places to stay in this area.

Mossyrock

This mountain village remains so remote today, its hard to imagine what it must have been like for early fur trappers and loggers, who floated goods downriver to Kelso-Longview or packed them in and out on horseback. Small by many standards, it's still the biggest pocket of civilization on the route to Mt. Rainier.

PARKS, BEACHES, AND RECREATION AREAS

19 Ike Kinswa State Park

🐾🐾 (See Southwest Washington map on page 182)

Mayfield Lake has a lot of shoreline—46,000 feet—and 454 acres spread out along that shoreline is slim, with just enough room for the 1.5-mile Mayfield Trail that follows the water's edge and a .5-mile guided interpretive trail through the woods. The designated swimming beach and playground are off-limits to dogs. Let's see, that leaves about 45,400 feet of shoreline that's A-okay.

From I-5, take Exit 68 and drive east on U.S. Highway 12 for 14 miles. Turn north on State Route 122, which loops around Mayfield Lake, travel 1.9 miles, take a right at the fork in the road, and travel another 1.9 miles. Parking is $5.

PLACES TO EAT

Red Barn Café: The Dachsie Twins have good luck with roadside restaurants that have red-and-white-checkered tablecloths on sidewalk tables. Sure enough, people have been known to drive from Yakima, 100 miles away, for this restaurant's meatloaf, pot roast, and steak, and double that distance for a piece of homemade pie. 206 E. State St.; 360/983-3021.

PLACES TO STAY

Seasons Motel: This big motel in a small town allows one pet per room if large, two if portable. The rooms are huge and very nice. Rates range $60–80. The pet fee is $10. 200 Westlake Ave.; 360/496-6835; www.whitepasstravel.com/seasons.htm.

Stormking Spa: The pet-friendly cabin available at this mountain retreat is actually about 30 minutes from Morton/Mossyrock in Ashford, but Coop 'n' Isis had to include it. The circa-1920s Bear Cabin is awesome, built of old-growth fir, hemlock, and cedar. The dogs know you'll also appreciate the resort's full line of spa services. One dog, who's older than six months, house-trained, and knows not to get on the bed or furniture, is permitted for a $15 pet fee. The cabin rate is $175, with a four-night minimum June–September. 37311 Hwy. 706, Ashford; 360/569-2964; www.stormkingspa.com.

Kelso-Longview

Situated at the confluence of three rivers, the Columbia, Cowlitz, and Toutle, this area is a prime location for an international deep-water port with an active riverfront industry. If you want to get to the Oregon Coast from Washington, without the hassles of Portland traffic, the Lewis and Clark bridge from Longview crosses over to U.S. Highway 30 in Oregon, where it's a quick hour at most to Astoria.

PARKS, BEACHES, AND RECREATION AREAS

20 Lake Sacajawea

🐾🐾🐾🐾 (See Southwest Washington map on page 182)

This city park is a stunning walkers' park. You know that every detail of this formal park was planned, yet it all looks so effortless. Around the long, thin lake is a wide, level crushed-gravel trail, surrounded by lawns good enough to eat and stately mature trees. The visual delights just keep coming: water fountains, an island Chinese garden over an arched bridge, and totem poles, all surrounded by handsome homes on quiet boulevards. Here and there are restrooms and playgrounds, benches, and picnic tables. At every long block, there is a bridge across the lake, so you can custom tailor the length of the loop you walk. The path is illuminated at night by antique-reproduction lamp-posts. It is the park city residents are most proud of, and you'll meet many of them and their canines jogging or walking the lake. Coop 'n' Isis spent such a relaxing afternoon here meeting the locals, they granted it four paws, even though swimmers of either species are not allowed to break the smooth water's surface.

From I-5, take Exit 39 onto State Route 4, and follow the road four miles as it crosses a bridge, zigs, and changes names to become Ocean Park. Turn south on Kessler or Nichols Boulevards and park along the street where signs allow.

PLACES TO STAY

Hudson Manor Inn and Suites: The innkeepers have taken what could have been a very ordinary place and turned it into something special with deck chairs, tables, and potted trees outside every room, and elegant furnishings inside. Little extras include a coffee room for guests, a business center with wireless Internet, and a free guest pass to the Three Rivers Athletic Club. As they say, only nice people get to stay, and two dogs under 40 pounds each may join you. Angus, the corgi of the manor, will greet you and request a scratch on the hind end. Rates range $55–79; plus a $10 flat fee per room for pets. 1616 Hudson St.; 360/425-1100; www.hudsonmanorinn.com.

More Accommodations: Please look under Chain Hotels in the Resources section for additional places to stay in this area.

Battle Ground

This fast-growing community got its ironic name from a battle that never took place; disagreements between Native Americans and Fort Vancouver soldiers were settled peacefully in 1855.

PARKS, BEACHES, AND RECREATION AREAS

21 Moulton Falls Park

🐾🐾🐾 (See Southwest Washington map on page 182)

This 300-acre regional park has lots of bells and whistles. At the confluence of the East Fork of the Lewis River and Big Tree Creek, there are two waterfalls, Moulton and Lucia, and two bridges, one an arched bridge more than three stories high over the Lewis and the other a rare swing bridge over Big Tree.

From Moulton, you can take the two-mile Bells Mountain Trail to Lucia, and eventually, the trail will connect nine miles south to the Cold Creek Campground. You might be interested to know that you'll pass volcanic rock formations from early lava flows and historic Indian meeting grounds. Your hiking partner will concern herself more with the Douglas firs and the riparian route, which Isis learned means "on the banks of a natural course of water."

Take the Lewisville Highway, State Route 503, north from Battle Ground. Turn right on N.E. 152nd Avenue, follow it as it curves right and then left, and take the left fork in the road onto N.E. Lucia Falls Road, directly to the park on your right. Open 7 A.M.–dusk. 27781 Lucia Falls Rd.; 360/696-8171.

Vancouver

Vancouver, Washington, is three hours south of Seattle, and Vancouver, British Columbia, is three hours north of Seattle. On the border of the Columbia River, within drooling distance from Portland, *this* Vancouver is the state's oldest and fourth-largest city. Cooper and Isis like to come here to be reunited with their buddies Kona and Murphy, who moved down from Seattle to be advance dog scouts for the Dachsie Twins. The website for Vancouver's parks, and greater Clark County parks in general, is an excellent resource (www.vanclarkparks-rec.org). The city tells a tale of two trails, one in the city and one outside, allowing you and your dog to get up close and personal with the mighty Columbia River.

PARKS, BEACHES, AND RECREATION AREAS

22 Frenchman's Bar Trail

🐾🐾🐾 (See Southwest Washington map on page 182)

This 2.5-mile riverfront trail is a 12-foot-wide asphalt path connecting Vancouver Lake to Frenchman's Bar on the Columbia River. A narrow wood-chip path, designed for equestrians, parallels the main trail. In tree clearings, you'll have close views of commercial ship traffic passing on the river.

Dogs of the land say pass on the pavement, and walk up over the berm to the mile-long sandy beach, yeah baby. Avoid the north end, too close for comfort to the volleyball courts and lawn chairs. Soggy dogs come grinning up over the hill from the south.

From I-5, take Exit 1D onto Fourth Plain Boulevard, State Route 501, and follow it as it becomes N.W. Lower River Road out of town. Instead of paying for parking at the main entrance, we recommend the smaller lot at the south end of the trail system, 5.5 miles from the highway exit on the left side of the road. Caution: We found out the hard way that those teeth stuck in the road, to prevent you from entering the wrong way, really do slice and dice tires. Go in the *first* entry point to your left. Open 7 A.M.–dusk. 9612 N.W. Lower River Road; 360/735-8838.

23 Columbia Renaissance Waterfront Trail

🐾🐾 (See Southwest Washington map on page 182)

This four-mile, 14-foot-wide promenade is the shining symbol of Vancouver's extensive efforts to restore an industrial waterfront into an attractive and functional public space. The sidewalk and boardwalk path hugs the river the entire way, allowing you to watch how amazingly active the boat traffic is on the Columbia. You'll pass other civic projects including sculpture, fountains, the Renaissance Promenade, and Ilchee Plaza, plus some upscale condos and a couple of coffee shops. Grass, trees, benches, picnic tables, and landscaping are available every few blocks. Come mid-morning to catch the Mom-and-stroller crowd, watch downtown Vancouver escape cubicle life at lunch time, and spend time with the sunbathers in the afternoon.

From I-5, take Exit 1C onto Mill Plain Boulevard, travel five blocks, turn left on Columbia Street, and follow it under the highway and railroad trestle as it curves to the left. The trail starts at the Red Lion at the Quay, the first convenient parking is about a block farther at Waterfront Park.

PLACES TO EAT

Pepper's Taqueria: This colorful and festive restaurant has five hand-hewn picnic tables outside that are extra long, which is necessary because Pepper's is the home of the four-foot burrito. Standard-sized dishes include Mexican standards, combo plates, and delicious tortilla soup. 800 Main St.; 360/737-0322.

Tiger's Garden Take-Out: There are almost as many Thai food places in the Pacific Northwest as there are coffee shops, yet this Laotian and Thai restaurant manages to stand out from the rest. The flavors are bolder, the ingredients fresher, and the stars hotter. 312 W. 8th St.; 360/693-9585.

Tommy O's Aloha Café: The Hawaiian specialties at Tommy's will make you long for famous surfing and tropical beaches, the names of which grace the breakfast omelettes and sandwiches. Slow-roasted kalua pork quesadillas, coconut crunchy shrimp, and panko-crusted calamari top the list of tastes you should try. Tommy's has four sidewalk tables. 801 Washington St.; 360/694-5107.

PLACES TO STAY

Homewood Suites: This Hilton-owned hotel allows two dogs over 80 pounds to a room, more if everybody but you weighs in at less than 80 pounds. In addition to impeccable rooms, there's a full breakfast bar for the humans and afternoon social with snacks. For the dogs, the hotel is couple of blocks from the waterfront trail. Rates range $89–139; plus a flat $25 pet charge; 701 S.E. Columbia Shores Blvd.; 360/750-1100 or 800/225-5466; www.homewoodsuites.com.

Camas and Washougal

The camas is a type of lily bulb, a staple in the diet of the Native Americans of this region. In contrast to the industrialism of the Georgia Pacific paper mill in town, Main Street in Camas is a tree-lined boulevard with a profusion of hanging flower baskets. Neighbor to Camas, Washougal is the second-largest wool-producing region in the states. At the factory store for the Genuine Pendleton Woolen Mill, you can buy rugs for your dog to sleep on and slippers for him to chew.

PARKS, BEACHES, AND RECREATION AREAS

24 Lacamas Lake Park

🐾🐾🐾 (See Southwest Washington map on page 182)

From one parking spot and trailhead, you can walk four different trail systems through old-growth forests, along creeks and lakes, past fancy lakeside homes and golf courses, and alongside one water ditch, hand-dug by Chinese laborers in 1884 for paper mill production. Along the way, your dog's smart nose can pick up the distinctions between up to 100 different species of wildflowers.

The trail systems are: Lacamas Park Trails, the Lacamas Creek Trail, the Heritage Trail, and the Mill Ditch Trail. All of the trails are unpaved, of three miles or less one-way, and have interpretive brochures available in a rack at Camas City Hall's lobby, at 606 N.E. 4th Avenue. The best comprehensive trail map is the City of Camas Parks, Trails, and Open Space brochure.

From I-5, take State Route 14 east to the Union Street/State Route 500 exit, a left exit. Go straight on Union and carefully follow the signs to weave through town to stay on State Route 500/Everett Street for 2.5 miles. The parking lot and park entrance are immediately before you cross the bridge over the lake. Parking lot is open 7 A.M.–dusk. There's a $250 fine if you don't pick up after your pet or keep her on leash. Ouch.

PLACES TO EAT

Downtown Deli and Catering: This deli serves hot sandwiches and daily specials that'll warm you up from the inside out. How long has it been since you've had a Reuben or French Dip or meatball and provolone hoagie? There are breakfast sandwiches and platters with home fries and biscuits, too. No outdoor seating is available; order to go. Open Monday–Friday; 212 N.E. 4th Ave.; 360/834-1204.

Skamania

If you see Bigfoot picking huckleberries while you're hiking the backcountry trails of Skamania, don't bug him—he's been granted official protected status by the Skamania County Board of Commissioners. He's allowed to harvest his annual allotment of three gallons of berries, like anybody else. Sasquatch sightings are rare, but according to the Bigfoot Field Researchers Organization, he's been seen in this county more than anywhere else in Washington, except at Seattle Supersonics basketball games, where he is the mascot, and goes by the name S'quatch.

From Skamania, the Bridge of the Gods is a $1.00 toll bridge to Cascade Locks in Oregon.

PARKS, BEACHES, AND RECREATION AREAS

25 Sam's Walker Trail

🐾🐾🐾 (See Southwest Washington map on page 182)

Ahhh, for a trail even a Westie can love, this 1.7-mile universal access walk has two loops through conifer forests and meadows. It's easy and level throughout, with peeks at wildflowers, wildlife, and waterfalls, specifically Horsetail Falls across the Columbia River on the Oregon side of the Gorge. It's not too heavily used, either, giving you and your dog the opportunity for some quiet, quality time together.

Turn south at the west end of Skamania Landing Road, a loop road, cross the railroad tracks and travel .3 mile to the parking lot on your right.

PLACES TO STAY

Dolce Skamania Lodge: This internationally esteemed golf course hotel often ranks on the Northwest's most romantic lists. The contemporary lodge allows pets in four rooms on the first floor with outdoor exits that can take you to three miles of trails on the property. A $50 nonrefundable pet fee per stay is nonnegotiable, but the blow to your pocketbook is softened a bit by the big bag of goodies, including treats, a toy, bowl, towel, and leash that you are welcome to keep. A letter to the pet clarifies the lodge's expectations, including not running on the course or eating golf balls. Rates range $99–189. 1131 S.W. Skamania Lodge Way; 509/427-7700 or 800/221-7117; www.skamanialodge.dolce.com.

Stevenson

The most frequently sighted form of wildlife in Stevenson are boardheads, the windsurfers and kiteboarders who come to Bob's Beach or Swell City or The Hatchery to ride the Columbia. The colorful patterns of their sails and boards are fun to watch on the water.

For those of you who find it hard to leave the office or chat room behind, the entire town of Stevenson is a free wireless Internet hot spot. Pick up an instruction sheet with the user name and password at the visitors center or most downtown stores.

PARKS, BEACHES, AND RECREATION AREAS

26 Beacon Rock

🐾🐾 (See Southwest Washington map on page 182)

This 848-foot monolith is the core of an extinct volcano, named by Lewis in his journals alternating as Beacon Rock or Beaten Rock, the latter probably after he climbed it. To make it possible for people to climb, a guy named

Henry Biddle bought the rock and built a trail, completed in 1918. Dogs are not allowed on the rock itself, since they lack the opposable thumbs to hold onto the railings and rope ladders required to ascend.

At 4,650 acres and 9,100 feet of riverfront shoreline, there's still more than enough territory for a dog to chronicle in his scent journals. Across the highway from the rock, there's a hill you can drive up or hike up, to picnic tables looking out over the rock. Overall, there are nine miles of trails in the park. Your pal probably wouldn't mind sniffing along the shore while you fish for sturgeon, salmon, and steelhead below the Bonneville Dam.

Beacon Rock and the park entrance are at milepost 36 on State Route 14. Parking is $5. Coop can't recommend the campground. There's too much train and highway noise.

PLACES TO EAT

Crab Shack: Isis wishes her doghouse was as nice as this so-called shack, which serves all kinds of seafood in soups, salads, and sides for lunch, and surf, turf, and pasta for dinner. Your dog will want to join you on the deck, but she'll have to settle for a spot on the lawn in the park next door, where you can keep an eye on her. 130 S.W. Cascade Ave.; 509/427-4400.

PLACES TO STAY

Columbia Gorge Riverside Lodge: Eight individual theme units share four modern log cabins on the banks of the river, in the middle of two popular parks. The rooms are decorated with authentic art and hand-carved furniture, and each has a gas fireplace, equipped kitchenette, and private or shared deck hot tubs. Your laid-back host Angus welcomes dogs and sailboarders and doesn't believe in unnecessary rules or high, variable room rates. His only request is no dogs on the furniture or beds. Units are $69 or $89, a phenomenal price for the quality and features. The dog fee is $10. 200 S.W. Cascade Ave.; 509/427-5650 or 866/427-5650; www.cgriversidelodge.com.

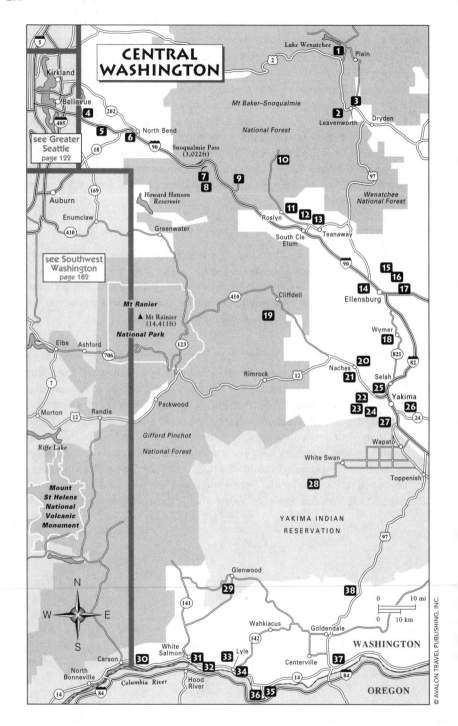

CENTRAL WASHINGTON

Lake Wenatchee

1 Plain

Kirkland

Bellevue

3

Mt Baker–Snoqualmie

2 Leavenworth

Dryden

see Greater
Seattle
page 122

North Bend

National Forest

Snoqualmie Pass
(3,022ft)

10

Wenatchee
National Forest

Auburn

Enumclaw

Howard Hanson
Reservoir

Greenwater

Roslyn

11

12

13

Teanaway

South Cle
Elum

see Southwest
Washington
page 182

Mt Ranier

▲ Mt Rainier
(14,411ft)

National Park

Cliffdell

19

15

16

14

17

Ellensburg

Elbe

Ashford

Rimrock

Packwood

Wymer

18

20

Naches

21

Selah

25

Yakima

22

23

24

26

27

Morton

Randle

Gifford Pinchot

National Forest

Wapato

Riffe Lake

White Swan

Toppenish

28

**Mount
St Helens
National
Volcanic
Monument**

YAKIMA INDIAN

RESERVATION

Glenwood

N

29

38

W   E

0   10 mi

S

0   10 km

Wahkiacus

Goldendale

WASHINGTON

Carson

White
Salmon

31

33 Lyle

Centerville

37

North
Bonneville

30

32

34

36 **35**

Columbia River

Hood
River

OREGON

© AVALON TRAVEL PUBLISHING, INC.

CHAPTER 8

Central Washington

Seattleites and their dogs love the fact that they can hit the slopes of the Central Cascades for sport activities within a half-hour's drive of the city east on Interstate 90. The Mt. Baker–Snoqualmie National Forest cuts a wide swath down the entire state, and I-90 and U.S. Highway 2 are the only major roads that give you entry into this otherwise remote world. Trees easily outnumber people a hundred to one, a thought that gets a dog's entire body wagging.

On the east side of the Cascades, the Yakima Valley rests on lava fields covering 200,000 square miles in Washington, Oregon, and Idaho. Layers of basalt in the cliffs have been measured at up to 10,000 feet thick. It's hot out here in the valley, with an average 300 sunny days per year, and summer temperatures up to 100°F. The combination of rich volcanic soil, endless sun, and extensive man-made snowmelt irrigation combine to produce a fertile agricultural plain. More than six billion apples a year come from the area's 65,000 acres of orchards. Beer drinkers will also get a kick out of knowing that 75 percent of the nation's total hops are grown here. And, though it extends beyond the scope of this book, it'd be a doggone shame not to mention that

PICK OF THE LITTER—CENTRAL WASHINGTON

BEST PARKS
Randall Park, Yakima (page 230)
Conboy Lake Wildlife Refuge, Trout Lake (page 235)

BEST HIKES
Boulder Cave, Chinook Pass (page 226)
Cowiche Canyon Trail, Yakima (page 229)

BEST PLACE TO EAT
Sassy's Kitchen, Naches (page 228)

BEST PLACES TO STAY
House in the Trees, Snoqualmie (page 219)
Inn of the White Salmon, Bingen-White Salmon
(page 237)

there are almost 50 wineries along I-82 headed east. Stops along roadside fruit stands are fruitful indeed.

You and your furry traveling companions can hike your way through the Cascades on enough trails to fill dozens of books. You can savor the bounty of the valley while you enjoy its well-irrigated parks. At the southern border, you'll both find something to appreciate in the striking Columbia Gorge, whose walls span 80 miles and descend up to 4,000 feet, past waterfalls and explosions of wildflowers. The Columbia River, separating Washington and Oregon, is one of the world's top destinations for sailboarders, with regular wind gusts up to 85 mph and swells of 3–8 feet.

NATIONAL FORESTS AND RECREATION AREAS

Alpine Lakes Wilderness

Nearly 700 lakes are tucked into the mountain peaks and valleys of this 394,000-acre wilderness jointly managed by the Mt. Baker–Snoqualmie and Wenatchee National Forest Districts. There are 47 trailheads that access 615 miles of trails. You may need permits, maps, and advice on weather and trail conditions before you head into the backcountry. Start at the Snoqualmie Ranger District office in North Bend, 42404 S.E. North Bend Way; 425/888-1421.

Wenatchee National Forest

The Cle Elum and Naches Ranger Districts of the 2.2 million-acre Wenatchee forest are in this region. Pick up hiking and campground lists and directions for the White Pass and Chinook Pass Corridors. Snow closure information is most important in the winter, and campfire restrictions and trail closures due to lightning-ignited fires are vital in the summer. Cle Elum: 803 W. 2nd St.; 509/852-1100; www.fs.fed.us/r6/wenatchee.

Yakima Box Canyon Recreation Area

Between the cities of Ellensburg and Yakima, the Yakima River runs through valley walls of a deep box canyon. Along Canyon Road, State Route 821, the Umtanum Creek, Roza, Lmuma Creek, and Big Pines recreation sites are popular for fishing, camping, and floating the river. Daily parking fees range $2–5, and camping is free or $5 per day, depending on the site and season. Dogs are required to be on leashes not longer than six feet. For information, contact the Wenatchee Resource Area (509/665-2900) or pick up campground and river access maps at the Naches Ranger Station (10237 Hwy. 12; 509/653-1400).

Leavenworth

Leavenworth is a huge destination, voted the #1 Holiday Town U.S.A. in 2003 by Arts and Entertainment TV. When all other sources of income dried up or moved on, new life for this ailing town began as a controversial idea, a way to draw visitors 90 miles into the mountains, where the only other major sign of civilization is the Stevens Pass Ski Area. Citizens reached back to common German roots and set about creating a replica of a Bavarian Village in the heart of what some call the "American Alps." Today, every building in the village, including the golden arches, must meet strict, legitimate Bavarian building codes.

Leavenworth is at its finest during the winter holidays, when all of the intricate baroque woodwork is decked out to become the Village of Lights, chestnuts are roasted on open fires, Father Christmas and St. Nick wander through town smiling for photo ops, and at dusk, everyone gathers to sing "Silent Night" in the town square. It doesn't hurt that the community is surrounded by the peaks, crags, glaciers, alpine lakes, and meadows of the Snoqualmie and Wenatchee National Forests.

PARKS, BEACHES, AND RECREATION AREAS

1 Lake Wenatchee State Park

🐾🐾🐾 (See Central Washington map on page 210)

Mountain peaks, 489 acres of state park land, and thousands of acres of national forest land surround this glacier-fed lake high in Cascade Country.

The state park has two distinct areas, one for swimming and boating, and another more rough and ready area for camping and hiking—lots and lots of hiking. The North River Trail and North Lake Loop are less than two miles each, plus there's the Riverview Loop Trail, interpretive trails, hiking-only trails, hiking and biking trails, forest service trails, and so on. There's a simplified map posted at the North Entrance, and more precise maps are available at the host's site in the campground for the state park. For surrounding forest service trails, the Lake Wenatchee Ranger Station is four miles up the road from the park. Dogs are required to be on leash in the state park; however, dogs are allowed under voice control on national forest lands in this district.

From U.S. Highway 2, turn north on State Route 207. The south entrance, to the swim beach and boat launch, is 3.5 miles up the road; the north entrance, for camping, picnicking and hiking, is another mile beyond the first entrance. Parking is $5. A Sno-Park permit is required during the winter recreation season, when sledding and snowshoeing replace hiking and swimming.

◻ "The Dog Beach"

🐾🐾🐕 (See Central Washington map on page 210)

We put the name of this spot in quotes, because it isn't officially "dog" anything. On Wenatchee National Forest land, there's a lovely little beach on the Wenatchee River with a latrine and gravel parking lot. It has no name, and it is not marked except by a tiny brown Day Use Only, No Overnight Parking sign tacked to a tree. Local dog owners have adopted the beach, and they voluntarily maintain it in good condition in exchange for the privilege of having a swimming hole for all creatures great and small. In the Lake Wenatchee Ranger District, dogs are allowed off leash if they are under continuous voice control.

Watch carefully for the dirt road banking steeply down the hill, .3 mile east of milepost 97 on U.S. Highway 2, before you get into Leavenworth proper.

◻ Waterfront Park and Blackbird Island

🐾🐾 (See Central Washington map on page 210)

Make no mistake, the Dachsie Twins love the oompah-band music piped through town. The peace and quiet of this tree-lined riverfront promenade is a nice contrast, that's all. On property once occupied by a sawmill operation, there are viewing benches and picnic tables, sandy beaches, a playground, and a river viewing platform. Short and sweet dog-walking trails are across a concrete bridge to the island, a pile of silt that accumulated in the river and sprung to life with trees and vegetation. Spend some quality time with your pup as she paws through the sand in search of the mythical treasure of Blackbird Island, not that your dog ever needed an excuse to paw through the sand.

As you enter Leavenworth on U.S. Highway 2 from Seattle, get in the right lane after Icicle Road to turn into the town loop on Front Street. From Front

Street, turn right on 8th Street, and right on Commercial, two and a half blocks to the park. There's no visible sign, so look for the angled dirt parking on the left.

PLACES TO EAT

Echos Bistro and Biergarten: What a treat to walk into the beer garden and see a big Dogs Welcome in the Garden sign. This is your most elegant option for outdoor dining with your pets, featuring authentic German and French cuisine with wine and beer. Some days, there are as many dogs as people at the 20 outdoor tables on the lawn behind the white picket fence. We'll drink a toast to that, *eins, zwei, drei, g'suffa!* 911 Commercial St.; 509/548-9685.

The Gingerbread Factory: Cooper and Isis would have gladly changed their names to Hansel and Gretel to get their paws on this sweet shop's gingerbread cookies. Such drastic measures proved unnecessary. Owner Anita puts out bowls of water for the dogs and gives them free gingerbread dog biscuits because she doesn't like bad doggie breath and ginger is good for dog's tummies. If dog breath is all it takes, Isis is golden. In addition to a lovely case of goodies, the Factory manufactures pasta salads and fantastic hot chicken and vegetable pockets in flaky crusts with cranberry sauce and sour cream. There's abundant outdoor yard and patio seating. 828 Commercial St.; 509/548-6592.

Uncle Uli's Pub: Fondue, baby back ribs, hot broiler sandwiches, and salads are the specialties of the house at this restaurant with outdoor seating tucked into alley picnic tables. 902 Front St.; 509/548-7262.

PLACES TO STAY

Der Ritterhof Motor Lodge: This motel is a good bet if you want to stay in town. Practically speaking, up to two large pets can join you comfortably for an extra $10 per pet, per night. Rates range $78–99. 509/548-5845 or 800/255-5845; www.derritterhof.com.

Destination Leavenworth: These higher-end rental properties allow pets in five of the cabins and homes. The management prefers only one pet but will make exceptions for two well-behaved dogs with advance notice. These vacation destinations are gorgeous, hidden all over the canyon. Rates range $100–175; the pet fee is $15. Office: 940 Hwy. 2; 509/548-4230 or 866/904-7368; www.destinationleavenworth.com.

Natapoc Lodging: Usually one pet is allowed, two with special exceptions, in each of the six lodges on 17 acres of riverfront property. These stunning log homes are all on the Wenatchee River in the woods 15 miles from Leavenworth. Special items are set out for pets, such as treats, pick-up bags, and a policy sheet, and crates are available to borrow. Dogs may be unleashed if under voice control, and the community beach on the river is awesome. The owners know and love dogs, and they have had many of their own. Skookum is the current dog overseer. You'll often see him riding the tractor with his dad, patrolling the grounds. Rates range $200–375 per night, with an additional $25 pet fee. 12348 Bretz Rd.; 509/763-3313 or 888/628-2762; www.natapoc.com.

More Accommodations: Please look under Chain Hotels in the Resources section for additional places to stay in this area.

Issaquah

This desirable mountain town at the foot of the "Issaquah Alps" is growing faster than a Great Dane puppy. The so-called alps are Tiger Mountain, Cougar Mountain, and Squak Mountain, together providing more than 150 miles of hiking and biking trails within a half hour's drive from Seattle.

PARKS, BEACHES, AND RECREATION AREAS

4 Lake Sammamish State Park

🐾🐾 (See Central Washington map on page 210))

Dogs are denied the pleasure of swimming on the beaches in Washington's state parks. Smarty pants that she is, Isis hasn't figured out how to swim and be on leash at the same time anyway. That doesn't keep them from enjoying this park's trails, along Issaquah Creek, nor from lounging on its large lawns watching the boaters and water skiers on the huge lake, which is more than a mile wide and 10 miles long. The two trails worth a tail wag are the .8-mile Meadow Trail following one side of the creek and the .7-mile Homestead on the other. Both are level, effortless meanderings.

From U.S. Highway 90, take exit 15 and go east on East Lake Sammamish Parkway N.E.; at the next light turn left onto N.W. Sammamish Road. To avoid paying $5 for parking at the main entrance, turn right into the next driveway for the Homestead Trail. To take the Boat Launch Trail to the Meadow Spur, stay on East Lake Sammamish Parkway, to the boat launch, 20606 S.E. 56th St.; 425/455-7010.

5 Tiger Mountain State Forest

🐾🐾🐾 (See Central Washington map on page 210))

When the Wonder Wieners discovered this mountain, they didn't hike anywhere else for a year. It is the golden child of the alps and the largest, at 13,000 acres and 80 miles of trails. There are three peaks—East, West, and South. West is favored by hikers, East by the mountain bikers, and South is the least frequented and most remote. You can tell immediately which trails are not frequently used, as the ferns and moss quickly claim the ground. Cooper's favorite trail starts at the High Point Way trailhead and goes up to Poo Poo Point, one of the country's top hang gliding and paragliding points.

In September, we nicknamed it Spider Mountain, for the plump arachnids weaving in the ferns, which Cooper finds a delicious protein supplement once they stop tickling his nose.

From U.S. Highway 90, take Exit 20, south on 270th Ave S.E., and turn right immediately onto S.E. 79th Street to High Point Way. You'll see many cars parked along this road, and there is a large parking area farther up a gravel road with facilities and maps.

PLACES TO EAT

Issaquah Distillery and Public House: A brewpub and producer of Rogue beers, the Issaquah Public House has a permit for outdoor seating each year from May through September. If there is a scene in this foothills town, this is it. The food is reliable and Rogue beers, originally from Oregon, go down nice and easy. 35 Sunset Way; 425/557-1911; www.rogue.com/locations-issaquah.html.

XXX Root Beer Drive-in: It is a doggone shame that a persnickety health inspector has declared this institution's patio off-limits to dogs. It's the last of its kind in the world, and its homemade brew, a smooth root beer produced with cane sugar instead of corn syrup, is named one of the Top 10 root beers in the United States. Get a burger, fries, and root beer float to go, or better yet, take a gallon jug home with you and have a party. Nothing you eat here is good for you. We'll drink a float to that. 98 N.E. Gilman Blvd.; 425/392-1266; www.triplexxxfamilyrestaurant.com.

PLACES TO STAY

In this area, chain hotels offer the best choices for dogs and their owners; please look under Chain Hotels in the Resources section.

Snoqualmie and North Bend

Fans of the TV show *Twin Peaks* will recognize Snoqualmie Falls and Salish Lodge that sits perched above the cascade from the opening credits sequence. Dogs are not allowed on the two-acre grounds of the falls nor at the lodge. You should make a pit stop to see the 270-foot waterfalls on your way to playing at the lake or at least look at them online at www.snoqualmiefalls.com.

Snoqualmie Valley Trail: This crushed-rock and original ballast rail trail extends 36 miles through the valley, from North Bend to Duvall. You'll pass over former railroad trestles, to which handmade decks and rails have been added. Access and parking are available at McCormick Park in Duvall and at Rattlesnake Lake in North Bend/Snoqualmie. www.metrokc.gov/parks/trails/snoqv.htm.

PARKS, BEACHES, AND RECREATION AREAS

6 Rattlesnake Lake

🐾🐾🐾🐾 ✖ (See Central Washington map on page 210)

When the kids are rattling your nerves, it's time to roll on over to the lake for some light hiking and swimming. Take to the Lake Trail, a 1.5-mile paved loop along the southeast side of the lake that is level and easy for all abilities.

Even better is the two-mile Rattlesnake Ledge Trail, a steeper gravel trail up to 1,175 feet above the Snoqualmie Valley. You'll share the trail with mountain bikers and the occasional equestrian. The lake itself has a couple of good ball-throwing areas and, of course, the water.

Microsoft has funded an educational center at the site that has a rainwater drum circle, an exhibit where the drums are played by choreographed rain spouts when it's dry outside, and by nature's hand when it rains. It's cool.

In addition, the gravel trail that begins across the road from the first parking lot is the Snoqualmie Valley Trail, leading 30 some-odd miles to Duvall for long-distance dogs. Finally, if that's not enough for your irondog athlete, the 100-mile John Wayne State Trail starts across the street from the lake.

Technically, there is no rule requiring a leash at Rattlesnake Lake. The ranger asks that you reign in your dog, by leash or voice control, when passing others on the trail. You will be asked to leash up on beach areas during busy summer weekends, and you should always walk with your dog on leash through the visitors center grounds.

From U.S. Highway 90, take Exit 32, go south on 436th Avenue S.E., and continue on the road, which will become Cedar Falls Road for 2.8 miles to the first parking lot on your right, parking for the Rattlesnake Ledge Trail. The John Wayne Trail is on your left at 3.0 miles, and the Cedar River Watershed Education Center is at 3.5 miles. Gates to the center lot close at 6 P.M. Other trailheads are open until dark. There are no parking fees at Rattlesnake Lake trailheads, parking is limited to two hours at the Center lot, and it is $5 per day to park at the John Wayne trailhead.

PLACES TO EAT

Gordy's BBQ: Great ribs and steaks pack people into Gordy's BBQ next to the Cascade Golf Course. Tee off with smoky St. Louis pork ribs or a flank steak at picnic tables out back, while you watch some poor sod shank a ball into the evergreens. No dogs on the course greens, please. 14303 436th Ave S.E.; 425/831-2434; www.gordysbbq.com.

Jeani's Sunshine Café: This tiny eclectic place has excellent soups, salads, and chili. A patio with plastic chairs has been carved out of the parking lot to create a little haven for casual outdoor dining. Buy 10 bowls of chili or soup and get one free. 247 E. North Bend Way; 425/888-6978.

PLACES TO STAY

House in the Trees: Dogs are welcome in both romantic rooms of this bed-and-breakfast, although you and your dog will find it hard to stay in your room. The sunroom, the indoor/outdoor pool, the hot tub, the gardens, and the 20 acres of room to roam will beckon you to get out and enjoy the valley. Ask owner Owen to show you his Dolman, a Celtic stone structure that pre-dates pyramids and Stonehenge. Rooms are $95 per night, including breakfast. There is no dog fee. 35909 S.E. 94th St.; 425/888-2349; www.bethabarafarms.com.

Snoqualmie Inn: This relaxed bed-and-breakfast welcomes a couple of small dogs in all but the wedding suite for $10 per pet, per night. The Inn is also the home of Woodslake Winery and la Cascina Ristorante, and the grounds have lots of fenced room to run out back by the grape-press building. One downstairs room is ADA-equipped for people with service dogs. Rates are $99, including breakfast. 9050 384th Ave. S.E.; 425/888-9399; www.snoqualmieinn.com.

More Accommodations: Please look under Chain Hotels in the Resources section for additional places to stay in this area.

Snoqualmie Pass

This mountain pass is only a 45-minute drive from Seattle, with popular Sno-Parks and ski slopes in the winter, hiking and mountain biking in the summer. Trails are muddy and variable, and you should be prepared for unexpected turns for the worse in weather at any moment.

PARKS, BEACHES, AND RECREATION AREAS

🐾 Asahel Curtis Nature Trail

🐾🐾 (See Central Washington map on page 210)

In 1897, nature photographer Asahel Curtis took 3,000 glass plates into the wilds of Washington and Alaska to document the Klondike Gold Rush. He was a strong advocate for the protection and responsible development of forest areas, especially Mt. Rainier. The hike named in his honor is an easy 1.25-mile loop through a rare old-growth forest, crossing Humpback Creek on wooden bridges several times and heading into a grove that includes western red cedar, western hemlock, and Douglas fir. It gives you a feel for the moist nature of Northwest hiking, the kind that cultivates large ferns, mosses, and lichens and draws out the banana slugs that repel humans and attract dogs.

Take Exit 47 from I-90, go south and turn left on Forest Road 55, .5 mile to the trailhead parking lot. The trail starts at the east end of the parking lot.

🖪 Alpine Lakes Wilderness–Annette Lake

 (See Central Washington map on page 210)

The Annette Lake trail is up the gravel road from the Asahel Curtis trail, and several notches up on the difficulty scale. This hike is a challenging 3.5 miles one-way, uphill, gaining 1,600 feet of elevation along the way. The trail can be rocky and narrow, and you'll slop through mud and errant streams along the way. The toughest switchbacks are in the first two miles, then the slope mercifully levels out for the last mile. For fit dogs and humans, the reward is a crystal clear, icy lake at the top, surrounded by glacier-capped mountains. Cooper picked this trail out of the many available in the wilderness as one of the easiest to get to and one with fairly reliable conditions.

Take Exit 47 from I-90, go south and turn left on Forest Road 55, .5 mile to the Asahel Curtis parking lot. At the east end of the lot, go past the first trail, up and to the left.

Easton

Crumbling buildings and rusted railway cars are common sights in Easton, visible reminders of the town's history as an 1880s logging camp and the last station where trains could be serviced before climbing over the mountains. Although there's little commerce left, Easton is a great place to access the John Wayne Pioneer Trail. Like the legend it is named after, the trail is larger-than-life, capturing the biggest and best of the Northwest mountains (look in the Resources chapter for more information).

PARKS, BEACHES, AND RECREATION AREAS

🖬 Lake Kachess

(See Central Washington map on page 210)

This photogenic lake is popular with the canoeing and kayaking crowd, if you can call a couple of silent boats gliding along the water a crowd. Only four miles from the highway, the picnic area has perfect vistas of the lake surrounded by the mountain peaks, without development to spoil the scenery. It's easy to get down to the shore for a quick dip in the water and a few short trails wander through a nearby campground. Perhaps your dog is like Sweetheart, a playmate of Isis who loves to sit in the canoe between her people, watching them do all the work. It brings new meaning to the phrase dog paddling.

From I-90, take Exit 62 at Stampede Pass, follow the signs to the lake, and go past the Gayle Creek campground loop to reach the day-use area. Parking is $5.

PLACES TO EAT

Elly's: Folks at Elly's are very dog-friendly. "Heck," said the gal behind the counter, "everybody in town's got at least one dog." Visiting dogs can join the locals for croissant sandwiches and French toast for breakfast, brats and chicken for lunch, and steak dinners. Outdoor seating is a picnic table out front. 1941 Railroad Ave.; 509/656-2600.

Mountain High Hamburgers: There's indoor and outdoor seating and a drive-through at the home of the Mt. Rainier burger with double meat, double cheese, and double bacon; 31 flavors of shakes; and blended ice cream and candy shakes called Avalanches. All the scrumptious burgers are named after local peaks, and they loom almost as large. Veggie burgers, fish and chips, a chicken club, and fried zucchini lighten up the menu, if only a little bit. 2941 W. Sparks Rd.; 509/656-3037.

PLACES TO STAY

Silver Ridge Ranch: There's one room with a shared bath at this bed-and-breakfast that accepts dogs, the Ghost Room, and it looks as no-nonsense as you'd expect it to on a working horse ranch. Instead of frills, they've spent money on the good stuff, including a big screen TV in the great room, a sunken tub in the bath, and picture windows with views of the two dozen or so horses roaming the pastures. Boarding horses are welcome, and snowmobile rentals are available in winter. The rate of $75 includes a ranch hand–sized breakfast. 182 Silver Ridge Ranch Rd.; 509/656-0275; www.silverrideranch.com.

Salmon La Sac

PARKS, BEACHES, AND RECREATION AREAS

🔟 Wenatchee National Forest–Cooper River Trail

🐾🐾🐾 (See Central Washington map on page 210)

You're never very far from the sight or sound of the river along the four miles of this popular trail for day trekkers, starting with the series of running rapids within the first .25 mile. You'll roughly follow the river for 2.5 miles, descend deeper into the woods for a mile, then join up with a dirt road another .25 mile to Cooper Lake. Thick brush makes it challenging to get into the river, but once you reach the lake, head north of the Owhi Campground and boat ramp to find a few picnic tables and several convenient spots to take a dip. There's another three-mile trail around the lake, but it is rough going, not nearly as well maintained as the river segment.

Take Exit 80 off I-90, turn left on State Route 903, go east through Roslyn and 17 miles to Salmon La Sac. The trailhead is .5 mile on the dirt road past the campground. Parking is $5.

Roslyn

Before Roslyn played the part of Cicely, Alaska, in the quirky TV show *Northern Exposure*, it was a sleepy ghost town, the remnants of a coal mining community. The Coal Miners' Memorial on Pennsylvania Avenue is a powerful reminder of hard times, and the preserved "Cicely's Store" of better days. Now that the show has ended, the historic district benefits from its 15 minutes of fame, enjoying a modest celebrity status that brings in curious tourists looking for the moose on the wall of Roslyn Café at the corner of 2nd and Pennsylvania.

PARKS, BEACHES, AND RECREATION AREAS

🐾 Roslyn City Park

🐾🐾🐾 (See Central Washington map on page 210)

Cooper and Isis love city parks like this one, with a huge, empty field they can run in. Technically speaking, there is a leash law in town, but Lisa the dogcatcher only responds to complaints, so as long as you're not one of them, you should be okay. There's a pretty gazebo that provides the only shade other than two covered picnic tables. On the west side of the field is a wooden bridge that connects you to the middle of the Coal Mine Trail.

As you're coming east into town on State Route 903, turn left on Nevada Avenue and right on 3rd Street (3rd is after 6th—don't look for 4th and 5th, as they are elsewhere!). Idaho Ave. and 3rd St. 509/649-3105.

PLACES TO EAT

Leftie's Eats: Thank goodness there's a place that offers healthy, organic, vegetarian choices. Even better that they taste good enough to fool the dogs, especially the no-chicken nuggets, black bean burritos, and vegan "tuna"—not to mention the fresh-squeezed juices, smoothies, ice cream, and thick cookies. Adirondack chairs out front make for comfortable, if messy, eating. 107 Pennsylvania Ave.; 509/649-2909.

Cle Elum

Nearby Cle Elum's population swelled when the TV crews moved in to Roslyn, but times are quieter now. Cle Elum has a ranger station for the Wenatchee National Forest: 803 W. 2nd St.; 509/852-1100; www.fs.fed.us/r6/wenatchee.

PARKS, BEACHES, AND RECREATION AREAS

12 Cle Elum City Park

 (See Central Washington map on page 210)

It'll do as a picnic spot, with lots of tall pine trees and unusual playground equipment, including a Model-T car and a climbing centipede designed and welded by hand. If you want an upper body workout, the do-it-yourself swing, where you pump with your arms to generate momentum, is big enough for grown ups. Tree stumps are made into tables with colorful tops. Keep dogs on leash to avoid problems with 2nd Street, the busy mainline between Roslyn and Cle Elum. Alpha Ave. and W. 2nd St.; 509/674-2262.

13 Coal Mine Trail

🐾🐾🐾 (See Central Washington map on page 210)

As if the John Wayne Trail isn't enough, the former mining towns of Ronald, Cle Elum, and Roslyn are joined by another excellent trail, 4.7 miles one-way. It's tidy, easy gravel and dirt, with a slight incline as you head west. It alternates between open sun and deep shade, through forests and past town parks. It's a popular hangout. You'll meet lots of local dogs out for exercise with their owners along the way.

Trailheads and parking are located in all three towns, at the Ronald Fire Station, in Roslyn behind the City Park, and at Cle Elum's Flagpole Park. 509/674-5958.

PLACES TO EAT

Thorp Fruit and Antiques: This big warehouse on the side of the road carries everything you need to put together an amazing picnic lunch. In addition to fruit, they specialize in locally made gourmet food products, including Anna's Honey. It's about 10 minutes past Cle Elum, on the highway to Ellensburg. 1503 Gladmar Rd., Thorp; 509/964-2474.

PLACES TO STAY

Aster Inn: Pets are welcome without restrictions or charges at this tiny inn with lots of character that comes from individually decorated rooms furnished with brass beds, clawfoot tubs, and antiques (which are for sale). Most rooms have kitchenettes at unbeatable prices of $45–60 and only $85 for a Jacuzzi room! All rooms are nonsmoking. 521 E. 1st St.; 509/674-2551 or 888/616-9722.

Cascade Mountain Inn: You can relax at this modern hotel with huge rooms and an equally massive fireplace in the lobby. Rates range from $60 for standard rooms to $120 for suites with spas, plus $10 per pet, per night. 906 E. 1st St.; 509/674-2380.

Ellensburg

It is a four-legged animal of a different breed, the horse, that is most lauded in the famous annual Ellensburg Rodeo, held every Labor Day weekend since 1923. Cooper believes the annual Dachshunds on Parade, held in June, will soon become just as big a draw, pardner. To attend the former, call 509/962-7831 or visit www.ellensburgrodeo.com. You can find information on the latter at the visitors center (609 N. Main St.; 509/925-2002; www.ellensburg-chamber.com) as well as a self-guided Historic Ellensburg Walkabout Guide to the eclectic mix of 1889 brick buildings and preserved early 20th century architecture. An Ellensburg Outdoor Recreation Guide lists a dozen regional hikes, most a bit more ambitious than those the easily winded Wieners have listed here. For unique dog and cat collectables, visit **Wind River** (1714 Canyon Rd.; 509/933-4438; www.windrivergifts.com), one of the largest and best gift shops we've encountered on our travels.

PARKS, BEACHES, AND RECREATION AREAS

🐾 Irene Rinehart

🐾🐾🐾 (See Central Washington map on page 210)

The Yakima River runs thick and full past Ellensburg, and Rinehart is the city's woodsy riverfront park. From the southern entrance, there's a .5-mile gravel trail called Howard's Way that will keep your dog happily occupied. Birds rustle in the trees, yellow marmots scurry through the bushes, and there are plenty of convenient put-in spots on the river. Know your pet's limits; the currents are strong all summer.

Dogs are not allowed on the people beach or the groomed grass. This policy is strictly enforced by frequent police car patrols through the park.

From I-90, take Exit 109 to Canyon Road, take the first left turn on Umptanum Road, crossing under I-90 to the park entrance on the right. Turn left immediately into the south parking lot.

🐾 Reed Park

🐾🐾 (See Central Washington map on page 210)

This sunny sliver of a city park is at the top of the hill, on a crescent lawn carved out of the property next to the city's gigantic water tower. It's an ideal spot to catch some rays, along with fantastic views of the valley from a row of benches. A strategically placed doggie bag dispenser reminds you to do your part to maintain the public green space.

From Main Street, go east on 3rd Street 11 blocks to Alder Avenue. Turn left up the hill through a residential area to the center of the park, in front of the American Legion Post.

16 Mountain View

 (See Central Washington map on page 210)

Any day is a good day for a dog at this two-block city park, even hot, hazy days with no mountain in sight. Your toughest decision will be whether you should take your lunch basket to the park's gliding bench swing or spread out on a blanket under one of several maple trees. Then it's up to your pup to decide where to wander in the bunches of sweet-smelling grass. Kids have the toughest choice of all: swing sets and playgrounds or the tennis courts converted to an in-line skate park?

From Main Street, turn east on Monitoba Avenue and go 10 blocks to Maple Street.

17 Olmsted Place

(See Central Washington map on page 210)

In 1875, Samuel and Sarah Olmsted crossed the Cascade mountains on horseback to homestead in the Kittitas Valley. For almost a hundred years, their dairy cows' butter was a prized commodity on the Seattle market, and their crops yielded hay, wheat, and oats. In 1968, their granddaughters Leta and Clareta deeded the 217-acre farm to Washington State Parks, to be maintained as a living historical farm for future generations to visit and study. On the property, their 1908 home is furnished as the family left it!

Even pampered city pets can experience what a working dog's life must have been like on the farm, walking with you through the hay and corn fields, past the cow and horse pasture, in the rose garden, and on the .75-mile path following Altapes Creek.

The farm is designed for kids to watch and participate in some of the farm chores, collecting eggs from chickens in the morning, threshing wheat, churning butter, and picking vegetables in the garden. Free hay wagon rides run noon–4 P.M., Saturday and Sunday, Memorial Day–Labor Day. No animals in the buildings, please.

Take Exit 115 from I-90, four miles east of Ellensburg in the town of Kittitas. Follow signs through Main Street, turn left on Patrick Avenue, go three miles, and turn left on Ferguson. Parking is $5.

18 Yakima Box Canyon–Umtanum Creek

(See Central Washington map on page 210)

This BLM recreation site is a favorite high desert hiking trail. Sunglasses, sunscreen, bug spray, and drinking water are essential carry-ins. At the start of the hike, you'll cross a swaying wood and cable bridge over the river and some unmarked railroad tracks. After that, the hike is pretty straightforward. You'll follow and occasionally cross the creek, which attracts flowers, birds, and butterflies to the water from the parched surrounding hills. Be on the lookout for rattlesnakes.

The turnout to the trailhead is marked, 10 miles south of I-90 on State Route 821. Parking is $5 per day.

PLACES TO EAT

Ellensburg Pasta Co.: The Pasta Co.'s covered patio keeps you, your dog, and your salad greens from wilting in the heat as you dine on hearty portions of classic red- and white-sauce pasta dishes, soups, and spumoni ice cream. 600 N. Main St.; 509/933-3330.

Smo'kin Joe's Bar-BQ: Your pal can rub elbows with other carnivores in hog heaven at Joe's, eating meat, potato salad, beans, and sweet potato pie at colorful outdoor tables, crafted from painted cable spools stood on end. 702 N. Main; 509/925-RIBS (509/925-7427).

Sweet Memories: Your dog will fondly recall any tidbits you sneak to her under the table from your sun-dried tomato and turkey sandwich, roasted chicken salad, or soup with incredible breadsticks. More power to you if you can keep your paws off the platter-sized cookies. 319 N. Pearl St.; 509/925-4783.

PLACES TO STAY

Ellensburg Inn: Nice lobby, nice colors, nice bedspreads. A nice place located conveniently near Exit 109. Rates range $64–88, plus a $6 pet fee and your signature on a reasonable pet policy. 1700 Canyon Rd.; 509/925-9801.

More Accommodations: Please look under Chain Hotels in the Resources section for additional places to stay in this area.

White Pass and Chinook Pass

On the way up and over 4,500-foot White Pass, you'll pass through parts of the Wenatchee, Mt. Baker–Snoqualmie, and Gifford–Pinchot National Forests. To the north, Chinook Pass is an even higher and more scenic destination at 5,430 feet in elevation. There are abundant hiking and mountain biking trails for you and your ambitious pups. The Naches Ranger Station has a long list of hikes and campgrounds along the White Pass and Chinook Pass Corridors (10061 Hwy. 12; 509/653-1416). Furry breeds would enjoy the area's winter recreation as well, including groomed cross-country skiing trails, the downhill slopes at White Pass Ski Area, and designated snowmobiling Sno-Parks.

PARKS, BEACHES, AND RECREATION AREAS

19 Boulder Cave

🐾 🐾 🐾 🐾 ◖ (See Central Washington map on page 210)

Boulder Cave is home to the only known population of Pacific Western big-eared bats. Bats?! Don't worry—they only use the cave as a place to hibernate in the winter. The trail and cave are closed Oct. 31–Apr. 1 to let them get their beauty sleep.

The remainder of the year, you and your dog can hike the easy, clear path 1.5 miles to the bat cave and back. Bring a flashlight for the 350-foot-long by 30-foot-wide cave. Don't be shy—we've seen babes in strollers manage it without fears or tears.

For those who prefer staying out in the open, a .75-mile fully accessible loop follows along the Naches River from the same trailhead. Resting benches and footbridges encourage lingering. The riverside picnic area is a pretty area for relaxing, pre- or post-spelunking.

The entrance to Boulder Cave is clearly marked, west of American River on State Route 410, 30 miles from Naches on Chinook Pass. Parking is $5, payable to a private management agency.

PLACES TO STAY

Game Ridge Motel: Although the room furnishings are humble in this mountain lodge, the important things are done right, such as hot tubs on decks with views of the Tieton River, cool cotton bed quilts, and in-room refrigerators, TV/VCR, and coffeemakers. There are picnic tables, barbecue pits, and a tepee for the kids to play in out back by the river. Non-view rooms start at $55, view rooms at $115, up to a full cabin that sleeps eight for $195. All rooms are nonsmoking. Pets under 65 pounds only, at $10 per pet, per night. 27350 Hwy. 12; 509/672-2212 or 800/301-9354; www.gameridge.com.

Naches

The correct pronunciation of this historic agricultural center is na-CHEES. The town's name, and the area's language, culture, and cuisine, are strongly influenced by the fact that 25 percent of Yakima county's population is Hispanic American. They are the majority labor force working to harvest the apple, pear, and other fruit orchards.

PARKS, BEACHES, AND RECREATION AREAS

20 Eschbach Park

🐾🐾🐾 (See Central Washington map on page 210)

This county park is a little rough around the edges, barely recovered from its wild state. From all appearances, this only serves as a greater attraction to the kids and dogs who see it as one big adventure. There's no formal parking, and the dirt roads are not safe for car traffic. The ball fields have reverted to just fields, and the water, at the shallow end of the Naches River, looks decidedly brown. Even so, it was the liveliest place in town the day the dogs came to visit, with Latin music blaring from boom boxes, buses of day-care kids unloading, kids floating and swimming in the river, and older folks chatting and eating among the scattered picnic tables. It reminded the dogs' mom that being messy can be the most fun.

From U.S. Highway 12 in Naches, turn south on S. Naches Road and travel 5.5 miles through apple orchard country to the park on your left, halfway between Yakima and Naches. Open 9:30 A.M.–dusk. 4811 S. Naches Rd.; 509/574-2435.

PLACES TO EAT

Sassy's Kitchen: Let's talk turkey, real turkey, carved for your sandwich—you won't find pressed and machine-sliced deli meat here. As though you were in her home, Sass makes everything for breakfast and lunch from scratch while she chats with you over the counter. Your dogs will have to beg directly from Sass herself. They'll go hungry hoping you'll part with even one bite of yours. Sassy's has four sidewalk tables protected under an awning. 217 Naches Ave.; 509/653-1700.

PLACES TO STAY

Cozy Cat Bed and Breakfast: Well-behaved dogs on leashes are welcome at this comfy-casual home, as long as they don't find it necessary to chase the resident cats or go fishing for the koi in the pond. The desert foothills beckon from the inviting front porch, and a trail out back leads through the pines to the Naches River. The Burgundy Cat room is $75 and the Mini-Suite is $85. 12604 S.R. 410; 509/658-2953.

Yakima

The valley's advanced farm irrigation techniques extend to Yakima's parks. Lawns are lush and trees are tall, a good trick in a desert valley where average summer temperatures easily reach 100°F. The name of the city, county, and valley are derived from the native tribe inhabiting the region, who use the spelling Yakama.

Yakima Greenway: This 10-mile, paved path follows the river and loops halfway around the city, through three parks, two lakes, and three boat landings. A map from the Visitors Center shows eight parking access points and distances from point to point. Open 6 A.M.–9 P.M.; some areas are safer walked in groups. Greenway Foundation; 509/453-8280.

Powerhouse Canal Pathway: Using old transit corridors and irrigation rights of way, this convenient multi-use trail bisects the city, 2.5 miles west to east. Parking is available at McGuinness Park at 1407 Swan Ave. (east) and Chesterley Park at the intersection of N. 40th Ave. and River Rd. (west). Open 6 A.M.–10 P.M. Yakima Parks and Recreation; 509/575-6020.

DIVERSION

There are nearly 50 wineries in this region, and all of them have award-winning *this* and tasting medal *that,* but only one has Bung the Wonder Dog, the Aussie living at the **Bonair Winery** in Zillah, between Yakima and Toppenish. He'll saunter out to greet you as you arrive, or on a hot, lazy afternoon, allow you to come and greet him on the front porch. The Puryears entice you to visit their "little hobby that got out of hand." Bring your dogs and stroll through the vineyard, bring a lunch and picnic near a koi pond, and bring your thirst and some extra cash for a bottle or two of mead. Open daily 10 A.M.–5 P.M.; weekends only Dec.–Feb. 500 S. Bonair Rd.; 509/829-6027 or 800/882-8939; www.bonairwine.com.

The **Maryhill Winery** is another vintner that welcomes social and well-behaved pets, at their discretion. The staff reserves the right to request that you leave your dogs in the car if they appear aggressive or territorial, or there are too many other kids or dogs around. Maryhill is open for wine-tasting, picnicking, and music on the deck, and they have what they call a "doggie railroad," a fenced dog run for visiting pets to stretch their legs and take care of life's necessities. Regrettably, dogs are not allowed on the lawn for the summer concert series. The tasting room is open 10 A.M.–6 P.M.; 9774 Hwy. 14; 509/773-1976; www.maryhillwinery.com.

PARKS, BEACHES, AND RECREATION AREAS

21 Cowiche Canyon Trail

🐾🐾🐾🐾 (See Central Washington map on page 210)

No dog bones about it, this is a spectacular trail. It's Coop's kind of walk, wide and level, with no elevation gain unless you hike out of the Canyon on the viewpoint spur. Along the three-mile one-way gravel road, you'll follow the course of Cowiche Creek, crossing over 11 sturdy wooden bridges built on former Burlington-Northern railroad trestles. You're close to the city, but you'd never know it, in a private universe of lush vegetation near the river, starkly contrasted by steep shale walls. There are places where your dog can sneak into the creek for a quick dip, and he'll get a kick out of testing the echo of his bark against the hillside. The Wieners walked the trail at sunset, with the moon rising on one side, and the sun burnishing the rocks to a bright gold on the other. For the first time in her life, Isis was speechless.

Bring drinking water, keep alert for rattlesnakes in hot weather, and stay away from poison ivy.

Take exit 33 off I-82 onto Yakima Avenue, jog north on 7th Avenue to Summitview. Travel seven miles past 40th Avenue in Yakima, turn right on Weikel Road, and go another .25 mile to the trailhead parking.

22 Gilbert Park

🐾🐾🐾 (See Central Washington map on page 210)

At this city park, Cooper learned the difference between a maze and a labyrinth. In the classic sense, a labyrinth is a stone path, where you can see the whole pattern, meant to be walked with a certain meditation in mind—prayer, calmness, gratitude, a concern, energy, hope, or just for fun. We suspect Coop walked it praying for a treat. Isis was distracted from her mantra by a bulldog in his own deliberations with a beach ball. The stone path is on the front lawn of an arts center, and the center's backyard is a gently sloping lawn, dotted with huge trees and tables. It's a simple park for a reflective afternoon.

From downtown Yakima, follow Lincoln Avenue past 40th Avenue to the park on the left at N. 50th Avenue and Lincoln Street. Open 6 A.M.–10 P.M.

23 Randall Park

🐾🐾🐾🐾 (See Central Washington map on page 210)

Cooper and Isis are impressed with the pedigree of Yakima's parks, especially at Randall, where the emerald lawns and ancient timbers are cultivated as carefully as the valley's grapes, apples, and hops. The dogs are glad park planners chose a sprinkler system over, say, Astroturf, for Randall's football-sized field on a plateau. The paved pathway around the park weaves through the tree canopy. Don't miss the section south of the parking lot down by the creek—it is the prettiest picnic area.

From I-82, take Exit 34 west on Nob Hill Boulevard to 48th Avenue, and go south on 48th to the park. Open 6 A.M.–10 P.M.

24 Emil Kissel Park

🐾🐾 (See Central Washington map on page 210)

Everything still has that new park smell in this city plot that's so fresh it didn't make the press deadline for the 2004 tourist brochure. There won't be any sun protection for a few years from the young trees and shrubs that have been landscaped. For the present, come to undiscovered Kissel to avoid the crowds or if you're lacking in vitamin D and are in need of southern exposure.

From I-82, take Exit 34 west on Nob Hill to 32nd Avenue, head south on 32nd to the park at S. 32nd Avenue and Mead Road. Open 6 A.M.–10 P.M.

25 Byrd Dog Park

🐾 🐕 (See Central Washington map on page 210)

These meager couple of acres have the barest essentials necessary for an off-leash park, that is, a five-foot chain link fence with a gate, a picnic bench, and a garbage can. It was kind of Norman and Nellie Byrd to provide the funding for a dog park in 2000, and surely it looks better in a dog's eyes than a human's. Where we see parched dirt, rocks, and bushes that leave seeds and burrs in fur, they see a place in the sun to run and nature to inspect. While we struggle to find the @#$% place, they experience only the sweet agony of anticipation. While we lug in toys, water, and poop bags, they look at us with ultimate trust, knowing we'll always provide the good stuff for them. Finally, while we swelter in the shimmering heat, they pant and grin lopsidedly. Sometimes, it's good to see the water bowl as half full.

The dog park is at the Rotary Lake access point on the Yakima Greenway. Turn north on 1st Street from Yakima Avenue, and turn right on R Street. Turn left on onto the frontage road immediately before R Street dead ends into the parking lot of Trail Wagons RV and Truck Sales. This dirt road curves around under the highway and then parallels it on the opposite side for about .25 mile before the park on your right. Parking is past the field on the left. Open sunrise–sunset.

26 Yakima Sportsman Park

🐾 🐾 🐾 (See Central Washington map on page 210)

Every dog can have his day at this 246-acre state park, created by the Yakima Sportsman Association for better game management, pollution reduction, and preservation of natural resources. These days, the only hunting you'll do is for the entrance to the river trail (between campsites 22 and 23). The park is expansive and grand, richly green and forested with deciduous trees. Built on a floodplain of the Yakima River, it is a green zone in an otherwise desert environment. It's also a bird-watcher's delight; at least 140 different avian species have been identified on the grounds. On the property, the Juan O. Alvarez Wetlands Trail is paved and accessible, with full-color photographs of the animals and plants you might encounter on the .1-mile path to a wetland viewing platform. No dog paddling in the wetlands! There are many species your dog could harm, and a few that could give her trouble.

From I-82, take Exit 34 east on Nob Hill Boulevard for a mile, turn left on Keys Road, and go another mile past the KOA campground to the park entrance. Open 8 A.M.–dusk. Parking is $5. 904 Keys Rd.; 509/575-2774.

PLACES TO EAT

Marketplace Deli: If you can't find what you're craving on the list of 30 specialty sandwiches, you can always have it made to order. For a $10 minimum, they'll deliver. 304 E. Yakima Ave.; 409/457-7170.

Mercedes and Family: If you like it *caliente y picante* (hot and spicy), Mercedes' take-out window is the place for you. Grab authentic combination plates of tacos, tamales, chilis rellenos, or sopitos (a fat tostada), with rice and beans for $5 each on your way to Gilbert Park. At the corner of 56th and Tieton; 509/965-9193.

Some Bagels: Like Charlotte spinning "Some Pig" in her web for Wilbur, this bagel joint spins an intricate array of yummy bagel concoctions for breakfast and lunch. For a snack, buy a bag of bagel holes on your way to Randall Park. 610 S. 48th Ave.; 509/965-3218.

PLACES TO STAY

Apple Country Bed and Breakfast: The proprietors try to accommodate dogs whenever possible in their Picker's Cottage, a romantic hideaway steps away from the orchards. Call ahead and talk to Shirley to see what she can do for you. Unique perks include breakfast served outdoors in a hand-carved gazebo and the chance to pick and eat whatever is in season from the crops. The weekend rate is $85; weekdays are $75. 4561 Old Naches Hwy.; 509/965-0344 or 877/788-9963; www.applecountryinnbb.com.

Sun Country Motel: Free snacks—like popcorn, cherries, apples, and cookies—are always out for guests at this convenient motel with big, cool rooms and an outdoor pool. Rates range $45–57, plus a $5 pet fee. 1700 N. 1st St.; 509/248-5650.

More Accommodations: Please look under Chain Hotels in the Resources section for additional places to stay in this area.

Union Gap

Union Gap is where Yakima used to be. When some settlers refused the railroad's demands in 1884, Northern Pacific routed its trains four miles north and offered to move any businesses or residences to its new community. At least 50 city buildings were moved on log rollers over the trail, some doing business as they rolled. Old-timers still refer to Union Gap as Old Town Yakima.

PARKS, BEACHES, AND RECREATION AREAS

27 Youth Activities Park

😊😊😊 (See Central Washington map on page 210)

With a name like that, you'd expect the park to be a sports complex, but it is mostly 74 acres of heavenly tree-shaded picnic grounds; it could just as easily be called Dog Activities Park. It is the most heavily used park in the region, but even when big gatherings have reserved all 10 areas for groups of 50–200, there's still enough room for big dogs to run as long as you can keep up with them on your end of the leash.

Take your pick among the well-tended lawns, in the shade or the sun, around the BMX bike track, volleyball sand pits, playground, and tennis courts. The water tower and barn remain from the park's former use as a farm labor camp.

Take Exit 36 off of I-82/U.S. Highway 12 to Valley Mall Boulevard. Go west, and then turn south on Main Street, turn west again on Ahtanum Road. Open 9 A.M.–dusk. 1000 Ahtanum Road.

PLACES TO STAY

Quality Inn: This hotel lives up to its name, with a long list of desirable conveniences including free full breakfast, wireless Internet, HBO, and an outdoor pool. Rates range $69–99, plus a $10 pet fee. 800/510-5670; www .qualityinnyakima.com.

Toppenish

Downtown Toppenish relishes its history in the Northern Pacific Railway Museum, the American Hops Museum, and the Yakama Nation Cultural Heritage Center (509/865-2800), which celebrates the people of the Yakama Indian Reservation, which covers 39 percent of the valley. The city's most famous historical record is chronicled outdoors, where you can enjoy it on a walk with your pet, accompanied by piped country-and-western music. As of 2004, there were 65 larger-than-life murals painted on the buildings down-town, and at least one new mural is added every year.

PARKS, BEACHES, AND RECREATION AREAS

28 Fort Simcoe Heritage Site

🐾🐾 (See Central Washington map on page 210)

This state park is a reminder of a positive chapter in the long struggle between Native Americans and settlers in the Pacific Northwest. Although the Army chose the camping ground of the Yakama people for the construction of a fort in 1856, it was peacefully abandoned in 1859 and turned over to the Bureau of Indian Affairs, serving instead as a Native American school and training facility. Ownership was returned to the Yakamas, and in 1956, they signed a 99-year lease with the state to allow the public entry to the site. Five of the original structures have been restored, several have been reconstructed, and the others are noted by markers around the 420-foot square parade ground.

NATURE HIKES AND URBAN WALKS

The town of Toppenish, Washington, is called the **City of Murals** for its 65 (and counting) larger than life pictorials of pioneer days on downtown buildings. Artists come from all over the world to paint these full-color scenes. The Toppenish Mural Society occupies the same building as the visitors center, where you can get a free map to guide yourself through a colorful history lesson. Toppenish Ave.; 800/596-3982; www.toppenish.net.

Across the border, in The Dalles, Oregon, they one-up Toppenish with **Talking Murals.** You can purchase a key for $5 to unlock the talk box for each picture at the Chamber of Commerce office (404 W. 2nd St.; 541/296-2231 or 800/255-3385; www.thedalleschamber .com). Though the mayor may not have given you the actual key to the city, you get to keep your souvenir.

If your dog doesn't get enough exercise walking the grounds with you, there is a trail around the fort, although it's hot and dry. Your pal can enjoy the shade, playground, and picnic area if you decide to tour the officer's quarters, 10:30 A.M.–3:30 P.M., April–September. The park is open 6:30 A.M.–dusk daily in the summer; weekends and holidays only October–March.

Fort Simcoe is 30 miles west of Toppenish in White Swan on the Yakima Indian Reservation. The drive out is through fields of hops, grapes, and orchards. From U.S. Highway 97, turn west on Fort Road, left on Signal Peak Road, and right on Fort Simcoe Road. There is no fee for parking; donations are accepted to support historic preservation. 5150 Ft. Simcoe Rd.; 509/874-2372.

PLACES TO STAY

In this area, chain hotels offer the best choices for dogs and their owners; please look under Chain Hotels in the Resources section.

Trout Lake

There's a Trout Creek in Trout Lake, but no Trout Lake. This is the last stop on State Route 141 before it dead-ends into the base of Mt. Adams. Climbing permits, information, and human waste pack-out kits are available at the Mt. Adams Ranger Station (2455 Hwy. 141; 509/395-2501), because there's no place to go on the rocks and snow above tree line. Secretly, your dog will get a chuckle out of seeing you carry your own poop in a bag for a change. A climb to the summit requires technical equipment.

PARKS, BEACHES, AND RECREATION AREAS

29 Conboy Lake Wildlife Refuge

🐾🐾🐾🐾 (See Central Washington map on page 210)

An early homestead returning to the wild, Conboy delivered immediately on its promise as a hoot owl ushered us into the gravel parking area for the Willard Springs Foot Trail. Every red-blooded quadruped we know would love this three-mile walk through big-sky country, on leash in case the distractions prove too tempting. The soft pine needles are easy on the paws, there's wild scat to smell, marshes and field grasses to explore, and the sights and sounds of multiple bird and ground species. The scenery is equally easy on the eyes. The interpretive trail is a test of your photographic memory; there's a list of the markers posted at the entrance, but no brochures to take with you through it. There are restrooms and a makeshift picnic table. Bring drinking water.

The signs will guide you to the shortest route, also the most confusing. We vote instead for taking State Route 141 a little farther into Trout Lake, taking the right fork in the road, turning right on Sunnyside Road toward Glenwood, and following it 10.8 miles to Wildlife Refuge Road. It's another mile on the gravel to the parking area by the trailhead.

PLACES TO STAY

Kelly's Trout Creek Inn Bed and Breakfast: The hospitality is as long as its name at this lovely creekside home. The patio, where breakfast is served (weather permitting), has a soothing view of Trout Creek, with a swimming hole and paths along the water for dog paddling and dog walks. Rooms are $65, plus $5 per kid to cover breakfast; there's no dog fee. Some rooms share a bath; private baths are also available. Your hostess's pressed flower art adorns the walls. 25 Mt. Adams Rd.; 509/395-2769; www.kellysbnb.com.

Carson

PARKS, BEACHES, AND RECREATION AREAS

30 Dog Mountain Trail

🐾🐾🐾 (See Central Washington map on page 210)

Never mind that this trail is a real paw-bruiser, the Wonder Wieners would include this 3.1-mile climb on the merit of its name alone. We won't tell them it was named as such because starving early pioneers ate their dogs to survive. An explosion of wildflowers in the spring and summer, and views of Mt. Hood, Mt. Adams, and Mount St. Helens make your panting worth the while. The trail doesn't make you go all the way to the 2,948-foot summit, merely from the starting point at 60 feet above sea level to 2,800 feet.

The scenic route has better views and better meadows for the price of a steep, direct ascent. There's another trail that is a kindler, gentler route, adding .6 mile each way, and leading you through more forests than fanfare, also more prone to rattlesnake crossings. To follow the pack leader and gut it out on the scenic route, stay to the right at the fork in the trail at .5 mile. Foot traffic is very heavy mid-May through June and on summer weekends.

The trailhead is 13 miles east of Stevenson on State Route 14. The sign and the gravel parking area come up quickly between mileposts 53 and 54, so watch for them. For map reference, this is USFS Trail #147. Parking requires a Northwest Forest Pass or $5 daily.

Bingen-White Salmon

Bingen is named for its sister city in Germany and White Salmon for the color the fish turn as they die after spawning, as described in the journals of Meriwether Lewis. Immediately west is the Hood River Toll Bridge, where 75 cents gets you over to said town on the Oregon side. West of that, exactly .1 mile west of Mile Marker 56, is Dog Creek Falls. From a marked gravel pullout, a quick walk down a few feet of rocky path leads you to the base of the falls and right into the streambed, if anyone in your expedition party is feeling the call of the water.

PARKS, BEACHES, AND RECREATION AREAS

31 Daubenspeck Park

 (See Central Washington map on page 210)

As near as we can figure it, *Daubenspeck* roughly translated from the German means Bacon Stick, a name that thrilled the Dachsie Twins, who immediately set about looking for one to fight over. The playground doubles as a baseball field, and there are various picnic tables in the shade of wind-breaking poplars and under a covered shelter. A big log and the remains of a tree trough remind you of the town's sawmill history while you hang out and ham it up.

When State Route 14 becomes Steuben Street through town, look for Willow Street and turn north a half-block to the park.

32 Sailboard Park

 (See Central Washington map on page 210)

The Bingen Marina, in the Port of Klickitat, is a major dog hangout after their people get off from work in the late afternoon. As long as you have control of your dog, voice or otherwise, local leash enforcement is relaxed. The sniff-and-greet area is a long strip of lawn, which is also a landing pad for hang gliders. A rough dirt ramp leads down to a rocky shoreline. About the only

DIVERSION

The **Happy Tails Boarding Kennel** in White Salmon, Washington is so close to the Hood River Bridge that you can take advantage of its services whether you're on the Washington or Oregon side of the Columbia Gorge.

Each dog has an individual 5- by 10-foot inside run and a 5- by 5-foot outdoor romp. All are welcome to participate in exercise and playtime in the group play yards, and every pup is given individual love and affection by resident staff in an American Boarding Kennel–certified facility.

Rates are $18 per dog, per night for one pet or $15 per dog, per night for two pets who share the same kennel. A bath and blow dry is $20, $30 if you include a flea dip for Fido. 70 Acme Rd.; 509/493-4255.

thing not going on in Sailboard Park is sailboarding; enthusiasts prefer the windier conditions and easier put-in at Doug's Beach.

From State Route 14, turn south on Maple Street into the port industrial area, turn left on Lakeview Boulevard, right on N. Harbor Drive, and left on E. Bingen Point Way at the Sailboard Park sign.

PLACES TO EAT

Bingen Station: This coffeehouse and deli proves that low-carb doesn't have to be no taste, with a mesquite chicken wrap with cilantro-lime mayo and other equally flavorful combinations. One two-seater table and a couple of benches provide shade for a quick bite. Give her a few nibbles of your roast beef, and your dog will wait while you look at the antiques that are a sideline business. 213 W. Steuben; 509/493-1121.

The Creamery: For $.81, you can get your pup a scoop of ice cream on a plain cone, which is probably as much dairy as any dog should have, regardless of what he'll tell you. A triple-scoop waffle cone with fudge, whipped cream, and nuts will run you a few bucks more. This ice cream shop also has panini sandwiches and two café tables in front. 121B E. Jewett; 509/493-4007.

PLACES TO STAY

Inn of the White Salmon: This European-styled bed-and-breakfast has welcomed guests since 1937. It looks like it might have belonged to a rich Great Auntie, and every effort has been made to retain the original charm of the brick building with patterned wallpaper, designer wool carpets, period photos, brass beds, and furnishings that would make an antique hunter's eyes light up. There's a parlor for guests to share and a back patio with hot tub. Civilized rules include no smoking, no barking, leashing your pet, picking up his calling cards, and not leaving the room without him. Rates range $106–143; the pet fee is $10 per stay. 172 W. Jewett; 509/493-2335 or 800/972-5226; www.innofthewhitesalmon.com.

Lyle

Lewis and Clark are believed to be the first white men to visit this area along the Columbia, named for the town's 1876 postmaster, James O. Lyle. Lyle's economic mainstay over the years has been sheep and wool-shipping. Lyle's parks are wonderful for wheelchair users.

PARKS, BEACHES, AND RECREATION AREAS

33 Catharine Creek Universal Access Trails

🐾🐾🐾 (See Central Washington map on page 210)

Other than being too steep in a couple of sections for in-line skates (yes, we tried), these two hillside loops are excellent for anything with wheels, feet, or footpads. The trail is a combination of asphalt and wooden bridges, and each loop is .75 mile. It is an ideal nature stroll, with gorge views and wildflowers for humans, and nature and wildlife sightings crowded up against the trail for dogs. There are no facilities.

From State Route 14, turn north at the west entrance to Old Highway No. 8, immediately west of Rowland Lake, and travel 1.5 miles to the gravel parking area on your left and the trailhead on your right.

34 Balfour-Klickitat Park

🐾🐾🐾 (See Central Washington map on page 210)

This mile of riverfront and the surrounding hillsides were purchased in 1892 by English Lord Balfour, in need of a sunny break from his dreary homeland. He planted orchards and vineyards and built a castle on the hill. Only his name survives in this park, opened in June 2004. The nubby fruit of the Osage orange trees in the park are reported to be the first botanical sample the Lewis and Clark Expedition sent back to President Jefferson.

By its full name, the Balfour-Klickitat Columbia River Gorge National Scenic Area is on the west side of the muddy-brown Klickitat River. The parking lot, vault toilet, and beautifully smooth asphalt loop are easy for all users to navigate through the native ground cover to bluff picnic tables, watching river and train traffic along the gorge. The hills are alive at this community park, with prairie dogs piping, green dragonflies buzzing, and who knows what scurrying through the high grass, providing distractions for your dog. It's our favorite quick escape on this side of the river.

From State Route 14 west of Lyle, turn north at the east entrance to Old Highway No. 8, and go up the hill .2 mile to the park entrance on your right.

PLACES TO STAY

Lyle Hotel: There are no TVs or phones at this tiny 1904 historic property, so you'll have to be self-entertaining. Your hosts can lead you to leash-free water play or a long walk on the 13-mile Klickitat Trail. In the European fashion, hallway bathrooms are shared. The rate is $64 for two people, including breakfast. The pet fee is $10. 100 7th St.; 800/447-6310; www.lylehotel.com.

Dallesport

PARKS, BEACHES, AND RECREATION AREAS

35 Columbia Hills State Park

😺😺😺 ◀● (See Central Washington map on page 210)

When the rising waters of the floodplain created by the Dallas Dam buried thousands of Native American petroglyphs on the canyon walls, a few examples were taken out and stored in the dam complex. They were eventually returned to the tribes, who graciously put them on display for everyone to see and appreciate at this state park. A cooperative effort between the Yakima Nation, Umatilla Reservation, Nez Percé, and tribes of the Warm Springs Reservation created the *Temani Pesh-wa* (Written on the Rock) Trail. You can see a few pictographs along an accessible pathway, but you would need to make advance reservations for the guided tour of the longer .5-mile trail, Friday and Saturday at 10 A.M., April–October.

You can enjoy the 338 acres of cool canyon cliffs, green picnic lawns protected by planted poplars, and 7,500 feet of Columbia riverfront all year. At milepost 58 on State Route 14, near Maryhill. Open 6:30 A.M.–dusk. Parking is $5 per day. Call 509/767-1159 for tour reservations.

36 Spearfish Park

😺😺🐕 (See Central Washington map on page 210)

The dogs wanted to include this hole-in-the-wall park because there are no leash rules to keep your dog from jumping in the lake to cool off in this dry hill country. There's not much infrastructure other than a boat ramp and a vault toilet. If you don't need anything more, you can catch a big trout for dinner and set up camp here free, with a four-day limit.

Turn east on Dock Road, from U.S. Highway 197, immediately north of the bridge to The Dalles. The paved road will become gravel as you travel through the Klickitat County Industrial Port. When you come to an unmarked fork in the road, take the left fork down a slight hill into the park.

Maryhill

No need to rub your eyes with your paws, for that is indeed a full-size replica of Stonehenge sitting on the bluff. It is America's first memorial to soldiers lost in World War I, built 1918–1929 by eccentric Quaker pioneer and engineer Sam Hill. Your dog may walk around and through it with you while it is open to the public between 7 A.M.–10 P.M. Sam Hill is also responsible for the classical building housing the Maryhill Museum of Art, built as a castle for his daughter Mary, on the hill. His visionary structures are the only part of Maryhill to survive; his hopes for a thriving Quaker community were never realized.

PARKS, BEACHES, AND RECREATION AREAS

37 Maryhill State Park

🐾🐾🐾 (See Central Washington map on page 210)

This is a wide, friendly park on the shores of the Columbia River at the easternmost point on the Gorge. Its lawns are a shockingly bright green in a sea of rolling brown hills, thanks to extensive watering. Check the sprinkler schedule on the board before you lay down a blanket if you don't want an unexpected shower. On the other hand, with temperatures often in the 90-degree range, you might not mind.

It's easy enough for you and your dog to dodge the sailboarders setting up and taking off from the beach into the wide, windy channel of the Columbia River. The sunny lawns are expansive and the shady trees are tall, and dogs aren't allowed in the designated beach area anyhow. The restrooms have private changing facilities. Maryhill has camping, but we can't recommend it due to highway and train noise.

Follow the signs from State Route 14 going east or U.S. Highway 97 south from Goldendale. The park is 12 miles south of Goldendale. Open 6:30 A.M.–dusk.

PLACES TO EAT

Gorge Gourmet To Go: The only "restaurant" in Maryhill is in a turquoise blue RV. It has oven-roasted turkey, herbed ham, and smoked salmon wraps; spinach or pepperoni calzones; smoothies and sweets; and two picnic tables surrounded by pretty flower baskets. Closed Wednesday. In the parking lot of Maryhill State Park; no phone.

Goldendale

The golden dales of this farming community are 35,000 acres of alfalfa and 25,000 acres of wheat. It's a good idea to fuel up your bodies and automobiles in Goldendale; if you're headed north, the next services are 50 miles away and almost 100 miles east. Just south of town on I-97 is a viewpoint where you can see the tip of Mt. Rainier and Mount St. Helens, all of Mt. Adams, and most of Mt. Hood.

There are no clouds to get in the way of the view from one of the country's largest public telescopes at Goldendale Observatory. Summer hours are 2–5 P.M. and 8 P.M.–midnight, Wed.–Sun.; winter hours are 1–5 P.M. and 7–9 P.M., Sat. and Sun. Call 509/773-3141 for information.

PARKS, BEACHES, AND RECREATION AREAS

38 Brooks Memorial Park

🐾🐾 (See Central Washington map on page 210)

This state park has nine miles of infrequently used hiking trails through high and dry alpine forests. Cooper seemed happy to let his webbed paws air out in a region that averages only 16 inches of rainfall per year, in contrast to Seattle's 36 inches on average. The picnic meadow is wide, with a couple of covered shelters. You'll catch glimpses of the Little Klickitat River and, if you make it to the top, views of Mt. Hood. It's more popular for camping than as a day-use area. November through April, the park is a snowy playground for winter sports.

It's located 13 miles north of Goldendale on U.S. Highway 97.

PLACES TO EAT

St. John's: Proceeds from this bakery, coffeehouse, and gift shop benefit the sisterhood of the St. John's Greek Orthodox Monastery. You benefit from phenomenal handmade Greek food and desserts, including stuffed grape leaves, gyros, hummus and pita, coconut cake, and baklava. Eat at patio tables, then browse the gift shop for items made by the sisters and bring some pastries home for your lucky family and friends. 2378 Hwy. 97; 509/773-6650; www.stjohnmonastery.org.

PLACES TO STAY

Brooks Memorial Campground: This camping spot with 23 utility sites and 22 tent sites is unremarkable but for one notable exception—it is blissfully quiet, whereas almost every other campground along the Gorge has trains running by on one side and a highway on the other. It's only 12 miles inland and a good night's sleep away. 2465 Hwy. 97; 888/CAMPOUT (888/226-7688); www.camis.com/wa.

Ponderosa Motel: Dogs are illogically charged by the pound at the Ponderosa; it's $7 for small, $9 for medium, and $14 for large. If he sits and smiles sweetly at the manager, perhaps your dog will look lighter than he really is. The rooms are fair, with kitchens or kitchenettes, and fairly priced at $49–65. 775 E. Broadway; 509/773-5842.

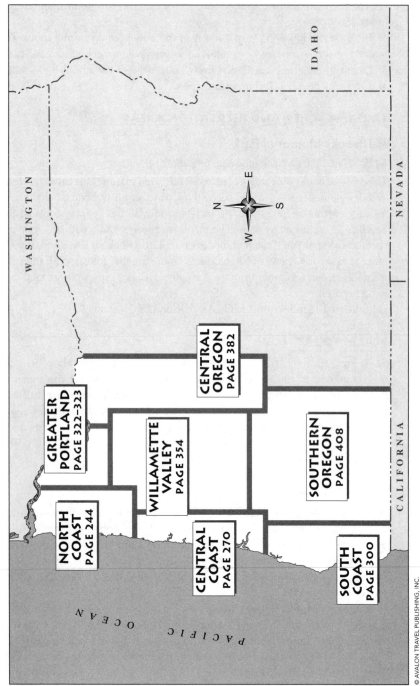

WASHINGTON

IDAHO

NEVADA

CALIFORNIA

PACIFIC OCEAN

N
E
S
W

GREATER PORTLAND
PAGE 322–323

NORTH COAST
PAGE 244

CENTRAL OREGON
PAGE 382

WILLAMETTE VALLEY
PAGE 354

SOUTHERN OREGON
PAGE 408

CENTRAL COAST
PAGE 270

SOUTH COAST
PAGE 300

OREGON

"Oregon is dogs' country," said a park host at a tiny county oasis in the Coquille River Valley. Well, if dog utopia is measured in trees, he's right—nearly 60 percent of Oregon, about 30 million acres, is forested. If dog heaven includes room to roam, Oregon wins again, with a population that's little more than half of Washington state's. There are extensive wilderness areas and rural farmlands. Extremely tough standards protect all of the state's natural resources.

Water dogs seeking paradise will be beside themselves to learn that every inch of Oregon's 360 miles of beaches are public lands. The beaches fall under the jurisdiction of the State Park system, which requires pets to be on leashes of six feet or less. This rule is ABSOLUTE in the campgrounds, but you'll see much more freedom of movement on the beach. Oregonians are split on the issue of keeping dogs leashed on the beach. Many feel that because they are public lands, they should be allowed to do as they please. Others argue that the beaches are crowded and dogs should be leashed to give everyone the opportunity to enjoy the waterfront. Most often, you'll be left to use your own judgment.

There are thousands of miles of riverfront waterways for swimming, boating, whitewater rafting, and the state's seemingly most popular pastime, salmon and steelhead trout fishing. Perhaps to avoid gender complications, the word fisherman has been universally replaced in Oregon with the word angler. If dogs had opposable thumbs, surely they would be anglers.

With the exception of the I-5 Highway Corridor, all roads are head-out-the-window, tongue-hanging-out scenic. Add in 14 national forests, almost 200 state parks, and dozens of dog events, and it sure is starting to sound like somebody up above had canines in mind when designing Oregon.

Humans enjoy a few extra perks in the Beaver State, too. Most recreation areas have park hosts in the summer, valuable resources to answer your questions and help you with things like campfire wood and trail maps. In Oregon, all shopping is free of sales tax, and you don't have to pump your own gas. Actually, state law requires that attendants pump gas for you (New Jersey is the only other state to have such a law).

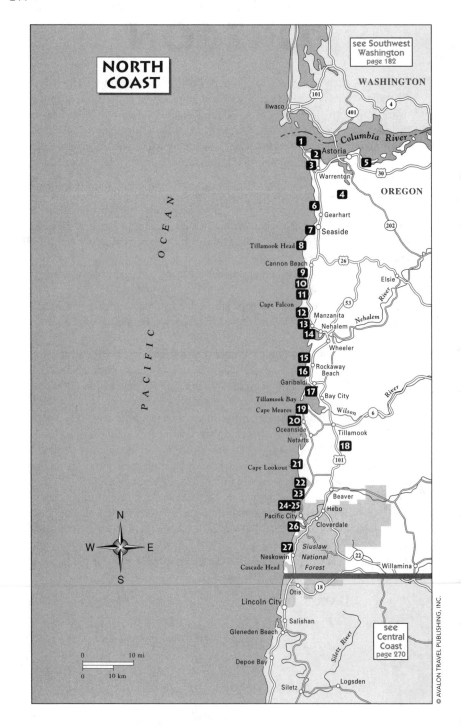

CHAPTER 9

North Coast

Though they are die-hard Washingtonians, Isis and Cooper will be the first to admit that Oregon's coast is the most beautiful place to play near big water. To keep the shores looking their best, more than 5,000 residents gather twice a year for massive beach cleanup work parties. Go to www.solv.org for more information if you'd like to participate in the Great Beach Cleanup.

There are so many fun parks and beach access points that the coast had to be split into three chapters. Even then, the dogs had an agonizing time choosing only the best. Basically, you can't lift a leg along the coast and miss a state park or public beach. Access to them may be limited in areas where uplands are private property, but once you are on the sand, there's nothing to stop you other than high tides, cliffs, and rocks. Well, that and the snowy plover. For such a tiny bird, this creature has stirred up a larger-than-life controversy between conservationists and people trying to preserve Oregon's tourist economy. Because the snowy plover is on the endangered species list, and because it makes its nest in the soft, dry sand, your dog's freedom may be restricted in marked areas March–September.

PICK OF THE LITTER—NORTH COAST

BEST PARKS
Ecola State Park, Cannon Beach (page 253)
Cape Lookout, Netarts (page 264)

BEST BEACHES
Oswald West, Cannon Beach (page 255)
Manhattan Beach, Rockaway Beach (page 259)

BEST EVENT
Dog Show at the Beach, Cannon Beach (page 266)

BEST PLACES TO EAT
Blue Heron French Cheese Company, Tillamook (page 262)
Whiskey Creek Café, Netarts (page 265)

BEST PLACES TO STAY
Ocean Lodge, Cannon Beach (page 256)
Coast Cabins, Manzanita (page 257)
Inn at Cape Kiwanda, Pacific City (page 268)

You don't have to wait until summer to enjoy the quintessential coast experience. Winter storms produce shows of power and drama. Rare finds, such as Japanese glass floats and agates, are more likely to wash ashore during these turbulent times. If you get chilled, it is legal to have campfires on Oregon beaches unless a fire restriction is posted. On the coast, you should be prepared for wet weather and ocean squalls at any time. Oregon's average coastal rainfall is actually higher than Seattle's, if you can believe that.

Of the 11 lighthouses on the coast, nine are on the National Register of Historic Places, seven of them open for public viewing and tours. Two are privately built and individually owned, open to the public only as sneak peaks from roadside viewpoints.

Astoria-Warrenton

Astoria is rich in history as the oldest settlement west of the Rocky Mountains. In 1792, explorer Robert Gray entered the mouth of the Columbia River, naming it after his ship, the *Columbia Rediviva.* It was here in 1805, where the

Lewis and Clark Expedition wintered at Fort Clatsop, waiting out the rain and preparing for their return journey. In 1811, American John Jacob Astor financed a trading post in what is now Astoria. As you walk through town, you can see the past in more buildings per square foot on the National Historic Register than any other Oregon location.

The Astoria Sunday Market along 12th Street, 10 A.M.–3 P.M., Mother's Day–October, has a long-standing reputation as a dog-friendly event.

PARKS, BEACHES, AND RECREATION AREAS

🗹 Fort Stevens

🐾🐾🐾 (See North Coast map on page 244)

At the tip of the Oregon Coast, this state park starts things off with a bang. Constructed during the Civil War, it remained an active military post until after World War II. Eight concrete gun batteries are the focal point of a self-guided tour of the abandoned fort, the tip of the iceberg in this 3,700-acre park.

There are five major parking areas to reach miles of windswept beach. Parking Lot A is primarily for equestrian access, Lot C has an excellent long-range viewing platform for watching the kiteboarders and surfers, and Lot D reaches the most protected area around the bend where the Columbia River meets the ocean. It's the lot without a letter, however, that's the most popular. The southernmost access point takes you to the wreck of the *Peter Iredale*. The rusting hulk of this English sailing ship remains onshore, almost a hundred years after it ran aground.

NATURE HIKES AND URBAN WALKS

The **Fort Clatsop National Memorial** is a national park where dogs *are* allowed, except in the buildings. According to the park ranger, you may keep your traveling companion with you because Meriwether Lewis was never far from Seaman, his faithful Newfoundland, on his journey.

Together, you can walk the grounds and peek into the cramped spaces of this life-size replica shared by the 31 men, Sacagawea, and her papoose, from December 7, 1805 until March 23, 1806. The fort was re-created according to exact specifications described in Lewis's journals. At a site in nearby Seaside, the men made salt to preserve meats for the return journey, hunted, sewed moccasins, and traded frequently with Chinook and Clatsop Native Americans. True to form for this region, it rained every day but 12 of their winter stay.

Open 9 A.M.–5 P.M. Entrance is $3 per person. Pets are free. 92343 Fort Clatsop Rd.; 503/861-2471; www.nps.gov/focl.

For some, the beach is too windy and exposed. They prefer to take to the seven miles of bike trails or five miles of hiking trails in the park, especially the two-mile, hikers-only loop around Coffenbury Lake. Isis has just one beef with this park—it's crowded, crowded, crowded.

Take U.S. Highway 101 four miles south of Astoria. Turn west on Warrenton Road and follow the signs another five miles to the park. Parking is $3. 503/861-1671.

❷ Cathedral Tree Trail

 (See North Coast map on page 244)

From 28th Street and Irving in downtown Astoria, you and your pup can climb up past lofty Cathedral Tree to Coxcomb Hill and the Astoria Column. Or, you can start and the top and wander down into town. Where you start depends on whether you want to go uphill first or last, and if you have someone to pick you up at either end. It is a pleasant, manageable walk, 1.5 miles one-way. There are stairs and boardwalks for the steep parts, and plenty of benches for resting along the way. The tree is about halfway through if you want to shorten the trip using it as a turnaround. Or, to lengthen your excursion, additional short trails spur off to the sides.

Street parking is very limited in town. You'll have better luck if you pay the buck to park at Astoria Column.

❸ Astoria Column

 (See North Coast map on page 244)

The park is called Astor Park, but it is known by its main feature, the 125-foot-tall Astoria Column, patterned after Rome's Trajan Column and Paris' Vendome. The bas-relief art of the column combines paint and plaster carvings to tell the story of Astoria's early white explorers and settlers.

Visitors crowd the column, leaving more room on the hillsides where your dog may better enjoy himself at view picnic tables and benches. The view from Coxcomb Hill, where the column sits, has always been stunning. It encompasses the wide mouth of the Columbia River, the grand Astoria-Megler Bridge, and the start of the Pacific Coast Scenic Highway, U.S. Highway 101. Naturally, it is the best place in town to watch sunsets.

From U.S. Highway 30, Marine Drive in town, turn north on 16th Street and follow the stencils of the column on the road. A parking permit is $1, good for a full calendar year. Open daylight–10 P.M.

❹ Youngs River Falls

(See North Coast map on page 244)

Captain Patrick Gass of Lewis and Clark's Corps of Discovery recorded happening upon these 65-foot falls during a hunting expedition in March of 1806. Today, this county park is an undeveloped picnic area with a gravel road and a few steps down to the bottom of the falls on the western fork of the Youngs River. Dogs can splash right into this local swimming hole and do some light hiking up and around the top of the cascade.

From U.S. Highway 30 in Astoria, take State Route 202, 10 miles to Olney and turn south on Youngs River Falls Loop Road for another 3.8 miles.

5 Bradley Viewpoint

😸 (See North Coast map on page 244)

This is a gem of a park, a tiny State Scenic Viewpoint with an incomparable vista of the Columbia Gorge from Clatsop Crest, 650 feet above sea level. It was one of the first parcels of land donated through the Oregon Highway Commission as a rest stop in 1922. There was a designated pet area, but unfortunately, it is no longer off-leash because a dog bit a little girl in the face. It's no secret that kids and dogs can be an unpredictable combination, regardless of who is or isn't at fault. At this point, think of it as a potty stop with superb scenery.

PLACES TO EAT

Bow Picker Fish and Chips: Order a half order or full order of fish and chips right off the boat—only this 1956 wooden boat is moored in a field at the corner of 17th and Duane, across from the Maritime Museum. They serve seasonally, usually May–October, with a couple of picnic tables under a tree and beverages in a cooler. Cash only. No phone.

Gunderson's Cannery Café and Wine Bar: The only thing casual about this fancy surf and turf restaurant are the dogs relaxing with their people on the outdoor patio with a riverfront view. The salads are fabulous. A wine and beer bar and Internet espresso counter share the building and the Gunderson name. Restaurant reservations are encouraged. Sixth Street Dock; 503/325-8642.

Paniolo Hawaiian: At Paniolo, they roll up the garage doors on the store-front, roll out the grill, and start slow-cooking the kalua pig, shoyu chicken, curried shrimp, and barbecued pork for you to put on rice or a Bahn Mi roll and wash down with mango, guava, or coconut juice. The smells wafting down the sidewalk past their picnic tables are torturously good for humans, much less a dog! 247 11th St.; 503/325-6674.

T. Paul's Urban Café: This bistro dishes up gourmet food and an "unclassic" sandwich menu in a relaxed atmosphere at large sidewalk tables, with fancy desserts, wine, and beer. They spin old standards in new ways, such as quesadillas with jerk chicken, tenderloin steak salad, and Cajun prawns on angel hair pasta. 1119 Commercial St.; 503/338-5133; www.tpaulsurbancafe.com.

PLACES TO STAY

Clementine's Bed and Breakfast: Judith welcomes dogs, has three of her own, and is happy to go with you on daily dog walks around town and lead you to the secret spots in the woods nearby. Her only request is that your dogs don't pee on her beautiful flowers—there's a park a few blocks away. Pets are allowed in the two rooms of the Moose Temple Lodge, next door to the main inn. The rate is $135 per night, plus a $15 cleaning fee per stay to cover all your pets. 847 Exchange St.; 503/325-2005; www.clementines-bb.com.

Crest Motel: There are no pet fees at this Scandinavian-themed motel, and the only rules are that you keep your pet leashed on the property and don't leave them unattended in the rooms. Rates range from $63 for non-view queens to $124 for a view suite. 5366 Leif Erickson Dr.; 503/325-3141 or 800/421-3141; www.crest-motel.com.

Fort Stevens Campground: This campground is a city with 174 full-hookup, 302 electrical, and 19 tent sites in 14 loops. Rates are $13–21. Believe it or not, vacancy goes fast in the summer. You'll need reservations. 100 Peter Iredale Rd.; 800/452-5687; www.reserveamerica.com.

More Accommodations: Please look under Chain Hotels in the Resources section for additional places to stay in this area.

Gearhart

Golf is the biggest attraction in this otherwise sleepy town, a tasteful and quiet oceanfront community that has been compared to old Cape Cod.

PARKS, BEACHES, AND RECREATION AREAS

🐾 Del Ray Beach

🐾🐾🐾 (See North Coast map on page 244)

At this State Recreation Site, you can experience the wonderful feeling of watching the rest of the world disappear. Once you climb over the sand dune that hides the parking lot, the only sight before you is the ocean and miles of flat, pristine beach. Light fog often obscures the town of Seaside and Tillamook Head, and even though cars are allowed on the wide, hard-packed sand, you'll watch the few that pass by shrink and fade in the distance. When the rest of the world seems too crowded and noisy, come to Del Ray to expand your horizons. Dogs appreciate the blissful simplicity of Del Ray's empty beach in the same way they can chase a single slobbery tennis ball until they drop.

From U.S. Highway 101, two miles north of Gearhart, turn west on Highlands Lane and continue straight onto the beach, or follow the left fork in the road until it dead-ends in the parking lot. There are no facilities at this beach.

PLACES TO STAY

Gearhart Ocean Inn: The cottage units at this 1941 restored inn are cool, crisp, and refreshing. The prices, ranging from $45–105, are equally refreshing, only five blocks to the nearest beach. A maximum of two pets are allowed in units #3–5, 7, and 8 for $15 per pet, per night. 67 N. Cottage Ave.; 503/738-7373; www.gearhartoceaninn.com.

Seaside

This classic beach town has attracted visitors for 150 years, and the antics of the seals at Seaside's famous aquarium have entertained people for more than 60 of those years. You can feel the old-timey character of Oregon's first resort town along Broadway, a crowded arcade street with bumper cars, carousel rides, and cotton candy and ice cream shops. For those times when only modern retail therapy will do, there are 25 factory outlet stores north of downtown.

Sunset Boulevard, immediately south of downtown, is an aptly named place to park and watch the day descend into twilight, along a rocky, driftwood-scattered section of the beach. While in Seaside, your canine companion might enjoy a side trip to Oregon's largest tree, a 750-year-old behemoth that's also the largest Sitka spruce in the United States. The pullout is on U.S. Highway 26, 1.5 miles east of the junction with U.S. Highway 101.

PARKS, BEACHES, AND RECREATION AREAS

7 Seaside Promenade

😸😸 (See North Coast map on page 244)

The city's famous sidewalk promenade, the Prom, has been an institution since 1908. The original was a boardwalk, replaced with a wide concrete structure in 1920. The aquarium marks the north end of the Prom, and on the south you'll pass the site of Lewis and Clark's Salt Camp, with a historic re-creation of the seawater boiling operation. In the middle is an automobile turnaround commemorating the end of the Lewis and Clark Trail. There are excellent views of crashing waves all along the 1.5-mile one-way walk. Many resident and visiting canines cruise the boardwalk, along with walkers, joggers, bikers, and skaters. You can get down onto the beach at the turnaround.

Downtown public parking is easiest to find in the Trend West Tower at the intersection of 1st Avenue and Columbia Street. A one-block walk from there to the beach puts you right in the middle of the Prom.

PLACES TO EAT

Big Foot Pub 'N' Grub: Patio dining at this bar and grill requires an extra level of vigilance. No matter how well-mannered, any canine culprit is going to be tempted to do a grab-and-dash, taking off with the juicy slab of prime rib that Big Foot is deservedly famous for serving. 2427 S. Roosevelt Dr.; 503/738-7009.

Dog Water Café: The folks at this premium pet place in the Seaside Factory Outlet Center invite you to "share a meal with a friend" at picnic tables, complete with treats and water bowls for Bowser. You'll be distracted from deciding what to eat by all of the fun dog pictures on the walls, making it even tougher to choose among clam chowder, quesadillas, pizza, and fresh deli sandwiches. 1111 N. Roosevelt Dr.; 503/738-0180.

PLACES TO STAY

Lanai Oceanfront Condos: These comfortable condos are inches away from the beach, with great views of the ocean and downtown Seaside. Four individually owned, decorated, and maintained units allow small pets for a $10 fee. You and your dog can sit on the patio and pretend you own oceanfront property for $98 per night. All nonsmoking; 3140 Sunset Blvd.; 503/738-6343; www.seasidelanai.com.

Seaside Inn Bed and Breakfast: This colorful oceanfront inn excels in whimsy, each room decorated no-holds-barred to its theme. Pets 40 pounds and under are allowed in the Sports Corner, Captain's Quarters, and Mountain Cabin. Dog lovers who can appreciate this quirky, lovable attention to detail are asked to read and abide by a reasonable set of pet policies, including leashing or carrying your dog when outside of the guest rooms. Rates range $95–185, plus a $25 flat fee per visit. 581 S. Promenade; 503/738-6403 or 800/772-7766; www.theseasideinn.com.

More Accommodations: Please look under Chain Hotels in the Resources section for additional places to stay in this area.

Cannon Beach

Named for a cannon washed ashore in 1846 from the wreck of the schooner *Shark*, this booming community is the busiest destination on the North Coast. It has a reputation for its dramatic sea stack rock formations, first-class lodging, and art from more than two dozen galleries and studio artists in a few short city blocks. The town bulges at the seams in the summer from the pressure of visitors and a growing number of permanent residents. For outdoor recreation with your dogs in and around Cannon Beach, the Dachshund Duo recommends the quiet season, October–April.

DIVERSIONS

Beach Dog Supply, in Pacific City on the Three Capes Scenic Loop, has everything you'll need to prepare your pet for a rough-and-tumble day at the beach. You'll find essentials for protection, such as life vests, raincoats, mesh paw water booties, and dog goggles for those sand-swept days. There's also a great selection of gifts and toys that only the hardest of hearts may not think are essential. Little extras include a hitching post in front of the store, a dog run with bags out back, and the **Rufus and Joe** espresso stand next door, for coffee and treats for canines and humans. 34950 Brooten Rd.; 503/965-6455.

In Cannon Beach, **Wags and Rags** is another absolute must-stop for dog lovers. People come into this boutique for dog raincoats when they get caught in the area's frequent squalls, then they get caught up in buying all kinds of other wonderful goodies. 123 S. Hemlock; 503/436-8887.

PARKS, BEACHES, AND RECREATION AREAS

8 Ecola Sate Park

🐾🐾🐾🐾 (See North Coast map on page 244)

Coop 'n' Isis decided that Ecola smelled like a four-paw park from the moment we drove through its 1,300 acres of forest, climbing up Tillamook Head to emerge at the first of many viewpoints at the Ecola Point parking lot. The whole park is nine miles of ocean frontage, from Cannon Beach to Indian Head, following the coastal exploratory routes of Lewis and Clark.

The first hike you might want to try extends 1.5 miles from Ecola Point to Indian Head Beach, alternating between forests of mythical proportions and cliffside ocean views. You can also drive straight to Indian Head Beach for a more relaxing trip, or to save your strength for more hiking.

The Clatsop Loop Interpretive Trail heads two miles north from Indian Head, with a brochure that traces the tale of a whale, where the Corps of Discovery, led by Lewis and Sacagawea, came upon Clatsop Indians carving and rendering whale blubber. At 1.5 miles, there is a hikers' camp, with three-sided bunk cabins, a fire ring, water, and restrooms. Beyond the camp, the trail leads to the Tillamook Rock Lighthouse Viewpoint. All of the trails have areas of steep cliffs; leashes are a must.

Twelve miles out to sea, the Tillamook Rock Lighthouse is the coast's most unusual in many ways. It is the only one to sit completely offshore. The poor lightkeepers in this precarious spot were so battered by waves that the sentinel earned the nickname Terrible Tilly. It is the only registered historical lighthouse to be privately owned. It serves the unique purpose of being a Columbarium, a storage place for ashes of the deceased.

From U.S. Highway 101, turn off at the north Cannon Beach Loop exit onto Sunset Boulevard, bear right on 5th Street for a few blocks, and follow the signs to turn off on Fir Street into the park. Open 6 A.M.–10 P.M. Parking is $3. 503/436-2844.

9 Tolovana Beach Wayside

 (See North Coast map on page 244)

This State Recreation Site is the largest beach access point in the city, giving beach walkers an entry point for a seven-mile stretch of active waterfront. Haystack Rock, the universal symbol of Cannon Beach, sits onshore. The 235-foot monolith is a National Wildlife Refuge, home to a large colony of bright tufted puffins. Between April and August, when the birds are nesting, you have to keep your distance. The rest of the year, you can investigate the tidepools around the other sea stacks, called the Needles. Your dog can pal around with the many other dogs who'll be on the beach.

There's a lot of action at Tolovana Beach. You can grab a cup of chowder at Mo's or catch a game of pickup volleyball. Strong winds make for good kite flying; in fact, you can tie a kite to your lawn chair and it'll fly itself. Although Cannon Beach city municipal code states that dogs are only required to be under good voice control, crowds may necessitate the dreaded leash.

From U.S. Highway 101, turn west on Hemlock Street, also called the Cannon Beach Loop. After .4 mile, turn left into the wayside parking lot. Open 5 A.M.–10 P.M.

10 Arcadia Beach

(See North Coast map on page 244)

From the gravel lot, you can park and sit and look at the ocean through the trees, for starters. After a short walk and a few wooden steps, your dog will love feeling the soft sand in his paws and the water lapping at his forelegs in this pretty cove. You might as well leave your shoes in the car, too. The odd sandal or sock left on the sand is a frequent sight, evidence of the irresistible urge to let loose on the beach and leave your cares behind. The waves crashing against offshore rocks have a hypnotic effect, inducing deep states of relaxation.

There is a restroom and a picnic table on a patch of lawn at this day-use only State Recreation Site, three miles south of Cannon Beach on U.S. Highway 101. Open 6 A.M.–10 P.M.

🐾 Hug Point

🐾🐾🐾 (See North Coast map on page 244)

You can trace the remnants of a treacherous stagecoach route carved into the cliffs that hugs the point on the north end of this glistening beach. You're free to walk along the historic roadbed, explore a couple of caves, and hike to a waterfall around the headland, but only at ebb tide. It's critical to know the tide table for the day, available free at the visitors center or most merchants in town, or you could find yourself stranded on the rocks as travelers of old often were.

The highway parking lot has drinking water and a vault toilet. This State Recreation Site is 4.3 miles south of Cannon Beach on U.S. Highway 101. Open 6 A.M.–10 P.M.

🐾 Oswald West

🐾🐾🐾🐾 (See North Coast map on page 244)

Oswald West, Oregon's Governor from 1911 to 1915, is the man responsible for designating all of the state's beaches as public lands, preserving the coastal playground for all to enjoy. This 2,474-acre State Park does him proud in honoring his memory and foresight.

As you drive into the park on U.S. Highway 101, there are a series of viewpoints as the road winds up and around Neah-Kah-Nie Mountain. From the southern parking lot, a .5-mile spur trail leads you down to Short Sands Beach, tucked into lush Smugglers Cove, a highly prized destination for surfers and boogie boarders chasing endless summer. The multiple waterways of Kerwin, Necarney, and Short Sands Creeks splash down the hillsides of Neah-Kah-Nie Mountain and Cape Falcon, the two headlands protecting the crescent beach. High-rise old-growth cedars, hemlocks, spruce, and firs hide a tent city of 30 hike-in sites; you can pass within feet of the campground and not see it.

From Manzanita to Arch Cape, a 13-mile stretch of the Oregon Coast Trail traverses the park. For you and your pup, two excellent trail sections break off from the beach spur. Cape Falcon is the easier trail, rising 300 feet in two miles to the tip of the headland to view the spectacle of the ocean below. The Neahkahnie Mountain Trail starts across a woozy suspension bridge, climbs switchbacks to a meadow, then crosses the highway on the way up to the summit at 1,631 feet. Up in this rarified air, every few footsteps lead you to another ocean vista.

Trail maps, wheelbarrows to transport camping gear, restrooms, and a drinking fountain are located in a second, larger parking lot on the east side of the highway. Oswald West is on U.S. Highway 101, 10 miles south of Cannon Beach. 503/368-3575.

PLACES TO EAT

Clark's: The brick patio easily seats 50 at this pub, where you can wash down a good burger or wood-fired pizza with a draft beer or wine by the glass. 264 E. 3rd St.; 503/436-8944.

PLACES TO STAY

Inn at Arch Cape: This intimate retreat is perfectly placed between Hug Point and Oswald West. Rooms recall an earlier, gracious era when the well-to-do summered at the coast. Each has tongue-and-groove pine interiors and beach rock fireplaces, with wood provided. Two dogs are allowed in rooms #3–6, for $15 per pet, per night. Rates vary $75–145 seasonally. 79340 Hwy. 101; 503/738-7373 or 800/352-8034; www.innatarchcape.com.

Ocean Lodge: This motel is sparkling and modern, nearly perfect. The management doesn't care if your pet is as big as a Mack truck, as long as he is well behaved. Treats and bags are provided, and there's a pet shower on the lawn along the beach path. There are eight non-view pet rooms, six of which have king-size beds and Jacuzzis, and six oceanfront pet rooms available. Rates range $189–289 for two–four people, plus $15 per pet, per night; there is a two-pet maximum. All rooms are non-smoking; 2864 S. Pacific; 503/426-2241 or 888/777-4047; www.theoceanlodge.com.

Oswald West Campground: For a more pristine camping experience, try one of 30 walk-in tent sites. It's about a third of a mile down to the campground, and you can borrow a wheelbarrow for no charge. There are restrooms and drinking water, but no showers. Open March–October on a first-come, first-served basis. Rates are $10–14. 503/368-3575.

Shaw's Oceanfront Bed and Breakfast: From the back deck at Shaw's, you and your dog can step into the fenced backyard, through the gate, and onto the beach. This casual home includes a separate bedroom, living room, and kitchen for preparing meals and snacks, except for breakfast, which is made for you. The entire two-bedroom suite is yours for $170 a night, $145 per night if you book for two or more nights. Pets are an additional $30 per stay. 79924 Cannon Rd.; 503/426-1422 or 888/269-4483; www.shawsoceanfrontbb.com.

St. Bernards Bed and Breakfast: There are no St. Bernards at this chateau, just a Maltese who thinks she is one. Pre-screened dogs may be permitted in the Provence Room, an intimate suite on the garden level with its own entrance through elegant French doors. It's the only room with a terrace and a Jacuzzi tub. Darn. The rate is $209 per night; there's no pet fee. 31970 E. Ocean Rd.; 503/436-2800; www.st-bernards.com.

Surfsand Resort: This large, cheerful resort openly brags about their pet-friendliness by sponsoring Cannon Beach's annual Dog Show on the Beach. Dogs are welcome in all types of rooms except waterfront Jacuzzi suites, for a $12 pet fee. Pet-friendly condos and vacation rental homes are available as well. Your dog will receive a basket of goodies at the front desk and there are puppy pick-up papers everywhere for your convenience. Room rates range $139–289; see the website for home selection and pricing. 147 W. Gower; 800/547-6100; www.surfsand.com.

Manzanita

This smaller beach community at the foot of Neah-Kah-Nie Mountain is so popular with the canine crowd, it has earned the flattering nickname Mutt-zanita. There are a few choice shops, cafés, and a lovely beach on a loop off the beaten highway.

PARKS, BEACHES, AND RECREATION AREAS

13 Neah-Kah-Nie Beach

🐾🐾🐾 (See North Coast map on page 244)

The name of this city beach is sometimes simplified to Neahkahnie, and more often just Manzanita Beach. There are tales of buried treasure, of a Spanish galleon strayed off course and wrecked at the foot of the mountain. No one has unearthed gleaming gold bullion, but artifacts such as a wine cup and a beeswax candle prove at least part of the story. As for beach treasures, the early bird gets the best pick of seashells, agates, and driftwood, or, seaweed, flotsam, and jetsam, as your dog may prefer. Beachcombers are allowed to take the treasures they find—including driftwood, shells, sand dollars, and agates—unless in a protected refuge area or marked signs indicate otherwise. Because your dog may be tempted to stray, it is wiser to stay leashed on this hectic beach.

From U.S. Highway 101, turn west on Laneda Avenue through town, and turn onto Ocean Road. Park at any one of several roadside areas and walk straight onto the beach.

PLACES TO EAT

Marzano's Pizza Pie: This restaurant's takeout pizza wins Cooper's vote for best on the coast. The cooks at Marzano's take great pride in their house-made spicy Italian sausage. Cash, checks, and credit cards accepted. 60 Laneda Ave.; 503/368-3663.

PLACES TO STAY

Coast Cabins: Isis would like to hire the interior decorator and landscaper for these exceptional cabins, which would be right at home in the pages of *Metropolitan Home* magazine. A package of goodies will await your pet, who is allowed in all five cabins. The property is a few blocks from the beach. Ah, but such luxury is worth the walk. Rates range $125–245, plus $20 per pet, per night. All non-smoking; 635 Laneda Ave.; 503/368-7113; www.coastcabins.com.

Manzanita Rental Company: This agency rents 22 pet-friendly vacation homes with a wide variety of capacities and rates. Each listing on its website clearly states whether or not pets are allowed. There's a $15 per pet nightly charge at all homes, and some may have limits on the number of pets depending on the size of the property. It's easiest to call and discuss your desires and dog situation with an agent; they'll know exactly what they've got that will meet your needs. 686 Manzanita Ave.; 503/368-6797 or 800/579-9801; www.manzanitarentals.com.

Ocean Inn: It's out the door and onto the beach for you if you stay at these airy oceanfront cottages, which allow a maximum of two pets in units 2, 3, and 4. Rates range $135–165, plus $10 per pet, per night. All non-smoking; 32 Laneda Ave.; 503/368-7701 or 866/368-7701; www.oceaninnatmanzanita.com.

Wheeler and Nehalem

When the railroad completed a link between Wheeler and Portland in 1911, the town quickly became the site of the largest sawmill on the coast. Even as the logging industry dried up and fishing declined, Wheeler retained a modest level of fame thanks to the Rinehart Arthritis Clinic and Dr. Rinehart's "miracle cure." Protected by Nehalem Bay, Wheeler is sometimes called *pukalani,* the hole in the sky, staying sunny when it's raining everywhere else.

PARKS, BEACHES, AND RECREATION AREAS

14 Nehalem Bay

🐾🐾🐾 (See North Coast map on page 244)

It's easy to get to this ultra-popular State Park, and there's plenty to do once you've arrived. On the four-mile spit enclosing Nehalem Bay, there's a landing strip for fly-in campers, six miles of horse trails and a separate camp for equestrians, and two miles of paved, wheelchair-accessible trails for pedestrians and cyclists.

Any noise from the airstrip and the hectic campground fades away completely once you've climbed over a substantial dune to the ocean. Four miles of soft white sand and ocean views stretch along the Nehalem Spit to the south, and Neah-Kah-Nie Mountain towers overhead. Small dog warning: Winds here are strong. A kite tied to a collar will fly itself and Toto just might get whisked off to Kansas.

If beachcombing isn't your thing, the waters are quieter on the east side of the spit. A boat ramp provides access to kayaking, crabbing, and fishing.

From U.S. Highway 101, the turnoff to the park is .8 mile north of the center of town in Nehalem, and another 1.2 miles to the entrance, marked with an unmistakable timber archway. Open 6:30 A.M.–10 P.M. Parking is $3. 503/368-5154.

PLACES TO EAT

The Bunkhouse Restaurant: The owners are relaxed about allowing dogs on the porches while you eat. At worst, if someone on the front porch would rather not eat with a dog nearby, they may ask you to move to the back porch. After you're finished with your heaping plate of comfort food, you won't feel like moving anywhere for a while. 36315 Hwy. 101; 503/368-5424.

Mom's Beach House Café: The Dachsie Twins wish their mother could cook food that tastes this good. The soups, salads, sandwiches, chowder, and baked goods are made from scratch daily. For diners and dogs on a budget, a bowl of rice and beans is only $1. 495 Nehalem Blvd. (Hwy. 101); 503/368-3719.

PLACES TO STAY

Nehalem Bay Campground: This campground is a parking lot of 267 electrical sites, one big block party with a changing cast of characters. Pets of every breed abound. Sites are $16–20, and summer reservations are a necessity. 800/452-5687; www.reserveamerica.com.

Wheeler on the Bay: This non-smoking lodge and marina is a lively place to stay. In addition to the best boat-watching dock on the bay, it has video rentals, kayaks, charter fishing, and on-site massage. The property managers have a sideline business selling bird kites, the most aerodynamic flyers you'll find anywhere. Room rates range $80–135 for homey cottages, plus $10 per pet, per night. In the busy summer, they allow pets of 20 pounds or less; there's more leeway for big pets in the off-season. 580 Marine Dr.; 503/358-5858; www.wheeleronthebay.com.

Rockaway Beach

This resort community emerged as a getaway for Portlanders in the 1920s, focusing on the seven miles of sandy beach accessible from the center of town.

PARKS, BEACHES, AND RECREATION AREAS

15 Manhattan Beach

🐾🐾🐾🐾 (See North Coast map on page 244)

This State Recreation Site is thoroughly relaxing. The beach is secluded, the parking lot is protected from the highway, and the picnic tables are sheltered from the wind in groves of shore pine. There are restrooms and one main path of about 50 feet to the beach. Once onshore, there's no development on the hill behind you, and nothing to interrupt the glorious view before you. The Wonder Wieners prefer this type of beach wayside—one without an attached campground and not in a city center.

Turn west on Beach Street from U.S. Highway 101, two miles north of Rockaway Beach, and immediately turn left onto the park access road.

16 Rockaway Beach City Wayside

😺😺 (See North Coast map on page 244)

This city park provides beach access, pure and simple. There's a parking lot with room for about 50 cars, although it's not well protected from traffic. Amenities include a drinking fountain and restroom, outdoor shower, volley-ball beach setup, and a few picnic tables and viewing benches in the parking lot area. The beach extends for seven miles along the homes, hotels, shops, and restaurants of town.

From U.S. Highway 101, turn west on S. First Street into the park.

PLACES TO EAT

Dragonfly Sisters Café: Dogs and kids love this place, with its sandbox, lawn, and picnic tables crammed out back in the alley behind the store. The café offers the traditional soup, salad, and sandwich selections, yummy baked goods, and ice cream and espresso. 127 Miller St.; 503/355-2300.

PLACES TO STAY

Tradewinds Motel: One pet per room is allowed in six of the oceanfront suites at this motel with big rooms and even bigger views. Rates range $77–134, plus $10 per night for your dog, up to a maximum of $40 per stay. There's a lawn in the back with picnic tables and barbecue grills by the beach. 523 N. Pacific St.; 503/355-2112 or 800/824-0938; www.tradewinds-motel.com.

Garibaldi

Captain Robert Gray was the first known U.S. explorer to spend time in this area on what is now Tillamook Bay. His crew of 12 men arrived on the Sloop *Lady Washington* in 1778 and left hastily in a week after a skirmish with Native Americans onshore. A replica of his tall ship moors and sails from harbor in Aberdeen, Washington.

The pace of life is calm in this fishing and oystering village. The Boat Basin at the mouth of the Miami River is the primary hive of activity, for commercial and sport anglers. To see the boats in the harbor, and perhaps get some fresh fish or crab for dinner, turn west on 7th from U.S. Highway 101 to Mooring Basin Road.

PARKS, BEACHES, AND RECREATION AREAS

🐾 Barview Jetty County Park

🐾🐾 (See North Coast map on page 244)

The Barview Jetty protects the boats entering and exiting Tillamook Bay, a rich estuary nicknamed the Ghost Hole. The nickname comes either from the ghost shrimp harvested in the bay, a sought-after bait for anglers; from the elusive 1,000 pound sturgeon who lives forever out of reach of anglers' lines; or for the ghost of a disgruntled early settler who was crushed to death by a log he tried to move on the hillside.

It's fun to watch the waves crash against the jetty wall and the boats entering and exiting the harbor while your dog sniffs around the beach extending north. You'll have to time your beach walks for low tide, although you can meander through the sand dunes and campground anytime. 503/322-3477.

PLACES TO STAY

Barview Jetty Campground: The brave windblown trees on this beach jetty provide a decent amount of privacy in this 245-site county campground with hot showers and heated restrooms. Tent sites are $15, RV hookups are $20, and pull-through sites are $25. For reservations, call and leave a message at 503/322-3522 with your name, address, phone number, site request, and dates.

Bayshore Inn: The simple rooms at this motel offer all the standard amenities at the pocketbook-protecting rate of $50–70 per night, plus a $7 pet fee. It's conveniently located a block from the city park. 227 Garibaldi Ave.; 503/322-2552.

Tillamook

At Tillamook, the Pacific Coast Scenic Highway heads inland for a short detour through rich dairy valleys, through countless cows to the Tillamook Cheese Factory, the Pacific Northwest's most famous purveyor of cheese and ice cream.

PARKS, BEACHES, AND RECREATION AREAS

🐾 Munson Creek Falls

🐾🐾🐾 (See North Coast map on page 244)

It's an easy .5-mile out-and-back trot through ancient Sitka spruce and western red cedar to see the 319-foot falls, the highest in the Coastal Range. You'll follow rippling Munson Creek and pass by the world's second-largest recorded spruce, 260 feet tall and eight feet in diameter. It's a beautiful walk through this State Natural Site. Cooper only wishes it was longer.

From U.S. Highway 101, six miles south of Tillamook, turn west on Munson Creek Road. After .7 mile, the road becomes gravel, and you'll follow the signs to take first a left fork in the road, then a right, to reach the circular driveway at 1.5 miles.

PLACES TO EAT

Blue Heron French Cheese Company: The hens, roosters, turkeys, and pheasants are running amok in Tillamook, all over the grounds of this farmstead converted into a fantastic deli and gourmet food store. You can put together an amazing picnic basket full of food to go or eat in their picnic area, but keep your pet leashed to prevent him from chasing his own dinner. Kids like to buy oats in the store to feed the farm animals. 2001 Blue Heron Dr.; 503/842-8281; www.blueheronoregon.com.

Tillamook Cheese Factory: Although she would dearly love to join you, your dog will have to wait outside while you take the self-guided tour through the factory, but you'll be forgiven instantly if you sneak a couple of cheese curd samples into your pocket for her. There's a gourmet gift shop, ice cream counter, and deli in the factory, and you can share together after the tour on the lawn of the visitors center next door. 4175 Hwy. 101; 503/815-1300; www.tillamookcheese.com.

PLACES TO STAY

In this area, chain hotels offer the best choices for dogs and their owners; please look under Chain Hotels in the Resources section.

Cape Meares

Separating from Highway 101 in Tillamook, the Three Capes Scenic Loop—to Cape Meares, Cape Lookout, and Cape Kiwanda—presents a quieter side of the Oregon Coast. Rush hour might be the morning launch of the dory fishing boats into the surf, and traffic congestion probably means there are cows blocking the road. This is life in the slow lane, where you can pull over to the side of the road to watch a blue heron nabbing fish in Netarts Bay or an oysterman hauling nets out of the mud.

PARKS, BEACHES, AND RECREATION AREAS

🔟 Cape Meares State Scenic Viewpoint

🐾🐾🐾 (See North Coast map on page 244)

Your dog will get her exercise as you visit each of this cape's unique attractions, situated on a bluff 200 feet above the ocean. The paved path to the lighthouse is a quick .2-mile roundtrip. Next, a .4-mile out-and-back gravel loop leads to the Octopus Tree, a many-trunked Sitka spruce. Immediately to the north of the entrance is a .25-mile quickie that loops around another giant Sitka in this protected coastal old-growth forest. On all the trails, you can see the many bird species that nest in Cape Meares National Wildlife Refuge to the north and on the rock formations at sea, including peregrine falcons, a species slowly recovering from near extinction. There's a picnic meadow to the south of the parking area, a neat surprise tucked between a rock alcove and the well-protected, fenced bluff.

If all the sightseeing hasn't worn you out, there's a moderately difficult, two-mile trail down to a deserted beach that takes you through and under fallen old growth. For your dog's enjoyment, we can practically guarantee that this path will be muddy and plastered with giant banana slugs.

The Cape Meares Lighthouse is puny by most standards, only 38 feet tall. It was illuminated in 1890 and wasn't replaced with an automatic beacon until 1963. It has a gift shop and is open for tours April–October. Call 503/842-2244.

From the intersection of State Route 6 and U.S. Highway 101 in Tillamook, follow the signs for the Three Capes Scenic Loop, which begins on Netarts Highway. You'll bear right at Bayocean Road and travel four miles, then left on Cape Meares Loop for another two miles.

Oceanside

Look up! It's a bird…it's a plane…it's—actually, it's probably a hang glider, riding the wind currents down from this hillside community to the beach below. In this quiet community, the most strenuous activities are usually hang gliding, paragliding, and kite flying.

PARKS, BEACHES, AND RECREATION AREAS

20 Oceanside Beach

🐾 🐾 (See North Coast map on page 244)

Located in town, the beach at this State Recreation Site offers some of the best agate-hunting on the coast in the winter storm season when outgoing currents strip away the sand. Agates are colorful gemstones, rounded by the sea and tossed onto the sand. They can be opaque in white, carnelian, red, blue-black, and dark green. Many are translucent, and crystal formations can be seen inside when they are held up to the sun. Look for them in loose gravel at the tide line.

Year round, Oceanside has great views of the Three Arch Rocks National Wildlife Refuge. These offshore rock formations support Oregon's largest colony of tufted puffins and the largest colony of common murres outside of Alaska. The barking you'll hear isn't from dogs, but from the Oregon Coast's only breeding grounds for Stellar sea lions. The beach extends about a mile and a half in either direction. There are two parking levels, restrooms, and a hillside picnic table.

Oceanside is 11 miles west of Tillamook on the Three Capes Scenic Loop. You can approach from the south on Netarts Highway or from the north on Bayocean Road.

Netarts

PARKS, BEACHES, AND RECREATION AREAS

21 Cape Lookout

🐾 🐾 🐾 🐾 (See North Coast map on page 244)

Of the three trails available from the Cape Lookout Trailhead, the moderate, 2.5-mile Cape Trail is the most popular. For a nice change of pace, the trail starts at the highest point and begins with a gradual descent 400 feet to the tip of the cape, rambling through a coastal forest. When you reach the ocean, your grand view encompasses the ocean to the horizon, Cape Kiwanda to the south, and Cape Meares to the north. The South Trail is steeper, winding 1.8 miles down to a secluded beach south of the cape and the 2.3-mile North Trail leads to the campground and the beach at Netarts Bay. There are steep drop-offs on all of the trails. Protect your dog by keeping her on a short leash at this state park.

If your dog would rather head right for the water, continue north of the trailhead entrance to the campground. There's a large day-use parking area, sheltered and viewpoint picnic tables, and a gorgeous beach.

From Sand Lake Road on the Three Capes Scenic Loop, turn onto Cape

Lookout Road for 3.5 miles to the trailhead parking lot and another 2.5 miles to the campground. Open 7 A.M.–9 P.M. Parking is $3. 503/842-4981.

PLACES TO EAT

Whiskey Creek Café: This down-home café's reputation reaches far and wide, pulling people in with homemade pie, chowder and cioppino soups, and oysters fresh from Netarts Bay. The word will spread quickly throughout the dog community that there's also a fat jar of dog cookies at the door and picnic table seating with views of Netarts Bay around the side. A stack of magazines and family board games encourages you to relax and sit a spell. No credit cards; 6060 Whiskey Creek Rd.; 503/842-5117.

PLACES TO STAY

Cape Lookout Campground: At this state park, sites closer to the sea are more open, in trees stripped bare of leaves by rough shore breezes. For privacy head to loops C and D. There are 38 RV and 173 tent sites, for $12–20. Summer reservations are wise. 800/452-5687; www.reserveamerica.com.

Pacific City

Imagine a fishing village without docks, marinas, piers, or a wharf. On the south end of the Three Capes Loop, Pacific City is the home of the oceangoing Dory fishing fleet, flat-bottomed boats that launch directly into the surf. When they've caught their load for the day, they return by running the boats full-throttle onto shore to a sand-slide stop. They have right-of-way, so you and your pooch better watch out!

Your dog will get a kick out of Pacific City's large population of domestic bunnies who have taken to the wild, hopping all over town.

PARKS, BEACHES, AND RECREATION AREAS

22 Sand Lake

 (See North Coast map on page 244)

Sand Lake is a playground for all-terrain vehicles (ATVs), spinning and spitting their way through the sand dunes at the East Dunes and West Winds sites on the northwest side of the lake. For quiet dune hikes with your dog and playtime in the water, turn to the left as you enter the recreation area to the Fisherman Day-Use Area, where ATVs are not allowed. At high tide, there really is a lake, but when the tide is out, you can fool around on the mushy lake of sand and walk .75 mile out to the ocean.

From Sand Lake Road on the Three Capes Scenic Loop, turn southwest on Galloway Road for 2.3 miles.

DOG-EAR YOUR CALENDAR

Your darling doesn't have to be a purebred to participate in the **Dog Show at the Beach** in Cannon Beach on the second Saturday in October. Pedigree isn't the point at this event, which features 1st, 2nd, and 3rd place ribbons in more than 20 categories—everything from biggest ears to best tail wag. The event is graciously sponsored by the Surfsand Resort and Nutro Pet Products. There's no fee to enter, and any donations you wish to make will go to the Clatsop County Animal Shelter. Buy lots of raffle tickets! For more information or to make a donation, call 503/426-2274 or 800/547-6100; www.cannonbeach.org.

Farther south, Beach Dog Supply in Pacific City hosts **Paws in the Snow: A Canine Christmas Carnival** with dog massage, a cake walk for canines, toenail painting, and pictures with Santa Paws. All proceeds benefit the Tillamook Animal Shelter. Dates vary between late November and early December each year. Call 503/965-6455 for more information.

23 Clay Myers

🐾🐾🐾 (See North Coast map on page 244)

The 180 acres of Whalen Island became a state park in 2000, one of the most significant new State Natural Areas in 30 years. From a small, gravel parking loop, you can walk straight to a bayfront beach or to estuary and wetland overlooks on short, wheelchair-accessible trails. Cooper recommends going the long way around on an easy, level wood-chip trail that loops 1.4 miles through Sitka spruce, shore pine, and salal dripping with moss. At low tide, you can dig for sand shrimp or walk .75 mile along the tidelands to the ocean. In this pristine ecosystem, you can watch the salmon returning to spawn in the fall and the salmon smolts struggling back to the ocean in the spring. Whether or not you are a fan of state lotteries, you can thank the people of Oregon for voting to use lottery funds to purchase this public treasure.

The site is maintained simply, with a vault toilet and trail map. From Pacific City, follow the Three Capes Scenic Route north on Sand Lake Road for 5.5 miles and turn left at the sign for Whalen Island–Clay Myers.

24 Tierra del Mar Beach

🐾🐾 (See North Coast map on page 244)

Sometimes there's a bit too much going on at Cape Kiwanda with the dory boats crashing on shore and cars driving on the beach, so families and picnickers come the tiniest bit north to this beach access point to escape the ruckus.

Vehicles are prohibited on the beach to the north May–September, and on weekends and holidays all year. Tierra del Mar is on Kiwanda Drive a bit less than a mile north of Cape Kiwanda.

25 Cape Kiwanda

🐾🐾🐾 (See North Coast map on page 244)

The golden, wave-carved sandstone cliff of Cape Kiwanda, jutting a half mile out to sea, is of one Oregon's most frequently photographed natural wonders. It is the smallest of the three capes, yet it's usually the most exciting. Heading north from the parking area, carefully climb to the top of the dune. From this perch, you can get a better view of the haystack rock and watch the surfers, boogie boarders, and dory boats launching into the ocean. At low tide, the beach extends south for four miles to the tip of Nestucca Spit. Beachcombers on the cape often come away with a great selection of sand dollars.

On the same site as this State Natural Area, Tillamook County maintains the parking lot, a restroom, and a wheelchair-accessible ocean viewing deck. Cars are allowed on the beach during certain times of the year.

From U.S. Highway 101, take the Pacific City exit at Brooten Road. Follow it for 2.8 miles into town, and turn left on Pacific Avenue across the bridge. Turn right at the stop sign onto Cape Kiwanda Drive, and follow it another mile.

26 Bob Straub State Park

🐾🐾🐾 (See North Coast map on page 244)

This undisturbed beach on the Nestucca River sand spit is a wonderful spot for a scenic beach walk. To the south, you can see Porter Point and Cannery Hill, behind you are the uninterrupted dunes you climbed over to reach the beach, and to the north is a haystack rock formation with good potential for watching wave action and nesting birds. On the bay side of the spit, the Nestucca River is the stuff of fishing legend, where it's not uncommon to hook a 50-pound Chinook salmon.

From Pacific City, turn west at the only four-way stop in town, go straight through the next intersection, and turn left immediately into the park. The park has restrooms and a drinking fountain.

PLACES TO EAT

Village Coffee Shop: If Pacific Northwesterners weren't so obsessed with coffee, this café might have a more descriptive name, such as the Village Home of the World's Largest Chicken-Fried Steak. At patio picnic tables, dogs are treated to free toast scraps while they wait for the leftovers from your large portions of steak and eggs or clam chowder. 34910 Brooten Rd.; 503/965-7635.

PLACES TO STAY

Inn at Cape Kiwanda: Every warm, light-filled room at the inn has an ocean-view balcony and a gas fireplace. In the Jacuzzi rooms, the ocean view is from the tub! The beach and the pub are right across the street, and there's a bag dispenser, washing station, and dog walk on the north side of the building. Treats and extra blankets are provided at check-in. Room rates range $109–179, up to $249 for Jacuzzi rooms. The pet fee is $20. This is an all non-smoking facility. 33105 Cape Kiwanda Dr.; 503/965-7001 or 888/965-7001; www.innatcapekiwanda.com.

Sand Lake Campgrounds: The U.S. Forest Service operates three campgrounds. East Dunes and West Winds are open all year, with $10 camping on open lots and $5 camping on the sand. There are 101 sites at Sandbeach Campground; 60 require reservations, the other 41 are on a first-come, first-served basis. Sites are $16. Sandbeach closes for the winter. 877/444-6777; www.reserveusa.com.

Sea View Vacation Rentals: This pet-friendly agency has an easy-to-navigate website, which clearly lists the properties in Pacific City and Neskowin that allow pets. 6335 Pacific Ave.; 503/965-7888 or 888/701-1023; www.seaview4u.com.

Whalen Island Campground: All 30 county park sites are beachfront, on the quiet estuary of this park adjacent to Clay Myers State Natural Area. This primitive campground with vault toilets is appropriate for small RVs or tents only. Sites are $10. For reservations, call and leave a message at 503/322-3522 with your name, address, phone number, site request, and dates.

Neskowin

After heading inland through Tillamook, the Pacific Coast Scenic Highway meets up with the ocean again in this tiny town with posh cottages, two golf courses, a general store, and a restaurant. Slightly north, you can canoe and kayak in Nestucca Bay's estuary waters through strands of spruce and ocean views. It's a beautiful spot that escapes the tourist frenzy.

PARKS, BEACHES, AND RECREATION AREAS

27 Neskowin Beach

🐾🐾🐾 (See North Coast map on page 244)

The beach cove at Neskowin is dominated by the island known as Proposal Rock. The history of the island's name is vague, with equal weight given to the stories that it was an Indian Chief's daughter or an early Postmaster's daughter who received a proposal here. There's no mistaking the profile of the rock, partially onshore and partially in the water, topped with a hairdo of tall spruce trees.

After crossing the parking lot, which has a couple of picnic tables and a restroom, and carefully walking across Hawk Street, you'll walk to the beach on a sidewalk that starts out paved and rapidly becomes engulfed in the deep, silky sand of the shore. You'll share the tidepools and surf with local dogs who wander about and people from the nearby inn, but few others. It is a pleasant place to while away the hours—a pursuit dogs have mastered.

Turn west at the sign for Neskowin Beach Wayside on Hawk Street from U.S. Highway 101 in Neskowin.

PLACES TO EAT

Hawk Creek Café: Although your dog can't join you on the deck, she can roll around on the lawn in front and chat with local dogs who regularly wander by. You can secure her leash to a large post in the middle of the yard while you tuck into harvest potatoes and pancakes or lunch sandwich-and-salad plates. 4505 Salem Ave.; 503/392-3838.

PLACES TO STAY

Proposal Rock Inn: Each room is individually owned and decorated at this inn. Some have fireplaces, most have kitchens, and what they all have in common are balconies and patios with views of Hawk Creek or the ocean and the rock. A bridge crosses the creek to the beach. Room rates are only $44–89; $135 for suites that sleep six. The best oceanfront prices on the coast get even better with 2-for-1 return customer discounts and Entertainment Book deals. The pet fee is $15. 48988 Hwy. 101 S.; 503/392-3115.

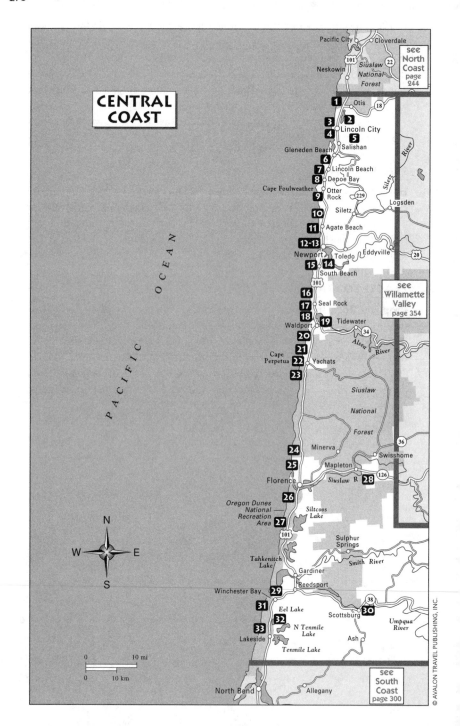

CENTRAL COAST

CHAPTER 10

Central Coast

Oregon's central coast is all about more— lodging options, beachfront parks, tourists, and infinitely more sand in the Oregon Dunes, an ever-changing landscape at the whim of the winds and tides. This section of the coast begins with dramatic capes and cliffs to the north that give way to the graceful dunes.

Even the surf is higher, and more dangerous, causing nine wrecks of significant historical record from 1852 to 1912. Four of Oregon's nine historic lighthouses cling to the rocks along Central Oregon, the sentinels to protect other mariners from similar fates. Two of them are in Newport at Yaquina Head and Yaquina Bay, one at Reedsport's Umpqua River, and the most famous at Heceta Head north of Florence.

For more than 30 pet-friendly properties for rent in Yachats, Waldport, Seal Rock, and other areas along the Central Coast, contact **Ocean Odyssey.** Pets are an additional $20 per pet, per stay with a maximum of two pets. Cleaning up after your pets is especially vital, as most of these are private homes. The office is in Clark's Market Plaza, 261 Hwy. 101, Yachats; 800/800-1915; www.ocean-odyssey.com (click the Pet Friendly button at the bottom of the home page).

PICK OF THE LITTER—CENTRAL COAST

BEST PARKS
Fogarty Creek, Lincoln Beach (page 279)
Oregon Dunes Overlook, Florence (page 294)

BEST TRAILS
Drift Creek Falls, Lincoln City (page 276)
Sweet Creek Falls, Mapleton (page 295)

BEST BEACHES
Beverly Beach, Newport (page 282)
Ona Beach, Seal Rock (page 286)
Driftwood Beach, Waldport (page 288)

BEST EVENTS
Easter Pet Parade, Gleneden Beach (page 278)
Mutt Masters Dog Show and Olympics, Lincoln City
(page 278)

BEST PLACES TO EAT
Sun Garden Café and Cyber Garden, Lincoln City (page 276)
Lighthouse Deli and Fish Co., South Beach (page 286)

BEST PLACES TO STAY
See Vue, Yachats (page 292)
Winchester Bay Inn, Winchester Bay (page 299)

NATIONAL FORESTS AND RECREATION AREAS

Siuslaw National Forest

The Siuslaw (Sigh-OOH-slaw) covers 630,000 acres from Tillamook to Coos Bay, bordered east-west by the Willamette Valley and the Pacific Ocean. Hardy Sitka spruce grow in the coastal zone, able to withstand ocean winds and dense fog. Inland, western hemlock grow under a thick canopy of Douglas fir. The Trip Planning section of the forest website, www.fs.fed.us/r6/siuslaw/recreation, is an excellent way to find trails, campgrounds, swimming, and horseback riding opportunities.

Oregon Dunes National Recreation Area (ODNRA)

The U.S. Forest Service manages a 47-mile sandbox between Florence and Coos Bay. While many will tell you that the dunes are a playground for off-highway vehicles (OHVs) or all-terrain vehicles (ATVs), approximately 27,200 of the park's 31,500 acres are reserved for people, dogs, and horses who feel otherwise. The ODNRA Ranger Station is in Reedsport (Junction of Hwy. 101 and Hwy. 38; 541/271-3495 or 800/247-2155; www.reedsportcc.org).

Lincoln City

This large coastal city is in the middle of everything. It's the halfway point between California and Washington, and it's on the 45th Parallel, the dividing line between the equator and the North Pole.

Lincoln City welcomes pets with open arms and good information about where to stay and local dog-oriented businesses. Call ahead for the Pet Friendly Vacation Guide, available at the visitors center (802 S.W. Hwy. 101; 541/996-1274; www.oregoncoast.org). You'll also want to grab a city map for 15 public beach access points along 14 miles of pristine beaches. The historic Taft District along S.W. 51st Street is a lively strip in town.

PARKS, BEACHES, AND RECREATION AREAS

🐾 Road's End

🐾🐾🐾 (See Central Coast map on page 270)

If you are on a mission to get to the beach, a couple of logs and some polished stones are all that separate you from the sand where the sidewalk ends. Then you're there, on the ocean, 14 miles of it south through Lincoln City. There's only one catch: You have to fight for the right to park on busy summer weekends. A few picnic tables are placed in the parking lot, functional as opposed to scenic.

This State Recreation Site commemorates the end of the road for the Old Elk Trail, a route used by Native Americans for thousands of years to reach summer fishing grounds on the Pacific Ocean.

From U.S. Highway 101, turn west on Logan Road and go to the end of the road. Open 6 A.M.–10 P.M.

🐾 Sand Point Park

🐾🐾🐾 (See Central Coast map on page 270)

Isis would be hard-pressed to choose a lakefront park when the ocean is so close, but this city park is a lovely place to enjoy the shores of Devil's Lake. There's a shady lawn—which you won't find on the beach—plus one picnic table in the sun and one in the shade. A wheelchair-accessible ramp leads

DIVERSION

A little absence now and then can make the heart grow fonder. Renew your puppy love by giving you and her a break at the **Critter Cottage** in Lincoln City. Doggie day care is $15 per pup for 1–5 hours, and only $20 for up to 10 hours from 8 A.M.–6 P.M., seven days a week and holidays. Overnight boarding is similarly well priced, and if she stays more than four days, they'll give your Bedlington a bath.

The same folks operate **Critter Comfort 'N' Care,** an at-home pet sitting service from Neskowin to Depoe Bay. Methods of payment are check with ID or cash only; 960 S.E. Hwy. 101; 541/996-7434.

down to a smidge of sand and a shallow swimming area. There's just enough room to launch a raft or do some dog paddling.

From U.S. Highway 101, turn at the north entrance to E. Devil's Lake Road and turn right onto Loop Road.

🗳 D River

🐾🐾🐾 (See Central Coast map on page 270)

At 120 feet, the shortest river in the Guinness Book of World Records doesn't need more than a single letter to name it. D River connects Devil's Lake to the ocean at this tremendously popular city beach. The parking lot is akin to the mall at the holiday season, with cars jockeying for position. There's so little room off the sand that people hold impromptu tailgate picnics out of their car trunks.

If you are looking for some action, this state wayside is your beach. There are kites flying, beach volleyball games, families, kids squealing and running in the surf, boogie boarding, bubble blowing—you name it. D River is so reliably windy that the world's largest kite festivals are held here every spring and fall. It is a fun place, one you can escape a little bit by walking up to seven miles in either direction. People are very good about having their dogs on leash in this unpredictable environment.

On U.S. Highway 101 in the middle of Lincoln City.

🗳 Siletz Bay

🐾🐾🐾 (See Central Coast map on page 270)

This city park is another people-packed destination. The gentle waters are protected by a sand spit, making them ideal for light canoeing, or for little tykes to toddle around in. Tough dogs can always walk around the bend to the north to reach the serious waves. It gets pretty muddy at low tide.

If you are lucky enough to find a spot, you can park along 51st Street, a pop-

DIVERSIONS

Along the Oregon Coast, people in the seaside towns make their livelihood from visitors, including four-legged ones. As a result, there are great little boutiques with toys, treats, gifts, and goodies for the dogs and dog lovers in your life. Cats, too. While full of frills, some don't have the essentials, like dog food.

Stop by these fine establishments so you can answer in the affirmative when your dog cocks her head and gives you that look that says, "Did you bring me something?"

Paws on the Sand: Pets are welcome to shop with their people at Patty's boutique, which has been in Lincoln City for 11 years. She carries premium food lines as well as an amazing selection of collars (one for every occasion), collar charms, bumper stickers, and signs that declare your canine tendencies to the world. 1640 N.E. Hwy. 101, Lincoln City; 541/996-6019; www.pawsonthesand.com.

Bella's Pet Boutique: Cashmere sweaters, beautiful necklaces, health and beauty aids, furniture, boating and camping equipment...yes, we're talking about a pet store, one that carries anything your little doggy's heart desires, and many wonderful things she never knew she desired. Bella's would be right at home on New York's 5th Avenue or L.A.'s Rodeo Drive. Lucky for you, it's in Oregon's Lincoln City, and online. 1688 N. Hwy. 101, SeaTowne Courtyard; 541/574-8600; www.bellaspetboutique.com.

Raindogs: Although mostly a people store, this great shop has a few toys and treats for your best friend, which is as good an excuse as any to come in for the unique jewelry, books, gifts, bath and body products, and so on for yourself. Raindogs has accumulated an eclectic selection that somehow just fits. 162 Beach St., Yachats; 541/547-3000.

Reigning Cats and Dogs: This shop carries an unashamed extravagance of pillows, towels, stationery, and anything you can think of geared toward humans' celebration of their pets, and the largest selection of breed-specific gifts. 1384 Bay St., Old Town Florence; 541/997-8982; www.shoprcd.com.

---

ular restaurant and shopping strip paralleling the north side of the bay. That way, you can grab some chowder at Mo's or an ice cream cone at Eleanor's Undertow. There is a tiny patch of lawn and a covered picnic table in the city park at the entrance to 51st Street.

The Siletz Bay National Wildlife Refuge extends nearly the entire length of the bay along the east side of the highway. Trails, viewing platforms, and other opportunities for public use are in the planning stages. In the meantime, you can enjoy views of the salt grasses and brackish marsh from the road.

5 Siuslaw National Forest—Drift Creek Falls Trail

🐾🐾🐾🐾 (See Central Coast map on page 270)

Everyone we talked to in town recommended this 1.5-mile trail as a great walk to do with your dog. The hike packs a big punch for little effort. It's the pride and joy of the Hebo Ranger District, well maintained with gravel and hard-pack. A mild slope takes you down to a 240-foot suspension bridge looking out over a 75-foot, free-flowing waterfall. Your dogs will love the journey and you'll appreciate the reward at the trail's destination.

The drive to get there takes all the work, along 10 miles of twisty, one-lane road. At least it's paved. From U.S. Highway 101, .25 mile south of Lincoln City, turn west on Drift Creek Road. For the next 12 miles, turn or bear left at every intersection and Y in the road to stay on Forest Road 17 until you see the large parking lot, vault toilet, and trailhead. Parking is $5. 503/392-3161.

PLACES TO EAT

Beach Dog Café: In a crafty display of double meaning, this joint serves dogs—bratwurst, kielbasa, kosher, and veggie—to humans, and welcomes dogs with homemade human-shaped treats. You can get your dogs with fix-in's, pastries, and espresso to go and stroll through the Taft District or eat at a sidewalk table. Stop by and see the picture of Coop 'n' Isis on the wall and chat with the owner, who sidelines as the local paper's food and wine critic. 1266 S.W. 50th St.; 541/996-9111.

Eleanor's Undertow: This café and ice cream parlor is hard to miss, with its bright pink building, 20-foot-tall candy canes, and mermaid fountain. The list of indulgences is long, including quarter-pound chocolate chip cookies, saltwater taffy, and anything you can make with ice cream. 869 S.W. 51st St.; 541/996-3800.

Sun Garden Café and Cyber Garden: This versatile two-sided shop has a soothing atmosphere to counteract all that caffeine and the hum of the computers in the cyber-section. The café side of the house serves fresh, vegetarian-only dishes. There is a tiny garden out back and abundant outdoor seating in front. 1816 and 1826 N.E. Hwy. 101; coffee house: 541/994-3067, café: 541/557-1800.

PLACES TO STAY

Coast Inn Bed and Breakfast: Pets are allowed in the Cordova Cottage Suite of this restored 1930s Craftsman-style home, with a private entrance from the front lawn. The room embraces the beach theme with light periwinkle walls, a ceiling fan, and a tropical scene painted on the wall. It's $135 per night, with a refundable $25 cleaning deposit. 4507 S.W. Coast Ave.; 541/994-7932 or 888/994-7932; www.oregoncoastinn.com.

Ester Lee Motel: Each vintage 1940s unit is unique at this homespun property that proudly advertises its pet-friendliness as far away as Portland in the *Dog Nose News*. Up to two pets are allowed, in the cottages only, for $7 per pet, per night. Each unit has the comforts of kitchens, wood fireplaces, and fantastic views. Prices range from a low season $58 rate up to $153 in the summer. 3803 S.W. Hwy. 101; 541/996-3606 or 888/996-3606; www.esterlee.com.

Looking Glass Inn: The wood-shingled buildings, gazebo, and outdoor picnic area lend this little inn a warm, breezy feeling, matched by the exceedingly pet-friendly staff. Dogs are given a basket with extra towels, bones, and a monogrammed bowl that you can keep for $5. Spacious rooms are a block from Siletz Bay in the lively Historic Taft District. Room rates are $89–129; the dog fee is $10. 861 S.W. 51st St.; 541/996-3996 or 800/843-4940; www.lookingglass-inn.com.

Sea Horse Lodging and Vacation Rentals: If the fabulous views and feel-good comfort of the Sea Horse Motel don't do it for you, rent one of the private vacation homes with ocean views and/or private backyards. Its website has a description of the homes and restrictions. Motel rates are $75–105; limit two pets, $10 per pet, per night. Homes range from $110 to $180 per night and sleep four to six people. 2039 N.W. Harbor St.; 541/994-2101 or 800/662-2101; www.seahorsemotel.com.

More Accommodations: Please look under Chain Hotels in the Resources section for additional places to stay in this area.

Gleneden Beach

Gleneden is pronounced as though it were two words, Glen Eden, the latter the same as the garden of Adam and Eve. It is a fitting name for an idyllic ocean village and its pretty beach. On the north end of the Gleneden Beach loop, turn west on Laurel Street to the end to find a public beach access point with a couple of parking spaces.

PARKS, BEACHES, AND RECREATION AREAS

🐾 Gleneden Beach

🐾🐾🐾 (See Central Coast map on page 270)

Wet-suited surfers come out in the morning to catch the best waves at this State Recreation Site with a quieter, more serious reputation, a 10-minute drive away from the craziness of Lincoln City. The surf is strong and the drop-off into the water is fairly steep. Joggers and their dogs take to the level, coarse sand above the high-tide line. Seals bob in and out of the surf, searching for supper. Cascade Head looms to the north and flanking you on either side of the beach are ochre sandstone cliffs, a fitting backdrop for a foggy morning beach walk or lovely evening sunset. There's a big parking lot with restrooms and picnic tables on a fenced hillside and landscaped lawns. Cooper prefers this reflective solitude, reached by a paved path through a grove of shore pines.

From U.S. Highway 101 seven miles south of Lincoln City, turn west on Wessler Street, the Gleneden Beach Loop, and follow the signs.

PLACES TO STAY

Salishan Lodge: This luxury golf resort captures that particular Northwest flair for cedar and stone and muted colors that complement the lush green of the links and surrounding forest. Traditional rooms range $119–194 and Deluxe rooms with gas fireplaces and private balconies are $139–214. Pets, who are $25 each per stay, receive a letter from Stanley, the lodge's basset hound, with treats, a generous roll of bags, and a guide to the running loops, beach access points, and nature trails on the 350-acre property. 7760 Hwy. 101 N.; 541/764-2371 or 888/SALISHAN (888/725-4742); www.salishan.com.

DOG-EAR YOUR CALENDAR

If your pet enjoys the adoration she gets by being "So cute!" wearing bunny ears or a duck bill, she should participate in the **Easter Pet Parade** at Gleneden Beach in April. While the majority of participants are kids and dogs, there have been hedgehogs, parrots, rabbits, champion breeding ferrets, and lizards. 800/767-2064; www.coastvisitor.com.

The best dogsledders in the United States and Canada gather at the Oregon Dunes in March to show off their skills in the **Dune Musher's Mail Run.** Mini-teams of 3–4 dogs cover a "short" course of 55 miles in three days, and traditional 5–12 dog teams take on 72 miles in two days. Dogsled teams compete in this challenging event to send an Oregon musher to the Alaska Iditarod. For more information, contact the Reedsport/Winchester Bay Chamber of Commerce; 541/271-3495 or 800/247-2155; www.reedsportcc.org. There's a stopover in Winchester Bay, where the dogs rest while fans meet the teams.

Lincoln City's **Mutt Masters Dog Show and Olympics** celebrates our companions in ways that we can appreciate everyday, without having to worry about coiffure or conformation. Contests include best singing dog, coolest tricks, biggest ears, fastest eater, kid-dog look-alikes, and the so-ugly-you're-cute canine photo-op. Come, sit, and stay in Lincoln City the last weekend in April and strut your mutt at Mutt Masters. 541/996-1274 or 800/452-2151; www.oregoncoast.org.

Lincoln Beach

PARKS, BEACHES, AND RECREATION AREAS

7 Fogarty Creek

🐾🐾🐾🐾 (See Central Coast map on page 270)

A dog can learn to love this State Recreation Area, with acres of grass to sink his claws into and an abundance of bunny rabbits to chase. We like that it has large, protected areas of grouped picnic tables, places to get together with family, set up day camp, talk, and eat. The trouble with many other oceanfront parks is that there are no decent places to eat a decent meal and have a conversation without getting sand in your food and other places we won't mention. You can reach these picnic areas from two parking lots, over the creek on wooden footbridges, through the Sitka spruce and Western hemlock.

To top it all off, there is a trail to an ocean cove, where the creek meets the sea. The beach is famous for bird-watching and observing tidepools, and it has the allure of steep headlands on either side and offshore rock formations. There can be lots of seaweed onshore, which you may not adore, but will keep your saluki's snoot occupied for hours.

Turn east off U.S. Highway 101 into one of two parking lots, two miles north of Depoe Bay. Parking is $3. Open 6 A.M.–10 P.M.

PLACES TO STAY

Pana-Sea-Ah Bed and Breakfast: The two-bedroom cottage and the accessible Cozy Suite, also called the Tuscany, allow pets at this multilevel contemporary home across the street from Lincoln Beach access. The décor is refined, and sunsets through banks of windows in the drawing room are divine. Resident shih tzu Cookie is terribly shy, so please keep your pets downstairs on leash so they don't overwhelm her. The Cottage is $150, plus $20 per pet, pet night and a $100 refundable deposit. The Suite is $120, plus a $25 fee per pet, per stay. Your hosts will discuss the pet policies with you when you make your reservation. 4028 Lincoln Ave.; 541/764-3368.

Depoe Bay

The only beach access points are four miles north and south, so this seaside resort plays up the fact that you can watch migrating whales from vantage points along the city sidewalk on a rocky cliff above the ocean. Sure enough, Cooper and Isis saw their first gray whale nearby at Boiler Bay. In addition to gray whales that travel between summers in Alaska and winters in California, there are several hundred that hang out around the Oregon Coast year-round, not bothering to migrate.

Depoe Bay brags about having the smallest navigable port in the world, spouting water horns that shoot water geysers above the seawall promenade, and a street full of boutique shopping.

PARKS, BEACHES, AND RECREATION AREAS

8 Boiler Bay

😺😺😺 (See Central Coast map on page 270)

The rusting hulk of a boiler that lends its name to this State Scenic Viewpoint can be seen at low tide, where it rests after the 1910 explosion of the steam schooner *J. Marhoffer*. Before U.S. Highway 101 cut through the cliffs, these steam ships transported people along the coastline.

Coop 'n' Isis saw their first gray whale from this bluff, trolling the bay for its shrimp dinner. Averaging 45 feet long and 35 tons in weight, a gray is a baleen whale, with fringed plates in its mouth to gather and filter its food from the mud, sand, and water. The whale slurps up an area of the seafloor about the size of a desk, filters out the junk, and scoops the amphipods off the roof of its mouth with its tongue, much in the same way your dog sucks peanut butter off the roof of his mouth. If you train your binoculars to the north for a moment, you'll see Lincoln City.

Boiler Bay has restrooms, a sunny picnic meadow, and a loop parking lot, off U.S. Highway 101 a mile north of Depoe Bay.

PLACES TO EAT

Java Club: The scones are unbelievably good, the coffee is hot, and the club is a major dog hangout. Help yourself to the water bowl and jar of dog biscuits by the door and get your dog's picture taken for the Mutt Mug bulletin board. 26 N.E. Hwy. 101; 541/765-3023.

PLACES TO STAY

Inn at Arch Rock: Rooms at the inn are crisp and suitably beachy with light woods and wicker. Rooms 6–8 allow pets, for $119 per night, plus a $10 pet fee. It's a good price that includes a continental breakfast, ocean views, and wooden deck chairs on the lawn overlooking the bay. 70 Sunset N.W.; 541/765-2560 or 800/767-1835; www.innatarchrock.com.

Trollers Lodge: At this cheery hotel, each suite has a different personality, looking more like mini–summer homes than rooms. They accept pets in all suites except nos. 8, 9, and 11. Pets are $8 extra in rooms, $10 extra in ocean-front suites. Call ahead to find out which suite is appropriate for your size and number of pets. Rates are $75–95. All nonsmoking; 355 S.W. Hwy. 101; 541/765-2287 or 800/472-9335; www.trollerslodge.com.

Otter Rock and Cape Foulweather

Mother Nature was having a bit of a spat on March 7, 1778, when English explorer Captain James Cook rounded the headland and named it Cape Foulweather. His published accounts aroused interest in the area, and the fur trade came soon after. Now, everyone refers to this area by its most prominent offshore formation.

PARKS, BEACHES, AND RECREATION AREAS

🐾 Devil's Punch Bowl

🐾🐾 (See Central Coast map on page 270)

The various parts of this State Natural Area are spread out, offering more choices than are apparent at first glance, especially for dogs. After turning onto Otter Crest Loop and then west on 1st Street, everyone heads to the overlook to see the geological formation that churns, swirls, and foams with sea water during high tide, especially during winter storms. From the wind-blown picnic tables above, you can also catch the action of the surfers to the south on Beverly Beach. Across the street are Mo's Chowder House, a local winery tasting room, and an ice cream truck.

Once you've filled your stomach and absorbed the views, take your dog to the beach and tide pools. Turn right onto C Avenue before the viewpoint, and park at the lot at 2nd Street and C Avenue to find a paved path and stairs to the Marine Garden. At low tide, you can climb over the rocks into the Punch-bowl, where there are all kinds of sea creatures clinging to the rocks at dog nose level. A small lawn and restrooms are located on 1st Street between B and C Avenues.

From U.S. Highway 101, you can turn onto Otter Crest Loop from the north or south, approximately eight miles north of Newport.

PLACES TO EAT

Mo's West: People have been chowing down on Mo's clam chowder since the late 1960s. Today, the chain produces 500,000 gallons a year for various locations and grocery stores. Cups of the famous concoction come with every shrimp and oyster sandwich or dinner platter. Elbow your way through, get your food to go, and take your chowder hound across the street to Devil's Punchbowl. 122 1st St.; 541/765-2442; www.moschowder.com.

Newport

Newport is the largest city in the area, home of the Oregon Coast Aquarium and the Hatfield Marine Science Center. As it grew into a major commercial center, the character of some of original neighborhoods was preserved, including the Nye Beach promenade, with its art galleries, performing arts, and shops; and the Historic Bayfront, similar to San Francisco's Fisherman's Wharf, complete with a Ripley's Believe It or Not and a Wax Works.

PARKS, BEACHES, AND RECREATION AREAS

🔟 Beverly Beach

🐾🐾🐾🐾 (See Central Coast map on page 270)

This State Park is a zoo, no doubt because it is such a great beach. First of all, it is vast, extending from Yaquina Head to Otter Rock. The sand is soft and pliable for sandcastle building, the winds are strong and reliable for kite flying, and on the north end of the beach, the waves are prime for surfers and kiteboarders. On a typical day, entire clans set up camp above the high-tide line. If your dog enjoys all this added stimulus, camp in one of Beverly Beach's 277 spots and stay a while.

The day-use parking lot is to the left, just before the campground entrance. The few picnic tables are practically in the parking lot, intended mainly for gulping down a bologna and cheese sandwich before running back to the beach. For a change of pace, there is a .75-mile creek trail that starts behind the gift shop.

Beverly Beach is seven miles north of Newport on U.S. Highway 101. Open 6 A.M.–10 P.M. 198 N.E. 123rd St.; 541/265-9278.

🔟🔟 Yaquina Head

🐾🐾🐾 (See Central Coast map on page 270)

Yaquina Head (Yah-KWIN-nah) is an Outstanding Natural Area. No, that's not how the dogs rate it—that's its official name. It was formed by flowing lava around 14 million years ago, and the lighthouse perched on its outermost point is the tallest on the Oregon Coast, at 93 feet tall and 162 feet above sea level. The light, now automated, aids navigation along the coast and into Yaquina Bay. Call 541/574-3100 for visiting information.

There are five trails exploring the wildlife preserve, and your $5 pass is good for three days, so you should be able to do them all, except for the one around the lighthouse, which is off-limits to dogs. The walks are short, each less than a mile, and the steepest ones reward your efforts with great views.

Yaquina is full of noisy life, especially the thousands of squawking birds nesting on Colony Rock and the barking harbor seals on Seal Island. Another unique sound is the water tossing and tumbling beach cobbles, polished fragments of boiling hot lava that exploded upon impact with the cold water. About the time the Wieners hit Yaquina Head, they realized a common thread among all Oregon beaches: they are windy, very and often. Birds taking off into a headwind fly backwards.

Yaquina Head is about 3.5 miles north of Newport on U.S. Highway 101. Open dawn–dusk. 541/574-3100.

12 Don Davis Park

🐾 🐾 🐾 (See Central Coast map on page 270)

This city beach park was rated by *Sunset Magazine* as the most romantic on the coast. The dogs don't know so much about that; after all, their idea of romance is having you rub their tummies. For strolling couples, there are thought-provoking sculptures and built-in viewing benches along a stone paver pathway and rock wall that arches gracefully down to the beach. It's lighted at night by a host of lamps embedded along the walkway, which was built in honor of Vietnam Veterans.

The icing on the cake is an indoor ocean viewing conservatory, with wall-to-wall windows and cozy benches safe from the spray and freezing rain. It's the only public one on the coast, a choice place to watch sunsets and winter storms. Quiet, reflective dogs may join you in the rotunda.

From U.S. Highway 101, turn west on Olive Street to the end.

13 Yaquina Bay

🐾 🐾 (See Central Coast map on page 270)

This State Recreation Site is the place to come for views. Of course, there is the ocean, which you can see even from the loop drive and parking areas. From the viewing platform, you can watch sailboats, speed craft, and commercial vessels navigating a constructed jetty system at the outlet of the bay into the sea. Towering above you is the historic Yaquina Bay Bridge, built in 1936 and behind you on the top of the bluff is the lighthouse.

The Yaquina Bay Lighthouse was lit for a mere three years, from 1871 to 1874, before it was outshone by its brighter neighbor to the north, at Yaquina Head. It experienced a second life of fame in a *Pacific Monthly* story from 1899, when Lischen Miller wrote about resident ghost Muriel in "The Haunted Lighthouse." In years since, it has been called to service as a Coast Guard lifeboat station and is now open for tours. Call 541/574-3129 or visit www.yaquinalights.org for information.

Getting to the beach is a workout, first down a steep hill with several flights of stairs, and then through deep sand mounds before you reach the easygoing, hard-packed sand at the tide line. The park also has a playground, one of the few on the central coast, a fishermen's memorial sanctuary, and picnic tables in forested spruce and pine.

The entrance is immediately north of the Bay Bridge. Open 6 A.M.–10 P.M.

🔢 Mike Miller Park

🐾🐾🐾🐾 (See Central Coast map on page 270)

Cooper doesn't know if this former parks commissioner had dogs in mind when he planned this excellent county park, but he'd like to thank Miller personally for such a great trail that packs a bunch of stuff into a one-mile loop. The low-grade gravel path is an interpretive trail through a Sitka spruce forest, past old beaches, logging sites, and railway remains. While you read the brochure that corresponds to the numbered posts along the path, your dog will decipher the scent patterns left by local wildlife. In such a hustle-and-bustle beach town, this walk is a place of peace and quiet.

The educational trail is 1.2 miles south of the Yaquina Bay Bridge, at S.E. 50th Street on the east side of U.S. Highway 101. There's room for a couple of cars to park alongside the road.

PLACES TO EAT

Café Stephanie: Three mini picnic tables sit on the sidewalk outside this cute little café on the quaint Historic Nye Beach loop. The lunch menu is consistently good with hot and cold sandwiches, fish tacos, and turkey wraps. Breakfast changes daily, featuring quiches, breakfast burritos, crepes, and homemade granola. 411 Coast St.; 541/265-8082.

The Coffee House: This oddly tame name hides a wild menu of *bonzer tucker,* Australian slang for good grub. Tuck into kangaroo meat burgers and lasagna or Pacific Ocean bouillabaisse. Try Pavlova, a Down Under dessert of meringue nests with kiwi, strawberries, and passion fruit. It's a *ridgy didge, fair dinkum* treat for you and your dog. Oregon and Aussie beers and wines are poured if you are "as dry as a dead dingo's donger." We declined to ask for a direct translation of that one. 156 S.W. Bay Blvd., Historic Bayfront; 541/265-6263.

Nye Beach Scoop: Ice cream begs to be eaten outside, and your dog begs to be the one eating it. Sundaes, smoothies, and milkshakes are made with Eugene's Prince Puckler's gourmet ice cream, and there are dozens of flavors of Italian sodas. 613 N.W. 3rd St.; 541/265-2887.

Rogue Ales Public House: The vice president of this regionally famous brew pub is a black Lab named Brewer. Until the pub got called to the carpet by health inspectors, dogs were allowed everywhere. Now, your pal is limited to being hitched outside the beer garden fence. He'll still be treated as a special guest, with a personal water bowl and dog menu that includes pigs' ears, among other things. 2320 O.S.U. Dr., Historic Bayfront; 541/265-3188; www.rogue.com.

PLACES TO STAY

Agate Beach Oceanfront Motel: Owner Maynard calls his classic 1940s carport motel his little piece of paradise, with a $50,000 stairway to heaven down to the beach. It's a great discovery, with a protected lawn for room to run. Every unit welcomes one or two pets for an extra $10 per night. Says Maynard, "When people with pet allergies call, I simply apologize, because I can't turn down a friend with a pet in any of my rooms." Those rooms are lovingly restored and well kept, with ocean views, kitchens, and decks. Queen-size bed rooms are $49–69, suites are an unbeatable $89–139. 175 N.W. Gilbert Way; 541/265-8746 or 800/755-5674; www.agatebeachmotel.com.

Beverly Beach Campground: Sites are surprisingly private and quiet considering how huge the campground is, with an even split of 128 tent sites and 128 RV sites. Tent sites are in their own loops (C, D, and E) in the spruce to the east of the highway. Reservations well in advance are a must at this desirable park. Rates are $13–22; 800/452-5687; www.reserveamerica.com.

Hallmark Resort: This super-sized, cheerful, oceanfront resort prefers to put dogs and their people in first-floor rooms with walk-out patios to the backyard and immediate access to the beach trail. Deluxe rooms (fireplace, spas, and kitchens) are as low as $99–109 in the winter; standard rooms are $116–136 in the summer, plus a reasonable $5 dog fee. 744 S.W. Elizabeth; 541/265-2600 or 888/448-4449; www.hallmarkinns.com.

More Accommodations: Please look under Chain Hotels in the Resources section for additional places to stay in this area.

South Beach

PARKS, BEACHES, AND RECREATION AREAS

15 South Beach

🐾🐾🐾🐾 (See Central Coast map on page 270)

This state park has a lot going on. At the north end of the park are horse trails, as well as surfing, scuba diving, and windsurfing for the very advanced and skilled. For $15 per person, kayak tours are booked at South Beach, although the launching point is five miles south at Ona Beach. The Oregon Coast Aquarium and Hatfield Marine Science Center are within walking distance of the park, and a hospitality store and information center are on the grounds, as well as a campground with 227 sites for RVers and seven primitive tent sites that are first-come, first-served for $9 per night.

In a dog's world, the best things in the park are free: miles of windswept beach and multiple park trails to explore. After a bit of a drive from the highway, turn left to reach the picnic area, restrooms, and beach. The Cooper Ridge Nature Trail is a 1.75-mile, sandy loop around the perimeter of the campground. It's Cooper's favorite, not only because he's biased by its name. The South Jetty Trail is an accessible, 10-foot-wide paved pathway that's two miles to the bay wall and back through the dunes. The Old Jetty trail is the least traveled, a bit wilder path that picks its way through shore pine and beach grasses. The trails are the best way to escape the park's summer crowds, especially the school buses that spit out dozens of summer camp kids primed to get rowdy at the beach.

South Beach is two miles south of Newport on U.S. Highway 101. 5580 S. Hwy. 101; 541/867-4715.

PLACES TO EAT

Lighthouse Deli and Fish Co.: It's hard to get a snout in edgewise at this wildly popular seafood place with multicolored picnic tables on a parking lot patio. You're sitting next to the stew pots steaming with clams, oysters, mussels, and crabs—the food is that fresh. The folks at the Lighthouse also smoke their own salmon, albacore, and oysters. If you want something waiting for you at home, they ship next-day to anywhere in the United States. 3640 S.W. Hwy. 101; 541/867-6800; www.lighthousedeli.com.

PLACES TO STAY

Melva Company Vacation Rentals: Linda Lewis rents two absolutely stunning three-bedroom, two-bath vacation homes, one here in South Beach on a bluff, and another in Waldport directly on the beach. Both have fully fenced yards, and pets are welcome for no additional fee. Her business is too small to have a website, but if you call her, she'll mail you photographs, and we bet you'll be sold on them. Rates are $180 per night, less $10 per night for bookings of a week or more. 503/678-1144.

Seal Rock

The town of Seal Rock was platted in 1887, and a large hotel was built at the end of the Corvallis and Yaquina Bay Wagon Road, the first road to reach the coast from the Willamette Valley. None of the early development remains from land transferred over to the railroads in the 1890s and then by default to nature when the locomotives ceased their locomotion.

PARKS, BEACHES, AND RECREATION AREAS

16 Ona Beach

🐾🐾🐾🐾 (See Central Coast map on page 270)

Developed on a forested ocean flat around several tributaries of the Beaver Creek Estuary, this state park is a varied and interesting place to bring dogs. There's more room to relax than at most oceanfront parks. Pick your pleasure of the plentiful meadows under the protection of tall spruce trees, sheltered from the windy and wilder beach.

Ona has an accessible, paved trail to the ocean, ending in a wooden footbridge crossing above the creek. Where it empties into the river, the creek forms a shallow pool that's a good play place for younger children. Behind you and to the south are high sandstone cliffs.

Kayak tours of Beaver Creek are available. The boat launch is across the highway from the entrance to the park, on N. Beaver Creek Road. You can register and pay for the tours at South Beach State Park five miles north; call 541/867-4715.

Ona Beach is one mile north of Seal Rock on U.S. Highway 101.

17 Seal Rock

 (See Central Coast map on page 270)

There is no single rock formation at this State Recreation Site that is Seal Rock; there is, however, one known as Elephant Rock, the largest of many interesting geological formations with exposed faults sitting offshore. These outcroppings are home to seals, sea lions, and sea birds; a great place to observe the active wildlife is the paved path along a high cliff of the shoreline and from two accessible viewing platforms.

Dogs get bored with watching after a while, tending to tug you to the steep, switchback trail down to the beach. When the moon is full, pulling the tides farther out to sea, you can walk across the stones and driftwood to play among the rocks and get a closer look at the birds and the tidepool life. This is when the beach gets busier with people harvesting littleneck clams and seaweed, the good stuff that holds your sushi together. Otherwise, the slice of sand you can walk is somewhat cramped. The picnic area and restrooms are in a strand of shore pine, salal, and spruce.

Seal Rock is 10 miles south of Newport on U.S. Highway 101.

PLACES TO EAT

Bear's Cookie Den: You can shop the Whitmans' collection of thousands of teddy bears while they make you a deli sandwich, fresh salad, or soup of the day to go or to eat at courtyard tables. The owners are experts at recommending cookie pairings to complement your meal. 10563 N. Hwy 101; 541/563-5662.

Waldport

South of busy Newport is this quieter, gentler town where it's easy to enjoy yourself for little or no money. Fishing and clamming are popular, and there is a free crabbing dock. Stop at the Alsea Bay Bridge Interpretive Center to learn about Conde B. McCullough, Oregon's most famous engineer. He designed and built many art-deco bridges along the coast in the 1930s. All are still in use, except the Alsea Bay Bridge in Waldport, which has been reconstructed true to his artistic vision.

PARKS, BEACHES, AND RECREATION AREAS

18 Driftwood Beach

🐾🐾🐾🐾 (See Central Coast map on page 270)

If Cooper and Isis had to choose their favorite place to reach the beach between Waldport and Yachats, this would be the one. This State Recreation Site has the perfect combination of nature and nurture. The nature comes in the form of five miles of wide, flat, unspoiled beach from Seal Rock to Alsea Bay. Despite the name, there's not too much driftwood, just enough to find the ultimate fetch stick. Nurture is in the details: a wheelchair-accessible path to the beach, flush toilets with changing areas, a large parking lot set back from the road, and two view picnic tables. Even from the parking lot, you have an uninterrupted view of the ocean.

Driftwood Beach is three miles north of Waldport on U.S. Highway 101. Open 6 A.M.–9 P.M.

19 Robinson Park on Alsea Bay

🐾🐾 (See Central Coast map on page 270)

Pop in to this little park at Alsea Port at low tide and you might get to see the shrimp suckers in action. For 30 years, Alsea Bay's tidal flats have been a premier source of ghost shrimp, used not for human consumption, but as bait for steelhead and salmon fishing. It's fun to watch the suction pumps mine the mud for these fish-tempting delicacies. You also have a great view of the Alsea Bridge, the harbor seals, and the brown pelicans that call the bay home. The park, funded in part by the National Oceanic and Atmospheric Administration, has protected picnic tables and easy bay access.

Turn east on Route 34 from U.S. Highway 101 and look for the Port Area sign, turning north on Broadway and west on Port Street. The park is on the far west side of the port, past the ramp and boat trailer parking.

20 Governor Patterson Beach

🐾🐾🐾 (See Central Coast map on page 270)

The state has gone to the trouble of doing some landscaping at this Memorial State Recreation Site, providing your pal with a good-sized lawn to sniff if he gets bored with the beach. Follow your nose to find the hidden picnic tables, each tucked into a private grove of thick dune vegetation, and most with great sea views. Several rough, short walkways take you to another fabulous swath of sand, running south from Alsea Bay for miles. Some of the lawn areas are a little too close to the highway for comfort.

The Guv'nor is one mile south of Waldport on U.S. Highway 101. Open 6 A.M.–9 P.M.

PLACES TO EAT

Waldport Seafood Company: Same-day fresh shrimp, crab, oysters, and clams take center stage in soups, stews, sandwiches, and salads with home-made cocktail sauce and hot garlic toast. The tables out front are close to high-way traffic; take your spoils of the sea and your ice cream out back to Kealy City Wayside on the bay. It's a Wi-Fi Hotspot; 310 S.W. Arrow St. (Hwy. 101); 541/563-4107; www.waldport-seafood-co.com.

PLACES TO STAY

Blackberry Campground: Oregon is famous for fat, juicy blackberries in late July through August. At this campground, 18 miles east of Waldport on Route 34, the only place that isn't plastered with prickly berry bushes is the area cleared for the sites and the boat ramp. Campsites are $12; the day-use fee is $5 per car. Sites #15–30 are along the river. Make reservations and get maps at the Waldport Ranger Station, 1094 S.W. Hwy. 101; 541/563-3211.

Edgewater Cottages: Talk about location, location, location! If these nine cottages were any closer to the edge of the water, they'd be in it. Every one has a sliding glass door to a wind-protected sun deck, an ocean view, beach access, kitchen, and fireplace. They range from a tiny studio for two for $80 to a house that sleeps 14 for $415 per night, and any combination of people, rooms, and views in between. Every unique space welcomes pets who know not to get on the beds or the furniture. They're popular enough to require a two-night minimum stay in the winter, up to a 7-night minimum July–September. Pets are $5–10 per pet, per night. No credit cards. 3978 S.W. Hwy. 101; 541/563-2240.

Yachats

Yachats (YAH-hots) is a laid-back village of 600 or so full-time residents. This charming community calls itself the Gem of the Coast, and the dogs agree, although they might express it differently. The Beef Marrow Bone with Cheese and Peanut Butter of the Coast, perhaps. The mountain scenery is unspoiled by development along miles of uninterrupted beaches. There's less big-time tourist influence and more intimate lodging options and tiny shops with friendly owners. The largest events are the annual Smelt Fry in July, when thousands of sardine-like fish come into shore and jump into catcher's nets, and the Mushroom Festival in soggy October. The section of U.S. High-way 101 between Yachats and Florence to the south is full of cliff-hugging, jaw-dropping oceanfront vistas and multiple highway pullouts for stopping and taking it all in. While visiting area parks, stop by the Strawberry Hill and Bob Creek viewpoints.

PARKS, BEACHES, AND RECREATION AREAS

🐾 Smelt Sands

🐾🐾🐾 (See Central Coast map on page 270)

This turbulent section of coastline is designed not for playing in the surf, but for watching the surf play among the rocks and headlands. There are multiple blowholes, where waves crash up through holes carved in the rocks by thousands of years of water action.

At this State Recreation Site, your dog will be content to join you on your sightseeing tour along the 804 Trail, a .75-mile, fine gravel path that is accessible for all users. Concerned citizens saved this piece of the former Road #804 for public enjoyment, and enjoy it they do, in large numbers. It's mere feet away from the crashing surf, and your pooch will meet lots of other dogs walking their owners along the way.

In July, this is also the place to see the small, silvery relatives of the salmon called smelt jumping through the waves. Viewing benches along the trail give you front-row seats for divine ocean sunsets.

Turn west on Lemwick Lane from U.S. Highway 101 into the parking lot, on the north side of Yachats.

🐾 Cape Perpetua Scenic Area

🐾🐾🐾🐾 (See Central Coast map on page 270)

There are 10 scenic hiking trails in and around Cape Perpetua, from .25 mile to 10 miles long, with a little something for everyone. The Wonder Wieners recommend the .6-mile Captain Cook Trail and the .4-mile Restless Waters Trail for great views of an ocean spouting horn and chasm wave action, as well as for exploring tidepools. About the only thing you can't do at the Cape is get to miles of sandy beach, but you only need to go .25 mile south to Neptune for that.

The guide at the interpretive center, open 9 A.M.–5 P.M., recommends the longer 6.5-mile Cook's Ridge/Gwynn Creek Loop Trail to explore old growth Sitka, Douglas fir, and cedar trees. About 1.5 miles in on the trail is an area called the Dog Hair Forest, where the trees grow so close and thick it looks like the hair on a komondor's back from your vantage point.

The Cape Perpetua Overlook is the highest viewpoint on the coast, and the U.S. Forest Service brags that it's also the best. A 1930s stone shelter, built for scouting enemy ships and planes during WWII, is used as a whale-watching lookout. This overlook and the one at Devil's Churn were renovated in 2004 for wheelchair accessibility.

The entrance to the visitors center is three miles south of Yachats; it and the other areas of the park are well marked along U.S. Highway 101. Parking is $5.

23 Neptune Beach

🐾🐾🐾 (See Central Coast map on page 270)

Neptune North and South are one beach or two, depending on time and tide. At high tide, there are two slivers of sand to enjoy while you watch waves meet up with the reef. At low tide, which Isis prefers, you can walk from one beach to the other on firm, level sand, in and among the craggy formations. Just don't get caught in between as the tide is coming in!

The north parking lot of this State Scenic Viewpoint is not marked. It has one picnic table, a viewing bench, and a trail to the beach. The south parking lot is much larger, has restrooms, and stairs down to the sand. It is also set back farther from the highway and has a larger meadow for spreading out a blanket. Cummins Creek is a shallow stream that empties into the sea at the south beach.

You can walk as far as you want to on the 10-mile Cummins Creek Loop, Forest Road 1050. The trailhead is just north of the highway bridge between the two picnic areas. The turn-in for the longer, 18.6-mile Cummins Ridge Trail is just south.

Neptune is three miles south of Yachats on U.S. Highway 101.

PLACES TO EAT

The Joes' Town Center Café: The Joes, Joe and Joemma, are anti–fast food. They suggest you relax and unwind on the patio while they carefully prepare your Belgian hotcakes and omelettes for breakfast or burgers, hot sandwiches, and soups for lunch. This is a coastal favorite, crowded on weekends. 373 W. 4th St., corner of Hwy 101 & 4th; 541/547-4244.

Toad Hall: If you prefer your political discussion as heated as your coffee, stop into this java house, where your barista and the gal who runs the attached gift shop are known locally as the town's unofficial mayors. If our country's leaders could make mocha brevés this good, they'd have our vote. 237 W. 3rd St.; 541/547-4044.

PLACES TO STAY

Ambrosia Gardens Bed and Breakfast: The Carriage House, up the stairs above the garage of this contemporary home, is a kid- and dog-friendly place with a full kitchen. Mary is a fastidious housekeeper who requests that there be no smoking, no pets in the bedding, and no peeing on the flowers. Her green thumb nurtures almost three acres of gardens around the house, and National Forest land is to the east and south for hiking. You can take in the view of Sea Rose Beach across the highway from the outdoor hot tub. $125 per night; no pet fee. 95435 Hwy. 101; 541/547-3013; www.ambrosia-gardens.com.

See Vue: Each room is different in this eccentric, 10-room theme hotel. Some have kitchens; The Granny's Room has a tub and the rest have showers. What they all have in common are great prices ($50–85), astounding ocean views, and warm-hearted innkeepers. Pets are allowed in all but three of the rooms and are treated lavishly with extra sheets, towels, biscuits, bags, and a copy of *Dog Nose News*, all for a $5 pet fee. Isis is fond of The Princess and the Pea room with its raised bed of velvet and lace. All nonsmoking; 95590 Hwy. 101; 541/547-3227; www.seevue.com.

Shamrock Lodgettes: Pets are allowed in all of the cozy cabins, in the modern Danish-influenced Sherwood House, and in two of the substantial Bay View Redwood units. Yachats Ocean Road Park is right outside your door along the bay. Prices start as low as $59 per night, up to $159, plus a $6 pet fee. All nonsmoking. 105 Hwy. 101 S.; 541/547-3312 or 800/845-5028; www.shamrocklodgettes.com.

More Accommodations: Please look under Chain Hotels in the Resources section for additional places to stay in this area.

Florence

Florence is your spot for kitschy family fun. Break up the scenery and the history with family bonding activities such as bumper boats, dune buggy rides, putt-putt golf, sea lion caves, and other goofy stuff. The Shell gas station in the center of town has buckets of dog biscuits next to the pumps.

For more hikes and campgrounds than we have room to list, stop by the Mapleton Ranger Station of the Siuslaw National Forest (4480 Hwy. 101; 541/902-8526). Avoid the Siltcoos Lake Recreation Area. When the dunes of this section aren't overrun by ATVs, they're off-limits for snowy plover nesting. The best dune hikes are south of Florence. Keep in mind that distances are deceiving on the beach, longer than they look. Drink up! The wind wicks the moisture right out of you and your pets.

PARKS, BEACHES, AND RECREATION AREAS

24 Carl G. Washburn

🐾🐾🐾 (See Central Coast map on page 270)

What can you say? This Memorial State Park is yet another awesome beach along this stretch of coastline, a state park with 1,100 acres, a big parking lot, large restrooms with changing areas, and surprise picnic tables hidden in the stunted trees of the foredunes. U.S. Highway 101 bisects the park, with the campground to the east and the picnic area to the west. This beach is often foggy, with wisps of clouds clinging to the tops of the trees like cotton at Heceta Head to the south. You can take the China Creek Trail from the campground, which joins up with the Hobbit Trail and then the Heceta Head Trail, to travel the three miles down to the lighthouse.

This state park is located 14 miles north of Florence on U.S. Highway 101. 93111 Hwy. 101 N.; 541/997-3641.

25 Heceta Head Lighthouse

🐾🐾 ◂■▶ (See Central Coast map on page 270)

The Heceta (Huh-SEE-duh) Lighthouse is the most photographed structure on the coast. Operational in 1894, it is perched on the brink of a 205-foot outcropping on 1,000-foot-high headland. The former Keeper's Quarters are in an equally picture-perfect building below. Common murres lay their eggs directly on the rocks offshore, and gray whales and their calves pass close by in May on migrations to Alaska.

A half-mile trail, with a gradual uphill incline, takes you to the lighthouse, a designated State Scenic Viewpoint. Halfway up is a gift shop and the quarters, with a viewing bench that is perfect for a rest stop. Tucked into Devil's Elbow—the curve of land below the landmark—is a tiny crescent beach. Expect to share the trail and the beach with throngs of people in the summer and on weekends.

The lighthouse is open for tours Memorial Day–Labor Day, 11 A.M.–5 P.M. Call nearby Carl G. Washburn park for more information, 541/997-3641.

On U.S. Highway 101, 12 miles north of Florence. South of the park on the highway are several pullouts that offer the choicest areas to capture snapshots of the famous maritime building. Parking is $3.

NATURE HIKES AND URBAN WALKS

Up and down the Oregon Coast, there are so many geological formations named after the devil that Cooper and Isis wondered why the god of the underworld is so popular in Oregon. They may never know for sure, but they did hear a highly plausible explanation. The native inhabitants of the region believed that many spirits, evil and good, inhabited the natural world around them. The European settlers who arrived and began translating these Native American place names into their language had only one. So Beelzebub became the default evil spirit given credit for the wilder aspects of the coast. Here's a sample of the wicked places where you can walk your dog.

Devil's Churn, Yachats (page 290)
Devil's Elbow, Florence (page 293)
Devil's Kitchen, Bandon (page 310)
Devil's Lake, Lincoln City (page 273)
Devil's Punch Bowl, Otter Rock (page 281)
Seven Devils State Park, Bandon (page 309)

26 Jessie M. Honeyman

🐾🐾🐾 (See Central Coast map on page 270)

Jessie was a spunky Scottish woman, a tireless advocate for the protection of Oregon's natural resources. At her Memorial State Park, it's tough to choose between the two major lakes, Woahink and Cleawox, so you might as well stay longer and enjoy both. The dogs might vote for the East Woahink picnic area, with its huge, rolling lawns and lengthy beachfront access, plenty of room for a dog to be a dog. It can be crowded with water sport enthusiasts.

You might prefer the more scenic and quiet Cleawox Lake, to the west of U.S. Highway 101 near the campground. Picnic tables are shaded in the woods and surrounded by high sand dunes, two miles of them between the lake and the ocean. Kids grab plastic saucer slides and snow boards to ride the dunes. There's a foot-rinse station that doubles as a dog rinse.

Honeyman is two miles south of Florence on U.S. Highway 101. Parking is $3. Open 8 A.M.–8 P.M. 84505 Hwy. 101 S.; 541/997-3641.

27 Oregon Dunes Overlook

🐾🐾🐾🐾 🐾 (See Central Coast map on page 270)

The first marvel at this roadside stop are elevated platforms, with wheelchair-accessible ramps, that provide you with bird's eye views of the dunes and the ocean beyond. From there, a three-mile loop trail takes you first up and over the dunes, and then through coastal woods to the beach. The first half mile of this trail is also paved for accessibility. On the sand, the sky is so blue it hurts—think sunscreen, sunglasses, and extra water. Until you reach the forested foredune, the only way to know you're on the right path is to follow the posts topped with blue bands.

As little as a hundred years ago, the area was nothing but sand, until settlers planted the aggressive European beach grass in the 1920s to stabilize the shifting landscape. This led to quick development of the other vegetation you see today. If you're not accustomed to hiking through sand, you might need some sports cream for your calves later.

The overlook and trailhead are 10 miles south of Florence on U.S. Highway 101. Parking is $5.

PLACES TO EAT

Flying Tomato: It's almost impossible to find, an unassuming storefront on the end of a quickie car lube building a few blocks after you turn onto State Route 126. People search it out because it is far and away the best made-to-order deli sandwich place for miles, and it takes credit cards. Get 'em hot or cold to go. 2086 Hwy. 126; 541/997-8646.

Krab Kettle: It's a seafood market only, with fresh crab and fish, smoked salmon and halibut, shrimp, and other marine delights on ice in a case. Order a whole cooked crab and pick it apart while sitting at an outdoor picnic table. It's a messy affair. Your dog will be happy to give you a tongue bath afterwards. 280 Hwy. 101; 541/997-8996.

Souped-Up Sand-Witches Italian Cuisine: In case you're wondering, the owner's name is Glenda, and she let her grandchildren name the business. Her soups, sandwiches, and salads look good, but it's the chicken fettuccini Alfredo, portobello mushroom ravioli, and lasagna that Cooper goes for. 165 Maple St.; 541/997-2442.

PLACES TO STAY

Ocean Breeze: At this motel, the small rooms are sparkling and the crisp white building is a breath of fresh air. Decorator touches and a lawn with a picnic table out front help make this little motel very inviting for weary dune hikers. There are five pet rooms, all nonsmoking, for $64 and up, with an $8 pet fee. 85165 Hwy. 101 S.; 541/997-2642 or 800/753-2642; www.oceanbreezemotel.com.

Park Motel: Several rooms and two of the luxury cabins open their doors to pets at this classic 1950s lodge with genuine pine paneling in the rooms and pine trees out back. A disposal can and shovel are provided at a designated dog lawn. Standard rooms are $69–85; cabins are $127. The pet fee is $8. Friendly owner/manager Bob knows all the dog places to go in Montana if you're headed that direction anytime soon. 85034 Hwy. 101; 541/997-2634.

Mapleton

PARKS, BEACHES, AND RECREATION AREAS

28 Siuslaw National Forest—Sweet Creek Falls

🐾🐾🐾🐾 (See Central Coast map on page 270)

At a little over two miles out and back, this trail is an easy one to hike. The 20-foot falls at the end are a bit of an anticlimax, mostly hidden behind the rocks, but you won't be disappointed because there are dozens of rapids and falls in the gorge along the way. The whole trail is dazzling, and the elevated steel platforms, with bridges that cling to the hillside and carry you over the creek, are most exciting. It can be muddy, it can be buggy, and you must stay on the trail to avoid poison oak.

From Florence, travel 15 miles east to Mapleton on Highway 126. Shortly after town, you'll turn south on Sweet Creek Road and go another 10.2 miles to the marked trailhead. Bring your own drinking water; a latrine is available.

PLACES TO EAT

Alpha-bit: Books, gifts, and a health food café share a sunny space in a little strip of shops that are the center of town in Mapleton. Turkey and tuna are the only meats on the predominantly vegetarian and vegan menu. It's all light and delicious—even the ice cream is light enough to float in a tall, frosted glass of IBC root beer. A tiny county park out back has a picnic table waiting for you. 10780 Highway 126; 541/268-4311.

Reedsport

Reedsport is at the heart of the Oregon Dunes. If you come into town from State Route 38, pull into one of the Dean Creek elk viewing platforms, three miles east of Reedsport, to see if you can catch any of the reserve's 100 or so Roosevelt Elk in action.

PARKS, BEACHES, AND RECREATION AREAS

29 Umpqua Lighthouse

🐾🐾🐾 (See Central Coast map on page 270)

Cooper can think of three reasons to visit this state park—the lake trail, the lighthouse grounds, and the whale-watching station—all of which are wheelchair-accessible. The first is a fun, easy one-mile trail around Lake Marie beneath a tall forest with huckleberry bushes. The east half of the trail is paved; the west is gravel and dirt.

Dogs are allowed on the grounds of the lighthouse and Coast Guard station, and you can hear its distinctive two-tone foghorn anywhere in the park. The present lighthouse was operational in 1894 and still uses the original lenses crafted in Paris in 1890. Tour guides will take you, sans pooch, to the top Wed.–Sun., where visibility is 19 miles out to sea. Call 541/271-4631 for lighthouse museum and tour information.

Next to the lighthouse is a whale-watching station, with spotting scopes ($.50 for five minutes). Whales migrate anywhere between December and May, and you can watch the ATVs crawl over the sand from this lookout year-round.

Off U.S. Highway 101, six miles south of Reedsport. Open 7 A.M.–9 P.M. 460 Lighthouse Rd.; 541/271-4118.

PLACES TO EAT

Arbor Ice Cream: More than 40 flavors of BJ's Ice cream call your name from the dairy cases, and 70 some-odd flavors of colorful saltwater taffy tempt you from buckets along the walls. Broken cones and pieces are saved for dogs, and they'll add a tiny scoop of vanilla, free! 1061 Hwy 101; no phone.

Sugar Shack Bakery: We love a place that tells it like it is. Beyond enough baked goods, doughnuts, cookies, and fudge to send you into sugar shock, there are good deli sandwiches and daily soups. Order to go from the counter. 145 N. 3rd; 541/271-3514.

Scottsburg

Highway 38 is a great road, paralleling the Umpqua River from I-5 out to the coast at Reedsport. Somewhere along the way, you'll pass the town of Scottsburg before you even know it, but don't miss the park—it's a good 'un.

PARKS, BEACHES, AND RECREATION AREAS

30 Scottsburg Park

🐾🐾🐾 (See Central Coast map on page 270)

The rare Myrtlewood tree flourishes along the south shore of the Umpqua River at this county park, one of five tracts of land designated to protect the northern boundary of the Myrtlewood habitat. The park, with its playground, restrooms, and big grass plot is a beautiful and quiet setting for a break in your travels or a picnic. It's a popular fishing spot for Coho and Chinook salmon; the anglers get up early to put in from the boat ramp and floating docks.

The park is just west of Mile Marker 16 on State Route 38, about 15 miles inland from Reedsport.

Winchester Bay

From the center of Winchester Bay, Salmon Harbor Drive takes you to aptly named Windy Cove, a marina packed with thousands of recreational vessels, lodging, multiple beach access points, and some of the best food on the central coast. A mile south of Winchester Bay is a wayfinding point pullout, the only spot between Port Orford and Florence where you can get an unobstructed view of the Pacific Ocean. You'll spy the top of the Umpqua Lighthouse and the Triangle Jetty, where oysters and mussels are cultivated.

PARKS, BEACHES, AND RECREATION AREAS

31 ODNRA—Umpqua Dunes Recreation Area

🐾🐾🐾 (See Central Coast map on page 270)

The beach at Umpqua stretches far and wide, with sand the pleasing texture of superfine sugar. There are three large parking lots with beach access 20 feet from the pavement. Parking at the first lot is free, so you might as well stay there. There is a $5 fee to park in the second and third lots, used as staging grounds for off-highway vehicles. The only reason to go to the second lot is for a barrier-free beach trail with two excellent, accessible viewing platforms. The third lot has flush toilets and a covered picnic shelter, amenities not available at the others. ATVs are allowed on the dunes to the east of the access road; they are not allowed on the beach to the west, where you are headed.

From U.S. Highway 101, turn west on Salmon Harbor Road. Follow the Umpqua Dunes and Beach Road sign, past the marina and Windy Cove. Watch out for ATVs on the side of the road. Open 10 A.M.–6 P.M., until sunset in the summertime.

32 William H. Tugman

 (See Central Coast map on page 270)

If the beach is too windy and cold, this Memorial State Park provides good stomping grounds along the sheltered shores of 350-acre Eel Lake. It's big— big green lawns for fetch, big trees for naps in the shade, and a big lake you can paddle all around in, in a big canoe. On the north side of the picnic area is a trail that wanders about a mile, with several handy places for your dog to at least get his paws wet. Flush toilets and changing rooms make it nice if you or the kids decide to go for a swim. Your view of the lake from the handi- cap-accessible fishing dock isn't spoiled by any development, and there's no day-use fee at this state park. Eel Lake fishing nets crappie, largemouth bass, stocked rainbow trout, and steelhead and Coho salmon.

Off U.S. Highway 101, eight miles south of Reedsport. 72549 Hwy. 101; 541/759-3604.

33 ODNRA—John Dellenback Trail

(See Central Coast map on page 270)

This one-mile loop trail takes you to the highest dunes in the park, 500 feet tall or more, named in honor of someone instrumental in establishing the dunes as a recreation area. Our little dog goddess fancied herself Isis of Arabia as she climbed up to the top a view of the immensity before her. The northern half of the trail is through coastal woods, making the discovery of the dunes all the more exciting as you emerge from the trees. You continue through deep sand on the south to return.

For the ambitious and incredibly fit, there is a six-mile loop, 2.5 miles to the beach, .5 mile on the beach, and back. It is marked by posts topped with blue bands—the only way to tell if you're on the right track. This is a very difficult hike, slogging through deep sand and over high hills. We were also told that the last part of the trail may be under a foot or so of water during the rainy season. If you attempt the longer trail, we recommend dog goggles and boo- ties, gallons of water and sunscreen, and protective clothing for the sting of the sand whipped against your skin by the wind.

Watch for the entrance to trailhead parking on U.S. Highway 101, immedi- ately north of the turnoff for Lakeside. Parking is $5.

PLACES TO EAT

Bayfront Bar and Bistro: The four food groups at this European-style bistro are seafood, pasta, beer, and wine. There are two outdoor tables where you can sit and order calamari and clam appetizers, oyster shooters, scallops in cream sauce, and other supper entrées. 208 Bayfront Loop; 541/271-9463; www.bayfrontbistro.com.

Kitty's Kitchen is Christmas Forever: Dogs are welcome on the fantastic back patio of Kitty's, an eclectic diner and kitschy holiday gift shop. The cooks make whatever suits them that day—might be meatloaf, could be egg salad, and there's always chili dogs and homemade pies and cakes. 110 Bayfront Loop; 541/271-1919.

Old Anchor Seafood Café: At the Old Anchor, the namesake sits out front rusting near a couple of outdoor tables where you can sit and dine on the chef's award-winning smoked salmon chowder. Or, try Buffalo clam strips and chicken fried oysters, rare delicacies worthy of a Texan-sized appetite, with country gravy, French fries, coleslaw, and Texas toast. 75318 Hwy. 101; 541/271-5224.

Pah Tong's Thai Food: When you are craving the taste of Thai, no other flavors will do. Try Pah Tong's for a change of pace from the seafood all over the place. 460 Beach Blvd., Winchester Bay; 541/271-1750.

PLACES TO STAY

Umpqua Lighthouse State Park Campground: It may be a sand dune underneath, but it is a forest on top, enough to give each of 24 tent sites and 24 hookup sites decent seclusion. Rates are $16–20; 800/452-5687; www.reserveamerica.com.

Winchester Bay Inn: Pets are welcome to "be our guests" in all except four rooms of this bright, modern, squeaky clean motel. There are a wide range of prices and room types, including kitchenette rooms, suites, and spa rooms, $49–79, plus a $4 pet charge. 390 Broadway; 541/271-4871 or 800/246-1462; www.winbayinn.com.

More Accommodations: Please look under Chain Hotels in the Resources section for additional places to stay in this area.

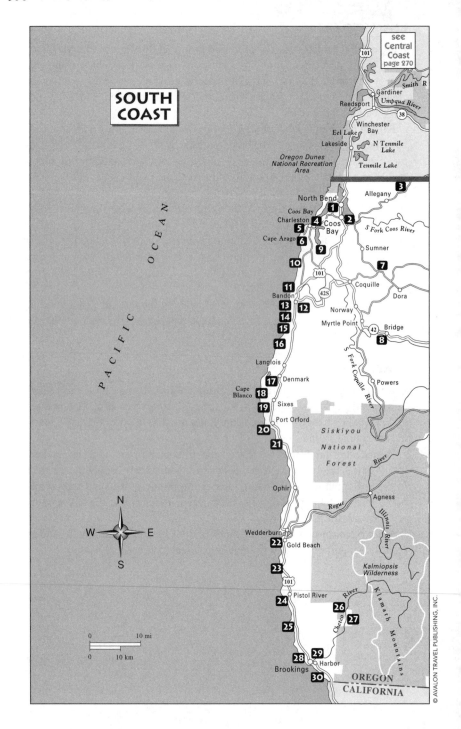

SOUTH COAST

see
Central
Coast
page 270

PACIFIC OCEAN

Smith R
Gardiner
Umpqua River
Reedsport
38
Winchester
Bay
Eel Lake
Lakeside
N Tenmile
Lake
Oregon Dunes
National Recreation
Area
Tenmile Lake

Allegany
3
North Bend
Coos Bay
1
Charleston
2
Cape Arago
5 4 Coos
Bay
S Fork Coos River
6 9
Sumner
10
7
101
Coquille
Dora
11
425
Bandon
13 12
Norway
14
Myrtle Point
15
42 Bridge
16
8
Langlois
Powers
17 Denmark
Cape
Blanco
18
19 Sixes
20 Port Orford
21

Siskiyou

National

Forest

River

Ophir
Rogue
Agness

Illinois River

Wedderburn
22 Gold Beach

Kalmiopsis
Wilderness

23
101
24 Pistol River
Chetco River
26
27
25
Klamath Mountains

29
28 Harbor
Brookings
30
OREGON
CALIFORNIA

N
W E
S

0   10 mi
0   10 km

© AVALON TRAVEL PUBLISHING, INC.

CHAPTER 11

South Coast

The southern coast of Oregon is also called America's Wild Rivers Coast, where all of the major waterways that begin in the Cascades—Smith, Chetco, Pistol, Elk, Sixes, and mighty Rogue and Umpqua—empty into the sea, creating interesting lakes, estuaries, and Oregon's Bay Area, Coos Bay, along the way. The towns and recreation areas become less touristy the farther south you go. There's less saltwater taffy and more saltwater, exactly the kind of thing a dog pricks up her ears to hear.

In the forests south of the Umpqua River, your pet will have the pleasure of encountering the Oregon Myrtlewood, a tree she's probably never smelled before. Famed for its multicolored burled wood and fragrant dark leaves that smell similar to bay, it grows only in this region of Oregon and the Holy Land in Israel.

If you travel in May and June, another exotic species your pup will meet is the *Vellela Vellela* (By the Wind Sailor), a member of the jellyfish family pushed ashore by west winds in massive numbers. Their fins are translucent, their bodies are cobalt blue, and, fortunately for curious wet noses, they don't have stingers or tentacles.

PICK OF THE LITTER—SOUTH COAST

BEST PARKS
Sunset Bay, The Bay Area (page 304)
Cape Blanco, Port Orford (page 313)

BEST BEACH
Seven Devils, Bandon (page 309)

BEST TRAIL
Oregon Redwood Nature Trail, Brookings-Harbor (page 319)

BEST EVENT
Afternoon Concerts in Azalea Park, Brookings-Harbor (page 318)

BEST PLACES TO EAT
Bandon Fish Market, Bandon (page 311)
The Crazy Norwegian, Port Orford (page 315)
Scampi's Fish Wagon, Brookings-Harbor (page 321)

BEST PLACES TO STAY
Coos Bay Manor Bed and Breakfast, The Bay Area (page 306)
Castaway By the Sea, Port Orford (page 315)

The Bay Area

The Bay Area of Oregon refers to the city of Coos Bay and suburbs North Bend and Charleston. Coos Bay is Oregon's largest bay, a significant commercial passage first for coal at the turn of the 19th century, and later lumber and seafood. A stroll along Coos Bay's Boardwalk gives you the opportunity to shop quaint stores and gawk at the marina's working boats and pleasure craft. North Bend is the shopping district, and Charleston on the west is a fishing village, still one of the state's commercial fishing ports that also serves as the main gateway to three state parks, with their promontories and protected bays famous for blazing sunsets. Flower lovers come to the 743 acres of Shore Acres Botanical Gardens, with its wheelchair-accessible paths; however, this state park is off limits to dogs.

PARKS, BEACHES, AND RECREATION AREAS

❶ Empire Lakes/John Topits Park

 (See South Coast map on page 300)

These woodsy lakes are surrounded by strip malls and superstores, but you'd never know it from walking or fishing along the forested paths of their shores. Tourists usually miss this 120-acre destination, so the friendly dogs you meet and greet are probably locals. The 1.25-mile path around the lower lake is paved and wheelchair-accessible, and there are additional unpaved and primitive trails around Upper and Middle Empire. These bayous are full of what dogs think of as everything nice: bugs, frogs, birds, and bumper stickers on trucks that read, "A bad day fishing is better than a good day at the office."

From Newmark Street, the main east-west thoroughfare in North Bend, turn north on Hull Road to find the parking lot, trailhead, and restrooms. 541/269-8918.

❷ Mingus Park

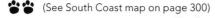 (See South Coast map on page 300)

Mingus is a truly lovely city park, with immaculate Japanese and rhododendron gardens surrounding a pond complete with water fountains (lighted from underneath at night), lily pads, and waterfowl. Even if you start out in a hurry, the peaceful grounds tempt you to stop to smell the flowers. The paved, accessible path around the pond is .4 mile, passing by viewing benches and crossing over a traditional arched bridge. There is a covered picnic gondola at the far end and a few minor wooded trails in an arboretum beyond.

From U.S. Highway 101, turn west onto Commercial Avenue and turn north on 10th Street. Pass the ball field and the skate park and cross the street to Chosi Gardens. 541/269-8918.

❸ Golden and Silver Falls

 (See South Coast map on page 300)

Two trails, less than a half mile each, head off in opposite directions through an old-growth forest of maple, alder, Douglas fir, and Myrtles to these cascades on Silver and Glenn creeks. They are stunning, easy hikes. The 160-foot Silver Falls appears to rain straight out of the sky, and Golden Falls is only slightly less impressive. If your energetic pup needs more exercise, there is a .9-mile trail that climbs the edge of a steep cliff (leashes please) and gives you views of both falls. To reach the longer trail, head to the right from the parking lot, over a bridge, then left at the first trail junction.

The 24-mile drive inland from the coast to this State Natural Area is a roller coaster ride. From the Y intersection on the south end of Coos Bay, follow the sign to Allegany. Cross the bridge, turn north on 6th Avenue for .5 mile, and

DOG-EAR YOUR CALENDAR

Didn't have time to make a float? Don't have a pet? No problem! Kids with pets—of the live or stuffed animal variety but preferably *not* of the taxidermy kind—are encouraged to participate in the **July Jubilee Parade** at the **Dawg Days of Summer,** presented by the Pacific Cove Humane Society in Coos Bay–North Bend. Awards are given in various categories, and entries are generously "judged" on creativity and the inclusion of at least one animal in the theme.

There is a $5 entry fee. Parade entry forms and rules and regulations are available at the Coos Bay or North Bend visitors centers, or call 541/756-6522 or email topdog@coosnet.com.

turn east on Coos River Road. The closer you get, the less of a road it is, and the last five miles are unpaved. Just when you're convinced that you can't possibly be on the right road, you'll see the sign to Glenn Creek Road indicating you only have three more miles to go. 541/888-3778, ext. 26.

🞄 Bastendorff Beach

🐾🐾🐾 (See South Coast map on page 300)

No pets are allowed in the picnic area of Bastendorff Beach County Park, and camping is nicer at Sunset Bay anyway, so Coop 'n' Isis suggest driving right past the county park and straight to the beach. The sun rises early on these shores, which curve two miles around to the north and east. You can park steps away from the beach in multiple places along a mile of road below the Coos Head U.S. Naval Facility. Walk your dog on the superfine sand for miles, from the jetty access to Coos Bay at the north end on down.

Take Cape Arago Highway west from U.S. Highway 101 and turn right at the sign for the county park onto Coos Head Road. 541/888-5353.

🞄 Sunset Bay

🐾🐾🐾🐾 (See South Coast map on page 300)

Partially enclosed by high sandstone bluffs and a narrow sea passage, this state park once played safe haven to vessels during storms, and as local lore has it, pirate ships waiting to spring on unsuspecting ships passing in the night. Waves are gentle behind the protected breakwall, and the water is shallow, making it a great place to play. The tidepools send dogs' noses and kids' imaginations into overdrive checking out the hermit crabs, sea anemones, starfish, limpets, urchins, and so on. The sealife is for your eyes only, no licking or nudging with paws.

For hiking, you can pick up a two-mile section of the Oregon Coast Trail between Sunset Bay and Shore Acres. You'll find the trail marker tucked behind the right side of the restroom in the picnic area. The park meadow is big enough for a hot-air balloon, as proved by Malcolm Forbes in 1973 when he took off on his successful transcontinental flight.

On Cape Arago Highway, 12 miles southwest of Coos Bay. 541/888-4902.

6 Cape Arago

🐾🐾🐾 (See South Coast map on page 300)

It is rewarding enough to simply drive or walk the loop at the road's end, gawking at incredible views, explosive surf, and sunsets beyond compare from a wheelchair-accessible lookout. Your dog will certainly appreciate it if you look more closely for multiple pullouts and markers for trails that wind through this state park. The Pack Trail, for example, is a 2.25-mile trip that gains 400 feet in elevation past WWII bunkers to the end of the cape. From another trail, you can catch a glimpse of the Cape Arago Lighthouse perched on the edge of the cliffs. It is not open to the public, but you can hear its unusual foghorn. Another paved switchback trail leads down to the South Cove, a sliver of beach with lots of smelly detritus washed onshore. (Oh boy! Oh boy!) If your dog thinks his bark is loud, he ought to get a load of the chorus of pinnipeds—that's seals and sea lions to us lay dogs—along Simpson Reef. Hundreds to thousands of them haul out on the rocks of Shell Island Refuge offshore to bask, bark, and breed in the sun.

Think "'ere I go" to correctly pronounce Arago, and to get there, take the Cape Arago Highway west from U.S. Highway 101, and watch for signs that say Charleston-State Parks. Cape Arago is at the end of the road, 14 miles southwest of Coos Bay. Open 7 A.M.–6 P.M., until 9 P.M. in the summer. 541/888-3778, ext. 26.

PLACES TO EAT

Blue Heron Bistro: This restaurant specializes in two distinctly different types of cuisine: seafood and German food. If the shrimp, bacon-wrapped oysters, or blackened salmon sandwiches don't tempt you, perhaps the bratwurst, knockwurst, and sauerkraut will. You can squeeze into one of a couple of tiny sidewalk tables for lunch or dinner. 100 Commercial Ave.; 541/267-3933; www.blueheronbistro.com.

Charleston Station Donuts and Bagels: ...and ice cream, and pies, and Italian sodas, and croissants, cider, teas, chocolate, sandwiches, fresh bread, and soups. Closed Monday and Tuesday. 91120 Cape Arago Hwy., Charleston; 541/888-3306.

Taylor Maid Do-nuts: "One or a thousand," reads the sign at this been-around-forever bakery. There's a brisk drive-through business in dairy, too—cones, parfaits, shakes, malts, and sundaes. Isis double-dog-dares you to order a thousand donuts. 1091 Hill St.; 541/269-0411.

Top Dog Espresso: With a name like that, of course this drive-through serves dog biscuits to canine backseat drivers. Try the espresso milkshake; it's good enough to growl for. 3636 Tremont (Hwy. 101 S.), North Bend; 541/756-6135.

Willett's Chowder House: Bring your appetite along with your preferably large dog to the covered patio at Willett's, where all meals come with a cup of chowder, a vegetable, garlic cheese bread, and fries. That's in addition to your pork chops, chicken, steak, prawns, scallops, or salmon. Cooper the Hoover did his best to test the theory that it's possible to eat more than one's own body weight in a single sitting. 63048 Hwy. 101; 541/266-0922.

PLACES TO STAY

Coos Bay Manor Bed and Breakfast: Pam and Bill Bate welcome mannerly dogs with open arms (and no extra fees!) in all five rooms of their home, a stunning example of neo-Colonial architecture on the National Register of Historic Places. The original owner was a paper-pulp mill baron named Nerdrum, who settled in Coos Bay from Finland in 1912. Many famous families have sheltered on the portico and front porch since, where you and your pets are welcome to hang out with Bark Lee, the Bates' transplanted Texan shih tzu. Rooms are $80–100, including breakfast and optional history lessons and tours. 955 S. 5th St.; 541/269-1224 or 800/269-1224; www.coosbaymanor.com.

Edgewater Inn: Coos Bay's only waterfront motel has big, ground-level rooms with sliding glass doors out to a nice strip of lawn by the bay. Rates range $78–89, plus a $10 pet fee. 275 E. Johnson Ave.; 541/267-0423 or 800/233-0423; www.edgewater-inns.com.

Sunset Bay Campground: You'll need reservations for the 29 hookup, 36 electrical, and 66 tent sites in a sheltered cove, each with decent privacy thanks to tall trees and shrubbery. Spaces are $12–20, which includes free admission to nearby Shore Acres Botanical Gardens, where, alas, dogs are not allowed. 89526 Cape Arago Hwy.; 800/452-5687; www.reserveamerica.com.

More Accommodations: Please look under Chain Hotels in the Resources section for additional places to stay in this area.

Coquille and Myrtle Point

These two towns are off the radar, inland 20 miles from Bandon on the coast, and their combined population is probably less than 5,000. The countryside is serene, most notable for large groves of the exotic Myrtle tree and the multiple winding forks of the Coquille River.

PARKS, BEACHES, AND RECREATION AREAS

7 LaVerne Park

 (See South Coast map on page 300)

When it's time to leave behind the tourist frenzy on the beaches and escape into the countryside, come to this beautiful county park. A broad playfield is bordered by tall Douglas firs and Myrtlewood trees set on the banks of the North Fork of the Coquille River. The park has been around awhile and has matured nicely into a pleasant rural getaway. No dogs are allowed on the designated swimming beach, which isn't much to brag about anyway. There are other spots along the river where your dog could sneak in for a quick swim.

From State Route 42 in Coquille, follow the signs to turn on West Central Boulevard, and east on Fairview Road 14 miles to the Upper North Fork Road. 541/396-2344.

8 Sandy Creek Covered Bridge Wayside

 (See South Coast map on page 300)

Just west of a town called Remote, 42 miles from Roseburg on State Route 42, is a covered bridge built in 1921 beside a circle of lawn, some good-sized pine trees, and a latrine. It may come in handy on the ride out to the coast if your backseat companion is giving you that special whine and you've got your legs crossed. If nothing else, you both can get out and stretch your legs while you look at the map of Coos County parks on display.

PLACES TO EAT

Figaro's Italian Kitchen and Sub Express: We bet your black-and-tan coonhound would happily serenade you with the famous refrain from the opera *Barber of Seville* for this Figaro's hot fajita or cool ranch chicken wrap. At the drive-through or on the wraparound porch, the restaurant's pizza, subs, calzones, ice cream, and frozen yogurt are tasty enough to entice your minstrel mutt to sing for his supper. 29 W. 1st St., Coquille; 541/396-5277.

PLACES TO STAY

LaVerne County Park Campground: The camping pads at LaVerne are gravel, and most sites have river views. The park host recommends leaving the place to the locals on crowded Memorial Day and Labor Day weekends. Tent sites are $11, full hookups are $16; local checks only, so bring cash. Reservations: 541/396-3121, ext. 354.

Bandon

The official name of this cute village is Bandon-by-the-Sea. The first settlements were destroyed by fire in 1914 and again in 1936 and now, Old Town Bandon is generally what the place looked like after the latter, and hopefully last, fire. Bandon is also a sweet town, home of the best fudge on the coast (Big Wheel General Store; 130 Baltimore; 541/247-3719) and Cranberry Sweets, a company that makes a huge variety of jelly-fruit candies and gives out free samples! Cooper's mom likes shopping in town, but, fortunately for him, the parks and beaches are plentiful and pup-friendly. Turn onto Beach Loop Drive, starting south of Bandon and ending in Old Town, for a scenic byway that takes you past most of the lodging and beach parks.

PARKS, BEACHES, AND RECREATION AREAS

⑨ South Slough National Estuarine Research Reserve

🐾 🐾 (See South Coast map on page 300)

With a mouthful of a name that is easily shortened to South Slough, this 19,000-acre estuary is only a fraction of the larger 384,000 protected acres of the Coos Bay Estuary. An estuary is a rich wetlands environment where freshwater meets and mixes with saltwater, creating a biological stew perfect for infinite varieties of marine-, plant-, and birdlife. The Ten-Minute Loop trail gives you a quick look at the local flora, labeled for easy identification. There are a variety of other trails and boardwalks, from .75 mile to three miles, for you and your curious pet to explore a variety of marshes full of frogs and snails and puppy dogs' tails (just kidding about

that last one). They were all underwater when we visited; call ahead to the interpretive center for their status before you visit. 61907 Seven Devils Rd.; 541/888-5558; www.southsloughestuary.org.

10 Seven Devils

🐾🐾🐾🐾 (See South Coast map on page 300)

The Wonder Wieners give this State Recreation Site high marks for sticking to the KISS principle. You have instant access to the beach, the whole beach, and nothing but the beach. A narrow strip of meadow is protected by cliffs that rise to either side, and a smattering of picnic tables have outstanding views. At seven miles off the highway, it doesn't get much action other than a few rockhounders looking for agates. Come up here and get away from the hubbub for a purist beach experience. Restrooms are available.

From U.S. Highway 101, 14 miles north of Bandon, turn west another seven miles onto Seven Devils Road. The approach to Seven Devils from the south is paved; north of the wayside, the road becomes a precarious, one-lane, dirt forest road. Poor Cooper got carsick.

11 Bullards Beach

🐾🐾 (See South Coast map on page 300)

This state park has multiple picnic areas and parking lots along the wide mouth of the Coquille River as it dumps into the sea. The campground is a mile from the beach along a paved trail, and the three-mile Cut Creek Trail is a dirt track through flat grassland out to the Coquille River Lighthouse, built in 1896. The smallest lighthouse on the coast, it was officially decommissioned in 1939 and restored in 1979 with a solar-powered light in the tower to re-create the visual effect. Call 541/347-2209 for the lighthouse interpretive center.

The best access to Cut Creek is between corrals #7 and #8 in the horse camp. If you're not interested in hoofing it alongside the horses, a road with parking leads directly to the beach and lighthouse. The campground at Bullards Beach is designed for RVs and horse trailers rather than tent campers. The turnoff is two miles north of Bandon on U.S. Highway 101. 541/347-2209.

12 Bandon City Park

🐾🐾🐾 (See South Coast map on page 300)

Bandon is the only beach town we know of that has a dog park! The rules sign on the secure gate includes a notation that your dogs owe their thanks to Edith Leslie for her donation that made possible the designated and fenced play area. There are a couple of picnic tables, a water faucet, trash can, and bag dispenser in an uneven acre of meadow with a stand of trees in the middle. In short, the OLA is a little piece of dog delight.

The larger city park is an oval, and traffic is routed one-way westbound on the north, eastbound on the south. The OLA is on the south, eastbound side of the loop. From U.S. Highway 101, turn west on 11th Street, go past Jackson Avenue, make the loop around the park, and look to your right. The Russ Sommers Memorial Playground is worth a detour to the north side of the park, dogs on leash, if you have kids.

Bandon Marsh National Wildlife Refuge

 (See South Coast map on page 300)

The mouth of the Coquille River forms the Bandon Marsh NWR at Coquille Point. It's more informative from a human's perspective, with paved walkways leading to a series of interpretive signs telling the story of the mammal, marine, and aviary species who take up residence in a marsh. For your darling dog, sauntering along the windy bluff at your side has to be worth a tail wag or two. From U.S. Highway 101, turn west on 11th Street to the end.

14 Face Rock Wayside

(See South Coast map on page 300)

Don't be embarrassed if you can't see her face at first. It's like one of those Rorschach inkblots, where once someone points the picture out to you, you can't *not* see it. Nah-So-Mah Tribe legend says that the woman rising out of the water is Ewanua, a chief's daughter who swam into the sea and was turned to stone when she refused to look into the face of the spiteful god Seatka. When her faithful dog Komax swam out to rescue her, the monster petrified him as well (now that's evil), and her cats and kittens, creating the string of rocks to the northwest.

The rock formations are viewed from a paved walkway above, and a long series of steps leads down to the beach proper. It's a favorite spot of joggers, beachcombers, and people who like to peer into the busy marine goings-on of tidepools. Challenge your dog to see how many sea creatures she can sniff out stuck to the sides of the rocks.

From U.S. Highway 101, turn west on Beach Loop Road, one mile south of Bandon to this State Scenic Viewpoint.

15 Devil's Kitchen

 (See South Coast map on page 300)

Bandon State Natural Area is this park's official name; Devil's Kitchen is the colloquialism. At the southernmost Beach Access Road, you have to cross an ankle-deep river to reach the ocean. The trail down to the beach is on the north end of the parking lot, hiding behind some rocks. The second wayside has a shady picnic meadow, but the beach is over a very steep dune, covered with prickly bushes and spiky trees. The dachshunds never made it, having been distracted by turquoise dragonflies.

Of the three waysides, the northernmost gives you the easiest path to the sand, by way of a partially paved trail and series of wooden steps. It's also the largest and most developed, with rolling meadows, restrooms, picnic tables, and fire pits. The rock formations include a haystack rock, but it is not *the* Haystack Rock everyone talks about, which is farther north in Cannon Beach.

From U.S. Highway 101, five miles south of Bandon, turn on Beach Loop Road and follow the signs to reach the three park waysides.

16 New River ACEC

😸 😸 😸 (See South Coast map on page 300)

An ACEC is an Area of Critical Environmental Concern, land granted federal status for the protection unique ecosystems and wildlife. In this park, a reserve for globally important birding, three miles of trails take you through a variety of habitats, across a meadow, past ponds, into a forest, along the sand, and among marsh grasses. The trail surface varies, but is always easy and clear, and a small portion is paved for wheelchair accessibility. The New River separates you from the ocean, but as you approach you can hear the surf pounding and catch a glimpse of it from the top of the boat ramp. Car and boat access is restricted March 15—September 15 to protect the snowy plover. Trails are open all year, along with the Ellen Warring Learning Center, where kids can touch and explore exhibits about the creatures that live in the park (dogs not allowed inside the center). Isis and Cooper saw a brace or two of birds but were more impressed by the abundance of bunnies.

From U.S. Highway 101, 8.5 miles south of Bandon, turn west on Croft Lake Lane for 1.7 miles down a somewhat bumpy dirt road, and bear right at the fork in the road marked by a small brown sign with binoculars to reach the Storm Ranch Entrance. Trail maps are available at the center. Open sunrise–sunset.

PLACES TO EAT

Bandon Fish Market: The rockfish fish-and-chips baskets, seafood cocktails, fish tacos, and chowder in sourdough bread bowls all taste amazing, especially when you're seated at outdoor tables with spiffy blue-and-white checkered tablecloths. There's a dog dish outside and a bucket o' biscuits at the counter, and if you're feeling flush, splurge and buy your best friend a $2 dried salmon stick. "They feed you too much," said one patron, who obviously didn't have a dog to take the excess off of his hands. 249 1st St. S.E.; 541/347-4282; www.bandonfishmarket.com.

Bandon Gourmet: This excellent deli specializes in omelettes for breakfast, made-to-order sandwiches for lunch, and whole pizza pies for early dinner (open until 6 P.M.). That doesn't even begin to touch the rows of cakes and baked goods behind the display glass and loaves of bread to take home. 92 2nd St.; 541/347-3237.

Port O' Call: Owners of the largest breeds may want to keep an eye out for the dangerous combination of curious noses and paws around the claws of the live lobsters and crabs in the tanks at this authentic seafood market. Order your crustaceans steamed or served up in tomato broth for a spicy soup called cioppino, while you sit at the outdoor oyster bar and sip bottled beer and wines by the glass. 155 1st St.; 541/347-2875.

PLACES TO STAY

Driftwood Motel: There are no ocean-view rooms at this all nonsmoking motel, unless you count the original painted ocean landscapes on the walls above the beds. Hues are soothing grays and blues to invoke the right mood, and the $55–80 rates won't make you blue or gray at the gills. Except for resident dogs Brett and Osa, pets are charged $10 per night. 460 Hwy. 101; 541/347-9022 or 888/374-3893.

Sunset Oceanfront: In the trade, ocean view means you can catch a glimpse of the ocean from your window and oceanfront means you can reach the beach from your door. This motel has both, and both new and older rooms, all facing Face Rock. Oceanfront rooms range $80–135; ocean views are noticeably cheaper at $56–79; all require a $10 pet fee. 1865 Beach Loop Dr. S.W.; 541/347-2453 or 800/842-2407; www.sunsetmotel.com.

Table Rock Motel: Table Rock is a tiny motel, where dogs are allowed in six of the 14 rooms. Rooms are refreshing, with pretty cotton quilts on the beds, and refreshingly priced at $60–80, especially for Room #12, with an ocean view. Small dogs are $5, large are $10. 840 Beach Loop Rd. S.W.; 541/347-2700 or 800/457-9141.

More Accommodations: Please look under Chain Hotels in the Resources section for additional places to stay in this area.

Port Orford

After much strife with the land's earlier inhabitants, this port became the oldest European settled town on the coast in 1851. The coast's oldest continuously operating lighthouse is at nearby Cape Blanco, commissioned in 1870 to aid the ships transporting gold and lumber from the region.

PARKS, BEACHES, AND RECREATION AREAS

17 Boice-Cope at Floras Lake

🐾🐾 (See South Coast map on page 300)

In 1910, there were about 400 people living here on a developer's promise to build a canal connecting the lake to the ocean to create a thriving sea port. When they discovered the lake is at a slightly higher elevation, and thus would drain out into the ocean if linked, the plan dried up and so did the people. The windsurfers don't mind a bit, making the lake a favorite place to practice because winds are steady at 15–25 knots, it's shallow, and water temperature averages 68°F.

You can walk around the lake on a sandy trail, and up over a single dune to the ocean on the far side from the parking lot/campground. Campsites at this county park are all together in a big meadow, $12 for tents, $16 for RVs.

Turn onto Floras Lake Loop from U.S. Highway 101, west onto Floras Lake Road, and west again on Boice-Cope Road. Parking is $2 per day. 541/247-7011.

18 Cape Blanco

🐾🐾🐾🐾 (See South Coast map on page 300)

Among some pretty stiff competition, Cape Blanco manages to stand out as a superb state park, the tip of which sticks out as the westernmost spot in the contiguous 48 states. It's got everything a dog dreams of: beach access along the south, picnicking in fields along the Sixes River, and eight miles of trails through a wide variety of ecosystems, from forest to tall grass dunes. For the people in your party, the views of the ocean surrounding three sides of the landmass are unbeatable. History buffs will appreciate the tours of the 245-foot Cape Blanco Lighthouse, the Victorian Hughes House on the National Register of Historic Places, and the remains of the church and cemetery. The lighthouse is the southernmost in Oregon, and the first to have a Fresnel lens installed in 1870. Call 541-765-0100 for information about hours and tours for the lighthouse and Hughes House, both of which have wheelchair-accessible areas.

The easiest beach access point is through the campground, next to site #A32. You can drive or walk down a winding lane that eventually crumbles right onto the beach, with a few parking places just before the sidewalk ends.

From U.S. Highway 101, nine miles north of Port Orford, go west on Cape Blanco Road to the end. 39745 S. Hwy. 101; 541/332-6774.

19 Paradise Point

🐾🐾 (See South Coast map on page 300)

Paradise, in this instance, is a coarse sand beach that extends several miles from the Port Orford Heads to Cape Blanco. Look closely, and you'll see that the beach is actually billions of tiny pebbles that have yet to be ground to the fine texture of sand. In most places, it is a steep slope of sand down to the water, making it tricky to walk long distances without feeling lopsided.

For Paradise Point, there's no State Park sign on U.S. Highway 101. Look for the turnoff to Paradise Point Road about one mile north of town. Don't let the Dead End signs scare you, the road dead-ends into the State Recreation Site.

20 Port Orford Heads

🐾🐾🐾 (See South Coast map on page 300)

From 1934 to 1970, this state park was one of the busiest Coast Guard Stations on a stretch of treacherous water. The Heads are prominent landmasses jutting over the ocean, providing the best viewpoint for sighting ships in trouble on the rocks. Now, they give you some fantastic views. Trails in the park are well groomed in soft wood-mulch that's easy to walk. The half-mile Headland Trail leads out onto the edge of the bluff, and from there, you can connect to the .75-mile Loop Trail that takes you past the site of the former lookout tower and the boat house where rescuers launched into the rough seas. While you read the placards telling the stories of the search-and-rescue station and check out the restored lifeboat on display, your watchdog can keep his eyes peeled for the black-tailed deer common to the area. You can't reach the beach at the Heads, but you can look out over it for miles in every direction.

From U.S. Highway 101, follow the signs to turn west on 9th Street, and then south on Coast Guard Road. Open 6 A.M.–8 P.M.

21 Humbug Mountain

🐾🐾🐾 (See South Coast map on page 300)

Rottweilers, get ready to rumble. Pull out those paw booties and take on the challenge of Humbug Mountain, a six-mile loop trail that climbs from the beach up to the summit at 1,748 feet. As you rest along the way, your pal can sniff out the subtle differences between myrtle, maple, and old-growth Douglas firs. If you make it, you'll be treated to a northward viewpoint of Redfish Rocks and Port Orford and another south to Gold Beach. Trailhead parking is just north of the campground entrance. Isis has a tricky back that wasn't quite up to the rigors of the trail, but she did enjoy herself on the park's coarse gravel beach, north of the mountain, accessible along the banks of a creek starting near campsite #C7. The waves crash against the base of the mountain, and the surf has a wicked undertow.

To the south of the mountain is a picnic area, with its own parking and a meadow the length of a football field that looks fun to run around on. Walk down the paved pathway along the stream to find it.

This state park is unmistakable, even before you get there on U.S. Highway 101, six miles south of Port Orford. Open 6 A.M.–10 P.M. 39745 Hwy. 101; 541/332-6774.

PLACES TO EAT

Bread Zeppelin: Go through the drive-through for the basics—espresso, chai tea, fresh-squeezed juices and smoothies, bagels, scones, brownies, muffins, cookies, and cinnamon rolls. Go inside for a moment for the more exotic stuff like take-and-bake pizza and calzones and made-to-order sandwiches and salads. Dog treats are available at the drive-through! 1035 Oregon St.; 541/332-0587.

The Crazy Norwegian: As honorary Norwegians (on their step-maternal side), Isis and Cooper can say with tongue firmly in cheek that putting "crazy" and "Norwegian" together is a bit redundant. The cook will make you some insanely good fish-and-chips, salads, homemade cookies, burgers, sandwiches, and chowder to go. While you wait, you can experience the dry Scandinavian sense of humor, reading the menu and learning the various meanings of the expression "Uff Da," including "Having a mouse crawl up your leg on a hay ride," and "Waking yourself up in church with your own snoring." 259 Hwy. 101; 541/332-8601.

PLACES TO STAY

Cape Blanco Campground: A few of the 53 electric/water sites at this state park have water views, but most are neatly hidden from the water, and each other, widely spaced among the thick woods. It's miles to the main road through farm country; the only sounds you'll hear are the other campers, neighing from the neighboring horse camp, and the surf. Rates are $12–16 for first-come, first-served sites. 39745 S. Hwy. 101; 541/332-6774.

Castaway By the Sea: This motel did major renovations in 2004, but you probably won't notice because you'll be spending all of your time on the private, enclosed sun porch enthralled by the fantastic views. No dogs on the furniture, please. A variety of room sizes are priced at $45–135. Pets are $15 each per night. 545 W. 5th St.; 541/332-4502; www.castawaybythesea.com.

Holly House Inn Bed and Breakfast: Blinky the Staffordshire bull terrier welcomes you to one of two units in her home. The upstairs apartment has two bedrooms, a huge kitchen, and a living room with a woodstove. The downstairs is a smaller one-bedroom unit with a laundry room. "We are not delicate and refined here," says owner Francie, "we're much more user-friendly." In other words, you won't have to worry whether you're allowed to sit in the antique chairs. Roughhousing is also acceptable in the good-sized backyard. Both units require stairs and are not wheelchair-accessible. 600 Jackson St.; 541/332-7100; www.hollyhouseinn.com.

Gold Beach

This coastal community is where Oregon's most famous river, the Rogue, meets the Pacific Ocean. Ocean fishing and river charters for salmon and steelhead are at your beck and call. Coop 'n' Isis claim that the strip of beach between Brookings and Gold Beach is the best and most accessible on the Southern Coast. South Park and Kissing Rock provide two wheelchair-accessible ocean viewpoints, the former on the far south end of town, and the latter a mile south, on the south side of Hunter Creek.

Although the dogs couldn't technically list it as a park, there's a rest stop nine miles north of Gold Beach on U.S. Highway 101 that gives you instant access to miles of unspoiled sand between Nesika Beach and a spot known as Sisters Rocks. All that, plus a potty, pay phone, and picnic tables.

PARKS, BEACHES, AND RECREATION AREAS

22 Buffington Park

 (See South Coast map on page 300)

While everyone else is getting sand in their muzzles on the beach, you can escape to this cute community park in the center of town, with clean restrooms, covered and open picnic tables, and a Kid Castle playground.

From Ellensburg Avenue (Hwy. 101) in town, turn on E. Caughell at the sign pointing to the Library and Community Park. Open sunrise–sunset.

23 Cape Sebastian

(See South Coast map on page 300)

The cape is a cliff you can climb for the widest ocean, shore, and mountain views on the lower coast. There are two parking lots, 200 feet above sea level, where you can park to take in the expanses—40 miles to the north and Humbug Mountain and 50 miles as far south as California. From the second lot, there is a 1.5-mile trail leading to more panoramic vistas. The first half mile is paved, a real treat for wheelchair patrons (just about the best accessible views on the coast), and then it settles into a softer, paw-pleasing dirt trail through Sitka spruce with frequent clearings. It's essential to keep your pal on leash to avoid him going over the edge in his enthusiasm.

This State Scenic Corridor is seven miles south of Gold Beach on U.S. Highway 101. 800/541-6949.

24 Pistol River Sand Dunes

(See South Coast map on page 300)

In 1856, an infamous Native American–U.S. Army battle was fought here, and the park's name comes from a militia soldier rumored to have dropped his gun in the river in the heat of the fight. It'll be a slightly different park every time you visit. The sand dunes shift and grow in the summer, and the river has changed course several times in recent years. The big, bold surf is different every day. You'll often see windsurfers practicing for the Pistol River Wave Bash, the U.S. national championships, held here since 2000. After a short climb over the sand dunes, you reach an open stretch of beach between Brookings and Gold Beach.

The pullout for parking is directly off U.S. Highway 101, 11 miles south of Gold Beach. There are no amenities at this State Scenic Viewpoint, only sand, sea, and sky.

PLACES TO EAT

The Cannery: This building is home to a bunch of lunch options including the Coffee Dock for espresso, pastries, and teas; Cone Amor for ice cream and sweets; and Fisherman Direct Seafoods, a cooperative of local boat operators offering live and cooked crab, shrimp cocktail, smoked salmon, and other fresh treasures from the sea. 29975 S. Harbor Way; 541/247-9494.

Marty's Lunchbox Express: The folks at this drive-through are as friendly as all get out. They'll chat you up while they make burgers, cold and hot subs (including meatball, veggie, and pastrami), burritos, Italian sausage, daily specials, and cookies. Cash or checks only. 29471 Ellensburg Ave.; 541/247-6336.

PLACES TO STAY

Huntley Park Campground: This privately owned campground is a super secret, seven miles up the Rogue River from Gold Beach. Spacious sites in a deep myrtle grove are only $7 each, $5 in the winter. Bring quarters for the hot showers; firewood and blocks of ice are also available for a small fee. 96847 Jerry's Flat Rd.; 541/247-9377.

Inn of the Beachcomber: For people with pets, availability is limited to a second building behind the main building. Now, before you get your hackles up, keep in mind that these rooms are all on the ground floor, farther away from the noisy street, and closer to the beach. Out back, there's a big lawn and access trail. Pets are limited to two per room for a fee of $15–25, depending on size. Rates vary widely, $55–130. 29266 Ellensburg Ave.; 541/247-6691 or 888/690-2378; www.beachcomber-inn.com.

Ireland's Rustic Lodges: There's a surprising amount of room in the real log cabins, each one unique, with separate bedrooms and living rooms with fireplaces. Pets are allowed in cabins #2–8, but Cooper prefers the Hobbitish rooms out back (#25, #26, #27) because they have sliding glass doors out to a huge lawn and the beach trail. The price is more than right at $55–70 per night. Pets over 50 pounds are $10 per night; those under are $5. 29330 Ellensburg Ave.; 541/247-7718 or 877/447-3526; www.irelandsrusticlodges.com.

More Accommodations: Please look under Chain Hotels in the Resources section for additional places to stay in this area.

Brookings-Harbor

Only four miles north of the California border, Brookings benefits from weather patterns that give it the warmest average temperatures on the coast. The town is famous for its flowers, especially azaleas and Easter lilies, producing about 75 percent of all Easter lily bulbs grown in the United States. Vast fields of the tall white flowers are in full bloom in July, and the bulbs are shipped worldwide. You can reach this southernmost Oregon town only by coming down from U.S.

Highway 101, or by dipping into California from Grants Pass and back up again on the famed Redwood Highway, U.S. Highway 199.

If the parks and trails listed here are too tame for your taste, the **Kalmiopsis Wilderness,** with 197,000 acres of solitude and wildlife, is 30 miles inland from Brookings. The Chetco Ranger Station in Brookings can give you all the details (539 Chetco Ave.; 541/412-6000).

PARKS, BEACHES, AND RECREATION AREAS

25 Samuel H. Boardman

🐾🐾🐾🐾 (See South Coast map on page 300)

Sam Boardman was Oregon's first Superintendent of Parks, a visionary who led the effort to build a phenomenal system of preserved public lands. The acquisition of this State Scenic Corridor named in his honor was successfully negotiated as his last triumph before retiring. It's not so much a park as an adventure—a 12-mile long forest on rugged cliffs punctuated by small beaches. As you drive through the park on U.S. Highway 101, there are viewpoints, picnic areas, 300-year-old Sitka spruce trees, and beach access. If you'd rather explore the park on foot, 27 miles of the Oregon Coast Trail wind through its forests and along the coast.

The dynamic duo got a kick out of seeing how fast they could exhaust their mother, hopping in and out of the car at every viewpoint and wayside of the 1,471 acres. Of them all, the Whalehead Beach Trail is the paws-down winner. A narrow path winds through thick brush for about a half mile (in the spring, before feet have trampled down the brush, parts of the path are almost invisible). Undaunted trailblazing bulldogs are rewarded with the largest, most fabulous beach in the park.

DOG-EAR YOUR CALENDAR

Pack a picnic, grab a blanket or lawn chair, harness up your pup, and head to **Afternoon Concerts in Azalea Park** in Brookings. The summer concert series, Sundays at 1 P.M., May–September, is free of charge. No alcohol, please. Singing along with the music is strongly discouraged for dogs and tone-challenged humans. Call the Chamber of Commerce for more information at 541/469-3181.

Big dogs, little dogs, and dogs who walk on stilts (now that's something Cooper would like to see) are encouraged to attend Brooking's annual **Canine Capers** to benefit the South Coast Humane Society. The festivities take place on the Boardwalk at the Port in mid-September. There are obedience training demonstrations and all kinds of contests that require no training whatsoever. Call the Humane Society for information at 541/469-0325.

You can't miss the park—U.S. Highway 101 drives straight through the middle, beginning four miles north of Brookings. You'll see signs for stops, including a good picnic area at Lone Ranch Beach and great viewpoints at Cape Ferrelo, House Rock, and Indian Sands. On your way, you'll cross over the tallest bridge in Oregon.

26 Oregon Redwood Nature Trail

😸😸😸😸 📣 (See South Coast map on page 300)

This awe-inspiring one-mile trail takes you through the Pacific Coast's northernmost grove of redwood trees. You'll get a crick in your neck as you wonder at these giants, estimated to be between 600 and 800 years old. The path is generally easy, with a few steep, rocky, and narrow sections. Your pooch may not appreciate the height of the trees, but she'll certainly enjoying sniffing around their girth and pestering the harmless spiders living in the equally large ferns on the forest floor. Pick up an interpretive map at the trailhead, which leads you counterclockwise around the trail.

Parking at the trailhead is $5 per day, but if you are up to it, you can park free at Alfred A. Loeb State Park and take the .7-mile Riverview Trail connecting to and from this trail.

27 Alfred A. Loeb

😸😸😸 (See South Coast map on page 300)

If you've worked your way down the coast, overdosing on ocean vistas, this state park deep in the woods is a welcome change of pace. Dozens of secluded picnic areas are tucked into a 200-year-old Myrtlewood grove. The meadows and trails and woods are next to the banks of the Chetco River, here a swift-moving, shallow stream in a wide bed of river rocks.

From the picnic area, the Riverview Trail travels .7 mile along the shore, connecting you to another great hike, the Redwood Trail, in the Siskiyou National Forest. Cooper highly recommends camping here in the peaceful forest by crystal-clear waters. Isis comes for the amazing variety of birds living in the grove. Note to dogs: Don't eat or play with the orange newts in the region—their skin secretes a deadly toxin. Note to humans: Don't worry too much, as the newts are fast and can probably out-scamper your scamp.

From U.S. Highway 101, follow the signs to the state park, 10 miles in on the North Bank Chetco River Road. Open 7:30 A.M.–10 P.M. 541/469-2021.

28 Harris Beach

😸😸 (See South Coast map on page 300)

You begin to see the wonders of the ocean from the minute you drive into this state park. Unique rock formations loom from several pullout viewpoints, including Goat Island, the coast's largest offshore island. From this area, you can reach the first section of beach on the short Sunset Beach Trail.

Keep driving, and you'll pass the campground to reach the looped parking lot for the main picnic area and a second crescent of silky sand. Picnic tables are well placed for maximum views on a terraced hillside, wheelchair-accessible along a paved path. In between them is an outdoor shower where you and pup can rinse off after a frolic on the small beach. Cooper can't recommend camping here because the sawmill next door makes too much noise at night.

Harris Beach is directly off of U.S. Highway 101, just north of the main section of Brookings. Parking is $3 per day. Open 8 A.M.–8 P.M. 541/469-2021.

29 Azalea Park

 (See South Coast map on page 300)

This beautiful and unique city park is at its peak in mid-May, when the azaleas are in full bloom. Imagine the nuances a dog's nose must smell among 1,100 bushes of three species, some up to 300 years old. There are aspects of the park for you and your pets to appreciate all year: rolling hills, an accessible sidewalk and paths through the trees, sand-pit volleyball courts, viewing benches, and hidden picnic tables. Dogs are allowed to pull up a patch of lawn and enjoy summer concerts with you at the Stage Under the Stars and on the big playground called Kid Town. The fragrance from the riot of flowers is most heady in the center of the park, from the observation tower. There are no restrictions except to keep your pet on leash in the ball fields. Like Dorothy and her companions in the poppies, a drowsy afternoon here may lull you to sleep. The park is easy to find by following the signs from U.S. Highway 101 just after you cross the bridge over the Chetco River.

30 McVay Rock

(See South Coast map on page 300)

This windy, brisk picnic spot is off the beaten path, a quieter place for your dog to explore the local flora and fauna while you take in the endless ocean views. From a gravel parking lot and a petite lawn, a very steep but short trail will take you down to the beach. It's mostly gravel, without water access because of the large rocks in the surf. The rock itself sits several stories tall behind you in someone's field of veggies. There are no signs directing you to this State Recreation Site, so watch for Ocean View Drive on U.S. Highway 101, two miles south of Brookings. Turn left there, travel about a mile, and turn left again on Seagull Lane.

PLACES TO EAT

Homeport Bagels and Sandwiches: On the back of the menu, you can read the amusing story of the Bagel Boy who used his bagel as a lifesaver when the listing S.S. *Laura* was lost at sea. On the front you can order one of 14 custom bagel sandwiches, or make your own, for breakfast and lunch. Juice smoothies, green salads, and soups are made from scratch daily, just like the bagels. 1011 Chetco Ave.; 541/469-6611.

Scampi's Fish Wagon: Scampi, the Pomeranian with a haircut, is something of a local celebrity, thanks to having his own lunch wagon with a bunch of picnic tables under an awning down by the harbor. His mom and dad serve really good seafood at an unbelievably low price. Choose from fish caught daily, homemade clam chowder, and scallops, prawns, and oysters in tacos or in baskets with fries or onion rings. Cash or check only. Lower Harbor Rd.; 541/412-9530.

PLACES TO STAY

Alfred A. Loeb Campground: There are 48 electrical sites with water, flush toilets, and hot showers by the Chetco River in a grove of Myrtlewood trees. Summer rates are $16 per site, in the off-season it's a measly $12. All sites are on a first-come, first-served basis. North Bank Chetco River Road, 10 miles northeast of Brookings. 541/469-2021.

Harbor Inn: South of town on U.S. Highway 101, this motel is done in soothing colors of rose and light blue with comfy pillow-top beds, microwave, refrigerator, and cable in every room. Top-floor rooms have distant ocean views. Rates are $58–78, plus a $12 per pet nightly fee. 15991 Hwy. 101 S.; 541/469-3194 or 800/469-8444; www.harborinnmotel.com.

Sea Dreamer: Every homey room is different at this bed-and-breakfast in the blue Victorian house, built by hand in 1912 of California redwoods. Most rooms have ocean views, and pets have a nice yard to explore. Pet fee varies depending on the size and behavior of the dog(s); please call ahead to discuss with the owners. Rates are $60–70. 15167 McVay Lane; 541/469-6629 or 800/408-4367.

More Accommodations: Please look under Chain Hotels in the Resources section for additional places to stay in this area.

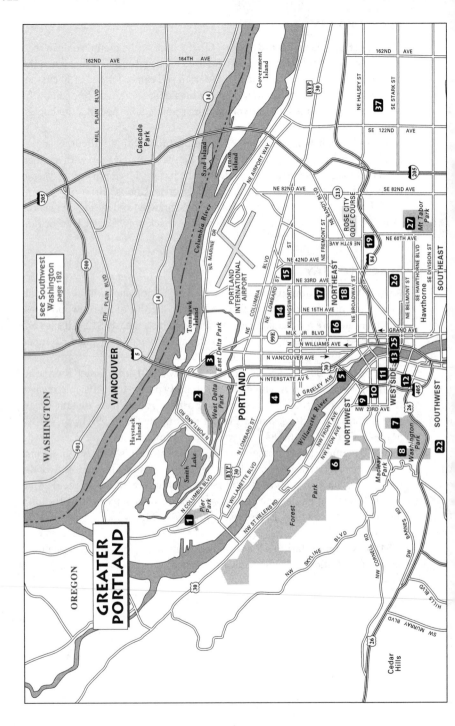

GREATER PORTLAND

OREGON

WASHINGTON

see Southwest Washington page 182

VANCOUVER

PORTLAND

NORTHWEST

NORTHEAST

WEST SIDE

SOUTHWEST

SOUTHEAST

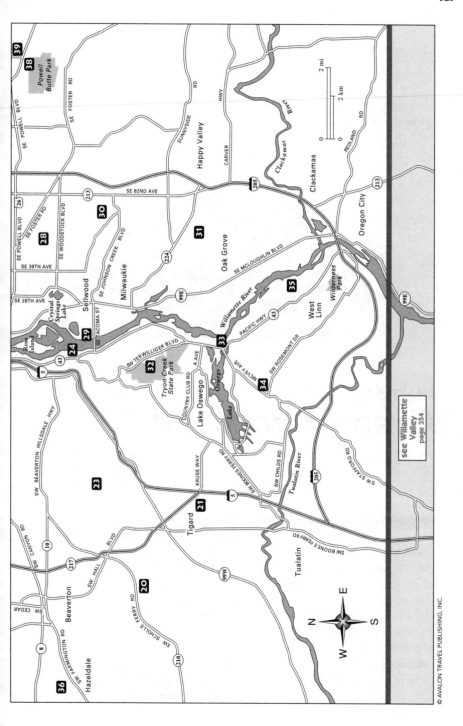

see Willamette
Valley
page 354

© AVALON TRAVEL PUBLISHING, INC.

CHAPTER 12

Greater Portland

The *Dog Nose News,* Portland's free monthly publication for animal lovers, estimates that 30 percent of the city's households have pets in the family. Such a high canine census makes sense in a metro area with 37,000 acres of parks and green spaces. Despite an annual rainfall that rivals Seattle's, Isis and Cooper can testify that Portlanders will tolerate wet dog smells and muddy paw prints to take advantage of the outdoors under any weather conditions.

When not braving the elements, the city's diverse populations cluster in ever-present neighborhood coffee houses and bookstores, the greatest of which is Powell's City of Books, the country's largest independent bookseller, with more than a million volumes on shelves that take up an entire city block (1005 W. Burnside; 503/228-0540 or 866/201-7601; www.powells.com). When not drowning in mud, Portland natives also like to drown their sorrows in one of the city's 25 craft breweries.

On a serious note, Portland had a very public tragedy involving dogs in city parks in 2003. Seventeen dogs were deliberately poisoned by pieces of sausage tainted with a toxic herbicide, placed in bushes of a park known for ongoing

PICK OF THE LITTER—GREATER PORTLAND

BEST PARKS
South Park Blocks, Downtown (page 333)
Laurelhurst Park, Southeast Portland (page 344)

BEST DOG PARKS
Chimney Park, North Portland (page 326)
Gabriel Park, Southwest Portland (page 341)
Luscher Farm Dog Park, Lake Oswego (page 349)
Hazeldale Park, Beaverton (page 351)

BEST EVENTS
Dog Daze of Summer (a dogs-only pool swim), Milwaukie (page 343)
Dogtoberfest Dog Wash, Southeast Portland (page 343)

BEST PLACES TO EAT
St. Honoré Boulangerie, Northwest Portland (page 330)
South Park, Downtown (page 334)
Berlin Inn, Southeast Portland (page 346)
Lucky Lab Brewing Co., Southeast Portland (page 346)

BEST PLACES TO STAY
Hotel Lucia, Downtown (page 334)
Mallory Hotel, Downtown (page 335)

leash-law skirmishes. Two more poisoning incidents occurred in 2004, one in a Portland park and one at a northern Oregon Coast beach. Protect your dog by being aware of his activities at all times, by leashing up in unpredictable environments, and by being a good canine citizen to promote better relations.

In the hopes that something good could come out of the bad, the Parks and Recreation Department put a new off-leash program on the fast track, designating off-leash hours in specific areas of 30 city parks. These SHARED (Seasonal Hours At REserveD sites) sites give dogs a place to exercise and play in open areas not designed for other uses. By the same token, non-dog people know when and where to recreate without interaction with dogs. In each park, look for the Exercising Your Pet Off-Leash sign. Unless we note otherwise in the park description, SHARED site hours are 5–9 A.M. and 8 P.M.–closing,

May–Oct.; 5–9 A.M. and 4 P.M.–closing, Nov.–April. These time-limited areas are available in addition to the city's six full-time off-leash areas, called YES sites (Year-round Exercise Sites).

Cooper and Isis have included as many SHARED sites in this chapter as possible—meaning you can find it and there's at least some parking—for several reasons. First, the dogs want to encourage responsible usage of these OLAs to persuade the city to continue the program and to inspire other metropolitan areas to follow suit. Secondly, the dogs hope you'll go on a dog park tour of the city, exploring historic neighborhoods you might not see otherwise. Of course, if you're only in town for a day or two, there's plenty to do in Northwest Portland and Downtown. Portland Parks and Recreation 503/823-DOGS (503/823-3647); Dogs In Parks at www.parks.ci.portland.or.us.

North Portland

North Portland is a heavy industrial area, with a couple of historic neighborhoods experiencing modest revitalization. With so few attractions to distract you, your dog hopes you'll have no alternative but to spend hours with her in the district's big off-leash areas.

PARKS, BEACHES, AND RECREATION AREAS

1 Chimney Park

🐾🐾🐾🐾 🦴 (See Greater Portland map on pages 322–323)

Dogs are having a field day at the city's largest YES site. It's only a four-mile trip from downtown to get to this full-time 16-acre dog park. Two separately enclosed and gated plots are dedicated to dogs from the crack of dawn until it's too dark to see. The north side is a well-groomed, gently sloping hill with large, mature shade trees. It's also the side with a picnic table, poop bag supplies, and a garbage can. The south side is an uneven field of wildflowers infrequently mowed over. The groomed side is occasionally closed to give the grass time to breathe. Don't look for a tall landmark to guide you; the city's incinerator smokestack that gave the park its name has been removed. Bring your own water.

From I-5 northbound, take exit 306A. Go east on N. Columbia Boulevard for 4.5 miles. Turn left at the sign for the Stanley Parr Archives and Records Center. There's plenty of gravel parking behind the building. Open 5 A.M.–midnight. 9360 N. Columbia.

2 West Delta Park

🐾 🦴 (See Greater Portland map on pages 322–323)

The West Delta YES site is being monitored as an experimental site to determine its long-term worth as an off-leash area. It's definitely got some quirks.

The grounds may flood in the rainy season, the area is used for overflow parking for Portland International Raceway events, and the winter wild geese population can overrun the field and leave a whole mess of poop behind. Last, and most bizarre, the place smells like stinky cheese on hot days. It's an empty, three-acre field of scrubby bush, protected by a fence on the north and separated only by a guardrail on the south. There are no amenities.

Why do we bother to mention it? One, the only other OLA in the immediate vicinity closes November–April. Two, it's usually not crowded. And, three, even a bad day at a mediocre dog park is better than a good day at the office.

From I-5, take exit 306B and follow the signs to Portland International Raceway. From N. Expo Road, turn left onto N. Broadacre Street. Gravel parking is available along Broadacre. Open dawn–dusk.

🔢 East Delta Park

😋😋🐕 (See Greater Portland map on pages 322–323)

East is better equipped than West as a dog park, but sadly, this YES site isn't really year-round. It's only open May—October. Across the street from a massive sports complex, the five-acre off-leash area is fully fenced and reserved for unfettered romping. Three gates lead into the rectangular area that features rough grass, a few trees, scattered water bowls, and a couple of picnic tables in the shade.

Other areas of the park make for good sunbathing and picnicking, but dogs must be leashed, and they are not allowed in the playgrounds, on paved trails, or on the sports fields.

From I-5, take Exit 307 and follow signs to Delta Park and Marine Drive East. Take a left on N. Union Court. The dog park is on the left. Open dawn–dusk, May–October.

🔢 Arbor Lodge

😋🐾 (See Greater Portland map on pages 322–323)

As in many of the city's SHARED sites, the off-leash area at Arbor Lodge is an unfenced, tree-filled section of a pretty city park. Although partially bounded by tennis courts, basketball courts, and paved pathways, you must have excellent voice control of your pet to protect him from residential traffic on all four sides. The parks department relies on you to provide bags and water for your dog. The people's potty is in the center.

From I-5, take Exit 304. Go west on N. Portland Boulevard .75 mile, turn right on N. Greeley Avenue, and right on N. Bryant Street. The SHARED area is on the northwest corner of the park. Street-side parking is available on parts of Bryant. Morning off-leash hours are shortened to 5–8 A.M. at this park.

5 Overlook Park

 (See Greater Portland map on pages 322–323)

The SHARED site at this city park overlooks the industrial workings of a busy city port and railyards, the Fremont Bridge, and the downtown skyline. More suited to people than pets, the off-leash area is a tiny triangle at the south end of the park. The view is the upside; the downsides are scarce parking, an unenclosed area without amenities, and a busy medical center next door. It's a panoramic potty stop and not much more.

From I-5, take Exit 303, and turn right on N. Alberta Street. Turn left at the next light, and continue south on N. Interstate Avenue for .7 mile. You can pass Overlook Boulevard and turn right on N. Fremont Street to park in the cul-de-sac next to the SHARED area, if you're lucky enough to score a spot. Or, you can turn right on Overlook Boulevard, find easier street parking and walk south on leash until you see the OLA sign.

PLACES TO EAT

Craftsman Café: The Afghan hound who lives upstairs at the architectural restoration firm is willing to share *her* dog treats from the simple coffee and sandwich shop downstairs. 4231 N. Interstate Ave.; 503/528-2025.

PLACES TO STAY

In this area, chain hotels offer the best choices for dogs and their owners; please look under Chain Hotels in the Resources section.

Northwest Portland

In this metro quadrant, there is a city park so large that a man and his daughter lived quite well in its woods for four years before anyone noticed. For hounds who love to hike, the words Forest Park may earn a place in the dog linguistic hall of fame alongside treat, ball, car, dinner, and walk.

PARKS, BEACHES, AND RECREATION AREAS

6 Forest Park

 (See Greater Portland map on pages 322–323)

As if the 5,000 acres of Forest Park weren't enough, its most popular hiking trail doesn't even start within its borders! The 28-mile hikers-only Wildwood Trail begins near Washington Park's rose garden and wanders up through Hoyt Arboretum before it enters the deep woods of this city wilderness. From the moment you step onto any of Forest Park's trails, Oregon's largest city might as well not exist. Total hiking mileage on developed trails tops out near 60 miles, not including the cross-country trekking people also enjoy in the park. Leif Erickson Drive is the former road that winds 11 miles through the center, providing the widest and most visible path. It rises gently uphill and has handy markers every .25 mile to let you know how far you've come. You'll have to share Leif Erickson with mountain bikers; leashes are required and helpful. There's a trail map and a water fountain at the start of Leif Erickson Drive.

From I-405, take Exit 3 and follow the N.W. Vaughn Street exit ramp. Get in the second to the right lane, and turn left on N.W. 23rd at the bottom of the exit. Go one block and turn right on N.W. Thurman Street and follow it 1.4 miles to the end. Limited angled parking is available in front of the trailhead gate.

7 Washington Park—International Rose Test Garden

(See Greater Portland map on pages 322–323)

No proper visit to the City of Roses would be complete without a visit to the garden that started it all. Portland's International Rose Test Garden in Washington Park is one of the largest and oldest gardens in the country dedicated to the fragrant blooms of the romantic flower. Almost 600 varieties are represented in 4.5 acres, on a hilltop with city views. Picture-taking, stopping to smell the flowers, and walking on leash are encouraged, whereas pruning or digging is punishable by a $500 fine. There is a rose gift shop, and for a dog who thinks a rose by any other name wouldn't smell as sweet as a hot dog, there is a snack bar.

Beyond the rose garden, Washington Park includes many non-dog activities and sites, including the Oregon Zoo, the World Forestry Education Center, the Children's Museum (CM2), and a Japanese Botanical Garden.

Go west through downtown on W. Burnside Street. Although you'll see several signs to Washington Park, wait until S.W. Tichner Drive to make a sharp left-hand turn up the hill, then turn right on S.W. Kingston, following the more specific signs to the rose garden. 400 S.W. Kingston Ave.; 503/823-3636.

8 Hoyt Arboretum

(See Greater Portland map on pages 322–323)

The $2 fee is a small price to pay for the map that provides peace of mind in this 185-acre tree museum's maze of vaguely marked trails. Twelve miles of hiking opportunities wind through about 1,100 species of trees, grouped by horticultural family. Starting at the visitors center, where a water bowl is thoughtfully provided for pets, the wheelchair-accessible Overlook Trail will take you and your dog to the dogwood collection. The rest of the park's trails are soft-surface. Cooper recommends a seasonal approach to the Hoyt, visiting tree families at their showiest times of the year.

From U.S. Highway 26, 1.8 miles west of downtown, take Exit 72. Turn right on S.W. Knights Boulevard, pass the zoo and the forestry center, and turn right on S.W. Fairview to the parking lot. Grounds are open 6 A.M.–10 P.M.; visitors center hours are 9 A.M.–4 P.M. 4000 S.W. Fairview Blvd.; 503/228-8733; www.hoytarboretum.org.

PLACES TO EAT

St. Honoré Boulangerie: The car turned, seemingly of its own will, toward this French café, as we headed up to Forest Park. The soups, salads, and rows of éclairs and croissants are all stunning, and there's ample outdoor seating at umbrella-shaded tables. 2335 N.W. Thurman St.; 503/445-4342; www.sainthonorebakery.com.

Nob Hill

This high-profile neighborhood is also called the Northwest District or the Alphabet District, because the streets progress alphabetically north from Burnside. Its north–south avenues, especially 23rd and 21st, are full of trendy shops and the city's largest concentration of outdoor eats. Your dog is sure to get extra pats and leftovers in this sophisticated and pet-perfect area to walk, window shop, and dine.

PARKS, BEACHES, AND RECREATION AREAS

9 Wallace Park

🐾🐾 🐕 (See Greater Portland map on pages 322–323)

For years, Wallace Park has been known as the place to go for a pickup game of basketball. Since implementation of this park's SHARED site, a new breed of ball players are dribbling in the northeast corner, and the pickup action is equally hot. The whole park is only five acres, so the off-leash area is small, perhaps a tad larger than a regulation half-court. It has a chicken wire fence on three sides to protect it from busy side streets and the fourth side is open to the interior of the park, with covered and open picnic tables for spectators. Bring your own bags; water and trash can are provided.

Go west on W. Burnside Street from downtown, turn right on N.W. 23rd Avenue, left on N.W. Pettygrove Street, and right on N.W. 25th Avenue. The SHARED area is on the northeast corner at the intersection of 25th and Raleigh. Limited parking is available on side streets. Morning off-leash hours are shortened to 5–8 A.M. at this park.

10 Couch Park

😋 😺 (See Greater Portland map on pages 322–323)

Rarely has so small a space received so much gleeful use by the four-legged patrons who call Couch Park home. And, oh boy, does it get muddy in the winter! The small, unsecured SHARED area is squished between a terraced play structure and a walkway on a slight slope. It's hectic day and night in and around the park, across the street from a private school and only two blocks from one of the hottest street scenes in the city. Only the most civilized and completely voice-controlled dogs should be allowed off leash. Barking and street parking are at a premium in Couch Park.

Go west on W. Burnside Street from downtown, turn right on N.W. 21st Avenue, and right on N.W. Hoyt Street. The SHARED area is on the north side on the park on Hoyt between the 19th and 20th Avenue blocks. Morning off-leash hours are shortened to 5–8 A.M. at this park.

PLACES TO EAT

Alotto Gelato: The only thing served at this storefront counter is gelato, up to 30 flavors of ice cream and sorbets, every day a little different. The line often goes around the block, and that's just the dogs. 931 N.W. 23rd Ave.; 503/228-1709.

McMenamins Blue Moon Tavern: People and their pets have been gathering at the sidewalk picnic tables of this hot spot since 1933 to drink pints of ale and down great burgers and fresh-cut fries. The Terminator Stout should impress even Guinness fans. 432 N.W. 21st Ave.; 503/223-3184; www.mcmenamins.com.

Papa Haydn: This sidewalk café is a Sunday brunch tradition. The small selection of lunch and dinner items is far outstripped by a dessert menu of profanely rich cakes. 701 N.W. 23rd; 503/228-7317.

Yuki: This Japanese restaurant's menu is a struggle for the indecisive. The sushi menu alone takes up four pages and that doesn't include the yakisoba noodles, teriyaki, tempura, and combinations of all of the above. Bento boxes are the perfect compromise, and they look interesting, too. 930 N.W. 23rd Ave.; 503/525-8807.

PLACES TO STAY

Park Lane Suites: This suites hotel is perfect for longer stays. Each unit is apartment-style, with full kitchens, living rooms with TV, onsite laundry, and business desks. It accepts dogs under 25 pounds for a $10 per night fee (negotiable for longer stays). It's in a desirable neighborhood surrounded by restored mansions, a block away from chic 23rd Street. Rates range $89–119. 809 S.W. King Ave.; 503/226-6288 or 800/532-9543; www.parklanesuites.com.

More Accommodations: Please look under Chain Hotels in the Resources section for additional places to stay in this area.

Downtown and Historic Waterfront

Downtown Portland is ideal for dog-walkers. Built on a European model, using half-size city blocks, the city encourages exploration on foot. Smaller lots have left more room for pocket parks, water gardens, plazas, and plenty of foliage. Drinking water, too, is plentiful downtown in Benson Bubblers, 20 elegant freshwater drinking fountains commissioned at the turn of the 19th century by wealthy lumber baron and teetotaler Simon Benson.

Portland's enhanced status as a pedestrian city may be due partially to the fact that getting around by car can be complicated. With the Willamette River cutting a wide swath north–south, and the Columbia River dividing Oregon and Washington, going across town requires crossing one of the area's 17 major bridges.

To take in the city in a nutshell, hang out with your dog in Pioneer Court-house Square, Portland's outdoor living room. Walk along the waterfront park for the Portland Saturday Market under the Burnside Bridge, for more than 250 crafts booths, food, and music on Saturday (and Sunday), March–December 24th.

Spend time in the recently gentrified Pearl District, industrial warehouses reborn into sleek loft apartments and galleries. On a rainy afternoon in The Pearl, you can sit indoors—yes, indoors—with your dog at **Urban Fauna's Barking Bistro** (235 N.W. Park; 503/223-4602; www.urbanfauna.com) sipping tea or coffee while she munches on treats made especially for her. You can have her groomed and bathed while you buy her a bed, new collar, and a coat in the retail section. Should you choose to skip away for an afternoon to Powell's City of Books or an art gallery, she can make new friends at Urban Fauna's puppy playground. This boutique is a must for any pampered city pet.

PARKS, BEACHES, AND RECREATION AREAS

11 North Park Blocks

🐾🐾 (See Greater Portland map on pages 322–323)

These six park squares in The Pearl are close to the majority of downtown's vintage hotels, a handy place to walk your dog. If you see dogs veering automatically to the west at the corner of N.W. Everett Street, it's because they know treats await them at Urban Fauna. Also in the North Blocks, Portland dogs have their very own Benson Bubbler, a bottomless brass bowl of water on the west side north of N.W. Davis Street.

The North Park Blocks are on Park Avenue between W. Burnside Street and N.W. Hoyt Street. Metered street parking is $1.50 for up to 90 minutes.

12 South Park Blocks

🐾🐾🐾 (See Greater Portland map on pages 322–323)

Leave plenty of time for walks along the city's South Park Blocks, an even dozen lawn-carpeted squares lined with aged elms from Salmon Street to Jackson Street on Park Avenue. You'll pass through Portland State University and the heart of the cultural district, including the Portland Center for the Performing Arts, Arlene Schnitzer Concert Hall ("The Schnitz"), classical Portland Art Museum, historic First Congregational Church, and the Oregon Historical Society, with its multi-story, elaborate *trompe l'oeil* mural. You'll see all walks of life, and many manners of breeds, on your perambulations.

If you're slaving away at the computer, but your dog is waiting at your feet with his leash in his mouth, make a compromise. Check your email or surf the Internet from any park bench in the South Blocks—the whole area is a free Wi-Fi Hotspot.

Parking is practically nonexistent along the South Park Blocks. Find a long-term lot downtown and walk.

13 Governor Tom McCall Waterfront Park

🐾🐾 (See Greater Portland map on pages 322–323)

Waterfront Park must be Portland's most expensive park. The mile-long sidewalk promenade is built on top of Portland Harbor Wall, the single most expensive piece of infrastructure built by the city. It replaced the rotting docks and dilapidated pier buildings as part of an urban renewal project in the 1920s. Buried within is the first sewer system on the west side of the river. From 2003 to 2006, another 1.2 billion dollars is being spent on the "Big Pipe" project, to update the sewer system to handle modern population pressures. The project will wreak a bit of havoc in the park. The city is keeping it to a minimum by blocking off short sections at a time. The wide lawns along the promenade also take a beating from Portland Saturday Market booths and frequent city festivals held on the grounds.

It's still one of the best waterfront walks you can take with your dog, especially if you cross the Hawthorne or Steel Bridges to join up with the Eastbank Esplanade. The south end of Waterfront Park expands to a grassy slope down to the beach. Stay on leash and watch out for goose droppings. North of the Burnside Bridge, the Japanese Historical Plaza deserves a quick look-see.

Tom McCall Waterfront Park is on N.W. Front Avenue/Naito Parkway, between N.W. Glisan Street and S.W. Clay Street. The closest parking is in a Smart Park Lot on Front Avenue between N.W. Davis and N.W. Everett Streets.

PLACES TO EAT

Carafe: With an owner from Paris, this French bistro is as authentic as it gets. It serves escargot, smelly cheeses, and confit of duck, and *pomme frites* come with mayo, not ketchup. The outdoor seating is also traditional European, with all seats facing out toward the park plaza to observe the pulse of the city. 200 S.W. Market St.; 503/248-0004; www.carafebistro.com.

Good Dog/Bad Dog: It was the fascinating array of handmade sausages that drew us in, but it was the Good Dog/Bad Dog T-shirt and hat that followed us home. 708 S.W. Alder; 503/222-2410.

Pearl Bakery: This bakery and bistro excels in the French tradition of foods that make the difficult look easy and taste simply delectable. Try their meltingly rich brioche, chiffon cake, and eggplant-red pepper-mozzarella sandwiches. 102 N.W. 9th Ave.; 503/827-0910.

South Park: Reservations are a must for dinner at this seafood grill and wine bar in the midst of the cultural center of town. You and your well-mannered dog will compete for patio tables with the crowds from the symphony, theater, and the college. South Park combines fresh local produce and catch-of-the-day in creative ways, and its list of wines by the glass is excellent. 901 S.W. Salmon St.; 503/326-1300; www.southpark.citysearch.com.

PLACES TO STAY

Heathman Hotel: *Condé Nast Traveler* and *Travel + Leisure* have rated this luxurious hotel among their top favorites in the world, perhaps because its list of services and amenities is longer than a Great Dane's legs. The Heathman is perhaps most famous for doormen dressed like the guy on the Beefeater gin bottle. Pets under 70 pounds (probably not that Great Dane) are welcome for a $25 pet fee. Rates range $159–189. 1001 S.W. Broadway; 503/241-4100 or 800/551-0011; www.heathmanhotel.com.

Hotel Lucia: Cooper and Isis get into a tiff when we travel to Portland, because he wants to stay at this modern masterpiece of serene, minimalist Zen, while she prefers the old-world charm of The Mallory. Although opposites in character, the hotels are owned by the same group, one that welcomes pets without restrictions or fees. Hotel Lucia's art collection alone is worthy of a visit, including 679 photographs of Pulitzer Prize–winner David Hume Kennerly. The dog bowls are on loan only, but you may keep the Aveda products and the jazz CD from your room. Bedheads will love the pillow menu, with choices from the softest down to the firmest fiber. Rates range $125–195. 400 S.W. Broadway; 503/225-1717 or 877/225-1717; www.hotellucia.com.

Hotel Vintage Plaza: Lovely and luxurious, this upscale hotel is cared for as though it is a well-loved antique. The ambience is inspired by a French vineyard, bright enough to make you thirsty for a sip of the grape, and relaxing enough for you to nap peacefully afterwards. Rates range $139–259; there is no fee for pets. 422 S.W. Broadway; 503/263-2305; www.vintageplaza.com.

Mallory Hotel: This 1912 boutique hotel near the PGE Stadium wins with a triple-play: no pet fee (rare), free continental breakfast (rarer), and free and secured parking (unheard of!). With rates ranging $100–155, it's also the most reasonable of Portland's vintage hotels. You'll save a bundle on a charming place to stay, steeped in a tradition of gracious eccentricity, well loved by its loyal human and dog clientele. 729 S.W. 15th Ave.; 503/223-6311 or 800/228-8657; www.malloryhotel.com.

Mark Spencer Hotel: The Spence was a famous hotel from 1907 to the 1960s, then apartments, and now a hotel again, with a rooftop garden and the tiny appliances and walk-in closets left over from its apartment era. The hotel's slightly frumpy Bohemian air is favored by the arts and theater crowd. 409 S.W. 11th Ave.; 503/224-3293 or 800/548-3934; www.markspencer.com.

RiverPlace Hotel: Isis never knew that the royal treatment—bottled water, porcelain bowls, dog biscuits, and personalized note cards delivered on a tray to the room—is standard for all canine guests. Humans are equally spoiled. Request a riverside or courtyard room for the best views. All rooms are open to dogs without size restrictions, except for a 30-pound limit in 10 condo units. A Doggie Diner menu is available from room service. If you're nice to Charles, the longtime chief concierge, he may be able to arrange in-room dog-sitting by a staff member for a reasonable rate. Waterfront Park is the hotel's backyard. There is a $50 nonrefundable pet cleaning fee, with rates ranging $149–189. 1510 Southwest Harbor Way; 800/227-1333; www.riverplacehotel.com.

More Accommodations: Please look under Chain Hotels in the Resources section for additional places to stay in this area.

Northeast Portland–Airport

Northeast Portland provides room for the large facilities that can't be crammed into the downtown core on the Westside, such as the Portland International Airport and the Convention Center. Lloyd Center, Oregon's largest shopping mall, has 200 retail stores encircling an indoor ice rink. Only a few blocks farther out, the historic neighborhoods of Northeast Portland have distinct personalities, from the blowsy Hollywood area to upstanding Laurelhurst. The many wonderful city parks in Northeast Portland also share a signature look of rolling hills, thick carpets of grass, and a treasure trove of stately, mature deciduous trees that have guarded the city since its infancy.

NATURE HIKES AND URBAN WALKS

Penitent pups may walk by your side on leash at **The Grotto,** The National Sanctuary of Our Sorrowful Mother, in Northeast Portland at the intersection of N.E. 85th Street and Sandy Boulevard. In a deep pocket of mature forest, this holy Catholic place of solitude, peace, and prayer allows dogs on the plaza level only, walking through the stations of the cross and to Our Lady's Grotto, a rock cave carved into the base of a 110-foot cliff with a marble replica of Michelangelo's Pietà. Isis was pleasantly surprised to see religious-themed pet tags at the onsite gift shop. There is no fee, but donations are welcome. Hours change with the seasons; call ahead at 503/254-7371 or go to www.thegrotto.org.

PARKS, BEACHES, AND RECREATION AREAS

🐾 Alberta Park

🐾🐾🐾🦀 (See Greater Portland map on pages 322–323)

The SHARED area at Alberta is comfortable and roomy. The lawn is soft, punctuated by big trees widely spaced apart. The off-leash area is unsecured, its borders marked by park pathways, along a fairly quiet side of the street. Restrooms, trash cans, water, and poop bag dispensers are available, although the latter are frequently empty. The sheltered basketball court and ball fields at Alberta get only moderate use, often leaving the park to the dogs.

From I-5, take Exit 303 and follow signs to N.E. Killingsworth Street, go east a little more than a mile and turn left on N.E. 22nd Avenue. The SHARED area is on the east side of the park. Limited street parking is available alongside. Morning off-leash hours are shortened to 5–8 A.M. at this park.

🐾 Fern Hill Park

🐾🐾🐾🦀 (See Greater Portland map on pages 322–323)

The SHARED area at Fern Hill Park is a vague amorphous blob in the center of a 24-acre greenspace. Your dog will have her choice between gently rolling hills and gently rolling hills lightly covered with venerable trees. She's likely to meet new friends among the large group of local dogs who come to Fernhill. There are no boundaries or fences of any kind to mark the off-leash area. However, it is big enough to stay a safe distance from the residential streets and the school sports fields. There are restrooms, water fountains, and playground areas. Bring your own bags. Heck, always bring your own bags.

From I-5, take Exit 303 and follow signs to N.E. Killingsworth Street, go east almost two miles, turn left on N.E. 42nd Avenue, and left on N.E. Ainsworth Street. Street parking is available between Ainsworth Street and Ainsworth Court.

16 Irving Park

🐾🐾 🐕 (See Greater Portland map on pages 322–323)

Irving Park is built on one of Portland's four defunct racetracks converted into city parks. Neighborhood dogs cut some racing tracks of their own on the park's hilly SHARED area, bordered by the horseshoe pits and the basketball courts. Although not secured, the off-leash area is a couple of blocks removed from the busiest side street. Irving is another park that is rich and green, sporting a healthy crop of tall trees. There are garbage cans and water fountains; as ever, bring poop bags.

From Hwy. 99 E, go west on N.E. Fremont Street, right on N.E. 7th Avenue and left on N.E. Siskiyou Street. The safest parking is available on N.E. 8th, 9th, and 10th Avenues, which dead-end into the south side of the park. The SHARED area is on the west side of the park along 47th.

17 Wilshire Park

🐾🐾🐾 🐕 (See Greater Portland map on pages 322–323)

Portland's mature trees are alive and well in Wilshire Park in the SHARED area bordered by park walkways. Most Portland parks have paved walkways,

DIVERSION

There are times, no matter how close you are to your canine, that you will need or want to hop on a plane without her. For such times, the **AirPet Hotel** is a stroke of genius. This dog day care and boarding service is located five minutes from the Portland International Airport and offers discounted rates at nearby park-and-fly lots, with shuttle services to your flight terminal. Board your dog, park your car, and board your flight—it's that easy.

For a reasonable $24 per day (20 percent discount for multiple dogs), the AirPet Hotel offers what the owner calls "cageless boarding." Your pet sleeps in a comfy indoor kennel overnight, and during the day she gets to play in a supervised indoor playpen with dogs of similar temperament and size, and she is taken outside for at least five 10-minute potty breaks. She'll fall asleep each night exhausted, well fed, and happy.

Although normal business hours are 6 A.M.–10 P.M., the facility is staffed 24 hours a day. You can arrange early or late drop-off and pickup times by appointment for those red-eye flights. For once, your pet might not mind being left behind. AirPet Hotel; 6212 N.E. 78th Court; 503/255-1388; www.airpethotel.com.

but Wilshire's jogging paths are wood-chip, more pleasing to the paws for leashed walks. Wilshire has the characteristic look of parks in this area: huge shade trees, evenly spaced on lush lawns. The open, off-leash area is a good size, near picnic tables and a children's play area. The nearby streets are not too busy, and the park doesn't get heavy traffic from other users. You are on your own for water and bags, and the nearest garbage can is quite a walk away.

From I-5, take Exit 303, go east on N.E. Killingsworth for 1.25 miles, turn right on N.E. 33rd Avenue, go .6 mile, turn left on N.E. Skidmore Street and right on N.E. 37th Avenue. The SHARED area is on the northeast corner of the park, bordered by Skidmore and 37th. Street parking is available.

18 Grant Park

 (See Greater Portland map on pages 322–323)

This park is named in honor of the 18th president of the United States, Ulysses S. Grant, who began his career at nearby Fort Vancouver and continued to visit the city throughout his presidency. A celebrity in its own right, the park's setting has inspired many scenes in Beverly Cleary's children's books. There are so many varied activities going on at this community centerpiece that there's not much room left over for the SHARED dog site. It occupies a tiny, unsecured sliver on the north end at 35th Avenue and Knott Street. Coop 'n' Isis almost enjoyed a leashed stroll on park's paved walkways more than spending time in the off-leash area. Almost.

From Hwy. 99 E/Martin Luther King Jr. Boulevard, go east on N.E. Knott Street. Turn right on N.E. 35th Place and park along this dead-end; you'll be directly in front of the SHARED area. Morning off-leash hours are shortened to 5–8 A.M. at this park.

19 Normandale Park

(See Greater Portland map on pages 322–323)

Double your pleasure and double your fun at this city park's identical twin YES sites. The two separately gated and fenced areas are both open in the summer, and one side or the other will close periodically in the rainy season for "turf restoration." The re-greening of these high-traffic dog sites is a lost cause. Lately, the city has resorted to dumping piles of sand and wood chips in an attempt to mitigate the mud. Messy conditions do nothing to dampen Normandale's popularity; it's the closest full-time off-leash area to the city center. These dog parks are a 50–50 balance of open areas and tall conifers, and the sites share water and garbage facilities just outside the front gates. Bring your beloved to bond and smell butts in a lively canine social circle and join in on the turf wars.

From I-84, take Exit 2 into the right-most lane to go west on N.E. Halsey Street. Turn south on 57th to the parking lot at the intersection of N.E. 57th Avenue and N.E. Hassalo Street. Open 5 A.M.–midnight.

PLACES TO EAT

Dahlia Café: This neighborhood café has healthy and filling food concentrating on vegan and vegetarian dishes, and the biggest bowl of dog biscuits the Dachsie Twins had ever seen. It has its own picnic tables and is near Alberta and Fernhill parks. 3000 N.E. Killingsworth; 503/287-4427.

PLACES TO STAY

Country Inn and Suites: We didn't hear any plane noise in our comfortable room at the comfortable price of $79–89, plus a $10 pet fee. They put out a nice complimentary breakfast spread, including make-your-own waffles. 7025 N.E. Alderwood Rd.; 800/456-4000; www.countryinns.com.

Portlander Inn: This motel is a city unto itself. You get a great room for a great rate of $60–67 per night, and you have access to a movie theater, shoe repair, laundromat, deli, country and western bar, gift shop, visitors center, gas station, chiropractor, convenience store, medical clinic, and hair salon. Long-haul truck drivers think of it as a second home. The pet fee is $10 per night for up to two pets, no more than $40 per stay. 10350 N. Vancouver Way; 800/523-1193; www.portlanderinn.com.

More Accommodations: Please look under Chain Hotels in the Resources section for additional places to stay in this area.

Tigard

PARKS, BEACHES, AND RECREATION AREAS

20 Summerlake Dog Park

😊😊😊🐕 (See Greater Portland map on pages 322–323)

Suburban dogs idle away their days at Summerlake, one of the newest additions to Portland-area dog parks. It's a mid-sized field, a couple of acres, one of a few excellent off-leash areas created and maintained by the Tigard Dog Park Committee. Summerlake's off-leash area is crowded and friendly, with a large covered shelter that makes for a nice people-hangout while the dogs go about their business. It's got all the goods, including garbage cans, pooper-scoopers and bags, running water, a secured fence with double-gated entry, and just enough tree cover for a bit of shade and a couple of suicidal squirrels.

From State Route 217 southbound, take Exit 4B (Exit 4 northbound), and go west on Scholls Ferry Road for a mile. Take a left onto 130th Avenue, and go .4 mile, straight through a couple of stop signs, until the road becomes S.W. Winter Lake Drive. The OLA and the parking lot will be on your left, past the sports courts and the restrooms. Open dawn–dusk. 503/639-2931; www.ci.tigard.or.us/community/parks.

21 Potso Dog Park

😊😊😊🐾 (See Greater Portland map on pages 322–323)

Potso pups long for summer evenings and winter weekends, when this great part-time dog park is open to them for unleashed play. Potso is open 4:30 P.M.– dusk, Monday–Friday, May–Oct.; and dawn–dusk on weekends and holidays all year. Cooper and Isis were so busy having a ball chasing balls in the open field's healthy green grass, they didn't even mind that they missed meeting Potso, the poodle for whom the park is named.

Potso comes well equipped with poop bags, running water, garbage cans, and sheltered picnic tables. It is completely fenced, with a double gate, and as an extra bonus, has a separate off-leash area for smaller dogs (yip, yip, yippee!).

From State Route 217 southbound, take Exit 7, make a right onto 72nd Avenue, follow the cloverleaf and immediately turn left on S.W. Hunziker. Turn left on Wall Street in front of the Coe Manufacturing building. Parking for Spot is in designated spots with giant paw prints painted on them. 7930 S.W. Hunziker. 503/639-2931.

Southwest Portland

Southwest Portland is green with money as well as trees. The real estate taxes in this area climb in direct proportion to the elevation, all the way to the city's highest point at Council Crest.

PARKS, BEACHES, AND RECREATION AREAS

22 Marquam Nature Trail and Council Crest Park

😊😊😊🐾 (See Greater Portland map on pages 322–323)

On a really, really clear day at the 1,043-foot summit of Council Crest, you can see the city, and the Mounts of Hood, Adams, Jefferson, St. Helens, and even Rainier. And, if you time it right, your dog can enjoy the SHARED area at the park, although the off-leash area is steep and does not have a fence or dog amenities.

The tip of Council Crest is panoramic in every direction, but the point of including this park in the book, according to Cooper, is to access the Marquam Nature Trail. It's a great city escape through a primal fern-filled canyon forest. On this steep, lung-capacity-stretching hike, there are so many things outdoor dogs love: trees, wildflowers, squirrels, and plump banana slugs, whose slime creates a favorite hair gel for Isis. For stretches of the trail's 1.5-mile length, you'll feel lost in the woods, until you see the West Hill Mansions tucked here and there in the green space. On the trail, use the leash, pick up the poop, and don't pick up the purple trilliums.

Many guidebooks recommend starting at Marquam, allowing you to finish downhill rather than up. Imagine the accomplishment you'll feel ending at the top of the city! Besides, driving directions are easier to Council Crest. To corkscrew up the hill, take S.W. Broadway Drive south through downtown, stay in the far right to avoid the Barbur Boulevard/99W interchange, and follow Broadway another 1.3 miles. Turn left on S.W. Greenway Avenue, go another .7 mile, and take the right fork onto S.W. Council Crest Drive. The SHARED area is on the southeast hillside. Council Crest's official hours are 10 A.M.–8 P.M.; dogs enjoy it off-leash before and after 5–9 A.M. and 8 P.M. until dark (and often after, with glow-in-the-dark toys).

🐾 Gabriel Park

🐾🐾🐾🐾🐕 (See Greater Portland map on pages 322–323)

The grass is soft and green on the rolling hills of Gabriel Park—yes, even in the fully fenced YES area. The trees are big and shady—and we're talking some serious trees here—and the benches and chairs are comfy. It's definitely one of Portland's fanciest off-leash areas. The only drawback is that there are separate summer and winter areas to allow the turf to recover in the off-season. The summer area is bordered by the tennis courts, which had Isis doing the Wimbledon head wobble watching the balls go to and fro.

The two-acre winter site, dubbed "Little Gabriel," is unfenced, with fewer amenities, and it's a bit hard to find. Walk south of the summer area, down wooden steps and across a bridge to the paved path. When you come into a clearing, you are there, bordered by a baseball diamond and the community garden. The rest of the park's 90 acres provide amiable on-leash walks.

From I-5, take Exit 297, and continue straight onto S.W. Bertha Boulevard. Turn left on S.W. Vermont Street, pass the park, and turn left on S.W. 45th Avenue. There's a parking lot that's often full. To better your chances, continue south on 45th, turn left on S.W. Multnomah Boulevard, left on S.W. 40th Avenue, and left on S.W. Canby Street to park by the winter YES area and sneak in the back way. Open 5 A.M.–midnight.

🐾 Willamette Park

🐾🐾🐟 (See Greater Portland map on pages 322–323)

Willamette has a choice waterfront location, south of the city. The unfenced SHARED site is good-sized, half open and half shaded. The grass is thick and green, a nice playground for those with paws. Soccer fields occupy the south end of the park, so the best time to enjoy this spot is midday weekdays, when there are no games. The only other users are boaters headed straight for the water; you can watch them unload and take off down the river while you play. If your loved one smells too much like a dirty dog after a day at this off-leash area, the Wiggles and Wags Dog Wash is across the street (6141 S.W. Macadam; 503/977-1775).

From I-5, take Exit 299A and go south on S.W. Macadam Avenue and turn right on S.W. Nebraska Street. The OLA is on the north end of the park, to your left past the pay booth at the entrance. This park has a rare parking lot, which costs $3 per day.

PLACES TO EAT

Fat City Café: This owners of this country café have four dogs, and they wish they could provide outdoor seating, but the sidewalk's too narrow and the codes are too strict in Historic Multnomah Village. They'll provide a water bowl and treats for your pet while he waits for you outside, or you can order to-go and take your homemade, good lovin' cookin' to Gabriel Park around the corner. 7820 S.W. Capitol Hwy.; 503/245-5457.

PLACES TO STAY

Hospitality Inn: Motel rooms are cheery and large at the inn, and the complimentary continental breakfast spread is not too shabby either. Rates range $63–78, plus a $10 pet fee. 10155 S.W. Capitol Hwy.; 503/244-6684 or 800/929-4442.

Southeast Portland

Southeast Portland is perhaps best described as bohemian, honoring the hippie more than the hip. Hawthorne Boulevard and Belmont Street are the places to find an eclectic mix of retro storefronts, dining, and avant-garde theater. If you or your kids are science buffs, drop your pal at doggie daycare for a half-day and visit the Oregon Museum of Science and Industry (OMSI). A stop into The Lucky Lab Brewing Co. is a must for dog lovers.

PARKS, BEACHES, AND RECREATION AREAS

25 Eastbank Esplanade

🐾 🐾 (See Greater Portland map on pages 322–323)

Located between the historic Hawthorne and Steel Bridges, this 1.7-mile waterfront promenade hugs the eastern banks of the Willamette River. It provides a superb unobstructed look at the city skyline and boasts a series of sculptures celebrating Portland's history. On the north end, a lower deck on the Steel Bridge provides bicycle and pedestrian access to Waterfront Park. The park's 1,200-foot floating dock is the longest in the United States, supported by 65 concrete pylons.

Your only hope for parking is on Carruthers Street, south of the Hawthorne Bridge. From I-5, take Exit 300, and get in the right lane to exit at OMSI/Central Eastside Industrial District. Turn right onto S.E. Water Street, go .7 mile, and turn right on S.E. Carruthers Street to the dead end.

DOG-EAR YOUR CALENDAR

The equines donate their home for a day to raise money for their friends, the canines, at the **Tail Wag,** a party to benefit the Oregon Humane Society. In the Portland Police Mounted Patrol Barn, along the shores of the Willamette River, humans only gather to bid on silent auction items, dine on appetizers from Portland restaurants, and imbibe cocktails, wine, and beer. 503/285-7722, ext. 327; www.oregonhumane.org

Oregon State Parks hosts the Annual **Oregon State Barks Day** at Rooster Rock the last Saturday in July. There's a dog walk, free nail clipping, agility courses, flyball and disc demonstrations, pets available for adoption, and discussions about training, tracking, dealing with aging and adopted pets, and more. While you're there, you can visit the off-leash area at this big state park, located off Hwy. 84 at Exit 25. 503/695-2261, ext. 228; www.prd.state.or.us.

You know the drill—the lifeguard blows his whistle and shouts, "No running by the pool!" Well, it's probably a moot point at the **Dog Daze of Summer,** a one-day, dogs-only swim at the North Clackamas Aquatic Park in Milwaukie. Dogs get the rare chance to swim in an indoor pool before it's drained for annual maintenance. Sessions are rated as Freshwater, noon–2 P.M.; Semi-fresh Water 3–5 P.M.; and Not-So-Fresh Water 6–8 P.M. Early swims are $6 per dog or $8 per multiple-dog family, with a $1 discount off each for later sessions with lower water-quality standards. Your dog certainly doesn't care. 7300 S.E. Harmony Rd.; 503/557-7873; www.pdxsurf.com.

Dogtoberfest, otherwise known as the dog wash at the Lucky Lab, celebrated its 10th year in 2004. The record is 600 dogs washed and $4,000 raised in one day to benefit local Dove Lewis Animal Hospital. Festivities include T-shirts, music, and a special brew, Dog Wash Pale Ale. Drink some suds while celebrity dog-washers suds up your pup on the third Saturday in September. 503/236-2555; www.luckylab.com.

It's a dog-eat-dog world at the Berlin Inn's annual **Barktoberfest,** where the pooch sausage-eating contest is about technique, not quantity. On the second weekend in September, this restaurant hosts dog events and activities all weekend, complete with beer and bratwurst for canine chaperones. Funds raised benefit the humane society, Dog Rescue, and No Kill Shelters. 3131 S.E. 12th; 503/236-6761; www.berlininn.com.

Beaverton has a beautiful dog park, and the city wants to keep it that way. Every August it holds a **Dog Day Afternoon** fundraiser at the Hazeldale Dog Park. There are vendor booths, a raffle, blessing of the animals, and contests and demos for lure coursing, agility, and flyball. Be a vendor, donate raffle items, or come and participate to raise rent and maintenance money for a great regional dog park. Email dogdaysraffle@yahoo.com for more information.

26 Laurelhurst Park

🐾🐾🐾🐾 🐕 (See Greater Portland map on pages 322–323)

Laurelhurst is a city institution. Emanuel Mische of the famed Olmsted Brothers landscape firms created the park in 1912, the electric lights were lit for the first time in 1915, and, in 1919, it was named the most beautiful park on the West Coast. In 2001, it became the first city park to be listed on the National Register of Historic Places. The park is straight out of an impressionist painting, complete with ladies carrying parasols on the arms of dapper gentlemen on walkways under antique lighting fixtures. The pond has elegant swans and blue herons nesting under a weeping willow. The leaves fall gently on the walkways as a yellow Lab runs screaming by after stealing a toy from his Doberman playmate. Yes, friends, as genteel as it may seem on the surface, Laurelhurst has had a regular base of boisterous canine clientele.

Dogs are fortunate to have an off-leash area in such a high-profile park as part of the city's experimental program. To help keep the privilege, it's critical that you and your dog respect the area's boundaries and limited hours and remain leashed while walking the rest of the park.

From Hwy. 99 E, go east on E. Burnside Street to S.E. 39th Avenue, the eastern border of the park. Turn right on S.E. Oak Street. The SHARED area is in the center of the park on the south side, along Oak Street, defined by the walkways. Parking is ad hoc, on the streets bordering the park perimeter.

27 Mt. Tabor Park

🐾🐾🐾 🐕 (See Greater Portland map on pages 322–323)

Mt. Tabor is an extinct volcano, which probably hasn't been active for about three million years. The dog scene, on the other hand, is very active at this city park. Only a tiny sliver of the 196-acre mountain is designated as a limited-hours SHARED site, and it isn't even where the canines tend to congregate. The city is trying to discourage the impromptu social hour on the west side of the mountain, above the largest reservoir, because the grass gets torn up, leading to runoff problems. You can help by sticking to the official area, on the south side near the Harrison Street entrance.

You can join the cruising dogs, hanging out of car windows, on the loop drive to the 643-foot summit. For buns of steel, you and your Bernese can try climbing the stairs, essentially straight up. Multiple dirt paths cross and climb the point, and you can make up a different route every time you go—past the park's three reservoirs, through the Douglas fir, around the crater amphitheater, and so on. Mt. Tabor is a gathering place in the heart of Southeast Portland, and you and your dog can make many friends while you take in the great city views, especially on Wednesday, when the roads are closed to vehicles for walkers.

From I-84, take Exit 5 and turn right at the stop sign at the bottom of the exit ramp. Go one block and turn left on S.E. 82nd Avenue, go 1.1 miles, turn right on S.E. Yamhill Street, go .3 mile, turn left on S.E. 76th Avenue, go .5 mile, turn right on S.E. Harrison Street, and follow the signs into the park. There is angled parking.

28 Woodstock Park

🐾🐾🦮 (See Greater Portland map on pages 322–323)

There are a bunch of neighborhood dogs who take advantage of the SHARED site at Woodstock City Park. It's slightly hilly and has neat green grass and big deciduous trees. In response to a problem complying with waste pickup laws, the city has cabled giant, blue plastic trash cans to each of the trees bordering the off-leash area as a major hint. There is no fence around the area and you need to stay well clear of busy Steele Street. Playgrounds, a wading pool, and the restrooms are near the SHARED area.

From Hwy. 99 E, go east on U.S. Highway 26, S.E. Powell Boulevard, turn right on S.E. 52nd Avenue, right on S.E. Steele Street, and left on S.E. 47th Avenue. The SHARED area is on the west side of the park along 47th Avenue south of Steele. Street parking is available along 47th. Morning off-leash hours are shortened to 5–8 A.M. at this park.

29 Sellwood Riverfront Park and Oaks Bottom Trail

🐾🐾🦮 (See Greater Portland map on pages 322–323)

The SHARED site at Sellwood carves out a healthy center section of the nine-acre city park. It is a nice, open lawn, with no fencing or dog amenities. You'll need excellent voice control of your dog, as there are no natural features to separate the off-leash area from other park uses.

Many parts of Sellwood are worth exploring on leash. The riverfront part of the park's name is easy to reach by means of a ramp, and it extends around the bend all the way to Portland's historic Oaks Amusement Park, operating since 1904. The views of the city and Sellwood Bridge are excellent.

Sellwood also connects to the Oaks Bottom Trail, a 1.5-mile, soft-surface hike through a wildlife refuge packed with more than 140 species of birds, mammals, reptiles, and amphibians. You're most likely to see great blue herons, beavers, and muskrats in addition to the usual geese and ducks. It's a level, easy, and shady walk with blackberries free for the picking in late summer.

From I-5, take exit 297 south on S.W. Terwilliger Boulevard for .9 mile, turn left onto S.W. Taylors Ferry Road for one mile, and right on S.W. Macadam Avenue .5 mile to the Sellwood Bridge. Cross the bridge and immediately turn left on S.E. 7th Avenue to S.E. Oaks Parkway. The SHARED area is in the center of the park at the intersection of S.E. Spokane and Oaks Parkway.

30 Brentwood Dog Park

😊 🐕 (See Greater Portland map on pages 322–323)

The YES site at Brentwood City Park is a muddy patch of rectangular earth carved out of an existing park. The tiny off-leash area sits in a depression, gathering runoff from the sprinklers on the sports fields. After 15 minutes with her beloved soccer ball ("The ball, the ball, PUULEEEZ the ball!"), Isis came away with enough earth caked in her fur to bake four-and-twenty blackbirds into a mud pie. She suggests you give in to it—let yourself get covered head-to-toe. As any dog will tell you, that whole cleanliness is next to godliness thing is overrated. The park is fenced and gated with a single tree in the middle and a garbage can. Bring your own bags, water, and a stack of towels.

From I-205, take Exit 17 west toward S.E. Woodstock, turn left at the next intersection on S.E. 92nd Avenue, then right on S.E. Duke Street, and left on S.E. 62nd. The YES site is on the southeast corner of 62nd Avenue and S.E. Rural Street. Street parking is on 62nd, south of S.E. Cooper Street. Open 5 A.M.–midnight.

PLACES TO EAT

Berlin Inn: Dogs, that's *hunds* in German, have their very own Patio Pooch Menu for dining in the *biergarten* at this upscale Bavarian restaurant. Canine connoisseurs can select from items such as Lollipups, a peanut butter biscuit on a rawhide stick; a Bag-O-Bones sampler of treats; or Mutt Mix, two turkey hot dogs sliced and tossed with biscuits. Humans are treated to filling gourmet fare, fine wines, and, of course, German beer. 3131 S.E. 12th; 503/236-6761; www.berlininn.com.

Caffé Destino: We're destined to return again and again to this coffeehouse. The mug of the shop's mascot, a rottweiler-mix named Espresso, graces the frequent-buyer coffee card (buy 10, get one free). Tiny sidewalk tables provide just enough room to eat your bagel or grilled panini sandwich. If your dog can spare a bone or two, there's a jar on the counter for dog biscuit donations to the local humane society. 1339 N.E. Fremont; 503/284-9455.

Dingo's Fresh Mexican Grill: Dingo's has dozens of picnic tables, a full bar, sit-down service, and inventive Mexican food, all on a hip street within a few blocks of Mt. Tabor Park. The restaurant is popular for tequila samplers and breakfast, although perhaps not together. 4612 S.E. Hawthorne Blvd.; 503/233-3996; www.dingosonline.com.

The Lucky Lab Brewing Co.: Some people would have a tough time choosing between beer or their dog as their truest best friend. Fortunately, they can have both, and decent grub, at a big, covered outdoor patio with dozens of picnic tables. Inside, the walls are lined with photos of the many Labs and other breeds who have paid a visit to this pub that's famous in canine social circles. Add a little extra to your beer money to buy a Lucky Lab T-shirt or hat; we bet you'll want one. And, don't forget a photo of your furry loved one to add to the wall. 915 S.E. Hawthorne Blvd.; 503/236-3555; www.luckylab.com.

Milwaukie

Between Portland and historical Oregon City, this City of Dogwoods is a taste of small-town charm, close to the city. Before it closes for fall maintenance, the state-of-the-art North Clackamas Aquatic Park has a dogs-only swim day, an extremely rare opportunity for your dog to get a taste of indoor pool water.

PARKS, BEACHES, AND RECREATION AREAS

31 North Clackamas Park

🐾🐾🐕 (See Greater Portland map on pages 322–323)

This fenced off-leash area is a prized privilege for Milwaukie dogs, even though it's smallish, a bit under two acres. Word of mouth says it can get really crowded on weekends, and there's a local gang of Akitas who act tough in the after-work hours, which can be intimidating.

It's a wood-chip area, a bit dusty in summer and certainly muddy the rest of the year. Through the double-gated entry, you'll find picnic tables and a peaked-roof rain shelter for human counterparts. Although the Portland metro area has plenty of off-leash opportunities, this is one of a treasured few that are securely fenced. Bring bags and water.

From Hwy. 99 E, take State Route 224, the Milwaukie Expressway, turn south on S.E. Rusk Road, and when this arterial road curves around to the left, continue straight to enter the park. To find the OLA, turn right at the Area A&B sign, pass the Milwaukie Center, and park behind the peaked-roof picnic shelter. Walk a few hundred feet west to the fenced area on your right. 5440 S.E. Kellogg Creek Dr.; 503/794-8002.

PLACES TO EAT

Bob's Red Mill: From the Milwaukie Expressway, you can't miss Bob's big red barn. This specialty mill grinds whole-grain, organic flours for sale at health food grocery stores around the country. There is a deli, whole-grain store, and visitors center on site. Kids can watch the water wheel turn and sample Bob's breads and cookies. The patio is iffy for pets; get your hearty whole-grain sandwiches to go. 5209 S.E. International Way; 503/654-3215; www.bobsredmill.com.

Lake Oswego

As you approach this well-to-do bedroom community, you'll see forested landscapes and expansive views of the Willamette River, along with formal landscapes and expansive homes. The few blocks of downtown have a dense concentration of trendy shops, galleries, and a sculpture garden on A Avenue along the Millennium Plaza Park.

PARKS, BEACHES, AND RECREATION AREAS

32 Tryon Creek

🐾🐾🐾 (See Greater Portland map on pages 322–323)

There are eight miles of hiking tails in this 645-acre State Natural Area, plus three miles reserved for equestrians, and another three-mile paved path along the east edge. Pick any trail in the ravine, and you'll enjoy plenty of shade among the cedar, fir, and big leaf maples, while your dog appreciates the mixed bouquet of the forest and the occasional horse puck. If there's anyone in your group who thinks the last one in the creek is a rotten egg, the fastest route to the water is along the Middle Creek Trail from the nature center to High Bridge, returning on the Old Man Trail to make a quick one-mile loop. Many lunchtime and after-work joggers take to Tryon's hills; the park is strict about enforcing leash laws on the tight and narrow trails. The .4-mile Trillium Trail is fully accessible. There are drinking fountains and restrooms at the nature center, at the main entrance.

From I-5, take Exit 297, and stay in the right lane to cloverleaf around south onto S.W. Terwilliger Boulevard. The park entrance is 2.5 miles down on your right. Open 7 A.M.–dusk. 503/636-9886.

33 George Rogers Park

🐾🐾 (See Greater Portland map on pages 322–323)

Life is pretty relaxed on the swimming beach at this city park. Many of the park's 26 acres are taken up by baseball diamonds, tennis courts, a children's play area, and the formal, landscaped Memorial Garden. Pass all of that up and head down the hill to the sandy banks of the Willamette River to mingle with the geese at a natural open-space area.

George Rogers is the site of Oregon's first iron smelter in the 1890s. You can view the preserved historic chimney behind a fence on the grounds.

From I-5, take Exit 299A and travel south on State Route 43, S.W. Macadam Avenue, into Lake Oswego. The road becomes N. State Street through downtown; a few blocks later, watch closely for Ladd Street. Turn left, past the athletic fields, and then right at the Main Parking Lot sign. Open 6 A.M.–10 P.M. 611 State St.; 503/797-1850.

34 Luscher Farm Dog Park

🐾🐾🐾🐾🐾 🐕 (See Greater Portland map on pages 322–323)

There's no getting up at the crack of dawn to milk the cows and feed the hens on this farm. The only chores you're likely to face are throwing a slimy ball a hundred times for your happy-go-lucky farm animal and picking up the fertilizer he leaves in the field. Dogs will find any excuse to escape to the countryside if it means coming to this popular off-leash park. A secure fence and gate protect a broad, gently sloping hill of several acres, with generous field grass and a wood-chip trail around the inside perimeter. There's a cluster of shady trees in the upper corner by the entry gate, with scattered seating for humans to sit and shoot the breeze. It can be hectic, but you can get 40 dogs inside the fence and still have room to run. Cleanup bags are available; B.Y.O. water.

From I-205, take Exit 3 north on S.W. Stafford Road for two miles. A gravel parking lot is on the right. If you continue north on this road, it becomes McVay Avenue into downtown Lake Oswego.

PLACES TO EAT

Port City Pasta Co.: Get your turkey sandwich to go, one block south to George Rogers Park, and relish every bite of the focaccia bread that *Gourmet* magazine called "the Best in the West." Your dog would rather have bits of the turkey filling anyway. 333 S. State St.; 503/699-2927.

Zeppo: The salads are so gorgeous at this fine Italian eatery, you may never make it to the thin-crust pizzas, al dente pastas, or low-carb dinners. Your pup may join you on the *piazza*, a sunny brick plaza. 345 First Street; 503/675-2726; www.zepporestaurant.com.

PLACES TO STAY

Crowne Plaza: This swank property, favored by business executives, places pets in rooms on the second floor, saving other floors for those who may have allergies. Rates range $129–156; the pet fee is $20. 14811 Kruse Oaks Dr.; 503/624-8400; www.crowneplaza.com/lakeoswegoor.

More Accommodations: Please look under Chain Hotels in the Resources section for additional places to stay in this area.

West Linn

With a median household income comfortably in the $80K range, this affluent suburban city survived fires and floods in the early years to emerge as a comfortable place to live and play. With a descriptive nickname, "The City of Hills, Trees, and Rivers," West Linn has no established commercial downtown, which doesn't hurt a dog's feelings at all. **The Dog Club** in West

Linn is posh and well equipped for a day of play, a wash or groom, or to pick up quality chow, toys, and accessories. 18675 Willamette Dr.; 503/635-3523; www.dogclub4u.com.

PARKS, BEACHES, AND RECREATION AREAS

35 Mary S. Young

🐾 🐾 🐕 (See Greater Portland map on pages 322–323)

If your dog is stir-crazy but you don't have time for a drive to the country, take her to the trails and the pet exercise area at this State Recreation Site. The off-leash area is a couple of acres, protected by a ring of trees on three sides. It's wide open and unfenced, yet remote enough to feel reasonably secure. There's some shade at picnic tables huddled in one corner, restrooms, and a water pump for dog drinking and bathing. Bring your own pickup bags.

The trail system is a bit vague in the forested section of the park. The city narrows it down to somewhere between five and eight miles of trails through the fir, maple, and alder. The paths you can easily find begin across the parking lot from the dog run, leading down to the southwest bank of the Willamette River.

From I-205, take Exit 8 north on Willamette Drive (State Route 43). Turn left toward Lake Oswego and go two miles. To find the OLA, drive past the athletic fields to the end of the circular parking loop. Open 7 A.M.–dusk. Mary S. Young is owned by Oregon State Parks and managed by West Linn Parks and Recreation, 503/557-4700.

PLACES TO STAY

Rivershore Hotel: Not only does this lovely hotel take dogs, but they've had a chimpanzee stay once. The only four-legged creatures they turn away are those with hooves. While your livestock may have to lodge elsewhere, your dog is welcome to join you for a $5 fee per night, soaking up Willamette River views from the balcony. Although technically in Oregon City, it is just across the river, and the highway, from West Linn. Rates range $78–89. 1900 Clackamette Dr.; 503/655-7141 or 800/443-7777.

Beaverton

Beaverton is Oregon's fifth-largest city. Seven miles southeast of Portland, it is the heart of the state's "Silicon Forest," an economic artery pumping capital into a healthy business environment. Silicon or no, this forest is worthy of a side trip from Portland for its dog park.

DIVERSION

Biscuit lovers in Beaverton have got it made, with no fewer than three bakeries dedicated to fulfilling doggie dessert dreams.

Throw a party for your dog's next birthday, and order a "cake" by phone or online from the **Animal Lover's Birthday Bakery.** Cake-sized hard dog treats are baked with your dog's name and age in 93 different breed-specific shapes and two flavors, liver or bacon. Squeaky toys in the shape of wrapped presents and hand-tied bags of smaller treats make great party favors for invited dog guests. 503/259-2203; www.animalloversbakery.com.

A dog is not well and truly spoiled until she's joined the Treat-of-the-Month Club at the **Great Dog Bakery.** Healthy treats, made in flavors such as peanut butter, chicken, ginger, and mint, are shipped door-to-dog-door the first week of each month. Isis bets that Beaverton dogs are nice to their mailmen. 15365 S.W. Beaverton Creek Ct.; 503/626-3600 or 877/292-1113; www.greatdogbakery.com.

When you're out running errands, don't forget to stop at **All Pooches Bakery** for unique gifts and homemade treats for your pet. Twice a year, this bakery brings in a trained pet communicator to help humans have a meeting of the minds with their pets. 8154 S.W. Hall Blvd.; 503/526-8781; www.allpoochesbakery.com.

PARKS, BEACHES, AND RECREATION AREAS

36 Hazeldale Park

🐾🐾🐾🐾🐕 (See Greater Portland map on pages 322–323)

This full-time off-leash complex devoted to the art of being a dog deserves all four paws, one for each of its four separate, fully fenced areas. There are two dog runs for the big boys and two for the little fellas. They're used in pairs, one set each for the summer and winter, allowing the opposites to repair themselves naturally for half the year.

Each area is long and thin. There's some openness, but most of the space is covered with short, stocky pine trees for games of hide and seek. They are beautifully equipped. The fences are high and secure and there are double gates to create leash-transition zones. There are picnic tables, bags tucked in the fence, and water brought in bowls and buckets from elsewhere in the park. Perhaps best of all, the people and dogs are exceptionally friendly and take great pride in maintaining the OLA in tip-top shape.

From U.S Highway 26, exit to State Route 217, then exit on State Route 10 westbound and follow it past Beaverton until you see signs for Aloha. Turn right on S.W. 192nd Avenue, then turn left on the third street, Prospect Street.

There's plenty of parking. Everyone is vigilant about keeping their dogs on leash until inside the gates. Managed by Tualatin Hills Parks and Recreation, 503/645-6433.

PLACES TO EAT

Krispy Kreme: People are as loyal to these doughnuts as dogs are to their owners. How could they not be? When the neon "HOT" light is on, you can step into the store and watch your doughnut glide through a waterfall of sugary glaze only moments before it touches your lips. It's possible to down a dozen before you even realize what you've done. 16415 N.W. Cornell Rd.; 503/645-2228; www.krispykreme.com.

PLACES TO STAY

Sweetbrier Inn and Suites: This suburban highway motel manages to be quite personable, with its own wooded park for a quick jog, walk, or reflective moment with your pawed companion. It's about 10 miles south of downtown Portland. Rates range $79–95, and there is a $25 refundable pet deposit. 7125 S.W. Nyberg Rd.; 503/629-5800 or 800/551-9167; www.sweetbrier.com.

More Accommodations: Please look under Chain Hotels in the Resources section for additional places to stay in this area.

Gresham

While these parks are still technically within Portland city limits, they are far enough east to use the heavy retail suburb of Gresham as a home base.

PARKS, BEACHES, AND RECREATION AREAS

37 Glenfair Park

🐾🐾🐾 (See Greater Portland map on pages 322–323)

This city park's SHARED site encompasses almost the entire park, roughly in the shape of a massive triangle defined by the park's circular driveway on one side, and school property fences on the other two. It's really big, nice and green, and completely open, except for a few pine trees clustering at the extreme southern tip. Bring dogs who are into long-distance running, the free-throw fetch, Frisbee, and other sports that require room to spread out. You are on your own for bags, water, and even a convenient trash can.

From I-84, take Exit 13 and go south on 181st Avenue for 1.5 miles. Turn right on E. Burnside Street and right on S.E. 154th Avenue at 1.2 miles. The SHARED area is the southern two-thirds of the park. Street parking is available along the Couch Street circular drive. Morning off-leash hours are shortened to 5–8 A.M. at this park.

38 Powell Butte Nature Park

🐾🐾🐾 (See Greater Portland map on pages 322–323)

Pick a day when the mountains will be out to head to the top of this 570-acre park, an extinct volcano with a nine-mile trail system for hikers, cyclists, and equestrians. In addition to the indigenous forest, trees include old apple, pear, and walnut orchards from the 1900s farm of Henry Anderegg. Powell Butte is exceedingly popular with mountain bikers, and you'll have to tolerate them buzzing by you at the beginning of the trail until you can break off onto a walkers-only path. There's a gravel parking lot with restrooms, a drinking fountain, and a trail map at the start. At the top is a rolling meadow where Anderegg's cattle used to graze within sight of Mt. Hood and the tips of a few other peaks. Underneath it all is a 500-million-gallon reservoir, part of the Bull Run system, the primary water source for the Portland metro area.

From I-205, go east on S.E. Division Street for 3.5 miles. Take a right on S.E. 162nd Avenue and continue .7 mile to the park entrance. Open 7 A.M.–8 P.M.

39 East Lynchwood Park

🐾🐾🦴 (See Greater Portland map on pages 322–323)

The Wonder Wieners will be the first to admit that this park is obscure. Its remote location and lack of other specific use are the very things that make it an ideal SHARED site. A large grove of trees forms a semi-circle around the flat field, protecting it from the only adjacent road, which isn't a very busy street. The other three sides of the rectangle are enclosed by residential and school fences. You'll feel like this off-leash area is your own secret discovery. Benches in the trees are the only amenities. You should go potty before you leave the house and bring anything you'll need, including bags, water, and your pooch's favorite UFO.

From I-205, go east on S.E. Division Street for four miles, take a right on S.E. 174th Avenue, and a right on S.E. Haig Street. The SHARED area is on the east side of the park. Park along Haig where it dead-ends. Morning off-leash hours are shortened to 5–8 A.M. at this park.

PLACES TO EAT

Subs on Sandy: This tiny corner shop in the strip mall makes enough fat, messy sandwiches to order a different one every day of the month and teriyaki on weekends. An outdoor picnic table looked weary; the ones at nearby Glenfair Park are next to the off-leash area. 13912 Sandy Blvd.; 503/252-SUBS (503/252-7827).

PLACES TO STAY

In this area, chain hotels offer the best choices for dogs and their owners; please look under Chain Hotels in the Resources section.

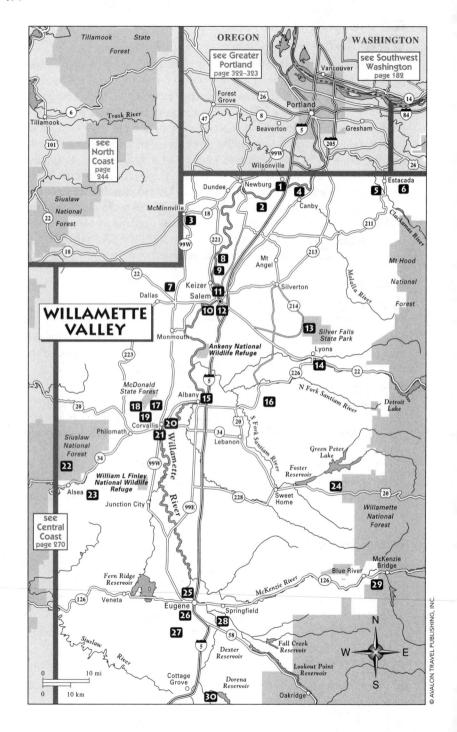

CHAPTER 13
Willamette Valley

From 1843 to 1869, a half million pioneers hitched up their wagons and traveled the 2,000-mile Oregon Trail from Missouri to reach the promised land of the Willamette Valley. As you travel through, you can see why they came—and reap the fruits of their labors. Tucked between the Cascade and Coastal mountains, the abundant valley sits on the same latitude as France's Burgundy wine region and is perfect for growing grapes. Dogs are welcome in the picnic areas of Anne Amie Winery (6580 N.E. Mineral Springs Rd.; 800/248-4825), Duck Pond Cellars (23145 Hwy. 99 W; 503/538-3199; www.duckpondcellars.com), and Sokol Blosser (5000 Sokol Blosser Ln.; 503/864-2710; www.sokolblosser.com).

The climate is also ideal for hazelnuts, also called filberts, producing 99 percent of the nation's entire supply. Tree farms and nurseries line the rolling hillsides, with thousands of identical conifers in soldierly order. The valley's abundance includes a cornucopia of fantastic off-leash areas as well, within state parks and in the region's three major college towns of Eugene, Salem, and Corvallis.

PICK OF THE LITTER—WILLAMETTE VALLEY

BEST PARKS
Willamette Mission, Salem (page 364)
Silver Falls, Silverton (page 368)

BEST DOG PARKS
Champoeg State Park, Newberg (page 358)
Milo McIver State Park, Estacada (page 362)
Alton Baker Dog Park, Eugene (page 377)

BEST EVENTS
Silverton Pet Parade, Silverton (page 365)
Bark in the Park, Brownsville (page 365)

BEST PLACES TO EAT
Butteville General Store, Newberg (page 358)
Oregon Tea Garden, Silverton (page 369)

BEST PLACES TO STAY
Avellan Inn, Newberg (page 359)
A' Tuscan Estate, McMinnville (page 360)
Wayfarer Resort, Blue River (page 380)

Water is the source of life in the valley, and its rivers and reservoirs are the primary source of recreation. To cross the multiple tributaries of these major rivers, Oregon pioneers built bridges with wooden buildings around them to protect the wooden trusses from accelerated decay in rainy weather. The state has preserved the largest number of historical covered bridges west of the Mississippi, most of them in the Willamette Valley, each county featuring a different design. Covered bridge tour maps from city visitors centers are an excellent way to explore scenic roads.

The top two tourist attractions in Oregon are in the Willamette—the Champoeg and Milo McIver Pet Exercise Areas. No, actually they are Spirit Mountain Casino (www.spirit-mountain.com) and the upscale outlets at Woodburn Company Stores (www.woodburncompanystores.com), but dogs may beg to differ.

NATIONAL FORESTS AND RECREATION AREAS

Willamette National Forest

This playground has more than 80 developed campgrounds and 1,700 miles of hiking trails. The forest service's interactive Trip Planning Map online is a great way to find recreational opportunities far beyond what we have room to mention in this book. For the McKenzie River Recreation Area, along State Route 126, stop into the ranger station in McKenzie Bridge (57600 Hwy. 126.; 541/822-3381). The Sweet Home Ranger District also publishes an excellent free guide to the hikes around the Santiam Area, along U.S. Highway 20 from Albany east to Sisters (3225 Hwy. 20; 541/367-5168; www.fs.fed.us/r6/willamette).

Wilsonville

This fast-growing city hosts corporate biggies like Xerox and Hollywood Entertainment. At the same time, it has a Tree City USA designation to keep it green.

PARKS, BEACHES, AND RECREATION AREAS

❶ Memorial Bark Park

🐾🐾🐾🐕 (See Willamette Valley map on page 354)

This popular off-leash area is where local dogs come to blow off steam after a hard day's nap waiting for their humans to come home from work. The city says the park has been left in its natural state except for the occasional mowing, but the Dachshund Duo found it to be in much better shape than many parks they've seen. Gopher holes are the main hazard, also providing something to stick a nose in for a snout full of rodent spoor. There's no long list of rules, merely the statement that only good dogs are allowed.

A chicken-wire fence surrounds a couple of acres with tables in either corner and gates on both ends. There are a few shade trees along one side and bag dispensers, which were all empty. Bring your own bags and water.

From I-5, take Exit 283 and go east on Wilsonville Road for .3 mile, turn right on Memorial Drive and almost immediately turn left. The OLA is around the corner to your left past the sports fields, down a short path from a gravel parking area. Open dawn–dusk.

PLACES TO EAT

Country Grains Bread Co.: It's only a couple of blocks from Memorial Bark Park, but you may want to eat at this deli's picnic tables to avoid mass begging. In addition to sandwiches and low-carb choices, there's chili to go by the quart. 8553 S.W. Main St., in the Village at Main Street; 503/682-5857.

PLACES TO STAY

In this area, chain hotels offer the best choices for dogs and their owners; please look under Chain Hotels in the Resources section.

Newberg

This city was the boyhood home of Herbert Hoover, the 31st president of the United States. It's a popular stop along the "Wine Highway," State Route 99 W, 25 miles southwest of Portland.

PARKS, BEACHES, AND RECREATION AREAS

🛛 Champoeg State Park

😺😺😺😺🐾 (See Willamette Valley map on page 354)

After her first visit to the pet exercise area at this State Heritage Area, your dog's tail will start wagging if you even think the word Champoeg (sham-POO-ee). The park's designated off-leash area is a five-acre field that seems much larger, in the middle of 615 acres of white oak forests, fields, and wetlands along the Willamette River. The pet area is not secured, but it is far enough removed from everything else to present no problems for well-managed dogs. The park sits on the site of the ghost town of Champoeg, where Oregon's first provisional government was established. The town was destroyed in an 1861 flood and abandoned after more floods in 1890.

There are other activities to enjoy with a leashed pooch. The Riverside Picnic Area is nearby, and if you walk on the trails west of the Pioneer Mother's Cabin, there are a few informal areas along the river to catch the drift. There is a four-mile paved trail from the park to the Butteville General Store, where you can rent bicycles for the day. A large campground, visitors center, historic buildings, hiking trails, and disc golf course occupy other areas of the large park.

We say phooey to the convoluted signs to Champoeg. Instead, take the Charbonneau Exit (282B) from I-5, go west on winding Butteville Road for five miles, then bear right onto Champoeg Road for another three miles. To find the OLA, turn down the hill to the left toward the Riverside Area and Pioneer Mother's Cabin and go .7 mile to parking along a gravel lane at the far end of the field. Parking is $3. 503/678-1251.

PLACES TO EAT

Butteville General Store: First opened in 1863, Oregon's oldest continually operating store carries on the tradition of being the social center of a rural community. It's a deli, an art gallery, a historical museum of local photographs, a venue for local musicians, and a bicycle rental shop for treks to nearby Champoeg. Plan your vacation to coincide with pizza or gourmet burger nights. Pets are warmly welcomed on the front porch or in garden seating. 10767 Butte St.; 503/678-1605; www.buttevillegeneralstore.com.

PLACES TO STAY

Avellan Inn: This exquisite bed-and-breakfast is a haven of country peacefulness. Once you've lain down on the downy featherbeds, sat in a swinging chair on your private enclosed deck, and eaten the homemade hazelnut truffle left on your pillow, you may never want to leave. Neither will your dog feel any desire to part from the hazelnut orchards and fields of the 12-acre property, where he's free to roam off-leash. The only thing making your departure easier to bear is the bag of homemade cookies Carol hands you when you leave. Emily's Room, $125 per night or $145 if you add the suite area, has a private entrance for pet people. The pet fee is $10. Children are welcome. 16900 N.E. Hwy 240; 503/537-9161; www.avellaninn.com.

Champoeg Campground: There are 79 RV sites for $16–20, and six walk-in tent sites for $12–16 at this state park in a remote setting on the plains by the Willamette River. 800/452-5687; www.reserveamerica.com.

More Accommodations: Please look under Chain Hotels in the Resources section for additional places to stay in this area.

DIVERSION

Take your dog to a drive-in movie, before this endangered species becomes extinct. The **99W Drive In Theatre** in Newberg runs double features of first-run titles, with real-butter popcorn and original, restored 1950s trailers before the show and between features. Cash only; 503/538-2738; www.99w.com.

The drive-in's pet policy is so priceless, we requested permission to print it in its entirety:

Question: Can I bring my dog/cat/ferret/elephant? **Answer:** Yes, as long as the animal is harmless to the customers and our operation. Management reserves the right to refuse any animal (including human) admission. Elephants and other larger animals will be charged a single-occupant car admission due to the fact they would take up a car space by themselves. You will be solely responsible for damage caused by your animal to the drive-in, yourself, other drive-in patrons or property. You must keep your animal secured to your vehicle/parking space. NOTE TO ELEPHANTS AND GIRAFFES: Our ticket window height clearance is 8 feet.

McMinnville

Historic downtown McMinnville, along 3rd Street, is an enjoyable place to stroll, shop, and eat. It's the hub for wine country tours of the valley, catering to travelers with its quaint bed-and-breakfast inns and a pretty city park.

PARKS, BEACHES, AND RECREATION AREAS

🐾 McMinnville City Park

🐾🐾 (See Willamette Valley map on page 354)

Conveniently located at the end of the downtown historic district, this city park has two levels. The upper park has a gigantic wooden play castle for the kids, sandwiched between the library and city pool. The lower level is more informal and dog-friendly, with a short walking path and picnic tables along Cozine Creek.

As you enter town from the north, State Route 99W becomes Adams Street southbound. The park is located at the intersection of 3rd and Adams Streets. If you are entering from the south, 99W merges onto Baker Street northbound. At Third Street, turn left on 3rd, one block to Adams.

PLACES TO EAT

Harvest Fresh Grocery and Deli: Hearty soups, fresh salads, and sandwiches of substance including tempeh, tarragon chicken, and turkey meatloaf are only the beginning at the deli side of this health food grocery store a couple of blocks from the city park. The fresh vegetable and fruit juice blends are refreshing, sipped at a sidewalk table. 251 E. 3rd St.; 503/472-5740.

PLACES TO STAY

A' Tuscan Estate: This bed-and-breakfast has the perfect combination of opulent romance and practicality. For example, there's a doggie shower and wash tub downstairs to clean up your canine before you head up to your plush room with the saturated, warm colors of an Italian villa. Rooms are $125 a night. Pets are welcome in the Portofino or Napoli rooms for an additional $35 per stay. The home is close to everything, including historic downtown, the city park, and walking trails. Kids are also welcome. 809 N.E. Evans St.; 503/434-9016 or 800/441-2214; www.a-tuscanestate.com.

More Accommodations: Please look under Chain Hotels in the Resources section for additional places to stay in this area.

Canby

Canby sits in the state's garden spot for flax, floral, nursery, and dairy farming, most visible in the summer at the Swan Island Dahlia Farm, the nation's largest dahlia grower. Other local landmarks include the Canby Depot Museum, one of the oldest remaining railroad stations in Oregon, and the Canby Ferry across the Willamette to Wilsonville.

PARKS, BEACHES, AND RECREATION AREAS

◻ Molalla River

🐾🐾🐕 (See Willamette Valley map on page 354)

The Dachsie Twins give the off-leash area at this State Park one paw, with an extra paw thrown in for the riverfront trails. Unfenced and smallish, the main problem with the pet exercise area is that it's rarely mowed. Any dog with hair longer than a Chinese crested is likely to come away with half the park's native groundcover stuck to his fur. Starting west of the boat ramp, opt instead for a .75-mile hike, along the Willamette River to where it joins with the Molalla then loops back around through the woods for a total of about 1.5 miles. A quarter mile downstream from the park is the Canby Ferry across the Willamette; pedestrians and bicycles cross for no charge, cars are $1.25 each way. For information, call 503/650-3030.

From 99E in Canby, turn north on Grant Street, go two blocks, turn right on 2nd Avenue, go one block, turn north on Holly Street, and travel 2.2 miles. The park entrance comes up suddenly on the left after a bend in the road. Open 7 A.M.–dusk.

PLACES TO STAY

In this area, chain hotels offer the best choices for dogs and their owners; please look under Chain Hotels in the Resources section.

Estacada

Estacada is the gateway city to the Clackamas River Recreation Area of the Mt. Hood National Forest. Ask at the Ranger Station for a long list of scenic hikes and river boat ramps (595 N.W. Industrial Way, 503/630-6861). Despite early years of logging and dam development to supply nearby Portland with hydroelectric power, the area remains beautiful for hiking, fishing, camping, and hounding around.

PARKS, BEACHES, AND RECREATION AREAS

5 Milo McIver State Park

😊 😊 😊 😊 🐾 (See Willamette Valley map on page 354)

Sometime in the 1970s, according to a local historian, this state park hosted its first and only government-sponsored concert event called Vortex. Supposedly, the goal was to keep all the hippie activists happy and busy, away from Portland while President Nixon was in town. Local farmers were reputedly paid to drop off bags of food and smokable plants for the 35,000 people.

While the flower power days of the '70s may be over, at least your dog can enjoy a carefree existence at Milo McIver's off-leash pet exercise area. Even though the area is not fenced, the rest of the park's designated areas are miles away in this 951-acre sprawling park on the Clackamas River. There's a garbage can, a bag dispenser, and a huge, wide open field of tender, green grass—real grass, not dirt or wood chips. You can enjoy the shade of one gigantic tree and an amazing view of Mt. Hood while developing a case of tennis elbow tossing a ball with one of those fling-things.

It's easy to spend an entire vacation at this pet-friendly park and not get bored. There are miles of Milo along the riverbanks, hiking trails with long beaches and convenient splash points. Rafting down the river from Milo McIver to Barton Park is another popular pastime, plus there are equestrian trails, a campground, a fish hatchery, and several picnic areas.

From Estacada, travel southwest on State Route 211 for a mile, turn right on Hayden Road, and right on Springwater Road for another mile. The off-leash area is to the right along the main park road. Open 7 A.M.–sunset. Parking is $3. 503/630-7150.

6 Eagle Fern

😊 😊 😊 (See Willamette Valley map on page 354)

The county's largest and most doggone divine park is tucked deep in the woods in one of the few remaining old-growth timber stands in the valley. There is an excellent kiosk of information presented by the forest service to give you an idea of the treescape around you. Each of many individual picnic areas along Eagle Creek has convenient water and garbage cans nearby. Across a bouncy suspension bridge are short and sweet hikes, from .5 mile to 1.25 miles each, through towering Western red cedars, Douglas firs, hemlocks, and maples. The water is inviting for fishing and dog paddling. It is a relaxed and relaxing atmosphere for people with pets.

From State Route 224, four miles north of Estacada, follow the sign to Eagle Fern Park/Dover District, turning on Wildcat Mountain Road and traveling two miles to bear right onto Eagle Fern Road and another 2.3 miles to the park. Open 6 A.M.–9 P.M., May–Sept., until 6 P.M. in the winter. A $3 parking fee is charged weekends and holidays, Memorial Day–Labor Day. 503/353-4414; www.co.clackamas.or.us/dtd/parks.

PLACES TO EAT

Cada Corner: Estacada's first and only liberal coffee shop is affectionately called the town's living room, with a TV, Internet, live music, and games. With your dog in tow, you'll have to get your breakfast and lunch to go. Coop couldn't talk them into adding outdoor bark-o-loungers. 458 S.W. 2nd; 503/630-2323.

PLACES TO STAY

Clackamas Inn: This friendly highway stop in Clackamas (Exit #12 off I-205) is the closest motel to Estacada. Management caters to seniors and pet owners, and non-smoking rooms are available. Rates range $59–109, plus a $10 pet fee. 16010 S.E. 82nd Dr.; 503/650-5340 or 800/874-6560; www.clackamasinn.com.

Milo McIver Campground: The 44 electric sites at Milo are friendly for RVs or tents, for $13–17. There are also nine primitive tent sites available for a measly $6–9 per night. 800/452-5687; www.reserveamerica.com.

Dallas

Dallas, done Oregon style, is a town of historic county government buildings, surrounded by rolling hills at the base of the Coast Mountain Range, 13 miles west of Salem.

PARKS, BEACHES, AND RECREATION AREAS

⑦ Baskett Slough National Wildlife Refuge

😊😊😊 (See Willamette Valley map on page 354)

The trails of the slough are a meditative place to walk, perhaps to contemplate where you are going in life as you watch endangered dusky Canada geese headed to Canada, with a friend beside you who trusts implicitly that where *she's* going in life is wherever you are. Seven miles of walking trails through the 2,492-acre preserve might lead you to songbirds, ducks, black-tailed deer, great blue herons, and Fender's blue butterfly, a species thought to be extinct until rediscovered here. Whether or not it leads you to a personal epiphany is up to you, and your dog will enjoy herself regardless. Much of the hikes are in open areas without shade, and you'll need to bring water.

The slough sits on a triangle of land formed by the intersection of State Routes 22 and 99W. The wildlife-viewing platform is along State Route 22. The easiest trailhead access is off 99W; turn left on Colville Road, a gravel road, and drive 1.4 miles to the fenced parking area and a lone picnic table huddled under a tree. Trail maps area available at the trailhead. Open sunrise–sunset, May–September. 10995 Hwy. 22; 503/623-2749.

PLACES TO STAY

In this area, chain hotels offer the best choices for dogs and their owners; please look under Chain Hotels in the Resources section.

Salem–Keizer

In 1864, the capital of Oregon was moved from Oregon City, near Portland, to its present location in Salem. Perhaps they realized how convenient this centrally located city is to all that the valley has to offer in Marion and Polk counties.

The gardens around the Salem suburb of Keizer are well known as the center of the world's iris industry. May and June are the months to see this tall flower in bloom.

PARKS, BEACHES, AND RECREATION AREAS

🖪 Willamette Mission

🐾 🐾 🐾 🐾 🐾 (See Willamette Valley map on page 354)

This 1,600-acre state park is a time capsule and a hands-on agricultural lesson, with an off-leash dog park thrown in for good measure. The history is visible against the sky in the form of ghost structures, metal sculptures that trace the outlines of original Methodist mission, established in 1834 by Rev. Jason Lee. You can hike up to 12 miles through vineyards, fields of hops, mission roses, and habitat restoration projects, and in the fall, you can gather hazelnuts in the picnic orchards. (Don't pick them off the trees; they're not ripe until they fall.) For $1.35, you can ride across the Wheatland Ferry, the first to carry a covered wagon across the Willamette in 1844. For ferry information, call 503/588-7979.

As for the real reason you came here, to find the pet exercise area, turn left at the entry booth, and go a mile toward the picnic facilities, to the parking lot for the nation's largest black cottonwood tree. To your left is an unfenced off-leash area, another orchard with many trees to inspect. There's a garbage can and a bag dispenser. The OLA is close to group picnic areas, providing an opportunity to practice tough love to keep your German shepherd from snagging a bratwurst off someone's grill.

From I-5, take Exit 263 and drive two miles west on Brooklane Road. After a right turn on Wheatland Road, it's another 2.5 miles through hazelnut orchards and hops fields to the park entrance. Parking is $3. Open 7 A.M.–sunset. 503/393-1172.

🐾 Spong's Landing

 (See Willamette Valley map on page 354)

You'd never suspect that such a great countryside watering hole can be found five minutes from the commercialism of the main drag in Keizer. There is some serious running around going on, on the fields of Spong's Landing. It's also an excellent hidden river spot with bark dust trails down to a little beach on a wide bend in the Willamette River. Officially, as a county park, dogs are to be on leash. That's all we'll say about that.

DOG-EAR YOUR CALENDAR

In the summertime, the canine event calendar heats up in the Willamette Valley.

The **Silverton Pet Parade,** on the third Saturday in May, is the longest running pet parade this side of the Mississippi. It was started by the American Legion as a way to get kids out for some fun after the Great Depression and has blossomed into a way to promote an animal-friendly community. The parade is free to enter and free to watch. The lineup starts at Coolidge McClaine Park and wanders through downtown Silverton. 503/873-5615.

In Salem, dogs take to the city streets for the **Dog Days of Summer** on the first Wednesday in August. A Downtown Dawg parade leaves KeyBank at the corner of Liberty and State Streets every half hour from 5–8 P.M. to strut past the costume contest judges while local retailers hand out biscuits. Humans snoop in galleries, bargain hunt, listen to music in the streets, and take in the scene. Look up Salem's First Wednesday at www.downtownsalem.org, or contact Valerie Sovern, 503/373-3848.

People get in free and dogs pay $3 for a bandana entitling them to participate in activities and contests at the **Marion County Dog Fest**. While your dog participates in dancing, treat hide-and-seek, and water retrieval contests from the pool, you'll be raising money to benefit the Marion County Dog Shelter. First Saturday in August, 10 A.M.–4 P.M.; Bush's Pasture Park in Salem; http://commissioners .co.marion.or.us/dog_fest.

Brownsville Bark in the Park honors the special relationships between humans and dogs on the third Saturday in September, 10 A.M.–5 P.M. at Pioneer Park. Almost everyone heads home with a blue ribbon, awarded for human look-alike contest, best costume, tail wagging, and more. Participants say the relays are the most fun. Dogs are $5, humans are free. See if you qualify for the award for Furthest from the Dog House. 541/466-3394.

From River Road, turn west on Lockhaven Drive for .9 mile, right on Windsor Island Road for .7 mile, and left on Naples for .6 mile. Opens at sunrise; closes a half hour after sunset.

10 Minto Brown Island Park

😖😖😖 🐕 (See Willamette Valley map on page 354)

Today, the former farmsteads of Isaac "Whiskey" Brown and John Minto have been combined into an 900-acre park with a 20-acre off-leash area. Through cooperative use agreements, some of the land continues to be farmed, while 12 miles of paved and soft-surface trails wind through the remaining wildlife areas. If there's a dog in your life who needs some space, this is an ideal place to bring him. The dog run at Minto Brown is just that, a long field, not fenced or secured, separated from the park road by a row of trees and large boulders. There's not much traffic to worry about in the middle of an island surrounded by low-usage orchards, gravel pits, timber, dense underbrush, and grassy meadows. Trash cans are provided, bring your own bags and water. The nearby trails, the Blue and Green Loops, are both under two miles.

Regular volunteer park patrols have significantly diminished the park's reputation as an unsafe place in the 1990s. It's still best to stick to the daylight hours in this remote area.

From I-5, take Exit 253 west on Mission Street. Turn left on Commercial Street and shortly thereafter, turn right on Owens Road. Then you'll bear left onto River Road, and right onto Minto Island Road. The park entrance is a mile from the turn onto Owens Road. The dog run is between parking areas #2 and #3, .6 mile into the park. 503/588-6336.

11 Salem Riverfront Park

😖😖 🐾 (See Willamette Valley map on page 354)

We'll admit to the dogs up front that this park plaza is included primarily for your people. The main attraction is the Riverfront Carousel, with $1.25 rides on its colorfully restored horses. Wet-nosed ones won't mind the stroll along the Willamette River, down to the *Willamette Queen* sternwheeler paddleboat and the Eco Globe, a former acid tank for the Georgia Pacific paper mill transformed into a work of art using 86,000 mosaic tiles. The luxurious grass of the elevated amphitheater steps is tailor-made for picnic blankets.

From I-5, take Exit 256 and go west on Market Street through town and turn left on Front Street. The park is immediately south under the bridge to State Route 22.

12 Bush's Pasture Park

🐾🐾🐾 (See Willamette Valley map on page 354)

You can go for a long walk on the gentle bark dust trails of 95-acre Bush's Pasture. As the joggers pass you, you'll pass wide fields, mature oak trees and apple orchards, and a playground designed specifically for handicapped users. You'll skirt Willamette University's stadium and historic Deepwood Estate and Bush House Museums. You can detour through a 2,000-bloom rose garden and along Pringle Creek. Also at this city park, Salem is one of the few cities in the nation to have a track dedicated to Soap Box Derby racing. For a serious dose of lighthearted fun, check the schedule at www.salemsbd.com, and catch a race. There's more here, but you get the idea. Salem dogs are lucky to have such a diverse urban park, and the Dachsie Twins thank them for sharing.

From I-5, take Exit 253 west on Mission Street, less than a half mile to the park on your left. Turn into the first parking lot for trail access. To find the Municipal Rose Garden, continue on Mission and turn left on High Street. Open 5 A.M.–midnight.

PLACES TO EAT

Arbor Café: In the heart of the Capitol Mall area, this deli and bakery serves a half dozen daily specials in addition to a long list of delicious sandwiches and salads. Your eyes might glaze over as you gaze at the glazed tarts in the pastry case. There's plentiful courtyard seating. 380 High St.; 503/588-2353.

Gerry Frank's Konditorei: You can't miss the big sign that reads "Extravagant Cakes Etc." on your way to Minto Brown park. The etc. stands for traditional soups, salads, and sandwiches, but Isis couldn't take her eyes off the rotating pastry case of those aforementioned extravagant cakes. 310 Kearney S.E.; 503/585-7070.

La Margarita Express: This Mexican restaurant with colorful umbrella tables may very well be your elected government representative's favorite lunch haunt. It'll win your vote with vegetarian specialties and a light menu. 515 Chemeketa St.; 503/371-7960.

PLACES TO STAY

Salem Inn: The staff at this motel are extra welcoming and friendly, and that extends to your pets. The oversize rooms are clean and quiet. An extensive breakfast for you and doggie bags for your dog (the kind for leavings, not leftovers) are included. Rates range $79–89. The pet fee is $10. If you pay for the room with cash, a $50 refundable damage deposit is required. 1775 Freeway Ct. N.E.; 503/588-0515 or 888/305-0515; www.saleminn.net.

More Accommodations: Please look under Chain Hotels in the Resources section for additional places to stay in this area.

Silverton

On your way to Silver Falls State Park, enjoy Silverton's excellent galleries, boutiques, and antique stores along its historic main thoroughfare, Water Street. The **Gibson Girl,** an antique furniture gallery and pet boutique, always has an overflowing jar of dog biscuits and bowls of water waiting to occupy your dog while you shop for that special furry someone (107 N. Water St.; 503/873-4681). Stop in the visitors center to ask about the story of Bobby the Wonder Dog, whose statue, doghouse, and mural are located in town.

The internationally renowned **Oregon Garden** is located on 80 acres in Historic Silverton. Pets who won't pee on the flowers and people who pick up after their pets are welcome to walk together through 20 specialty gardens and around Oregon's only house designed by Frank Lloyd Wright (879 W. Main St.; 503/874-8100 or 877/674-2733; www.oregongarden.org).

PARKS, BEACHES, AND RECREATION AREAS

13 Silver Falls

🐾🐾🐾 🦴 🐟 (See Willamette Valley map on page 354)

There's no doubt that dogs will enjoy a hike on any stretch of the 18 miles of trails open to pets in the 8,700 acres of Oregon's largest state park. Yet, for their humans, it's a bit of a cruel tease, because pets are not allowed on the park's most famous trek, the seven-mile Canyon Trail loop, a.k.a. the Trail of Ten Falls. It is simply too crowded and too precipitous to allow dogs. As a condolence, there is an unfenced off-leash pet exercise area in the South Falls day-use area.

Despite the restrictions, you shouldn't pass up this park. You can see South Falls, the most popular, and two other falls from viewpoints accessible by car or along the 2.7-mile Rim Trail, where dogs are allowed. If possible, bring some friends and tag team it, a couple of you hanging with the dogs while the others take to the trail. The waterworks are truly spectacular, and you can walk behind four of the falls for the full sound-and-spray experience.

From downtown Silverton, the drive out State Route 214 to the park passes through beautiful farm country, rolling hills of tree farms and grass seed fields. After the park, the road loops down to intersect with State Route 22 in Salem. Park hours vary widely with the seasons; call 503/873-8681. Parking is $3.

PLACES TO EAT

Oregon Tea Garden: You will feel so very civilized enjoying traditional high tea in cushy chairs under the leaves with your canine. Sample tea sandwiches, salads, daily soups, cream scones, and bread pudding drenched in butterscotch-orange-raisin sauce and choose from at least 50 kinds of tea to complement your meal. Isis ordered the Queen of Sheba cake, but her mother was forced to eat the French chocolate cake with espresso buttercream frosting for her. 305 Oak St.; 503/873-1230.

PLACES TO STAY

Silver Falls Campground: There are 47 electrical sites open year round for $16–20 and 46 tent sites open May–Oct. for $12–16. 800/452-5687; www.reserveamerica.com.

Lyons

PARKS, BEACHES, AND RECREATION AREAS

🐾🐾🐾 John Neal Memorial Park

🐾🐾🐾 (See Willamette Valley map on page 354)

This county park has all the ingredients for a perfect afternoon except for a bucket of chicken and some lemonade. When not eating at sheltered tables or crawling on the playground setup, most kids and pets can be found floating, swimming, and fishing on the North Santiam River. For a walk, head to the Beaver Addition, marked by two logs immediately outside the park gate. From there, a .5-mile pathway leads through the beaver dams, also home to blue herons, raccoons, and turtles sunning themselves on the logs. It emerges by site #22 in the campground. It's a peaceful place, ideal for a making a quick getaway from city grime.

Camping is available Apr. 15th–Oct. 15th, on a first-come, first-served basis. For $11 a night, you get a quiet riverside plot, potable drinking water, real flush toilets, and instant hot-water showers.

From State Route 226 in Lyons, continue straight onto Lyons-Mill City Drive, and turn north on 13th Street, which dead-ends into the park. Open dawn–dusk. 541/967-3917.

PLACES TO EAT

The Gingerbread House: Sure, it looks like a typical drive-through order window with burgers and fries, until you try the warm gingerbread with vanilla ice cream sprinkled with nutmeg. A blue "X" taped in the window is the secret code for the days when there's fresh banana bread. There are lounge chairs with side tables lined up out front. 21935 Gingerbread St.; 503/859-2247.

Albany

Despite a difficult economy, residents of this historic town are working to restore the Victorian homes and the high concentration of covered bridges surrounding the city, reminders of a vital role this central town played in the trade and commerce of the early valley. Call 541/929-6230 for your copy of *Seems Like Old Times,* the self-guided tour brochure that will take you time traveling, walking or driving through the town's historic districts, including the Monteith House Museum, said to be the most authentic restoration project in Oregon.

PARKS, BEACHES, AND RECREATION AREAS

15 Takena Landing—Eagle Trail

🐾🐾 (See Willamette Valley map on page 354)

The picnic area and restrooms of this city park are under a highway overpass, but you lose the traffic noise after about .25 mile on the Eagle Trail, named by default as the ongoing project of the local Eagle Scout troop. This 1.7-mile one-way walk parallels the Willamette River on the opposite shore from the city. The scouts are doing a good job maintaining the hard pack and trimming back the blackberry bushes just enough to give you peek-a-boo water views. As for getting into the water, where there's a will, there are pathways. Your companionable river walk should be shady, serene, and private.

The park is a mile from State Route 99E. Turn west on Lyon, which crosses the river and curves around to U.S. Highway 20, and turn left onto North Albany Road. Open 6 A.M.–10 P.M.; 541/817-7777; www.cityofalbany.net/parks.

16 Larwood Wayside

🐾🐾🐾 (See Willamette Valley map on page 354)

On a Linn County covered bridge tour, pause at this countryside gathering place to soak up the timeless fun of a dog day afternoon. The park looks much as it must have more than 60 years ago, when the Larwood Covered Bridge was wet with whitewash in 1939. Farm kids hang off the sides of the bridge, wave at passing cars, then jump into the water. Others float by on inner tubes past the ruins of the water wheel power plant on the riverbank. For sustenance, there's a U-Pick blueberry field two miles down the road.

From State Route 226 east of Albany, Larwood is 6.7 miles down Fish Hatchery Road.

PLACES TO EAT

Loafers: By day, Loafers is an over-the-counter Bread and Bistro. At the magic hour of 5 P.M., it morphs into After Dark, a surf-and-turf restaurant, heavy on the turf. Park on the street, because the lot has been taken over by steakhouse seating for 40 people and their dogs. 222 S.W. Washington St.; 541/926-8183.

PLACES TO STAY

In this area, chain hotels offer the best choices for dogs and their owners; please look under Chain Hotels in the Resources section.

Corvallis

Corvallis is the home of Oregon State University and their mascot the Beavers. It's fairly difficult to live in Oregon without being a rabid fan of the Beavers or of their rivals, the University of Oregon Ducks.

All city parks are open 6:30 A.M.–10 P.M. The Dachsie Twins applaud Corvallis for having six off-leash areas, although most of them can only be described as having rough ground cover, and they leave a bit to be desired in terms of creature comforts like shade, water, seating, and human facilities. On the other side of the coin, dogs are prohibited in Chintimini, Central, Franklin, Lilly, and Washington city parks. For heavier-duty hiking than the Wieners can manage, on primitive trails in the foothills, contact the OSU Research Forest Department regarding hiking trails in Dunn and McDonald State Forests, 541/737-4452.

One thing the dogs love about college towns is that there's a great variety of restaurants to serve a hungry student body. The highest concentration of prime outdoor eating is along 1st Street downtown, across from Riverfront Commemorative Park, and a block over on 2nd Street. For legit dog food and other goodies, visit **Animal Crackers** pet supply (949 N.W. Kings Blvd.; 541/753-4559; www.animalcrackerspetsupply.com).

PARKS, BEACHES, AND RECREATION AREAS

🐾 Chip Ross Park

🐾🐾🐾🐕 (See Willamette Valley map on page 354)

This city park is composed of 125 acres of savannah, oak, and upland prairie in the foothills north of town. A 1.5-mile loop takes you through, and your sidekick will be thrilled to discover that he's allowed off-leash on the trail. It's a bit of climbing to reach the summit, where you can connect to the Dan Trail in the McDonald Forest if, for example, your vizsla hasn't yet exhausted his supply of boundless energy. Cooper opted to rest and absorb the vistas of Coast and Cascade Mountains from summit benches before returning to a couple of picnic tables at the trailhead for a bite of bologna and cheese sandwich. You may pass horses and their riders along the hot, sunny trail. There are portable potties; bring your own drinking water.

From 3rd or 4th Streets, the main north-south thoroughfares through town, go west on Harrison Avenue to 10th Street. Follow 10th northeast through town until it turns north and becomes Highland Drive, and continue until the road starts to climb. Turn left on Lester Avenue, which dead-ends into the park. Closed Nov. 1–Apr. 15 for snow conditions.

🐾 Walnut Park

🐾🐾🐕 (See Willamette Valley map on page 354)

At first, the designated off-leash area at Walnut is as clear as mud. From the parking lot, head due south about three-quarters of the way through a field. On the right, you'll see a painted brown wooden bridge and a Public Urban Stream Corridor sign. Cross the bridge and follow the gravel path, and you'll break out into a clearing with a post marking the dog area. It is effectively secured by the surrounding woods and a stream with the added bonus of a landscaped private garden on the southern, fenced border. Once you've run the gauntlet to find it, you are rewarded with big meadows of wildflowers and field grass to play in, at least part of which have been mowed to dachshund height. There are no amenities other than a lonely shaded bench. A gravel path bisects the area, leading you back to the north end by the parking lot.

From 99W, turn west on Walnut Boulevard. The park is on the right as the road swings to the south, immediately as it becomes 53rd Street.

🐾 Woodland Meadows

🐾🐕 (See Willamette Valley map on page 354)

Rough and tumble pups only need apply at this city park. The off-leash area is essentially the back forty of the farm, behind the historic Corl House. The field grass is like hay, and it's rarely, if ever, mowed. The hilly area is not secured in any way, marked only by signposts. Things like shade, or a bench, or water have probably escaped the tight budgets of city planners. Avoid the side of the hill along Circle Avenue, a busy arterial street, and bring a wide-brimmed hat for self-made shade. The park on the west side of Circle Avenue only is off-leash, past the perimeter around the historic house.

From 99W, turn west on Circle Boulevard to the park. Turn north on Witham Hill Drive and right at the Corl House sign to the gravel parking lot.

20 Riverfront Commemorative Park

🐾🐾   (See Willamette Valley map on page 354)

The banks of the Willamette River have served as the focus for commerce in Corvallis since the 1860s. Flour mills, grain warehouses, sawmills, rail lines, and even the city jail occupied the lots along the 11 city blocks of what is now the downtown core. In order to create a place for people to gather, the city had to remove 110,000 pounds of concrete rubble, asphalt, scrap metal, car bodies, and other debris as part of the riverfront restoration project.

The results speak for themselves. Even the garbage cans double as flower planters along this beautiful city parkway. You and your mutt mate can stroll the promenade, day or night, to take in the gardens, artwork, and views of the river. Across the street are excellent restaurants, many with outdoor seating where your dog is allowed. The Aquathusiasts Boat Ramp is on the north end, and Riverfront Park connects to Pioneer Park and Avery Park on the south. Dogs must be leashed, especially enthusiastic water dogs, to keep them from jumping into the spray fountain and scaring the toddlers.

The park is along 1st Street, from Washington to Van Buren. There's a large, free parking lot and restrooms south of the intersection of 2nd Street and B Avenue, and metered parking along the walk.

21 Willamette Park

🐾🐾🐾🐾🦴   (See Willamette Valley map on page 354)

Coop 'n' Isis had encountered so many wonderful off-leash areas in the valley that they had become critical and jaded by the time they reached Corvallis—until they came here. At this big park close to downtown, the city has found a way for "civilized man" and "beast" to co-exist. It is the slightest bit complicated, so check the map at the north entrance information kiosk if you're unsure. Willamette is three parks in one. Dogs are always allowed off-leash on Willamette Park trails, east along the river and in the Kendal Nature Park, trails to the west of the sports fields. Dogs are allowed seasonally off-leash on the open Crystal Lake Sports Fields, Nov. 7–Apr. 10, when fields are not in play for intramural sports. Dogs are not allowed off-leash in the campground, south of Goodnight Avenue in the playground, or north of Fisher Lane by the boat ramps. Basically, stick to the trails until the whole park goes to the dogs in the winter. Behind the kiosk, only a short run from the parking lot, is a wide dirt ramp straight down into the wonderful Willamette River.

The off-leash areas, and more importantly the map, are easiest to reach from the north entrance to the park. From 99W, which is 4th Street downtown, turn left on Crystal Lake Drive, the opposite direction from Avery Avenue on the west. Curve around past the Evanite Glass Fiber factory and left into the park on Fisher Lane. 541/766-6198.

PLACES TO EAT

American Dream Pizza: Make your pizza dreams come true with a huge list of meat and veggie combos served by the slice at a couple of picnic tables. 214 S.W. 2nd St.; 541/753-7373. For delivery of whole pies to most of Corvallis, call the campus branch of the Dream at 541/757-1713.

Chippery: In this case, the chip referred to is of the potato variety, up to 20 crunchy exotic flavors fresh daily, including lemon-dill, ketchup, malt and salt, and banana. Every sandwich and salad comes with a quick-fix bag of potato chips in your chosen flavor. The outdoor seating is on the riverfront. 130 S.W. 1st St.; 541/75-CHIPS (541/752-4477); www.chipperyusa.com.

Fox and Firkin: What we didn't know was that a firkin is a type of wooden keg. What we do know is that a menu of pub grub, including shepherd and vegetable pot pies, tastes best when washed down with one of the 46 beers on tap or 32 single malt scotches. The Fox has more seating outside than in, along the riverfront. 202 S.W. 1st St.; 541/753-8533.

Iovino's Ristorante: It's always a treat to see a civilized, full-service restaurant offer sidewalk seating so that your dog may partake of robust antipasti, salads, thin pizzas, and pasta dishes with you. We suggest you keep the wine list to yourself. 125 S.W. 1st St.; 541/738-9015.

New Morning Bakery: This shop is so much more than a bakery. It delivers the one-two punch, first with a glass case full of beautiful salads, then with one of even more beautiful desserts. 219 S.W. 2nd St.; 541/754-0181; www.newmorningbakery.com.

Sunnyside Up: Breakfast is the dogs' favorite meal of the day, especially when it is served all day at this café. The Sunnyside concentrates on organic, wholesome food served in very large portions, which shouldn't be a problem when you have a four-legged food disposal device sitting at your feet. Outdoor seating and wireless Internet; 116 N.W. 3rd St.; 541/758-3353.

PLACES TO STAY

Hanson Country Inn: People flock to this former poultry farm for its rural setting, still within city limits. Molly and Charlie, the dogs of the city's oldest and classiest bed-and-breakfast, are often out front to greet arrivals. Smaller or particularly well-mannered pets may be allowed in the posh, restored 1928 main house. The only slightly more rustic detached cottage is suitable for more rambunctious Rovers. There are extensive fields to roam if your dog is careful not to disturb the neighbors' sheep and chickens. Rates range $95–145. 795 S.W. Hanson St.; 541/752-2919; www.hcinn.com.

More Accommodations: Please look under Chain Hotels in the Resources section for additional places to stay in this area.

Alsea

PARKS, BEACHES, AND RECREATION AREAS

22 Siuslaw National Forest—Mary's Peak

😾😾😾 🐾 (See Willamette Valley map on page 354)

Even if you don't hike any of the 12 miles of trails on this peak, you owe it to yourself and your dog to visit Observation Point at the top of the 4,097-foot mountain, the highest in the coastal range. If you want to hoof it, come in at the north end, off U.S. Highway 20, to the Woods Creek Trailhead. From there, it is a challenging 5.8-mile climb to the top on the North Ridge Trail. If you'd rather stick your heads out the window and drive 9.5 miles to the top, enter from the south, off State Route 34, to Mary's Peak Road. From the parking lot, it's a short, easy .5-mile walk to the tip-top. Once there, you'll be so inspired by the 360-degree vistas you may want to circle the peak on the Meadowledge Trail, an easy 1.6-mile loop near the summit. Come for sunsets over the ocean, and if you decide to stay overnight, there are two primitive, first-come, first-served campgrounds on the peak.

The signs are clear at the north entrance on Forest Road 2005, Woods Creek Road, and on the south from Forest Road 30, Mary's Peak Road. Mary's Peak Road is closed at milepost 5.5 Dec.–Apr.; foot traffic is welcome in the snow. Parking is $5. 541/563-3211.

23 Alsea Falls

😾😾😾 (See Willamette Valley map on page 354)

The coastal forest at the Alsea Falls Recreation Site is thick enough to grow in an arch over the road. As you hike along the South Fork of the Alsea River, .5 mile in one direction to the campground or a mile the opposite way to Green Peak Falls, you can see the remains of old growth, last logged in 1945. Life persists, reclaiming the forest in thick carpets of springy moss, giant ferns, red vine maple and new Douglas firs. The sun filters through the trees in dapple patterns, lending an air of enchantment.

The falls are a short series of segments tumbling over a wide ledge. At the end of the summer, when the water has slowed, we've seen people picnicking on the rock ledge right next to water. Picnic areas are hidden within their own private groves. On a hot day, Alsea offers cool relief in the river and a popular picnic spot. Camping at the falls is on a first-come, first-served basis, for $10 a night.

From the town of Alsea on State Route 34, turn south on State Route 201 for one mile and left on the Back Country Byway for nine miles, two of which are on a nicely graded gravel road. 503/375-5646.

Sweet Home

PARKS, BEACHES, AND RECREATION AREAS

🐾 Cascadia

🐾🐾🐾 (See Willamette Valley map on page 354)

This state park captures much of what makes the Pacific Northwest such a great outdoor destination. There's a quiet 25-tent campground in the woods behind the South Santiam River. The East Picnic Area has a wide, sunny field. The West Picnic Area is shaded under big trees. The paved Soda Springs Trail follows the springs, which divides the park east to west, and then down to the river. A 1.5-mile out-and-back trail runs along the creek to Soda Creek Falls. It's an easy magical mystery tour through a dense forest of ferns, moss, and old growth, a quintessential Northwest forest.

Cascadia is off U.S. Highway 20, 8.5 miles east of Green Peter Dam. The first-come, first-served campground, $14 per night, and East Picnic Area are open May–September. The West Picnic Area and the trails are open year-round. 541/367-6021.

Eugene–Springfield

In Eugene, and incidentally in Corvallis too, people and their dogs are running around and bicycling everywhere. Both cities have consistently been rated among the most bicycle-friendly cities in the country. There are marked bicycle paths on 95 percent of the streets within city limits, and paved multi-use paths parallel scenic routes throughout the valley, with Bicycle Guides available at visitors centers.

Eugene is also the birthplace of Nike (now headquartered in Beaverton), with a long-running tradition of long-distance runners that dates back to the 1970s, when Steve Prefontaine, or Pre as they affectionately call him, broke every record in the world for races of 2,000 meters and above. Needless to say, there's no shortage of places for your dog to get her exercise in the hometown of the University of Oregon Ducks. When it's time for a little time apart, pack Fido off to **Dogs at Play** for the day (590 Wilson St.; 541/344-3647).

In downtown Springfield, step into the alley on 5th Street between Main and A Streets to give your pet a moment to commune with the 11-foot by 16-foot mural titled *Bob the Dog Visits the Old Growth*.

PARKS, BEACHES, AND RECREATION AREAS

25 Alton Baker Dog Park

🐾🐾🐾🐾🐕 (See Willamette Valley map on page 354)

It is not easy to get to Alton Baker. Once there, you could try your dog's suggestion of never leaving, and, thus, never having to worry about trying to find your way back. This wonderful off-leash area has everything a dog park should. Its big, grassy fields are fenced with double gates for leash maneuvers. It has covered picnic tables, shady benches, and hefty trees. There's water galore in the form of drinking fountains, water pumps, and wading pools to dunk in. Garbage receptacles and bags are plentiful. Outside the gates, you can connect to miles of Ruth Bascom's Riverbank Trail, paved multi-use pathways that follow the Willamette and Steve Prefontaine's four-mile soft jogging trails. As you can imagine, its popularity sometimes makes it a crazy place. The only time it's not good to visit is prior to and after a sporting event; get a list of game dates for the stadium to avoid rowdy sports fans.

From I-5, take Exit 194B to I-105/State Route 206. Take Exit 2 to Coburg Road/Autzen Stadium. Take the right fork of the exit, then immediately get in the left lane. Here's where it gets tricky. Don't take the hard left at the light onto Coburg Road, take the soft left and then carefully follow the signs to MLK Boulevard/Autzen Stadium. Immediately west of the stadium, turn right on Leo Harris Boulevard behind the stadium to park at the Alton Baker Park Eastern Natural Area lot. Cross the wooden bridge to the dog area. Whew.

If you're already in downtown Eugene, it's much easier to get to the park. Take 5th Street downtown heading east, follow the signs for I-105/206/Coburg Road, cross the bridge, and peel off to the right at the sign for Autzen Stadium/MLK Boulevard and right on Leo Harris Boulevard.

26 Amazon Dog Park

🐾🐾🐾🐕 (See Willamette Valley map on page 354)

"Our dog has such a high ball drive, I don't know what we'd do without a dog park," said the owner of a 16-month old black Lab Cooper met at Amazon's off-leash park. Indeed, this off-leash area is perfect for a game of toss. The wide field is level and open, fenced, and gated. In between rounds, there is a water station and plastic wading pools for cooling off. Our new friend warned us that the park can get a little rough. People come to cluster around the single covered picnic table and chew the fat, and sometimes they don't pay enough attention to what their dogs are doing. If you're worried about the pack mentality getting out of hand, it wouldn't hurt to go up and introduce yourselves first and ask people to watch their charges around your new or smaller dog.

From 6th and 7th Streets, the main east-west thoroughfares downtown, turn south on Pearl Street and stay in the right lane until the road merges onto Amazon Parkway. Continue in the right lane until 29th Street, then turn left into the parking lot behind the bus terminal. It's a total of two miles from the center of downtown.

27 Morse Ranch Dog Park

🐾🐾🐾🐕 (See Willamette Valley map on page 354)

This off-leash area is the place to perfect the precision of your throw to avoid tossing your dog's favorite ball or toy into the fenced-off, protected natural areas in the middle of the park. There are two large, fenced pastures and lots of grass at Morse Ranch, with several gated entry points and natural bridges to cross in between. The ground in both sections is uneven and hilly; the west side has big trees, and the east is more open. Your Aussie can pretend he's patrolling the farm and then reward himself with a quick swim in the wading pools. There are historic buildings outside the OLA, several of which house Willamette Wildlife Rescue.

From 7th Street, eastbound downtown, turn south on Willamette Street and go 2.2 miles, then take a hard right up the hill on Crest Drive, and go another .4 mile to the parking lot at the intersection of Crest and Arden, past the fenced-off areas. The West Pasture, with some lighting, is open 6 A.M.–11 P.M.; the East Pasture 8 A.M.–8 P.M.

28 Howard Buford Recreation Area—Mt. Pisgah

🐾🐾🐾🐕 (See Willamette Valley map on page 354)

You can see the mound of Mt. Pisgah as you drive into HBRA, named for the Biblical summit from which Moses sighted the Promised Land. We say "Hallelujah!," for dogs are allowed to hike off-leash on five of this 2,363-acre county park's seven trails. Only on Trails #1 and #2 are pups required to wear an eight-foot or shorter tether. Hikes are .7 to 3.9 miles in length, and some to the 1,531-foot summit tougher than others that circle the base. Cooper can't promise your pet a religious experience, but he finds off-leash hiking to be nothing short of a revelation. Maps are available at visitors centers in town or at the bulletin board by the Arboretum entrance. Hiking on the hill can be hot and dry. Bring plenty of water and poop bags.

From I-5, take Exit 189 to the east and go a block north on the frontage road. Turn right on Franklin Road for .4 miles, and left on Seavey Loop Road for 1.8 miles. Parking is $2 May–Sept.; free in the off-season. www.co.lane.or.us/Parks/MtPisgahPage.htm.

PLACES TO EAT

Café LN: The LN stands for Lucky Noodle, a takeout restaurant that blends Asian and Italian cuisine, highlighting the slippery string in its various incarnations. Your mutt can *mangia* with you at outdoor tables, or you can get it to go home and pop *The Lady and the Tramp* in the DVD player while you slurp. 207 E. 5th Ave.; 541/484-4777.

Steelhead Brewing Co.: When the brewpub garage door is rolled up, it reveals a sidewalk sports bar, complete with TVs, homebrews on tap, and plenty of room for dogs to sit at their owners' elbows. The only thing missing is your lumpy couch. 199 E 5th Ave.; 541/686-2739; www.steelheadbrewery.com.

PLACES TO STAY

Campbell House: You really have to want to stay at this bed-and-breakfast, with a steep dog fee of $50 per pet, per night; plus tariffs (that's British for rates) of $119 per night for the Frazer Room, and $245–345 for the Celeste Cottage, the two rooms where pets are allowed. If you can swing it, you'll be a temporary resident at the most elegant address in town, a four-diamond property a few blocks from the desirable 5th Street Public Market. 252 Pearl St.; 541/343-1119 or 800/264-2519; www.campbellhouse.com.

Village Inn: Just outside of town, this motel impressed us with the high quality of its rooms, a fountain courtyard with tables and a lawn, and the fact that no pet fee is charged. Room rates range $62–82, a great price for the amenities it offers. 1875 Mohawk Blvd.; 541/747-4546 or 800/327-6871; www.villageinnspringfield.com.

More Accommodations: Please look under Chain Hotels in the Resources section for additional places to stay in this area.

Blue River and McKenzie Bridge

From Eugene, State Route 126 leads you to the McKenzie River Recreation Area, 60 miles of swimming, boating, and fishing pleasure. If you forgot anything for your road trip along the river, **Harbick's Country Store** has it, including pet provisions (91808 Mill Creek Rd.; 541/822-3575).

The **McKenzie River National Recreation Trail** runs 27 miles along the whitewater tumbling down from the Cascades. From 11 well-marked parking areas, you can access 600-year-old stands of trees, waterfalls and turquoise pools, log bridge crossings, and hardened lava flows. The first trailhead is 1.5 miles east of McKenzie Bridge. Sahalie and Koosah Falls and Tamolich Pool are two highly recommended hikes. Directions and maps are available at the ranger station, 57600 S.R. 126, 541/822-3381.

PARKS, BEACHES, AND RECREATION AREAS

🐾 Delta Old Growth Trail

🐾🐾 (See Willamette Valley map on page 354)

This half-mile stroll through old-growth forest is a synopsis of the unique features of a Pacific Northwest temperate rainforest. Soft, pine needle–carpeted trails and three wooden bridges take you past giant hemlock, fir, and cedar trees draped in moss. Your footsteps are hushed by the surrounding undergrowth of lichen and thick ferns. This trail is at the northern end of the Aufderheide Scenic Byway, a 19-mile drive through the Willamette Forest skirting the edge of the Three Sisters Wilderness. You can pick up a narrated CD or cassette of the journey at Harbick's Country Store; there's no charge if you return the borrowed disc or tape.

From State Route 126 east of Blue River, turn on Forest Road 19, and shortly thereafter, turn right into the Delta Campground. The trail is at the very end of the campground, 1.3 miles from the turnoff. Parking is $5.

PLACES TO EAT

Blue River Sweet Shoppe and Deli: This ice cream parlor added a deli by popular demand because there wasn't anything else in town. The place is nicknamed the Squeeze-In (what you have to do to eat inside), but you and your Great Dane have no worries, chilling with your cones on a deck bigger than the entire shop. They suggest you eat dessert first, then finish with comfort food, maybe chili and cheese Fritos pie, chicken and dumplings, or a French dip sandwich. 51745 Blue River Dr.; 541/822-3144.

PLACES TO STAY

McKenzie River Inn: Dogs may run free in the orchard and along 500 feet of riverfront at this bed-and-breakfast, as long as they are on leash in and around the buildings and other guests. The cabins are best for dog owners, with separate entrances and river-view decks, ranging $89–125 per night; $60–90 Oct.–April; no pet fee. 49164 McKenzie Hwy.; 541/822-6260; www.mckenzieriverinn.com.

Wayfarer Resort: Across a covered bridge and into the woods are 12 dog-friendly cabins, much too luxurious to be called cabins, on a 10-acre property surrounded by the McKenzie River and Martin Creek. Rates range from $65–90 for studios for two on up to a house that sleeps six for $260 per night; there is a three-night minimum Memorial Day–Labor Day; $10 dog fee. Ironically, the only unit dogs are not allowed in is The Dogwood unit. There's a stocked pond for the kids to fish, tennis and basketball courts, resident dogs Bella and Rags to play with, and easy river access. Quiet dogs may be left unattended if crated. 46725 Goodpasture Rd; 541/896-3613 or 800/627-3613; www.wayfarerresort.com.

Cottage Grove

This township is proud of its claim to fame as the location where Buster Keaton starred in the film *The General* in 1926. Today, it is known more as the starting point for a Covered Bridge Scenic Tour featuring five of Oregon's oldest covered bridges.

PARKS, BEACHES, AND RECREATION AREAS

30 Row River Trail

 (See Willamette Valley map on page 354)

The river got its name from a row over cows, a dispute between two pioneer men over cattle-grazing rights in the 1850s. You can take it fast or slow on the paved 15.6-mile trail, originally the line of the Oregon, Southern & Eastern railway nicknamed the "Old Slow and Easy." There are nine trailheads to reach trail segments from Cottage Grove to the mining and lumber towns of Dorena and Culp Creek. The most scenic part of the trail begins at Mosby Creek, three miles outside of town, passing the shores of Dorena Reservoir.

A trail map from the Cottage Grove visitors center shows restroom and water stops, trailheads, camping parks, and historic covered bridge sites along the trail. To reach the Mosby Creek Trailhead, take Exit 174 from I-5 and turn east at the bottom of the exit ramp onto Row River Road. Drive three miles and turn left onto Layng Road. Open dawn–dusk.

PLACES TO EAT

Café Sheilagh: This bistro serves elegant meals and a fabulous Sunday brunch at sidewalk tables in a prime downtown location. In European fashion, they serve wine, beer, and cappuccino with meals and allow your pets to be by your side as you dine. 616 Main St.; 541/942-5510.

PLACES TO STAY

Relax Inn: This small motel has decent rooms at a price that's hard to beat, $38–48 a night, with a $5 pet fee. 1030 Hwy. 99N; 541/942-5132.

More Accommodations: Please look under Chain Hotels in the Resources section for additional places to stay in this area.

WASHINGTON

see Southwest
Washington
page 182

Portland

see Greater
Portland
page 322–323

Troutdale Corbett

OREGON

Sandy

Columbia River

Cascade
Locks

Hood
River

The Dalles

Lost Lake

Parkdale

Mt Hood
(11,235ft)

Government
Camp

Zigzag

Trillium
Lake

Timothy
Lake

Pinhead Buttes
(5,585ft)

Silver Falls
State Park

Breitenbush
Springs

Olallie
Lake

WARM   SPRINGS

INDIAN

RESERVATION

Maupin

Deschutes River

Kah-Nee-Ta

Warm
Springs

CENTRAL
OREGON

North Santiam River

Detroit

see Willamette
Valley
page 354

Detroit
Lake

South Santiam R.

Green Peter
Reservoir

Foster
Reservoir

Sweet
Home

Marion
Lake

Three Fingered Jack
(7,841ft)

Blue
Lake

Hoodoo Butte
(5,721ft)

Clear
Lake

Mt Washington
(7,800ft)

Suttle Lake

Belknap Crater
(6,877ft)

McKenzie
Bridge

Vida

McKenzie River

Cougar
Reservoir

The Husband
(7,520ft)

South Sister
(10,358ft)

Mt Jefferson
(10,495ft)

Metolius River

Black Butte
(6,415ft)

Lake Billy
Chinook

Haystack
Reservoir

Culver

Madras

Sisters

Deschutes R.

North Sister
(10,085ft)

Middle Sister
(10,047ft)

Broken Top
(9,152ft)

Sparks Lake

Redmond

Bend

0   10 mi

0   10 km

Fall Creek
Reservoir

Lowell

Oakridge

Elk Lake

Cultus
Lake

Cultus
Mountain
(6,756ft)

Mt Bachelor
(9,060ft)

Lava
Lake

Little
Lava Lake

Sunriver

N
W   E
S

© AVALON TRAVEL PUBLISHING, INC.

CHAPTER 14

Central Oregon

From the high desert of the Oregon Outback in the south, to Mt. Hood and the Columbia River Gorge up north, Central Oregon is expansive and majestic, full of the kind of splendor that makes nature photographers drool like dogs. While traveling in this dry and sunny region, you'll often encounter more wildlife than people. Watch for deer on the road, elk in the mountains, and squirrels and chipmunks everywhere. Cooper has developed a deep, abiding love affair with the golden-mantled ground squirrel, small and striped like a chipmunk, numbering in the billions in Central Oregon's mountains and high plains.

The top boundary of the region is the Columbia River, fourth largest in the United States, with a water volume twice the Nile in Egypt. Before multiple dams and development, it is believed to have had the largest salmon runs in the world, between 6 and 10 million per year.

PICK OF THE LITTER—CENTRAL OREGON

BEST PARK
Mt. Hood National Forest—Lost Lake, Lost Lake
(page 392)

BEST DOG PARKS
Rooster Rock State Park, Corbett (page 386)
Big Sky Park, Bend (page 405)

BEST EVENT
Fourth of July Pet Parade, Bend (page 403)

BEST PLACES TO EAT
Pasquale's Ristorante, Hood River (page 391)
Elliot Glacier Public House, Parkdale (page 397)
Astro Lounge, Bend (page 406)

BEST PLACES TO STAY
Columbia Gorge Hotel, Hood River (page 391)
Old Parkdale Inn, Parkdale (page 397)
Cricketwood Country's Pet-Friendly Cottage, Bend
(page 407)

NATIONAL FORESTS AND RECREATION AREAS

Columbia River Gorge National Scenic Area

Columbia River residents brag that their gorge is gorgeous, and they're not suffering from delusions of grandeur. In the 292,500-acre protected area, you can walk under waterfalls, wade through wildflowers, and retrace the route of Oregon Trail settlers in two states. You can windsurf until your lips turn blue and ski until you're blue in the face, on the same day. Nearly every hike is a bun-buster. You are, after all, hiking up out of a gorge that's 80 miles long and up to 4,000 feet deep. Hood River Ranger Station; 541/386-2333; www.fs.fed.us/r6/columbia.

Deschutes National Forest

The Deschutes invites eight million people annually to come out and play in its 1.6 million acres (that's twice the size of the state of Rhode Island). Its diverse regions include the Crooked River National Grassland, Newberry

National Volcanic Monument, eight wilderness areas, wild and scenic rivers, and the Pacific Northwest's largest ski area at Mt. Bachelor. Its recreation opportunities could fill a library, much less a book. Where does a dog begin? In addition to our suggestions, try the World Wide Web at www.fs.fed.us/r6/centraloregon or call the main line at 541/383-5300.

Mt. Hood National Forest

At the summit of 11,235-foot Mt. Hood, the largest mountain in Oregon, is the grave of Ranger, a dog who was said to have climbed the volcano 500 times in his life from 1925 to 1938 with his owners and friends. At only 20 miles from Portland, this national forest is an easy recreation area for you to reach, following in Ranger's footsteps to create your own feats of athleticism on more than 1,200 miles of trails. Powder hounds can schuss and skijor on Mt. Hood's five ski areas. Sandy Ranger Station; 503/668-1700; www.fs.fed.us/r6/–mthood; or Mt. Hood Chamber of Commerce; 503/622-3017; www.mthood.org.

Troutdale

This period town welcomed travelers in their new-fangled Model Ts when the Columbia River Highway opened in 1915. Travelers rested up in auto courts, predecessors to today's motels, before their adventures on the King of Roads. Merchants in Troutdale sold tires, fuel, and parts, now replaced by antiques, gifts, and clothing boutiques. Check out the dog on the "Hitchin' a Ride" bronze sculpture at the corner of Dora Avenue on Main Street.

Dogs are prohibited at Glenn Otto, Oxbow Regional, Blue Lake Regional, and Dabney State parks.

PARKS, BEACHES, AND RECREATION AREAS

◘ Lewis and Clark State Recreation Site

🐾🐾🐾 🐕 (See Central Oregon map on page 382)

About a third of the grounds at this State Recreation Site is designated as a pet exercise area. While there are no fences to separate the space, signs clearly mark where your dog may be off-leash. It's hemmed in on three sides by bushes, an inviting place to spend a leisurely afternoon on the grass under the shade trees by Sandy River. There are restrooms, picnic tables, and interpretive signs for the Lewis and Clark Trail.

Across the street from the park is the easiest access to the Sandy River. You'll see cars parked in the dirt and in the roadside pullout before the Troutdale bridge. Portlanders bring their dogs here to walk along the river and go for a swim off-leash.

From I-84, take Exit 18 and turn left at the bottom of the cloverleaf exit ramp. You'll see the recreation area to your left around the bend under the railroad trestle. Closes at 9 P.M.

PLACES TO EAT

Celebrate Me Home: Several of Troutdale's downtown shops do double-duty as cafés; this home décor boutique with sidewalk seating also fixes up excellent daily pasta and green salads, stuffed brioche, lasagna, and chicken and veggie wraps. 319 E. Historic Columbia River Hwy.; 503/618-9394.

Columbia River Cellars: As one of the nicer places in town with outdoor seating, this bistro has wines by the glass, a small selection of sandwiches and sides, and a kids' menu. 125 E. Historic Columbia River Hwy.; 503/674-4921.

PLACES TO STAY

In this area, chain hotels offer the best choices for dogs and their owners; please look under Chain Hotels in the Resources section.

Corbett

For the best gorge views, the curviest section of the Historic Columbia Gorge Highway, and the highest concentration of waterfalls in the United States, take Exit 22 from I-84 and follow the signs to Corbett. Your first stop should be the Portland Women's Forum, and then you'll rise to Crown Point and the Vista House.

PARKS, BEACHES, AND RECREATION AREAS

2 Rooster Rock State Park

😾😾😾🐕 (See Central Oregon map on page 382)

Dogs are allowed off-leash in this state park, as are people without clothes, as Rooster Rock is one of Oregon's two public clothing-optional beaches. There are some restrictions: Dogs are not allowed on the nude beaches to the far east of the park, and nude sunbathers are not allowed in the dog area to the far west of the park. The dogs definitely got the better end of the deal.

The off-leash area is a lengthy, hefty field, partially shaded by old-growth trees, yet open enough to break into a run after a ball. The only oddity is that the state is waiting for funds to replace the decayed wooden tops and benches of the picnic tables, leaving the concrete bases as mini-monoliths for your dog to sniff and lift a leg on.

From I-84, Exit 25 is an exclusive road into the park. Parking is $3. Park closes at 10 P.M.

3 Larch Mountain

😾😾🦴 (See Central Oregon map on page 382)

On a clear day at the Sherrard Viewpoint picnic area, at an elevation of 4,055 feet, you can see Mt. Rainier, Mount St. Helens, Mt. Adams, Mt. Hood, Mt. Jefferson, and the Columbia River Gorge. It's as if you're in an airplane with

NATURE HIKES AND URBAN WALKS

On the Historic Columbia River Highway, between Exit 22 and Exit 35 from I-84, you can drive or walk to 10 **Columbia Gorge Waterfalls.** Your dog will feel the rush if you stop at picnic areas and hiking trails along the way. Half of them require fancy footwork to see; the rest are visible from highway stops.

Upper and Lower Latourell: It's a short walk from the parking lot viewpoint to the base of 249-foot Lower Latourell Falls. A 2.3-mile circuit takes you to 100-foot Upper Latourell, where you can walk behind the falling water and through the peaceful picnic area of Guy W. Talbot Park. On Highway 30, 3.4 miles west of Exit 28 from I-84.

Shepperds Dell: Two tiers of falls can be viewed from the bridge crossing. The upper tier is a straight plunge of 35 feet, the lower is a horsetail formation, falling 60 feet. From I-84, take Exit 28, 2.0 miles west on Highway 30.

Bridal Veil: There's a mile hike down steep switchbacks and stairs to the base of Bridal Veil, which plunges twice rapidly—first 100 feet, then another 60 feet. The basalt formation Pillar of Hercules can be seen from a separate wheelchair-accessible path around the cliff above Bridal Veil. The falls is in a state park that includes a picnic area and restrooms. Near milepost 28 on Highway 30, accessed from I-84 at Exit 28.

Wahkeena: These 242-foot fantail falls are described by the Yakima tribe's word meaning "most beautiful." They can be seen from a picnic area, or you can walk .2 mile to a bridge viewpoint, close enough to feel the spray. Picnic gates close at 8 P.M. Wahkeena is .5 mile west of Multnomah Falls on Highway 30.

Multnomah: The highest and most famous of the falls, Multnomah cascades 620 feet in two sections from the top of Larch Mountain to the Columbia River. Two million people crowd the .2-mile trail to the bridge viewpoint each year. A few hardy souls climb the 1.2 miles from the visitors center to the top of the falls, and those of you with buns of steel may want to tackle the six-mile trail to the top of Larch Mountain or trek the equally long loop to Wahkeena Falls and back. Multnomah has a lodge, restaurant, gift shop, and snack bar. Exit 31 from I-84; 503/695-2372.

Horsetail and Ponytail: This 176-foot swisher can be seen from a turnout on Highway 30, 2.5 miles east of Multnomah Falls. Viewing the smaller Ponytail Falls requires a short, steep hike.

Oneonta and Triple Falls: Starting at Horsetail Falls Trailhead (#438), it's a mile uphill to Oneonta Falls, with the added treat of a footbridge over Oneonta Gorge on the way. From there, it's another 1.7-mile climb on Trail #424 through wild canyon scenery to the log bridge viewpoint of Triple Falls, parallel chutes ranging from 100 to 135 feet. Round trip is 5.4 miles.

a much bigger window. From the parking area, it's only a .25-mile climb to the picnic spot.

For a true test of endurance, you can hike 6.6 miles straight up Larch Mountain from Multnomah Falls to this glorious spot. Bring plenty of water and protein bars.

From I-84, Take Exit 22 and follow the signs to Highway 30. Go east from Corbett to Larch Mountain Road, turn right and follow the main road 14 miles to the viewpoint sign.

Cascade Locks

If you get as excited by technical marvels as you do by wonders of nature, let the dogs take a backseat and drive through the grounds of the Bonneville Locks and Dam and watch the fish play chutes and ladders.

Native American oral history tells of a natural bridge across the Columbia created by a landslide, but evidence of the crossing was lost by the time Lewis and Clark arrived, and the explorers had to portage over a difficult section of rapids. The new Bridge of the Gods is a steel toll bridge, costing $1 to drive over to Stevenson, Washington.

PARKS, BEACHES, AND RECREATION AREAS

4 Marine Park

🐾 🐾 (See Central Oregon map on page 382)

This scenic city park is the site of frequent weddings and also the port for Sternwheeler paddleboat cruises along the gorge. There's a rose garden, pristine lawns, and seawall walk along a fishing canal. The coolest part of this park is the trek over to Thunder Island, a man-made berm once part of an elaborate and expensive boat locks system that was never fully successful. A historical museum and interpretive signs tell the saga of humans' attempts to control the forces of nature, from the Lewis and Clark expedition to the crossing of Oregon Trail pioneers and the debacle of building and tearing down the locks.

From Wa Na Pa Street in Cascade Locks, turn north on N.W. Portage Road, down the hill and under a tunnel with a 12-foot clearance to enter the park. Open a half hour before sunrise to 10 P.M.

PLACES TO STAY

In this area, chain hotels offer the best choices for dogs and their owners; please look under Chain Hotels in the Resources section.

Hood River

Vibrant and outdoorsy, this city is a magnet for young and energetic sail-boarders and kiteboarders pumped to ride the crests of the Columbia River. To hang out and watch the boarders, ask for directions to The Hook or The Spit. Between town and the mountains is an agricultural valley you can tour with a Fruit Loop brochure from the visitors center (405 Portway Ave.; 541/386-2000; www.hoodriver.org). While most places prefer you leave pets in the car, your dogs can mingle with the dogs at Draper's Farms (6200 Hwy. 35; 541/352-6625; www.drapersfarm.com) and relax in the picnic area at Hood River Winery while you enjoy free wine-tasting (4693 Westwood Dr.; 541/386-3772).

The **Gorge Dog** is a great store in town for accessories for your best friend. They can also recommend great hiking in the area. Check their website for pet-friendly services in the area (410 Oak Ave.; 541/387-3996; www.gorgedog.com).

PARKS, BEACHES, AND RECREATION AREAS

5 Tucker Park

🐾🐾🐾 (See Central Oregon map on page 382)

Tucker is tucked into a bend in Hood River, offering camping with showers and flush toilets, which is pretty swank for a county park. When views of the river simply won't suffice, there's a quickie river trail across the picnic meadow from the parking lot. Water dogs will find several swimming holes while picking their way along the sandy and rocky trail. Tent sites are $13 a night.

From Oak Street, turn south on 13th Street, which will merge into Tucker Road. The park is 5.5 miles from the Oak Street turnoff.

6 Port Marina Park—Port of Hood River

🐾🐾 (See Central Oregon map on page 382)

The port's a busy place, with boat builders, surfboard rentals, docks, and the Hood River County Historical Museum. All the activity makes for good people-watching...novice sailboarders trying to take off from a nearby sand spit, toddlers with water wings splashing in the shallow cove, a Chihuahua swimming on leash as her owner wades alongside. The picnic tables are in front of the surfboard shop, and a huge lawn by the museum is popular with the Frisbee crowd.

From I-84, take Exit 64 and turn north toward the river. Before you cross the Hood River Bridge, turn left into the marina and follow the signs to the left. Closes at 10 P.M.

◪ Wilson Park

 (See Central Oregon map on page 382)

"There are always dogs at Wilson," said Jessie at the visitors center. There's a little bit of shade and a little bit of sun on an Irish-green lawn, with primary-colored playground equipment and just enough room to throw a ball around. The park is out of the way on a quiet residential street with a fence along one side.

From Oak Street, turn south on 13th Street and left on May Street to 2nd Street.

◨ Mark O. Hatfield–Mosier Twin Tunnels Trail

🐾🐾🐾 (See Central Oregon map on page 382)

Before this old section of the Historic Columbia River Highway was restored and paved, trail users were 80 percent dogs off-leash and 20 percent mountain bikes. Now, it's 80 percent bicycles and 20 percent dogs *on* leash. Either way, you get 100 percent of the best views in the gorge. Dog activists in town are trying to secure a couple of off-leash hours per day; so far, no luck. We say, if you can't beat 'em, join 'em. Rent a bike at Mt. View Cycles in Hood River (205 Oak St.; 541/386-2453) and pedal the 10-mile roundtrip with your dog jogging alongside. You'll pass through two radically different climate zones from lush forest to arid desert, two rock tunnels with windows on the gorge, and an engineering marvel designed to keep rocks from falling and crushing trail users.

The two trailheads are named for Senator Mark O. Hatfield, who was active in promoting highway restoration and park projects. From I-84, take Exit 69 and turn left on Rock Creek Road to the East Trailhead. In Hood River, take Exit 64 and turn right at the Historic Columbia River Highway State Trail sign for the West Trailhead. Plentiful parking is $3 per day, and there are restrooms and water at both ends. This trail is excellent for wheelchair users.

PLACES TO EAT

Hood River City Market: Passionate foodies will be in heaven in this gourmet store and deli. Salads have dreamy combinations such as spinach and pears, pralines and chicken, and Asian noodle and oriental cabbage. Sandwiches are dressed in the likes of curried chicken or cranberry and hazelnut cream cheese with turkey. Wraps, cookies, and pastries are available, plus daily specials and shelves of delicacies for you to pack your own picnic. Pass the Grey Poupon. 406 Oak St.; 541/386-9876.

Mike's Ice Cream: Mike's Adirondack chairs, picnic tables, and glass-topped café tables rest on a corner lawn that is probably the busiest patch of turf in town. You and your malamute have it made in the shade, slurping down ice cream, shakes, malts, and floats. 504 Oak St.; 541/386-6260.

Pasquale's Ristorante: Pasquale's large patio tables are cool and covered, the ideal spot to people-watch as you dine for lunch or dinner at the fanciest restaurant in the gorge. The chef's menu of free-spirited creations changes periodically, leaning toward the Mediterranean, the Moroccan, and the exotic. Isis recommends the pomegranate-glazed salmon or lamb with Turkish spices and citrus tahini. It's all so very civilized, especially in light of the fact they allow your dogs to join you on the patio and partake of your leftovers. 102 Oak St.; 541/386-1900.

PLACES TO STAY

Columbia Gorge Hotel: This 1921 grande dame is the Hope Diamond of hotels, voted the most romantic in Oregon year after year, and the site of more than 100 weddings annually. According to the personalized postcard every dog receives upon check-in, Tux the black Lab is the owner of the 40-room boutique mansion, and everyone else works for him. For $25 per stay, dogs receive treats stored in a Waterford crystal jar, blankets, and a dog dish to keep. An original Otis Elevator, with an operator, whisks you to your elaborate, antique-filled room with a Mt. Hood or Columbia River view. The price of your room, ranging $199–279, includes a five-course farm-style breakfast and afternoon champagne and caviar. The grounds are a park in themselves with 208-foot Wah Gwin Gwin Falls and lavish formal gardens. Go on, your dog deserves it! 4000 Westcliff Dr.; 541/386-5566 or 800/345-1921; www.columbiagorgehotel.com.

Hood River Hotel: The best rooms in this historic hotel are reserved for dogs—three ground-floor suites that have been graciously restored into vintage masterpieces with antique reproductions, wood floors, and four-poster beds. Suite rates are $89–169; the pet fee is $15. 102 Oak St.; 541/386-1900 or 800/386-1859; www.hoodriverhotel.com.

Hood River Vacation Rentals: The great thing about renting a house is that you can find one with a fenced yard if you'd like to sneak away for a movie or to shop without your terrier in tow. This property listing service has eight dog-friendly homes from two to four bedrooms, in a variety of price ranges, available nightly or weekly. Dog fees are $8 per night or $50 per week. 541/387-3113 or 877/260-2519; www.hrvacations.com.

Meredith Gorge Motel: This highly stylized motel is a blast from the past, with reproduction '50s furniture and décor. It's fun, and the views of the gorge are just as beautiful as hotels four times the price. Rates range $49–74, $69–84 for the mini-suite; dogs are a flat fee of $10 per night. 4300 Westcliff Dr.; 541/386-1515; www.lodging.gorge.net/meredith.

Pheasant Valley Bed and Breakfast: Dogs who can be sociable with resident dogs, cats, and namesake pheasants can stay with you in The Cottage, a stylish two-bedroom apartment in the pear orchard of this winery, farm, and inn. The private deck can be securely fenced to give your dog a comfy place to hang out. Nightly rate is $135, and there's no pet fee as long as they don't have to clean up after your dog. 3890 Acree Dr.; 541/386-2803 or 877/386-2337; www.pheasantvalleywinery.com.

More Accommodations: Please look under Chain Hotels in the Resources section for additional places to stay in this area.

Lost Lake

PARKS, BEACHES, AND RECREATION AREAS

🐾 Mt. Hood National Forest—Lost Lake

🐾🐾🐾🐾 (See Central Oregon map on page 382)

This destination deep in the woods is full of perks for humans and canines, from spectacular views of the lake and Mt. Hood to pockets of old-growth cedars and firs and plenty of places to take a swim. The hike around the alpine lake is an easy 3.2 miles on soft dirt track and alternating boardwalks, starting from the viewpoint parking lot. There's a general store, paddleboat rentals, cabins, and camping at the lake as well. It's peaceful; motorboats are strictly prohibited and cell phones stop working about a quarter mile before the park. The picnic area closes at 9 P.M. Maps are available at the general store for a half dozen additional hikes in the area.

From Oak Street in Hood River, turn south on 13th Street, which merges onto Tucker Road. Follow Tucker as it becomes State Route 281 into Dee. From there, the only way to avoid getting lost on your way to Lost Lake is to carefully follow the signs as Lost Lake Road twists and turns 28 miles to your destination. Parking is $6 per day; the Northwest Forest Pass does not apply. Closed Oct.–May.

PLACES TO STAY

Lost Lake Resort: Lost Lake has private tent sites available for $15 per night, $20 if you want a lake view on F loop. All campsites are on a first-come, first-served basis. Showers are coin-operated. If you'd rather stay warm and dry, dogs are allowed in the seven cabins, $50–100 per night; no dog fee. They are various sizes, sleeping 2–10 people, and guests must provide their own cooking utensils and bedding. There's a two-night minimum on weekends and holidays. 541/386-6366; www.lostlakeresort.org.

The Dalles

We're pretty sure this is the only city in the United States that officially has the word "the" as part of its name. The French translation of the town's unusual moniker means "river rapids flowing swiftly through a narrow channel over flat, basaltic rocks." The rapids have disappeared, drowned in the rising waters of The Dalles Dam, locks, and irrigations systems. The dam visitors center is open 10 A.M.–5 P.M. Wed.–Sun., Apr.–Oct. 541/296-1181.

Cars can pick up another segment of the Historic Columbia River Highway from The Dalles to the east in Mosier. It's another stunner, with a terrific viewpoint at the Rowena Crest Overlook. From this apex, you'll descend again in loops that Agent 007 would love to take on in his Aston Martin.

PARKS, BEACHES, AND RECREATION AREAS

🔟 Sorosis Park

🐾🐾🐾🐾 (See Central Oregon map on page 382)

Never mind that it sounds like that disease of the liver—drinking in the intoxicating sights and smells in this city park can only be good for you. The buzz starts right in front of the park, at the Kelly Viewpoint, with a panoramic vista that includes the Columbia River and Gorge and the city of The Dalles below. It continues at the park entrance with a fragrant and beautiful rose garden, in the center of which is a towering water fountain, given to the city in 1911 by Maximillian Vogt. Kids will get giddy just looking at the Treetop Play Park, one of those gigantic playground castles that'll keep them occupied for days. Finally, it's the soft grass and the trees—immensely tall and fat pines thickly grouped together—that make dogs dizzy with delight. We're not sure how they managed it, but it looks like the city cleared 15 acres of forest floor and laid a carpet of sod, without touching a single tree.

From the city center on 3rd Street westbound or 2nd Street eastbound, turn south on Union Street, right on 9th Street, and left on Trevitt. Continue on Trevitt past 17th Street, where it becomes W. Scenic Drive, winding up several

NATURE HIKES AND URBAN WALKS

At the start of the **Lewis and Clark Riverfront Trail** in The Dalles, there are authentic covered wagons to fuel your imagination as you travel what was a treacherous final section of the Oregon Trail for thousands of pioneers. Your journey along the Columbia River should be a much easier one, up to five miles one-way on a smooth asphalt path, and you won't have to lug provisions other than plenty of drinking water. The starting point is the Columbia Gorge Discovery Center, and the trail ends at the Boat Basin downtown, near Riverfront Park. It's also a great way to observe the present, watching the commercial freighters and tugs navigate the river.

From I-84, take Exit 82 and go west on U.S. Highway 30 to Discovery Drive. 541/296-8600.

spirals into the foothills before you'll see the park on your right and the viewpoint on your left. Open 6 A.M.–dusk.

Celilo Park

🐾 (See Central Oregon map on page 382)

It seems like an unremarkable park, a seven-acre plot with the usual complement of restrooms, picnic tables, scarce trees, and a boat ramp down to a rocky beach. An interpretive marker is the only indication of the tremendous significance and turbulent history of Celilo Falls. Archeological digs have established this site as the most productive fishing grounds for Northwest tribes for at least 10,000 years. A vertical drop of 20 feet between sheer bluffs forced the river into seething rapids, which teemed with literally millions of salmon that were caught, pounded, and dried into year-round food supplies and highly prized trade goods. The Treaty Fish Access Site, where Native Americans were granted permanent rights to the fishing grounds in 1855, remains next to the public park. However, when the Dalles Dam was completed in 1957, the flood basin waters rose to submerge the falls, eliminating the precise conditions that fostered the fish runs.

From I-84, take Exit 97 and follow the park signs west onto State Route 206.

PLACES TO EAT

Four C's Catering and Café: Cooper is betting the Cs are croissants, corn chowder, crab cakes, and Cobb salad. In any case, this café creates daily soups, specialty salads, heroic sandwiches, and indulgent desserts to eat at sidewalk tables or under an awning in the shade. Lunch only; 11 A.M.–2 P.M. 414 Washington; 541/298-1714.

Holstein's Coffee and Café: Who knew three pages of specialty drinks could come from a bean and an udder? If the Holy Cow, with three shots of espresso with ground chocolate and steamed milk, doesn't take you to a higher plane, nothing will. For lunch, try one of 10 paninis, and as many salads, soups, and pastries. While chewing your cud, check your email on wireless Internet. Moo if you like outdoor seating! 303 E. 3rd St.; 541/298-2233.

PLACES TO STAY

Cousins Country Inn: On the outside, this motel invokes the relaxed comfort of a country home with a big red barn replica housing the lobby and restaurant. Inside, it's fairly standard. They have no official restrictions, but said, "Please don't bring herds." Rates are $62–102; pet fee is $10. 2114 W. 6th St.; 541/298-5161 or 800/848-9378; www.cousinscountryinn.com.

More Accommodations: Please look under Chain Hotels in the Resources section for additional places to stay in this area.

Mt. Hood

In the Mt. Hood Territory, you can start a hike to Mexico on the Pacific Northwest Trail or watch the birds migrate there on the Pacific Flyway. You can water ski in the morning on the Columbia River and snowboard in the afternoon on the largest night ski area in the nation. Dogs are not allowed to stay at the historic Timberline Lodge, but if you *had* to leave your loved ones at home and need a fix, stop by and pet the lodge's Saint Bernards Bruno and Heidi. Or, take a romantic dogsled tour around the winter wonderland of Frog Lake (Mt. Hood Sled Dog Tours; 503/622-5879; www.mthoodsleddogtours.com). Each village has its own name—ZigZag, Rhododendron, Welches, Government Camp, Brightwood—but ask even Portland natives where Welches is, and they'll scratch their heads. It's all Mt. Hood to them.

PARKS, BEACHES, AND RECREATION AREAS

12 Wildwood Recreation Site

🐾🐾🐾 (See Central Oregon map on page 382)

There is something for every ability and interest at this family-oriented interpretive nature site. The biggest draw for the kids is the underwater fish-viewing window on the .75-mile Cascade Streamwatch Trail. Adults may enjoy the Wetland Boardwalk Trail more, suspended over the ponds and marshes. Both trails are wheelchair-accessible, and picnicking spots are nearby. If you and your dog are looking for a better workout, the Boulder Ridge trail climbs 4.5 miles one-way up steep and narrow switchbacks into the Mt. Hood wilderness. Open 8 A.M.–sunset May–September. Parking is $3. 503/622-3696; www.or.blm.gov/salem.

13 Trillium Lake

🐾🐾🐾 (See Central Oregon map on page 382)

Mt. Hood towers in all its glory above the crystal-clear lake, easily one of the best views of the mountain in the region. Only two miles off State Route 35, this mountain gem has an easy mile loop around the lake, alternating between hard pack, pavement, and boardwalks. There are dog-paddling opportunities galore. Drive past the Day Use/Boat Ramp sign to another parking lot by the dam to reach the lake loop trailhead.

The lake entrance is .25 mile west of the junction of State Route 35 and U.S. Highway 26. Parking is $3. Winter use of the Trillium Sno-Park for snowmobiling and cross-country skiing requires a separate permit Nov. 15–Apr. 30.

PLACES TO EAT

The Soup Spoon: Gourmet soups and daily specials are served in a pretty garden setting behind the Heart of the Mountain gift shop. Shop and slurp and go home happy. Well-behaved dogs are welcome. 67898 E. Hwy. 26; 503/622-0303.

PLACES TO STAY

Old Welches Inn: A hundred years old, the town's original hotel is a sparkling bed-and-breakfast that allows pets in Lutie's Cottage, if they are on a flea program and have had a recent bath. They'll charge extra only if your dog causes a problem, but you must call ahead and discuss your dog's demeanor with the innkeepers. 26401 E. Welches Rd.; 503/622-3754; www.mthood-lodging.com.

Resort at the Mountain: The Scottish were the first to play golf, so it's appropriate that this resort on the grounds of the first golf resort in Oregon (a nine-hole hayfield in 1928) has a Scottish theme. Thankfully, the tartan isn't overdone, nor is the snob factor. The older Croft Rooms allow two pets for a $25 fee per stay; rates are $89–99. In 2004, the resort opened a few fancier rooms to pets, ranging in price $99–185. 68010 E. Fairway Ave.; 503/622-3101 or 800/669-7666; www.theresort.com.

More Accommodations: Please look under Chain Hotels in the Resources section for additional places to stay in this area.

Parkdale

PARKS, BEACHES, AND RECREATION AREAS

🐾 Mt. Hood National Forest—Tamanawas Falls Loop

🐾🐾🐾🐾 (See Central Oregon map on page 382)

Dog owners at both the Gorge Dog boutique and the visitors center recommended this moderate trail through a cool forest glade along Cold Spring Creek to the falls viewpoint. It's four miles round-trip, with only a few huff-and-puff sections. First, you cross a springy suspension bridge over the East Fork of the Hood River, then turn right after the bridge. Stay to the left at the remainder of the trail junctions to stay on the Tamanawas Trail #650A. The hike is typically doable April–November. It's a beautiful hike, one that's easy to get to, and it provides several places where your dog can go for a quick swim in the creek.

From I-84, take Exit 64 and go south on State Route 35 for 25.3 miles to a gravel parking area on the right side of the road. The trailhead entrance is .2 mile north of the Sherwood Campground.

PLACES TO EAT

Elliot Glacier Public House: It's dog central on the lawn out back by the patio seating of this brewpub, where your pal can hang with the local ruff-raff. The food tastes great and it's cheap; Monday night is $1 taco night! Don't miss the porter brownies. 4945 Baseline Rd.; 541/352-1022.

PLACES TO STAY

Old Parkdale Inn: Mary puts out a whole spread for dogs, including bowls, bags, blankies, treats, and a letter of behavioral expectations. The gorgeous Monet Suite has a kitchen, and breakfast can be served in your room, so you don't have to worry about leaving your pal unattended. Dogs are allowed free on the acre property, but please stay out of the pond and away from the resident cats. The room is $125 per night; no dog fee. 4932 Baseline Rd.; 541/352-5551 or 877/687-4669; www.hoodriverlodging.com.

Maupin

The main draw in Maupin is the Deschutes River Recreation Area for life-vest-wearing, rubber-raft-carrying crowds intent on fording the river's low-level rapids and fishing its swells. None of the local companies allow Rover to raft with you. (Try Ferron's Fun Trips on the Rogue in the Southern Oregon chapter.) For rafting, fishing, horseback riding, camping, and hiking along the banks of the Deschutes, check out the Bureau of Land Management's information center at 7 N. Hwy. 97; 541/395-2778.

PARKS, BEACHES, AND RECREATION AREAS

15 White River Falls

🐾🐾 (See Central Oregon map on page 382)

The river lives up to its name in the hottest months as melting glacial water deposits silt and sand into the water. This turbulent waterfall is the site of a former hydroelectric plant, built in 1901 to power the gristmill of the Wasco Warehouse Milling Company, grinding the grain of local farmers into flour. In the picnic area above the falls, each tree guards its own picnic table, providing precious shade. Your dog's reward for waiting patiently while you look at the falls lies across a wooden bridge and down a rough, short trail to a swimming hole below, near the stone remains of the mill. As they obviously note, rattlesnakes in the area don't make good playmates for your dog, so leashes are vital.

From U.S. Highway 197 in Maupin, travel 10 miles north and turn east on White River Road for 3.8 miles to the State Park.

PLACES TO EAT

Imperial River Company: This business is a triple-treat of white-water rafting rental company, excellent restaurant, and great lodge. Dogs are not allowed in the picnic area of Maupin City Park, so walk on over to the picnic tables on the lawn or backyard patio tables, where you and your dog will be warmly welcomed and well fed with steaks, burritos, chicken, pastas, and other big-appetite pleasers. 304 Bakeoven Rd.; 541/395-2404; www.deschutesriver.com.

PLACES TO STAY

Imperial River Company: Dogs are allowed in the five ground-floor rooms of this all nonsmoking lodge. The Bunkhouse for $110 per night, and the Imperial Suite with kitchen, TV, fireplace, and private deck for $150, are modern with a western flair, as big as the open prairie. Your pet can play with lodge dog Key, who believes people were put on the earth for the sole purpose of throwing a disc for him. The pet fee is $10. 304 Bakeoven Rd.; 541/395-2404; www.deschutesriver.com.

Madras–Culver

A drive along U.S. Highway 197 through the golden wheat fields of this arid desert region is a cure for feeling overcrowded. It looks like the plains extend to the Cascades without interruption, and until you're right on the brink of it, you can't see the immense Crooked River Canyon extending from Madras to Culver. For better canyon views, less traffic, and quicker park access, drive the **Cove Palisades Tour Route.** Maps are available in Madras (366 5th St.; 503/475-2350).

PARKS, BEACHES, AND RECREATION AREAS

16 Round Butte Overlook

😺😺 (See Central Oregon map on page 382)

Thanks to the Portland General Electric Company, park visitors can look into the workings of the dam and the hydroelectric power it produces and learn much about the history of the Warm Springs Indians, including Billy Chinook and Chief Simtustus. Next to the free educational center, there's probably more exquisite shade on the spruced-up grass than in the rest of the valley combined.

From Madras, turn west on Belmont Lane, and south on Mt. View Drive, following the signs to the park. Open 10 A.M.–8 P.M. Thurs.–Mon.

🖈 Cove Palisades

🐾🐾🐾 🐕 (See Central Oregon map on page 382)

It took a darn big dam to create this watery playground in the Crooked River Canyon. The majority of people come to this state park for the water sports on Lake Billy Chinook, named for the Tribesman and scout to Captain John C. Fremont on his explorations of the Oregon Country in 1843. Water sport rentals of all kinds are available at the marina.

This is a big, 5,200-acre park with two campgrounds and its own pet exercise area. The off-leash area is a fenced and gated acre of rarely mowed field, simple and desirable for a leisurely stroll and sniff. There's no immediate parking; park at the Upper or Lower Deschutes day-use areas and walk a short ways on a trail to the dog area.

After you drive your way down into the canyon, you can hike your way back out on the Tam-a-Lau Trail. It's a difficult, steep, hot hike topped off with seven stunning mountain peaks, one for each mile of the seven-mile loop. There are thousands of harmless whiptail lizards living in the area—an added bonus and distraction for dogs.

From U.S. Highway 97, turn west onto State Route 361, the Culver Highway, and follow signs six miles to the park. Parking is $3. 7300 Jordan Rd.; 541/546-3412.

PLACES TO EAT

Beetle Bailey Burgers: The restaurant selection isn't huge in Culver. This burger shed on the way to Cove Palisades is about it, which is probably why the half dozen picnic tables out front are always packed. 403 W. 1st, Culver; 541/546-8749.

PLACES TO STAY

Cove Palisades Campground: Cooper highly recommends sites #B18–#B22 in the Deschutes River Campground, five miles into the park. They are pleasantly shady, and, most importantly, they line up against the fence off the off-leash area. There are a total of 92 tent sites and 82 hookups in Crooked River and the Deschutes Campgrounds, both in the park. $13–21; 800/452-5687; www.reserveamerica.com.

Hoffy's Motel: Hoffy's rooms are decent, comfortable, and inexpensive at $38–48, plus $5 per pet, per stay. 600 N. Hwy. 26; 541/475-4633.

Sisters

The Three Sisters—Faith, Hope, and Charity—are mountains, tremendous and snow-capped year-round. In the valley below, the town has cultivated the western frontier look, where you might expect the sheriff to stroll around with his six-shooters and shiny star. It is the gateway to the Metolius River Recreation Area and the Three Sisters Wilderness.

Grizzly, the handsome standard poodle who is the visitors center mascot, is anything but bearish. He met us at the door with a toy in his mouth and begged relentlessly to be petted. He's a local dog dignitary, appearing regularly in town parades. He recommends the Best Western Ponderosa Lodge, where humans go out of their way to cater to visiting dogs.

PARKS, BEACHES, AND RECREATION AREAS

Village Green

🐾 (See Central Oregon map on page 382)

In the village of Sisters, population 1,080, this block of picnicking green is a welcome respite from the heat. It's got restrooms, picnic tables…and a good sprinkler system, as Coop 'n' Isis unexpectedly found out early one morning.

The park is on Elm Street, two blocks south of State Route 20/126, which is Cascade Avenue through town.

PLACES TO EAT

Depot Deli: We'd call this more of a diner than a deli, a beloved, been-around-forever diner with a big selection of favorites for breakfast, lunch, and dinner. 250 W. Cascade St.; 541/549-2572.

Martolli's: Order hot subs, calzones, and authentic, hand-tossed pizza by the slice, or create your own pie to wolf down at the restaurant's outdoor tables, for takeout, or to take and bake yourself. 220 W. Cascade St.; 541/549-8356.

PLACES TO STAY

Aspen Meadows Lodge: The lodge is a hybrid between a motel and a bed-and-breakfast. Each Native American–themed room has a private entry and bath, and a full country breakfast is served. Dogs are welcome in all five rooms, for no extra fee. The nine-acre property is a menagerie for birders, in a stand of quaking aspen trees along Squaw Creek. Dogs, no chasing the deer, please. Winter rates range $59–89, summer $89–119. 68733 Junipine Ln.; 541/549-4312 or 866/549-4312; www.sisterslodging.com.

Conklin's Guest House Bed and Breakfast: Small dogs under 25 pounds are allowed in the Forget-Me-Not room at this elegant turn-of-the-20th-century home that's right out of the pages of *Country Living* magazine. The house is set against a backdrop of two acres of gardens, a gazebo on a pond, and the Sisters Mountains. The rate is $130, plus a $10 pet fee. 69013 Camp Polk Rd.; 541/549-0123 or 800/549-4262; www.conklinsguesthouse.com.

Swallow Ridge Bed and Breakfast: On the ridge, your Eagle's Nest is a 500-square-foot upstairs studio apartment with inspiring 360-degree views, private access, and a fully stocked fridge and kitchen to make your own breakfast at your leisure. It's casual, with no fussy details, at the unfussy price of $50 per night for two adults for two or more nights ($70 for a single night's stay), plus $5 per pet and $5 per kid. 657 Twin Bridges Rd.; 541/389-1913; www.swallowridgebandb.com.

More Accommodations: Please look under Chain Hotels in the Resources section for additional places to stay in this area.

Redmond

Redmond is the second-largest city in the county, and growing, because home prices are generally lower than in Sisters or Bend. While it may not be as glamorous or desirable, it is a central location to use as home base for exploring the region. It's also the site of Central Oregon's only commercial airport. On your way through, stock up on chow at **The Feed Barn** in Redmond. 2215 Hwy. 97; 541/923-FEED (541/923-3333); www.feedbarn.net.

PARKS, BEACHES, AND RECREATION AREAS

19 Smith Rock

😼😼 (See Central Oregon map on page 382)

Energetic people are crawling all over the walls at this internationally famous technical rock-climbing destination. Canines tag along with their rappelling buddies to any of several thousand staked and marked pitches for every skill level. You can skip the chocks and cams if you just want to relax at the viewpoints and picnic areas. There's a jumbled maze of hiking and horse trails that don't require equipment around the multi-colored rock formations and down into the Crooked River Canyon. We suggest you grab a trail map and double your water rations before you head out—the rim of the developed hike is called Misery Ridge for a reason. Also, you should know that the local ranger's biggest pet peeve is an off-leash dog and he won't hesitate to slap you with a $94 fine if your terrier is caught off his tether.

Turn east onto Smith Rock Way from U.S. Highway 97, nine miles north of Redmond in Terrebonne. Follow the signs to turn north on 1st. Parking is $3. Closes at 10 P.M. 9241 N.E. Crooked River Dr.; 541/548-7501.

20 Cline Falls

😼 (See Central Oregon map on page 382)

It ain't easy being green in the high desert, which makes this flourishing rest stop along the Deschutes River an especially desirable locale for a basket lunch and a pickup game of flag football or fetch. Waterfront picnic tables are close to fishing access on the river if you want to swing a line to catch your supper.

This rest stop is on State Route 126, four miles west of Redmond.

🐾 Dry Canyon

🐾🐾🐾 (See Central Oregon map on page 382)

The Dry Canyon cuts through the middle of the city, providing a three-mile paved path that you'll share with cyclists and in-line skaters out for exercise or their morning commute. Dogs may prefer the narrow dirt track that parallels the main trail to the west. This single track will give your dog a more interactive experience with the gully's natural environs. It's not marked, but you'll easily see it leading from the south end of the trailhead parking lot. There are no restrooms or water in the gulch. However, right about mid-point in the trail is a road that leads up to West Canyon Rim Park. It's the only green space to relax, water, and refresh yourselves before descending again from the rim.

From U.S. Highway 97 north of Redmond, turn west on Pershall Way and travel a mile to the trailhead entrance sign on your left by the City of Redmond Water Pollution Control.

PLACES TO STAY

Eagle Crest Resort: Owners and their refined canines enjoy the finer things in life at this well-appointed resort that includes a golf course, spa, and equestrian center. All rooms and chalets are nonsmoking, with mission-style furniture. Room rates range $75–150, chalets $150–335, plus a $10 pet fee. 1522 Cline Falls Rd.; 541/923-2453 or 800/682-4786; www.eagle-crest.com.

Bend

Locals who moved here years ago to get away to a quiet mountain town are bemoaning the fact that Bend is quickly becoming the "Aspen of Oregon." Nothing this good stays hidden for long, and Bend's proximity to the Cascade Lakes Recreation Area draws as many mountain bikers, hikers, and anglers in the summer as nearby Mt. Bachelor calls boarders and skiers to the slopes in winter. Upscale shops and restaurants pull people into the hip downtown core. For fanciful dog treats, toys, and accessories, pop into **Biscuits of Bend** (1033 N.W. Brooks St., Brooks and Newport; 541/318-3333).

Dogs are allowed in all city parks as long as they are on a leash and you pick up after them. To assist you in this task, Bend Parks and Recreation has installed what they call Dog E Rest Stops, bag dispenser stations with a witticism borrowed from Smokey the Bear: "Only *you* can prevent dog piles."

Cascade Lakes Recreation Area: From Bend, Century Drive leads to State Route 46, also called the Cascade Lakes National Scenic Byway. The nonprofit organization Scenic America has named it one of the Top 10 most important byways in the country, with extravagant views of mountain peaks, and access to alpine lakes, campgrounds, hiking, and skiing at **Mt. Bachelor** (541/382-7888; www.mtbachelor.com). From the Deschutes National Forest website, www.fs.fed.us/r6/centraloregon, click the High Cascade Lakes button under

Recreational Activities. Easier yet, stop by the Bend–Ft. Rock ranger station; 1230 N.E. 3rd St.; 541/383-4000.

PARKS, BEACHES, AND RECREATION AREAS

22 Tumalo

🐾🐾 (See Central Oregon map on page 382)

At less than a half mile out and back, the trail that leads from the day-use area at this state park is just the right length for a morning constitutional. It follows the Deschutes River and provides a couple places to slip into the water for a quick swim or to fish for rainbow trout. Riverside picnic tables are shaded by pines, junipers, and alder trees. Cooper recommends it as a scenic picnic spot, but too much road noise keeps him from endorsing the campground.

From U.S. Highway 97/20 North, follow the signs to Tumalo on O.B. Riley Road. Parking is $3.

23 Sawyer Park

🐾🐾 (See Central Oregon map on page 382)

Robert W. Sawyer River Park, which was a state park and is now part of the City of Bend, is a sampler platter of regional recreation. It has interesting rock formations, picnic benches under ponderosa pines, a bridge over the

DOG-EAR YOUR CALENDAR

If your pup is feeling patriotic, she can prance in the annual **Fourth of July Pet Parade** in Bend. The organized chaos starts at Drake Park at 9 A.M. and winds through downtown on Bond and Wall Streets. In 2004, more than 6,000 walkers and another 6,000 onlookers participated in a tradition that dates back to the 1930s.

Although dogs are the primary species, there have been lizards, rats, goldfish, cows, donkeys, llamas, and more on parade with kids walking, pulling wagons, and riding bicycles and tricycles. Everyone is welcome to come in costume, and kids can join in with a stuffed animal if there are no live, tame animals in the family. All participants get a collector's button and Popsicle at the finish line. There's no registration, no fees, and no solicitation—it's a free-for-all in every sense. 541/389-7275.

Also in Bend, January 2003 was the first run of the **Atta Boy 300,** bringing top dogsled racers in from around the world. The tradition continues, and onlookers can see the event at various stops along the cities of Bend, Sunriver, LaPine, Sisters, Prineville, and at the start and finish on Mt. Bachelor. 541/350-3049; www.attaboy300.com.

Deschutes river, and an outstretched circle of turf over the hill with a Dog E Bag dispenser. A piece of the Deschutes River Trail follows the water, past squirrels and wildlife popping in and out of ground holes. You can get your fill and be wanting more a few hours later.

From U.S. Highway 97/20 North, turn left on O.B. Riley Road and left into the park.

24 Shevlin Park

🐾🐾🐾 (See Central Oregon map on page 382)

This hillside of shady pines became a city park in 1920, the same year as Drake Park. Its six miles of looped paths are a popular spot for trail runners and joggers. Mountain bikers take their cycles for a spin on parallel, separate tracks. Tumalo Creek rambles through the park, with bridges to cross here and there. Shevlin is on the outskirts of town, but not for long. As high-profile housing developments pop up around it, its sampling of the Oregon Outback topography will be appreciated even more by canines who prefer parks to pavement.

Turn west on Business 20 from U.S. Highway 97. Stay in the right lane to remain on Newport, which leads to Shevlin Park Road. The park is 4.8 miles from the turnoff onto Business 20. 18920 Shevlin Park Rd.

25 Drake Park

🐾🐾🐾 (See Central Oregon map on page 382)

Isis thinks this gorgeous park, named for Bend founder Alexander M. Drake, should be renamed Mrs. May Arnold Park, for it was she and early women of Bend who were responsible for its establishment in 1920. They gathered 1,500 signatures in a fledgling town of 5,400 to convince the city council to purchase the land.

No mere asphalt will do for the people and dogs strolling the greens centered around Mirror Pond—the walking paths are of intricate flagstone. Over an arched wooden footbridge in the middle of the 13-acre park is Harmon Park, which Isis mentions because it has a playground for kids and placards telling the early history of the pond's famous Swan Pageant. The pageant is no more, but the swans and geese remain, as does their prodigious poop.

Dog E Rest Stops are found on the Harmon end of the footbridge and the west end of the park, which is where the dogs tend to hang out, a bit farther away from downtown.

Follow the signs from U.S. Highway 97 to downtown and turn west on Franklin Avenue from Wall Street. If you can't find street parking, there is a public lot on the east side of the park. It's free for the first two hours, $1 per hour thereafter.

26 Pilot Butte

🐾🐾🐾 (See Central Oregon map on page 382)

About 19,000 years ago, a cinder cone erupted, leaving this peak in the middle of the flats. Civilization has overtaken the butte, and now it's an oddly located State Scenic Viewpoint in the middle of a busy suburban area on auto row. There are two ways to hike to the top of Bend's natural answer to the Stairmaster: alongside the road on a one-mile trail, or up the shorter but steeper .8-mile nature trail. You'll see all of the city and the mountains beyond. It's a fine place to catch the high country's colorful sunsets.

For dogs who would rather stick their heads out of the window on a drive to the top, the summit access road is .75 mile east of the trailhead entrance.

From U.S. Highway 97, turn east on Greenwood Avenue and follow it to Summit Drive and the Trailhead Parking signs.

27 Big Sky Park

🐾🐾🐾🐾 (See Central Oregon map on page 382)

In 2004, the Park Department's board voted 5–0 to move forward with a 10-acre, fenced off-leash area up at Big Sky on the far east side of town. It'll be a rough-and-tumble, natural park among the juniper trees and sagebrush behind the youth sports complex, slated for completion in spring 2005. Another park, at Hillside, is scheduled for 2006.

Meanwhile, Coop 'n' Isis went on an advanced scouting party. The area is dry and dusty, prickly and brambly, overrun by chipmunks, and there's an irrigation pond to root around in. In short, they loved it. While development plans for an acre of groomed lawn, irrigation, and a half-mile jogging trail may tame some of the park's wilds, you're still likely to come away coated in fine red dust in the summer and rich mud after a rain.

Before its official opening, you can take your dog off-leash once you're past the playgrounds, BMX track, and ball and soccer fields to the end of the parking lot marked with large rocks.

Turn east on Olney from 3rd Street/Business 97. Continue onto Penn, which becomes Neff Road. Follow Neff until you see the park, 3.5 miles from the turnoff at 3rd. Call ahead to the Parks and Recreation Department for the status of the park before you arrive. 21690 Neff Rd.; 541/389-7275.

28 Upper Deschutes River Trails

🐾🐾🐾🐾 (See Central Oregon map on page 382)

You can walk a little or a lot on this easy, family-friendly trail system closely following the banks of the tumbling Deschutes. There are seven trailheads, two picnic areas, three waterfalls (Dillon, Lava Island, and Benham), and one really exciting stretch of whitewater called Big Eddy along a 10-mile stretch from Bend south to Sunriver. Hiker, biker, and horse trails are separated to give you room to spread out, but dogs have to be on leash May–September, darn it, because the trails are so popular. The drier and hotter the weather, the more you'll come away with a fine sheen of red dust on your skin or fur from the dusty paths.

To reach the Meadow Picnic Area, travel six miles west of U.S. Highway 97 on Century Drive (follow the signs toward Mt. Bachelor). Immediately before the Widgi Creek Golf Course, turn left on the gravel road with the little brown park sign. For other trailheads, continue on Century Drive and turn left on Forest Road 41. Parking is $5 at all marked trailheads: Lava Island, Aspen Falls, Big Eddy, Dillon Falls, and the Slough.

🐾 Newberry National Volcanic Monument—Lava Cast Forest

🐾🐾◀● (See Central Oregon map on page 382)

It's not every day that you get to walk on a lava field, especially if you're not going to Hawaii anytime soon. A mile-long interpretive trail takes you through a forest where the trees are gone, but their impressions, molded in lava, remain. The trees acted as casts around which the molten lava surged when the Newberry Volcano erupted about 6,000 years ago. The path is paved, but the nine-mile road to the site is not. For the price of a bumpy ride on a washboard dirt road and a $5 parking fee, you're treated to one of the most unusual geological sites you're likely to see. The peaks of the Cascades accentuate the stark beauty, and in the spring, fiery Indian paintbrush and purple prairie lupine flowers contrast with the hardened black lava. Your dog will be too busy enjoying her leashed stroll to question the point of going to a treeless forest.

Travel south on U.S. Highway 97 and turn east on Forest Service Road 9720, directly across from the Sunriver exit. The trail is wheelchair-accessible. Closed due to snow cover in winter. 541/593-2421.

PLACES TO EAT

Astro Lounge: Also known as The Bend Distillery, this is the IT night spot in Bend for a dizzying list of specialty martinis, and everything from chi-chi appetizers of brie and fruit to comfort food interpretations. Patrons 21 and over only, please—that's about three in dog years—at the sidewalk tables. 147 N.W. Minnesota Ave.; 541/38-0116.

Merenda Wine Bar: Please your palate with more than 60 wines by the glass, and hors d'oeuvres and small plates with interesting combinations like fennel, grapefruit, and avocado salad or asparagus and prosciutto pizza. It's sidewalk dining at its finest. 900 N.W. Wall St.; 541/330-2304.

Mother's Juice Café: Mother wants to make sure you eat your apple a day, provided with every sandwich. But the health-conscious flock to Mother's mainly for the list of more than 30 fruit juice and smoothie blends, made from whole, fresh fruit. An impressive list of Metabolic Accessory Nutrients, stuff like spirulina, psyllium, echinacea, and ginseng, can be added for that extra performance punch. 1255 N.W. Galveston St.; 541/318-0989.

Papayas Tropical Grill: At this Mongolian grill jury-rigged onto a corner hot dog stand, you'll find Atkins-friendly cuisine with a variety of fresh flavors in healthy tortilla wraps. Wraps include cheese, chicken, fresh spinach, rice, and fruit with various sauces. Try the Thai Tango with mango and teriyaki sauce or the Mona Kona with pineapple and a squeeze of lemon. At the corner of Oregon and Wall Streets; 541/390-7144.

Soba Asian Bistro: Everything is made to order and served in a bowl, be it a rice dish, a noodle dish, or a salad. Recipes are from all regions of Asia; there's sure to be something your shar-pei will love. You'll love the shaded sidewalk tables and cold Asian beer or ginger-peach iced tea on a hot day. 945 N.W. Bond St.; 541/318-1535; www.eatsoba.com.

Victorian Café: There's usually a dog or two hanging out on the lawn beside glass-topped patio tables where people enjoy a comfy-casual menu of breakfast scramblers with thick hobo potatoes and hot sandwiches and fresh salads for lunch. 1404 N.W. Galveston St.; 541/382-6411.

PLACES TO STAY

Cricketwood Country's Pet-Friendly Cottage: The name says it all. The cottage is a self-contained getaway on a property that a guest once described as "Disneyland for Dogs." Your pal can cavort in the hayfield and jump in the pond by the barn on a fenced, rural property down a dirt road with very little traffic. A rate of $125 per night covers you and all your dogs, within reason, including a full kitchen, gas fireplace, and satellite dish with 150 channels, but not breakfast. Your dog is welcome to fertilize the fields, but please pick up in the yard. 63520 Cricketwood Rd.; 541/330-0747 or 877/330-0747; www.cricketwood.com.

Entrada Lodge: You can feel your stress level decrease a notch or two as soon as you enter the warm, fuzzy lobby of this quiet lodge on the west side of town, mere steps away from the Cascade Lakes Scenic Byway and the Deschutes National Forest. Rates range $69–119. There's a short list of reasonable pet rules and a $5 pet charge. Continental breakfast is included. 19221 Century Dr.; 541/382-4080; www.entradalodge.com.

Riverhouse Resort: This extensive, popular hotel is always busy thanks to superior service and Danish-influenced rooms with sliding glass doors onto patios overlooking the Deschutes River. If you sign a simple pet policy, there is no charge for your pets. Rates range $79–115, higher for suites. 3075 N. Business Hwy. 97; 541/389-3111 or 800/547-3928; www.riverhouse.com.

Westward Ho: No sled teams, please. Of the inexpensive motels along U.S. Highway 97 (3rd Street through town), this one is the dog-friendliest. Rates range $38–44; no pet fee. 904 S.E. 3rd; 541/382-2111 or 800/999-8143; www.westwardhomotel.com.

More Accommodations: Please look under Chain Hotels in the Resources section for additional places to stay in this area.

Fern Ridge Lake

Springfield

Vida

126

Venata

Eugene

126

see
Willamette
Valley
page 354

5

58

Lookout Point
Reservoir

Cascade Range

see
Central
Oregon
page 382

Cottage
Grove

Dorena
Reservoir

Curtin

Oakridge

Wickiup
Reservoir

Elkton

38

Cottage Grove
Reservoir

Hills Creek
Lake

Waldo Lake

Davis
Lake

99

138

SOUTHERN
OREGON

Idleyld Park

Steamboat

58

Crescent

23 **24**

Crescent
Lake

3

Glide

138

Diamond
Lake

1

Roseburg

2

Tenmile

42

Umpqua

National

Forest

230

25

138

Crater Lake
National
Park

97

Canyonville

Tiller

227

Crater
Lake

22

Union
Creek

21

Kirk

Lost Creek
Reservoir

19

Prospect

62

26

5

20

Trail

Fort Klamath

27

Galice

4

Merlin

Shady Cove

Rogue River

5

Grants
Pass

62

National

Upper
Klamath
Lake

Winema
National
Forest

6 **7**

White
City

11

Lakecreek

Forest

238

8

Jacksonville

Medford

14

140

Algoma

199

9 **12**

Phoenix

13

Applegate

10

Ruch

15

Howard
Prairie
Reservoir

28

Klamath
Falls

29

Cave
Junction

Ashland

16

17 **18**

66

Siskiyou National
Forest

Rogue River
National Forest

Pinehurst

Lower
Klamath
NWR

OREGON
CALIFORNIA

N

Klamath National Forest

W   E

S

Happy
Camp

5

0   10 mi

0   10 km

97

Lower
Klamath
Lake

Yreka

© AVALON TRAVEL PUBLISHING, INC.

CHAPTER 15

Southern Oregon

The mighty Rogue and Umpqua Rivers, named for regional Native American tribes, are the source from which fun flows in Southern Oregon. The rivers begin high in the Cascade Mountains, winding and tumbling down to the ocean, providing hikes, campgrounds, and water sports of infinite variety along the way. Salmon, trout, and steelhead fishing and white-water rafting on the Rogue draw people from all over the world. Even so, except for a few hot spots, Southern Oregon is not as crowded as, say, the Oregon Coast. Rules are more relaxed, areas more open, and the lifestyle resonates in a lower key. While visitors crowd Crater Lake and the Oregon Caves National Monument—both places where dogs are *not* allowed—you can recreate unhampered in the backwoods.

The rivers connect to lakes, literally hundreds of them, and dozens of those have lake resorts. In addition to providing lodging or camping or both, they are complete destinations, offering boat and bicycle rentals, general stores, restaurants, and more places to picnic, play, and hike. The topography shifts from fertile valleys in the west to the Cascade Mountains as you head east. Be

PICK OF THE LITTER—SOUTHERN OREGON

BEST PARK
Whistler's Bend, Roseburg (page 412)

BEST DOG PARKS
Bear Creek Dog Park, Medford (page 421)
Ashland Dog Park, Ashland (page 422)

BEST OFF-LEASH BEACHES
**Crescent Lake Recreation Area—Simax and Contorta
Point,** Crescent Lake (page 428)

BEST TRAIL
Rogue Gorge Trail, Union Creek (page 427)

BEST EVENT
Puss 'n' Boots Costume Ball, Ashland (page 423)

BEST PLACES TO EAT
Blue Stone Bakery and Coffee Café, Grants Pass (page 416)
Allyson's of Ashland, Ashland (page 424)

BEST PLACES TO STAY
Sutherlin Inn, Roseburg (page 413)
Jacksonville Inn, Jacksonville (page 419)
CrystalWood Lodge, Fort Klamath (page 432)

prepared with traction tires and/or snow chains for any elevation above 1,000 in the winter months, and ask for local road conditions before traveling.

NATIONAL FORESTS AND RECREATION AREAS

Rogue River–Siskiyou National Forests

The 1.6 million acres of the Siskiyou and the Rogue are managed together, and cover parts of Southern Oregon and Northern California. Biologists will tell you that it's the most floristically diverse forest in the nation and includes the carnivorous *Darlingtonia californica*, the fly-eating Cobra Lily. As this guide went to press, the status of many recreation opportunities in this national forest were in question. In 2002, more than 500,000 acres and

318 miles of forest trails were involved in the Biscuit Fire, Oregon's largest in recorded history. By 2004, the Forest Service and the Bureau of Land Management had approved a plan for recovery, but the forest will take time to heal. For recreation in unaffected areas, try the Prospect ranger station: 47201 Hwy. 62; 541/560-3400; and the Ashland ranger station: 645 Washington St.; 541/552-2900; www.fs.fed.us/r6/rogue or www.fs.fed.us/r6/Siskiyou.

Umpqua National Forest

The Umpqua covers almost a million acres on the western slope of the Cascade Mountains. This forest's most popular recreation opportunities are Diamond Lake, included in this chapter, and a 34-mile hiking trail following the North Umpqua wild and scenic River. Playing with the interactive North Umpqua Trail Map online is almost as much fun as hiking the trail itself, through floodplain and riparian areas, meaning the habitats on the banks of a natural course of water. The North Umpqua ranger station is in the tiny town of Glide: 18782 N. Umpqua Highway; 541/496-3532; www.fs.fed.us/r6/umpqua.

Winema National Forest

On the eastern slope of the Cascades, the 1.1 million acres of the Winema are wild and rugged, with fewer developed recreation opportunities. The two main trails, sections of the Pacific Crest Trail and the Mount McLoughlin Trail, are in Winema's wilderness. Mt. McLoughlin isn't so much of a trail as it is a rock scramble guided by unreliable spray paint markers on loose boulders. You and your experienced trail dog really need to know what you are doing to wander in the Winema. The ranger station in Klamath Falls has more information: 1936 California Ave.; 541/883-6714; www.fs.fed.us/r6/winema.

Roseburg

Roseburg is the center point of The Land of Umpqua, a major river system that provides public parks, hiking trails, and campgrounds that are a source of dog delights in every form. The Roseburg visitors center (410 SE Spruce St.; 800/444-9584; www.visitroseburg.com) publishes a self-guided tour map that takes you in four directions, literally and figuratively—Historic South, Wine West, Cultural North, and Scenic East. Isis pointed her paw east for the best outdoor adventures.

PARKS, BEACHES, AND RECREATION AREAS

1 Singleton Park

😺😺 (See Southern Oregon map on page 408)

The story goes that would-be farmer George Singleton had his eye on a plot of land owned by farmer Charles Curry. Charles finally relented and sold it to George, when George did him a favor by fixing a cantankerous Curry farm tractor. Not a bad way to become landed gentry, especially of such a choice plot at the confluence of the North and South Umpqua rivers. This postage-stamp-sized park was the first land purchased by Douglas County in 1951. A jug of wine, a loaf of bread, and dog need be your only companions as you rest in the shade of the dark green leaves of the myrtlewood trees.

Part of the park's appeal is that it's out a ways, past vineyards, orchards, and farms. Take Garden Valley Parkway west, turn left on Curry Road and right on North Curry Road to the end.

🐾 Riverside Park

🐾🐾 (See Southern Oregon map on page 408)

When everyone is hot, sweaty, and tired from driving the super slab of I-5, you can all dog-pile out of the car onto the shady green laws of this park in the backyard of the Roseburg visitors center. The grass slopes to the water, but your entrance is blocked by thick brush and trees, so you'll have to enjoy the river simply for its cooling breezes and refreshing sound. The gardens surrounding the park and center are full of rhododendron bushes, especially pretty in bloom in May.

From I-5, take Exit 124 onto State Route 138 and turn right on S.E. Oak Street, following the signs to the visitors center. Open dawn–dusk.

🐾 Whistler's Bend

🐾🐾🐾🐾 (See Southern Oregon map on page 408)

Like Cooper, your dog may gleefully and vocally greet the many sheep, wild deer, and turkeys you'll encounter on the rolling foothills surrounding this county park. The Wonder Wieners highly recommend this remote, beautiful spot along the North Umpqua River. The picnic area is on the north side of the bend, with front row seats on the wide, strong water. Watch the current carefully if you or your dog decide to take a dip. The swings and slides are shaded by myrtlewood and pine trees, which are also used as obstacles for a very challenging disc golf course. The only flush toilets are in the campground, around the bend on the south side, far enough away that you'll want to hop in the car to reach them.

The road to the park is 12 miles east of Roseburg on State Route 138. Follow the sign to turn on Whistler Park Road and travel patiently until it dead-ends into the park.

PLACES TO EAT

Anthony's Italian Café: Dine out or takeout, lunch and dinner at this pasta place features at least 20 specialty dishes, plus pizzas, subs, soups, antipasto, and salads. Sip Chianti or bottled and tap beer with your meal on the large concrete patio. You won't regret accepting the challenge to save room for Mama Carole's cheesecake. 500 S.E. Cass Ave.; 541/229-2233.

Gay '90s Ice Cream and Deli: Dogs don't know or care if the name of this café is referring to the 1890s or the 1990s, as long as you feed them bits of your sandwich and legendary Umpqua ice cream at one of three outdoor tables. 925 W. Harvard Ave.; 541/672-5679.

PLACES TO STAY

Holiday Motel: Dogs are welcome at this motel as long as you declare them upon arrival rather than try to sneak them in. There's a $10 one-time fee for up to two pets. It's a plain place that does something unusual, charging a flat $44 rate, regardless of the season. The bathrooms have starlight Formica countertops; those of us with a few more dog years may remember the pattern fondly. 444 S.E. Oak Ave.; 541/672-4457.

Sutherlin Inn: Although it's at least a half hour south of Roseburg, we had to include this spotless motel, which offers the best quality for the price in the region. Rooms are spare, modern, and clean, and the beds are extra comfortable—"chiropractor-approved!" A lawn out back is handy for pit stops. Rates start at $40, plus a $10 pet fee. 1400 Hospitality Pl., Sutherlin; 541/459-6800 or 800/635-5425; www.cloud9inns.com.

More Accommodations: Please look under Chain Hotels in the Resources section for additional places to stay in this area.

Merlin and Galice

These two villages mark a section of the wild and scenic Rogue River that is most famous for rafting and salmon and steelhead fishing. Drive the historic Rogue River Loop between Exits 61 and 71 off of I-5, to trace the struggles between early pioneers and native inhabitants during the Rogue Indian Wars of 1852–1856. The battles erupted largely due to The Oregon Donation Land Act, passed by congress to allow settlers to stake claims to Native American lands without consent or treaties. Today, the river remains as turbulent as the area's history. Dozens of scenic pullouts line the waterfront, with fishing access near river *riffles,* which Isis learned is waterfolk lingo for miniature rapids. However, as a miniature dachshund, she does not feel it is appropriate to call her a diffle.

PARKS, BEACHES, AND RECREATION AREAS

❹ Indian Mary Historic Reservation

🐾🐾🐾 (See Southern Oregon map on page 408)

What was once the smallest Native American reservation in the United States is now a 61-acre, well-kept county park. Indian Mary filed a homestead application in 1884 and was granted the land in honor of her father, known as Umpqua Joe, who had warned settlers of a planned massacre, saving the lives of settlers and Native Rogues. The county purchased Mary's property from her descendants in 1958.

It is a showpiece park with lawns of golf-course green perfection. Wet noses go into overdrive sniffing the many varieties of trees, including Japanese fern, maple, flowering cherry, Port Orford cedars, pines, fir, oak, walnut, and Pippin apple trees from an old orchard. Isis spent most of her time inspecting the tall grape arbor that divides the RV sites from the tent camping area. The park is on the banks of the Rogue River, with the picnic area closest to the water, and the campground loops above. The hosts who care for this park obviously take great pride in keeping it well maintained. Its level spaces are excellent for handicapped users. There are accessible camping plots and an ADA-rated fishing platform.

From I-5, take Exit 61 and follow Merlin-Galice Road five miles north of Galice.

ⓓ Griffin Park

 (See Southern Oregon map on page 408)

Despite the Swim at Your Own Risk signs, the river is long and calm beside this quiet, cozy park. And, leash laws aside, we saw dogs chasing Frisbees at their own risk, as well. Griffin pales in comparison to Indian Mary, but then again, it's not as crowded. Plastic climbing equipment and a wooden bridge over a tributary creek provide the kind of simple pleasures kids and dogs appreciate.

From U.S. U.S. Highway 199, go north on Riverbanks Road for six miles and turn right on Griffin Road.

PLACES TO EAT

Backroad Grill: The quality and variety of the gourmet food available at this restaurant comes as a bit of a surprise is such a tiny, unassuming town. Even better yet, if you are staying at a place with an oven, many dishes area available in individually sized take and bake options. Try Chinese Pork with peppers, pineapple, and water chestnuts; chicken Divan with Mornay sauce and Parmesan; or eggplant moussaka with feta, tomato and béchamel sauce. After roughing it on the Rogue River, it doesn't get any better than this. 330 Galice Rd.; 541/476-4019.

Galice Resort: Lunches are simple and filling at this roadside stop. Try a famous river burger, for example, the Widowmaker, with Swiss cheese and jalapeño peppers. The dinner menu adds great choices like vegetarian lasagna, breaded fantail shrimp, and homemade strawberry shortcake. In the summer, there's a big barbecue spread Friday and Saturday nights and a famous Sunday brunch buffet. 11744 Galice Rd.; 541/476-3818.

PLACES TO STAY

Indian Mary Campground: This county park has been named one of the 10 best camping spots in Oregon. There are 91 spaces, 35 of which are for tents on amazingly level, tidy plots. Tent sites are $13 in the off-season and $15 April–October. If you call ahead for reservations, and you'll need to in the summer, there is an additional $5 fee. 541/474-5285. www.co.josephine.or.us/parks/.

Grants Pass

An 18-foot-tall caveman welcomes you to this city on the lawn of the visitors center (1995 N.W. Vine St.; 800/547-5927; www.visitgrantspass.org), commemorating the oldest inhabitants of the area. Grants Pass brags about its ideal climate that gets warmer earlier than the rest of the valley but stays cooler as the summer heat beats down farther south. Parks in and around the city showcase the Rogue River, the whitewater rafting capital of Oregon. For a change of pace and more local color, travel the Rogue River Highway (State Route 99), which roughly parallels I-5 through the area.

PARKS, BEACHES, AND RECREATION AREAS

6 Schroeder Park

🐾🐾🐾 (See Southern Oregon map on page 408)

Schroeder County Park is a great destination that manages to give off a country vibe, even though it's within whistling distance of downtown. Separate areas of the park are neatly divided by rows of towering trees, hills, fences, and

DIVERSION

Ferron, Sue, and Junior the mostly black Lab are co-owners of the only rafting guide service along the Rogue River that allows you to bring your dog along for the ride. **Ferron's Fun Trips** are aptly named, as long as you don't mind getting wet. You can rent your own floating craft or take a tour guided by Junior and Ferron, which Cooper highly recommends. Ferron is a character who knows much about local wildlife, ecosystems, and history. Junior is an experienced guide dog who has been featured on an *Animal Planet* TV special. Take a fishing expedition for gamefish, steelhead, and Chinook salmon or a mild Class 2 whitewater trip on the infamous Rogue. Guided raft trips are $50 per person for a half day, $70 for a full day, and include lunch. 541/474-2201 or 800/404-2201; www.roguefuntrips.com.

sculpted shrubs, adding to the secluded feel. The sports fields and playground are first, fenced off and with a separate parking lot. Next is the campground, a loop with a large lawn in the center designed for croquet or badminton. Most dogs make a beeline for the picnic area, with about the dimensions of a football field, down the hill and alongside the river. There's a barrier-free fishing platform for anglers with special access needs.

From U.S. Highway 199 west of the city, turn right on Willow Lane for a mile to Schroeder Lane.

🐾 Riverside and Baker Parks

🐾🐾🐾 (See Southern Oregon map on page 408)

Several recreation areas along the Rogue River share the Riverside name, but this one is the coolest among them, especially for a picnic. The grass goes on for 26 acres, mature trees provide soothing shade, and the river burbles alongside.

The grounds include the Josephine County Peace Memorial, a rose garden, decent restroom facilities, and plenty of picnic shelters to go around. The big playground has a real tractor, scoop truck, and steamroller to climb on. Wheelchair-accessible pathways wind through the trees, and there are ample parking places. Across the parking lot, Baker Park adds a public boat ramp and more restrooms into the appealing mix.

From I-5, take Exit 58 to State Route 99, which becomes N.W. 6th Street through town. Cross the river and turn onto E. Park Street. Open 7 A.M.– 10 P.M.

PLACES TO EAT

Blue Stone Bakery and Coffee Café: The Blue Stone's menu is more extensive and healthier than a typical coffeehouse, with fabulous soups and choices like stuffed potatoes, chicken burritos, and the *Yougonnalikeit,* a deluxe sandwich that approximates a Thanksgiving dinner between two slices of bread. Okay, so the pastries, cakes, and puddings aren't exactly healthy, but they are so fine! Outdoor seating and free wireless Internet are available. 412 N.W. 6th St.; 541/471-1922.

La Burritta: This restaurant serves large portions of all your Tex-Mex favorites, plus a wide selection of Mexican beers and margaritas, at your covered patio table. The management requests that you sit with your dog along the edge of the deck. The menu features an entire page of fajita and seafood specialties with plenty of zing. 941 S.E. 7th St.; 541/471-1444.

Rosso's Trattoria: This Italian answer to lunch serves 10 wondrous salads and twice as many fantastico specialty sandwiches on focaccia or sourdough French bread, plus soups and select pastries. Order a cappuccino, and relax at sidewalk tables downtown on the main drag. 225 W. 6th; 541/476-8708.

PLACES TO STAY

Redwood Motel: There are so many different room options at this neat motel that prices range widely, $30–105 per night. Rooms are big, the TVs are huge, and the grass out back is wide and soft. The pet fee is $10, which buys a couple of biscuits at check-in. 815 N.E. 6th St.; 541/476-0878 or 888/535-8824; www.redwoodmotel.com.

Riverside Inn: This resort is a grand affair, covering three city blocks. It's the only lodging on the river in town, and all 12 pet-friendly rooms have river views. Front desk receptionist David is an international championship disc winner with his Border collie, Chico—he can tell you where to go and play with your champion. Standard rates are $99–150, but there are often specials. The dog fee is $10. 971 S.E. 6th St.; 541/476-6873 or 800/334-4567; www.riverside-inn.com.

Schroeder County Park Campground: This is a serene and outdoorsy campground close to the city with 54 sites, 22 of them designated for tents in a separate loop. $15 for tents or $20 for hookup sites; 541/474-5285; www.co.josephine.or.us/parks/.

More Accommodations: Please look under Chain Hotels in the Resources section for additional places to stay in this area.

Jacksonville

This well-preserved historic district was founded in 1852 by gold prospectors. When the railroad bypassed the town in the 1890s, so did commercial development, leaving it captured in time. Citizens with excellent foresight began preserving and restoring this history in the 1960s, and now more than 100 of its buildings are listed on the National Historic Register. You might want to avoid the town on Britt Music Festival Nights (www.brittfest.org), when throngs of concertgoers, without dogs in attendance, take up all the parking spots in town. Otherwise, dogs are welcomed here by a big water dish in front of the visitors center (Oregon and C Streets), where you can pick up a Jacksonville Trails Map, listing 14 walking paths and woodland trails around the city, from .3 mile to a mile each.

PARKS, BEACHES, AND RECREATION AREAS

🐾 Sarah Zigler Interpretive Trail

🐾🐾🐾 (See Southern Oregon map on page 408)

This mile-long trail follows the Jackson Creek, where gold was first discovered in 1851. An excellent and extensive brochure and map is available. It's a good idea to follow the city's request to keep your dogs on leash, because poison oak grows heartily in the area (remember, "Leaves of three, let it be").

Coop saw lots of poop on the trail, so please do your part not to add to the problem.

From Oregon Street southbound into Jacksonville, turn right on C Street. The trail begins across the street from the visitors center parking lot, at the entrance to Britt Park.

9 Albert "Doc" Griffin Park

🐾 (See Southern Oregon map on page 408)

Dogs don't mind tagging along on trips to this tidy and pretty park, designed mainly with kids in mind. Those kids will tell you that the "bestest" part of Doc's is the Spray Park, custom-designed for water play on hot summer days. Dogs will have to settle for stray spray while sitting on the nearby lawn. There's also a big playground, a picnic pavilion, and clean restrooms.

On Pine Street between 4th and 5th Streets.

10 Cantrall-Buckley

🐾🐾🐾🐾 (See Southern Oregon map on page 408)

Don't rely on first impressions to judge this county park in the country. The initial pull-out is an uninspiring dirt lot, with a single picnic table hidden in tall grass and a sandy riverbank down to a swimming hole. That's just a tease. Keep going, across a single-lane bridge, and you'll come to a campground on the left and an 88-acre picnic area on the right.

You'll want to go all the way down past the group picnic shelters to the South Lawn on the banks of the Applegate River, where there's fun play equipment, bathrooms and showers, a trail, and shade trees. It wouldn't be surprising to find a rope swing somewhere out over the 1.75 miles of river frontage.

Take State Route 238 west from Jacksonville, turn left on Hamilton Road, for about a mile. Parking is $3. Open 10 A.M.–dusk.

PLACES TO EAT

Lutrell's Mustard Seed Café: A rose garden marks the entrance to Lutrell's outdoor patio. The food is named after family and friends; Pop's Covered and Smothered is hashbrowns and biscuits with sausage gravy, Renee has her own chicken burger, Joel's BLAT is a BLT with avocado, and Millie has a killer Philly. 130 N. 5th St.; 541/899-2977.

MacLevin's Whole Foods Deli, Bakery, and Ice Cream Parlor: This authentic Jewish deli is the place to nosh on pastrami, knishes, and potato latkes, oy vey! All-day breakfast and lunch are served at a couple of outdoor tables. Or, you could take your matzo ball soup, herring in sour cream, borscht, and lox to go. 150 W. California St., 541/899-1251.

NATURE HIKES AND URBAN WALKS

When gold was discovered in Rich Gulch in 1851, the town of Jacksonville sprang up around the prospectors and the gold diggers hoping to profit from them. Development and modernization passed by when the railroads bypassed the town in favor of Medford, and the early character of Jacksonville remained largely unchanged as surrounding communities grew. In 1966, the charm of the city was permanently preserved when the entire town was designated as a National Historic Landmark.

Walk through the past on the **Jacksonville Historic Landmark Walking Tour,** with a brochure from the visitors center (N. Oregon and C Streets). People have thoughtfully placed water bowls outside the homes and businesses along the tour to refresh your thirsty pup. 541/899-8118; www.jacksonvilleoregon.com.

PLACES TO STAY

Cantrall-Buckley County Park Campground: It costs $10 to overnight at this quiet county campground, not including quarters for the coin-operated showers. The 42 first-come, first served sites are well shaded, but too close together to be private. 541/774-8183. www.jacksoncountyparks.com.

Jacksonville Inn: Cooper and Isis are on their very best behavior at this glamorous inn. It is rare that an establishment of this caliber accepts pets, and they'd like to keep it that way. Eight guest rooms and four cottages combine tasteful Victorian opulence with modern conveniences in the heart of town. The owner requests that she be allowed to meet every dog, that they sleep in their own beds—not hers—and that they not be left alone in the room, which goes without saying. The inn has an elegant restaurant, casual bistro, and wine shop. Rooms are $145–189; decadent cottages are $250–375. You get what you pay for. 175 E. California St.; 541/899-1900 or 800/321-9344; www.jacksonvilleinn.com.

Stage Lodge: Nicholas the Lhasa apso is Lord of the Lodge, and, yes, you may kiss his paw. Pets under 40 pounds are welcome at this "anti-motel" with real colonial furniture and designer bath fixtures. Rooms are all nonsmoking. Rates are $88–98; suites with fireplaces and jetted tubs are $165. 830 N. 5th St.; 541/899-3953 or 800/253-8254; www.stagelodge.com/right.html.

Medford

The working-class cousin of Ashland, Medford is the largest and most commercial city in Southern Oregon. It is surrounded by a rich agricultural valley dominated by pear orchards and vineyards. Many of the region's delectable goodies can be found at famous **Harry and David** (1314 Center Dr.; 541/864-2278; www.harryanddavid.com). Medford is a good central location from which to explore the Applegate Valley, named for pioneers Jesse and Lindsay Applegate, trailblazers of Southern Oregon in 1846. Not as quaint as Ashland or Jacksonville, Medford has its merits in less expensive lodging and winery tours.

North of Medford in Eagle Point is the oldest and largest training facility for hearing-assistance dogs in the nation. Tours of **Dogs for the Deaf** are free, but you are welcome to make a donation to the privately funded facility. See how rescued pups are trained for a higher calling as service dogs for the deaf and hearing-impaired. There are areas where your pup can wait for you; visiting dogs would be too disruptive to those in training (10175 Wheeler Rd.; 541/826-9220; dogsforthedeaf.org).

PARKS, BEACHES, AND RECREATION AREAS

11 Tou Velle

🐾🐾🐾 (See Southern Oregon map on page 408)

So much of this region calls for activity—trails to hike, mountains to climb, rivers to navigate—that it is refreshing to come across a park tailor-made for doing little other than lying in the shade of a tree alongside a quiet river. This State Recreation Site is one of the few places where the Rogue calms down, gliding past the foot of the Table Mountains. Large trees shade the rolling grassy slopes dotted with picnic tables. Even when busy, there's plenty of room for everybody. Relaxation runs rampant.

From State Route 62, turn west on Antelope Road and right on Table Rock Road. Parking is $3 per day.

12 Alba Park

🐾🐾 (See Southern Oregon map on page 408)

It's easy to imagine this lovely little park as the social center of downtown Medford. Dedicated to the city by Charles and Callie Palm in 1934, it has the formal quadrangle design of that era, with a gazebo and a fountain in the center of diagonal sidewalks. Next to the fountain is a statue of a young man—surely it's Charles—kneeling to pet two Irish setters. The thick maple trees lining the square lawn must have been around since the beginning. As the historic heart of downtown Medford is rapidly being restored, Alba revels in its former glory. This rarified atmosphere is appropriate for a walk, but probably not for mutts who want to mess around.

Alba Park is at the corner of Holly and Main Streets.

13 Hawthorne Park

🐾🐾🐾 (See Southern Oregon map on page 408)

There's room to roam at Hawthorne, enough for Friends of the Animal Shelter to hold a benefit parade annually on the expansive lawn. Picnic tables are smartly placed under the few shade trees. Isis adores the elaborate rose garden, where No Pruning signs admonish humans tempted to take flowers home. Dogs, that means no digging, either.

The park is across the street from Medford Center Mall, which has a Cold Stone Creamery ice cream shop. At the corner of Jackson and Hawthorne Streets. Open 6 A.M.–10:30 P.M.

14 Bear Creek Dog Park

🐾🐾🐾🐕 (See Southern Oregon map on page 408)

Bear Creek Park is a 100-acre expanse of rolling hills with a litany of fancy amenities, including a skate park, amphitheater, playground, tennis courts, barbecue areas, a BMX bicycle track, and restrooms. Best of all, it is the location of Medford's only off-leash area, a good-sized two acres, secured all around by a sturdy, tall fence with a double-entry gate. A blend of open field and tree-covered shade, bushes to sniff, and a dirt path around the perimeter suit every dog's needs. There's a garbage can, a picnic bench, and water to sip, but we didn't see a bag dispenser, so come prepared. We visited at the peak of the dry season, yet the grass was still lush, watered, and maintained.

The main parking lot is on Siskiyou Boulevard, but there's a back way to sneak in directly to the off-leash area. From I-5, take Exit 27 east onto Barnett Road. Turn left immediately on Alba Drive in front of the Dairy Queen and park at the Little League field. Follow the signs across a wooden footbridge to reach the dog park entrance. Hours are 6 A.M.–10:30 P.M.; 541/774-2400.

PLACES TO EAT

Sonny's Downtown Café: Enjoy breakfast and lunch in Vogel Plaza at an outdoor table near the restored Craterian Ginger Rogers Theatre. The omelettes are extra fluffy, any burger can be made with a veggie patty, and the Rueben has lots of oomph. Try the BLATCHO (bacon, lettuce, avocado, tomato, and cheddar on grilled sourdough). 210 E. Main St.; 541/245-1616; www.sonnyscafe.net.

PLACES TO STAY

In this area, chain hotels offer the best choices for dogs and their owners; please look under Chain Hotels in the Resources section.

Ashland

This cultured, artistic town is world famous thanks to a guy named Bill who wrote great plays. Founded in 1935, the Oregon Shakespeare Festival has grown and evolved to present music, dance, and theater far beyond the Bard. The Plaza, a triangle in the center of town, is the hot spot for theater, shopping, and an entire row of restaurants with "Creekside Dining," essentially a block-long outdoor patio. It's public space, where dogs can join you while you dine.

Ashland is iffy when it comes to dog-friendliness. Dogs are not allowed in city parks, and we found that you couldn't trust the lodging brochures. Accommodations that say they allow pets often have only one room, or don't allow pets in the high season, or stick them in smoking rooms. Cooper and Isis have selected the few that really are dog-friendly.

PARKS, BEACHES, AND RECREATION AREAS

15 Ashland Dog Park

🐾🐾🐾🐕 (See Southern Oregon map on page 408)

It has no official moniker, but this off-leash area by any other name would smell as sweet. It's completely fenced, grassy, and graced by shade trees and scattered bushes. There's a covered shed (with a couch inside!) for waiting out the rain, and a plastic swimming pool and water fountains for both species. A dozen or so lawn chairs are scattered around for impromptu seating in addition to a couple of picnic tables. Smack dab in the middle is a built-in trash bin with a bunch of garden shovels leaning against it. Why bother with bags or mitts when you can simply shovel the you-know-what?

The OLA is actually two parks in one: a two-acre, sloping lawn for the big boys, and a separately fenced, little spot with its own entrance for small or timid dogs. Cooper figures that now is as good a time as any to reveal his darkest secret: He is afraid of dog parks. Gasp! How can it be? For starters, practically everybody is bigger than he is and, sadly, his scars bear witness to prior dog attacks before he was rescued. What a treat to have his own space, complete with a miniature copse of trees for him to anoint.

From the center of town, turn east onto Oak Street for about a mile, turn left on Nevada, and right onto Helmann, which looks like a driveway past the Ashland Greenhouses. You can also connect to the Bear Creek Greenway Trail from this location. Open dawn–dusk. 541/488-5340.

DOG-EAR YOUR CALENDAR

The Friends of the Animal Shelter (FOTAS) in Ashland host an annual **Puss 'n' Boots** costume ball and silent auction to benefit the Jackson County Animal Shelter in nearby Phoenix, Oregon. The event is typically held in October. Cost is a worthwhile $20 per person, with all funds raised going to pay the salary of a full-time coordinator who wrangles more than 100 volunteers to keep the shelter running smoothly.

In nearby Jacksonville, the annual **Mutt Strut** parade is held in May, sponsored by the Jacksonville Animal Hospital, with all funds raised also going to FOTAS. 541/552-1079; www.fotas.org.

16 Siskiyou Mountain Park

🐾🐾🐾 (See Southern Oregon map on page 408)

If you enjoy the nightlife, shopping, and culture of staying in Ashland *and* you want to do some more serious hiking, you're in luck. Above the city on the west side are 270 acres of single-track trails connecting the Pacific Crest Trail and the Creek to Crest Byway.

The tourist brochure recommends that you access the trails from Park Street, but there's no parking in that residential area. Coop 'n' Isis have a better idea: on either side of Lithia Park (where dogs are not allowed), there is a loop formed by Granite and Grandview Streets. After the paved road ends, there are several locations for trailhead parking, maps, and signs directing you through the maze of hiking opportunities. Even if you don't make it to the trails, this dirt road above town provides a bird-dog's-eye view of the city. It is frequented by local joggers and their sidekicks.

From State Route 99 southbound into town, turn right on Granite Street, one street north of the Plaza.

17 Emigrant Lake

🐾🐾🐾🐕 (See Southern Oregon map on page 408)

Word on the street is that Emigrant Lake is packed with local dogs on weekends. The catch is that they're not allowed in the County Recreation Area, a.k.a. the RV park. Go past the park entry and you'll see several dirt roads with Parking Area and Shoreline Access signs. The roads are rough, you're lucky if there's a latrine, and parking is a dirt patch. Yet, persevere! There are no leash restrictions; there *are* meadows filled with wildflowers and lots of comfortable entry points along the lake for dog paddling; and you don't have to pay the $3 to park that dogless people are paying in the RV park.

From I-5, take Exit 14 west on State Route 66 to the lake. Park closes at sunset.

18 Hyatt Lake

🐾🐾🐾🐾 (See Southern Oregon map on page 408)

The Hyatt Lake Recreation Complex is located a dizzying mile above sea level, so unless you're from Colorado, don't be alarmed if you're a little out of breath. Here's another tip: The higher you go in altitude, the less alcohol it takes to get buzzed. The lake is crystal clear, remote, and surrounded by wilderness and snow-capped peaks. The playground and picnic areas are rudimentary except for a large fire ring, ideal for a bonfire and weenie roast. Isis suggests you spend time hiking the section of the Pacific Crest Trail that parallels the west side of the lake, accessible from behind the park office.

From Ashland, take State Route 66 east for 17 miles, past the top of Green Springs Pass. Turn onto Hyatt-Prairie Road and follow the signs. Parking is $3.

PLACES TO EAT

Allyson's of Ashland: It's predictable in this town for things to be named after Shakespearean characters, and Allyson has followed suit in dubbing her sandwiches MacBeth, Shylock, King Lear, etc. That's the only thing clichéd about them—they are otherwise exciting and really good. Daily specials are even better, such as chicken and pumpkin tortellini. Order downstairs and they'll bring your food to your sidewalk table. 115 E. Main St.; 541/482-2884.

Greenleaf Restaurant: Of all the restaurants on the plaza, Isis favors this one. The menu is five pages long, with something for even the pickiest palates. Food dishes lean toward the healthy side, and it's all fresh and delicious. 49 N. Main St.; 541/482-2808.

Pangea Grills and Wraps: Meals wrapped in tortillas make for handy, on-the-go lunches. Get your taste buds tingling with Greek and Mediterranean flavors, then cool down with a mango or peach smoothie. Order at the counter and relax at a sidewalk table. Your food is brought to you, along with a water dish and some dog biscuits for your dining companion. 272 E. Main St.; 541/552-1630.

Water Street Café: It's a great concept, well suited to a resort town—open air dining with healthy food ordered from an outdoor bar. Salads, wraps, smoothies, and espresso soothe the savage stomach. Downtown at the corner of Water and Main Streets; 541/482-0206.

PLACES TO STAY

Ashland Patterson House: At this classic, craftsman-style bed-and-breakfast, dogs of all shapes and sizes are welcome in the cozy cottage, and innkeeper Vivienne occasionally allows smaller dogs in one of the rooms in the main house. Everything feels elegant without being the least bit stuffy. Weather permitting, breakfast is served on the patio so that your pals may join you (vegetarian meals upon request). Rates range $70–140, plus a $10 pet fee. 639 N. Main St.; 541/482-9171 or 888/482-9171; www.patterson-house.com.

Green Springs Inn: The road to get here, halfway between Ashland and Klamath Falls, is worth the price alone. State Route 66 winds through deep forests above green valleys to arrive here at the top of Green Springs Mountain at about 4,000 feet. The delicious food served at the restaurant and the lodge rooms with decks and jetted tubs are icing on the cake. Plain old rooms are $69, tub and deck rooms are $99, and there's no pooch tariff. 11470 Hwy. 66; 541/482-0614; www.greenspringsinn.net.

Hyatt Lake Campground: Tent sites are on an opposite shore from the RV sites, with walk-in or drive-in availability. Sites are deeply wooded and widely spaced apart for privacy. Most have views; #T15 is the best. Available June–October. Fees are $12 Mon.–Thurs. and $15 Fri.–Sun. Hyatt-Howard Prairie Rd. off Hwy. 66; 541/482-2031; www.or.blm.gov.

Plaza Inn and Suites: The Plaza is a sophisticated, modern choice in downtown Ashland. Dogs under 60 pounds are allowed in a second building, smaller but equally fancy. Deluxe Room rates range $79–159 and include a European breakfast. The pet fee is $10. 98 Central Ave.; 541/488-8900 or 888/488-0358; www.plazainnashland.com.

More Accommodations: Please look under Chain Hotels in the Resources section for additional places to stay in this area.

Shady Cove and Prospect

These tiny burgs are mere spots of community along the Rogue-Umpqua Scenic Byway (State Route 138), also known as the Highway of Waterfalls, leading to the wilderness, forests, and high mountain lakes of the Oregon Cascades. The area has drawn famous anglers, including western novelist Zane Grey, to its fishing holes and nature trails. Pick up U.S.F.S. maps for the hikes along the Rogue River at the Prospect ranger station (47201 Hwy. 62; 541/560-3400).

PARKS, BEACHES, AND RECREATION AREAS

19 Lost Lake Trail

🐾🐾🐾 (See Southern Oregon map on page 408)

The Dachsie Twins prefer skipping the crowds at Joseph Stewart and traveling the far side of the lake on this trail instead. It's 2.4 miles from this trailhead to a viewpoint called The Grotto. Pick up a U.S. Army Corps of Engineers map of all the trails around Lost Creek Lake at the state park on your way. On the back of the map is a species list of hundreds of birds, mammals, flora, and fauna you may see. While you should leash your dog to keep her paws out of the poison ivy, there are places where she can slip into the water for a quick dip.

Start at the Lewis Road Trailhead, reached by traveling north of the state park on State Route 62, and turning left onto Lewis Road for a mile.

20 Joseph H. Stewart

🐾🐾 (See Southern Oregon map on page 408)

This State Recreation Area is the place to go for family reunions and big gatherings. The whole place is like one big, happy family in the summer anyway, parked on wide, open plains aside Lost Creek Lake. It's a big park, mostly taken up by endless campsites. Dogs will undoubtedly prefer the separate day-use area, southwest of the campground, with room to roam along the lake and a store, café, marina, and boat launch. There are 5.5 miles of trails in the park along the south shore, from the dam to the picnic area and up to the campground.

Take State Route 62 from Shady Cove northeast to Lost Creek Lake. Parking is $3. Open 6 A.M.–7 P.M.

PLACES TO EAT

Phil's Frosty: Bunches of umbrella-shaded picnic tables are outside the order window. Inside is the standard fare you're supposed to eat on summer vacation. There are dogs, burgers, burritos, fries, and onion rings for the main course; doughnuts and hard and soft ice cream are for dessert. 22161 Hwy. 62, Shady Cove; 541/878-2509.

PLACES TO STAY

Edgewater Inn: The Rogue River runs right past your room at this spiffy motel, and your pooch can do the same at the dog run in the back. The rooms are fresh and simple with white pine furniture and Danish accents. Continental breakfast is included. Rates range from $67 for parking lot views up to $138 for a room with a king-size bed, spa, and patio on the river. The pet fee is $7. 7800 Rogue River Rd., Shady Cove; 541/878-3171 or 888/811-3171; www.edgewaterinns.com.

Prospect Historical Hotel/Motel and Dinnerhouse: Behind the original 1892 stagecoach inn is a simpler motel that is more suitable for families with dogs and children. Well-behaved, clean pets are allowed in the motel rooms at no charge (even gorillas, according to the policy). Dog treats are provided at check-in with a map of where to play and potty, in a huge groomed field with a little creek to wade in. Rooms are $50–90. 391 Mill Creek Dr., Prospect; 541/560-3664 or 800/944-6490; www.prospecthotel.com.

Union Creek

Pick a trail, any trail, and you can't go wrong. All of them follow the splashy spectacle of the Rogue River and Union Creek, through rapids and waterfalls, lava tubes, beaver dams, and log jams. Some lead you to volcanic rock formations and pumice flats, or deep into canopies of Douglas fir. The trails can be accessed reliably June–October; during winter months, the region is a popular snowmobile and cross-country skiing playground. While hiking, you'll probably need to exercise restraint, otherwise known as a leash, to keep your dog out of the water. The adjectives used to describe the river—such as wild, raging, and swift—do not exaggerate, and no one wants to see their dog get swept away by strong currents.

PARKS, BEACHES, AND RECREATION AREAS

21 Rogue Gorge Trail

🐾🐾🐾🐾 🐕 (See Southern Oregon map on page 408)

On a .25-mile paved loop, there are four scenic viewpoints that demonstrate the power of water over time to slice through solid rock. It is simply spectacular, even more so during spring runoff in June. A 3.5-mile trail starts at the southern end of the loop, traveling along the east side of the river down to the Natural Bridge area. The sometimes rocky, mostly level trail is easy, featuring rock formations called potholes, carved by churning river currents. Your dog will get a kick out of watching you drool for a change, your mouth agape, awed by the scenery.

Travel north on State Route 62 approximately 12 miles from Prospect to the parking lot. A latrine is the only amenity.

22 Natural Bridge Trail

🐾🐾🐾🐾 🐾 (See Southern Oregon map on page 408)

The Natural Bridge is a lava tube, carved through rock by the molten flow. The Rogue River now follows the same path, disappearing underground for several hundred yards before emerging in a roiling rage downstream. Viewpoints around the formation are accessible on a paved walkway. Near the viewpoint bridge is a trailhead that leads to a 3.5-mile trail following the Upper Rogue River south to Woodruff picnic area. Much of the time, you'll be treading on mossy lava rock, alternating between sheltering old-growth forest and open brush.

Travel nine miles north on State Route 62 from Prospect and look for signs to the Natural Bridge Viewpoint. If you crave more, continue south another 4.6 miles to the River Bridge campground, along a section known as the Takelma Gorge Trail.

PLACES TO EAT

Beckie's Restaurant: Although they are tasty, no one would blame you if you skipped past the burgers, sandwiches, and chicken-fried steak and went straight to the homemade pies. Dogs feel no guilt when eating dessert first, nor for chowing down on steak and eggs for breakfast, and they've been doing it here for more than 80 years. Order to go and eat at the tables in front of the ice cream shop next door. 56484 Hwy. 62; 541/560-3563.

Crescent Lake

If dogs awarded sainthood to humans, Ronda Bishop would be on the short list. As the Recreation Program Manager for the Crescent Ranger District of the **Deschutes National Forest,** she has designated eight off-leash play areas around the beach at Crescent Lake. For more information than we've listed below, stop by the office in the town of Crescent, or call her at 541/433-3200.

Winter activities in the area include Alpine and Nordic skiing at the Willamette Pass Ski Area and miles of roads and trails for snowmobiling, snow shoeing, and skijoring. Crisp air and warm summer days are ideal for fishing, hiking, swimming, and taking to all those trails on a mountain bike.

PARKS, BEACHES, AND RECREATION AREAS

23 Deschutes National Forest—
Crescent Lake Recreation Area

🐾🐾🐾🐾 🐕 (See Southern Oregon map on page 408)

Do doubt about it, this is dogtopia. Cooper and Isis had to pinch each other to make sure they hadn't died and gone to doggy heaven. Crescent Lake is a

4,000-acre, crystal-clear, glacially fed water playground surrounded by silky sand beaches and mountain peaks that make you want to sing, "The hills are alive!" Ronda has put so much effort into designating and clearly marking the dog-use areas; please return the favor by keeping your pets off non-designated beaches and on leash when they are in the campgrounds. Day-use areas are open 6 A.M.–10 P.M. Wear your mosquito dope in June and July.

Take the Crescent Cut-Off Road from the center of town in Crescent on U.S. Highway 97, turn right toward Oakridge on State Route 58 and go 3.5 miles to Road 60, to Crescent Lake Campgrounds-Resort-Marina. It's another 2.2 miles to the Y junction that is the start of all recreation around the lake. From Eugene, the lake is 70 miles southeast on State Route 58. The Off-Leash Areas (OLAs) are:

North Simax: This is the only OLA on the south shore. There is paved parking, a latrine, picnic tables, and the most beautiful wide and long beach you can imagine with a gentle slope into the water. Go straight to the left when the road forks right to the campground.

Crescent Lake Campground: This OLA is only practical if you are staying in the campground. It is small and steep, to the right of the old boat launch. It's.3 mile to the right of the Y junction. There is a $5 parking fee at this area.

Day-Use Areas: There is limited, dirt parking in two pullouts. If you're the first ones there, you'll probably get to keep the area to yourselves. No facilities. Go right at the Y intersection, 3.3 miles.

Tranquil Cove: The cove has picnic tables, garbage, gravel parking, a potty, and a designated swimming beach marked by posts driven into the ground. The OLAs are to the outsides of the pylons, left and right. Head right at the Y, four miles.

Tandy Bay: Walk a few yards through the woods at this bay to the beach, to a single picnic table with a phenomenal lake view and a peek at Diamond Peak behind you. The whole area is off-leash. Right at the Y, 4.5 miles.

Spring Campground: This is the last access area off of the paved road. The OLA is to the right of the boat launch. In addition to a lovely crescent of beach, there are high grass fields for olfactory exploration. Right at the Y, 5.5 miles. There is a $5 parking fee at this area.

Contorta Point: The lake saves its best for last. This beach is an interesting mix of sand and crumbly volcanic pumice. Views of Diamond Peak take up the entire skyline. As of press time, there was no charge to stay at the undeveloped campground. Right at the Y, 7.5 miles, left at Cortorta Point turnoff, and .5 mile to the first campground road and OLA. The last two miles are on a dirt road.

24 Diamond Peaks Wilderness—Fawn Lake Trail

🐾🐾🐾 (See Southern Oregon map on page 408)

The official distance to Fawn Lake from the trailhead was three miles on the sign, but someone had crossed that out and written in four. It sure seems longer, perhaps because of the continuous elevation gain and hot, dusty trail. The higher you go, the better the views get, so the moderately steep trail isn't the only thing that will take your breath away. Signs will direct you if you want to branch off in the direction of Pretty Lake, Stag Lake, and Diamond Peak Lake for even more mileage and vistas. Water and some form of bug deterrent are essential traveling companions.

Park at the Crescent Lake Campground and watch for the busy road you must cross at the beginning of the hike. Parking is $5.

PLACES TO EAT

KJ's Café: Sure, dogs are allowed on the covered porch, where they can plead earnestly for a bite of your omelette or pancakes, burger, sandwich, or salad. KJ's also has a lengthy kids' menu, great chili, ice cream, and milk shakes. Milepost 69, Hwy. 58; 541/433-2005.

PLACES TO STAY

Crescent Lake Campground: Of the 44 tent/RV sites, #37 is the choicest spot with direct access to the off-leash beach. Fees are $13 for premium lakefront sites and $11 for the rest, on a first-come, first-served basis. Follow the signs to the campground from Road 60. 503/433-2234.

Willamette Pass Inn: This inn, seven miles east of the ski area, looks like a snow lodge should. It has a timber exterior and spacious rooms with hand-carved log bed frames, kitchenettes, stovepipe fireplaces, and futon second beds or bunk beds for the kids or your ski buddies. Rates start at $68 for weekdays, $78 for weekends. The pet fee is $5. Milepost 69, Hwy. 58; 541/433-2211; www.willamettepassinn.com.

Diamond Lake

Diamond Lake has the most developed National Forest facilities in Oregon. For more information before you go, call the visitors center at 541/793-3310.

PARKS, BEACHES, AND RECREATION AREAS

25 Umpqua National Forest—Diamond Lake

🐾🐾🐾 (See Southern Oregon map on page 408)

The crystal waters of the lake sparkle at 5,182 feet, a mile above sea level. As they say, it's a recreation paradise. For sea dogs, there are boat rentals of all breeds—pedal boats, patio boats, dinghies with dinky motors, kayaks, canoes, and bumper boats. For landlubbers, an 11-mile paved, multi-use trail circles the entire lake. Humans can rent bicycles at the lake's resort to do the double-digit mileage. Resort management is low-key about allowing dogs off-leash to run around the ball field and go swimming, but the trail passes through several government-managed campgrounds where you should leash up. Winter recreation includes inner-tubing, ice skating, and snowmobiling.

Diamond Lake is five miles north of Crater Lake on State Route 138.

PLACES TO STAY

Diamond Lake Resort: Dogs are welcome in both the durable cabins and rooms in the lodge for $5 each per night. Thick-furred animals will do fine in the cabins, heated only by woodstoves. Italian greyhounds and Chihuahuas might prefer the warmer lodge. The resort includes restaurants, a general store, and boat and bicycle rentals (snowmobile and Snocat tours in winter). Motel rooms are $75–80, cabins are $145–185 for up to six people. 350 Resort Dr.; 800/733-7593; www.diamondlake.net.

Fort Klamath and Crater Lake

Crater Lake is Oregon's only National Park, and as such, your dog is not allowed on trails or in buildings. She can still experience the best part of this natural wonder with you, a 33-mile Rim Road drive encircling the 4,000-foot-deep basin, the remnants of the Mount Mazama volcano that erupted an estimated 7,700 years ago. You have to travel the route slowly as the curves hug the mountains and the water, leaving lots of time for her to hang her head out the window and take in the territory. The full drive is open only during the warmest summer months; the southern entrance and a short drive up to a lake viewpoint and historic lodge are open year-round. The entrance fee is $10 per vehicle.

PARKS, BEACHES, AND RECREATION AREAS

26 Jackson F. Kimball

🐾🐾 (See Southern Oregon map on page 408)

Locals will tell you that the best time to visit this State Recreation Site is in September, after the first hard frost kills off the mosquitoes that will drink you dry during spring and summer. A 50-foot path leads to the Wood River Headwaters; on one side is a creek not much wider than a road, and on the other is a panorama of snow-capped mountains and towering pines that our host at CrystalWood Lodge said was "straight out of a John Wayne western." Despite including a river and a marsh, it is called a dry camp, because none of the water is drinkable. Bring some with you on this short, sweet stop.

From State Route 62, north of Fort Klamath, turn west on Dixon Road and left at the T intersection onto Sun Mountain Road.

PLACES TO STAY

CrystalWood Lodge: Every detail of this DB&B (Dinner, Bed, and Breakfast) is designed to welcome dogs. After all, owners Liz and Peggy have 21 dogs of their own! You are welcome to meet the troops, who are in training for the 2008 Iditarod dogsled races in Alaska. Copies of *Fido Friendly* and *Bark* magazine are in every room, as are kennels, lint-hair remover brushes, and designer doggie bag holders. You are not required to use the kennels—extra sheets are provided if your dogs sleep in bed with you! The property encompasses 130 acres, with five miles of trails your hosts have cleared and access to the 10-mile Klamath Lake Canoe Trail. The lodge, an original homestead, is also a phenomenal place for bird-watchers, anglers, and hunters. It's easy to reach, yet secluded between the Winema National Forest and the Upper Klamath National Wildlife Refuge.

You won't mind being sent to the doghouse here, full of games for kids and a self-service dog-wash station. The room rates, ranging $195–245, are worth every penny, as they not only include unparalleled hospitality, but breakfast and a massive gourmet dinner as well, served by a chef trained at the California Culinary Academy. There's more, but we're running out of room, so look it up on the Web. In short, Coop 'n' Isis think it's the best place for dogs to stay in the region. 38625 Westside Road; 541/381-2322 or 866/381-2322; www.crystalwoodlodge.com.

More Accommodations: Please look under Chain Hotels in the Resources section for additional places to stay in this area.

Klamath Falls

In the Oregon High Country, the only way you and your dog will get cabin fever is by staying in too many of them. Between the Rogue Valley and Klamath Falls are the Cascade Mountains, famous for more than 100 alpine lakes, at least a dozen of which have cabin resorts on their shores.

Klamath County is a high-desert region. You'll leave behind the dreary, drippy Pacific Northwest with an average of 300 days of sunshine yearly. The heat rises up through the ground as well, as most of the city is warmed by underground geothermal energy, a pleasant reminder of an explosive volcanic legacy. In the winter, when it's not sunny, it's snowing. Keep traction tires or chains on hand.

DIVERSION

You don't have to roam the wilds of Alaska to experience the once-in-a-lifetime adventure of dogsled racing. At **Briar's Patch Sled Dogs,** veteran musher Liz Parrish and her team of long-distance racing dogs will take you on an extreme sport wilderness trip, where you get to enjoy all of the excitement without doing any of the work. These Huskies and their handlers are pros, in training for the 2008 Iditarod.

You won't forget the thrills—from the tension-building moment the dogs are harnessed, bootied, and put into position, to the bedlam that erupts as the command is given to "GO!" After whooshing through the forest, you'll return with rosy cheeks and a serious case of perma-grin. Even in the summer, these eager working dogs are happy to pull you in a rugged, all-terrain cart.

One-hour rides ($45 adult/$25 child) include warm refreshments; half-day ($125 adult/$60 child) and all-day ($225 adult/$110 child) excursions also include lunch. Talk to Liz about dog-sitting for your pups while you're out.

Mush puppy wanna-bes can attend twice-yearly training camps to learn the ropes of dogsledding; call for more information. 38625 Westside Rd. (based at CrystalWood Lodge); 541/381-2203; www.briarspatchsleddogs.com.

PARKS, BEACHES, AND RECREATION AREAS

27 Collier Memorial

 (See Southern Oregon map on page 408)

The main attraction at Collier is the logging museum, with the largest collection of equipment in the country on 147 acres of state park land. The museum is outdoors, allowing your dogs to enjoy it with you. Self-guided tour brochures are available. The rusting hulks of machinery are left in situ, rain or shine, although it doesn't rain much in this high, dry country. Across the highway, the poor trees in the campground look thirsty and scrawny. The picnic area is greener, with watered lawns leading to the banks of the Williamson River and Spring Creek. Cooper was driven to an ecstatic frenzy by the excess of chipmunks and tiny prairie dogs in the park. If he hadn't been on leash, Isis doubts she would have ever seen him again.

Collier is 30 miles north of Klamath Falls on U.S. Highway 97. Open dawn–dusk. 541/783-2471.

28 Link River Nature Trail

🐾🐾🐾 (See Southern Oregon map on page 408)

In the summer, a morning stroll along this 1.7-mile gravel trail is best, before it gets too hot to enjoy the meandering river and the many birds. For longer walks, the Link Trail connects to the Lake Ewauna Wingwatchers Nature Trail for another mile. You might see blue herons, white pelicans, mallards, and red-winged blackbirds.

To reach the trailhead parking lot, turn west on Nevada Avenue from U.S. Highway 97. The small, gravel parking area is on the left, shortly after the road becomes Lakeshore Drive and before you round the bend and cross the bridge. If you reach Moore Park (where dogs are not allowed), you've gone too far.

29 Veterans Memorial Park

🐾🐾 (See Southern Oregon map on page 408)

In this hot, dry town near the California border, this city park may be the only place where you can picnic in the shade of large trees. The football-sized lawn also has steps for sitting in the sun, restrooms, and big steam engine trains on display.

It's on the south end of downtown at the bottom of Main Street, which has a couple of great places to grab a picnic lunch before heading to the park.

PLACES TO EAT

Café Paradise: Mexican food and American fare sit side-by-side on the extensive menu, and it's all good. Cooper is biased toward the Mexican side of the border, with to-drool-for quesadillas and deep-fried ice cream. There's easy ordering through a to-go window. 1401 Esplanade; 541/850-2225.

The Daily Bagel: The custom bagel sandwiches, named after big-city U.S. newspapers, are so fat they're almost impossible to fit your mouth around. You're highly likely to drop sandwich filling, and nothing would please your pooch more. It's a cash-only establishment with sidewalk tables, also offering daily soups and Ben & Jerry's ice cream bars. 636 Main St.; 541/850-1809.

PLACES TO STAY

Maverick Motel: This downtown establishment prefers to accept dogs for a couple of days only, not weeks or months. Each pet is $5 per stay, and rates are $39–59. Rooms are crisp and clean, with a full list of amenities including continental breakfast and afternoon cookies and milk. Afternoon naps are also encouraged. 1220 Main St.; 541/882-6688 or 800/404-6690; www.maverickmotel.com.

Running Y Ranch Resort: If you enjoy running with a high-brow crowd, as Isis certainly does, you'll love this upscale western ranch on the grounds of Oregon's only Arnold Palmer–designed golf course. Everything is as nice as you'd expect, from the leather furniture, timbered ceilings, and flagstone floors to the views of the greens and surrounding mountains. Rates are $139–179 per night, plus a $20 pet fee. 5500 Running Y Rd.; 541/850-5500 or 888/850-0275; www.runningy.com.

Spring Creek Ranch: At this motel, the rooms and cabins are spartan with tile floors and cement walls, on 25 acres of sweet nothing. Regulars come for Spring Creek, a fascinating natural phenomenon in the back yard. It's a three-mile river fed from an unknown subterranean source. It never varies from 38°F, never rises or lowers more than an inch, and is so clear you can read a newspaper at the bottom from 50 feet above. They stock the river every summer weekend with 1,200 trout. Rooms are $50–65, cabins are $80, and there's no charge for pets. Live-in hounds are Caesar, who will greet you, and Molly, who will try to herd you. 47600 Hwy. 97, Chiloquin; 541/783-2775.

More Accommodations: Please look under Chain Hotels in the Resources section for additional places to stay in this area.

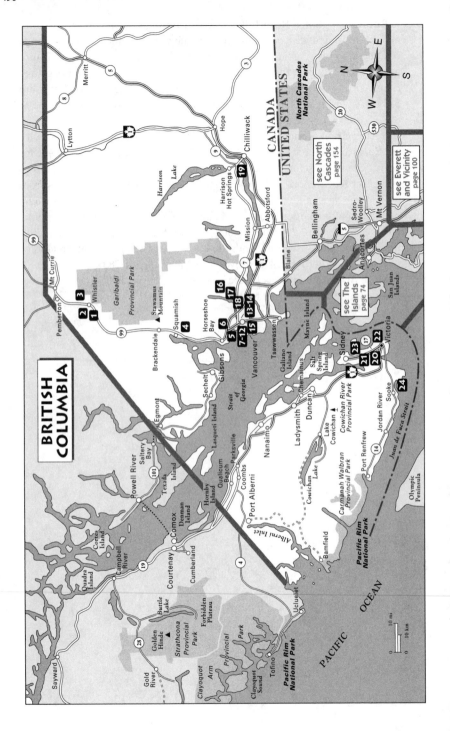

BRITISH COLUMBIA

CANADA

To a Dachshund, which is pronounced DASH-hound up north, Canada seems like an awfully big place. So much of the Great White North requires sled dogs to visit, and taking your mush team on vacation is a subject for a different book entirely. Knowing you'd have your paws full with Washington and Oregon, the Wonder Wieners decided to include only three key destinations in the province of British Columbia this go-around: Whistler, Vancouver, and Victoria. Even then, in these incredibly dog-friendly cities, their stubby little legs only got them so far, hardly scratching the surface of the region's dog parks and other recreation possibilities.

In general, Canada is very dog-friendly and more relaxed than the States. In many parks, having your dogs under voice control is comparable to having them on leash. Restaurants were the only places where the Dachsie Twins found Canada to be as strict as the United States; British Columbia health code does not allow dogs on restaurant patios.

It was nearly impossible to pin down rates for hotels in Vancouver. Rates change drastically between seasons and even more dramatically based on how full they often are in this popular international destination. All rates for hotels and other expenses are listed in Canadian dollars.

If your canine wants to blend in like a true Canuck, she can start by adding the expression "eh?" at the end of every bark. For example: "Sure is good Canadian maple syrup, eh?" or "I'm renting my house out for the 2010 Olympics for ten grand. Good idea, eh?" By the way, if you do want to go anywhere near Vancouver or Whistler in the winter of 2010, book now. The Olympics will be there, and everything will be gone soon, probably from Portland, Oregon, on up.

Prior to 9/11, crossing the border from the United States to Canada was a more casual affair, usually only requiring a driver's license or picture ID. Today the rules are strict and uniformly enforced. United States travelers must have either a Passport *or* a Birth Certificate and Photo ID *or* a Naturalization Certificate, *or* a Citizenship Certificate. For canines crossing the border from the United States to Canada, proof of rabies vaccination is required. Bring proof of other shots and a health certificate from your dog's veterinarian, just in case.

CHAPTER 16
British Columbia

In Canada, there are provinces instead of states, and thus, provincial parks instead of state parks. In the province of British Columbia, with the exception of parks listed here, check in advance before visiting regional or provincial parks. Some parks prohibit dogs in the high season, generally May–August, and most prohibit dogs on public beaches June 1–September 15.

The best times for a dog to visit British Columbia are April–May and September 16–October. Lodging establishments call this the shoulder season, and room rates are significantly cheaper than in the high season. This is when provincial parks open up beaches to dogs, but the weather isn't uniformly gray. Vancouverites and Victorians insist they don't get as much drizzle as Seattle; Isis might raise an eyebrow at that, if she had one.

Vancouver and Victoria are within easy reach of the United States, the former a three-hour drive from Seattle, and the latter by a ferry ride from Seattle; Port Angeles, Washington; or Vancouver. Whistler, farther into the imposing mountains, is about a six-hour drive from Seattle, the latter part on the Sea to Sky Highway, a twisty two-lane road sandwiched between the cliffs and

PICK OF THE LITTER— BRITISH COLUMBIA

BEST PARKS

Stanley Park, West End (page 450)

Belcarra Regional Park, Tri-Cities Area (page 457)

BEST DOG PARKS AND BEACHES

Ambleside Beach and Dog Park, West Vancouver (page 445)

Vanier Dog Beach, Kitsilano (page 447)

Buntzen Lake Dog Beach, Tri-Cities Area (page 457)

Dallas Beach in Beacon Hill Park, Victoria (page 463)

BEST PLACES TO EAT

Val D'Isere Brasserie, Whistler (page 442)

The Urban Barkery, Tri-Cities Area (page 458)

Waddling Dog Bar and Grill, Sidney-Saanich (page 462)

BEST PLACES TO STAY

Pacific Palisades Hotel, Downtown Vancouver (page 452)

Pacific Spirit Guest House, Cambie (page 455)

Annabelle's Cottage, Victoria (page 466)

Sooke Harbour House, Sooke (page 469)

the water. This road's dangerous beauty requires attentive driving, preferably in the daytime, although improvements are being made to accommodate the 2010 Olympics. Tires and snow chains are required in winter.

Whistler

The resort municipality of Whistler is an internationally famous ski and golf destination, and everything is priced accordingly. Whistler Village is compact, designed to explore on foot, with a pedestrian-only Village Stroll leading to all the shops, restaurants, and resorts.

Schussing and slicing are two activities not particularly high on a dog's wish list, due to the technical difficulties. To allow you to engage in skiing fun without puppy guilt, Whistler has a good dog day-care option. Try the **Puppy Zone Dog Day Care and Adventure Centre** (4295 Blackcomb Way #117; 604/905-6704; www.puppyzone.com) open 8 A.M.–6 P.M., 365 days

DOG-EAR YOUR CALENDAR

Did you ever see the cell phone commercial where a ranch hand ordered 200 oxen and got 200 dachshunds instead? If you are a dachshund fan and your travel plans are taking you anywhere near British Columbia in mid-August, you can experience more than 200 wieners first-hand at the **Annual Picnic and Wiener Walk** organized by The Western Dachshund Club at Winskill Park in Tsawassen, B.C. Since 1998, these hot dogs have been coming—many in costume—to show off in a parade and play games. Stampede! Find out more on the unofficial Canadian Dachshund Lovers' Web page at www.wienerdogs.org.

In the resort town of Whistler, **DogFest** is held every April, the last weekend of the TELUS World Ski and Snowboard Festival. There's a dog parade, booths, contests, raffles, and general merrymaking and mayhem to support Whistler Animals Galore (WAG) and the Canadian Avalanche Rescue Dog Association (CARDA, www.carda.bc.ca). Money is raised by donations. Contact the main sponsor and organizer, the Puppy Zone, for more information, 604/905-6705; www.puppyzone.com.

In Vancouver, *Pet Lovers Digest* magazine holds its annual **Pet Lovers Digest Celebration** every September, although the exact dates and locations vary. The pet party includes booths, agility courses, hot dogs, games, music, fashion, and a fun kid zone. The kids and dogs are free, adults are $5, to benefit the Pacific Assistance Dog Society and the Network for Animals in Distress. 604/702-3352; www.petloversdigest.com.

a year. Puppy Zone will hotel-sit after hours and take dogs overnight by special arrangement.

Whistler resorts spoil pets, as does the abundance of open space and fresh mountain air, not to mention a few treats and pats from shops in town. Dogs are required to be on leash in the municipality. They are not allowed on beaches, except ones reserved for them, and they are not allowed on trails on Whistler Mountain or in nearby Garibaldi Provincial Park.

Valley Trail: This paved multi-use path connects all things throughout the valley, including the parks a dog might wish to visit. You can rent bikes and strollers in Whistler Village if walking the 30 kilometers (19 miles) gets too long. There are excellent trail markers at all points along the trail, and most maps of Whistler include the path.

PARKS, BEACHES, AND RECREATION AREAS

🐾 Alpha Lake Park

🐾🐾 (See British Columbia map on page 436)

A leashed stroll around this small lake is an attractive option for a walk, across a suspended bridge and through light wooded areas. Children get a charge out of the treehouse playground, a focal point of the park. Dogs are allowed in the picnic area, but not on the main beach.

For dogs, water access at Alpha Lake is a fluid concept: Sometimes there is a designated dog area, and sometimes there's not. Occasionally, there's a dog beach with limited hours. It depends on the season, the crowds, and the number of complaints the municipality gets from residents. Watch for any signs, and behave accordingly. Facilities include restrooms and a doggy bag dispenser.

Alpha Lake Park is located in Creekside, 2.5 miles south of Whistler Village. From Highway 99, turn west on Lake Placid Drive, around the bend only about .1 mile to the gravel parking area on your right. You can reach the park from the Valley Trail.

🐾 Barking Bay at Rainbow Park

🐾🐾🐕 (See British Columbia map on page 436)

Rainbow Park is on the west side of Alta Lake, a large lake south of Whistler Village with several parks. Along Alta, there are long, sandy beaches with walk-on docks, picnic areas with barbecue grills, volleyball courts, and a heritage site with three log cabins. Lucky dogs will find their reward at the end of the Rainbow, at Barking Bay, a private, miniature dog beach and picnic area. The bay has a couple of petite lawns with tables and a sliver of sandy beach. Dock dogs will love their private floating pier. Beyond Barking Bay, dogs must leash up. If it gets too busy during the summer, dog beach hours may be limited; watch for signs.

There are multiple walking and hiking options starting at Rainbow Park. One of the most scenic sections of the paved Valley Trail travels between Rainbow Park and Meadow Park, following the river of golden dreams. For serious hikers, the five-mile Rainbow Falls–Rainbow Lake trail starts on the west side of Alta Lake Road, just north of the park. It links to another good choice, the Madley Lake Route, a 5.5-mile climb winding through the fir trees.

From Highway 99, 2.7 miles south of the center of Whistler Village, turn west on Alta Lake Road and travel three miles to the paved parking lot. To reach the off-leash beach, go the right from the parking lot, through the Railway Crossing bars, across the wide wooden footbridge, and to the right around the lake a few hundred feet.

❸ Canine Cove at Lost Lake Park

🐾🐾🐾🐕 (See British Columbia map on page 436)

Within walking distance from Whistler Village on the valley trail, Lost Lake Park offers barbecues, picnic areas, sandy beaches, a concession stand, plenty of grassy spots, floating docks, and walk-on docks from several locations around the lake.

The Lost Lake Loop, a wide gravel road, is a great walk. If you start on the trail, to the right around the lake from the main parking lot, you'll reach a private dog beach at about .25 mile. Canine Cove has a sandy beach, sitting logs, a bag dispenser, and its own floating dock with a ramp dogs can climb. This exclusive area is a real treat.

Cooper recommends Lost Lake as the most scenic of the three lakes near town, with the best unpaved, easy trails as well. You can get a map online or at visitors centers, but the soft-surface trails winding around south of the lake aren't very long, and eventually you'll hit the Lake Loop or the Valley Trail or Fitzsimmons Creek to get your bearings again. It's a relatively safe area in which to lose yourselves in the woods for a time. www.whistler.ca/recreation/hiking.html.

PLACES TO EAT

Citta Bistro: Ask a local for a friendly, not too stuffy place to eat in the Village, and you'll hear Citta 9 times out of 10. The menu changes regularly, leaning toward lighter fare. The patio is covered and heated for year-round outdoor eating, and dogs have their own hangout area nearby. 4217 Village Stroll; 604/932-4177; www.cittabistro.com.

Dubh Linn Gate Pub: This great Irish bar is one of the most crowded aprés-ski spots, right at the base of the mountain. The bar stocks 30 draft beers, 28 single-malt scotches, and without question, Guinness on tap. Although famed for its Crab and Guinness soup, the pub will serve you food without alcohol in it, if you insist. There's a large outdoor patio, and dogs can tie up nearby, within sight. Whistler Village, Pan Pacific Lodge; 604/905-4047.

Val D'Isere Brasserie: This full-service French restaurant is one of your most elegant dog-friendly choices in town, with patio tables in the summer season only. Ask to be seated around the border of the patio, where there is a low rock wall your dog can relax up against and a couple of lampposts where you could secure his leash if needed. 4314 Main Street; 604/932-4666; www.valdisere-restaurant.com.

Zogs Dogs: At summertime kiosk locations in Whistler Village and at the Sundial Lodge, Zogs serves a signature dog smothered in spaghetti sauce and mozzarella cheese (don't knock it until you've tried it), and "Beaver Tails" (fried dough in various cheesy and spicy flavors). There are picnic tables at the Whistler Village location. Village Stroll; no phone.

PLACES TO STAY

Chateau Whistler: This Fairmont property is high on the luxury scale. The pet fee is $25 total per night, and they'll allow a couple of pets, as they said, as long as there's no fighting among them! The hotel will send up biscuits, water bowls, and beds for pet guests. You'll lack nothing. Rates range $169–999 for standard rooms depending on the season. 604/938-8000 or 800/684-6344; www.chateauwhistler.com.

Crystal Lodge: This mid-range hotel is at the base of both Whistler and Blackcomb Mountains. Dogs are greeted with a welcome letter and pet beds, in rooms on two of the three floors. All rooms are nonsmoking. Rates range $125–310 for traditional rooms, higher for suites; the pet fee is $20. 4154 Village Green; 604/932-2221 or 800/667-3363; www.crystal-lodge.com.

Summit Lodge: The contemporary furnishings at this Kimpton boutique hotel are designed to help you and Rover relax and restore. A secluded walkway behind the hotel meanders along Fitzsimmons Creek. Dog lovers get treats and bags at check-in, and there are no pet fees or limits, but you must ask specifically for a nonsmoking room if you want one. Rates range $119–450. 4359 Main Street; 604/932-2778 or 888/913-8811; www.summitlodge.com.

Tantalus Lodge: The Tantalus Lodge has large, fully equipped, two-bedroom, two-bath suites, which are good for families, and 6.5 acres of property, good for pets. The Delta hotels in Whistler, including the Tantalus, go the extra mile to let people know they are pet-friendly, with a full set of pet goodies and convenience items listed on the website. Rates are based on four-person occupancy and range widely, based on season and demand, $149–689. There is a $15 one-time cleaning fee for pets. 4200 Whistler Way; 604/932-4146 or 888/633-4046; www.tantaluslodge.com.

Squamish

In a country legendary for outdoor recreation, this town's claim to be Canada's capital of outdoor recreation seems excessive. Then again, after climbing Stawamus Chief Mountain, you may feel like you've done all of Canada. When heading to Whistler, some people choose to stay in Squamish, about 45 minutes south, for cheaper accommodations and all kinds of hiking, biking, rafting, golfing, bird-watching, horseback riding, and other things you can do with dogs.

PARKS, BEACHES, AND RECREATION AREAS

4 Shannon Falls Provincial Park

🐾 🐾 🐾 (See British Columbia map on page 436)

People are falling all over themselves to get to Shannon Falls. At 335 meters (1,105 feet), it is British Columbia's third-highest falls, one of the most popular picnic spots along the Sea to Sky corridor. It's worth a look to see the spray foam and tumble over the smooth granite walls, even though your pup might feel the pinch of the crowds during all but the earliest days of spring or the last gasps of fall. There are 500,000 annual visitors in the park but only 50,000 on the hike up Stawamus Chief Mountain, a great place to take a fit canine if you want to cut the crowds.

This monolith is internationally famous among climbers, and its smooth granite face has appeared on more than its share of outdoor-type magazine covers. There are three summit points you can hike to, depending on how far—or rather how high—you choose to go. The hikes range from four to seven miles round-trip. The trails can be reached from the parking lot and viewpoint at Shannon Falls, where there is a basic and a topographic map of the trails. The hikes are all challenging, steady climbs that will really get your and your pooch's blood pumping.

Shannon Falls Provincial Park is located two miles (three km) south of Squamish and 16 miles (25 km) north of Horseshoe Bay on Vancouver's North Shore. Parking is $1 per hour or $3 per day by automated ticket machine. Open 7 A.M.–10 P.M.

PLACES TO EAT

Cheekye Bar and Grill: This restaurant is out there, out near the Cheekye River, close to great fishing and rafting at the Sunwolf Outdoor Centre. The owners always play blues music, frequently smoke their own salmon and chicken and make their own bread and burgers, and often seem to have dogs around the picnic tables in the garden below the outdoor deck. 70002 Squamish Valley Rd.; 604/898-4011.

PLACES TO STAY

Sunwolf Outdoor Centre: Come to the Sunwolf's cabins when you want to escape. This is where nightlife is a hoot owl and rush hour is the rushing waters of the Cheekye, Cheakamus, and Squamish Rivers. This mountain resort and river rafting tour company is situated on 5.5 acres of park and wooded land, where dogs get a new lease on life by being unleashed and by jumping into the water if the spirit moves them. The Sunwolf is an equal-opportunity pet facility, accepting snakes, cats, llamas, etc., in addition to good old Snoopys. Five cabins have kitchenettes, and all 10 renovated cabins have showers, cathedral ceilings, gas fireplaces, fir floors, and handcrafted pine furniture, nothing more or less than you need. The main lodge is a perfect place to meet, gather information, and plan an outing. Books, topographic maps, and friendly, experienced staff help you decide what to do and where to go. Come for the annual dog festival, It's a Dog's Life, every September. Basic cabins are $90 per night;

cabins with kitchenettes are $100. There is a flat $10 fee per visit for pets. 70002 Squamish Valley Rd.; 604/898-1537 or 877/806-8046; www.sunwolf.net.

West Vancouver

The city of Vancouver and surrounding cities and suburbs have an extensive network of full-time and part-time off-leash areas. These dog beaches and parks are rarely secured by fences or gates, reinforcing the expectation that you have complete voice control of your dog. You are required to pick up after your dog, carry a leash at all times, and observe the designated boundaries and time limits. There are excellent aerial photographs of the off-leash boundaries on the Vancouver Park Board website. Go to www.city.vancouver .bc.ca/parks/parks/index.htm and click the Dog Off-Leash Areas link. Of a few outstanding dog destinations, West Vancouver starts it all off with one of the best.

PARKS, BEACHES, AND RECREATION AREAS

5 Ambleside Beach and Dog Park

🐾🐾🐾🐾🐕 (See British Columbia map on page 436)

Half of this district park is off-limits to dogs, whether leashed or not. The other half is all for the dogs, whether leashed or not. The eastern half of Ambleside is a beautiful sandy off-leash beach, with extensive fields, bunches of trees, and a paved path for dogs' human companions with views of Vancouver, Stanley Park, Lions Gate Bridge, and Burrard Inlet. Your dog will agree it's a great place to watch sunsets over Vancouver Island, especially if you got there in time for sunrise the same day.

The off-leash area is bordered by the end of the parking lot, the pitch and putt course with a high fence, the railroad with a high fence, the Capilano River, and the Inlet.

Cross the Lions Gate Bridge through Stanley Park, turn left on Marine Drive, and left on 13th Street, down the hill and curving to the left into the park. To reach the off-leash area, you can stay on the road until you can't go any farther, and at the end of that parking lot will be the west end of the OLA. Or, you can turn left into the first parking lot you see, find the alley road at the end of the lot and take it until you can't go any farther, to the east end of the OLA, which is where the Dog Walk signs will direct you. There will be parking problems on sunny weekends and holidays.

THINK GLOBALLY, BARK LOCALLY

The British Columbia Society for the Prevention of Cruelty to Animals (BCSPCA) has six thrift stores in and around the Vancouver area that contribute valuable funds each year for the operation of animal shelters. The **SPCA Thrift Stores** receive donations, similar to Goodwill, and volunteers run the stores. For more information, go to www.spca.bc.ca/vancouver/thriftstores.htm. The locations in Vancouver are:

Vancouver (West)
Furniture: 3626 West Broadway;   Clothing: 3606 West Broadway
604/736-4136
Open 10 A.M.–6:30 P.M. Monday–Sunday

Vancouver (East)
5239 Victoria Drive (at 37th)
604/321-8144
Open 10 A.M.–6:30 P.M. Monday–Sunday

North Vancouver

PARKS, BEACHES, AND RECREATION AREAS

⑥ Capilano Suspension Bridge and Park

🐾🐾 ◀● (See British Columbia map on page 436)

The Capilano Suspension Bridge is Vancouver's biggest attraction, surrounded by the serenity of a 300-year-old West Coast rainforest. Even dogs with strong stomachs will appreciate that today's bridge is held up by steel cables, capable of supporting two fully loaded 747s, as opposed to the twisted hemp ropes used in the first bridge, built in 1889. Capilano Bridge is a dizzying 230 feet above the canyon floor and a dazzling 450 feet across. Each step creates a wave of action on the bridge surface. Relax—it's supposed to be fun!

Capilano Park continues to preserve and show the art and culture of First Nations artists, ever since Native people were invited to place totem poles and life-size red cedar statues in the park in the 1930s. The collection of totems and the ongoing work at the Big House Carving Centre are additional areas you shouldn't miss on a visit to the park. If you have kids of the two-legged variety, every area has extensive displays to teach and entertain them. The West Coast Rainforest trails, short walks through old-growth evergreens, will round out the adventure for Rover.

From downtown Vancouver, cross through Stanley Park over the Lions Gate Bridge and travel north one mile on Capilano Road. Dogs are allowed everywhere except the on the Treetop Adventure, in the gift shop, or in the Bridge House Restaurant. The park is open every day except December 25. Summer hours are 8:30 A.M.–dusk; winter hours are 9 A.M.–5 P.M. Cost is $23.50 per day for adults; dogs aren't charged. 3735 Capilano Rd.; 604/985-7474; www.capbridge.com.

PLACES TO EAT

Canyon Café and Logger's Grill: From May through September, this food stand in Capilano Park cooks up beef, chicken, and salmon burgers and feeds hungry park-goers with homemade pizza, muffins, and cookies. It's an over-the-counter affair, with plenty of open seating. 3735 Capilano Rd.; 604/985-7474; www.capbridge.com.

PLACES TO STAY

Lonsdale Quay Hotel: One pet is allowed in one room of this hotel, hidden on the third floor of a popular food and shopping market. Technically, the dog is supposed to be less than 50 pounds, although the staff is admittedly unscientific and liberal when applying the poundage policy. Rates are seasonally adjusted, $79–165. Your pet will add $25 to the nightly bill, for which she'll receive a basket with a loaner blanket and water bowl, treats, and scoop bags. 123 Carrie Cates Ct.; 604/986-6111; www.lonsdalequayhotel.com.

Kitsilano

"Kits" is one of the younger, hipper neighborhoods in Vancouver, with rows of California bungalows—craftsman-style homes—lining its fashionable streets. Our coverage of dog parks in Vancouver proper starts in this area, with a whopper of an off-leash beach.

PARKS, BEACHES, AND RECREATION AREAS

⑦ Vanier Dog Beach

😃😃😃😃🐾 (See British Columbia map on page 436)

Dogs are loving life at Vanier. As designated dog areas go, it doesn't get much better than this. The off-leash area of the park includes a large lawn on the bluff, a portion of the waterfront trail, and prime beachfront real estate, which is where you'll find all the barkers clustered. The leash-free zone is the area behind and to the west of the Vancouver Maritime Museum. The beach itself is down a short set of stairs—just follow the splashing sounds. Large driftwood logs give you a place to relax, close enough to the water to keep you from injuring your stick-throwing arm. From Vanier, you can leash up and walk along the water all the way through Hadden Park to Kitsilano Beach Park. Vanier Park hosts Bard on the Beach, Shakespearean outdoor theater, in the summer; however, dogs are not allowed in theater areas, not even those who can bark in verse.

From downtown, cross the Burrard Bridge and bear to the right onto Cornwall Avenue. Turn right almost immediately on Chestnut Drive to the end. It costs $1.25 per hour, maximum of four hours, to park in the museum lot in front of the OLA. If it's not too crowded, you may be able to find street parking by turning left on Ogden in front of the museum and left on Maple a block down.

Off-leash hours are 6–10 A.M. and 5–10 P.M., May–Sept. and 6 A.M.–10 P.M. Oct.–April. 1000 Chestnut Street; 604/257-8689.

🐾 Kitsilano Beach

🐾🐾 (See British Columbia map on page 436)

The city's fashionable people have been coming to Kits Beach for more than a hundred years to soak up the sun and, honestly, to check each other out. While dogs aren't allowed on the sand, canines are a trendy accessory for picnickers up on the wide lawns, judging by the number of fur-bearers basking alongside the bikini and board-shorts types. Walking along the waterfront around Kits, leash in hand, is a good way to meet Vancouver's young and restless. When your dog stops to sniff that cute stranger's dog, it's a natural segue to strike up a conversation about the great views of the North Shore mountains and downtown, the weather, your need for a knowledgeable tour guide while visiting the city...that sort of thing.

From downtown, cross the Burrard Bridge and veer to the right on Cornwall Avenue. Turn right on Arbutus Street. Parking is $1 for two hours, $3 all day, by automated machine. 1499 Arbutus Street.

PLACES TO EAT

Bean Brothers: Sidewalk seating is a natural at this casual café and coffee shop, serving light lunches and dinners and pizza by the slice. 2179 West 41st Ave.; 604/266-2185.

Incendio: The sidewalk café tables with colorful umbrellas lend such a European air to this brick-oven pizzeria and fresh pastaria that it has frequently been used for on-location TV and film shooting as "an unspecified city somewhere in Italy or France." It's easy for your dog to sit with you at the Kitsilano location, at 118 Burrard St.; 604/736-2220. A second Gastown location has an enclosed patio, where dogs would have to sit on the other side of the railing; 103 Columbia St.; 604.688.8694; www.incendio.ca.

The Smoking Dog: This classy restaurant wins accolades and awards for its authentic French cuisine. The outdoor dining scene is hot at *Le Chien Qui Fumé,* and neither you nor your dog have to light up to enjoy it. 1889 West 1st Ave.; 604/732-8811; www.thesmokingdog.com.

Three Dog Bakery: Cooper and Isis have no qualms about advertising this franchise, the original, and still one of the best, dog-exclusive bakeries in North America. The Vancouver location is at 2186 W. 4th Ave.; 604/737-3647 or 888/433-3647.

PLACES TO STAY

Kitsilano Guest Suites: This large home has three self-contained suites. Dogs are welcome in all suites, and the Garden Suite is the most convenient, with ground-level access to the property's beautiful gardens. All suites are stocked to the gills with amenities, including treats and toys to welcome pets. Resident cat Benny and boxer-Dane mix Lola can assist you with additional services, including dog-walking, sitters, day care, grooming, and vets. Rates are for up to four people, with a three-night minimum, starting at $190 per night. Pets may be subject to additional charges, but they'll decide on the details with you when you call to make arrangements. 2216 W. 14th Ave.; 604/734-5832; www.kitsguestsuites.com.

Point Grey

PARKS, BEACHES, AND RECREATION AREAS

🔢 Spanish Bank West Dog Beach

🐾🐾🐾🐕 (See British Columbia map on page 436)

As you pass miles of beach parks along West Point Grey—Jericho Beach Park, Locarno Beach Park, Spanish Bank East Park—your dog will be sorely tempted to jump out of the car and run to the water. At the very least, he'll beg to walk along the seaside trail, which he's welcome to do on leash. But if he can wait just a bit longer, he can taste freedom and be left to his own dog devices on the off-leash zones of Spanish Bank West.

In the off-leash area, across the wide lawns and picnic tables, past the willow trees, and beyond the paved waterfront walk is a long and narrow beach, with choice sand and gentle lapping waves. The park has great views of the water and mountains and is far enough from downtown to avoid the worst of the crowds, canine and otherwise.

From downtown, take the Granville Bridge, and go west on 4th Avenue W., past Jerico Beach Park. At the sign for Spanish Bank, bear right onto N.W. Marine Drive and patiently follow the road all the way to the end of the last parking lot you see before Acadia Beach and Pacific Spirit Regional Park. From there, the entire area in front of you is the OLA. Off-leash hours are 6 A.M.–10 P.M. 4801 N.W. Marine Dr.; 604/257-8689.

🔟 Pacific Spirit Regional Park

😊😊😊🐾 (See British Columbia map on page 436)

The Greater Vancouver Regional District takes the intelligent approach that dogs are great companions for exercise, safety, and socializing in parks. To welcome an average of 360,000 dog visits per year at Pacific Spirit Regional Park, the GVRD has created a Dog Management Pilot Program to designate leash-optional hiking options, to educate and enforce good canine etiquette, and to protect the park's sensitive areas and wildlife.

Sure, lots of dogs visit Pacific Spirit, but it's a big park, 1,800 acres with 34 miles of trails. Coop 'n' Isis applaud the spirit of allowing dogs off-leash on the park's hiking trails. In practice, it takes some studying of the park map before you can figure out where dogs are prohibited, where dogs are allowed on leash, and where dogs are allowed off-leash. Cooper likes to start on the north end of the park, from the small parking area immediately to the west of Spanish Bank Park. All the trails into the woods are leash-optional from this starting point.

Follow the directions to Spanish Bank West, going past the city's parking lot to a gravel lot for the GVRD park. Open 8 A.M.–7 P.M., as late as 11 P.M. in the summer. 604/224-5739; www.gvrd.bc.ca/parks/PacificSprit.htm.

West End

PARKS, BEACHES, AND RECREATION AREAS

1️⃣1️⃣ Stanley Park

😊😊😊😊 (See British Columbia map on page 436)

Stanley Park is Vancouver's first and finest park and North America's third-largest urban park. Stanley's 1,000 acres became an official park in 1888, and the elected committee set up to govern it has evolved into Vancouver's Board of Parks and Recreation, one of the only elected park management bodies in Canada. There are so many things to do and see in this city park, it shouldn't concern you that many of them don't involve dogs. The internal hiking trails, the gardens, and the lagoons can take days to explore, if you have the luxuries of time and stamina. Drawing an estimated eight million annual visitors, Stanley Park is never quiet—nothing this good ever is.

Cooper and Isis chose to get to the heart of what's best about the park by staying around its perimeter, on the 5.5-mile Seawall Promenade. To them, everything else is the white chocolate coating on the biscuit. It took nearly six decades to complete the seawall, from the 1920s to the 1980s. For most of the way, the paved trail is divided to separate pedestrians and leashed dogs from cyclists and in-line skaters. Every section of the trail adds another vista or attraction to the list, some of which can be enjoyed simply from a drive through the park.

From downtown, take Georgia Street W., Highway 99/1A, west to Stanley Park Drive, find the nearest parking lot, and start walking. Parking is $4 per day. Parking lots are open 6 A.M.–9 P.M. Apr.–Sept.; 7 A.M.–6 P.M. Oct.–March. 604/257-8400; www.city.vancouver.bc.ca/parks/parks/stanley.

Downtown Vancouver and Gastown

Of all the things to do in downtown Vancouver, shopping and dining on Robson Street hits the top of the list, followed in short order by a visit to Gastown, the birthplace of Vancouver and the location of Vancouver's most-photographed icon, the Gastown Steam Clock (www.seegastown.com).

PARKS, BEACHES, AND RECREATION AREAS

12 CRAB-Portside Dog Park

🐾🐾🐾 🦀 (See British Columbia map on page 436)

From your perch on a big rock, a driftwood log, or a bench, you can sit and reflect on life, watching the tugboats tug and the container ships being loaded and the few dogs running circles around each other. This medium-sized park has the closest off-leash area to the downtown core, but locals say it's not heavily used. It's nice enough, with gently sloping green lawns, a crushed-rock walkway, and restroom, water fountain, and garbage facilities. It could be underutilized because it's in an industrial area or because the water doesn't meet safety standards for people to swim in it. It serves a dog's purposes perfectly, as long as you're comfortable with your canine cavorting in an unfenced area.

Technically, the boundaries of the off-leash area stop short of the beach cove, along the gravel walkway. For the purposes of this book, the Dachsie Twins have to toe the official party line. What line your toes cross is up to you. When in Vancouver, do as the Vancouverites do.

From downtown, go north on Main Street, Highway 99A/1A, through Chinatown, over the bridge and around to the left onto Waterfront Road. The park will be to your right. The only parking for miles is a pay lot a block to your left. It's $2 per hour, or any part thereof, or only $4 per day. That little devil sitting on your shoulder, suggesting you might as well stay all day, looks surprisingly like your dog. No dogs are allowed within 15 meters (50 feet) of the playground. Off-leash hours are 6–10 A.M. and 5–10 P.M. 101 E. Waterfront Rd.; 604/257-8400.

DIVERSION

Rarely will you meet anyone with such a serious case of puppy love as dog photographer Tracy Lydiatt. Tracy says that no photo shoot is complete until she has nose prints on her lens and dog hairs on her person. "Dog slobber is my favorite camera accessory!" she declares with a straight face. We know mastiff owners who can't say as much.

Las Almas Photography will come to you, wherever your dog can most be herself, to deliver soulful pet photography in crisp, powerful black and white images. Tracy will spend about an hour and a half for a session and give you as little or as much creative input as you like when the prints come in, either digitally or viewed in person. On a visit to Vancouver, your dog's mug is a souvenir you'll treasure longer than a coffee mug. 604/649-5359; www.lasalmas.ca.

PLACES TO EAT

Brioche Urban Baking and Catering: This Italian-meets-West Coast casual eatery apologizes for its big selection and inventive daily specials, knowing that doesn't make it easier for you to choose between dashing in for a pastry and a cuppa' to go or a full meal made from scratch, relaxing with furry friends at summertime sidewalk tables. 401 W. Cordova St.; 604/682-4037; www.brioche.ca.

The Irish Heather: The manager says dogs are welcome in the back patio area as long as they buy their own drinks. Ha, there's no chance of that—mutts are consummate moochers! The bonny Heather is an authentic Irish public house, owned by Irish people who actually work in the bar. It leads the trend of "GastroPubs," i.e. pubs that serve fresh and fancy food in an unstuffy environment. 217 Carrall St.; 604/688-9779.

PLACES TO STAY

Georgian Court Hotel: All of this hotel's roomy quarters combine gracious, old-world style with newfangled amenities such as pillow-top mattresses and high-speed Internet. Small pets are welcome, for a flat $20 cleaning fee per visit. Nightly rates in high season (May 1–Oct. 15) range $165–360; low season (Oct. 16–Apr. 30) is $115–245. 773 Beatty St.; 604/682-5555 or 800/663-1155; www.georgiancourt.com.

Pacific Palisades Hotel: Located on trendy Robson Street in downtown Vancouver, the Pacific Palisades has South Beach Florida–inspired décor to brighten up those rainy, gray Vancouver days. Citrus-colored interiors look out to great views of the mountains, city, or harbor. This boutique embraces the legendary pet-friendliness of all Kimpton hotels, featuring a Four Paws Program. For a flat $25 fee, $5 of which will be donated to the local SPCA, dogs receive a Doggie Bag including freshly baked dog biscuits, plastic bags, souvenir orange flying disc, and discount coupons for Petcetera. Pet owners will receive a complimentary glass of wine and, through the concierge, can arrange for day care or an appointment at a local grooming salon (for their dogs or for themselves). Rates range $140–390. 1277 Robson St.; 604/688-0461 or 800/663-1815; www.pacificpalisadeshotel.com.

More Accommodations: Please look under Chain Hotels in the Resources section for additional places to stay in this area.

Granville Island

This hidden spot is a great place to spend a few hours. Dozens of outdoor shops and market stands sell seafood, jewelry, crafts, fresh fruit and vegetables, and cut flowers. There are food vendor kiosks where you can grab a bite to eat and sit on a bench to watch the other people and dogs go by. Several stores are dog-friendly, especially Blackberry Books, which offers dog treats.

Parking is tough on Granville Island, so your best bet is to take the inexpensive and fun False Creek Ferry. It's a short ride from downtown on the north to Granville, and as an added bonus, there's a tiny off-leash dog beach next to the north ferry terminal at Sunset Beach. Ferries run continuously 7 A.M.–10:30 P.M. in the summer, until 8:30 P.M. in winter. www.granvilleislandferries.bc.ca.

PARKS, BEACHES, AND RECREATION AREAS

🆔 Sutcliffe Park and the Island Park Walk

🐾 (See British Columbia map on page 436)

There's no chance Isis would allow your dog to be stuck on an island with no place to pee. For a dog who weighs 12 pounds soaking wet, she manages to wet more than her fair share of blades of grass in pursuit of the perfect piddle. She declares these petite gardens, ponds, and stone paver promenades will do nicely, thank you, discreetly hidden between the shops of Granville Island and the condos surrounding it.

As you drive onto Granville Island on Anderson Street, Sutcliffe Park and the Island Park Walk are to the right. The closest parking is near the Woofles and Meowz pet specialty diner, what a coincidence, or in front of The Cat's Meow.

PLACES TO EAT

The Cat's Meow: Vancouverites do indeed consider this diner with American flair to be the cat's meow. Your bow-wow can sit along the fringes of the patio, lassoed to a wooden railing, consoled with a water bowl. 1540 Old Bridge St.; 604/647-2287.

Dockside Restaurant: Dining al fresco is possible for more of the year at Granville Island Hotel's patio, with sun umbrellas, overhead gas heaters, garden flowers, and colorful tablecloths, plus views of False Creek, Vancouver City's skyline, and the Coastal Mountains. The transition from the patio to Granville Island's brick streets is pretty seamless, allowing dogs to sit nearby and graciously accept the water bowls and treats put out for them. 1253 Johnston St.; 604/685-7070.

Granville Island Brewery: The Taproom and gift shop at the GIB are dog-friendly, where you can taste limited release beers from Canada's first microbrewery. 1441 Cartwright St.; 604/687-2739; www.gib.ca.

Woofles and Meowz: This specialty store on Granville Island is where dogs and cats go to grab a bite to eat. Located in a caboose, still parked on a section of unconnected track, this pet deli prides itself on 100 percent natural treats and an unusual assortment of accessories and customized toys. 1496 Cartwright St.; 604/689-3647 or 877/WOOFLES (877/966-3537); www.woofles.com.

PLACES TO STAY

Granville Island Hotel: The pet-friendly rooms at this boutique hotel with a modern bent have marble floors, and most have views of Vancouver and the surrounding waters of False Creek. Rates range $150–230. The pet fee is $25. 1253 Johnston St.; 604/683-7373 or 800/663-1840; www.granvilleislandhotel.com.

Cambie

PARKS, BEACHES, AND RECREATION AREAS

14 Queen Elizabeth Park Dog Area

🐾🐾🐕 (See British Columbia map on page 436)

The top of this posh and straight-laced 130-acre city park is the highest point in the city, 505 feet above sea level. From the lookouts, about six million visitors a year admire the 360-degree view of the Vancouver skyline. These throngs then head to the North Quarry Garden to find nearly all trees native to Canada, exotic plants from other countries, and the Bloedel Conservatory's floral displays.

Meanwhile, on the south end of the park, and worlds away from the social awareness of the multitudes, local dogs and a few tail wags "in the know" happily romp in peace and quiet in QE's off-leash area. The designated dog area is a plain affair, an open plateau of grass bordered by a few small trees and protected by the ritzy homes of this desirable residential neighborhood. The OLA is kept hush-hush, not listed on the brochures or maps given to the general public. It'll be our little secret.

The off-leash area is bordered by 37th Avenue, the tennis courts, a pitch and putt course, and the driveway into the parking lot. There are minimal facilities in this section of the park.

From downtown Vancouver, take Cambie Bridge south and stay on Cambie Street until you see signs to the park. Turn left on W. 33rd Avenue, bear right on Kerrsland, turn left on W. 37th Avenue, and left into the parking lot east of Columbia Street. Off-leash hours are 6 A.M.–10 P.M. 4600 Cambie St.; 604/257-8689.

PLACES TO EAT

Meinhardt Fine Foods: This gourmet market gives the Dachsie Twins' Mom fits of pleasure. Put together a picnic or meal of your dreams from the store shelves. If you aren't in a do-it-yourself mood, get prepared delicacies from the deli counter or the affiliated mini-café, **The Picnic Table.** 3002 Granville St.; 604/732-4405; www.meinhardt.com.

PLACES TO STAY

Pacific Spirit Guest House: When Coop 'n' Isis were putting the book together, this bed-and-breakfast held the honor of being Vancouver's only certified pet-friendly facility, a new program in Canada that recognizes establishments where your pets are as welcome as you are. The Garden Room and the Cedar Room are West Coast casual and instantly comforting, sharing a living room with a wood-burning fireplace and a bath with a full tub. Pets are a total of $20 per night, which covers a list of Very Important Pet services too long to list and a $5 gift certificate to Three Dog Bakery. Plus, the Guest House is a block away from the regional park of the same name, the largest off-leash park in the city. The rate for either room is $90 per night. 4080 West 35th Ave.; 604/261-6837 or 866/768-6837; www.vanbb.com.

Kerrisdale

It's worth a quick stroll along West 41st Street in this district to find many cute cafés with outdoor seating, where you can stake out a prime people-watching spot. Vancouverite dogs socialize at the **Fetch** dog boutique during Yappi Hour, while their owners paw over the latest in all things dog-related (5617 W. Boulevard; 604/879-3647; www.fetchstore.ca).

PARKS, BEACHES, AND RECREATION AREAS

15 Fraser River Dog Park

🐾🐾🐾🐢 (See British Columbia map on page 436)

This neighborhood park allows dogs free reign over the whole park territory for select hours. The gigantic fields on the east end are well suited to any activity involving your dog's preferred UFO. Marsh boardwalks and docks and a waterfront trail are great for scenic walks, looking out on the north arm of the Fraser River, fashionable homes on the north side, and the Vancouver International Airport and container barges to the south. It's a good bird-watching spot, with blue herons that don't seem the least bit intimidated by the dogs.

The only drawback is a lack of convenient water access. Against the banks of the river are large granite boulders, called rip-rap, to act as channel and bank erosion control. The sharp rocks are too big and too plentiful to scramble over safely. There are convenient restrooms, water fountains, and garbage bins.

From downtown, take Granville Street south, turn right on 70th Avenue W., left on Barnard Street, and right on W. 75th Avenue to Angus Drive. Off-leash hours are 6–10 A.M. and 5–10 P.M. 8705 Angus Dr.; 604/257-8689.

PLACES TO EAT

Coco Pazzo: The literal translation of this neighborhood restaurant is Crazy Chef. A Tuscan influence flavors the food, and a converted bank vault houses a wide selection of local and Italian wines. From mid-May to September, the whole family can relax among cypress, palm trees, and flowering planters on the garden terrace. Reservations are always encouraged. 1864 W. 57th Ave.; 604/267-1864.

Moldovanos: It's all Greek and all good, and when the sun shines, the outdoor seating comes out to play. The prices are low, and the portions are large. Mind your dog to keep his distance if you order the Volcano for dessert, a mountain of sponge cake and strawberries flambéed with orange liqueur—nobody wants to go home with singed fur. 4432 Dunbar St.; 604/738-3186.

Tri-Cities Area

You might as well roll over and play dead if you come all the way up to Vancouver and don't go the extra kilometer to day-trip destinations in the Coquitlam, Port Coquitlam, and Port Moody area, some of the biggest and brightest dog and people parks in the region, about 18 miles outside the city.

PARKS, BEACHES, AND RECREATION AREAS

16 Buntzen Lake Dog Beach

🐾🐾🐾🐾 🐕 (See British Columbia map on page 436)

When dogs dream, they dream of Buntzen Lake, their legs churning in time to the count of the steps it takes to run from the gate to the water. The lake sure looks like a piece of heaven, with crystal-clear waters and clean sandy beaches with a mountain backdrop. You'd never suspect it's an artificial reservoir; it's even fooled the cameras for misty morning and late-night shots in *X Files* episodes.

Try not to be put off by all the Dogs Prohibited signs in the rest of the Recreation Area. It's hard to manage the wishes of the masses of petless people who also want to lap up the sun and water of Buntzen. The Designated Dog Beach is a special place, one of three off-leash options in the park. When you pass the park gates, go into the first parking lot to your right, to the end, to the trail leading to the off-leash beach. After a trot of maybe .1 mile, you'll see the gate. It's fenced on three sides, with the fences extending into the water to neatly divide dogdom from the Main South Beach area. The sand is soft, there are trees and picnic benches, and Buntzen Creek burbles through. Past the last main parking area is another off-leash section for dogs who would rather sink their claws into the turf, but it doesn't have quite the same curb appeal as the beach. There's a .6-kilometer out-and-back off-leash trail from the parking lot to the equestrian area. Skip it. Any part of the extensive hiking and biking system around the lake is better, and leashed dogs are welcome on all trails.

Exit the Trans-Canada Highway on Ioco Road and follow the signs to wind up and over on Heritage Mountain Boulevard, Parkside Drive, East Road, and Sunnyside Road. Turn right at the T intersection on Sunnyside Road to get to Buntzen. Hours change with the seasons. Avoid Buntzen and Belcarra on sunny summer days. The parks get so crowded, and there are quotas, so you'll likely be turned away at the gates. 604/469-9679; www.bchyrdo.com/recreation.

17 Belcarra Regional Park

🐾🐾🐾🐾 (See British Columbia map on page 436)

Covering more than 2,600 acres, this GVRD park is a huge destination for Vancouverites in every sense. Like nearby Buntzen, Sasamat Lake turns away all but the earliest arrivals from its crowded shores. Unlike Buntzen, there are no dog areas designated on the beach. Dogs are limited to leashed hikes on the many park trails, limits any dog we know would be willing to accept. Detailed maps are available from the park's concession stand. Cooper recommends the easy 1.5-mile Sasamat Lake Loop, the moderate four-mile Cod Rock Trail, and the moderately difficult three-mile Jug Island spur, the last only if you're up for the ups and down of hills and stairs. There are views everywhere you look.

Exit the Trans-Canada Highway to Ioco Road and follow the signs to wind up and over on Heritage Mountain Boulevard, Parkside Drive, East Road, and Sunnyside Road. Turn left at the T intersection on Sunnyside Road to Bedwell Bay Road. Signs will guide you the whole way. 604/432-6359; www.gvrd .bc.ca/parks/Belcarra.htm.

18 Rocky Point Park

🐾🐾🐕 (See British Columbia map on page 436)

For those dogs among us who need a little extra reinforcement to keep them nearby when allowed off-leash, and you know who you are, Cooper and Isis decided to toss in this little off-leash area, the only one included that is fenced and gated. The dog run has the full complement of necessary items, including a bag dispenser and garbage, benches, a double-gate with a leash-up area, and a water pump. The surface is dirt and sand, with grassy patches holding on for dear life in the corners. A few trees surround a natural gully where all the tennis balls end up, ensuring the balls are muddy *and* slobbery when you get them returned to you by helpful, eager retrievers.

For the scenic route from Vancouver, take Hastings Street E. from downtown all the way out. It will become Highway 7A. After you see the Port Moody signs, take the left exit onto Clark Street, turn left on Moody Street, cross the bridge and cloverleaf around, turn left on Murray Street, and travel .2 mile past the main park entrance and the skate park to the fenced OLA. There's room for three or four cars to park on the gravel.

PLACES TO EAT

Anducci's: It's a lovely day and you're looking for a patio, a place to enjoy the good life with your best friend. This authentic Italian restaurant hits the spot, with fresh salads and pastas, and different food and drink specials every day for lunch and dinner. 2729 Barnet Hwy.; 604/468-9002; www.anduccis.com.

The Urban Barkery: Sorry, kids, these bakery treats are for dogs only. The pastry case is full of lovingly handmade, all-natural treats, and the store carries raw and natural pet foods, stylish gear, and funky toys for your fuzzy buddy. 1410 Parkway Blvd.; 604/945-3647; www.urbanbarkery.com.

Chilliwack and Harrison Hot Springs

About an hour and a half east of Vancouver, Chilliwack is a popular vacation getaway for Vancouverites. In the hot springs resort town of Harrison, dogs are welcome anywhere on the lake except the small lagoon. The world's most talented sand sculptors come to Harrison Hot Springs every September to create new inventions for the annual World Championship Sand Sculpture Competition. With your dog, you can enjoy the sculptures from outside the fence; you'll have good views and you won't have to pay the entry fee.

PARKS, BEACHES, AND RECREATION AREAS

19 Bridal Veil Falls Provincial Park

🐾 (See British Columbia map on page 436)

To dogs, it's a little jaunt in the woods, capped by a 300-meter-high, cascading drinking fountain at the end. A half-mile looped dirt trail, uphill to the falls, downhill back, takes visitors to the park's signature feature. Worth seeing if you're a waterfall buff and for a photo op. Mom, who visited it with us, said it was her favorite part of the trip; if you're an active dog looking for a serious romp, maybe not. There were eight picnic tables near the foot of the trail, but with busloads of people pulling up to see the lacy falls, it's not a very secluded stop. Bridal Veil Falls is prone to freezing during colder winters, which results in the formation of an unstable ice wall. During this time, the base of the falls is a hazardous area.

The park is located on the south side of the Fraser River, 16 km east of Chilliwack. Take Exit 135 off the Trans-Canada Highway and follow the signs. http://wlapwww.gov.bc.ca/bcparks/explore/parkpgs/bridal.htm.

PLACES TO EAT

Harrison Pizza: The outdoor tables are naturally warmed by the heat coming from the pizza ovens. If you're not a pizza fan, go for the salads, ice cream, tasty fried chicken, and jo-jos (those thick fried potato wedges). 160 Lillooet, Harrison Hot Springs; 604/796-2023.

Miss Margarets: This to-go deli in the lobby of Harrison Hot Springs Resort shares outside tables with the hotel bar. Get your sandwich, salad, pastries, and drinks to go and sit at a table around the patio perimeter. 100 Esplanade Ave., Harrison Hot Springs; 800/663-2266.

Yaletown European Bakery: Display cases filled with pasta, fruit, and vegetable salads compete for your attention with soups, wraps, and made-to-order sandwiches, but save room for dessert! There are pastries, cakes, cookies, muffins, and floats. Take a just-baked loaf of Country Seed to go. Small dogs can be lifted over the fence on the side patio; big pals can stay near at a couple of tables under the awning out front, but keep your pal close, as it's on the busy main thoroughfare. A well-known TV and film animal trainer lives here; maybe your pug's mug will get discovered the way Lana Turner did. 46198 Yale Rd., Chilliwack; 604/703-0137.

PLACES TO STAY

Harrison Hot Springs Resort and Spa: This hot spot sits at the end of the road in a valley surrounded by mountains on the shores of Harrison Lake. It is gorgeous and unspoiled, and the views are stunning. The rooms are decent—nothing to write home about—but did we mention the views? The grounds of the resort include a fully fenced private garden with a fitness course trail and a trellis walkway that provide a good place for your Irish setter to stretch his legs. The three outdoor and two indoor pools fed by the springs are for humans only, but your dog doesn't need to feel left out—he can run right outside the entrance to the lobby and across the street for a quick dip in the chilly lake. Dogs under 50 pounds are allowed in designated rooms of the lodge for an additional $100 nonrefundable cleaning fee, but here's a secret: There are 10 tiny cabins out back, nestled against the hillside, that allow any size dog for no additional fee, and you have full use of all the facilities; one of them has a kitchenette. Rates range $129–370 in the main lodge; $150–220 for the cabins; 100 Esplanade Ave., Harrison Hot Springs; 800/663-2266; www.harrisonresort.com.

More Accommodations: Please look under Chain Hotels in the Resources section for additional places to stay in this area.

Sidney and the Saanich Peninsula

The charming town of Sidney-by-the-Sea is the largest community on the Saanich Peninsula, a thumb of land north of Victoria. Sidney is two kilometers south of Swartz Bay, where the Tsawassen Ferry from Vancouver arrives, and the Washington State Ferries to Anacortes and the San Juan Islands. The town got its start in 1894 when the Victoria–Sidney Railway began service. Downtown has shops, marinas, and diving facilities protected by its breakwater wall. The peninsula's regional parks allow unleashed dogs under voice control, except on beaches June–Sept. 15 and in other areas as signs indicate.

Lochside Regional Trail: The rails stopped carrying cars in 1924, and now the re-graded line carries people, bicycles, and in some places, horses, a total of 29 kilometers (18 miles) from Swartz Bay to Victoria. This civilized paved and gravel path traverses mostly urban areas and pastoral farmland. It connects to the Galloping Goose Trail, a wilder neighbor to the south in Victoria. For a good access point, with a couple of parking spaces, take Royal Oak Road west from Highway 17, and turn right down the dead end of Lochside Road. Please respect the No Parking signs near private property. www.crd.bc.ca/parks/lochside.htm.

PARKS, BEACHES, AND RECREATION AREAS

20 Francis/King Park

😊 😊 🐕 (See British Columbia map on page 436)

Freeman "Skipper" King, a local naturalist and scout leader, and homesteader Tommy Francis worked together to donate this farm to the community. Freeman designed and dedicated a 750-meter accessible nature trail for his wife Elsi, who spent her last years in a wheelchair.

The Elsi King Trail makes up a tiny fraction of the walking trails available in this nature park. Dogs must be leashed on this interpretive trail, and they should be leashed on the Moss Rock trail to protect the delicate plants. After that, they can be unleashed, as long as they return to you immediately upon command. The map on the diamond kiosk at the park entrance tallies up the trails to 11 kilometers (not quite seven miles). The longest, the Centennial Trail, is a moderate loop around the park that'll take about an hour for well-conditioned legs of either species.

From the Trans-Canada Highway, take Exit 8, west on Helmcken Road, turn left on Burnside and travel almost a mile, turn right on Prospect Lake Road, and take the left fork in the road to Munn Road, a total of another mile to the park entrance. Open 8 A.M.–9 P.M. 250/478-3344.

21 Elk and Beaver Lake Parks

😊 😊 😊 🐕 (See British Columbia map on page 436)

A thousand acres or so (442 hectares) is pretty big for a regional park, and this is one of the prettiest, with two lakes available for water sports. Any or all of the perimeter 10-kilometer (6.25-mile) trail is given high paws ratings by area dogs. It alternates between forest, fields, and wetlands, with bountiful lake views. Dogs may hike this trail off-leash under voice command, as well as the on the maze of short trails southeast of Beaver Lake. Near the Beaver Lake entrance, off to the right, is an unmarked field that's perfect for a game of fetch.

In the off-season of Sept. 15–May 31, dogs have the added bonus of free time on the lake's beaches and on the grassy slopes of the picnic areas. During the summer, pupsters may pass through on leash but are not allowed to remain in the picnic or beach areas.

From Highway 17, turn west on Haliburton Road, and for less crowded parking and better trail access, follow the frontage road south to the Beaver Lake parking area. 250/478-3344.

PLACES TO EAT

Sherlock's Restaurant and Waddling Dog Bar and Grill: At the Waddling Dog Hotel, Sherlock's is the formal restaurant for dinner, and the Waddling Dog Bar and Grill is the casual pub option. The two food establishments share sidewalk seating where your dog can fall in love with new foods, perhaps steak and kidney pie or salmon Wellington in a puff pastry. 2476 Mt. Newton Cross Road; 800/567-8466.

Stonehouse Pub: This cozy Old English stone house was built in 1935 and has housed a pub since 1985. It's tucked in a forest by the Canoe Cove marina, with room for your dog to relax on the lawn with a fresh bowl of water and some biscuits, courtesy of the management, near the covered, heated patio. You might want to avoid the insane weekend crowds. 2215 Canoe Cove Road; 250/656-3498; www.stonehousepub.com.

Third Street Café: This comfy diner is a long-standing favorite, with a huge list of breaky specialties (endearing Canadian slang for breakfast) and hot lunch sandwiches. The staff are professed dog lovers, giving scraps and pats to dogs. A bunch of sidewalk tables are up for grabs out front. 2466 Beacon Ave.; 250/656-3035.

PLACES TO STAY

The Cedarwood: The simple rooms of this motel, both standard units and suites with kitchens, are on landscaped grounds with a great beach walk right across the street. A small off-leash area at Tulista Park is right up the street. There are 10 nonsmoking pet rooms available, within five blocks of the specialty shops of Sidney's downtown. The website states small dogs only are allowed; in practice, the Cedarwood stretches the definition of small infinitely; up to three dogs per room are allowed. Rates range from $69–109 in winter to $109–$245 in summer. The dog fee is $15. 9522 Lochside Dr.; 250/656-5551 or 877/656-5551; www.cedarwoodinnandsuites.com.

Waddling Dog: "The Dog" is now a Quality Inn, but it retains a unique character, embracing a basset hound theme and going all-out with Tudor style and imported British antiques. It's close to Sidney and the ferries, and dogs have the added convenience of a fenced yard behind the property to run about with John III, the current resident basset. Guest dogs are not required to be bassets; all breeds are welcome for a $10 fee per pet, per night. Rates range $80–130. 2476 Mt. Newton Cross Road, Saanichton; 800/567-8466; www.qualityinnvictoria.com.

More Accommodations: Please look under Chain Hotels in the Resources section for additional places to stay in this area.

Victoria

The architecture and style of Victoria, with its afternoon high teas and double-decker buses, emphasizes the British in British Columbia. As of publication, the local dog advocacy group Citizen Canine (www.citizencanine.org) is submitting recommendations to add up to nine parks to the city's one existing off-leash area. In addition, Capital Regional District Parks allow dogs off-leash, as long as they are under control and stay on the trail, with the following exceptions: Elsi King Trail at Francis/King Regional Park and the Lochside Regional Trail. The regional park's definition of under control means that your dog returns to you immediately when called. See www.crd.bc.ca/parks/pets_in_parks.htm for more information.

Galloping Goose Regional Trail: This 55-kilometer (35-mile) trail passes through urban, rural, and wilderness scenery from Victoria to Sooke. Named for the ungainly, gas-powered passenger car that carried people and mail during the 1920s, the Goose is part of the Trans-Canada Trail System, linking large sections of the country, coast to coast. It connects to the Lochside Regional Trail. From downtown Victoria, you can start at the corner of Warf Street and Pandora Avenue, cross the Johnson Street Bridge in the pedestrian lane, and turn right on the paved path that intersects Harbour Road. The trail doesn't require dogs to be on leash, but it is heavily used by cyclists. For many more trailheads, download the brochure from www.crd.bc.ca/parks/galloping_goose.htm.

PARKS, BEACHES, AND RECREATION AREAS

22 Dallas Beach Dog Area in Beacon Hill Park

🐾🐾🐾🐾🐾 (See British Columbia map on page 436)

Beacon Park is as old as the hills, its 200 acres set aside in 1858 by governor James Douglas and officially established as a park in 1882. On a leashed stroll of this gorgeous city park, you and your pup may come across a strutting peacock, bald eagles, or a great blue heron among the lilies of Goodacre and Fountain Ponds. You might pass a horse-drawn carriage, children playing at the petting zoo, or a civilized game of cricket. You'll walk through exotic and native trees, including Garry oak, arbutus, Douglas fir, Western red cedar, birch, willows, and maples—to name a few.

But, wait, what is that sound interrupting your reverie? It could be the thundering paws of the scores of dogs beating a path to Dallas Beach, Beacon Hill's awesome off-leash area. Dogs can play where it all begins, at the Kilometer Zero marker for the Trans-Canada Highway, leading 7,349 kilometers to St. John's, Newfoundland. Victoria's dog park comes complete with a great view, on headlands where settlers erected twin beacons to guide seafarers around dangerous waters.

DIVERSIONS

In 1904, Jennie Butchart began a lifelong project to transform a barren limestone quarry into a garden. More than 100 years later, her vision has blossomed into 55 acres of world-renowned gardens on a 130-acre estate. If you are going to Vancouver Island, you really must go to **Butchart Gardens.** There's a different type of stunning floral explosion to see each month, although the staff suggests a late afternoon stroll, around 3 P.M., from mid-June to mid-September to best avoid crowds and enjoy pleasant weather. Pets on a six-foot leash are welcome anytime, except during fireworks displays on Saturday evenings, which they would probably hate anyway. Summer night strolls are magical, when one of the largest underground wiring installations in North America sets the gardens aglow. Entrance fees vary $14.50–21, depending on the time of year; there's no charge for your pet. Hours vary monthly, from 9 A.M.–3:30 P.M. in winter to as late as 10:30 P.M. in the height of summer. Inside the gardens are wonderful cafés with courtyard seating. Butchart Gardens are 12.5 miles north of Victoria; 800 Benvenuto Ave, Brentwood Bay; 250/652-5256 or 866/652-4422; www.butchartgardens.com.

On the mainland, leashed dogs may also join you at **Minter Gardens,** 32 acres of show gardens featuring 11 different themes, a labyrinth, and some surprising floral topiary sculptures. Spring highlights daffodils and 100,000 tulips imported from Holland. More than 1,000 rhododendron bushes explode in summer, and the rose garden blooms fragrantly through August. Autumn features chrysanthemums, blooming cabbages, and pansies. When you're weary, outdoor covered seating is available with an à la carte menu at The Garden Café. The gardens are open April–October. Hours vary seasonally. Admission is $12 for adults; $6.50 for youth 5–18; kids 5 and under are free. Complimentary umbrellas are provided for protection from the harsh sun or frequent rains. Exit #135 off Highway #1; 52892 Bunker Road, Rosedale; 888/646-8377; www.mintergardens.com.

If there's nothing more pleasing to your horticultural eye than row upon row of tidy vines hanging with bunches of plump fruit that will someday yield your favorite vintage, come picnic with your pup at the **Victoria Estate Winery.** Buy one of the winery's gourmet lunch baskets and a bottle or two of wine, and dine al fresco with Fido in one of two lovely picnic areas with views of the Saanich Peninsula and the vineyards. Before you get too far into it, you may want to pick someone other than your dog as designated driver. Dogs are not allowed in the buildings. Located between Butchart and Butterfly Gardens; 1445 Benvenuto Ave., Brentwood Bay; 250/652-2671; www.victoriaestatewinery.com.

Although it's called a beach, the largest land mass in the OLA are green fields of grass, divided by clumps of short trees and natural shrubs. There's a bunch of room for games involving your dog's flying object of choice. Be aware, as there are no dividers or fences separating your dog from a fairly busy road. From the bluff, careful footing is required to get down to a couple of beach coves, both rough and rocky. The cobble beaches have driftwood and other good stuff washed ashore to sniff. Once on the beach, your dog's not going anywhere; the steep headlands are behind you and cliff rocks on either side keep you tucked into a small area.

There are restrooms nearby, a water fountain, garbage cans, and benches. Your only responsibility is to bring bags. Before you wear him out completely, you might want to walk on leash with your dog around the full bluff trail for maximum views.

The Trans-Canada Highway and Provincial Highway 17 merge into Douglas Street a block before Beacon Hill Park. Follow Douglas until it dead-ends into Dallas and turn left onto Dallas. The off-leash area is located south of Dallas Road between Douglas and Cook Streets. Angled parking is available along the majority of Dallas Road.

23 Island View Regional Park

🐾 🐾 🐕 (See British Columbia map on page 436)

For four months out of the year, a walk along the dirt road trails of this regional park is good clean fun. It's a chance to hike above the beach, off-leash if you prefer, on a straight and level trail on Cordova Bay, looking out at James and Sidney Islands. You have far-reaching sight on the path, so you can see what's coming and leash up if necessary to pass other walkers and dogs.

September 15–May 31, Island View gets bonus points, because that's when dogs are allowed to get on the beach and get mucky in the water. The beach is sandy enough; it's just that saltwater somehow adds extra pungency to that wet dog smell.

From Victoria or Sidney, take Provincial Highway 17 to Island Drive Road and go east for 1.7 miles to the parking lot. Open 6 A.M.–11 P.M.

PLACES TO EAT

Murchie's: This venerable institution has been serving high tea in Victoria since 1894. The counter cases are filled with legendary cakes and tarts on one side and pasties, sandwiches, and savories on the other. Murchie's vegetable strata, in Italian veggie lasagna or Mexican styles, takes your taste buds to a new stratosphere. Murchie's sidewalk seating is along a popular people-watching boulevard. 1100 Government Street; 250/381-5451; www.murchies.com.

Ochre Grains: Ochre is a healthy option, with a menu of light vegetable salads and sandwiches. It would be easier for all of us to eat more fruits and veggies if they were always this tasty. The Ochre has lots of outdoor seating and water bowls for Bowser. 866 Yates St.; 250/381-5114; www.ochregrains.com.

PLACES TO STAY

Abbeymoore Manor: This mansion was built in 1912 and sits among the castles and gardens of Old Victoria, where governors, merchant barons, bankers, and architects built elaborate homes to show off their wealth. Pets are welcome in the Garden Suites only, and please let them know you have pets when making reservations, which you should always do to ensure that your pets will get along with the resident pets. There is a $25 flat fee, which includes a freshly washed pet blanket, food bowls, and gourmet doggie treats. Rates range $129–179. 1470 Rockland Ave.; 250/370-1470 or 888/801-1811; www.abbeymoore.com.

Abigail's Hotel: This hotel is a five-star bed-and-breakfast accommodation, frequently rated Victoria's best small hotel by Frommers Travel Guides. It's a warm and comfortable Tudor-style house with country furnishings and English gardens. Dogs were welcomed for the first time in late 2004, in the Coach House Suites, three rooms on one floor that do require navigating narrow stairs. Abigail's is four blocks from Dallas Off-Leash Dog Beach. Rates range $309–389. The pet fee is $25 per dog, per stay. 906 McClure Street; 250/388-5363 or 800/561-6565; www.abigailshotel.com.

Annabelle's Cottage: Annabelle is a lovely bichon frise who would like to invite your dogs to stay in her Lavender or Rosemary Bed-and-Breakfast Suites, and she will graciously allow you to accompany them. For only $10 per stay, each pet receives home-baked biscuits, a dog sheet for the bed, and a towel for coming back from the off-leash beach, only two blocks away. The suites are sunny and cheerful, with all kinds of wonderful amenities, and the Rosemary is wheelchair-accessible. Rates are $99–155. 250/384-4351; www.annabellescottage.com.

Dashwood Manor: If you want to give your dog the experience of a lifetime, stay for a month at the apartment in this bed-and-breakfast and go across the street every day to Dallas Beach OLA. You'll soak up a month's worth of ocean and Olympic mountain views and the comfort of the Piccadilly Suite. Monthly rentals are $1350–1750. If the suite is available in the summer, you can sample a night's worth for $125, plus a $25 for one large or two small pets, by prior approval only. One Cook St.; 250/385-5517 or 800/667-5517; www.dashwoodmanor.com.

Paul's Motor Inn: This motel has a bright copper roof and rooms that are retro-hip, even more hip because the retro is original. It's right downtown, within walking distance of everything. Paul's has won awards for genuine hospitality at an unbeatable price. Pets under 30 pounds are allowed in 14 rooms, for a $15 per stay fee. Children under 12 stay for free, and two adults can stay for $49–89. 1900 Douglas Street; 250/382-9231 or 866/333-PAUL (866/333-7285); www.paulsmotorinn.com.

DIVERSIONS

For awesome holiday cards, get an old-time photo made with your whole family, including your well-behaved dogs, at **Grandpa's Antique Photo Studio.** You pick the costumes, which usually fit over street clothing or fur, for all ages and sizes. Prices start at $39 for two people, no extra charge for dogs, for an 8x10 or two 5x7 photos. Choose from Old West, Victorian Era, Military, and other themes and get your prints in 10 minutes in sepia-tone, black and white, full color, or aged color. 1252 Wharf Street; 250/920-3800.

Get along, little doggy, on a **Victoria Carriage Tour** of beautiful Beacon Hill Park and the historic buildings of downtown Victoria. Calm, leashed, lap dogs are welcome to join you on 30-minute or 90-minute guided horse-drawn carriage tours starting at $70 for the entire carriage, which holds four to six people. Carriages usually run daily 9 A.M.–midnight, weather permitting. 877/663-2207; www.victoriacarriage.com.

Prior House Bed and Breakfast: The Prior House Inn accepts pets with well-behaved owners, providing dogs with treats, walk bags, and most importantly, a welcome environment in a lavish home with ocean views. There are three suites set aside for pets, the Hobbit Garden Studios, unique with private outside entrances and furnished patios on a secluded lawn surrounded by award-winning gardens. There is a $5 per day pet fee, and the basic courtesies apply: pet owners are responsible for damages, pick up after dog nuisances when walking the gardens or the neighborhood, and do not leave pets in the room unattended. Pet-sitting can be arranged with advance notice. Rates range $125–310. 620 St. Charles; 250/592-8847 or 877/924-3300; www.priorhouse.com.

More Accommodations: Please look under Chain Hotels in the Resources section for additional places to stay in this area.

Sooke

PARKS, BEACHES, AND RECREATION AREAS

24 East Sooke Regional Park
🐾🐾🐾🐾 (See British Columbia map on page 436)
This park's coastline trail, pocket peaches, timeless woods, and tidepool coves come with a lot of caveats. This is a wilderness park, a rugged experience you can enjoy if you are confident of your hiking skills and the capabilities of your canine. Let's just say that East Sooke's 1,463 hectares—that's 3,511

acres—are more than a walk in the park. To handle any of this regional park's 50 kilometers (30 miles) of trails, come prepared with maps and backcountry essentials, and allow more time than usual to return to your vehicle before dark. Imagine your dog's embarrassment if the rangers have to send a rescue dog to find him!

Anderson Cove is the starting point for hiking trails to the uplands, Babbington Hill and Mount Maguire. You and your dog might share views of the Strait of San Juan de Fuca and the Olympic Mountains with bald eagles, turkey vultures, and red-tailed hawks. Pike Road, the westernmost access point, is the best place to pick up the Coast Trail, a vigorous, seven-hour hike to private beaches, rocky bays, and tidepools for hours of exploring.

In a park where only voice control is required, leashes are still highly desirable, due to a greater likelihood of running into deer, black bears, and cougars. We'll let you off with one more warning: Do not allow your dog to swim in an area where seals or sea lions are present. It can disrupt the pinnipeds' breeding patterns, and, more importantly, the sea mammals will attack and can kill. Cooper and Isis don't want to scare you away from Sooke; they merely want you to come fully prepared to safely enjoy this spectacular experience.

From the Trans-Canada Highway starting in Victoria, take Exit 10 to Colwood. Go to your left to follow the Old Island Highway, which becomes Sooke Road. From Sooke Road, turn left on Gillespie Road. When you reach the T intersection on East Sooke Road, turn right to reach the park entrances at Anderson Cove and Pike Road, or turn left to Aylard Farm, off Becher Bay Road. Dogs are never permitted *in* Aylard Farm pond and they are not allowed on the Aylard Farm beach and picnic area June 1–Sept. 15. Open 7 A.M.–sunset. www.crd.bc.ca/parks/east_sooke.htm.

PLACES TO EAT

Mom's Café: Fellow restaurateurs teasingly refer to it as the clichéd hole in the wall, yet this diner has been around, garnering awards and loyal followers, since 1963. You can be sure your dog will loyally follow you around to the picnic tables on the lawn as long as you've got leftovers, or even a plate to lick, from Mom's homemade pies and hot meals. 2036 Shields Rd.; 250/642-3314; www.momscafe.net.

17 Mile House Pub and Restaurant: The lanterns of 17 Mile House welcome you as you round the bend from East Sooke Regional Park, not much changed from 1894, when weary gold panhandlers and settlers rode up on horseback. The hitching post is still there, and the pub sticks to its traditional purpose to quench the thirst of weary travelers with cold beer, wine, ciders, coolers, spirits, and liqueurs. It also fills empty bellies with salads, a couple of sandwich selections, pastas, and burgers. At the owner's discretion, dogs are allowed to sit at outdoor tables nearest to the lawn. Come into the restaurant and ask a server how to get around back to the patio. Takeout is also available all day, seven days a week. 5126 Sooke Road; 250/642-5942; www.17milehouse.com.

Mead Tasting Room, Tugwell Creek Farm: This honey farm and meadery keeps things laid-back and friendly, allowing leashed dogs who can keep a respectful distance from the hives and goats, mainly so they don't get stung or kicked. The latest and greatest product of the honey farm is mead, a heady brew made from honey and local berries. Sample the brew and buy honey products noon–4 P.M. Wed.–Sun. 8750 West Coast Rd.; 250/642-1956; www.tugwellcreekfarm.com.

PLACES TO STAY

Amazing Vacation Homes and Cottages: This rental agency has a spectacular selection of oceanfront vacation homes and cottages, the only rental properties in the area that allow pets. These houses and cottages all have acres of land surrounding them and feature such goodies as private hot tubs, fireplaces, large sun decks with panoramic views, private beaches, lovely gardens, fully equipped gourmet kitchens, and washers and dryers. Rates range $125–400 per night; weekly, monthly, and low season rates are also available. Children are welcome, as well as pets. All homes have a fee of $10 per pet, per night; ask about pet fees for longer-term rentals. 250/642-7034 or 877/374-8944; www.amazingvacationhomes.com.

Sooke Harbour House: Art, natural beauty, and artful food will surround you and your spoiled pets at this phenomenal property. Pets are allowed in all 28 rooms—take your pick from ocean views or garden rooms with antiques, original paintings and sculpture, and extravagant amenities. The remote location, scenery, and walks on Whiffen Spit will restore your spirit. It's a feast for all the senses. After you've stayed a day or two, leaving may be the hardest thing you ever do. Dogs are allowed on leash everywhere on the property, except around the world-famous cafés. Rates range $335–575; the pet fee is $30. 1528 Whiffen Spit Rd.; 250/642-3421; www.sookeharbourhouse.com.

RESOURCES

Emergency Veterinary Clinics

For better geographic coverage, this list includes clinics that have an emergency veterinarian on call in addition to 24-hour animal clinics.

Washington

OLYMPIC PENINSULA

Angeles Clinic for Animals: Doctor on call. 1134 E. Front St., Port Angeles; 360/452-7686.

Olympic Veterinary Clinic: Doctor on call. 1417 E. Front St., Port Angeles; 360/452-8978.

Pacific Northwest Veterinary Hospital: Doctor on call. 289 W. Bell St., Sequim; 360/681-3368.

Sequim Animal Hospital: Doctor on call. 202 N. 7th Ave., Sequim; 360/683-7286.

Veterinary Center for Family Pet Care: Doctor on call. 2201 W. Sims Way, Port Townsend; 360/385-0512.

KITSAP PENINSULA

Animal Emergency and Trauma Center: Weekday nights and 24 hours on weekends. Poulsbo Village Shopping Center, 19494 F 7th Ave N.E., Poulsbo; 360/697-7771.

Animal Emergency and Trauma Center: After hours and weekends only; Bremerton; 360/475-3077.

Animal Hospital of Central Kitsap: 24-hour clinic. 10310 Central Valley Rd. N.E., Poulsbo; 360/692-6162.

Kitsap Veterinary Hospital: 3036 Bethel Rd.; Port Orchard; 360/876-2021.

THE ISLANDS

Animal Hospital on Midway: Doctor on call. 250 N.E. Midway Blvd., Oak Harbor, Whidbey Island; 360/240-8888.

Ark Veterinary Clinic: Doctor on call. 262 Weeks Rd.; Lopez Island; 360/468-2477.

Islands Veterinary Clinic: Doctor on call. 700 Mullis St., Friday Harbor, San Juan Island; 360/378-2333.

Orcas Animal Clinic: Doctor on call. 429 Madrona St., Eastsound, Orcas Island; 360/376-7838.

EVERETT AND VICINITY

Alderwood Companion Animal Hospital: Doctor on call. 19511 24th Ave. W., Lynnwood; 425/775-7655.

Animal Emergency Clinic Of Everett: 24-hour clinic. 3625 Rucker Ave., Everett; 425/258-4466.

Veterinary Specialty Center: 24-hour emergency and critical care, plus a referral service. 20115 44th Ave. W., Lynnwood; 425/697-6106 or 866/872-5800.

GREATER SEATTLE

After-Hours Animal Emergency Clinic: 24-hour clinic. 2975 156th S.E., Bellevue; 425/641-8414.

Animal Critical Care And Emergency Services: 24-hour clinic. 11536 Lake City Way N.E., Seattle; 206/364-1660.

Animal Emergency Services East: After-hours clinic open 6 P.M.–8 A.M., Mon.-Fri.; until 12 P.M. Sat.; and all day Sunday until 8 A.M. Monday morning. 636 7th Ave., Kirkland; 425/827-8727.

Auburn Veterinary Hospital: After-hours and weekend clinic. 718 Auburn Way N., Auburn; 253/833-4510.

Emerald City Emergency Clinic: After-hours and weekend clinic. 4102 Stone Way N., Seattle; 206/634-9000.

NORTH CASCADES

Animal Emergency Care: Open nights, weekends, and holidays. 317 Telegraph Rd., Bellingham; 360-758-2200.

SOUTHWEST WASHINGTON

Animal Emergency Clinic: 24-hour clinic. 5608 S. Durango, Tacoma; 253/474-0791.

Camas-Washougal Animal Hospital: Doctor on call. 401 6th St., Washougal; 360/835-7240.

Clark County Emergency Veterinary Service: Open nights, weekends, and holidays only. 6818 E. Fourth Plain Blvd., Vancouver; 360/694-3007.

St. Francis 24-Hour Animal Hospital: 12010 N.E. 65th St., Vancouver; 360/253-5446.

Willapa Veterinary Services: Doctor on call. 231 Ocean Ave., Raymond; 360/942-2321.

CENTRAL WASHINGTON

Airport West Animal Clinic: Doctor on call. 5804 W. Washington Ave., Yakima; 509/966-8460.

Alpine Animal Hospital: 24-hour pet hospital. 888 NW Sammamish Rd.; Issaquah; 425/392-8888.

Mt. Stuart Animal Hospital: Doctor on call. 807 E. 8th Ave., Ellensburg; 509/925-2332.

Oregon

NORTH COAST

Bayshore Animal Hospital: Doctor on call. 325 S.E. Marlin Ave., Warrenton; 503/861-1621.

Cloverdale Veterinary Clinic: Doctor on call. 34610 Hwy. 101, Cloverdale; 503/392-3322.

Pioneer Veterinary Hospital: Doctor on call. 801 Main Ave., Tillamook; 503/842-8411.

Reigning Cats and Dogs Animal Hospital: Doctor on call. 1109 Main Ave., Tillamook; 503/842-2322.

The Tillamook Veterinary Hospital: Doctor on call. 1095 N. Main St., Tillamook; 503/842-7552.

CENTRAL COAST

Animal Medical Care Of Newport: Doctor on call. 159 N.E. 10th, Newport; 541/265-6671.

Oceanlake Veterinary Clinic: Doctor on call. 3545 N.W. Hwy. 101; Lincoln City; 541/994-2929.

Osburn Veterinary Clinic: Doctor on call. 130 E. Railroad Ave., Reedsport; 541/271-5824.

Osburn Veterinary Clinic: Doctor on call. 1730 Kingwood, Florence; 541/902-2013.

SOUTH COAST

Bandon Veterinary Hospital: Doctor on call. June Ave. & Hwy. 101, Bandon; 541/347-9471.

Gold Beach Veterinary Clinic: 94211 3rd St., Gold Beach; 541/247-2513.

Hanson Animal Hospital: Walk-in only, no appointments. Doctor on call after hours. 45 E Lockhart Ave., Coos Bay; 541/269-2415.

Morgan Veterinary Clinic: Doctor on call. 230 Market Ave., Coos Bay; 541/269-5846.

Ocean Boulevard Veterinary Hospital: Doctor on call. 1710 Ocean Blvd. N.W., Coos Bay; 541/888-6713.

Town & Country Animal Clinic: Doctor on call. 15740 Hwy. 101 S., Brookings; 541/469-4661.

GREATER PORTLAND

Dove Lewis Emergency Animal Hospital: 24-hour clinic. 1984 N.W. Pettygrove, Portland; 503/228-7281.

Southeast Portland Animal Hospital: 24-hour clinic. 13830 S.E. Stark, Portland; 503/255-8139.

WILLAMETTE VALLEY

Dallas Animal Clinic: Doctor on call. 135 Fir Villa Rd., Dallas; 503/623-3943.

Emergency Veterinary Hospital: After-hours and weekends only. 103 Q St., Springfield; 541/746-0112.

Newberg Veterinary Hospital: Doctor on call. 3716 Hwy. 99W. Newberg; 503/538-8303.

Salem Veterinary Emergency Clinic: After hours and weekends only. 3215 Market St. N.E., Salem; 503/588-8082.

Willamette Veterinary Clinic/Animal Emergency and Critical Care Center: 24-hour clinic. 650 S.W. 3rd St., Corvallis; Daytime: 541/753-2223; After-Hours Emergency: 541/753-5750.

CENTRAL OREGON

Animal Emergency Center: After hours and weekends. 1245 S. Hwy. 97, Bend; 541/385-9110.

Blue Sky Veterinary Clinic: Weekdays and Saturday. 61575 American Ln., Bend; 541/383-3833.

Sisters Veterinary Clinic: Doctor on call. 371 E. Cascade Ave., Sisters; 541/549-6961.

SOUTHERN OREGON

Animal Emergency Service: Doctor on call. 2726 S. 6th St., Klamath Falls; 541/882-9005.

Basin Animal Clinic: Doctor on call. 1776 Washburn Way, Klamath Falls; 541/884-4558.

Grants Pass Veterinary Clinic: Doctor on call. 585 S.W. Lincoln Rd., Grants Pass; 541/476-7769.

Medford Animal Hospital: Doctor on call. 619 Market St., Medford; 541/772-2222.

Siskiyou Veterinary Hospital: Doctor on call. 100 W. Stewart Ave., Medford; 541/773-1335.

Valley Animal Hospital: Doctor on call. 400 N.E. E St., Grants Pass; 541/955-9655.

Canada

BRITISH COLUMBIA

Animal Emergency Clinic: After hours and weekends only. 6337 198th St., #103, Langley; 604/514-1711.

Animal Emergency Clinic: 24-hour emergency clinic. 1590 W. 4th Ave., Vancouver; 604/734-5104.

Central Victoria Veterinary Hospital: 24-hour clinic. 760 Roderick St., Victoria; 250/475-2495.

Coast Mountain Veterinary Services: Doctor on call. 2011 Innsbruck Dr., #201, Gateways Plaza, Whistler Creek; 24-hour emergency number: 604/932-5391.

Elk Lake Veterinary Hospital: Doctor on call. 4975 Pat Bay Hwy., Sidney-Saanich; 250/658-5922.

Granville Island Veterinary Hospital: Doctor on call. 1635 W 4th., Vancouver; 604/734-7744.

Langley Animal Clinic Ltd.: Doctor on call. 5758 203rd St., Langley; 604/534-4813.

Pet-Friendly Chain Hotels

The following chains are generally pet-friendly; but not every location of every chain allows dogs. If a specific location is listed below, you can expect a warm welcome for your weimaraner; for any unlisted location, call ahead and check with management before arriving with your dog in tow.

ACCENT INNS

This Canadian chain is uniformly pet-friendly. Two small to medium-sized pets are allowed per room. The pet fee is $10 total per night. Pet-friendly rooms are all on the ground floor; smoking and nonsmoking are available. 800/663-0298; www.accentinns.com.

British Columbia

Victoria: $69–109; 3233 Maple St.; 250/475-7500.
Vancouver: $69–109; 10551 St. Edwards Dr.; 604/273-3311.

BEST WESTERN
This is the largest hotel chain in the world. Not all Best Westerns take pets, and their fees and regulations vary. 800/528-1234; www.bestwestern.com.

Washington

Bellingham, WA–Lakeway Inn: There are only four pet-friendly rooms; call ahead for availability. Two-dog limit, under 20 pounds; $87–131; $10 pet fee; 714 Lakeway Dr.; 360/671-1011.

Chehalis, WA–ParkPlace Inn and Suites: Two dog limit, under 20 pounds; $82–126; $10 pet fee; 201 S.W. Interstate Ave.; 360/748-4040.

Enumclaw, WA–Park Center Hotel: Four dog limit, under 25 pounds; $83–94; $10 pet fee; 1000 Griffin Ave.; 360/825-4490.

Everett, WA–Cascadia Inn: Two dog limit, under 20 pounds or one dog over 20 pounds; $65–142; $10 flat fee per stay; 2800 Pacific Ave.; 425/258-4141.

Gig Harbor, WA–Wesley Inn: Very pet-friendly! Pet package with treats given at check-in. Jack, a chow/lab mix, and Parker, a Maltese mix, are resident dogs. Two dogs, no weight limits; $120–214; $10 per dog, per night or $50 per dog, per week; 6675 Kimball Dr.; 253/858-9690; www.wesleyinn.com.

Kirkland, WA–Kirkland Inn: No restrictions; $83–107; $50 refundable damage deposit; 12223 N.E. 116th St.; 425/822-2300.

Monroe, WA–Baron Inn: Field behind hotel. Two dog limit, no weight restrictions; $83–143; $15 flat fee for pets; 19233 Hwy. 2; 360/794-3111.

Mount Vernon, WA–College Way Inn: Dogs not allowed in pool area and must be kept on leash at all times in public areas. Two dog limit, no weight restrictions; $70–96; $10 pet fee; 300 W. College Way; 360/424-4287.

Mount Vernon, WA–Cottontree Inn: Third floor only; two dogs, no weight restrictions; $98–109; $25 per stay flat fee; 2300 Market St.; 360/428-5678.

Olympia, WA–Aladdin Motor Inn: Unlimited size and number of dogs, at the discretion of management; $72–79; $5 pet fee; 900 Capitol Way S.; 360/352-7200.

Puyallup, WA–Park Plaza: Goodie bag at check-in. Two small dogs or one large dog; $124–146; $25 flat fee; 620 S. Hill Park Dr.; 253/848-1500.

Seattle, WA–Evergreen Inn: Two dogs, no weight restrictions; $80–164; $10 pet fee; 13700 Aurora Ave N.; 206/361-3700.

Snoqualmie Pass, WA–Summit Inn: One large or two small dogs; $120–219; $25 flat fee per room; 603 Hwy. 90; 425/434-6300.

Tacoma, WA–Lakewood Motor Inn: No restrictions; $61–85; $10 flat fee; 6125 Motor Ave. S.W.; 253/584-2212.

Tacoma, WA–Tacoma Inn: Smoking rooms only; two dog limit, no weight restrictions; $76–120; $20 flat fee per stay; 8726 Hosmer St.; 253/535-2880.

Toppenish, WA–Lincoln Inn: Two dog limit, under 15 pounds; $87–131; $10 pet fee; 515 S. Elm St.; 509/865-7444.

Tumwater, WA–Tumwater Inn: Four dog limit, no weight restrictions; $77–94; $10 pet fee; 5188 Capitol Blvd. S.; 360/956-1235.

Union Gap, WA–Ahtanun: One dog, under 50 pounds; $109–131; $10 pet fee; 2408 Rudkin Rd.; 509/248-9700.

Yakima, WA–Peppertree Yakima Inn: Two dog limit, under 10 pounds; $65–164; $10 pet fee; 1614 N. 1st St.; 509/453-8898.

Oregon

Albany, OR–Pony Soldier: No restrictions; $87–98; $10 pet fee; 315 Airport Rd.; 541/928-6322.

Ashland, OR–Bard's Inn: Two dog limit; $90–200; $15 pet fee; 132 N. Main St.; 541/482-0049.

Ashland, OR–Windsor Inn: No restrictions; $87–153; $15 pet fee; 541/488-2330.

Astoria, OR: Three dog limit, at managers discretion for size and temperament; $75–330; $10 pet fee; 555 Hamburg Ave.; 503/325-2205.

Bandon, OR–Inn at Face Rock: Dog rooms do not have ocean view, but the beach is dog-friendly. No restrictions; $97–280; $15 for the first dog, $5 each additional dog, per stay; 3225 Beach Loop Rd.; 541/347-9441.

Beaverton, OR–Greenwood Inn: Nonsmoking dog rooms are available on the first floor. No restrictions; $77–120; pet fee $20 flat fee per stay; 10700 S.W. Canyon Rd.; 503/643-7444.

Bend, OR: No restrictions; $87–142; pet fee $10, $50 if not declared; 721 N.E. 3rd St.; 541/382-1515.

Brookings, OR–Beachfront Inn: No restrictions; $109–215; $5 pet fee; 16008 Boat Basin Rd.; 541/469-7779.

Cascade Locks, OR–Columbia River Inn: No restrictions; $71–142; $10 pet fee; 735 Wanapa St.; 541/374-8777.

Coos Bay, OR–Holiday Motel: Two dog limit, 35 pounds or less; $82–175; $10 pet fee; 411 N. Bayshore Dr.; 541/269-5111.

Cottage Grove, OR–Village Green Inn: Super dog-friendly! Hotel has an entire building for dog owners include singles, doubles, smoking and non-smoking rooms. Grounds include 14 acres to walk on leash. Treats and other specials given at check-in. $76–120; no pet fee except $50 penalty if dog is not declared at registration; 725 Row River Rd.; 541/942-2491.

Creswell, OR–Creswell Inn: No restrictions. Small off-leash area on property. $76–131; $10 flat fee for all dogs; 345 E. Oregon Ave.; 541/895-3341.

Dallas, OR–Dallas Inn and Suites: One dog limit, 20 pounds max, smoking rooms only. $87–98; $10 pet fee; 250 Orchard Dr.; 503/623-6000.

The Dalles, OR: Small dogs only, two dog limit; $69–98; $10 pet fee; 112 W. 2nd St.; 541/296-9107.

Eugene, OR–Greentree Inn: Two dog limit, small pets only, special treat bag given at check-in. $88–104; refundable $30 deposit per dog, depending on room condition; 1759 Franklin Blvd.; 541/485-2727.

Eugene, OR–New Oregon: Two dog limit, do not leave dog unattended, special treat bag given at check-in. $88–104; refundable $30 deposit per dog, depending on room condition; 1655 Franklin Blvd.; 541/683-3669.

Forest Grove, OR–University Inn and Suites: No restrictions; $76–109; $10 pet fee; 3933 Pacific Ave.; 503/992-8888.

Grants Pass, OR–Grants Pass Inn: Content, well-behaved dogs may be left unattended for short periods, such as dinner. Biscuits given at check-in. No restrictions; $81–128; $10 flat fee per stay; 111 N.E. Agness Ave.; 541/476-1117

Grants Pass, OR–Inn at the Rogue: Grassy hill for on-leash walks. No restrictions; $66–132; Under 20 pounds, $10 per dog, per night and $30 refundable deposit; Over 20 pounds $20 per dog, per night, and $50 refundable deposit; 8959 Rogue River Hwy.; 541/582-2200.

Gresham, OR–Pony Soldier Motor Inn: Small and medium dogs only; $87–108; no pet fee; 1060 N.E. Cleveland; 503/665-1591.

Hood River, OR–Hood River Inn: Treats given at check-in. No restrictions; $87–153; $12 pet fee; 1108 E. Marina Way; 541/386-2200.

Klamath Falls, OR–Klamath Inn: No restrictions; $86–90; no pet fee; 4061 S. 6th St.; 541/882-1200.

Lake Oswego, OR–Sherwood Inn: Two dog limit; $49; $10 pet fee; 15700 S.W. Upper Boones Ferry Rd.; 503/620-2980.

La Pine, OR–Newberry Station: Dogs under 25 pounds only; $98–131; $25 pet deposit, $10 is nonrefundable; 16515 Reed Rd.; 541/541/536-5130.

Madras, OR–Rama Inn: Treat bag given at check-in. Four dog limit, no pit bulls; $76–98; $20 per dog, per stay; 12 S.W. 4th St.; 541/475-6141.

Medford, OR–Horizon Inn: Across the street from Medford's off-leash dog park. $75–91; flat $10 fee per night for all dogs; 1154 Barnett Rd.; 541/779-5085.

Newport, OR–Agate Beach Inn: Treats, dog sheets/bedding given at check-in. Two dog limit; $87–164; $15 per dog, per stay; 3019 N. Coast Hwy.; 541/265-9411.

Oakridge, OR–Oakridge Inn: No restrictions; $76–98; $10 pet fee; 47433 Hwy. 58; 541/782-2212.

Portland, OR–Inn at the Meadows: Biscuits available at front desk. Two dog limit, 50 pounds or less per dog; $87–109; $20 flat fee per stay; $79–89; 1215 N. Hayden Meadows; 503/286-9600.

Portland, OR–Northwind Inn: Four dog limit, each less than 30 pounds, at discretion of front desk staff; $84–99; $10 pet fee; 16105 S.W. Pacific Hwy.; 503/431-2100.

Reedsport, OR–Salbasgeon Inn: Two dog limit, less than 70 pounds each; large, well-behaved dogs allowed for an extra fee at staff discretion; $81–182; $10 flat fee per stay, $40 if dog is undeclared; 1400 Hwy. 101 S.; 541/271-4831.

Roseburg, OR–Garden Villa: Bags are available at the front desk and there is a walking trail behind hotel; $76–104; $15 per dog, per stay, plus credit card or $125 cash refundable deposit; 760 N.W. Garden Valley Blvd.; 541/672-1601.

Salem, OR–Mill Creek Inn: One dog limit, less than 20 pounds; $94–110; $10 pet fee; 3125 Ryan Dr. S.E.; 503/585-3332.

Salem, OR–New Kings Inn: No restrictions; $80–94; $12 pet fee; 1600 Motor Ct. N.E.; 503/581-1559.

Salem, OR–Pacific Highway Inn: Two dog limit; $79–98; $20 pet fee up to $40 maximum per stay; 4646 Portland Rd. N.E.; 503/390-3200.

Sandy, OR–Sandy Inn: Two dog limit; $90–126; $10 pet fee, no charge for service dogs; 37465 Hwy. 26; 503/668-7100.

Seaside, OR–Oceanview Resort: Treat bags given at check-in. Dogs not permitted in whirlpool suites; $77–413; $20 pet fee; 414 N. Prom; 503/738-3334.

Sisters, OR–Ponderosa Lodge: Very pet-friendly! Doggie basket given at check-in with sheets, towels, bags, and treats. Lodge is near Deschutes National Forest and has walking trails next to pet wing. Two dog limit; $87–186; $15 per dog, per visit; 500 Hwy. 20 W.; 541/549-1234.

St. Helens, OR: Four dog limit depending on size; $76–142; $10 per dog, per visit; 585 S. Columbia River Hwy.; 503/397-3000.

Wilsonville, OR–Willamette Inn: Two dog limit, under 25 pounds; $76–94; No dog fee; 30800 S.W. Parkway Ave.; 503/682-2288.

Woodburn, OR: Smoking rooms only; $83–127; $10 pet fee; 2887 Newberg Hwy.; 503/982-6515.

British Columbia

Garibaldi Highlands–Best Western Sea to Sky Hotel: Pets up to 15 pounds, smoking rooms only; $102–129; $15 pet fee; 40330 Tantalus Way; 604/898-4874; http://seatosky.isquamish.com.

COAST HOTELS

British Columbia

Vancouver, BC–Downtown: Four dog limit; $129–209, Internet rates may be cheaper; $20 per pet, per night, negotiable; 1763 Comox St.; 604/688-7711; www.coasthotels.com.

Vancouver, BC–Airport: $89–105; $20 per pet, per night; 1041 S.W. Marine Dr.; 604/263-1555; www.coasthotels.com.

COMFORT INN AND SUITES

Not all Comfort Inns allow pets, and each location's rules and fees vary. The fees assume payment with credit cards in case of damages. Cash transactions may require additional refundable deposits. 800/228-5150; www.comfortinn.com.

Washington

Ellensburg, WA: No restrictions. $70–155; $10 dog fee; 1722 Canyon Rd.; 509/925-7037.

Federal Way, WA: $69–149; $20 per week for 1–2 dogs totaling no more than 80 pounds; 31622 Pacific Hwy. S.; 253/529-0101.

Kent, WA: Limit one dog of 20 pounds or less; $69–149; $20 pet fee; 22311 84th Ave. S.; 253/872-2211.

Tacoma, WA: Up to three small dogs; $106–131; $15 per dog, per stay. 5601 Pacific Hwy. E.; 253/926-2301.

Vancouver, WA: $59–119; $10 for 1–2 dogs per night, $15 per night for three dogs; 13207 N.E. 20th Ave.; 360/574-6000.

Wenatchee, WA: Limit two dogs less than 50 pounds; $81–99; $10 per dog, per stay; 815 N. Wenatchee Ave.; 509/662-1700.

Yakima, WA: Limit three dogs, 15 pounds or under; $89–129; $10 per dog, per stay; 3702 Fruitvale Blvd.; 509/249-1900.

Oregon

Cottage Grove, OR: No restrictions; $59–79; $10 pet fee; 845 Gateway Blvd.; 541/942-9747.

Grants Pass, OR: Three small dogs or one large; $70–114; $100 refundable deposit; 1889 N.E. 6th St.; 541/479-8301.

Seaside, OR: No restrictions; $79–249; $10 flat fee per stay; 545 Broadway; 503/738-3011.

Sisters, OR: One dog under 60 pounds; $90–130; no pet fee; 540 Hwy. 20 W.; 541/549-7829.

Springfield, OR: Smoking rooms only; three dog limit, less than 50 pounds; $59–145; $10 pet fee; 969 Kruse Way; 541/746-5359.

The Dalles, OR: Limit two dogs under 20 pounds; $60–129; $10 pet fee; 351 Lone Pine Dr.; 541/298-2800.

Wilsonville, OR: Two dog limit; $60–100; $10 pet fee; 8855 S.W. Citizen Dr.; 503/682-9000.

British Columbia

Chilliwack: Comfort Inn by Journey's End, main floor only; caters to nearby dog shows, so allows many pets in one room; $89–99; pet fee is $5 flat fee per night; 45405 Luckakuck Wy.; 604/858-0636.

DAYS INN

Rules and regulations vary. 800/DAYS INN (800/329-7466); www.daysinn.com.

Washington

Auburn, WA: Limit one dog under 20 pounds; $59–79; $10 pet fee; 1521 D St. N.E.; 253/939-5950.

Bellingham, WA: Dogs under 30 pounds; $59–79; $7 pet fee; 125 E. Kellogg Rd.; 360/671-6200.

Everett, WA: No restrictions; $55–75; $10 pet fee; 1602 S.E. Everett Mall Way.; 425/355-1570.

Fife, WA: Limit two small to medium dogs; $49–59; $5 pet fee; 3021 Pacific Hwy. E.; 253/922-3500.

Lacey, WA: Limit two dogs under 50 pounds; $55–90; $10 pet fee; 120 College St. S.E.; 360/493-1991.

Mount Vernon, WA: Limit three dogs; $56–70; $10 pet fee; 2009 Riverside Dr.; 360/424-4141.

Port Orchard, WA: No restrictions; $69–109; $10 pet fee; 220 Bravo Terrace; 360/895-7818.

Seattle, WA: Limit one small dog; $59–99; $10 pet fee; Town Center, 2205 7th Ave.; 206/448-3434.

Tacoma, WA: Limit two dogs; $45–60; $30 per dog, per stay; 6802 Tacoma Mall Blvd.; 253/475-5900.

Vancouver, WA: Limit two dogs under 30 pounds; $45–69; $15 pet fee; 221 N.E. Chkalov Dr.; 360/256-7044.

Oregon

Albany, OR: Limit three dogs under 50 pounds; $54–75; $10 flat pet fee per stay; 1100 Price Rd.; 541/928-5050.

Corvallis, OR: No restrictions; $60–82;
$5 pet fee small dogs, $10 pet fee large dogs; 1113 N.W. 9th St.; 541/754-7474.

Eugene, OR: Two dog limit; $55–113; no pet fee, but no discounts or coupons with dogs; 1859 Franklin Blvd.; 541/342-6383.

Portland, OR–North: Four dog limit; $65–85; $15 flat fee per stay for pets; 9930 N. Whitaker Rd.; 503/289-1800.

British Columbia

Days Inn on the Harbour: Restrict to smoking rooms. Three pet limit; $69–213; $10 flat pet fee; 427 Belleville St.; 250/386-3451; www.days-innvictoria.com.

ECONO LODGE

Rules and regulations vary. 800/55 ECONO (800/553-2666); www.econolodge.com.

Washington

SeaTac, WA: Limit two dogs under 25 pounds; $54–79; $10 pet fee; 19225 International Blvd.; 206/824-1350.

Sequim, WA: One dog limit; $55–104; $10 pet fee; 801 E. Washington St.; 360/683-7113.

Woodland, WA: Three dog limit; $44–74; $10 per dog, per stay; 1500 Atlantic Ave.; 360/225-6548.

Oregon

Bend, OR: Limit three small or two large dogs; $56–99; $10 pet fee; 20600 Grandview Dr.; 541/318-0848.

Canby, OR: One dog limit; $55–75; $10 refundable deposit; 463 S.W. 1st Ave.; 503/266-5400.

Corvallis, OR: Two dog limit; $44–70; $5 pet fee; 345 N.W. 2nd St.; 541/752-9601.

Gold Beach, OR: No restrictions; $40–125; $10 pet fee; 29171 Ellensburg Ave.; 541/247-6606.

Lincoln City, OR:. Dogs under 40 lbs., but no rottweilers, Doberman pinschers, or pit bulls; $40–80; $10 pet fee; 1713 N.W. 21st St.; 541/994-5281.

Klamath Falls, OR: No restrictions; $41–48; no pet fees, but deposit required if paying with cash; 75 Main St.; 541/884-7735.

Newport, OR: Limit three small or two large dogs; $39–99; no pet fee; 606 S.W. Coast Hwy.; 541/265-7723.

Portland, OR–Northeast/Hollywood District: No restrictions; $40–70; $5 pet fee; 3800 N.E. Sandy Blvd.; 503/460-9000.

GUEST HOUSE INTERNATIONAL

Rules and regulations vary. 800/21-GUEST (800/214-8378); www.guesthouseintl.com.

Washington

Aberdeen, WA: Two dog limit; $70–150; $10 pet fee, plus a $50 refundable deposit; 701 E. Heron; 360/537-7460.

Kelso, WA: Limit three dogs; $66–190; $10 pet fee; 501 Three Rivers Dr.; 360/414-5953.

Tumwater, WA: Limit two dogs; $85–105; $15 pet fee; 1600 74th Ave. S.W.; 360/943-5040.

HOLIDAY INN, HOLIDAY INN EXPRESS

Pet room availability and rates may vary for special occasions. 800/HOLIDAY (800/465-4329); www.holiday-inn.com or www.ichotelsgroup.com.

Washington

Poulsbo, WA: Limit two dogs under 25 pounds; $69–89; $10 pet fee; 19801 7th Ave. N.E.; 360/697-2119.

SeaTac, WA: No restrictions; $99–134; $125 refundable deposit; 19621 International Blvd.; 206/824-3200.

Yakima, WA: Small dogs only; $55–85; $10 pet fee; 1001 East A St.; 509/249-1000.

Oregon

Astoria, OR: No restrictions; $79–179; $15 pet fee; 204 W. Marine Dr.; 503/325-6222.

Bend, OR: Four bodies per room (dogs and humans combined); $65–129; $10 pet fee; 20615 Grandview Dr.; 541/317-8500.

Corvallis, OR: Two dog limit; $89–109; $15 total per day; 781 N.W. 2nd St; 541/752-0800.

Cottage Grove, OR: Limit two dogs under 40 pounds; $64–89; $10 pet fee; 1601 Gateway Blvd.; 541/942-1000.

Grants Pass, OR: Four dog limit; $79–129; $5 pet fee; 105 N.E. Agness Ave.; 541/471-6144.

Klamath Falls, OR: Two dog limit; $93–142; $15 flat pet fee per stay; 2500 S. 6th St.; 541/884-9999.

Portland, OR–Airport: Limit two dogs under 25 pounds; $104–275; $20 flat fee per stay; 8439 N.E. Columbia Blvd.; 503/256-5000.

Roseburg, OR: Three dog limit; $69–94; $5 per room, per day; 375 W. Harvard Ave.; 541/673-7517.

Salem, OR: Limit four dogs under 25 pounds or three dogs over 25 pounds; $71–114; $15 per dog, per stay; 890 Hawthorne Ave. N.E.; 503/391-7000.

Springfield, OR: Limit three dogs under 50 pounds; $69–109; $10 pet fee; 3480 Hutton St.; 541/746-8471.

Wilsonville, OR: No restrictions; $79–124; $15 pet fee; 25425 S.W. 95th Ave.; 503/682-2211.

British Columbia

North Vancouver–Holiday Inn Hotel and Suites: Limit two dogs, under 25 pounds; $119–169; $20 pet fee; 700 Old Lillooet Rd.; 604/985-3111; www .hinorthvancouver.com.

Vancouver–Airport: Smaller dogs only; $109–169; no pet fee; 10720 Cambie Rd.; 604/821-1818.

Vancouver–Centre: Limit one medium-sized dog; $94–229; $20 pet fee; 711 W. Broadway at Heather; 604/879-0511; www.holidayinnvancouver.com.

Vancouver–Downtown Tower and Suites: Dogs allowed in smoking rooms only; $150–259; no pet fee; 1110 Howe St. at Helmcken; 604/684-2151.

KOA CAMPGROUNDS

Aggressive dogs of any breed are not welcome at any KOA. If your dog shows behavior that is protective and unfriendly to strangers, please leave it at home. If you bring your dog and it exhibits this type of behavior, the owner or management of the KOA will ask you to find other camping accommodations. KOA Kampgrounds have policies against accepting breeds that have been identified by its insurance provider as having a history of unfriendly and aggressive behavior to other dogs and humans, specifically pit bulls and pit bull mixes, rottweilers, and Doberman pinschers.

KOA does not charge pet fees. Dogs are not allowed in Kamping Kottages or Kabins. 406/248-7444; www.koa.com.

Washington

Anacortes/Burlington, WA: Tents $21–25; RVs $27–34; 6397 N. Green Rd.; 360/724-5511.

Bay Center/Willapa Bay, WA: Tents $21–25; RVs $25–32; 16 miles S. of Raymond on Hwy. 101; 360/875-6344.

Bellingham/Lynden, WA: Tents $20–31; RVs $25–37; 8717 Line Rd.; 360/354-4772.

Chehalis, WA: Tents $18–23; RVs $25–34; 118 Hwy. 12; 360/262-9220.

Concrete/Grady Creek, WA: Tents $19–23; RVs $24–32; 7370 Russell Rd.; 360/826-3554.

Ellensburg, WA: Tents $20–25; RVs $25–37; 32 Thorp Hwy. S.; 509/925-9319.

Leavenworth/Wenatchee, WA: Tents $21–34; RVs $26–41; 11401 Riverbend Dr.; 509/548-7709.

Port Angeles/Sequim, WA: Tents $21–28; RVs $21–38; 80 O'Brien Rd.; 360/457-5916.

Seattle/Tacoma, WA: Tents $28–31; RVs $33–50; 5801 S. 212th, Kent; 253/872-8652.

Yakima, WA: Tents $22–24; RVs $26–34; 1500 Keys Rd.; 509/248-5882.

Oregon

Albany/Corvallis, OR: Very dog-friendly! Tents $16–21; RVs $24–33; 33775 Oakville Rd. South; 541/967-8521.

Astoria/Seaside, OR: Tents $23–37; RVs $30–60; 1100 N.W. Ridge Rd.; 503/861-2606.

Bandon/Port Orford, OR: Tents $22–24; RVs $26–32; 46612 Hwy. 101; 541/348-2358.

Bend/Sisters, OR: Tents $20–40; RVs $20–40; 67667 Hwy. 20 W.; 541/549-3021.

Cascade Locks/Portland East, OR: Tents $20–24; RVs $22–45; 841 N.W. Forest Ln.; 541/374-8668.

Grants Pass/Redwood Highway, OR: Tents $20–24; RVs $23–30; 13370 Redwood Hwy. (Hwy. 199); 541/476-6508.

Grants Pass/Sunny Valley, OR: Tents $20–2; RVs $23–27; 140 Old Stage Rd.; 541/479-0209.

Klamath Falls, OR: Tents $20–24; RVs $23–30; 3435 Shasta Way; 541/884-4644.

Lincoln City, OR: Tents $22–28; RVs $24–32; 5298 N.E. Park Ln.; 541/994-2961.

Madras/Culver, OR: Tents $19–25; RVs $21–32; 2435 S.W. Jericho Ln.; 541/546-3046.

Medford/Gold Hill, OR: Tents $20–24; RVs $26–32; 12297 Blackwell Rd.(Gold Hill Exit 40); 541/855-7710.

Oregon Dunes, OR: Tents $15–29; RVs $20–45; 68632 Hwy. 101; 541/756-4851.

Waldport/Newport, OR: Tents $18–36; RVs $26–47; Alsea Bay Bridge, Waldport; 541/563-2250.

LA QUINTA
There are no restrictions or pet fees at the following locations, unless otherwise noted. 800/NU ROOMS (800/687-6667); www.laquinta.com.

Washington

Kent, WA: Limit one dog under 25 pounds; $49–79; $10 flat fee per stay; 25100 74th Ave. S.; 253/520-6670.

SeaTac, WA: Three dog limit; $85–109; 2824 S. 188th St.; 206/241-5211.

Seattle, WA: $69–149; 2224 8th Ave.; 206/624-6820.

Tacoma, WA: $89–119; 1425 E. 27th St.; 253/383-0146.

Wenatchee, WA: $74–99; a $50 refundable deposit is required for four or more dogs; 1905 N. Wenatchee Ave.; 509/664-6565.

Oregon

Albany, OR: $67–141; 251 Airport Rd. S.E.; 541/928-0921.

Ashland, OR: $69–139; 434 S. Valley View Rd.; 541/482-6932.

Bend, OR: $59–150; 61200 S. Hwy. 97; 541/388-2227.

Eugene, OR: $81–135; 155 Day Island Rd.; 541/344-8335.

Grants Pass, OR: Two dog limit; $60–130; 243 N.E. Morgan Ln.; 541/472-1808.

Newport, OR: $64–149; 45 S.E. 32nd St.; 541/867-7727.

Portland, OR–Airport: Limit two small or one large dog; $69–89; 11207 N.E. Holman St.; 503/382-3820.

Portland, OR–Lloyd Center: $72–129; 431 N.E. Multnomah St.; 503/233-7933.

Portland, OR–Northwest: $69–129; 4319 N.W. Yeon Ave.; 503/497-9044.

Tualatin, OR: $69–89; $10 flat pet fee per stay; 7640 S.W. Warm Springs Rd.; 503/612-9952.

Woodburn, OR: Two dog limit; $62–84; 120 N. Arney Rd.; 503/982-1727.

MARRIOTT
Rules and regulations vary. 800/228-9290; www.marriott.com.

Washington

Bellevue, WA– Residence Inn: Two dog limit; $89–179; $15 pet fee; 14455 N.E. 29th Pl.; 425/882-1222.

Kent, WA–TownePlace Suites: No restrictions; $75–95; $10 pet fee; 18123 72nd Ave. S.; 253/796-6000.

Lynnwood, WA–Residence Inn: No restrictions; $89–149; $10 pet fee; 18200 Alderwood Mall Pkwy.; 425/771-1100.

Mukilteo, WA–TownePlace Suites: Limit two dogs under 75 pounds; $79–99; $15 pet fee; 8521 Mukilteo Speedway; 425/551-5900.

Redmond, WA–Residence Inn: Limit two dogs under 60 pounds; $99–189; $10 per dog, per day, plus a $50 nonrefundable cleaning fee; 7575 164th Ave. N.E.; 425/497-9226.

Renton, WA–Springhill Suites: Two dog limit; $74–109; $15 per dog, per day or $150 flat fee per room if over four days. 300 S.W. 19th St.; 425/917-2000.

Seattle, WA–Residence Inn at Fairview: Three dog limit; $109–169; $10 pet fee; 800 Fairview Ave. N.; 206/624-6000.

Vancouver, WA–Residence Inn: No restrictions; $99–189; $75 nonrefundable fee; 8005 N.E. Parkway Dr.; 360/253-4800.

Oregon

Eugene-Springfield, OR–Residence Inn: No restrictions; $114–124; $75 nonrefundable fee; 25 Club Rd.; 541/342-7171.

Hillsboro, OR–Residence Inn: No restrictions; $99–159; $10 per dog, per day up to seven days or $75 flat fee per dog over seven days. 18855 N.W. Tanasbourne Dr.; 503/531-3200.

Hillsboro, OR–TownePlace Suites: No restrictions; $60–105; $10 pet fee; 6550 N.E. Brighton St.; 503/268-6000.

Lake Oswego, OR–Residence Inn: Two dog limit; $99–199; $75 nonrefundable pet fee; 15200 S.W. Bangy Rd.; 503/684-2603.

Portland, OR–Downtown RiverPlace Residence Inn: No restrictions; $89–229; $10 pet fee; 2115 S.W. River Pkwy.; 503/552-9500.

Portland, OR–Lloyd Center: No restrictions; $89–175; $50 nonrefundable fee; 1710 N.E. Multnomah St.; 503/288-1400.

Portland, OR–Marriott City Center: Three dog limit; $149–189; $25 per dog, per stay, $50 maximum; 520 S.W. Broadway; 503/226-6300.

MOTEL 6

All Motel 6 properties accept one dog under 80 pounds per room. There are no dog fees if you declare pets at check-in. There is a 10 percent discount for booking online. 800/4MOTEL6 (800/466-8356); www.motel6.com.

Washington

Bellingham, WA: $44–66; 3701 Byron St.; 360/671-4494.

Centralia, WA: $36–52; 1310 Belmont Ave.; 360/330-2057.

Everett, WA–North: $42–56; 10006 Evergreen Way; 425/347-2060.

Everett, WA–South: $44–56; 224 128th St. S.W.; 425/353-8120.

Fife, WA: $44–56; 5201 20th St. E.; 253/922-1270.

Issaquah, WA: $56–72; 1885 15th Pl. N.W.; 425/392-8405.

Kelso, WA: $42–63; 106 N. Minor Rd.; 360/425-3229.

Kent, WA: $46–60; 20651 Military Rd. S.; 206/824-9902.

Kirkland, WA: $56–68; 12010 120th Pl. N.E.; 425/821-5618.

Mountlake Terrace–Studio 6: $49 per night, weekly $249–319; 6017 224th St. S.W.; 425/771-3139.

SeaTac, WA–North: $46–58; 16500 International Blvd.; 206/246-4101.

SeaTac, WA–South: $46–58; 18900 47th Ave. S.; 206/241-1648.

Tacoma–South, WA: $46–64; 1811 S. 76th St.; 253/473-7100.

Tumwater, WA: $44–52; 400 W. Lee St.; 360/754-7320.

Yakima, WA: $36–48; 1104 N. 1st St.; 509/454-0080.

Oregon

Albany, OR: $50–56; 2735 E. Pacific Blvd.; 541/926-4233.

Bend, OR: $51–65; 201 N.E. 3rd St.; 541/382-8282.

Coos Bay, OR: $44–68; 1445 Bayshore Dr.; 541/267-7171.

Corvallis, OR: $49–58; 935 N.W. Garfield Ave.; 541/758-9125.

Eugene, OR: $46–62; 3690 Glenwood Dr.; 541/687-2395.

Gold Beach, OR: $47–78; 94433 Jerry's Flat Rd.; 541/247-4533.

Grants Pass, OR: $46–64; 1800 N.E. 7th St.; 541/474-1331.

Klamath Falls, OR: $42–64; 5136 S. 6th St.; 541/884-2110.

Lincoln City, OR: $48–75; 3517 N.W. Hwy. 101; 541/996-9900.

Medford, OR–North: $52–68; 2400 Biddle Rd.; 541/779-0550.

Medford, OR–South: $46–64; 950 Alba Dr.; 541/773-4290.

Portland, OR–Airport: $46–59; 9225 S.E.Stark St.; 503/255-0808.

Portland, OR–Central: $44–64; 3104 S.E. Powell Blvd.; 503/238-0600.

Portland, OR–North: $45–85; 1125 N. Schmeer Rd.; 503/247-3700.

Redmond, OR: $51–61; 2247 S. Hwy. 97; 541/923-2100.

Roseburg, OR: $46–56; 3100 N.W. Aviation Dr.; 541/464-8000.

Salem, OR: $44–64; 1401 Hawthorne Ave. N.E.; 503/371-8024.

Seaside, OR: $48–73; 2369 S. Roosevelt Dr. (Hwy 101); 503/738-6269.

Springfield, OR: $44–58; 3752 International Ct.; 541/741-1105.

Tigard, OR: $46–54; 17950 S.W. McEwan Ave.; 503/620-2066.

Troutdale, OR: $40–60; 1610 N.W. Frontage Rd.; 503/665-2254.

QUALITY INN

Rules and regulations vary. 800/228-5151; www.qualityinn.com.

Oregon

Bend, OR: Three dog limit; $59–99; $10 pet fee; 20600 Grandview Dr.; 541/318-0848.

Eugene, OR: Two dog limit; $50–108; $5 pet fee; 2121 Franklin Blvd.; 541/342-1243.

Klamath Falls, OR: No restrictions; $79–99; $10 pet fee; 100 Main St.; 541/882-4666.

Portland, OR–Airport: No restrictions; $65–125; $10 pet fee; 8247 N.E. Sandy Blvd.; 503/256-4111.

Roseburg, OR: No restrictions; $59–109; $7 pet fee; 427 N.W. Garden Valley Blvd.; 541/673-5561.

RAMADA INN

Rules and regulations vary. 800/2RAMADA (800/272-6232); www.ramada.com.

Washington

Bellingham, WA: No restrictions; $52–59; $10 pet fee; 215 N. Samish Way; 360/734-8830.

Fife, WA: Two dog limit; $45–83; $10 pet fee; 3501 Pacific Hwy. E.; 253/926-1000.

Longview, WA: No restrictions; $59–109; $15 flat fee for pets; 723 7th Ave.; 360/414-1000.

Seattle, WA–Northgate: No restrictions; $99–139; $10 pet fee; 2140 N. Northgate Way; 206/365-0700.

Sequim, WA: No restrictions; $49–119; $10 pet fee; 1095 E. Washington St.; 360/683-1775.

Tacoma/Lakewood, WA: No restrictions; $59–99; $25 flat fee for pets; 9920 S. Tacoma Way; 253/588-5241.

Oregon

Eugene, OR: No restrictions; $55–108; $15 flat fee; 225 Coburg Rd.; 541/342-5181.

Tigard, OR: No restrictions; $69–89; $10 pet fee; 17993 S.W. Lower Boones Ferry Rd.; 503/620-2030.

RED LION

There are no restrictions or fees for pets at these locations, unless stated otherwise below. 800/RED LION (800/733-5466); www.redlion.com.

Washington

Aberdeen, WA: $64–89; 521 W. Wishkah St.; 360/532-5210.

Kelso, WA: $49–79; $10 flat fee for pets; 510 Kelso Dr.; 360/636-4400.

Port Angeles, WA: $80–143; 221 N. Lincoln St.; 360/452-9215.

Seattle, WA–South: Two dog limit; $65–155; $35 deposit, $20 of which is refundable; 11244 Pacific Hwy. S.; 206/762-0300.

Vancouver, WA–Red Lion at the Quay: Two dog limit; $59–99; $25 per dog, per stay; 100 Columbia St.; 360/694-8341.

Wenatchee, WA: Two dog limit; $65–155; 1225 N. Wenatchee Ave.; 509/663-0711.

Yakima, WA: Three dog limit; $79–119; $10 pet fee; 818 N. 1st St.; 509/453-0391.

Oregon

Astoria, OR: Three dog limit; $69–129; $10 per dog, per stay; 400 Industry St.; 503/325-7373.

Bend, OR–North: $64–84; 1415 N.E. 3rd St.; 541/382-7011.

Bend, OR–South: $64–84; 849 N.E. 3rd St.; 541/382-8384.

Coos Bay, OR: $134–188; 1313 N. Bayshore Dr.; 541/267-4141.

Eugene, OR: $69–99; 205 Coburg Rd.; 541/342-5201.

Klamath Falls, OR: $62–89; 3612 S. 6th St.; 541/882-8864.

McMinnville, OR: $97–134; $10 pet fee; 2535 N.E. Cumulus Ave.; 503/472-1500.

Portland, OR–Airport: $69–99; $15 per dog, per stay; 5019 N.E. 102nd Ave.; 503/252-6397.

Salem, OR: $59–109; $10 pet fee; 3301 Market St. N.E.; 503/370-7888.

SHILO INNS

There are no restrictions or fees for pets at these locations, unless stated otherwise below. 800/222-2244; www.shiloinn.com.

Washington

Tacoma, WA: $55–99; $10 pet fee; 7414 S. Hosmer St.; 253/475-4020.

Vancouver-Hazel Dell, WA: $55–79; $10 pet fee; 13206 N.E. Hwy. 99; 360/573-0511.

Vancouver, WA: Limit one dog under 40 pounds; $55–79; $10 flat fee; 401 E. 13th St.; 360/696-0411.

Oregon

Beaverton, OR: Two dog limit; $55–109; $10 pet fee; 9900 S.W. Canyon Rd.; 503/297-2551.

Bend, OR: $69–195; $10 pet fee; 3105 O.B. Riley Rd.; 541/389-9600.

Grants Pass, OR: Three dog limit; $55–89; $10 flat fee; 1880 N.W. 6th St.; 541/479-8391.

Klamath Falls, OR: $79–149; $10 pet fee; 2500 Almond St.; 541/885-7980.

Medford, OR: $55–89; $10 flat fee; 2111 Biddle Rd.; 541/770-5151.

Newberg, OR: $59–99; $10 pet fee; 501 Sitka Ave.; 503/537-0303.

Newport, OR: $75–199; $10 pet fee; 536 S.W. Elizabeth; 541/265-7701.

Seaside, OR: Limit two dogs under 50 pounds; $59–169; $20 pet fee; 900 S. Holladay Dr.; 503/738-0549.

Springfield, OR: $59–119; 3350 Gateway; 541/747-0332.

The Dalles, OR: $59–139; $10 pet fee; 3223 Bret Clodfelter Way; 541/298-5502.

Tigard, OR: $59–99; $15 pet fee; 7300 S.W. Hazelfern Rd.; 503/639-2226.

Tigard, OR: $55–89; $10 pet fee; Washington Square, 10830 S.W. Greenburg Rd.; 503/620-4320.

Tillamook, OR: $59–129; $10 total pet fee per night; 2515 N. Main St.; 503/842-7971.

STARWOOD HOTELS

In 2003, all Starwood Properties, including Sherton, Westin, and W Hotels, made it corporate policy to accept and pamper pets after an independent study proved how loyal pet owners are to accommodations that accept their four-legged loved ones. Rules and regulations vary. www.starwood.com.

Washington

Seattle, WA–Westin: Very dog-friendly! Lots of treats and goodies, dog beds, and tips for owners. Dogs under 40 pounds only. $129–199; no pet fee; Downtown District, 1900 5th Ave.; 206/728-1000.

Tacoma, WA–Sheraton: No restrictions; $109–119; $50 refundable deposit authorized to your credit card; 1320 Broadway; 253/572-3200.

Oregon

Portland, OR–Sheraton Airport: $89–179; $25 nonrefundable pet fee; 8235 N.E. Airport Way; 503/281-2500.

Portland, OR–Sheraton Four Points Waterfront: No restrictions or fees; $79–159; 50 S.W. Morrison St.; 503/221-0711; www.fourpointsportland.com.

Portland, OR–Westin: $99–260; $50 nonrefundable pet fee; 750 S.W. Alder St.; 503/294-9000.

SUPER 8
Rules and regulations vary. 800/800-8000; www.super8.com.

Washington

Bremerton, WA: No restrictions; $58–81; $25 deposit per dog, $15 of which is refundable; 5068 Kitsap Way; 360/377-8881.

Ellensburg, WA: No restrictions; $60–95; $10 flat fee for pets; 1500 Canyon Rd.; 509/962-6888.

Federal Way, WA: No restrictions; $39–62; $10 per dog, per day, $30 maximum; 1688 S. 348th St.; 253/838-8808.

Ferndale, WA: No restrictions; $45–64; $10 flat fee; 5788 Barrett Ave.; 360/384-8881.

Kelso, WA: No restrictions; $44–71; $10 flat fee; 250 Kelso Dr.; 360/423-8880.

Lacey, WA: Two dog limit; $45–80; $25 deposit per room, $15 of which is refundable; 112 College St S.E.; 360/459-8888.

Long Beach, WA: Dog biscuits at front desk. No restrictions; $59–129; $5 pet fee; 500 Ocean Beach Blvd. S.; 360/642-8988.

Port Angeles, WA: Four dog limit; $57–93; $10 flat fee; 2104 E. 1st St.; 360/452-8401.

SeaTac, WA: Three dog limit; $59–89; $25 refundable deposit; 3100 S 192nd St.; 206/433-8188.

Union Gap, WA: No restrictions. $56–71; $25 refundable deposit; 2605 Rudkin Rd.; 509/248-8880.

Woodburn, OR: No restrictions; $43–66; $25 deposit, $15 of which is refundable; 821 Evergreen Rd.; 503/981-8881.

Oregon

Ashland, OR: One dog limit; $44–108; $10 per day fee; 2350 Ashland St.; 541/482-8887.

Bend, OR: Will decide size and quantity restrictions on an individual basis, so call ahead. $67–103; $5 pet fee; 1275 S. Hwy 97; 541/388-6888.

Grants Pass, OR: No restrictions or fees; $49–80; 1949 N.E. 7th St.; 541/474-0888.

Gresham, OR: Two dog limit; $49–69; $10 dog fee; 121 N.E. 181St Ave.; 503/661-5100.

Klamath Falls, OR: Three dog limit; $63–75; $25 refundable deposit; 3805 Hwy. 97 N.; 541/884-8880.

Portland, OR–Airport: No restrictions; $55–80; $25 refundable deposit; 11011 N.E. Holman St.; 503/257-8988.

Redmond, OR: No restrictions; $45–72; $10 flat fee for pets; 3629 S.W. 21st Pl.; 541/548-8881.

Roseburg, OR: Limit two dogs under 25 pounds; $46–65; no pet fee; 3200 N.W. Aviation Dr.; 541/672-8880.

Salem, OR: No restrictions; $54–76; $10 flat fee; 1288 Hawthorne Ave. N.E.; 503/370-8888.

Wilsonville, OR: Two dog limit; $38–64; $25 refundable deposit; 25438 S.W. Parkway Ave.; 503/682-2088.

TRAVELODGE

Rules and regulations vary. 800/578-7878; www.travelodge.com.

Washington

Auburn, WA: $59–99; $10 per pet, per night, but no more than $30 per pet, per week; 9 16th St. N.W.; 253/735-9600.

Edmonds, WA: Limit three small or two medium dogs; $59–109; $25 per dog, per stay; 23825 Hwy. 99; 425/771-8008.

Everett, WA: Limit two dogs under 75 pounds; $54–84; $5 pet fee; 3030 Broadway; 425/259-6141.

Fife, WA: No restrictions; $47–64; $50 deposit, refundable depending on length of stay and room condition; 3518 Pacific Hwy. E.; 253/922-0550.

Mercer Island, WA: Limit two dogs under 75 pounds; $66–79; $10 pet fee; 7645 Sunset Hwy.; 206/232-8000.

Renton, WA: Two dog limit; $45–79; $10 pet fee; 3700 E. Valley Rd.; 425/251-9591.

Seattle, WA–Space Needle: Limit two dogs under 30 pounds; $79–169; $10 pet fee; 200 6th Ave. N.; 206/441-7878.

Seattle, WA–West Seattle: This is the only motel in West Seattle, because zoning laws don't permit any more. Limit one dog under 30 pounds; $49–89; $35 fee per stay; 3512 S.W. Alaska St.; 206/937-9920.

Oregon

Grants Pass, OR: Limit one dog under 35 pounds; $59–69; $5 per day pet fee; 1950 N.W. Vine St.; 541/479-6611.

Hillsboro, OR: No restrictions; $38–42; $10 pet fee, $30 maximum per dog; 622 S.E. 10th Ave.; 503/640-4791.

Medford, OR: Limit one small dog; $59–99; no pet fee; 945 Alba Dr.; 541/773-1579.

Portland, OR: One dog limit; $59–99; $10 pet fee; 10450 S.W. Barbour Blvd.; 503/244-0151.

Roseburg, OR: Limit two dogs under 30 pounds; $60–89; $10 pet fee; 315 W. Harvard Ave.; 541/672-4836.

Salem, OR: Limit two dogs under 20 pounds; $49–69; $10 pet fee; 1555 State St.; 503/581-2466.

Troutdale, OR: Two dog limit; $38–59; $5 pet fee; 23705 N.E. Sandy Blvd.; 503/666-6623.

British Columbia

Sidney-Victoria Airport: Two dog limit; no alligators, boa constrictors, or tarantulas; $85–165; $10 pet fee; 2280 Beacon Ave.; 250/656-1176; www.airporttravelodge.com.

WINDMILL INNS

This is a very pet-friendly group of hotels. Windmill Inns are all nonsmoking facilities. It has a large number of designated pet rooms, gives out goodie bags, and has lists of area veterinarians and pet supply stores. No pet fees and no restrictions. 800/547-4747; www.windmillinns.com.

Oregon

Ashland, OR: $59–142; 2525 Ashland St.; 541/482-8310.

Medford, OR: $69–89; 1950 Biddle Rd.; 541/779-0050.

Roseburg, OR: $70–88; 1450 N.W. Mulholland Dr.; 541/673-0901.

Transportation

Washington

Guemes Island Ferry: A tiny ferry that takes about 10 minutes to go from Anacortes to Guemes Island, this county boat allows dogs in the car, or leashed on the open-air deck. Cost is $5.75 for vehicle and driver round-trip. 360/293-6356; www.skagitcounty.net, click on Guemes Island Ferry link.

Kenmore Air: This floatplane service flies to six airports in the San Juan Islands, leaving from floating airports on Lake Union and Lake Washington in Seattle. Dogs are welcome in the cabin with you and, if they are 23 pounds or under, can sit in your lap for no extra charge. Dogs 24 pounds and over are required to buy their own seats at child's fare rates. Kenmore will also transport animals in travel carriers without humans to accompany them; call for more information. Round-trip prices range $156–199 for adults, $149 for kids and dogs. 6321 N.E. 175th St., Kenmore, WA, 98028; 800/543-9595 or 425/486-1257; www.kenmoreair.com.

Victoria Clipper: The Clipper is a high-speed boat, passenger only, that goes between Seattle, Washington and Victoria, British Columbia. The ride takes 2.5 hours each way. Dogs are allowed in airline-approved kennels, and they are strapped to an outside deck. It could get a little chilly for them; bring their favorite blanket and put short-coated dogs in their coats. Cost for dogs is $10 each way; adult round-trip tickets range $106–133. 800/888-2535; www.victoriaclipper.com.

Washington State Ferry Association: This is the largest ferry system in the United States. There are 10 routes, served by 29 boats; all but one are car ferries, but you can walk on as a passenger or bicyclist on any of them:

• **Seattle to Bainbridge Island**

• **Seattle to Bremerton, Kitsap Peninsula**

• **Seattle to Vashon Island (passenger only)**

• **West Seattle to Vashon Island**

• **West Seattle to Kitsap Peninsula**

• **Edmonds to Kingston, Kitsap Peninsula**

• **Anacortes to the San Juan Islands and Sidney, B.C.**

• **Mukilteo to Whidbey Island**

• **Whidbey Island to Port Townsend, Olympic Peninsula**

• **Tacoma to Vashon Island**

Dogs can stay in the car or be on leash outside on the outer lower car deck. They can't go upstairs onto upper decks, even outside. Ferry schedules and pricing changes quarterly. 888/808-7977; www.wsdot.wa.gov/ferries.

Oregon

Broadway Cab: This taxi company in Portland will allow dogs if you call and let the driver know in advance. 503/227-1234.

British Columbia

BC Ferries: Pets are allowed on most of the BC ferries, including the route from Vancouver to Victoria. These ferries depart from Tsawassen, south of Vancouver, and arrive at Swartz Bay, north of Victoria near Sidney. Dogs are allowed on the open-air car deck and must stay in your car or tied in a designated pet area. Owners must stay with their pets. The travel time for this route is approximately an hour and 35 minutes. Guide dogs and certified assistance dogs are not required to stay on the car decks. From outside B.C.: 250/386-3431; from anywhere in B.C.: 888/BCFERRY (888/223-3779); bcferries.com.

Extended Trails

Regional

Pacific Crest Trail: Crisscrossing California, Oregon, and Washington on its way from Mexico to Canada, this American National Scenic Trail extends 2,650 miles. It transverses six ecozones, from high desert to old growth and arctic alpine. The Oregon section is typically wooded, generally the shortest and easiest terrain of the trail. Through the North Cascades, the Washington section boasts dramatic mountainous scenery and notoriously fickle weather patterns. The Pacific Crest Trail Association is in California: 5325 Elkhorn Blvd., PMB #256, Sacramento, CA 95842-2526; 916/349-2109; www.pcta.org.

Washington

Iron Horse State Park/John Wayne Pioneer Trail: Iron Horse is essentially 1,613 acres of easement through which the 100-mile-long John Wayne Trail passes from Vantage to North Bend. The trail is a wide dirt and gravel road that served as the right-of-way for the old Chicago–Milwaukee–St. Paul–Pacific Railroad. The mild grade is family-friendly, and it's easy to get to, never too far from the highway. Yet, you can disappear from civilization quickly into varied scenery and encounter cool things like high trestles and spooky tunnels (bring a flashlight). Along the way, you pass from mountains and valleys thick with forests to sagebrush desert and scrubland, as well as charming farm country. It intersects a handful of other state parks in the region where you can rest and camp and has campgrounds and trailheads of its own. In the summertime, you'll share the trail with horses and cyclists. In winter, bring paw booties, dog sleds, cross-country skis, and/or horseshoes to join snowmobiles on the trail. Dogs are welcome on an eight-foot or shorter leash.

You'll see signs that say Iron Horse State Park, John Wayne Pioneer Trail, or both. There is a $5 daily fee at all trailheads. While the trail is clearly marked and easy to follow, you can pick up maps for $2 at Lake Easton State Park, Exit 70 from I-90. Kiosks with trail information are located at Rattlesnake Lake in North Bend, and in Hyak, Easton, South Cle Elum, Thorp, and Kittatas. For trailhead directions, click the Iron Horse link on www.parks.wa.gov.

Oregon

Oregon Coast Trail: This is a 360-mile route from the tip of the state at the mouth of the Columbia River to the bottom at the California border. The majority of the trail is on the beach, sometimes so close you need a tide table to cross headlands when the tide is out. Some of it wanders inland through state forests and parks, and in between, landowners along the coast have generously provided easements and permits through property to make connections. Some of it is dirt and gravel, some paved, and some so narrow through brush you need a scent hound to pick up the trail. If you want to take on the whole thing, or major portions of it, buy a detailed point-to-point guide available at bookstores and magazine outlets. Contact the Trails Coordinator of the Oregon State Parks and Recreation Department for more information. 503/378-4168; www.oregonstateparks.org, type Oregon Coast Trail in the search bar.

OC&E Woods Line State Trail: At 100 miles long, this state trail is Oregon's longest linear park, stretching from Klamath Falls east to Bly and north to Sycan Marsh. The wide, level path is built on the rail bed of the Oregon, California, and Eastern Railroad (hence the OC&E). It's open to all nonmotorized travelers, so be prepared to yield right-of-way to horses and bicyclists, in-line skaters, and joggers. The farther you go, the more you'll run into the farm and ranch lands of the Klamath Basin, with great views of Mt. Shasta to the south. The first 15 miles of the trail is paved, but softer paws will prefer the wood-chip trail that parallels the asphalt. 800/551-6949; www.oregonstateparks .org/park_230.php.

Useful Organizations

Washington

Department of Fish and Wildlife: Contact this organization for fishing, shellfish gathering, and hunting licenses. Main Office: 360/902-2200; License Division: 360/902-2464; www.wdfw.wa.gov. Make license purchases online at www.greatlodge.com/wa.

Washington State Parks: All Washington state parks charge a $5 daily parking fee. Dogs are required to be on an 8-foot or shorter leash. State park camping costs $22 for RVs and $16 for tents, $1 less in the winter. For parks that require camping reservations, call 888/CAMPOUT (888/226-7688) or go to www.camis.com/wa.

KITSAP PENINSULA

Howe Farm Pets: An online Yahoo Group monitoring the development progress of an off-leash park at Howe Farm in Port Orchard; http://groups.yahoo.com/group/howefarmpets.

Kitsap Dog Parks, Inc.: A nonprofit organization working with Kitsap County to develop and maintain a peninsula dog park; www.kitsapdogparks.org.

THE ISLANDS

FETCH!: Free Exercise Time for Canines and their Humans is dedicated to providing Island County dog owners areas where they are free to exercise their pets without disturbing others. They promote and maintain five dog parks on Whidbey Island. 360/321-4049; www.whidbey.com/fetch.

GREATER SEATTLE

COLA: Citizens for Off-Leash Areas promotes and maintains city dog parks. www.coladog.org.

Puget Sound Pet: This free newspaper for pet owners is published quarterly and is available at individually owned pet stores around Seattle.

SODA: Serve Our Dog Areas is the off-leash group that manages and volunteers at Marymoor Off-Leash Area in Redmond and Grandview Dog Park in Kent. 425/881-0148; www.soda.org.

NORTH CASCADES

Grateful Dogs: What a great name for the organization that promotes responsible dog ownership and off-leash opportunities for canines in Bellingham. 360/671-4193; www.gratefuldogs.org.

Oregon

Department of Fish and Wildlife: Contact this organization for angling, shellfish gathering, and hunting licenses. Print an application online and fax to 503/947-6117. Main phone: 503/947-6000 or 800/720-6339; Licensing: 503/947-6100; www.dfw.state.or.us.

Oregon State Parks: Oregon calls its state parks by many names, and only a few charge a $3 daily parking fee. Camping fees vary by location. Dogs are required to be on a six-foot or shorter leash. Reservations are made by calling 800/452-5687 or through www.reserveamerica.com.

GREATER PORTLAND

C-SPOT: Citizens for Safe Parks with Off-Leash Territory works to find and preserve off-leash opportunities in Portland parks. 503/230-8131; www.cspotpdx.com.

Dog Nose News: This publication is a free monthly newspaper for animal lovers in the Portland Metro Area and beyond. Annual subscriptions are $20. 5519 NE 30th Ave., Portland, OR 97211; www.dognosenews.com.

Portland Pooch: This online guide to the Portland dog scene has great information and the best descriptions and directions to all of the area's dog parks. www.portlandpooch.com.

SOUTHERN OREGON

FOTAS: Friends of The Animal Shelter holds benefits and dog events in and around Ashland, Medford, and Jacksonville to raise funds for the county animal shelter. www.fotas.org.

SoftDawgs: This volunteer group was organized to educate dog owners about responsible dog stewardship to keep Bend parks dog-friendly. They hold De-Poop-Da-Park cleanup campaigns, monthly educational talks, and meetings. They are actively working with the Bend Parks Department to raise funds for and promote off-leash areas. SoftPaws, 1137 N.W. Federal St., Bend, OR 97701; 541/312-3766; www.softdawgs.org.

British Columbia

Citizen Canine: An off-leash advocacy group in Victoria; www.citizencanine.org.

RainCity Dogs: An online guide for Vancouver dogs; www.raincitydogs.com.

WAG: If you have a lost pet, or find one, in Whistler, B.C., contact Whistler Animals Galore at 604/905-7750.

INDEXES

Accommodations Index

Abbeymoore Manor (Victoria, BC): 466

Abigail's Hotel (Victoria, BC): 466

Accent Inn (Victoria, BC): 477–478

Ace Hotel (Seattle, WA): 139

Agate Beach Oceanfront Motel (Newport, OR): 284–285

Aladdin Motor Inn (Port Townsend, WA): 30

Alderbrook Resort (East Hood Canal, WA): 69

Alexis Hotel (Seattle, WA): 139

Alfred A. Loeb Campground (Brookings-Harbor, OR): 321

Amazing Vacation Homes and Cottages (Sooke, BC): 469

Ambrosia Gardens Bed and Breakfast (Yachats, OR): 291

Annabelle's Cottage (Victoria, BC): 466

Apple Country Bed and Breakfast (Yakima, WA): 232

Arlington Motor Inn (Arlington, WA): 105

Ashland Patterson House (Ashland, OR): 424–425

Aspen Meadows Lodge (Sisters, OR): 400

Aster Inn (Cle Elum, WA): 223

A' Tuscan Estate (McMinnville, OR): 360

Avellan Inn (Newberg, OR): 359

Bainbridge House (Bainbridge Island, WA): 62

Bartwood Lodge (Orcas Island, WA): 78–79

Barview Jetty Campground (Garibaldi, OR): 261

Bayshore Inn (Garibaldi, OR): 261

Bay View Campground (Mount Vernon-La Conner, WA): 174

Beach House, The (Poulsbo, WA): 54

Beach It Rental Houses (Long Beach Peninsula, WA): 201

Bellevue Club Hotel (Bellevue, WA): 151

Best Western: British Columbia 481; Oregon 479–481; Washington 478–479

Beverly Beach Campground (Newport, OR): 285

Big Red Barn (Port Townsend, WA): 30

Birch Bay Campground (Birch Bay, WA): 159

Bishop Hotel (Port Townsend, WA): 30

Blackberry Campground (Waldport, OR): 289

Blue Willow By the Sea (South Whidbey, WA): 97

Brauer Cove (Poulsbo, WA): 54

Breakers Motel and Condos (Westport, WA): 197

Brooks Memorial Park Campground (Goldendale, WA): 241

Camano Cottages (Camano Island, WA): 99

Camano Island State Park Campground (Camano Island, WA): 99

Campbell House (Eugene, OR): 379

Cantrall-Buckley County Park Campground (Jacksonville, OR): 419

Cape Blanco Campground (Port Orford, OR): 315

Cape Disappointment Campground (Long Beach Peninsula, WA): 201

Cape Lookout Campground (Netarts, OR): 265

Cascade Mountain Inn (Cle Elum, WA): 223

Castaway by the Sea (Port Orford, OR): 315

Castle Hill (Vashon Island, WA): 67

Cedarwood, The (Saanich Peninsula, BC): 462

Champoeg State Park Campground (Newberg, OR): 359

Charles Nelson Guest House (Long Beach Peninsula, WA): 201

Chateau Whistler (Whistler, BC): 443

Chautauqua Lodge (Long Beach Peninsula, WA): 201

Clackamas Inn (Estacada, OR): 363

Clark's Skagit River Resort (Rockport, WA): 178

Clementine's Bed and Breakfast (Astoria-Warrenton, OR): 250

Coast Cabins (Manzanita, OR): 257–258

Coast Hotels (Vancouver, BC): 482

Coast Inn Bed and Breakfast (Lincoln City, OR): 276

Columbia Gorge Hotel (Hood River, OR): 391

Columbia Gorge Riverside Lodge (Stevenson, WA): 209

Comfort Inn and Suites: British Columbia 483; Oregon 482–483; Washington 482

Conklin's Guest House Bed and Breakfast (Sisters, OR): 400

Coos Bay Manor Bed and Breakfast (Coos Bay, OR): 306

Cottages at Cayou Cove (Orcas Island, WA): 79

Country Inn and Suites (Northeast Portland, OR): 339

Country Inn (La Conner, WA): 174

Countryman Bed and Breakfast (Snohomish, WA): 117

Cousins Country Inn (The Dalles, OR): 394

Cove Palisades Campground (Madras-Culver, OR): 399

Cozy Cat Bed and Breakfast (Naches, WA): 228

Crescent Beach RV Park (Joyce, WA): 21

Crescent Lake Campground (Crescent Lake, OR): 430

Crest Motel (Astoria-Warrenton, OR): 250

Cricketwood Country's Pet-Friendly Cottage (Bend, OR): 407

Crowne Plaza (Lake Oswego, OR): 349

Crystal Lodge (Whistler, BC): 443

CrystalWood Lodge (Fort Klamath, OR): 432

Dashwood Manor (Victoria, BC): 466

Days Inn: British Columbia 484; Oregon 484; Washington 483

Deception Pass State Park
Campground (North Whidbey, WA):
92
Der Ritterhof Motor Lodge
(Leavenworth, WA): 215
Destination Leavenworth
(Leavenworth, WA): 215
Dew Drop Inn (Forks, WA): 33
Diamond Lake Resort (Diamond Lake,
OR): 431
Doe Bay Village (Orcas Island, WA): 79
Dolce Skamania Lodge (Skamania,
WA): 208
Driftwood Motel (Bandon, OR): 312
Dungeness Recreation Area (Sequim-
Dungeness Valley, WA): 25
Eagle Crest Resort (Redmond, OR):
402
Econo Lodge: Oregon 484–485;
Washington 484
Edgewater Cottages (Waldport, OR):
289
Edgewater Hotel (Seattle, WA): 139
Edgewater Inn (Coos Bay, OR): 306
Edgewater Inn (Shady Cove, OR): 427
Edmonds Harbor Inn (Edmonds, WA):
120
Ellensburg Inn (Ellensburg, WA): 226
Entrada Lodge (Bend, OR): 407
Ester Lee Motel (Lincoln City, OR): 277
Fairhaven Village Inn (Fairhaven, WA):
171
Fay Bainbridge State Park
Campground (Bainbridge Island,
WA): 62–63
Fidalgo Country Inn (Fidalgo Island):
90
Flowing Lake Park Campground
(Snohomish, WA): 117
Fort Flagler State Park Campground
(Marrowstone Island, WA): 30
Fort Stevens Campground (Astoria-
Warrenton, OR): 250
Friday Harbor Inn (San Juan Island,
WA): 83
Game Ridge Motel (White Pass-
Chinook Pass, WA): 227

Gearhart Ocean Inn (Gearhart, OR):
251
Georgian Court Hotel (Vancouver,
BC): 452
Gig Harbor Motor Inn (Gig Harbor,
WA): 72
Gracehaven (Rockport, WA): 179
Granville Island Hotel (Granville Island,
Vancouver, BC): 454
Green Springs Inn (Ashland, OR): 425
Grey Gull (Ocean Shores, WA): 45
Groveland Cottage (Sequim-
Dungeness Valley, WA): 25
Guemes Island Resort (Guemes Island
Resort, WA): 88
Guest House International Inn and
Suites: Aberdeen, WA 47; other
Washington 485
Hallmark Resort (Newport, OR): 285
Hanson Country Inn (Corvallis, OR):
374–375
Harbor Inn (Brookings-Harbor, OR):
321
Harrison Hot Springs Resort and Spa
(Harrison Hot Springs, BC): 460
Heathman Hotel (Downtown Portland,
OR): 334
Historic Sou'wester Lodge (Long
Beach Peninsula, WA): 201
Hoffy's Motel (Madras-Culver, OR): 399
Hogland House (Mukilteo, WA): 114
Holiday Inn/Holiday Inn Express:
British Columbia 486; Oregon 485–
486; Washington 485
Holiday Motel (Roseburg, OR): 413
Holly House Inn Bed and Breakfast
(Port Orford, OR): 315
Holly Lane Gardens (Bainbridge Island,
WA): 63
Homewood Suites (Vancouver, WA):
206
Hood River Hotel (Hood River, OR):
391
Hood River Vacation Rentals (Hood
River, OR): 391
Hospitality Inn (Southwest Portland,
OR): 342

Hotel Bellwether (Bellingham-Fairhaven, WA): 171

Hotel Lucia (Downtown Portland, OR): 334

Hotel Monaco (Seattle, WA): 139

Hotel Vintage Park (Seattle, WA): 139

Hotel Vintage Plaza (Downtown Portland, OR): 334–335

House in the Trees (Snoqualmie, WA): 219

Hudson Manor Inn and Suites (Kelso-Longview, WA): 204

Huntley Park Campground (Gold Beach, OR): 317

Hyatt Lake Campground (Ashland, OR): 425

Illahee Manor Vacation Rentals (Bremerton, WA): 59

Illahee State Park Campground (Bremerton, WA): 59

Imperial River Company (Maupin, OR): 398

Indian Mary County Park Campground (Galice, OR): 415

Inn at Arch Cape (Cannon Beach, OR): 256

Inn at Arch Rock (Depoe Bay, OR): 280

Inn at Cape Kiwanda (Pacific City, OR): 268

Inn at Gig Harbor (Gig Harbor, WA): 72

Inn at Port Gardner (Everett, WA): 112

Inn at Snohomish (Snohomish, WA): 117

Inn of the Beachcomber (Gold Beach, OR): 317

Inn of the White Salmon (White Salmon, WA): 237–238

Ireland's Rustic Lodges (Gold Beach, OR): 317

Iron Springs Ocean Resort (Copalis Beach, WA): 42

Island Country Inn (Bainbridge Island, WA): 63

Island Tyme (South Whidbey, WA): 98

Jacksonville Inn (Jacksonville, OR): 419

Kalaloch Campground (Kalaloch, WA): 36

Kalaloch Lodge (Kalaloch, WA): 36

Kayak Point Park Campground (Stanwood, WA): 104

Kelly's Trout Creek Inn Bed and Breakfast (Trout Lake, WA): 235

Kitsilano Guest Suites (Kitsilano, Vancouver, BC): 449

KOA Campgrounds: Oregon 487; Washington 486–487

La Quinta Inn: Oregon 488; Washington 488

Lakedale Resort (San Juan Island, WA): 83

Lake Quinault Historic Lodge (Lake Quinault, WA): 38

Lanai Oceanfront Condos (Seaside, OR): 252

LaVerne County Park Campground (Coquille, OR): 307

Lonsdale Quay Hotel (North Vancouver, BC): 447

Looking Glass Inn (Lincoln City, OR): 277

Lost Lake Resort (Lost Lake, OR): 392

Lyle Hotel (Lyle, WA): 239

Mallory Hotel (Downtown Portland, OR): 335

Manchester State Park Campground (Port Orchard, WA): 65

Manitou Lodge (Forks, WA): 34

Manzanita Rental Company (Manzanita, OR): 258

Mark Spencer Hotel (Downtown Portland, OR): 335

Marriott Hotels: Oregon 489; Washington 488–489

Maverick Motel (Klamath Falls, OR): 434

McKenzie River Inn (Blue River, OR): 380

Melva Company Vacation Rentals (South Beach, OR): 286

Meredith Gorge Motel (Hood River, OR): 391

Mike's Beach Resort (West Hood Canal, WA): 40

Millersylvania State Park Campground

(Olympia, WA): 194
Miller Tree Inn (Forks, WA): 34
Milo McIver Campground (Estacada, OR): 363
Moby Dick Hotel, Restaurant, and Oyster Farm (Long Beach Peninsula, WA): 201–202
Monte Square Motel (Aberdeen, WA): 47
Moran State Park Campground (Orcas Island, WA): 79
Motel 6: Oregon 490–491; Washington 489–490
Mountain View Inn (Granite Falls, WA): 107
Mount Walker Inn (West Hood Canal, WA): 40
Mt. Baker Lodging (Mt. Baker, WA): 164
Natapoc Lodging (Leavenworth, WA): 215–216
Nehalem Bay Campground (Nehalem, OR): 259
No Cabbages Bed and Breakfast (Gig Harbor, WA): 72
Northwest Manor (Port Angeles, WA): 22–23
Ocean Breeze (Florence, OR): 295
Ocean City State Park Campground (Ocean City, WA): 43
Ocean Inn (Manzanita, OR): 258
Ocean Lodge (Cannon Beach, OR): 256
Old Parkdale Inn (Parkdale, OR): 397
Old Welches Inn (Mt. Hood, OR): 396
Oswald West State Park Campground (Cannon Beach, OR): 256
Pacific Palisades Hotel (Vancouver, BC): 452–453
Pacific Spirit Guest House (Cambie, Vancouver, BC): 455
Palace Hotel (Port Townsend, WA): 30
Pana-Sea-Ah Bed and Breakfast (Lincoln Beach , OR): 279
Park Lane Suites (Northwest Portland, OR): 331
Park Motel (Florence, OR): 295

Paul's Motor Inn (Victoria, BC): 466
Penrose Point State Park Campground (Key Peninsula, WA): 73
Pheasant Valley Bed and Breakfast (Hood River, OR): 391–392
Plaza Inn and Suites (Ashland, OR): 425
Ponderosa Motel (Goldendale, WA): 241
Portlander Inn (Northeast Portland, OR): 339
Poulsbo Inn (Poulsbo, WA): 54
Prior House Bed and Breakfast (Victoria, BC): 467
Proposal Rock Inn (Neskowin, OR): 269
Prospect Historical Hotel/Motel and Dinnerhouse (Prospect, OR): 427
Puget View Guesthouse (Olympia, WA): 195
Quality Inn: Oregon 491; Saanich Peninsula, BC 462; Union Gap, WA 233
Rainbow Falls State Park Campground (Chehalis, WA): 196
Ramada Inn: Oregon 491; Washington 491
Rasar State Park Campground (Concrete, WA): 177
Red Lion: Oregon 492; Washington 492
Redwood Motel (Grants Pass, OR): 417
Relax Inn (Cottage Grove, OR): 381
Resort at the Mountain (Mt. Hood, OR): 396
Resort Semiahmoo (Blaine, WA): 159
Riverhouse Resort (Bend, OR): 407
River Meadows Campground (Arlington, WA): 105
RiverPlace Hotel (Downtown Portland, OR): 335
Rivershore Hotel (West Linn, OR): 350
Riverside Inn (Grants Pass, OR): 417
Robin Hood Village (East Hood Canal, WA): 70
Rockport State Park Campground (Rockport, WA): 179
Running Y Ranch Resort (Klamath Falls, OR): 435

Russell House Bed and Breakfast (Grayland-Tokeland, WA): 198

Salem Inn (Salem, OR): 367

Salishan Lodge (Gleneden, OR): 278

Sand Dollar Inn and Cottages (Pacific Beach, WA): 41

Sand Lake Campground (Pacific City, OR): 268

Sandpiper (Pacific Beach, WA): 41

Sandy Hook Beach Shack (Poulsbo, WA): 54

San Juan County Park Campground (San Juan Island, WA): 83

Schroeder County Park Campground (Grants Pass, OR): 417

Sea Dreamer (Brookings-Harbor, OR): 321

Sea Horse Lodging and Vacation Rentals (Lincoln City, OR): 277

Seaside Inn Bed and Breakfast (Seaside, OR): 252

Seasons Motel (Mossyrock, WA): 202

Sea View Vacation Rentals (Pacific City, OR): 268

See Vue (Yachats, OR): 292

Shamrock Lodgettes (Yachats, OR): 292

Shaw Island County Park Campground (Shaw Island, WA): 84

Shaw's Oceanfront Bed and Breakfast (Cannon Beach, OR): 256

Shilo Inns: Oregon 493; Washington 492–493

Silver Falls Campground (Silverton, OR): 369

Silver Lake Campground (Mt. Baker, WA): 164

Silver Ridge Ranch (Easton, WA): 221

Smuggler's Inn (Blaine, WA): 159

Snoqualmie Inn (Snoqualmie, WA): 219

Sooke Harbour House (Sooke, BC): 469

South Fork Marina Bed and Breakfast (Mount Vernon-La Conner, WA): 174

South Whidbey State Park Campground (South Whidbey, WA): 98

Spencer Spit State Park Campground (Lopez Island, WA): 86–87

Spring Creek Ranch (Klamath Falls, OR): 435

Stage Lodge (Jacksonville, OR): 419

Starwood Hotels: Oregon 494; Washington 493

St. Bernards Bed and Breakfast (Cannon Beach, OR): 256

Stormking Spa (Mossyrock, WA): 203

Summit Lodge (Whistler, BC): 443

Sun Country Motel (Yakima, WA): 232

Sunset Bay Campground (Coos Bay, OR): 306

Sunset Marine Resort (Sequim-Dungeness Valley, WA): 25

Sunset Oceanfront (Bandon, OR): 312

Sunwolf Outdoor Centre (Squamish, BC): 444–445

Super 8 Motel: Oregon 494–495; Washington 494

Surfsand Resort (Cannon Beach, OR): 256–257

Sutherlin Inn (Roseburg, OR): 413

Swallow Ridge Bed and Breakfast (Sisters, OR): 400–401

Swallow's Nest Guest Cottages (Vashon Island, WA): 67

Sweetbrier Inn and Suites (Beaverton, OR): 352

Table Rock Motel (Bandon, OR): 312

Tantalus Lodge (Whistler, BC): 443

Three Rivers Inn (Sedro Woolley, WA): 175

Tokeland Hotel (Tokeland, WA): 199

Tradewinds Motel (Rockaway Beach, OR): 260

Tradewinds-on-the-Bay Motel: (Grayland-Tokeland, WA): 199

TraveLodge: British Columbia 496; Oregon 496; Washington 495

Trollers Lodge (Depoe Bay, OR): 280

Twanoh State Park Campground (East Hood Canal, WA): 70

Umpqua Lighthouse State Park Campground (Winchester Bay, OR): 299

University Inn (Seattle, WA): 130
Vagabond Inn (Seattle, WA): 140
Val-U-Inn (Bellingham-Fairhaven, WA): 172
Village Inn (Springfield, OR): 379
Waddling Dog (Saanich Peninsula, BC): 462
Wayfarer Resort (Blue River, OR): 380
Welcome Motor Inn (Everett, WA): 112–113
Westerly Motel (Ocean Shores, WA): 45
Westward Ho (Bend, OR): 407

Whalen Island Campground (Pacific City, OR): 268
Wheeler on the Bay (Wheeler, OR): 259
W Hotel (Seattle, WA): 140
Willamette Pass Inn (Crescent Lake, OR): 430
Willows Lodge (Kirkland, WA): 148
Winchester Bay Inn (Winchester Bay, OR): 299
Windmill Inns: Oregon 496; Lynden, WA 160

Restaurant Index

Agua Verde Paddle Club and Café
(University District, Seattle, WA): 130
Allyson's of Ashland (Ashland, OR):
424
Alotto Gelato (Northwest Portland,
OR): 331
Alpha-bit (Mapleton, OR): 296
American Dream Pizza (Corvallis, OR):
374
Amici Italian Deli and Pizzeria
(Mukilteo, WA): 114
Anderson's General Store and Kitchen
(Guemes Island, WA): 88
Anducci's (Tri-Cities, BC): 458
AnneMarie's (Aberdeen, WA): 47
Anthony's Italian Café (Roseburg, OR):
412
Antique Sandwich Company (Tacoma,
WA): 189
Arbor Café (Salem-Keizer, OR): 367
Arbor Ice Cream (Reedsport, OR): 296
Astro Lounge (Bend, OR): 406
Backroad Grill (Galice, OR): 414

Bainbridge Bakers (Bainbridge Island,
WA): 62
Bandon Fish Market (Bandon, OR): 311
Bandon Gourmet (Bandon, OR): 311
Bayfront Bar and Bistro (Winchester
Bay, OR): 299
Beach Dog Café (Lincoln City, OR): 276
Bean Brothers (Kitsilano, Vancouver,
BC): 448
Bear's Cookie Den (Seal Rock, OR):
287
Beckie's Restaurant (Union Creek, OR):
428
Beetle Bailey Burgers (Culver, OR): 399
Berlin Inn (Southeast Portland, OR):
346
Big Bubba's Burgers (Hood Canal,
WA): 69
Big Foot Pub 'N' Grub (Seaside, OR):
252
Bilbo's Festivo (Orcas Island, WA): 78
Bingen Station (Bingen, WA): 237
Birdsview Burgers (Concrete, WA): 177

Blackberry House (Blaine-Birch Bay, WA): 158

Blue Heron Bistro (Coos Bay, OR): 305

Blue Heron French Cheese Company (Tillamook, OR): 262

Blue River Sweet Shoppe and Deli (Blue River, OR): 380

Blue Stone Bakery and Coffee Café (Grants Pass, OR): 416

Blu Water Bistro (Green Lake, WA): 128

Bob's Red Mill (Milwaukie, OR): 347

Bonney's Bakery (Port Angeles, WA): 22

Bow Picker Fish and Chips (Astoria-Warrenton, OR): 249

Bread Zeppelin (Port Orford, OR): 314–315

Brioche Urban Baking and Catering (Downtown Vancouver, BC): 452

Broadway New American Grill (Capitol Hill, Seattle, WA): 141

Bunkhouse Restaurant (Wheeler-Nehalem, OR): 259

Butteville General Store (Newberg, OR): 358

Byblos Deli (Bellevue, WA): 151

Cactus (Kirkland, WA): 148

Cactus (Madison, Seattle, WA): 142

Cada Corner (Estacada, OR): 363

Café Destino (Bremerton, WA): 58–59

Café LN (Eugene, OR): 378

Café Paradise (Klamath Falls, OR): 434

Café Septieme (Capitol Hill, Seattle, WA): 141

Café Sheilagh (Cottage Grove, OR): 381

Café Stephanie (Newport, OR): 284

Caffé Destino (Southeast Portland, OR): 346

Candy Depot and Depot Deli (Sequim-Dungeness Valley): 25

Cannery, The (Gold Beach, OR): 317

Canyon Café and Logger's Grill (North Vancouver, BC): 447

Carafe (Downtown Portland, OR): 334

Cascadian Farms (Rockport, WA): 178

Cat's Eye Café (West Seattle, WA): 145

Cat's Meow, The (Granville Island, Vancouver, BC): 453

Celebrate Me Home (Troutdale, OR): 386

Celebrations To Go (Magnolia, Seattle, WA): 133

Centralia Perk (Centralia, WA): 196

Charleston Station Donuts and Bagels (Charleston, OR): 305

Cheekeye Bar and Grill (Squamish, BC): 444

Chinoise (Queen Anne, Seattle, WA): 136

Chippery (Corvallis, OR): 374

Chuck's Seafood Grotto (Snohomish, WA): 116

Citta Bistro (Whistler, BC): 442

City Deli and Wine (Snohomish, WA): 116

Clark's (Cannon Beach, OR): 256

Coco Pazzo (Kerrisdale, Vancouver, BC): 456

Coffee Exchange, The (Kingston, WA): 51

Coffee House, The (Newport, OR): 284

Colophon Café (Bellingham-Fairhaven, WA): 170

Columbia River Cellars (Troutdale, OR): 386

Cone Heads (Sequim-Dungeness Valley): 25

Conway Skagit Barn (Mount Vernon-La Conner, WA): 174

Cookie Mill, The (Stanwood, WA): 104

Country Grains Bread Co. (Wilsonville, OR): 357

Crab Shack (Stevenson, WA): 209

Craftsman Café (North Portland, OR): 328

Crazy Norwegian, The (Port Orford, OR): 315

Creamery, The (Bingen-White Salmon, WA): 237

C Shop Summertime, The (Blaine-Birch Bay, WA): 158–159

Dahlia Café (Northeast Portland, OR): 339

Daily Bagel, The (Klamath Falls, OR): 434

Dee Bee's Sandwich and Soup Café (Snohomish, WA): 116

Deidra's Deli (Hoquiam, WA): 47

Depot Deli (Sisters, OR): 400

Dingo's Fresh Mexican Grill (Southeast Portland, OR): 346

Dish Urban Market (Ballard, WA): 132

Dockside Restaurant (Granville Island, Vancouver, BC): 454

Dock Street Sandwich Company (Tacoma, WA): 189

Doctor's Office, The (San Juan Island, WA): 82

Dog Water Café (Seaside, OR): 252

Dos Okies (Port Townsend, WA): 29

Double Barrel BBQ (Sedro Woolley, WA): 175

Downtown Deli and Catering (Camas-Washougal, WA): 207

Dragonfly Sisters Café (Rockaway Beach, OR): 260

Dubh Linn Gate Pub (Whistler, BC): 442

Dutch Mothers (Lynden, WA): 160

Echos Bistro and Biergarten (Leavenworth, WA): 215

Eleanor's Undertow (Lincoln City, OR): 276

Ellensburg Pasta Co. (Ellensburg, WA): 226

Elliot Glacier Public House (Parkdale, OR): 397

Elly's (Easton, WA): 221

Emmy's VegeHouse (Bainbridge Island, WA): 62

Essential Baking Company (Fremont, Seattle, WA): 135

Everybody's Store (Mt. Baker, WA): 164

Ezell's Famous Chicken (Lynnwood, WA): 121

Famous Black Diamond Bakery and Deli (Black Diamond, WA): 190–191

Famous Lynden Dutch Bakery (Lynden, WA): 160

Fatburger (Bellevue, WA): 151

Fat City Café (Southwest Portland, OR): 342

5th Avenue Grill (Edmonds, WA): 120

Figaro's Italian Kitchen and Sub Express (Coquille, OR): 307

Fish Club (Downtown Seattle, WA): 138

Flying Burrito, The (San Juan Island, WA): 82

Flying Tomato (Florence, OR): 294

Four C's Catering and Café (The Dalles, OR): 394

Fox and Firkin (Corvallis, OR): 374

Galice Resort (Galice, OR): 414

Gay '90s Ice Cream and Deli (Roseburg, OR): 413

Gerry Frank's Konditorei (Salem-Keizer, OR): 367

Gingerbread Factory, The (Leavenworth, WA): 215

Gingerbread House, The (Lyons, OR): 370

Good Dog/Bad Dog (Downtown Portland, OR): 334

Goodies (Bremerton, WA): 59

Gordy's BBQ (Snoqualmie-North Bend, WA): 218

Gorge Gourmet To Go (Maryhill, WA): 240

Granville Island Brewery (Granville Island, Vancouver, BC): 454

Greenbank Farm and Whidbey Pies Café (Central Whidbey, WA): 95

Greenleaf Restaurant (Ashland, OR): 424

Gunderson's Cannery Café and Wine Bar (Astoria-Warrenton, OR): 249

Harrison Pizza (Harrison Hot Springs, BC): 459

Harvest Fresh Grocery and Deli (McMinnville, OR): 360

Hawk Creek Café (Neskowin, OR): 269

Hideaway Café (Port Orchard, WA): 64

Holstein's Coffee and Café (The Dalles, OR): 394

Homeport Bagels and Sandwiches (Brookings-Harbor, OR): 321

Hood Canal Seafood and Dabob Café (Hood Canal, WA): 40

Hood River City Market (Hood River, OR): 390

Hotwire Café (Shoreline, WA): 125

Husky Ice Cream and Deli (West Seattle, WA): 145

Imperial River Company (Maupin, OR): 398

Incendio (Kitsilano, Vancouver, BC); 448

Iovino's Ristorante (Corvallis, OR): 374

Irish Heather, The (Downtown Vancouver, BC): 452

Issaquah Distillery and Public House (Issaquah, WA): 217

J'aime les Crêpes (Kingston, WA): 52

Java Club (Depoe Bay, OR): 280

Jeani's Sunshine Café (Snoqualmie-North Bend, WA): 218

Joes' Town Center Café, The (Yachats, OR): 291

Kelly's Café (Gig Harbor, WA): 71

Kelly's Deli and Chowder House (Long Beach Peninsula, WA): 201

Kitty's Kitchen is Christmas Forever (Winchester Bay, OR): 299

KJ's Café (Crescent Lake, OR): 430

Krab Kettle (Florence, OR): 295

Krispy Kreme Doughnuts (Beaverton, OR): 352

La Burritta (Grants Pass, OR): 416

La Margarita Express (Salem-Keizer, OR): 367

Langley Village Bakery (South Whidbey, WA): 97

Le Bistro (Gig Harbor, WA): 71

Leftie's Eats (Roslyn, WA): 222

Lehani's Café & Coffee: (Port Townsend, WA): 29

Le Pichet (Downtown Seattle, WA): 138

Liberty Bay Bakery and Café (Poulsbo, WA): 53

Lighthouse Café and Wine Bar (Silverdale, WA): 56

Lighthouse Deli and Fish Co. (South Beach, OR): 286

Lisa's Fresh Express Deli (Key Peninsula, WA): 73

Little Cheerful (Bellingham-Fairhaven, WA): 170

Loafers (Albany, OR): 371

Local Bar and Grill (Grayland-Tokeland, WA): 198

Love Dog Café (Lopez Island, WA): 86

Lucky Lab Brewing Co. (Southeast Portland, OR): 346–347

Lunch Box, The (Mount Vernon-La Conner, WA): 174

Lutrell's Mustard Seed Café (Jacksonville, OR): 418

Macadoo's Barbeque: (Port Townsend, WA): 30

MacLevin's Whole Foods Deli, Bakery, and Ice Cream Parlor (Jacksonville, OR): 418

Macrina Bakery and Café (Downtown Seattle, WA): 138

Magnolia Café (Poulsbo, WA): 54

Mallard Ice Cream and Café (Bellingham-Fairhaven, WA): 170

Marblemount Drive In Good Food (Marblemount, WA): 179–180

Marina Park Grill (Kirkland, WA): 148

Marketplace Deli (Yakima, WA): 232

Martolli's (Sisters, OR): 400

Marty's Lunchbox Express (Gold Beach, OR): 317

Marzano's Pizza Pie (Manzanita, OR): 257

McMenamins Blue Moon Tavern (Northwest Portland, OR): 331

Mead Tasting Room, Tugwell Creek Farm (Sooke, BC): 469

Meinhardt Fine Foods (Cambie, Vancouver, BC): 455

Mercedes and Family (Yakima, WA): 232

Merenda Wine Bar (Bend, OR): 406

Meyer's (Everett, WA): 112

Mighty O Doughnuts (Green Lake, WA): 128

Mike's Ice Cream (Hood River, OR): 390

Miss Margarets (Harrison Hot Springs, BC): 459

Moby Dick Hotel, Restaurant, and Oyster Farm (Long Beach Peninsula, WA): 201–202

Moldovanos (Kerrisdale, Vancouver, BC): 456

Mom's Beach House Café (Nehalem, OR): 259

Mom's Café (Sooke, BC): 468

Mo's West (Otter Rock, OR): 281

Mother's Juice Café (Bend, OR): 406

Mountain High Hamburgers (Easton, WA): 221

Mountain View Restaurant, Cocktail Lounge, and Robe Store (Granite Falls, WA): 107

Mount's Café (Ferndale, WA): 163

Murchie's (Victoria, BC): 465

New Morning Bakery (Corvallis, OR): 374

Norm's Eatery and Ale House (Fremont, Seattle, WA): 135

North Fork Brewery (Mt. Baker, WA): 164

Nye Beach Scoop (Newport, OR): 284

Ochre Grains (Victoria, BC): 465

Old Anchor Seafood Café (Winchester Bay, OR): 299

Old Milltown Pizza (Edmonds, WA): 120

Oosterwyk's Dutch Bakery (Marysville, WA): 106

Oregon Tea Garden (Silverton, OR): 369

Original House of Pizza (Westport, WA): 197

Pacific Pizza (Forks, WA): 33

Pah Tong's Thai Food (Winchester Bay, OR): 299

Pangea Grills and Wraps (Ashland, OR): 424

Paniolo Hawaiian (Astoria-Warrenton, OR): 249

Papa Haydn (Northwest Portland, OR): 331

Papayas Tropical Grill (Bend, OR): 407

Pasquale's Ristorante (Hood River, OR): 391

Pavé Bakery (Everett, WA): 112

Pearl Bakery (Downtown Portland, OR): 334

Peppermint Parlor (Ocean Shores, WA): 44

Pepper's Taqueria (Vancouver, WA): 206

Philly Ya Belly (Mukilteo, WA): 114

Phil's Frosty (Shady Cove, OR): 426

Picnic Table Bistro and Deli (Ocean Shores, WA): 44–45

Port City Pasta Co. (Lake Oswego, OR): 349

Port Gamble General Store (Port Gamble, WA): 52

Port O' Call (Bandon, OR): 311–312

Portofino Pizzeria (Orcas Island, WA): 78

Pot Belly Deli (North Whidbey, WA): 92

Prospect Historical Hotel/Motel and Dinnerhouse (Prospect, OR): 427

Qdoba (North Seattle, WA): 126

Red Barn Café (Mossyrock, WA): 202

River's Edge (La Push, WA): 35

Rockfish Grill (Anacortes, WA): 90

Rogue Ales Public House (Newport, OR): 284

Rosso's Trattoria (Grants Pass, OR): 416

Sand Castle Drive In (Ocean Shores, WA): 45

Sassy's Kitchen (Naches, WA): 228

Scampi's Fish Wagon (Harbor, OR): 321

17 Miles House Pub and Restaurant (Sooke, BC): 468–469

Sfoglio Gourmet and Fresh Pasta (South Whidbey, WA): 97

Sherlock's Restaurant and Waddling Dog Bar and Grill (Sidney-Saanich Peninsula): 462

60th Street Desserts and Delicatessen (University District, Seattle, WA): 130

Sluy's Poulsbo Bakery (Poulsbo, WA): 54

Smoking Dog, The (Kitsilano,

Vancouver, BC): 448
Smo'kin Joe's Bar-BQ (Ellensburg, WA): 226
Snohomish Pie Company (Snohomish, WA): 116
Soba Asian Bistro (Bend, OR): 407
Some Bagels (Yakima, WA): 232
Sonny's Downtown Café (Medford, OR): 421
Sound Food (Vashon Island, WA): 67
Souped-Up Sand-Witches Italian Cuisine (Florence, OR): 295
Soup Spoon, The (Mt. Hood, OR): 396
South Park (Downtown Portland, OR): 334
St. Clouds (Madrona, Seattle, WA): 142–143
Steelhead Brewing Co. (Eugene, OR): 378
St. Honoré Boulangerie (Northwest Portland, OR): 330
St. John's (Goldendale, WA): 241
Stonehouse Pub (Sidney-Saanich Peninsula): 462
Stray Dog Café (Vashon Island, WA): 66–67
Subs on Sandy (Gresham, OR): 353
Sugar Shack Bakery (Reedsport, OR): 297
Sun Garden Café and Cyber Garden (Lincoln City, OR): 276
Sunnyside Up (Corvallis, OR): 374
Surfer Sands (Long Beach Peninsula, WA): 201
Swan Café (Bellingham-Fairhaven, WA): 171
Sweet Memories (Ellensburg, WA): 226
Taco del Rey (Kent, WA): 186
Tatanka Take Out (Tacoma, WA): 189
Taylor Maid Do-nuts (Coos Bay, OR): 305
Third Street Café (Sidney-Saanich Peninsula): 462
Thorp Fruit and Antiques (Cle Elum, WA): 223
Three Crabs (Sequim-Dungeness Valley): 23

Three Dog Bakery (Downtown Seattle, WA): 138
Three Dog Bakery (Kitsilano, Vancouver, BC): 449
Tiger's Garden Take-Out (Vancouver, WA): 206
Tillamook Cheese Factory (Tillamook, OR): 262
Toad Hall (Yachats, OR): 291
Tommy O's Aloha Café (Vancouver, WA): 206
Top Dog Espresso (North Bend, OR): 306
Totem House (Ballard, WA): 132
T. Paul's Urban Café (Astoria-Warrenton, OR): 249
Traditions Café and World Folk Art (Olympia, WA): 194
Treehouse Café (Bainbridge Island, WA): 62
Truffles by the Sea (Blaine-Birch Bay, WA): 159
Uncle Uli's Pub (Leavenworth, WA): 215
Urban Bakery, The (Tri-Cities, BC): 458
Val D'Isere Brasserie (Whistler, BC): 442
Van Goes (Port Angeles, WA): 22
Verité Coffee (Madrona, Seattle, WA): 143
Victorian Café (Bend, OR): 407
Village Coffee Shop (Pacific City, OR): 267
Vita's Wildly Delicious (Lopez Island, WA): 86
Wagner's European Bakery and Café (Olympia, WA): 194
Waldport Seafood Company (Waldport, OR): 289
Waterfront Bakery and Café (Silverdale, WA): 56
Waterfront Coffee Company (Edmonds, WA): 120
Water Street Café (Ashland, OR): 424
Whale of a Cone (Westport, WA): 197
Whale's Tail, The (Olympia, WA): 194
Whidbey Coffee Company (Mukilteo,

WA): 114
Whiskey Creek Café (Netarts, OR): 265
Willett's Chowder House (Coos Bay, OR): 306
Woofles and Meowz (Granville Island, Vancouver, BC): 454
XXX Root Beer Drive-in (Issaquah, WA): 217

Yaletown European Bakery (Chilliwack, BC): 459–460
Yuki (Northwest Portland, OR): 331
Zany Zebra (Pacific Beach, WA): 41
Zeppo (Lake Oswego, OR): 349
Zogs Dogs (Whistler, BC): 442

General Index

A

Aberdeen: 45–47; parks 46–47; places to eat 47; places to stay 47
Admiralty Head Lighthouse: 95
agate-hunting: 264
agility courses: Patmore Pit 93–94; Portland 343; Vancouver 440
AirPet Hotel: 337
airplane travel: 9, 497
Albany: 370–371; parks 370–371; places to eat 371; places to stay 371
Alba Park: 420
Alberta Park: 336
Albert "Doc" Griffin Park: 418
Alfred A. Loeb State Park: 319, 321
All Pooches Bakery: 351
Allyn Waterfront Park: 68
Alpha Lake Park: 441
Alpine Lakes Wilderness: 212, 220
Alsea: 375–376; parks 375–376
Alsea Bay: 288
Alsea Falls: 375–376
Alta Lake: 441

Alton Baker Dog Park: 377
Amazon Dog Park: 377–378
Ambleside Beach and Dog Park: 445
American Camp: 82
American Legion Memorial: 108
Anacortes: 88–90; parks 88–90; places to eat 90; places to stay 90
Anacortes Community Forest Lands: 89–90
animal advocacy organizations: 501–503
Animal Crackers Pet Supply: 371
Animal Krackers Gala Dinner and Auction: 57
Animal Lover's Birthday Bakery: 351
Annapurna Center for Self Healing (ACSH): 26
Annette Lake: 220
Annual Picnic and Wiener Walk: 440
arboretums: Evergreen Arboretum and Gardens 108; Hoyt 329–330; Sehome Hill 167–168; Washington Park 141

Arbor Lodge: 327
Arcadia Beach: 254
Arlington: 104–105; parks 104–105; places to stay 105
Arlington Fly-In: 104
Arroyo Park: 168
Asahel Curtis Nature Trail: 219
Ashland: 422–425; parks 422–424; places to eat 424; places to stay 424–425
Ashland Dog Park: 422
Astoria: 246–250; parks 247–249; places to eat 249; places to stay 250
Astoria Column: 248
Atta Boy 300 dogsled race: 403
Azalea Park: 320

B

Babbington Hill: 468
Bainbridge Island: 59–63; parks 59–62; places to eat 62; places to stay 62–63
bakeries, dog: Beaverton 351; Seattle 139; Tri-Cities, BC 458; Vancouver, BC 449
Baker Lake Trail: 176–177
Baker Park: 416
Balfour-Klickitat Park: 238–239
Ballard: 130–133; parks 130–131; places to eat 132
Bandix Dog Park: 70–71
Bandon: 308–312; parks 308–311; places to eat 311–312; places to stay 312
Bandon City Park: 309–310
Bandon Marsh National Wildlife Refuge: 310
Bandon State Natural Area: 310–311
Bark!: 144
Barking Bay at Rainbow Park: 441
Bark in the Park (Everett baseball): 109
Bark in the Park (Seattle festival): 129
Barview Jetty County Park: 261
baseball: 109
Baskett Slough National Wildlife Refuge: 363

Bastendorff Beach: 304
bats: 226–227
Battle Ground: 204; parks 204
Battle Point Park: 60
Bay Area (Coos Bay and vicinity): 302–306; parks 302–305; places to eat 305–306; places to stay 306
Bay View State Park: 172, 174
Beach Dog Supply: 253
Beaches 1–4 (Kalaloch, WA): 36
Beacon Hill Park: 463–465
Beacon Rock: 208–209
Bear Creek Dog Park: 421
Beaver Lake Park: 461
Beaverton: 350–352; parks 351–352; places to eat 352; places to stay 352
Belcarra Regional Park: 457–458
Belfair State Park: 68
Bella's Pet Boutique: 275
Bellevue: 150–151; parks 150–151; places to eat 151; places to stay 151
Bellingham: 164–172; parks 165–170; places to eat 170–171; places to stay 171–172
Bend: 402–407; parks 403–406; places to eat 406–407; places to stay 407
Berthusen Park: 160
Beverly Beach State Park: 282, 285
Big Four Ice Caves: 106
Big House Carving Centre: 446
Big Sky Park: 405
Bingen: 236–238; parks 236–237; places to eat 237; places to stay 237–238
Birch Bay: 157–159; parks 157–158; places to eat 158–159; places to stay 159
Birch Bay State Park: 158, 159
bird-watching: Alfred A Loeb State Park 319; Bandon Marsh National Wildlife Refuge 310; Baskett Slough National Wildlife Refuge 363; Beacon Hill Park 463; Camano Island State Park 99; Cape Meares 263; English Camp 80; Fogarty Creek 279; Fraser River 456; Joseph Stewart Park 46; Kah Tai Lagoon 28;

Leadbetter Point 199–200; Link River Nature Trail 434; New River ACEC 311; Oaks Bottom Trail 345; Seal Rock 287; South Slough National Estuarine Research Reserve 308–309; Yakima Sportsman Park 231; Yaquina Head 282–283
Biscuits of Bend: 402
Blackbird Island: 214–215
Black Diamond: 190–191; parks 190; places to eat 190–191
Blaine: 157–159; parks 157–158; places to eat 158–159; places to stay 159
Bloedel-Donovan: 166
Blue Dog Pond: 146
Blue River: 379–380; parks 379–380; places to eat 380; places to stay 380
Bob's Red Mill: 347
Bob Straub State Park: 267
Bogachiel River Trail: 33
Boice-Cope at Floras Lake: 312–313
Boiler Bay: 280
Bonair Winery: 229
Bone-a-Fide Dog Ranch: 105
Boulder Cave: 226–227
Bradley Viewpoint: 249
Bremerton: 57–59; parks 57–58; places to eat 58–59; places to stay 59
Brentwood Dog Park: 346
Briar's Patch Sled Dogs: 433
Bridal Veil Falls (Oregon): 387
Bridal Veil Falls Provincial Park (British Columbia): 459
Bridge of the Gods: 207
Bridges Pets: 105
British Columbia: 438–469
Brookings: 317–321; parks 318–320; places to eat 321; places to stay 321
Brooks Memorial Park: 241
Brownsville Bark in the Park: 365
Buffington Park: 316
Bullards Beach: 309
Buntzen Lake Dog Park: 457
Burfoot County Park: 191–192
Burke-Gilman Trail: 124
Bush's Pasture Park: 367
Butchart Gardens: 464

Byrd Dog Park: 23

C

Camano Animal Shelter Association (C.A.S.A.): 98
Camano Island: 98–99; parks 98–99; places to stay 99
Camano Island State Park: 99
Camas: 206–207; parks 207; places to eat 207
Cambie: 454–455; parks 454–455; places to eat 455; places to stay 455
camping: Alfred A Loeb State Park 319, 320; Alsea Falls 375–376; Barview Jetty County Park 261; Bay View State Park 172, 174; Beverly Beach State Park 282, 285; Birch Bay State Park 158, 159; Brooks Memorial Park 241; Camano Island 99; Cape Blanco State Park 313, 315; Cape Disappointment State Park 200, 201; Cape Lookout State Park 264–265; Cascadia State Park 376; Champoeg State Park 358, 359; Cove Palisades 399; Deception Pass 91, 92; Dosewallips State Park 38–39; Dungeness Recreation Area 23–24, 25; Floras Lake 312–313; Fort Flagler State Park 32; Howard Miller Steelhead Park 178; Humbug Mountain State Park 314; Indian Mary Historic Reservation 413–414, 415; John Neal Memorial Park 369–370; Joyce 21; Kalaloch 36; Kayak Point 103, 104; Lakedale Resort 82; Lake Wenatchee 213–214; LaVerne Park 307; Manchester State Park 63, 65; Millersylvania State Park 193–194; Milo McIver State Park 362, 363; Moran State Park 77–78, 79; Mt. Baker 176–177; Mt. Hood National Forest-Lost Lake 392; Nehalem Bay 258–259; Obstruction Pass 78; Ocean City 43; Oswald West State Park 256; Pacific Beach 40–41; Penrose Point State Park

72, 73; Potlach State Park 39–40; Rainbow Falls State Park 195, 196; Rasar State Park 175–176, 177; River Meadows 104–105; Rockport State Park 177–178, 179; Sand Lake 265, 268; San Juan Island County Park 81, 82; Shaw Island County Park/South Beach 83–84; Silver Falls State Park (Silverton) 368–369; Silver Lake 163, 164; South Beach State Park 285–286; South Whidbey State Park 95–96, 98; Spencer Spit 85, 86–87; Sunset Bay State Park 304–305; Tucker Park 389; Twanoh State Park 68–69, 70; Umpqua Lighthouse State Park 296, 299; Wallace Falls 118; Whalen Island/Clay Myers State Natural Area 268; Willamette Park (Corvallis) 373–374

Camp 6 Logging Museum: 188
Canada: 436–469
Canby: 361; parks 361; places to stay 361
Canine Capers: 318
Canine Cove at Lost Lake Park: 441
Canine Fest: 187
Cannon Beach: 252–257; parks 253–255; places to eat 256; places to stay 256–257
Cantrall-Buckley County Park: 418
Canyon Trail: 368–369
Cape Arago: 305
Cape Blanco Lighthouse: 313
Cape Blanco State Park: 313, 315
Cape Disappointment State Park: 200, 201
Cape Foulweather: 281; parks 281; places to eat 281
Cape Kiwanda: 267
Cape Lookout State Park: 264–265
Cape Meares: 263; parks 263
Cape Meares Lighthouse: 263
Cape Meares State Scenic Viewpoint: 263
Cape Perpetua Scenic Area: 290
Cape Sebastian: 316
Capilano Suspension Bridge and Park:

446–447
Capitol Hill: 140–141; parks 140; places to eat 141
Capitol Lake Park: 193
Carl G. Washburn Memorial State Park: 292–293
Carl S. English Jr. Botanical Gardens: 131
carriage tours: 467
Carrie Blake Park: 24
Carson: 235–236; parks 235–236
car travel: 8, 9
Cascade Lake: 77–78
Cascade Lakes Recreation Area: 402–403
Cascade Locks: 388; parks 388; places to stay 388
Cascade Streamwatch Trail: 395
Cascade Trail: 174–175
Cascadia State Park: 376
casino gambling: 105
Catharine Creek Universal Access Trail: 238
Cathedral Tree Trail: 248
Celilo Falls: 394
Celilo Park: 394
Centennial Trail: 101–102
Centralia: 195–196; parks 195–196; places to eat 196; places to stay 196
Central Whidbey: 93–95; parks 93–95; places to eat 95
Champoeg State Park: 358, 359
Charleston: 302–306; parks 302–305; places to eat 305–306; places to stay 306
Chehalis: 195–196; parks 195–196; places to eat 196; places to stay 196
Chetco River: 319
Chetzemoka Park: 28
Chilliwack: 459–460; parks 459; places to eat 459–460; places to stay 460
Chimney Park: 326
Chinook Pass: 226–227; parks 226–227; places to stay 227
Chip Ross Park: 372
Christmas celebrations: Leavenworth 213; Pacific City 266

Chuckanut Mountain Trail System: 165
Church Creek Park: 103
Citizen Canine: 503
Citizens for Off-Leash Areas (COLA): 123, 129, 502
City of Murals: 234
Clay Myers State Natural Area: 266
Cleary, Beverly: 338
Cle Elum: 222–223; parks 223; places to eat 223; places to stay 223
Cle Elum City Park: 223
Cline Falls: 401
Clover Valley: 91
Coal Mine Trail: 223
Cold Spring Creek: 396
Collier Memorial: 433
Columbia Hills State Park: 239
Columbia Renaissance Waterfront Trail: 205–206
Columbia River: 383
Columbia River Gorge National Scenic Area: 384
Conboy Lake Wildlife Refuge: 235
concerts, outdoor: 318
Concrete: 175–177; parks 175–177; places to eat 177; places to stay 177
Contorta Point: 429
Cooper River Trail: 221
Coos Bay: 302–306; parks 302–305; places to eat 305–306; places to stay 306
Copalis Beach: 41–42; parks 42; places to stay 42
Coquille: 306–307; parks 307; places to eat 307; places to stay 307
Corbett: 386–388; parks 386–388
Cordova Bay: 465
Corvallis: 371–375; parks 372–374; places to eat 374; places to stay 374–375
Cottage Grove: 381; parks 381; places to eat 381; places to stay 381
Couch Park: 331
Council Crest Park: 340–341
Cove Palisades: 399
Covered Bridge Scenic Tour: 381
Cowiche Canyon Trail: 229–230

CRAB-Portside Dog Park: 451
Crater Lake: 431–432; parks 431–432; places to stay 432
Crescent Lake: 428–430; parks 428–430; places to eat 430; places to stay 430
Crescent Lake Recreation Area: 428–429
Critter Cottage: 274
C-SPOT (Citizens for Safe Parks with Off-Leash Territory): 502
Culver: 398–399; parks 398–399; places to eat 399; places to stay 399

D

Dallas: 363–364; parks 363; places to stay 364
Dallas Beach Dog Area in Beacon Hill Park: 463–465
Dallesport: 239; parks 239
Dalles, The: 392–394; parks 393–394; places to eat 394; places to stay 394
Damon Point: 43–44
Dash Point State Park: 186–187
Daubenspeck Park: 236
Dawg Days of Summer: 304
Deception Pass State Park: 91, 92
Del Ray Beach: 250
Delta Old Growth Trail: 379–380
Delta Park: 326–327
Denny's Pet World: 147
Department of Fish and Wildlife: Oregon 502; Washington 501
Depoe Bay: 279–280
Deschutes National Forest: 384–385, 428–429
Deschutes River: 397
Devil's Kitchen: 310–311
Devil's Punch Bowl: 281
Diamond Lake: 430–431
Diamond Peaks Wilderness: 430
Discovery Park: 132–133
Dog Beach: 214
Dog Club: 349–350
Dog Days of Summer Fun Run and Festival (Bellingham): 165

Dog Days of Summer (Salem): 365
doggie day care: AirPet Hotel 337;
    Critter Cottage 274; Dog Club 349–
    350; Dogs at Play 376; Downtown
    Dog Lounge Seattle 136; Puppy
    Zone 439–440; Urban Fauna 332
Dog Mountain Trail: 235–236
Dog Nose News: 324, 502
Dog-O-Ween: 129
Dogs at Play: 376
Dogs for the Deaf: 420
Dog Show at the Beach: 266
dog shows: Dog Show at the Beach
    266; Mutt Masters Dog Show and
    Olympics 278
dog sledding: 278, 403, 433
Don Davis Park: 283
Dosewallips State Park: 38–39
Double Bluff Beach Access: 96
Downtown Dog Lounge:136
Downtown Park: 150
Downtown Portland/Historic
    Waterfront: 332–335; parks 332–333;
    places to eat 334; places to stay
    334–335
Downtown Seattle: 136–140; parks
    137–138; places to eat 138–139;
    places to stay 139–140
Downtown Vancouver: 451–453; parks
    451; places to eat 452; places to
    stay 452–453
Drake Park: 404
Drift Creek Falls: 276
Driftwood Beach: 288
drive-in movie theaters: 359
D River: 274
Dr. Jose Rizal Park: 145–146
Dry Canyon: 402
Dune Mushers Mail Run: 278
Dungeness Recreation Area: 23–24

E

Eagledale Park: 61
Eagle Fern: 362
Eagle Trail: 370
Eastbank Esplanade: 342

Easter Pet Parade: 278
East Hood Canal: 67–70; parks 68–69;
    places to eat 69; places to stay
    69–70
East Lynchwood Park: 353
Easton: 220–221; parks 220; places to
    eat 221; places to stay 221
Eastside Dog: 148
East Sooke Regional Park: 467–468
Eastsound Waterfront Park: 77
Ecola State Park: 253–254
Elk Lake Park: 461
Ellensburg: 224–226; parks 224–226;
    places to eat 226; places to stay 226
Elliott Bay: 135–136
Emel House: 55
emergency veterinary clinics: 472–477;
    Canada 476–477; Oregon 474–476;
    Washington 472–474
Emigrant Lake: 423
Emil Kissel Park: 230
Empire Lakes: 303
English Camp: 80–81
Eschbach Park: 227–228
Estacada: 361–363; parks 362; places
    to eat 363; places to stay 363
etiquette: 6–8, 10–12
Eugene: 376–379; parks 377–378;
    places to eat 378–379; places to
    stay 379
Everett: 108–113; parks 108–112;
    places to eat 112; places to stay
    112–113
Everett Aquasox: 109
Evergreen Park: 58

F

Fairhaven: 164–172; parks 165–170;
    places to eat 170–171; places to stay
    171–172
F&W Boat Launch OLA: 161–162
Fawn Lake Trail: 430
Fay Bainbridge State Park: 59–60
Federal Way: 186–187; parks 186–187;
    places to stay 187
Fern Hill Park: 336–337

Fernandez, Tonita: 191
Ferndale: 161–163; parks 161–162; places to eat 163
ferries: 497–498; Granville Island 453; San Juan Islands 75–76; Wheatland 364
Ferron's Fun Trips: 415
festivals: Annual Picnic and Wiener Walk 440; Bark in the Park 129; Barktoberfest 343; Brownsville Bark in the Park 365; Canine Capers 318; Canine Fest 187; Dawg Days of Summer (Coos Bay) 304; Dog Day Afternoon 343; Dog Days of Summer (Salem) 365; Dog Days of Summer Fun Run and Festival (Bellingham) 165; DogFest (Whistler) 440; Dog-O-Ween 129; Dog Show at the Beach 266; Dogtoberfest 343; Dune Mushers Mail Run 278; Easter Pet Parade 278; Marion County Dog Fest 365; Mutt Masters Dog Show and Olympics 278; Oregon State Barks Day 343; Paws in the Snow: A Canine Christmas Carnival 266; Pet Lovers Digest Celebration 440; Silverton Pet Parade 365; Skagit Valley Tulip Festival 172
Fetch: 456
FETCH! (Free Exercise Time for Canines and Their Humans!): 93, 502
Fidalgo Island: 88–90; parks 88–90; places to eat 90; places to stay 90
Fidalgo Islanders for Dogs Off-leash (F.I.D.O.): 89
Firehouse Tails: 115
first aid: 12–13; emergency veterinary clinics 472–477
fishing: Hood Canal 39; Island Lake 56; Lakedale Resort 82; Lake Sylvia 46; Langus Riverfront Trail 108–109; Nestucca River 267; Ocean Shores 44; Rogue River 415; Shady Cove/ Prospect 426; Vance Creek 46–47; William H. Tugman Memorial State Park 298

floatplane service: 497
Floras Lake: 312–313
Florence: 292–295; parks 292–294; places to eat 294–295; places to stay 295
Fogarty Creek: 279
Forest Park (Everett): 110
Forest Park (Portland): 328–329
Forks: 32–34; parks 33; places to eat 33; places to stay 33–34
Forks Timber Museum and Loggers Memorial: 32
Fort Casey: 94–95
Fort Clatsop National Memorial: 247
Fort Ebey: 94
Fort Flagler: 31
Fort Klamath: 431–432; parks 431–432; places to stay 432
Fort Nisqually: 188
Fort Simcoe Heritage Site: 233–234
Fort Steilacoom Park: 188–189
Fort Stevens: 247–248
Fort Ward State Park: 61–62
Fort Worden: 27
Fourth of July Pet Parade: 403
Fragrance Garden for the blind: 161
Fragrance Lake: 169
Francis/King Park: 461
Frank Raab Municipal Park: 53
Fraser River Dog Park: 456
Fremont: 133–135; parks 134–135; places to eat 135
Frenchman's Bar Trail: 205
Friends of the Animal Shelter (FOTAS): 421, 423, 503
Furry 5K: 129

G

Gabriel Park: 341
Galice: 413–415; parks 413–414; places to eat 414; places to stay 415
Galloping Goose Regional Trail: 463
gardens: Azalea Park 320; Butchart Gardens 464; Carl S. English Jr. Botanical Gardens 131; Carrie Blake Park 24; Evergreen Arboretum and

Gardens 108; Fragrance Garden 161; George Rogers Park Memorial Garden 348; Lake Sacajawea 203; Mingus Park 303; Minter Gardens 464; Point Defiance Park Japanese garden 188; Priest Point Park 193; Queen Elizabeth Park 454–455; Rainbow Falls State Park 195; Scenic Beach 55; Shore Acres Botanical Gardens 302; Skagit Valley 172; Sorosis Park 393–394; Stanley Park 450–451; Volunteer Park 140; Washington Park-International Rose Test Garden 329
Garibaldi: 260–261; parks 261; places to stay 261
Gastown: 451–453; parks 451; places to eat 452; places to stay 452–453
Gas Works Park: 134–135
Gearhart: 250–251; parks 250; places to stay 251
Genesee Dog Park: 146
George Rogers Park: 348
Ghost Hole: 261
Gifford Pinchot National Forest: 185
Gig Harbor: 70–72; parks 70–71; places to eat 71; places to stay 72
Gilbert Park: 230
Gleneden Beach: 277–278; parks 277–278; places to stay 278
Glenfair Park: 352
Goat Island: 319
Gold Bar: 117–118; parks 117–118
Gold Bar Dog Park: 117
Gold Beach: 315–317; parks 316; places to eat 317; places to stay 317
Goldendale: 240–241; parks 241; places to eat 241; places to stay 241
Golden Falls: 303–304
Golden Gardens: 130–131
Gorge Dog: 389
Governor Patterson Beach: 288
Governor Tom McCall Waterfront Park: 333
Grand Avenue Park: 109
Grand Forest: 60–61
Grandpa's Antique Photo Studio: 467

Grandview Dog Park: 185–186
Granite Falls: 106–107; parks 107; places to eat 107; places to stay 107
Grant Park: 338
Grants Pass: 415–417; parks 415–416; places to eat 416; places to stay 417
Granville Island: 453–454; parks 453; places to eat 453–454; places to stay 454
Grateful Dogs: 502
Grayland: 198–199; parks 198; places to eat 198; places to stay 198–199
Grayland Beach: 198
Gray, Robert: 260
Grays Harbor: 197
Great Beach Cleanup: 245
Great Dog Bakery: 351
Green Cottage Pets: 70
Green Lake: 127–128; parks 127–128; places to eat 128
Green Lake Park: 127
Gresham: 352–353; parks 352–353; places to eat 353; places to stay 353
Griffin Park: 414
Griffiths-Priday State Park: 42
Grotto, The: 336
Guemes Island: 87–88; parks 87; places to eat 88; places to stay 88

H

H & 38th Reservoir Site Dog Park: 89
hang gliding: 263
Hansville: 50–52; parks 51; places to eat 51–52
Harbor: 317–321; parks 318–320; places to eat 321; places to stay 321
Harborview: 110
Harris Beach: 319–320
Harrison Hot Springs: 459–460; parks 459; places to eat 459–460; places to stay 460
Harry and David: 420
Hawthorne Park: 421
Haystack Rock: 254
Hazeldale Park: 351–352
health spas: Annapurna Center for Self

Healing (ACSH) 26
Heceta Head Lighthouse: 293
Hertz Trail: 167
highlights: British Columbia 439;
    Central Oregon 384; Central
    Washington 212; Everett 102; Kitsap
    Peninsula 50; North Cascades 156;
    Olympic Peninsula 20; Oregon
    Central Coast 272; Oregon North
    Coast 246; Oregon South Coast
    302; Portland 325; San Juan Islands
    76; Seattle 124; Southern Oregon
    410; Southwest Washington 184;
    Willamette Valley 356
Hiram M. Chittenden Locks: 131
historic homes: Corl House 372–373;
    Olmstead Place 225
Hoh Rainforest: 33
Hood River: 389–392; parks 389–390;
    places to eat 390–391; places to stay
    391–392
Hood River Winery: 389
Hoquiam: 45–47; parks 46–47; places
    to eat 47; places to stay 47
Horsetail Falls: 387
Hovander Homestead: 161
Howard Buford Recreation Area: 378
Howard Miller Steelhead Park: 178
Howarth Park: 109–110
Howe Farm: 64
Howe Farm Pets: 501
Hoyt Arboretum: 329–330
Hug Point: 255
Humbug Mountain: 314
Hyatt Lake: 424

I
ice cream cruise: 134
Ike Kinswa State Park: 202
Illahee State Park: 57–58
Indian Mary Historic Reservation:
    413–414, 415
International Rose Test Garden: 329
Interurban Trail: 101–102, 165
Irene Reinhart Park: 224
Iron Horse State Park: 499–500

Irving Park: 337
Island Lake: 56
Island Park Walk: 453
Island View Regional Dog Park: 465
Islehaven Books & Borzoi: 85
Issaquah: 216–217; parks 216–217;
    places to eat 217; places to stay 217

J
Jackson F. Kimball State Recreation
    Site: 431–432
Jackson House: 195
Jackson Park: 64
Jacksonville: 417–419; parks 417–418;
    places to eat 418; places to stay 419
Jefferson County Day-use Park: 32
Jennings Memorial and Nature Park:
    106
Jesse Webster Park: 22
Jessie M. Honeyman Memorial State
    Park: 294
Joemma Beach: 73
John Dellenback Trail: 298
John Neal Memorial Park: 369–370
John Topits Park: 303
Joseph H. Stewart State Recreation
    Area: 426
Joseph Stewart Park: 46
Joseph Whidbey State Park: 92
Joyce: 21; parks 21; places to stay 21
July Jubilee Parade: 304

K
Kah Tai Lagoon: 28
Kalaloch: 35–36; parks 35–36; places
    to stay 36
Kalmiopsis Wilderness: 318
kayaking: Ona Beach 287; South Beach
    285
Kayak Point: 103, 104
Keizer: 364–367; parks 364–367; places
    to eat 367; places to stay 367
Kelso-Longview: 203–204; parks 203;
    places to stay 204
kennels: AirPet Hotel 337; Bone-a-Fide

Dog Ranch 105; Critter Cottage 274; Happy Trail Boarding Kennel 237; Puppy Zone 439–440

Kent: 185–186; parks 185–186; places to eat 186; places to stay 186

Kerrisdale: 456; parks 456; places to eat 456

Kettles Park: 94

Key Peninsula: 72–73; parks 72–73; places to eat 73; places to stay 73

King Park: 461

Kingston: 50–52; parks 51; places to eat 51–52

Kirkland: 147–148; parks 148; places to eat 148; places to stay 148

kite-flying areas: Belfair State Park 68; Discovery Park 132–133; D River 274; English Camp 80; Fort Flagler 31; Gas Works Park 134–135; Nehalem 258; Ocean Shores 43; Tolovana Beach 254; Yaquina Head 282–283; Young's Park 85

Kitsap Dog Parks: 70–71, 501

Kitsap Humane Society fundraisers: 55, 57

Kitsap Live Steamers: 64

Kitsap Peninsula: 48–73

Kitsilano: 447–449; parks 447–448; places to eat 448–449; places to stay 449

Klamath Falls: 432–435; parks 433–434; places to eat 434; places to stay 434–435

KVI Beach: 65

L

Lacamas Lake Park: 207

La Conner: 172–174; parks 172–173; places to eat 174; places to stay 174

Lady Washington: 45

Lake Billy Chinook: 399

Lake Ewauna Wingwatchers Nature Trail: 434

Lake Kachess: 220

Lake Oswego: 348–349; parks 348–349; places to eat 349; places to stay 349

Lake Padden Dog Park: 169–170

Lake Quinault: 37–38; parks 37; places to stay 38

Lake Roesinger: 115

Lake Sacajawea: 203

Lake Sammamish State Park: 216

Lake Sylvia: 46

Lake View Cemetery: 140

Lake Washington Boulevard: 142, 148

Lake Wenatchee State Park: 213–214

Langus Riverfront Trail: 108–109

La Push: 34–35; parks 34–35; places to eat 35

Larch Mountain: 386–388

Larrabee State Park: 169

Larry Scott Memorial Trail: 28–29

Larwood Wayside: 371

Las Almas Photography: 452

Latourell Falls: 387

Laurelhurst Park: 344

Lava Cave Forest: 406

lava tube: 428

LaVerne Park: 307

Leadbetter Point: 199–200

leash laws: 5–6

Leavenworth: 213–216; parks 213–215; places to eat 215; places to stay 215–216

Lent Landing: 58

Leschi: 142–143; parks 142; places to eat 142–143

Lewis and Clark Riverfront Trail: 393

Lewis and Clark State Park: 195–196

Lewis and Clark State Recreation Site: 385

lighthouses: Admiralty Head 95; Cape Arago 305; Cape Blanco 313; Cape Disappointment 200; Cape Meares 263; Heceta Head 293; Mukilteo 113; North Head 200; Point No Point 51; Point Robinson 66; Tillamook Rock 253–254; Umpqua 296; Westport 197; Yaquina Bay 283

Lime Kiln Point: 81

Lincoln Beach: 279; parks 279; places to stay 279

Lincoln City: 273–277; parks 273–276;

places to eat 276; places to stay 276–277

Lincoln Park: 143

Link River Nature Trail: 434

Lisbuela Park: 66

Little Mountain City Park: 173

Little Squalicum Park: 165–166

Lloyd L. Good Memorial Park: 32

Lochside Regional Trail: 460–461

Loganberry Lane: 111–112

Long Beach Peninsula: 199–202; parks 199–200; places to eat 201; places to eat 201–202

Longview: 203–204; parks 203; places to stay 204

Lopez Island: 84–87; parks 84–86; places to eat 86; places to stay 86–87

Lord Hill: 116

Lost Creek Lake: 426

Lost Lake (Oregon): 392; parks 392; places to stay 392

Lost Lake Park (Whistler): 441

Lost Lake Trail (Southern Oregon): 426

Lowell Park: 110–111

Lowell Riverfront Trail: 111

Luscher Farm Dog Park: 349

Luther Burbank Park: 152

Lydiatt, Tracy: 452

Lyle: 238–239; parks 238–239; places to stay 239

Lynden: 159–160; parks 160; places to eat 160; places to stay 160

Lynnwood: 120–121; parks 121; places to eat 121; places to stay 121

Lyons: 369–370; parks 369–370; places to eat 370

M

Madison: 141–142; parks 141; places to eat 142

Madras: 398–399; parks 398–399; places to eat 399; places to stay 399

Madrona: 142–143; parks 142; places to eat 142–143

Magnolia: 132–133; parks 132–133; places to eat 133

Magnuson Park at Sand Point: 128

Manchester State Park: 63

Manhattan Beach: 259–260

Manzanita: 257–258; parks 257; places to eat 257; places to stay 257–258

Mapleton: 295–296; parks 295; places to eat 296

Marblemount: 179–180; parks 179; places to eat 179–180

Marguerite Brons Memorial Park: 97

Marina Park: 119–120

Marine Park: 388

Marion County Dog Fest: 365

Mark O. Hatfield Trail: 390

Marquam Nature Trail: 340–341

Marrowstone Island: 31–32; parks 31–32; places to stay 32

Maryhill: 240; parks 240; places to eat 240

Maryhill Winery: 229

Marymoor Park: 149

Mary's Peak: 375

Marysville: 105–106; parks 106; places to eat 106; places to stay 106

Mary S. Young State Recreation Site: 350

Mason Lake: 69

Maupin: 397–398; parks 397; places to eat 398; places to stay 398

Maury Island: 65–67; parks 65–66; places to eat 66–67; places to stay 67

McKenzie: 379–380; parks 379–380; places to eat 380; places to stay 380

McKenzie River National Recreation Trail: 379

McMinnville: 360; parks 360; places to eat 360; places to stay 360

McMinnville City Park: 360

McVay Rock: 320

Meadowdale: 118–119

Medford: 420–421; parks 420–421; places to eat 421; places to stay 421

meditation walking paths: 61, 230

Memorial Bark Park: 357

Mercer Island: 151–153; parks 152–153;

places to stay 153
Merlin: 413–415; parks 413–414; places
    to eat 414; places to stay 415
Mike Miller Park: 284
Millersylvania State Park: 193–194
Milo McIver State Park: 362, 363
Milwaukie: 347; parks 347; places to
    eat 347
Mingus Park: 303
Minter Gardens: 464
Minto Brown Island Park: 366
Molalla River: 361
Monte Cristo: 107
Montlake: 141–142; parks 141; places
    to eat 142
Moran State Park: 77–78, 79
Morse Ranch Dog Park: 378
Mosier Twin Tunnels Trail: 390
Mossyrock: 202–203; parks 202; places
    to eat 202; places to stay 202–203
Moulton Falls Park: 204
Mountain View: 225
Mount Maguire: 468
Mount Vernon: 172–174; parks 172–
    173; places to eat 174; places to
    stay 174
Mt. Adams: 234
Mt. Bachelor: 402–403
Mt. Baker: 163–164; parks 163; places
    to eat 164; places to stay 164
Mt. Baker-Snoqualmie National Forest:
    157, 176–177
Mt. Constitution: 77–78
Mt. Hood: 395–396; parks 395; places
    to eat 396; places to stay 397
Mt. Hood National Forest: 385, 392,
    396
Mt. McLoughlin: 411
Mt. Pisgah: 378
Mt. Tabor Park: 344–345
Mukilteo: 113–114; parks 113–114;
    places to eat 114; places to stay 114
Mukilteo Lighthouse Park: 113
Multnomah Falls: 387
Munson Creek Falls: 261–262
murals: 234
museums: Camp 6 Logging Museum
    188; Collier Memorial Logging
    Museum 433; Forks Timber Museum
    and Loggers Memorial 32; Museum
    of Glass 187; Tacoma Art Museum
    187; Washington History Museum
    187
Mutt Masters Dog Show and
    Olympics: 278
Mutt Strut: 423
Myrtle Edwards Park: 135–136
Myrtle Point: 306–307; parks 307;
    places to eat 307; places to stay 307
Myrtlewood tree: 301

N

Naches: 227–228; parks 227–228;
    places to eat 228; places to stay 228
national forests and recreation areas:
    Alpine Lakes Wilderness 212;
    Cascade Lakes 402–403; Columbia
    River Gorge National Scenic Area
    384; Deschutes National Forest
    384–385, 428–429; Gifford Pinchot
    National Forest 185; Mt. Baker-
    Snoqualmie National Forest 157,
    176–177; Mt. Hood National Forest
    385, 392, 396; Oregon Dunes
    National Recreation Area 273;
    Rogue River-Siskiyou National
    Forest: 410–411; Siuslaw National
    Forest 272, 276, 295, 375; Umpqua
    National Forest 411, 430–431;
    Wenatchee National Forest 156,
    213, 221; Willamette National Forest
    357; Winema National Forest 411;
    Yakima Box Canyon Recreation
    Area 213
national parks: Crater Lake 431–432;
    Fort Clatsop Memorial 247
national wildlife refuges: Bandon
    Marsh 310; Baskett Slough 363;
    Dungeness 23; Haystack Rock 254;
    Siletz Bay 275; Three Arch Rocks
    264; Willapa 199–200
Native American history: 31, 53, 172,
    233, 239, 394, 413–414

Natural Bridge Trail: 428
nature hikes: Concrete 176; Ocean
    Shores Public Beach Access Points
    44; Wescott Bay Reserve 80
Neah-Kah-Nie Beach: 257
Nehalem: 258–259; parks 258–259;
    places to eat 259; places to stay 259
Newhalem Bay State Park: 258–259
Neptune Beach: 291
Neskowin: 268–269; parks 268–269;
    places to eat 269; places to stay 269
Neskowin Beach: 268–269
Netarts: 264–265; parks 264–265;
    places to eat 265; places to stay 265
Newberg: 358–359; parks 358; places
    to eat 358–359; places to stay 359
Newberry National Volcanic
    Monument: 406
Newhalem: 180–181; parks 181
Newhalem Trails: 181
Newport: 281–285; parks 282–284;
    places to eat 284; places to stay
    284–285
New River ACEC (Area of Critical
    Environmental Concern): 311
Next to Nature: 144
99W Drive In Theatre: 359
92nd Street Park: 113–114
Nob Hill: 330–332; parks 330–331;
    places to eat 331; places to stay
    331–332
Normandale Park: 338
Northacres: 126
North Beach: 26–27
North Bend (Central Washington):
    217–219; parks 218; places to eat
    218; places to stay 219
North Bend (Coos Bay): 302–306; parks
    302–305; places to eat 305–306;
    places to stay 306
North Cascades: 154–181
North Clackamas Aquatic Park: 343
North Clackamas Park: 347
Northeast Portland: 335–339; parks
    336–338; places to eat 339; places
    to 339
Northern Exposure: 222

North Lake Whatcom Park: 167
North Portland: 326–328; parks
    326–328; places to eat 328; places
    to stay 328
North Seattle: 126; parks 126; places
    to eat 126; places to stay 126
North Vancouver: 446–447; parks
    446–447; places to eat 447; places
    to stay 447
Northwest Organization for Animal
    Health (NOAH): 173
Northwest Portland: 328–330; parks
    328–330; places to eat 330
North Whidbey: 90–93; parks 91–92;
    places to eat 92; places to stay
    92–93
nude beaches: 386
nutrition: 191

O

Oak Harbor: 91–92
Oaks Bottom Trail: 345
Obstruction Pass: 78
OC&E Woods Line State Trail: 500
Ocean City: 42–43; parks 42–43; places
    to stay 43
Ocean Odyssey: 271
Ocean Shores: 43–45; parks 43–44;
    places to eat 44–45; places to stay
    45
Oceanside: 263–264; parks 264
Oceanside Beach: 264
Octopus Tree: 263
Odlin County Park: 84
Old Fort Townsend: 29
Old Man House: 53
Olmstead Place: 225
Olympia: 191–195; parks 191–194;
    places to eat 194; places to stay
    194–195
Olympic National Forest: 20–21
Olympic Peninsula: 19–47
Ona Beach: 286–287
Oneonta Falls: 387
Orcas Island: 77–79; parks 77–78; places
    to eat 78; places to stay 78–79

Oregon: 242–435
Oregon Coast Trail: 255, 304–305, 500
Oregon Department of Fish and
    Wildlife: 502
Oregon Dunes National Recreation
    Area (ODNRA): 273, 297, 298
Oregon Dunes Overlook: 294
Oregon Humane Society: 343
Oregon Redwood Nature Trail: 319
Oregon Shakespeare Festival: 422
Oregon State Parks: *see* state parks,
    Oregon
Oregon State University: 371
Oswald West State Park: 255, 256
Otter Rock: 281; parks 281; places to
    eat 281
Overlook Park: 328

P

Pacific Beach: 40–41; parks 40–41;
    places to eat 41; places to stay 41
Pacific City: 265–268; parks 265–267;
    places to eat 267; places to stay 268
Pacific Crest Trail: 499
Pacific Pines: 200
Pacific Spirit Regional Park: 450
packing tips: 9–10
Padilla Bay Shore Trail: 172–173
parades: Annual Picnic and Wiener
    Walk 440; Easter Pet Parade 278;
    Fourth of July Pet Parade 403;
    Hawthorne Park Friends of the
    Animal Shelter benefit parade 421;
    July Jubilee Parade 304; Mutt Strut
    423; Silverton Pet Parade 365
Paradise Point: 313
Park Blocks: 332–333
Parkdale: 396–397; parks 396; places to
    eat 397; places to stay 397
Patmore Pit: 93–94
Paws in the Snow: A Canine Christmas
    Carnival: 266
Paws on the Sand: 275
paws scale: 4
Peace Arch Park: 157
Penrose Point State Park: 72, 73

permits: Washington Department of
    Fish and Wildlife for harvesting fish
    39
pet hospitals: 472–477; Canada 476–
    477; Oregon 474–476; Washington
    472–474
Peter Iredale: 247
PetsWALK Benefit: 57
photography studios: Grandpa's
    Antique Photo Studio 467; Las
    Almas 452
pick of the litter: British Columbia
    439; Central Oregon 384; Central
    Washington 212; Everett 102;
    Kitsap Peninsula 50; North
    Cascades 156; Olympic Peninsula
    20; Oregon Central Coast 272;
    Oregon North Coast 246; Oregon
    South Coast 302; Portland 325;
    San Juan Islands 76; Seattle 124;
    Southern Oregon 410; Southwest
    Washington 184; Willamette
    Valley 356
Picnic Point: 112
Pig War: 79–80
Pike Place Market: 123
Pilot Butte: 405
Pioneer Park: 153
Pistol River Sand Dunes: 316
PJ's Paws and Claws: 132
playgrounds: Albert "Doc" Griffin Park
    418; Alpha Lake Park 441; Azalea
    Park 320; Buffington Park 316;
    George Rogers Park 348; Jennings
    Memorial and Nature Park 106;
    Point Defiance Park 188; Scottsburg
    Park 297; Sorosis Park 393–394;
    South Whidbey Community Park 96;
    Wilshire Park 337–338
Point Defiance Park: 188
Point No Point Lighthouse: 51
Point Robinson Lighthouse: 66
poisoning, dog: 324–325
Ponytail Falls: 387
poop scooping: 6
Port Angeles: 22–23; parks 22; places
    to eat 22; places to stay 22–23

Port Gamble: 50–52; parks 51; places to eat 51–52

Port Hadlock: 31–32; parks 31–32; places to stay 32

Portland: 322–353; Beaverton 350–352; Downtown 332–335; Gresham 352–353; Historic Waterfront 332–335; Lake Oswego 348–349; Milwaukie 347; Nob Hill 330–332; Northeast Portland-Airport 335–339; North Portland 326–328; Northwest Portland 328–330; Southeast Portland 342–347; Southwest Portland 340–342; Tigard 339–340; West Linn 349–350

Portland Pooch online guide: 502

Portland Saturday Market: 332

Port Marina Park: 389

Port of Hood River: 389

Port Orchard: 63–65; parks 63–64; places to eat 64; places to stay 65

Port Orford: 312–315; parks 312–314; places to eat 314–315; places to eat 315

Port Orford Heads State Park: 314

Port Townsend: 26–30; parks 26–29; places to eat 29–30; places to stay 30

Post Point Lagoon and Dog Park: 168

Potlach State Park: 39–40

Potso Dog Park: 340

Poulsbo: 52–55; parks 53; places to eat 53–54; places to stay 54–55

Powell Butte Nature Park: 353

Powell's City of Books: 324

Powerhouse Canal Pathway: 228

Pressentin park: 179

Priest Point Park: 193

Proposal Rock: 268

Prospect: 426–427; parks 426; places to eat 426; places to stay 427

Protection Island: 43–44

Puget Sound Pet: 502

Puppy Zone Dog Day Care and Adventure Centre: 439–440

Puss 'n' Boots: 423

QR

Queen Anne: 135–136; parks 135–136; places to eat 136

Queen Elizabeth Park Dog Area: 454–455

Quinault Loop: 37

races: Atta Boy 300 dogsled race 403; Dog Days of Summer Fun Run and Festival 165; Furry 5K 129; PAWSwalk 129

rafting trips: 415

Railey's Leash & Treat: 144

Rainbow Falls State Park: 195, 196

Rainbow Park: 441

RainCity Dogs: 503

Raindogs: 275

Rainforest Nature Trail: 37

Randall Park: 230

Rasar State Park: 175–176, 177

Rattlesnake Lake: 218

Ravenna: 128–130; parks 128; places to eat 130; places to stay 130

Redmond (Oregon): 401–402; parks 401–402; places to stay 402

Redmond (Washington): 148–149; parks 149; places to stay 149

redwood trees: 319

Reed Park: 224

Reedsport: 296–297; parks 296; places to eat 296–297

Regrade Dog Park: 138

Reigning Cats and Dogs: 275

Resources: 471–503

Richmond Beach Saltwater Park: 125

Riverfront Commemorative Park: 373

River Meadows: 104–105

Riverside Park (Grants Pass): 416

Riverside Park (Roseburg): 412

Road's End State Recreation Site: 273

Robe Canyon Historic Park: 107

Robert W. Sawyer River Park: 403–404

Robin Hill Farm: 24

Robinson Park: 288

Robinswood Community Park: 150–151

Rockaway Beach: 259–260; parks 259–260; places to eat 260; places

to stay 260
Rockaway Beach City Wayside: 260
rock climbing: 401
Rockport: 177–179; parks 177–178;
    places to eat 178; places to stay
    178–179
Rockport State Park: 177–178, 179
Rocky Point Park: 458
Rogers Dog Park: 188
Rogue Gorge Trail: 427
Rogue River National Forest: 410–411
Rooster Rock State Park: 386
Roseburg: 411–413; parks 411–412;
    places to eat 412–413; places to
    stay 413
Roslyn: 222; parks 222; places to eat
    222
Roslyn City Park: 222
Round Butte Overlook: 398
Row River Trail: 381
Ruby Beach: 35

S

Saanich Peninsula: 460–462; parks 461;
    places to eat 462; places to stay 462
safety: 8–9; dog poisonings 324–325
sailboarding: Floras Lake 312–313;
    Hood River 389; Kayak Point 103;
    Pistol River 316
Sailboard Park: 236–237
Salem-Keizer: 364–367; parks 364–367;
    places to eat 367; places to stay 367
Salem Riverfront Park: 366
Salisbury Point: 51
Salmon La Sac: 221; parks 221
Salt Creek Recreation Area: 21
Sammamish River Trail: 124
Samuel H. Boardman State Scenic
    Corridor: 318–319
San Juan Island: 79–83; parks 80–82;
    places to eat 82; places to stay 83
San Juan Island County Park: 81, 82
San Juan Islands: 74–99
Sand Lake: 265, 268
Sand Point Park: 273–274
Sandy Creek Covered Bridge Wayside:

307
Santa photos: 55
Santiam River: 369
Sarah Zigler Interpretive Trail: 417–418
Sasamat Lake: 457–458
Sauk Mountain Trail: 178
Sawyer Park: 403–404
Scenic Beach: 55–56
Scottsburg: 297; parks 297
Scottsburg Park: 297
Scriber Park: 121
sculpture gardens: Blue Dog Pond
    146; Downtown Park 150; Wescott
    Bay Reserve 80
Seabeck: 55–56; parks 55–56; places
    to eat 56
Seal Rock: 286–287; parks 286–287;
    places to eat 287
Seaside: 251–252; parks 251; places to
    eat 252; places to stay 252
Seaside Promenade: 251
Seattle: 122–153; Ballard 130–132;
    Bellevue 150–151; Capitol Hill
    140–141; Downtown 136–140;
    Fremont 133–135; Green Lake 127;
    Kirkland 147–148; Leschi 142–143;
    Madison/Montlake 141–142;
    Madrona 142–143; Magnolia 132–
    133; Mercer Island 151–153; North
    Seattle 126; Queen Anne 135–136;
    Ravenna 128–130; Redmond 148–
    149; Shoreline 125; South Seattle
    145–147; University District 128–130;
    Wallingford 133–135; West Seattle
    143–145
Seattle Center Grounds: 137
Seattle Humane Society: 129
Seawall Promenade: 450–451
Sedro Woolley: 174–175; parks
    174–175; places to eat 175; places
    to stay 175
Sehome Hill Arboretum: 167–168
Sellwood Riverfront Park: 345
Semiahmoo Spit: 158
Sequim-Dungeness Valley: 23–25;
    parks 23–24; places to eat 25; places
    to stay 25

Serve Our Dog Areas (SODA): 149, 502
service dog training: 420
Seven Devils: 309
Seward Park: 147
Shady Cove: 426–427; parks 426;
    places to eat 426; places to stay 427
Shannon Falls Provincial Park: 443–444
SHARED sites: 325–326
Shark Reef Sanctuary: 85–86
Shaw Island: 83–84; parks 83–84;
    places to stay 84
Shaw Island County Park: 83–84
shellfish harvesting: Clay Myers
    266; Discovery Park 132–133; Fay
    Bainbridge State Park 59; Illahee
    State Park 58; Kayak Point 103; Seal
    Rock 287; Spencer Spit 85; Waldport
    287; Young's Park 85
Shepperds Dell Falls: 387
Shevlin Park: 404
shopping: Bend dog boutiques 402;
    British Columbia SPCA Thrift Stores
    446; Central Oregon Coast dog
    boutiques 275; Hood River dog
    boutiques 389; North Oregon Coast
    dog boutiques 253; Portland 332;
    Poulsbo 52; Seattle dog boutiques
    132, 144; Vancouver, BC dog
    boutiques 454, 456
Shoreline: 125; parks 125; places to
    eat 125
Sidney: 460–462; parks 461; places to
    eat 462; places to stay 462
Siletz Bay: 274–275
Silverdale: 55–56; parks 55–56; places
    to eat 56
Silver Falls (Coos Bay): 303–304
Silver Falls (Silverton): 368–369
Silver Lake: 163, 164
Silverton: 368–369; parks 368–369;
    places to eat 369; places to stay 369
Silverton Pet Parade: 365
Singleton Park: 411–412
Siskiyou Mountain Park: 423
Siskiyou National Forest: 410–411
Sisters: 399–401; parks 400; places to
    eat 400; places to stay 400–401

Siuslaw National Forest: 272, 276, 295,
    375
Skagit Valley Tulip Festival: 172
Skamania: 207–208; parks 208; places
    to stay 208
Smelt Sands: 290
Smith Rock: 401
Snohomish: 115–117; parks 115–116;
    places to eat 116; places to stay 117
Snoqualmie: 217–219; parks 218;
    places to eat 218; places to stay 219
Snoqualmie Pass: 219–220; parks
    219–220
Snoqualmie Valley Trail: 217
snowy plover: 43–44, 245
soap box derby racing: 367
SoftDawgs: 503
Sooke: 467–469; parks 467–468; places
    to eat 468–469; places to stay 469
Sorosis Park: 393–394
South Beach (Oregon Coast): 285–286;
    parks 285–286; places to eat 286;
    places to stay 286
South Beach (Shaw Island, WA): 83–84
South Beach State Park: 285–286
Southeast Portland: 342–347; parks
    342–346; places to eat 346; places
    to stay 346–347
South Indian Island Parks: 32
South Kitsap Community Park: 64
South Seattle: 145–147; parks 145–147
South Slough National Estuarine
    Research Reserve: 308–309
Southwest County Park: 119
Southwest Portland: 340–342; parks
    340–342; places to eat 342; places
    to stay 342
South Whidbey: 95–98; parks 95–97;
    places to eat 97; places to stay
    97–98
South Whidbey Community Park: 96
South Whidbey State Park: 95–96, 98
SPCA Thrift Stores: 446
Spearfish Park: 239
Spencer Spit: 85, 86–87
Spong's Landing: 365–366
Springfield: 376–379; parks 377–378;

places to eat 378–379; places to stay 379
Squamish: 443–445; parks 443–444; places to eat 444; places to stay 444–445
Squires Lake: 170
Stanley Park: 450–451
Stanwood: 102–104; parks 102–103; places to eat 104; places to stay 104
state parks, Oregon: 502; Alfred A Loeb 319, 320; Beverly Beach 282, 285; Bob Straub 267; Bullards Beach 309; Cape Arago 305; Cape Blanco 313, 315; Cape Lookout 264–265; Carl G. Washburn 292–293; Cascadia 376; Champoeg 358, 359; Ecola 253–254; Fort Stevens 247–248; Humbug Mountain 314; Jessie M. Honeyman 294; Milo McIver 362, 363; Nehalem Bay 258–259; Ona Beach 286–287; Oswald West 255, 256; permits 14; Port Orford Heads 314; Rooster Rock 386; Silver Falls 368–369; South Beach 285–286; Sunset Bay 304–305, 306; Umpqua Lighthouse 296, 299; William H. Tugman 298
state parks, Washington: 501; Bay View 172, 174; Belfair 68; Birch Bay 158, 159; Camano Island 99; Cape Disappointment 200, 201; Columbia Hills 239; Dash Point 186–187; Deception Pass 91, 92; Dosewallips 38–39; Fay Bainbridge 59–60; Fort Casey 94–95; Fort Ebey 94; Fort Flagler 31, 32; Fort Simcoe Heritage Site 233–234; Fort Ward 61–62; Griffiths-Priday 42; Ike Kinswa 202; Illahee 57–58; Iron Horse 499–500; Joemma Beach 73; Joseph Whidbey 92; Lake Sammamish 216; Lake Wenatchee 213–214; Larrabee 169; Lewis and Clark 195–196; Manchester 63; Millersylvania 193–194; Moran 77–78, 79; Obstruction Pass 78; Pacific Beach 40–41; Penrose Point 72, 73; permits 14;

Potlach 39–40; Rainbow Falls 195, 196; Rasar 175–176, 177; Rockport 177–178, 179; Scenic Beach 55–56; South Whidbey 95–96, 98; Tolmie 192; Twanoh 68–69, 70; Wallace Falls 118; Westport Light 197; Yakima Sportsman Park 231
Stawamus Chief Mountain: 444
Stevenson: 208–209; parks 208–209; places to eat 209; places to stay 209
Stillaguamish River: 104
Stray Dog Co.: 93
Summerlake Dog Park: 339
Sunday Fremont Ice Cream Cruise: 134
Sunrise Beach: 71
Sunset Bay: 304–305, 306
surfing: 277
Sutcliffe Park: 453
Sweet Creek Falls: 295
Sweet Home: 376
swimming: 343

T

Tacoma: 187–190; parks 188–189; places to eat 189; places to stay 190
Tail Wag benefit: 343
Takena Landing: 370
Tamanawas Falls Loop: 396
Tandy Bay: 429
taxis: 498
Tennant Lake: 161–162
Tennant Lake Wildlife Area: 162
theater: Oregon Shakespeare Festival 422; Vanier Park Bard on the Beach 447–448
Three Arch Rocks National Wildlife Refuge: 264
Thunder Island: 388
tidepools: Devil's Punch Bowl 281; Fogarty Creek 279; Haystack Rock 254; Kalaloch 36; Larrabee State Park 169; Neskowin Beach 269; Seal Rock 287; Twanoh State Park 68
Tierra del Mar Beach: 266–267
Tigard: 339–340; parks 339–340
Tiger Mountain State Forest: 216–217

Tillamook: 261–262; parks 261–262; places to eat 262; places to stay 263
Tillamook Rock Lighthouse: 253–254
Tillicum Park: 33
Tokeland: 198–199; parks 198; places to eat 198; places to stay 198–199
Tolmie State Park: 192
Tolovana Beach Wayside: 254
Toppenish: 233–234; parks 233–234; places to stay 234
totem poles: 446
Tou Velle State Recreation Site: 420
Trail of Ten Falls: 368–369
trails, extended: 499–500
train rides: 64
Trans-Canada Trail System: 463
transportation: 497–498
"Triangle of Death": 27, 31, 94–95
Tri-Cities Area: 457–458; parks 457–458; places to eat 458
Trillium Lake: 395
Triple Falls: 387
Troutdale: 385–386; parks 385; places to eat 386; places to stay 386
Trout Lake: 234–235; parks 235; places to stay 235
Tryon Creek: 348
Tucker Park: 389
Tugwell Creek Farm: 469
Tumalo: 403
Tuxes and Tails benefit: 129
Twanoh State Park: 68–69, 70

U

Umpqua Dunes Recreation Area: 297–298
Umpqua Lighthouse: 296, 299
Umpqua National Forest: 411, 430–431
Umtanum Creek: 225–226
Union Creek: 427–428; parks 427–428; places to eat 428
Union Gap: 232–233; parks 232–233; places to stay 233
University District (Seattle): 128–130; parks 128; places to eat 130; places to stay 130

University of Oregon: 376
Upper Deschutes River Trails: 405–406
Urban Dogs (Bellevue): 144
Urban Dogs (Tacoma): 187
Urban Fauna: 332
urban walks: Capitol Campus 192; Fairhaven Historic District 176; Jacksonville Historic Landmark Walking Tour 419; Port Gamble 52; Waterfront Trail, Port Townsend 27
Utsalady Point Vista: 98–99

V

Valley Trail: 440
Vance Creek: 46–47
Vancouver (British Columbia): 445–456; Cambie 454–455; Downtown/Gastown 451–453; Granville Island 453–454; Kerrisdale 456; Kitsilano 447–449; North Vancouver 446–447; Point Grey 449–450; West End 450–451; West Vancouver 445
Vancouver (Washington): 205–206; parks 205–206; places to eat 206; places to stay 206
Vanier Dog Beach: 447–448
Vashon Island: 65–67; parks 65–66; places to eat 66–67; places to stay 67
Veterans Memorial Park: 434
veterinarians: 472–477; Canada 476–477; Oregon 474–476; Washington 472–474
Victoria: 463–467; parks 463–465; places to eat 465–466; places to stay 466–467
Victoria Carriage Tours: 467
Victoria Estate Winery: 464
Vietnam Veterans memorial walkway: 283
Village Green: 400
Volunteer Park: 140

W

Wags and Rags: 253

Wahkeena Falls: 387
Waldport: 287–289; parks 288; places to eat 289; places to stay 289
Wallace Falls State Park: 118
Wallace Park: 330
Wallingford: 133–135; parks 134–135; places to eat 135
Walnut Park: 372
Warrenton: 246–250; parks 247–249; places to eat 249; places to stay 250
Washington: 17–241
Washington Department of Fish and Wildlife: 501
Washington Park Arboretum: 141
Washington Park (Fidalgo Island): 88–89
Washington Park (Portland): 329
Washington State Parks: see state parks, Washington
Washougal: 206–207; parks 207; places to eat 207
waterfalls: Alsea Falls 375–376; Bridal Veil Falls (British Columbia) 459; Bridal Veil Falls (Oregon) 387; Celilo Falls 394; Cline Falls 401; Drift Creek Falls 276; Golden and Silver Falls 303–304; Green Peak Falls 375; Horsetail Falls 387; Latourell 387; Moulton Falls 204; Multnomah Falls 387; Munson Creek Falls 261–262; Oneonta Falls 387; Ponytail Falls 387; Rainbow Falls 195; Shannon Falls 443–444; Shepperds Dell 387; Silver Falls State Park (Silverton) 368–369; Sweet Creek Falls 295; Tamanawas Falls 396; Triple Falls 387; Wahkeena 387; Wallace Falls 118; Whatcom Falls 166; White River 397; Youngs River Falls 248–249
Waterfront Park (Leavenworth): 214–215
Waterfront Park (Portland): 333
Wenatchee National Forest: 156, 213, 221
Wescott Bay Reserve: 80
West Canyon Rim Park: 402
Westcrest Dog Park: 144

West Hood Canal: 38–40; parks 38–40; places to eat 40; places to stay 40
West Linn: 349–350; parks 350; places to stay 350
Westport: 196–197; parks 197; places to eat 197; places to stay 197
Westport Light State Park: 197
West Seattle: 143–145; parks 143–144; places to eat 145; places to stay 145
West Vancouver: 445; parks 445
whale-watching: Depoe Bay 279–280; San Juan Island 81; Umpqua 296
Whatcom Falls Park: 166
Wheeler: 258–259; parks 258–259; places to eat 259; places to stay 259
Whidbey Animals Improvement Foundation (WAIF): 93
Whidbey Island: 90–98; Central 93–95; North 90–93; South 95–98
Whistler: 439–443; parks 441–442; places to eat 442; places to stay 443
Whistler Animals Galore (WAG): 503
Whistler's Bend: 412
White Pass: 226–227; parks 226–227; places to stay 227
White River Falls: 397
White Salmon: 236–238; parks 236–237; places to eat 237; places to stay 237–238
Wilcox Park: 121
wildlife areas/refuges: Conboy Lake 235; Tennant Lake Wildlife Area 162; see also national wildlife refuges
Wildwood Recreation Site: 395
Wildwood Trail: 328–329
Willamette Mission: 364
Willamette National Forest: 357
Willamette Park (Corvallis): 373–374
Willamette Park (Portland): 341–342
Willamette Valley: 355–381
Willapa National Wildlife Refuge: 199–200
Willard Springs Foot Trail: 235
William H. Tugman Memorial State Park: 298
Wilshire Park: 337–338
Wilson Park: 390

Wilsonville: 357–358; parks 357; places to eat 357; places to stay 358
Winchester Bay: 297–299; parks 297–298; places to eat 299; places to stay 299
windsurfing: Floras Lake 312–313; Hood River 389; Kayak Point 103; Pistol River 316
Winema National Forest: 411
wineries: Bonair 229; Hood River 389; Maryhill 229; Tugwell Creek Farm Meadery 469; Victoria Estate 464
Woodland Dog Park: 127–128
Woodland Meadows: 372–373
Woodstock Park: 345
Woofies and Meowz: 454

XYZ

Yachats: 289–292; parks 290–291; places to eat 291; places to stay 291–292
Yakima: 228–232; parks 228–231; places to eat 232; places to stay 232
Yakima Box Canyon: 225–226
Yakima Box Canyon Recreation Area: 213
Yakima Greenway: 228
Yakima Sportsman Park: 231
Yaquina Bay: 283
Yaquina Bay Lighthouse: 283
Yaquina Head Outstanding Natural Area: 282–283
YES sites: 326
Young's Park: 87
Youngs River Falls: 248–249
Youth Activities Park: 232–233

Acknowledgments

I'd like to extend my thanks to Jennifer, Jules, and Reggie for being my advance scouts in Canada; to Holly for checking into vet hospitals; and to Sheryl and Blue for their event expertise. I heap blessings upon Mom and Cindy for bringing Cooper into our lives and for helping to put Isis' butt back on. Indulge me for a moment, as I acknowledge indebtedness to our parents for financial flotation and gratefulness to my dad, who made me get directions to Jenny's house.

There are kudos due to the barista babes and brutes at Hotwire, my second office, for keeping me wired on caffeine, wireless on the Web, and sane.

Finally, this book would be greatly diminished if it weren't for the efforts of every dog advocate who campaigns for, creates, and cleans up off-leash areas.

Keeping Current

Note to All Dog Lovers:

While our information is as current as possible, changes to fees, regulations, parks, roads, and trails sometimes are made after we go to press. Businesses can close, change their ownership, or change their rules. Earthquakes, fires, rainstorms, and other natural phenomena can radically change the condition of parks, hiking trails, and wilderness areas. Before you and your dog begin your travels, please be certain to call the phone numbers for each listing for updated information.

Attention Dogs of the Pacific Northwest

Our readers mean everything to us. We explore the Pacific Northwest so that you and your people can spend true quality time together. Your input to this book is very important. In the last few years, we've heard from many wonderful dogs and their humans about new dog-friendly places, or old dog-friendly places we didn't know about. If we've missed your favorite park, beach, outdoor restaurant, hotel, or dog-friendly activity, please let us know. We'll check out the tip and if it turns out to be a good one, include it in the next edition, giving a thank-you to the dog and/or person who sent in the suggestion. Please write us—we always welcome comments and suggestions.

The Dog Lover's Companion to the Pacific Northwest
Avalon Travel Publishing
1400 65th Street, Suite 250
Emeryville, CA 94608, USA
email: atpfeedback@avalonpub.com

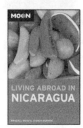